ASPECTS *of*
WESTERN CIVILIZATION

Problems and Sources in History

Seventh Edition

D0074291

Edited by
PERRY M. ROGERS

Prentice Hall

Boston   Columbus   Indianapolis   New York   San Francisco   Upper Saddle River
Amsterdam   Cape Town   Dubai   London   Madrid   Milan   Munich   Paris   Montréal   Toronto
Delhi   Mexico City   São Paulo   Sydney   Hong Kong   Seoul   Singapore   Taipei   Tokyo

Editorial Director: Craig Campanella
Executive Editor: Jeff Lasser
Editorial Project Manager: Rob DeGeorge
Senior Marketing Manager: Maureen E. Prado Roberts
Marketing Assistant: Marissa O'Brien
Senior Managing Editor: Ann Marie McCarthy
Project Manager: Lynn Savino Wendel; Debra Wechsler
Operations Specialist: Christina Amato; Sherry Lewis
Creative Director, Central Design: Jayne Conte
Cover Designer: Axell Designs
Manager, Visual Research: Beth Brenzel
Manager, Rights and Permissions: Zina Arabia
Image Permission Coordinator: Fran Toepfer
Manager, Cover Visual Research & Permissions: Karen Sanatar
Cover Photo: Portrait of a Young Woman, thought to be Sappho (c. 630–570 B.C.E.)/Art Resource, NY
Full-Service Project Management: Chitra Ganesan
Composition: GGS Higher Education Resources/A division of PreMedia Global Inc.
Printer/Binder: RRD Harrisonburg
Cover Printer: RRD Harrisonburg
Text Font: 10/12 AGaramond

*For Ann,
Elisa, Kit, and Tyler*

Credits and acknowledgments borrowed from other sources and reproduced, with permission, in this textbook appear on appropriate page within text.

Library of Congress Cataloging-in-Publication Data

Aspects of western civilization : problems and sources in history : volume i / edited by Perry M. Rogers.—7th ed.
   p. cm.
  Includes index.
  ISBN-13: 978-0-205-70833-8
  ISBN-10: 0-205-70833-1
 1. Civilization, Western—History.   2. Civilization, Western—History—Sources.   I. Rogers, Perry McAdow.
  CB245.A86 2010
  909'.09821—dc22

                                                     2009052325

10 9 8 7 6 5 4 3 2

Prentice Hall
is an imprint of

www.pearsonhighered.com

ISBN 10:   0-205-70833-1
ISBN 13:   978-0-205-70833-8

BRIEF CONTENTS

VOLUME 1
THE ANCIENT WORLD THROUGH THE REFORMATION

VOLUME 2

THE AGE OF THE RENAISSANCE THROUGH THE CONTEMPORARY WORLD

CONTENTS

PART III
THE ROMAN WORLD   **111**

THEMATIC CONTENTS

CHAPTER 13:   *"An Embarrassment of Riches"*: The Interaction of New Worlds   351

PREFACE

The Roman orator Cicero once remarked, "History is the witness of the times, the torch of truth, the life of memory, the teacher of life, the messenger of antiquity." In spite of these noble words, historians have often labored under the burden of justifying the value of studying events that are over and done. Humankind is practical, more concerned with its present and future than with its past. And yet the study of history provides us with unique opportunities for self-knowledge. It teaches us what we have done and therefore helps define what we are. On a less abstract level, the study of history enables us to judge present circumstance by drawing on the laboratory of the past. Those who have lived and died have left a legacy of experience through their recorded attitudes, actions, and ideas.

One of the best ways to travel through time and space and perceive the very humanness that lies at the root of history is through the study of primary sources. These are the documents, coins, letters, inscriptions, art, music, architecture, and monuments of past ages. The task of historians is to evaluate this evidence with a critical eye and then construct a narrative that is consistent with the "facts" as they have established them. Such interpretations are inherently subjective and therefore open to dispute. History is thus filled with controversy as historians argue their way toward the so-called truth. The only way to work toward an understanding of the past is through personal examination of the primary sources.

Yet for the beginning student, this poses some difficulties. Such inquiry casts the student adrift from the security of accepting the "truth" as revealed in a textbook. In fact, history is too often presented in a deceptively objective manner; one learns facts and dates in an effort to obtain the "right" answers for multiple-choice tests. But the student who has wrestled with primary sources and has experienced voices from the past on a more intimate level accepts the responsibility of evaluation and judgment. He or she understands that history does not easily lend itself to "right" answers, but demands reflection on the problems that have confronted past societies and that are at play even in our contemporary world. Cicero was right in viewing history as the "life of memory." But human memory is fragile, and the records of the past can be destroyed or distorted. Without the past, people have nothing with which to judge what they are told in the present. Truth then becomes the preserve of the ruler or government, no longer relative, but absolute. The study of history, and primary sources in particular, goes far in making people aware of the continuity of humankind and the progress of civilization.

Aspects of Western Civilization offers the student an opportunity to evaluate the primary sources of the past and to do so in a structured and organized format. The documents provided are diverse and include state papers, secret dispatches, letters, diary accounts, poems, newspaper articles, papal encyclicals, propaganda flyers, and trial testimony. Occasionally, the assessments of modern historians are included to lend perspective. All sources give testimony to human endeavor in Western societies. Yet this two-volume book has been conceived as more than a simple compilation of primary sources. The subtitle of the work, *Problems and Sources in History*, gives true indication of the nature of the book's premise. It is meant to provide the student with thoughtful and engaging material focused around individual units that encompass time periods, specific events, and historical questions. Students learn from the past most effectively when posed with problems that have meaning for their own lives. In evaluating the material from *Aspects of Western Civilization*, the student will discover that issues are not nearly as simple as they may appear at first glance. Historical sources often contradict each other, and truth then depends on logic and one's own experience and outlook on life. Throughout these volumes, the student is confronted with basic questions regarding historical development, human nature, moral action, and practical necessity. The text is therefore broad in its scope and incorporates a wide variety of political, social, economic, religious, intellectual, and scientific issues. It is internally organized around **seven major themes** that provide direction and cohesion to the text while allowing for originality of thought in both written and oral analysis:

1. *The Power Structure:* What are the institutions of authority in Western societies, and how have they been structured to achieve political, social, and economic stability? This theme seeks to introduce the student to the various systems of rule that have shaped Western civilization: classical democracy, representative democracy (republican government), oligarchy, constitutional monarchy, divine-right monarchy, theocracy, and dictatorship (especially fascism and totalitarian rule). What are the advantages and drawbacks to each? This rubric also includes the concepts of balance of power and containment, principles of succession, geopolitics, and social and economic theories such as capitalism, communism, and socialism.

2. *Social and Spiritual Values:* The Judeo-Christian and Islamic heritages of Western civilization form the basis of this theme. How have religious values and moral attitudes affected the course of Western history? Is there a natural competition between Church and State as two controlling units in society? Which is more influential, which legacy more enduring? How has religion been used as a means of securing political power or of instituting social change? To what extent have spiritual reform movements resulted in a change of political or social policy? Are ideas more potent than any army? Why have so many people died fighting for religions that abhor violence? Does every society need a spiritual foundation? Also included in this rubric are sources that express the values of particular societies, thus affording comparison with others.

3. *The Institution and the Individual:* What is the relationship between the institutions of society and the individual—between personal, creative expression in society and the governing political, religious, and social institutions of the age? How have writers, artists, and poets been variously employed through patronage systems to enhance political authority, perpetuate myths, and create heroes who embody the values of the age? What is the role of the rebel, the free thinker, who works against the grain and threatens the status quo by exploring new dimensions of thought or creative expression?

4. *Imperialism:* How has imperialism been justified throughout Western history, and what are the moral implications of gaining and maintaining an empire? Is defensive imperialism a practical foreign policy option? Is containment essentially a defensive or offensive policy? This theme is often juxtaposed with subtopics of nationalism, war, altruism, and human nature.

5. *Revolution and Historical Transition:* This theme seeks to define and examine the varieties of revolution: political, intellectual, economic, social, and artistic. What are the underlying and precipitating causes of political revolution? How essential is the intellectual foundation? Do technological and economic revolutions have a direct correlation to political or social revolutions? Does an artistic revolution stem from political change or a shifting of social realities? This theme focuses

on transition through historical or artistic periods and encourages students to debate and develop their own philosophies of historical change.

6. *The Varieties of Truth:* What is the role of propaganda in history? Many sections examine the use and abuse of information, often in connection with absolute government, revolution, imperialism, or genocide. What roles do art, architecture, poetry, and literature play in the "creation of belief" and in the successful consolidation of power? This theme emphasizes the relativity of truth and stresses the responsibility of the individual to assess the validity of evidence.

7. *Women in History:* The text intends to help remedy the widespread omission of women from the history of Western society and to develop an appreciation for their contributions to the intellectual and political framework of Western civilization. At issue is how women have been viewed—or rendered invisible—throughout history and how individually and collectively their presence is inextricably linked with the development and progress of civilization. This inclusive approach stresses the importance of achieving a perspective that lends value and practical application to history.

STRUCTURE OF *ASPECTS OF WESTERN CIVILIZATION*

The main strength of the text lies in its structure and in the direction given to the student through introductions to each primary source. Study questions promote analysis and evoke critical response. Each chapter follows the same format:

- *Timeline Chronological Overview:* These brief timelines are designed to give students a visual perspective of the main events, movements, and personalities discussed in the chapter. Each chapter also has a Key Events chronology for historical continuity.
- *Quotations:* These are statements from various historians, artists, philosophers, diplomats, literary figures, and religious spokespersons who offer

insight and give perspective on the subject matter of the chapter.

- *Chapter Themes:* Each chapter is framed by several questions that direct the reader to broader issues and comparative perspectives found in the ideas and events of other chapters. This feature acknowledges the changing perspectives of different eras while linking historical problems that emphasize the continuity of history.
- *General Introduction:* A general introduction then provides a brief historical background and focuses on the themes or questions to be discussed in the chapter.
- *Headnotes:* These are extensive introductions that explain in detail the historical or biographical background of each primary source. They also focus on themes and discuss interrelationships with other relevant primary sources.
- *Primary Sources:* The sources provided are diverse and include excerpts from drama and literature, short stories, speeches, letters, diary accounts, poems, newspaper articles, philosophical tracts, propaganda flyers, and works of art and architecture.
- *Study Questions:* A series of study questions conclude each source or chapter section and present a basis for oral discussion or written analysis. The study questions do not seek mere regurgitation of information but demand a more thoughtful response that is based on reflective analysis of the primary sources.

FEATURES AND INTEGRATED FORMAT

The study of history is necessarily an integrative experience. *Aspects of Western Civilization* provides insight into the interrelationships among art, music, literature, poetry, and architecture during various historical periods. Students are linked to relevant historical events, broader artistic movements, styles, and historiography through **four unique features** of the text:

1. *The Artistic Vision:* This feature emphasizes the creative processes and vision of an artist who embodies a dominant style of the period or

expresses the social or spiritual values of the age. This feature includes architecture as an expression of culture and presents a visual analysis of painting and sculpture, architectural floor plans, religious shrines, theaters, or other monuments that are important cultural expressions of a particular society.

2. ***Against the Grain:***   This feature focuses on those who don't fit or who are in conflict with their societies but embody the edge of creative change and set new artistic or historical parameters: the outsider, the radical mind, the free thinker. What impact does the individual have on the historical landscape? To what extent does progress depend on those who threaten the status quo and seek new directions outside the mainstream?

3. ***The Reflection in the Mirror:***   This feature offers an analysis of a focused moral or philosophical problem within a culture. It emphasizes the more abstract themes of progress and decline, arrogance and power, salvation, the impact of war and disease, the conflict between science and religion, the relationship between divinity and humanity, and the importance of human memory and creativity when juxtaposed with technological progress. This feature promotes thoughtful reflection at critical moments of change.

4. ***The Historian at Work:***   This is a feature of Volume 1 that provides a longer and more extensive analysis of the work of an historian who is a central source for our knowledge of the period. This feature allows students to view the creation of history by critically assessing method and understanding how the individual strengths and weaknesses of particular historians actually limit or enhance our perspective on the past and affect our assessment of truth.

USING *ASPECTS OF WESTERN CIVILIZATION*

Aspects of Western Civilization offers the instructor a wide variety of didactic applications. The primary purpose of the text is to develop in students a more refined sense of the value of history through a critical assessment of primary sources. Toward that end, *Aspects* is designed to supplement various textbooks

that provide a foundational historical narrative. Yet because of the introductory essays and detailed headnotes, *Aspects* provides an extensive historical framework so that student discussion and written analysis can always be achieved with perspective. The following suggestions should help instructors understand more clearly the full didactic structure and overriding intent of *Aspects of Western Civilization.*

Developing Historical Continuity: The chapters fit into a more or less standard lecture format and are ordered chronologically. There is a historical flow to each chapter that is structured from the outset with a ***Timeline*** for students who are more visual in their approach to learning. But each chapter is supplemented with an expanded ***Key Events chronology***. This is not just a list of dates, but a short explanation of the primary events of the historical period under discussion that should help the student focus information and gain clarity. The Key Events chronology is designed as a guidepost at appropriate moments in the chapter to act as a point of reference for a better understanding of historical periods and the essence of complex ideas.

Quotations: Presented at the beginning of each chapter or sometimes at the beginning of major chapter sections, the quotations are designed to spark interest and encourage class discussion as an intellectual supplement to the primary sources. Therefore, the quotations are selected for their controversial perspectives or their philosophical applicability to the historical themes at play in the chapter. They also demonstrate the eternal applicability of historical problems or issues across time. Several of the study questions refer to these quotations.

Study Questions: The study questions form the heart of this text and guide the student experience throughout. They are designed to establish a common foundation for discussion and critical assessment and to provide a framework for students to think and react in oral or written analysis. The study questions follow each source or chapter section and are divided into three separate types of questions, each numbered for easy reference and designed to develop a range of answers on several levels of complexity:

- *Consider This:* These questions are direct and pertain to individual sources. They are primarily designed to solicit specific information about the context and content of the primary source, and sometimes ask follow-up comparative questions that link sources. They are rather limited in focus but should provide a foundation for class discussion or a short paper. They demand some amount of regurgitation but do not neglect important analytical possibilities. This is how instructors can engage the discussion and easily determine the extent of student understanding.

- *The Broader Perspective:* These questions go beyond foundational information and frame the larger, more abstract problems and perspectives of historical analysis: moral responsibility, justifications of power, definitions of freedom, decline or progress. These questions are more complex and challenging, and they require more attention on the part of the instructor. But they stimulate discussions on a deeper level and seek to push students toward a more expansive awareness of the world around them.

- *Keep in Mind:* These questions occur at the beginning of primary sources contained only in the Features and help students analyze the source by providing a guidepost. They are designed to enhance discussion of a more complex topic.

The Written Assignment: Aspects of Western Civilization has been designed to promote both oral and written analysis. The study questions lend themselves to discussion, but the text has also been conceived as a vehicle for written assignments that are self-contained, are problem-oriented, promote reflection and analysis, and encourage responsible citation of particular primary sources.

- *The Short Paper:* This paper might run about two to four pages and might focus on particular primary sources, pulling from the "Consider This" questions or in combination with one or more "Broader Perspective" questions. Since each study question is numbered, instructors can easily assign various combinations to students that

would produce an engaged section analysis. This also works well for the framed debates in the Features: Students can focus on the historian Thucydides ("Bloodbath at Corcyra"), the artistic perspective of Eugène Delacroix ("The Greek Revolution of 1820"), perspectives on slavery with Olaudah Equiano and William Wilberforce ("The Horrors of the Slave Trade"), or freedom through the eyes of Nora Helmer in Ibsen's *A Doll's House* ("The Independent Woman").

- *The Term Paper:* For those instructors who are looking for a more extensive analysis of a topic or historical era, they might assign entire sections of particular chapters. For example, the chapter entitled "Democracy and Empire: The Golden Age of Athens" in Volume 1 is focused on the compatibility of democracy and empire: *From a moral standpoint, should a state that espouses freedom for all of its citizens control an empire that is maintained by fear and force? Is it even possible for a democratic government to rule an empire effectively? Finally, do the beauty and cultural worth of the monuments of a civilization justify the means of obtaining them? In other words, what price civilization?* These complex and abstract questions can be more easily understood by assigning the section on the Athenian Empire and choosing questions on specific sources like Pericles' Funeral Oration, the Mytilenian Debate, and the Melian Dialogue of Thucydides accompanied by the selection on *The Trojan Women* by Euripides. This could produce a longer paper of six to eight or eight to ten pages, depending on the selection. *Aspects* is also set up to produce thematic papers as well by comparing the treatment of women across time in the ancient, medieval, or Renaissance worlds; or by comparing the French and Russian revolutions; or by analyzing the Jewish Holocaust and the genocide in the Balkans during the 1990s.

Thematic Contents: Located after the table of contents, the Thematic Contents groups each primary source by chapter according to the seven themes listed in the Preface. Some sources are cross-referenced under multiple rubrics as application warrants. Sources are listed by author where appropriate and are grouped within each rubric according to their position in the chapter. The Thematic Contents allows instructors to assign discussion or written assignments along thematic lines across chapters and sections. For example, a comparative paper regarding women's roles or the treatment of women in different societies during the ancient, medieval, and modern worlds can be structured by identifying these sources in the Thematic Contents and assigning their accompanying study questions. Parenthetical citation of page numbers will establish credibility. Additional themes may be selected or blended to expand perspective.

NEW TO THIS EDITION

The seventh edition of *Aspects of Western Civilization* maintains a balanced coverage of historical periods while restructuring several chapters and enhancing coverage in particular areas. It also offers additional pedagogical resources for the instructor and guidance for students.

- *Structural Changes:* There are two new chapters in Volume 2 designed to help students better understand the development of nationalism and subsequent political unification movements during the nineteenth century ("Paths of Glory: Napoleon and the Romantic Movement" and "Fatherland: the Power of Nationalism"). Chapter 10 ("Fin de Siècle: The Birth of the Modern Era") has been restructured for greater continuity. There are also two new chapters added at the end of Volume 2 ("The Era of the Superpowers: Cold War Confrontation" and "The Dynamics of Change in the Contemporary World") in order to expand coverage of the Cold War from 1945 to 1990 and to focus in greater detail on events in the contemporary world from 1990 to 2010.

- *Enhanced Coverage:* Beyond the additional coverage from 1945 to 2010, several chapters in both volumes have been expanded to enhance the study of important topics: Hebrew prophets (Amos and Isaiah), early Greek literature (Sappho, Pindar, and Hesiod), values in the early and middle Roman Republic (Livy), and visions

of the New World (Thomas More and Michel de Montaigne) in Volume 1. Enhanced coverage in Volume 2 includes the American Declaration of Independence; Romantic poetry of Schiller, Goethe, and Byron; perspectives on the slave trade from Olaudah Equiano and William Wilberforce; additional nationalist sources from Alexis de Tocqueville and Theodor Herzl; and enhanced coverage of nineteenth-century feminist movements (Elizabeth Cady Stanton, Lucretia Mott, and Ibsen's *A Doll's House*). Several selections have also been added to the coverage of the Holocaust, and there are new sections on Serbian genocide in the Balkans in the 1990s, including the papal response. Coverage of the Cold War focuses on internal rebellion (Hungarian and Czechoslovakian revolutions), the Brezhnev Doctrine, and post–Cold War developments of Eastern European and Balkan states. Finally, a new section on the Islamic world and the West concentrates on economic relationships between Turkey and the European Union, and on Muslim relationships with France and the United States.

- *New Feature Selections:* Several new feature selections have been added to the seventh edition, including a new rubric in Volume 1 entitled "*The Historian at Work.*" This section introduces students to historiography as well as to critical method and provides longer excerpts from several of the most important historians of the ancient and medieval worlds (Herodotus, Thucydides, Livy, Tacitus, Josephus, Appian, and Usamah Ibn-Munqidh). New feature selections often focus on the integration of art and architecture into the political mainstream as revolutionary cultural elements (Giotto, Bernini and St. Peter's Basilica, Beethoven's Eroica Symphony, Francisco Goya and Napoleon, Eugène Delacroix and the Greek Revolution of 1820, the social perspective by train during the Industrial Revolution, the insular world of Edvard Munch, and the nightmare visions of Otto Dix during World War I). New features also include Theodor Herzl and the Zionist movement, excerpts from *A Doll's House* by Henrik Ibsen, Pope John Paul II on the

Serbian genocide, and President Obama's 2009 speech to the Muslim world in Egypt regarding "a new beginning" with the West.

- *New Pedagogical Aids:* Every effort has been made in the seventh edition to aid both instructors and students in using the text for discussions and class papers. **Opening chapter essays and introductions** to the primary sources have been reviewed and edited to establish a strong sense of historical continuity, and **study questions** have been clarified and refined to solicit specific information and to offer a broader perspective on the abstract implications of ideas and events. Additional **secondary sources** on the decline of the Roman Empire have been added and some questions on contending ideas under the rubric "Taking Sides" have been added. **Translations have been modernized** to clarify ideas and to bring older idioms into conformity with modern usage. **Study questions have been numbered** within each chapter for easier reference in class discussions and written assignments. **New Key Events chronologies** have been added to each chapter and placed near corresponding coverage. This should give students a solid historical reference point. Finally, a **new thematic table of contents** is available to instructors to assist in developing comparative ideas across time.

PEARSON mysearchlab www.mysearchlab.com Pearson's MySearchLab™ is the easiest way for students to start a research assignment or paper. Complete with extensive help on the research process and four databases of credible and reliable source material, MySearchLab helps students quickly and efficiently make the most of their research time.

ACKNOWLEDGMENTS

I would particularly like to thank friends and colleagues who contributed their expertise and enthusiasm to this book. Susan Altan lent her perspective and sensitive awareness of women's issues at critical moments when new avenues of thought were most needed. Daniel Hall and Thomas Tappan advised me on several scientific and technological matters that broadened the scope of the text immeasurably. Linda Swarlis and Mary Ann Leonard offered their unique perspectives regarding ethical issues, which often caused me to pause and certainly forced the introduction of new questions into the discussion. Marsha Ryan provided me with material and literary insight that added greatly to the accuracy of the text, and Jack Guy read drafts of some chapters, offering sterling commentary throughout. Thanks also to the students of Columbus School for Girls, who continue to test the chapters in this book with their typical diligence and hard work; the final product has benefited greatly from their suggestions and ideas. The following reviewers provided helpful suggestions and insights: Lisa Cox, Greenfield Community College, and Jessica Wyatt, Wilkes Community College. Finally, I owe an immeasurable debt to my wife, Ann, who suffered all the outrageous fortune and disruption that goes into writing a book of this kind over a period of years—she did it with me.

P. M. R.

Civilization in the Ancient Near East: Mesopotamia, Egypt, and Israel

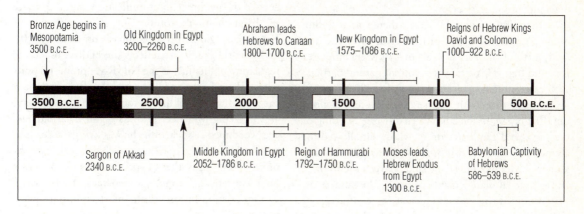

If a man destroy the eye of another man, they shall destroy his eye.

—Code of Hammurabi

You are a life span in yourself; one lives by you.

—Hymn to Aten

In the beginning, God created heaven and earth.

—Genesis 1:1

And what does the Lord require of you, but to do justly, and to love mercy, and to walk humbly with your God.

—Micah 6:8

CHAPTER THEMES

- **The Power Structure:** How did the monarchies in Mesopotamia, Egypt, and Israel differ from one another? What is the best form of government for primitive societies?

- **Social and Spiritual Values:** How did the belief systems of the ancient Near East contribute to the unity of society? In what ways were these societies primarily spiritual in nature? How radical a conception is monotheism?

- **Revolution and Historical Transition:** What were the main contributions of the early river valley societies to Western civilization? In what specific ways did civilization progress during this time?

- **The Big Picture:** What are the most important political, social, and spiritual characteristics that each society must possess in order to lay the foundations for the transmission of culture?

1

It is difficult to trace the origins of a culture and even more so to pinpoint the conditions that fostered the growth and development of Western civilization. Still, most historians agree that our contemporary world owes a great deal to the Near Eastern societies of Mesopotamia, Egypt, and Israel. We look to them for the conception of organized government, writing, law, complex religious ideas, and ethical values—the cornerstones of modern society.

Beginning about 3500 B.C.E., there was an influx of people into the region of the Fertile Crescent, the land north of the Persian Gulf that now encompasses Iran and Iraq. This area was devoid of natural barriers, such as mountain ranges, and so provided easy access for nomadic peoples. It was here that Western civilization first began, in the land watered by the flooding of the Tigris and Euphrates rivers, whose silt allowed for abundant harvests and prosperity. The region became known as Mesopotamia ("the land between the rivers"), and it fostered many distinct cultures. The Sumerians, who occupied the southern area at the confluence of the two rivers, assumed cultural leadership over the region by developing a syllabic writing script called cuneiform. Although conquerors would establish military control over the region, Sumerian literary and religious ideas and values proved a continuing influence.

Mesopotamia, at least initially, was organized on the basis of independent city-states. Each city had its own king and priests and conducted its own foreign policy, often in alliance with other city-states. The king's responsibilities included political and military leadership as well as supervision of the priests and their sacrifices to the gods. It is important to note that Mesopotamian kings were not considered to be divine themselves, but rather acted as representatives of the gods. The independence of the city-states often gave way to conquerors like Sargon the Great, who united the area briefly about 2300 B.C.E. Because of the open geographical access to the region, Mesopotamia was overrun by a succession of invaders, such as the Babylonians, Kassites, Assyrians, and finally Persians in the sixth century B.C.E. But the insecurity of the region did not limit the development of literature and law, which were its special contributions.

The second great civilization of the ancient Near East was Egypt. Whereas Mesopotamia suffered from the uncertainties of invasion and swift transition, Egypt was generally secure and isolated because of the surrounding, prohibitive deserts. Egypt remains a land with an aura of mystery, reinforced by a fascination for the colossal statues of Ramses II at Abu Simbel, the Temple of Karnak at Luxor, the overwhelming presence of the pyramids, mummification, and the wealth of Tutankhamon's tomb. But it is perhaps the Egyptian religion with its emphasis on death and the netherworld that most reflects the endless order and regulation of life. Just as the Nile River promotes unity within the country and its annual flooding symbolizes the recurring cycle of life, so too did the Pharaoh serve as a unifying presence. He was a god incarnate and was worshiped as such while he was living; in death he rose to the sky to be born anew each day with the cycle of the sun. Thus the Egyptians' close connection between state and religion, a theocracy of sorts, serves as a foundation for one of the more enduring themes in history.

Nowhere, however, did religion play a greater role than in the development of Hebrew civilization. The Hebrews were a nomadic people whose wanderings and eventual establishment in the so-called "promised land" of Canaan (modern-day Israel) form the narrative story of the Old Testament of the Bible. But more than this, the story concerns the relationship of Yahweh (or God) to his chosen people, the Hebrews. Many other Near Eastern conquerors held more land and ruled more people, but no one influenced the course of Western civilization more emphatically than the Hebrews. Their concern with moral law, right action, and adherence to monotheistic principles has formed the basis for Christianity and Islam in the modern world.

This chapter investigates the three main civilizations of the ancient Near East, with special concern for the relationships between kingship and religion. For it is through adherence to the principles of government and religion that society is ordered and civilization proceeds.

KEY EVENTS IN MESOPOTAMIAN HISTORY

3500 B.C.E.   The Bronze Age Begins
Bronze Age cultures develop in Mesopotamia, "the land between the rivers," soon followed in Egypt by about 3200 B.C.E.

3000 B.C.E.   The Sumerians
The first "Western" civilization develops in Sumeria, the southern portion of the Tigris and Euphrates River Valley near the mouth of the Persian Gulf. Sumerian culture advances with the development of writing and agriculture.

2340 B.C.E.   Sargon of Akkad
A Semitic king, Sargon of Akkad extends his empire over the city-state of Sumer to the "cedar forests of Lebanon," on the west coast of the Mediterranean.

2000 B.C.E.   The Epic of Gilgamesh
This is collection of stories about the Sumerian king of Uruk and is the first epic literature in Western civilization. Hittites, who were among the first to use iron, appear in Anatolia.

1792–1750 B.C.E.   Reign of Hammurabi
Hammurabi was the Amorite (Babylonian) king who ruled from Babylonia and established order in the region through the fullest and best-preserved law code extant from Mesopotamia.

Mesopotamian Civilization

The Reign of Sargon

The city-states that developed in the region of Mesopotamia after about 3500 B.C.E. were ruled by various kings who established local control. One of the first kings to conquer and control the region successfully was Sargon of Akkad, who ruled around 2300 B.C.E. The following excerpt from a tablet in the British Museum recounts his authority.

Sargon, King of Akkad, through the royal gift of Ishtar was exalted, and he possessed no foe nor rival. His glory over the world he poured out. The Sea in the East he crossed, and in the eleventh year the Country of the West in its full extent his hand subdued. He united them under one control; he set up his images in the West; their booty he brought over at his word. Over the hosts of the world he reigned supreme. Against Kassala he marched, and he turned Kassala into mounds and heaps of ruins; he destroyed the land and left not enough for a bird to rest thereon. Afterward in his old age all the lands revolted against him, and they besieged him in Akkad; and Sargon went forth to battle and defeated them; he accomplished their overthrow, and their wide-spreading host he destroyed. Afterward he attacked the land of Subartu in his might, and they submitted to his arms, and Sargon settled that revolt, and defeated them; he accomplished their overthrow, and their wide-spreading host he destroyed, and he brought their possessions into Akkad. The soil from the trenches of Babylon he removed, and the boundaries of Akkad he made like those of Babylon. But because of the evil which he had committed, the great lord Marduk was angry, and he destroyed his people by famine. From the rising of the sun unto the setting of the sun they opposed him and gave him no rest.

"The Reign of Sargon" is from George W. Botsford, ed., *A Source-Book of Ancient History* (New York: Macmillan, 1912), pp. 27–28.

The Code of Hammurabi

From 2000 to 1600 B.C.E., the city-states of Mesopotamia endured a period of nearly continuous warfare that saw shifting alliances and frequent chaos. The most dominant personality of the age, Hammurabi established his control over the region from about 1800 to 1750 B.C.E. and ruled from the city of Babylon. His great contribution to Western civilization was a series of laws that sought to establish justice within his empire. This concept of equity, which remedied a large number of abuses, influenced law codes yet to come, most notably those of Greece and Rome. In the following passages, note the continual emphasis on fairness in the regulation of property, trade, debt, family relations, and personal injury.

When the lofty Anu, king of the Anunnaki gods, and Enlil, lord of heaven and earth, he who determines the destiny of the land ... pronounced the lofty name of Babylon; when they made it famous among the quarters of the world and in its midst established an everlasting kingdom whose foundations were firm as heaven and earth; [they] . . . named me, Hammurabi, the exalted prince, the worshiper of the gods, to cause justice to prevail in the land, to destroy the wicked and the evil, to prevent the strong from oppressing the weak, to go forth like the sun over the black-headed people, to enlighten the land to further the welfare of the people. Hammurabi, the shepherd named by Enlil, am I, who brought about plenty and abundance; ... the powerful king, the sun of Babylon, who caused light to go forth over the lands of Sumer and Akkad; the king who caused the four quarters of the world to render obedience; the favorite of Ishtar, am I.

When Marduk sent me to rule the people and to bring help to the country, I established law and justice in the language of the land and promoted the welfare of the people. At that time [I decreed]:

1. If a man bring accusation against another man, charging him with murder, but cannot prove it, the accuser shall be put to death.
3. If a man bear false witness in a case, or does not establish the testimony that he has given, if that case be a case involving life, that man shall be put to death.
4. If he bear [false] witness concerning grain or money, he shall himself bear the penalty imposed in that case.
5. If a judge pronounce a judgment, render a decision, deliver a verdict duly signed and sealed, and afterward alter his judgment, they shall call that judge to account for the alteration of the judgment which he has pronounced, and he shall pay twelve-fold the penalty in that judgment; and, in the assembly, they shall expel him from his seat of judgment, and with the judges in a case he shall not take his seat.
22. If a man practice robbery and is captured, that man shall be put to death.
23. If the robber is not captured, the man who has been robbed shall, in the presence of god, make an itemized statement of his loss, and the city and the governor in whose province and jurisdiction the robbery was committed shall compensate him for whatever was lost.
24. If it be a life [that is lost], the city and governor shall pay one mina [about one pound] of silver to his heirs.
53. If a man neglects to maintain his dike and does not strengthen it, and a break is made in his dike and the water carries away the farmland, the man in whose dike the break has been made shall replace the grain which has been damaged.
54. If he is not able to replace the grain, they shall sell him and his goods, and the farmers whose

"The Code of Hammurabi" is from Robert F. Harper, trans., *The Code of Hammurabi* (Chicago: University of Chicago Press, 1904).

grain the water has carried away shall divide [the results of the sale].

55. If a man opens his canal for irrigation and neglects it and the water carries away an adjacent field, he shall pay out grain on the basis of the adjacent field.

109. If bad characters gather in the house of a wine seller and he does not arrest those bad characters and bring them to the palace, that wine seller shall be put to death.

110. If a priestess who is not living in a convent opens a wine shop or enters a wine shop for a drink, they shall burn that woman.

117. If a man be in debt and sell his wife, son, or daughter, or bind them over to service, for three years they shall work in the house of their purchaser or master; in the fourth year they shall be given their freedom.

128. If a man takes a wife and does not arrange a contract for her, that woman is not a wife.

129. If the wife of a man is caught lying with another man, they shall bind them and throw them into the water.

138. If a man wishes to put away his wife who has not borne him children, he shall give her money to the amount of her marriage price and he shall make good to her the dowry which she brought from her father's house and then he may put her away.

142. If a woman hates her husband and says, "You may not have me," the city council shall inquire into her case; and if she has been careful and without reproach and her husband has been going about and greatly belittling her, that woman has no blame. She may take her dowry and go to her father's house.

143. If she has not been careful but has gadded about, neglecting her house and belittling her husband, they shall throw that woman into the water.

168. If a man set his face to disinherit his son and say to the judges, "I will disinherit my son," the judges shall inquire into his record, and if the son has not committed a crime sufficiently grave to cut him off from sonship, the father may not cut off his son from sonship.

195. If a son strike his father, they shall cut off his hand.

196. If a man destroy the eye of another man, they shall destroy his eye.

197. If he break another man's bone, they shall break his bone.

199. If he destroy the eye of a man's slave or break a bone of a man's slave, he shall pay one-half his price.

200. If a man knock out a tooth of a man of his own rank, they shall knock out his tooth.

229. If a builder build a house for a man and does not make its construction sound, and the house which he has built collapses and causes the death of the owner of the house, that builder shall be put to death.

233. If a builder build a house for a man and does not make its construction sound, and a wall cracks, that builder shall strengthen that wall at his own expense.

[These are] the just laws which Hammurabi, the wise king, established and by which he gave the land stable support and good government. Hammurabi, the perfect king, am I. . . .

The great gods called me, and I am the guardian shepherd whose scepter is just and whose beneficent shadow is spread over my city. In my bosom I carried the people of the land of Sumer and Akkad; under my protection they prospered; I governed them in peace; in my wisdom I sheltered them.

In order that the strong might not oppress the weak, that justice be given to the orphans and the widow, in Babylon, . . . for the pronouncing of judgments in the land, for the rendering of decisions for the land, and to give justice to the oppressed, my weighty words I have written upon my monument, and in the presence of my image as king of justice have I established it.

CONSIDER THIS:

1-1. In the preface to the "Code of Hammurabi," why does Hammurabi feel justified in setting forth this law code? What are some of the penalties? Do they seem too harsh to be fair? Why is a law code such as this a sign of progress in civilization?

The Epic of Gilgamesh

The Sumerians who inhabited the southern region of Mesopotamia were the first people in Western civilization to produce epic tales about deities and human heroes. *The Epic of Gilgamesh* dates from about 2000 B.C.E. and is a collection of stories about the Sumerian king of Uruk. In the following passages, Gilgamesh, confronted with the reality of his friend Enkidu's death, sets out to find Utnapishtim, the only man to whom the gods have given eternal life. Gilgamesh discovers that he must accept the inevitability of his own death.

There follows the Mesopotamian tale of the Flood and the biblical account contained in the Old Testament. Flood epics were quite common in ancient literature and represented a cleansing of the community in accordance with a higher ethical law. But compare the two accounts closely, especially with regard to the attitudes and actions of the deities.

The Quest for Eternal Life

Bitterly Gilgamesh wept for his friend Enkidu; he wandered over the wilderness as a hunter, he roamed over the plains; in his bitterness he cried, "How can I rest, how can I be at peace? Despair is in my heart. What my brother is now, that shall I be when I am dead. Because I am afraid of death I will go as best I can to find Utnapishtim whom they call the Faraway, for he has entered the assembly of the gods." So Gilgamesh traveled over the wilderness, he wandered over the grasslands, a long journey, in search of Utnapishtim, whom the gods took after the deluge; and they set him to live in the land of Dilmun, in the garden of the sun; and to him alone of men they gave everlasting life. . . .

Gilgamesh said to him [Utnapishtim], "Why should not my cheeks be starved and my face drawn? Despair is in my heart and my face is the face of one who has made a long journey. It was burned with heat and with cold. Why should I not wander over the pastures? My friend, my younger brother who seized and killed the Bull of Heaven and overthrew Humbaba in the cedar forest, my friend who was very dear to me and endured dangers beside me, Enkidu, my brother whom I loved, the end of mortality has overtaken him. I wept for him seven days and nights till the worm fastened on him. Because of my brother I am afraid of death; because of my brother I stray through the wilderness. His fate lies heavy upon me. How can I be silent, how can I rest? He is dust and I shall die also and be laid in the earth for ever. . . . Oh, father Utnapishtim, you who

have entered the assembly of the gods, I wish to question you concerning the living and the dead, how shall I find the life for which I am searching?"

Utnapishtim said, "There is no permanence. Do we build a house to stand for ever, do we seal a contract to hold for all time? Do brothers divide an inheritance to keep for ever, does the flood-time of rivers endure? It is only the nymph of the dragon-fly who sheds her larva and sees the sun in his glory. From the days of old there is no permanence. The sleeping and the dead, how alike they are, they are like a painted death. What is there between the master and the servant when both have fulfilled their doom? When the Annunaki, the judges, come together, and Mammetun the mother of destinies, together they decree the fates of men. Life and death they allot but the day of death they do not disclose." . . .

The destiny was fulfilled which the father of the gods, Enlil of the mountain, had decreed for Gilgamesh: "In nether-earth the darkness will show him a light; of mankind, all that are known, none will leave a monument for generations to come to compare with his. The heroes, the wise men, like the new moon have their waxing and waning. Men will say, 'Who has ever ruled with might and with power like him?' As in the dark month, the month of shadows, so without him there is no light. O Gilgamesh, this was the meaning of your dream. You were given the kingship, such was your destiny, everlasting life was not your destiny. Because of this do not be sad at heart, do not be grieved or oppressed; he has given you power to bind and to loose, to be the darkness and the light of mankind. He has given unexampled supremacy over the people, in victory in battle from which no fugitive returns, in forays and assaults from which there is no going back. But do not abuse this power, deal justly with your servants in the palace, deal justly with the face of the Sun."

The Story of the Flood

Then Gilgamesh said to Utnapishtim, the Faraway, "I look at you now, Utnapishtim, and your appearance is no different than mine; there is nothing strange in your features. . . . Tell me truly, how was it that you came to enter the company of the gods and to possess everlasting life?" Utnapishtim said to Gilgamesh, "I will reveal to you a mystery, I will tell you a secret of the gods."

"You know the city Shurrupak, it stands on the banks of Euphrates? That city grew old and the gods that were in it were old. There was Anu, lord of the firmament, their father, and warrior Enlil their counselor, Ninurta the helper, and Ennugi watcher over canals; and with them also was Ea. In those days the world teemed, the people multiplied, the world bellowed like a wild bull, and the great god was aroused by the clamor. Enlil heard the clamor and he said to the gods in council, 'The uproar of mankind is intolerable and sleep is no longer possible by reason of the babel.' So the gods in their hearts were moved to let loose the deluge; but my lord Ea warned me in a dream. He whispered their words to my house of reeds, 'Reed-house, reed-house! Wall, O wall, hearken reed-house, wall reflect; O man of Shurrupak, son of Ubara-Tutu; tear down your house and build a boat, abandon possessions and look for life, despise worldly goods and save your soul alive. . . . These are the measurements of the barque as you shall build her: let her beam equal her length, let her deck be roofed like the vault that covers the abyss; then take up into the boat the seed of all living creatures.'

"When I had understood I said to my lord, 'Behold, what you have commanded I will honor and perform, but how shall I answer the people, the city, the elders?' Then Ea opened his mouth and said to me, his servant, 'Tell them this: I have learnt that Enlil is wrathful against me, I dare no longer walk in his land

nor live in his city; I will go down to the Gulf to dwell with Ea my lord. But on you he will rain down abundance, rare fish and shy wild-fowl, a rich harvest-tide. In the evening the rider of the storm will bring you wheat in torrents.'

"In the first light of dawn all my household gathered round me, the children brought pitch and the men whatever was necessary. . . . On the seventh day the boat was complete. . . .

"I loaded into her all that I had of gold and of living things, my family, my kin, the beasts of the field both wild and tame, and all the craftsmen. I sent them on board, for the time that Shamash had ordained was already fulfilled when he said, 'In the evening, when the rider of the storm sends down the destroying rain, enter the boat and batten her down.' This time was fulfilled, the evening came, the rider of the storm sent down the rain. I looked out at the weather and it was terrible, so I too boarded the boat and battened her down. . . .

"With the first light of dawn a black cloud came from the horizon. . . . One whole day the tempest raged gathering fury as it went, it poured over the people like the tides of battle; a man could not see his brother nor the people be seen from heaven. Even the gods were terrified at the flood, they fled to the highest heaven, the firmament of Anu; they crouched against the walls, cowering like curs. . . . The great gods of heaven and of hell wept, they covered their mouths.

"For six days and six nights the winds blew, torrent and tempest and flood overwhelmed the world, tempest and flood raged together like warring hosts. When the seventh day dawned the storm from the south subsided, the sea grew calm, the flood was stilled; I looked at the face of the world and there was silence, all mankind was turned to clay. The surface of the sea stretched as flat as a roof-top; I opened a hatch and the light fell on my face. Then I bowed low, I sat down and I wept, the tears streamed down my face, for on every side was the waste of water. . . . I threw everything open to the four winds, made a sacrifice and poured out a libation on the mountain top. . . . When the gods smelled the sweet savor, they gathered like flies over the sacrifice. . . .

"When Enlil had come, when he saw the boat, he was wrath and swelled with anger at the gods, the host of heaven, 'Has any of these mortals escaped? Not one was to have survived the destruction.' . . . Then Ea opened his mouth and spoke to warrior Enlil, 'Wisest of gods, hero Enlil, how could you so senselessly bring down the flood?

> 'Lay upon the sinner his sin,
> Lay upon the transgressor his transgression,
> Punish him a little when he breaks loose,
> Do not drive him too hard or he perishes;
> Would that a lion had ravaged mankind
> Rather than the flood,
> Would that a wolf had ravaged mankind
> Rather than the flood,
> Would that famine had wasted the world
> Rather than the flood,

> Would that pestilence had wasted mankind
> Rather than the flood.

It was not I that revealed the secret of the gods; the wise man learned it in a dream. Now take your counsel what shall be done with him.'

"Then Enlil went up into the boat, he took me by the hand and my wife and made us enter the boat and kneel down on either side, he standing between us. He touched our foreheads to bless us saying, 'In time past Utnapishtim was a mortal man; henceforth he and his wife shall live in the distance at the mouth of the rivers.' Thus it was that the gods took me and placed me here to live in the distance at the mouth of the rivers."

The Biblical Flood

God said to Noah, 'I have decided that the end has come for all living things, for the earth is full of lawlessness because of human beings. So I am now about to destroy them and the earth. Make yourself an ark out of resinous wood. Make it of reeds and caulk it with pitch inside and out. This is how to make it: the length of the ark is to be three hundred cubits, its breadth fifty cubits, and its height thirty cubits. . . .

'For my part, I am going to send the flood, the waters, on earth, to destroy living things having the breath of life under heaven: everything on earth is to perish. But with you I shall establish my covenant and you will go aboard the ark, yourself, your sons, your wife, and your sons' wives along with you. From all living creatures, from all living things, you must take two of each kind aboard the ark, to save their lives with yours; they must be a male and a female. Of every species of bird, of every kind of animal and of every kind of creature that creeps along the ground, two must go with you so that their lives may be saved. . . .' Noah did this, exactly as God commanded him. . . .

The flood lasted forty days on earth. The waters swelled, lifting the ark until it floated off the ground. . . . The waters rose higher and higher above the ground until all the highest mountains under the whole of heaven were submerged. . . . Every living

thing on the face of the earth was wiped out, people, animals, creeping things and birds; they were wiped off the earth and only Noah was left, and those with him in the ark. . . .

Then God said to Noah, 'Come out of the ark, you, your wife, your sons, and your sons' wives with you. Bring out all the animals with you, all living things. . . .' Then Noah built an altar to Yahweh and, choosing from all the clean animals and all the clean birds, he presented burnt offerings on the altar. Yahweh smelt the pleasing smell and said to himself, 'Never again will I curse the earth because of human beings, because their heart contrives evil from their infancy. Never again will I strike down every living thing as I have done. . . .' God blessed Noah and his sons and said to them, 'Breed, multiply and fill the earth.'

CONSIDER THIS:

1-2. What makes "*The Epic of Gilgamesh*" such an enduring story? Compare the two accounts of the Flood. Which account do you find more vivid or exciting? What are the reasons given for the Flood and what does it signify? Compare especially the roles of the deities. How does God of the Old Testament differ in manner and action from Enlil or Ea?

"The Biblical Flood" is from Genesis 6:13–9:1, from Alexander Jones, ed., *The Jerusalem Bible*, pp. 24–26. Copyright © 1966 by Darton, Longman & Todd, Ltd., and Doubleday, a division of Bantam, Doubleday, Dell Publishing Group, Inc. Reprinted by permission.

KEY EVENTS IN EGYPTIAN HISTORY

3200 B.C.E.   The Bronze Age in Egypt
Bronze Age cultures develop in Egypt, "the gift of the Nile."

3200–2260 B.C.E.   The Old Kingdom
Upper and Lower Egypt become unified under strong pharaonic authority. This is a secure, progressive period as reflected by the building of the pyramids, examples of great monumental architecture.

2052–1786 B.C.E.   The Middle Kingdom
Pharaonic authority was reestablished after civil war among nomarchs (regional governors) called the First Intermediate Period.

1575–1086 B.C.E.   The New Kingdom
After order is reestablished following the Second Intermediate Period, the New Kingdom is an era of Egyptian expansion and authority throughout the eastern Mediterranean, led by conquerors Thutmosis III (1490–1436 B.C.E.) and Ramses II (1301–1234 B.C.E.).

1367–1350 B.C.E.   The Reign of Akhenaten
The enigmatic Akhenaten disrupts this traditional culture by adopting monotheism and worship of the solar deity, Aten. His successor, King Tutankhamon, restores traditional polytheism but dies ca. 1350 B.C.E. at about nineteen years old. His unopened tomb, filled with artifacts and treasure, is discovered in 1922 by the archeologist, Howard Carter, who methodically catalogued the contents.

1287 B.C.E.   Battle of Cadesh
Massive confrontation between Egypt (Ramses the Great) and the Hittite Empire marks the beginning of decline for both powers.

1188 B.C.E.   Invasion of the "Sea Peoples"
A Massive attack on Egypt, repelled with great difficulty. Egyptian records on palace walls record invasion of "Sea Peoples" (Peleset). Could the "Sea Peoples" be Dorian invaders from north of Greece? Was the destruction of the Hittites and Egyptians the result of one invader, who also destroyed the Mycenaean settlements, or of several peoples on the move?

Egyptian Civilization

The Authority of the Pharaohs

The king of Egypt, or Pharaoh (meaning "Great House"), possessed an authority rarely achieved in World Civilization. He was regarded as a god incarnate who upon death rose to take his place in the sky as the deity Horus. In the Old Kingdom (3200–2260 B.C.E.), pharaonic authority was great, and the pyramids were built to house the body of the dead king. Egyptians considered preservation of the body essential for use in the afterlife, so they perfected the art of mummification. The following selections from the Greek historian Herodotus show the great authority of the Pharaoh in the Old Kingdom. Herodotus describes the commitment demanded by Cheops, for whom the Great Pyramid is named. An account of the process of mummification follows.

Building the Pyramids

HERODOTUS

After Cheops had ascended the throne, he brought the country into every manner of evil. First closing all the temples, he forbade sacrificing there, then ordered all the Egyptians to work for him. Some he told to draw stones from the quarries in the Arabian mountains about the Nile; others were ordered to receive them after they had been carried over the river in boats, and to draw them to the Libyan mountains. And they worked in groups of 100,000 men, each group for three months continually. Ten years of oppression for the people were required for making the causeway by which they dragged the stones. This causeway which they built was not a much inferior work to the pyramid itself, as it seems to me; . . . it is made of polished stones and engraved with the figures of living beings. Ten years were required for this, and for the works on the mound, where the pyramids stand, and for the underground chambers in the island, which he intended as sepulchral vaults for his own use, and lastly for the canal which he dug from the Nile. The pyramid was built in 20 years; it is square; each side measures 800 feet and its height is the same; the stones are polished and fitted together with the utmost exactness. Not one of them is less than 30 feet in length.

The pyramid was built in steps, in the manner of an altar. After laying the base, they lifted the remaining stones to their places by means of machines, made of short pieces of wood. The first machine raised them from the ground to the top of the first step; and when the stone had been lifted thus far, it was drawn to the top of the second step by another machine; for they had as many machines as steps. . . . At any rate, the highest parts were finished first, then the next, and so on till they came to the parts resting on the ground, namely the base. It is set down in Egyptian writing on the pyramid how much was spent on radishes and leeks and onions for the workmen; and I remember well the interpreter read the sum of 1600 talents of silver. Now if these figures are correct, how much more must have been spent on the iron with which they worked, and on the food and clothing of the workmen, considering the length of time which the work lasted, and an additional period, as I understand, during which they cut and brought the stones, and made the excavations.

Mummification

HERODOTUS

There are a set of men in Egypt who practice the art of embalming, and make it their proper business. These persons, when a body is brought to them, show the bearers various models of corpses made in wood, and painted so as to resemble nature. . . . The mode of embalming, according to the most perfect process, is the following: They take first a crooked piece of iron, and with it draw out the brain through the nostrils, thus getting rid of a portion, while the skull is cleared of the rest by rinsing with drugs; next they make a cut along the flank with a sharp Ethiopian stone, and take out the whole contents of the abdomen, which they then cleanse, washing it thoroughly with palm wine, and again frequently with an infusion of pounded aromatics. After this they fill the cavity with the purest bruised myrrh, with cassia, and every other sort of spice, except frankincense, and sew up the opening. Then the body is placed in natron [hydrated sodium carbonate] for seventy days, and covered entirely over. After the expiration of that space of time, which must not be exceeded, the body is washed, and wrapped round, from head to foot, with bandages of fine linen cloth, smeared over with gum, which is used generally by the Egyptians in the place of glue, and in this state

"Building the Pyramids" is from Herodotus, *History*, 2.124, in George W. Botsford, ed. *A Source-Book of Ancient History* (New York: Macmillan, 1912), pp. 6–8.

"Mummification" is from Herodotus, *History*, 2.86, 87, 90, in George Rawlinson, trans., *The History of Herodotus* (New York: E. P. Dutton, 1910), pp. 154–156.

it is given back to the relations, who enclose it in a wooden case which they have had made for the purpose, shaped into the figure of a man. Then fastening the case, they place it in a sepulchral chamber, upright against the wall. Such is the most costly way of embalming the dead.

If persons wish to avoid expense, and choose the second process, the following is the method pursued: Syringes are filled with oil made from the cedar-tree, which is then, without any incision or disemboweling, injected into the abdomen. The passage by which it might be likely to return is stopped, and the body laid in natron the prescribed number of days. At the end of the time the cedar-oil is allowed to make its escape; and such is its power that it brings with it the whole stomach and intestines in a liquid state. The natron meanwhile has dissolved the flesh, and so nothing is left of the dead body but the skin and the bones. It is returned in this condition to the relatives, without any further trouble being bestowed upon it.

The third method of embalming, which is practiced in the case of the poorer classes, is to rinse out the intestines and let the body lie in natron the seventy days, after which it is at once given to those who come to fetch it away. . . .

Whenever any one, Egyptian or foreigner, has lost his life by falling prey to a crocodile, or by drowning in the river, the law compels the inhabitants of the city near which the body is cast up to have it embalmed, and to bury it in one of the sacred repositories with all possible magnificence. No one may touch the corpse, not even any of the friends or relatives, but only the priests of the Nile, who prepare it for burial with their own hands—regarding it as something more than the mere body of a man—and themselves lay it in the tomb.

Ramses the Great

Ramses II (1301–1234 B.C.E.) was one of the greatest of all Egyptian Pharaohs. His reign has been immortalized by his magnificent construction projects, such as the temple of Karnak at Luxor and the enormous statues of Abu Simbel. In addition, his fame is recorded in the Old Testament as the Pharaoh under whom the Exodus of the Hebrews took place. His mummy has been remarkably well preserved; we can tell that he died in his nineties and that he suffered from acne, tuberculosis, and poor circulation of the blood. His tomb had been plundered by ancient grave robbers, and one can only imagine its former gold and splendor. The following passage is from an inscription found on the temple at Abu Simbel. In it, the god Ptah speaks to his son, Ramses.

Thus speaks Ptah-Totunen with the high plumes, armed with horns, the father of the gods, to his son who loves him. . . .

Num and Ptah have nourished your childhood, they leap with joy when they see you made after my likeness, noble, great, exalted. The great princesses of the house of Ptah and the Hathors of the temple of Tem are in festival, their hearts are full of gladness, their hands take the drum with joy, when they see your person beautiful and lovely like my Majesty. . . . King Ramses, I grant you to cut the mountains into statues immense, gigantic, everlasting; I grant that foreign lands find for you precious stone to inscribe the monuments with thy name.

I give you to succeed in all the works which you have done. I give you all kinds of workmen, all that goes on two or four feet, all that flies and all that has wings. I have put in the heart of all nations to offer you what they have done; themselves, princes great and small, with one heart seek to please you, King Ramses. You have built a great residence to fortify the boundary of the land, the city of Ramses; it is established on the

"Ramses the Great" is from George W. Botsford, ed., *A Source-Book of Ancient History* (New York: Macmillan, 1912), pp. 10–12. Translation modernized by the editor.

FIGURE 1.1 The temple of Ramses II at Abu Simbel is remarkable for its four colossal figures of the Pharaoh. They reflect the great authority of the famous Egyptian king (*Eugene Gordon/Pearson Education/Prentice Hall College*).

earth like the four pillars of the sky; you have constructed within a royal palace, where festivals are celebrated to you as is done for me within. I have set the crown on your head with my own hands, when you appear in the great hall of the double throne; and men and gods have praised your name like mine when my festival is celebrated.

You have carved my statues and built my shrines as I have done in times of old. You reign in my place on my throne; I fill your limbs with life and happiness, I am behind you to protect you; I give you health and strength; I cause Egypt to be submitted to you; and I supply the two countries with pure life. King Ramses, I grant that the strength, the vigor, and the might of your sword be felt among all countries; you cast down the hearts of all nations; I have put them under your feet; you come forth every day in order that foreign prisoners be brought to you; the chiefs and the great of all nations offer you their children. I give them to your gallant sword that you may do with them what you like. King Ramses, I grant that the fear of you be in the minds of all and your command in their hearts. I grant that your valor reach all countries, and that the dread of you be spread over all lands; the princes tremble at your thought, and your majesty is [evident]; they come to you as supplicants to implore your mercy. You give life to whomever you please; the throne of all nations is in your possession. . . .

King Ramses, ... the mountains, the water, and the stone walls which are on the earth are shaken when they hear your excellent name, since they have seen what I have accomplished for you; which is that the land of the Hittites should be subjected to your rule.... Their chiefs are prisoners, all their property is the tribute in the dependency of the living king. Their royal daughter is at the head of them; she comes to soften the heart of King Ramses; her merits are marvelous, but she does not know the goodness which is in your heart.

CONSIDER THIS:

1-3. Kingship and authority are major themes in ancient Near Eastern civilization. What do the readings reveal as being true indicators of the authority of the Egyptian Pharaoh?

THEME: THE POWER STRUCTURE

THE ARTISTIC VISION

The Great Pyramids of Egypt

The pyramid complex at Giza just outside of Cairo, Egypt, was considered to be one of the Seven Wonders of the ancient world. The Great Pyramid of Cheops is over 481 feet high, and its base covers about 13 acres. It is composed of 2,300,000 stone blocks averaging 2.5 tons each, and they were cut to within 1/50 of an inch. The stone was harvested from quarries miles up the Nile and floated down the river, where they were then moved on log rollers and sledges and pulled up ramps by thousands of workers to be set in place. This was truly an application of mathematics on the ultimate scale.

FIGURE 1.2 The Great Pyramids of Egypt (*Egyptian Tourist Authority*)

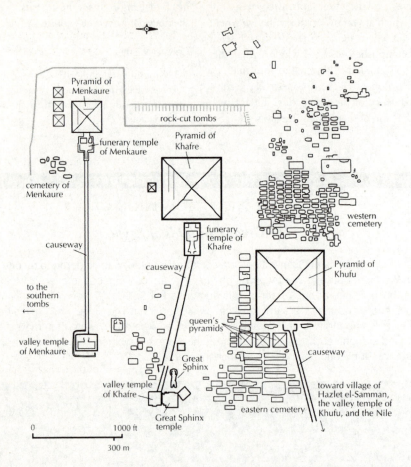

FIGURE 1.3 Diagram of the Pyramid Complex at Giza (*Pearson Education/Prentice Hall College*)

CONSIDER THIS:

1-4. How were the pyramids both religious monuments and testaments to the political power of the pharaoh in the Old Kingdom? What is a theocracy? Why did the pharaohs of the later Middle and New Kingdoms have rock tombs rather than pyramids built for themselves? What had changed—the religious values of the society or the political authority of the pharaoh?

THE BROADER PERSPECTIVE:

1-5. In the year 1682, the illustrious French divine-right monarch, Louis XIV, commented about his new palace at Versailles: "Those who imagine that these are merely matters of ceremony are gravely mistaken. The peoples over whom we reign, being able to apprehend the basic reality of things, usually derive their opinion from what they can see with their eyes." Was Louis correct? How important was it for a pharaoh or an absolute monarch to overawe his subjects and foreign kings alike with the majesty of architecture? Would you say the same holds true for the monuments to American democracy in Washington, D.C.?

Egyptian Religion and Values

Egyptian literature abounds with didactic writings intended to instruct an individual on right action or proper conduct in life. A sense of "limit" and thoughtful discretion pervades the following suggestions to a royal administrator named Kagemni from a sage whose identity is unknown. These maxims were found on a piece of papyrus dating from the Old Kingdom.

Instructions of Kagemni

The respectful man prospers,
Praised is the modest one,
The tent is open to the silent,
The seat of the quiet is spacious.
Do not chatter!
Knives are sharp against the blunderer,
Without hurry except when he faults.

When you sit with company,
Shun the food you love,
Restraint is a brief moment,
Gluttony is base and is reproved.
A cup of water quenches thirst,
A mouthful of herbs strengthens the heart,
One good thing stands for goodness,
A little something stands for much.
Vile is he whose belly covets when [meal]-time
    has passed,
He forgets those in whose house his belly roams.

When you sit with a glutton,
Eat when his greed has passed,
When you drink with a drunkard,
Take when his heart is content.
Don't fall upon meat by the side of a glutton,

Take when he gives you, don't refuse it,
Then it will soothe.
He who is blameless in matters of food,
No word can prevail against him;
He who is gentle, even timid,

The harsh is kinder to him than to his mother,
All people are his servants.
Let your name go forth,
While your mouth is silent,
When you are summoned, don't boast of
    strength
Among those your age, lest you be opposed.
One knows not what may happen,
What god does when he punishes.

The vizier had his children summoned, after he had understood the ways of men, their character having become clear to him. Then he said to them: "All that is written in this book, heed it as I said it. Do not go beyond what has been set down." Then they placed themselves on their bellies. They recited it as it was written. It seemed good to them beyond anything in the whole land.

The Pyramid Texts

The "Pyramid Texts" date from the Old Kingdom and were carved on the walls of the sarcophagus chambers of the pyramids at Saqqara. They were discovered in 1881, and their purpose was to promote the resurrection of the Pharaoh from the dead. Each utterance is

"Instructions of Kagemni" is from Miriam Lichtheim, trans. and ed., *Ancient Egyptian Literature: A Book of Readings*, vol. 1 (Berkeley: University of California Press, 1973), pp. 59–60. © 1973 The Regents of the University of California. Reprinted by permission.

Poems from the *Pyramid Texts* are from Miriam Lichtheim, trans. and ed., *Ancient Egyptian Literature: A Book of Readings*, vol. 1 (Berkeley: University of California Press, 1973), pp. 44, 49–50. Copyright © 1973 The Regents of the University of California. Reprinted by permission.

separated from the others by dividing lines and thus represents a self-contained prayer. The following incantations are from the pyramids of Pepi I, a king in the Sixth Dynasty (ca. 2400 B.C.E.).

The Pharaoh Prays for Admittance to the Sky

Awake in peace, O Pure One, in peace!
Awake in peace, Horus-of-the-East, in peace!
Awake in peace, Soul-of-the-East, in peace!
Awake in peace, Horus-of-Lightland, in peace!
You lie down in the Night-bark,
You awake in the Day-bark,
For you are he who gazes on the gods,
There is no god who gazes on you!

O father of Pepi, take Pepi with you
Living, to you mother Nut!
Gates of sky, open for Pepi,
Gates of heaven, open for Pepi,
Pepi comes to you, make him live!
Command that this Pepi sit beside you,
Beside him who rises in lightland!
O father of Pepi, command to the goddess
    beside you
To make wide Pepi's seat at the stairway of
    heaven!
Command the Living One, the son of Sothis,
To speak for this Pepi,
To establish for Pepi a seat in the sky!
Commend this Pepi to the Great Noble,

The beloved of Ptah, the son of Ptah,
To speak for this Pepi,
To make flourish his jar-stands on earth,
For Pepi is one with these four gods:
Imsety, Hapy, Duamutef, Kebhsenuf,
Who live by maat [truth],
Who lean on their staffs,
Who watch over Upper Egypt.

He flies, he flies from you as do ducks,
He wrests his arms from you as a falcon,
He tears himself from you as a kite,
Pepi frees himself from the fetter of earth,
Pepi is released from bondage!

The Pharaoh Prays to the Sky Goddess

O Great One who became Sky,
You are strong, you are mighty,
You fill every place with your beauty,
The whole earth is beneath you, you possess it!
As you enfold earth and all things in your arms,
So have you taken this Pepi to you,
An indestructible star within you!

The Book of the Dead: Negative Confession

The Book of the Dead is a collection of texts dating from the Middle and New Kingdoms that reflect a growing concern for the welfare of the dead and their search for eternal happiness. The Egyptians believed that on death, one was judged by Osiris, god of the underworld, who determined one's fate on the basis of truth (maat) and moral purity. The "negative confession" that follows was part of the summation of one's life in the presence of Osiris. The emphasis is not on one's positive accomplishments in life, but rather on the unrighteous acts that were not committed—hence the term "negative confession." The following selection is from the tomb of Nu, an administrator of the Eighteenth Dynasty (1570–1085 B.C.E.).

"The Book of the Dead: Negative Confession" is from E. A. Wallace Budge, trans., *The Book of the Dead According to the Theban Recension* (New York: E. P. Dutton, 1922), Ch. 125.

Homage to thee, O Great God [Osiris], . . . I have come to thee, O my Lord, I have brought myself hither that I may behold thy beauties. . . . In truth I have come to thee, and I have brought *maat* to thee, and I have expelled wickedness for thee.

1. I have not done evil to mankind.
2. I have not oppressed the members of my family.
3. I have not wrought evil in the place of right and truth.
4. I have had no knowledge of worthless men.
7. I have not brought forward my name for exaltation to honors.
8. I have not ill-treated servants.
9. I have not belittled a god.
10. I have not defrauded the oppressed one of his property.
11. I have not done that which is an abomination unto the gods.
14. I have made no man to suffer hunger.
15. I have made no one to weep.
16. I have done no murder.
17. I have not given the order for murder to be done for me.
18. I have not inflicted pain upon mankind.
22. I have not committed fornication.
26. I have not encroached upon the fields of others.
29. I have not carried away the milk from the mouths of children.
30. I have not driven away the cattle which were upon their pastures.
38. I have not obstructed a god in his procession. I am pure! I am pure! I am pure! I am pure!

CONSIDER THIS:

1-6. Compare the selections from the "Pyramid Texts" and *The Book of the Dead*. When were they written and what were they expected to accomplish? Can you draw any conclusions from your analysis? What do your conclusions say about Egyptian religion? Explain the term *negative confession*. What is the rationale behind this practice?

1-7. Compare Egyptian and Mesopotamian views of religion by analyzing the various views on the nature of the gods, death, and the afterlife shown in the selections. What general conclusions can you draw?

1-8. The geography of a region often influences the development of a civilization. In what ways did geography influence the religious outlooks of Mesopotamia and Egypt?

THEME: REVOLUTION AND HISTORICAL TRANSITION

AGAINST THE GRAIN

The Amarna Revolution

The Hymn to Aten

AKHENATEN

Egyptian civilization was noted for its tradition, respect for authority, and unchanging cycles, which gave unity and stability to the land for thousands of years. Yet one of the most radical changes in this pattern took place briefly during the reign of Amenhotep IV (1372–1355 B.C.E.). He changed the very essence of Egyptian religion by eliminating the several gods and goddesses that were the basis for Egyptian polytheism. He replaced them with one god, a solar disk he called Aten. In accordance with these new principles, Amenhotep IV ("Amon rests") changed his name to Akhenaten ("Aten is satisfied") and constructed a new capitol at Amarna. Systematically, the names of the old gods were erased from temple walls and public inscriptions. All worship was to be directed toward Aten, a universal deity. Thus Akhenaten sacrificed his own divinity to promote himself as the son and interpreter of Aten. The following prayer to Aten is the quintessential expression of Akhenaten's devotion to his universal god.

KEEP IN MIND . . .

1-9. Throughout this hymn, note the themes of regeneration and the regulation of life.

You rise in perfection on the horizon of the sky,
living [Aten], who started life.
Whenever you are risen upon the eastern horizon
you fill every land with your perfection.
You are appealing, great, sparkling, high over every
        land;
your rays hold together the lands as far as
        everything you have made.
Since you are Re, you reach as far as they do,
and you curb them for your beloved son.
Although you are far away, your rays are upon the
        land;
you are in their faces, yet your departure is not
        observed.

Whenever you set on the western horizon,
the land is in darkness in the manner of death.
They sleep in a bedroom with heads under the
        covers,
and one eye does not see another.
If all their possessions which are under their heads
        were stolen,
they would not know it.

Every lion who comes out of his cave and all the
        serpents bite,
for darkness is a blanket.
The land is silent now, because he who made them
is at rest on his horizon.

But when day breaks you are risen upon the
        horizon,
and you shine as the [Aten] in the daytime.
When you dispel darkness and you give forth your
        rays

the two lands are in festival,
alert and standing on their feet,
now that you have raised them up.
Their bodies are clean, and their clothes have been
        put on;
their arms are [lifted] in praise at your rising.

The entire land performs its works:
all the cattle are content with their fodder,
trees and plants grow,
birds fly up to their nests,
their wings [extended] in praise for your Ka.
All the kine prance on their feet;
everything which flies up and alights,
they live when you have risen for them.
The barges sail upstream and downstream too,
for every way is open at your rising.
The fishes in the river leap before your face
when your rays are in the sea.

You who have placed seed in woman
and have made sperm into man,
who feeds the son in the womb of his mother,
who quiets him with something to stop his crying;
you are the nurse in the womb,
giving breath to nourish all that has been begotten.

When he comes down from the womb to breathe
on the day he is born,
you open up his mouth [completely], and supply
        his needs.
When the fledgling in the egg speaks in the shell,
you give him air inside it to sustain him.
When you grant him his allotted time to break out
        from the egg,
he comes out from the egg to cry out at his
        fulfillment,
and he goes upon his legs when he has come forth
        from it.

How plentiful it is, what you have made,
although they are hidden from view,
sole god, without another beside you;
you created the earth as you wished,
when you were by yourself, [before]
mankind, all cattle and kine,
all beings on land, who fare upon their feet,
and all beings in the air, who fly with their wings.

> "You have set every man in his place,
> You have allotted their needs... And
> his lifetime is conted out"
>   —AKHENATEN

The lands of Khor and Kush
and the land of Egypt:
you have set every man in his place,
you have allotted their needs,
every one of them according to his diet,
and his lifetime is counted out.
Tongues are separate in speech,
and their characters as well;
their skins are different,
for you have differentiated the foreigners.
In the underworld you have made a Nile
that you may bring it forth as you wish
to feed the populace,
since you made them for yourself, their utter
        master,
growing weary on their account, lord of every land.
For them the [Aten] of the daytime arises,
great in awesomeness.

All distant lands,
you have made them live,
for you have set a Nile in the sky
that it may descend for them
and make waves upon the mountains like the sea
to irrigate the fields in their towns.
How efficient are your designs,
Lord of eternity:
a Nile in the sky [meaning "rain"] for the
    foreigners

and all creatures that go upon their feet,
a Nile coming back from the underworld for
        Egypt.

Your rays give suck to every field:
when you rise they live,
and they grow for you.
You have made the seasons
to bring into being all you have made:
the Winter to cool them,
the Heat that you may be felt.
You have made a far-off heaven
in which to rise
in order to observe everything you have made.

Yet you are alone,
rising in your manifestations as the Living [Aten]:
appearing, glistening, being afar, coming close;
you make millions of transformations of yourself.
Towns, harbors, fields, roadways, waterways:
every eye beholds you upon them,
for you are the [Aten] of the daytime on the face
        of the earth.

When you go forth
every eye [is upon you].
You have created their sight
but not to see [only] the body ...
which you have made.

You are my desire,
and there is no other who knows you
except for your son ...
for you have apprized him of your designs and
        your power.
The earth came forth into existence by your hand,
and you made it.
When you rise, they live;
when you set, they die.
You are a lifespan in yourself;
one lives by you.
Eyes are upon your perfection until you set:
all work is put down when you rest in the west.

When [you] rise, [everything] grows
for the King and [for] everyone who hastens on
    foot,
because you have founded the land
and you have raised them for your son
who has come forth from your body,
the King of Upper and Lower Egypt, the one
    Living on Maat,
Lord of the Two Lands . . .
son of Re, the one Living on Maat, Master of
    Regalia,
[Akhenaten], the long lived,
and the Foremost Wife of the King, whom he
    loves,
the Mistress of the Two Lands, . . .
living and young, forever and ever.

CONSIDER THIS:

1-10. What specific phrases from this Hymn to Aten
reflect the regeneration and regulation of life. If

Akhenaten's prayer to Aten emphasized stability
and security, why was it considered so threatening
to conservative Egyptian values?

1-11. What was the Amarna "revolution" and why was
it a radical change for Egyptians? What does the
Hymn to the Aten reveal about Akhenaten's conception of the deity? Compare this with Psalm
104 from the Old Testament. What are the simi-
larities? Can you make any conclusions?

THE BROADER PERSPECTIVE:

1-12. Akhenaten's monotheism has been hotly debated.
Some historians have regarded it as a unique and
creative approach to religion, which even influenced
later Hebrew monotheism; others have seen it as the
development of earlier Egyptian thought with new
elements included. In any event, Akhenaten's new
religion was considered a heresy and did not long
survive his reign. What does this tell you about the
process of change in Egyptian society?

KEY EVENTS IN HEBREW HISTORY

1800–1700 B.C.E. Hebrews Migrate to Land of Canaan
At the direction of Yahweh, Hebrew patriarch Abraham leads Jews from Ur in Sumeria into
the "promised land," the land of Canaan.

1400–1200 B.C.E. Hittite Empire
The aggressive Hittite people establish their empire in modern day Turkey and expand it
south to Syria. The Hittites are the first culture to use iron weapons, and they fight several
battles with Egyptian New Kingdom pharaohs.

1250 B.C.E. The Exodus from Egypt
At the direction of Yahweh, Moses leads Hebrews out of slavery in Egypt (Exodus) back to
the land of Canaan. Yahweh, through Moses, gives Hebrews the Ten Commandments.

1200 B.C.E. Widespread Mediterranean Destruction
Hittite culture in modern Turkey falls to an unknown force, as does the Mycenaean civilization in Greece. Egypt is attacked by "Sea Peoples" but repels invaders.

1100–900 B.C.E. Rise of Successor Civilizations
With the fall of the Hittites, several less powerful civilizations fill the power vacuum in the
region of modern Israel, Syria, and Lebanon. The Arameans, the Phoenicians, and most
importantly the Hebrews, who begin to establish kingdoms under the leadership of David

(ca. 1000–961 B.C.E.) and Solomon (961–922 B.C.E.). The latter establishes the Jewish Temple in Jerusalem.

732–722 B.C.E. Assyrian Conquest of Syria-Palestine
Northern Hebrew kingdom of Israel is destroyed (722 B.C.E.).

612–539 B.C.E. Neo-Babylonian Empire
Neo-Babylonian (Chaldean) Empire destroys Assyrian capital at Ninevah (612 B.C.E.) and King Nebuchadnezzar II conquers southern Hebrew kingdom of Judah (586 B.C.E.), thus removing Jews to Babylon (Babylonian Captivity).

559–530 Reign of Persian King Cyrus the Great
Founder of the Achaemenid dynasty, Cyrus establishes massive Persian Empire by conquering Lydia, Media, and Egypt. Cyrus destroyed the Neo-Babylonians in 539 B.C.E., thus freeing the Jews from captivity in Babylon.

Hebrew Civilization

Origins, Oppression, and the Exodus of the Hebrews from Egypt

Nowhere did religion play a greater role than in the development of Hebrew civilization. The Hebrews were a nomadic people whose wanderings and eventual settlement in the promised land of Canaan (modern-day Israel) form the narrative story of the Old Testament of the Bible. But more than this, the story concerns the relationship of Yahweh (or God) to his chosen people, the Hebrews. Many other Near Eastern conquerors held more land and ruled more people, but no one influenced the course of Western civilization more emphatically than did the Hebrews. Their concern with moral law, right action, and adherence to monotheistic principles has formed the basis for Christianity and Islam in the modern world.

The first few pages from Genesis in the Old Testament of the Bible contain some of the most powerful and influential ideas in world civilization. Genesis explains the origins of the universe by one omnipotent and omniscient God, who created human beings in his likeness, gave them dominion over nature, and endowed them with an inherent goodness. It is the story of the creation of woman, the origins of sin, and the fall from God's grace. This concept of monotheism and the ethical and social structures that derived from the development of these ideas were the primary contributions of the Hebrews to world civilization.

The story of the Hebrews in the Old Testament begins with the wandering patriarch Abraham, who led his family from Ur in Sumer around 1800 B.C.E. to the promised land of Canaan by about 1700 B.C.E. A group of Hebrews led by Joseph continued south to Egypt, where they were hospitably received by the Hyksos, a Semitic people like the Hebrews, who had conquered Egypt about 1710 B.C.E. Joseph, according to the Old Testament, actually ruled Egypt for a time. But by 1570 B.C.E., a resurgent Egypt had ended the Hyksos control, and the Pharaohs had enslaved the Hebrews and forced them to build new Egyptian cities. Shortly after 1300 B.C.E., Moses was directed by God to lead his people out of Egypt, across the Red Sea, and back to the promised land of Canaan.

The Creation of the World

In the beginning, God created heaven and earth. Now the earth was a formless void, there was darkness over the deep, with a divine wind sweeping over the waters.

God said, "Let there be light," and there was light. God saw that light was good, and God divided light from darkness. God called light "day," and darkness he called "night." Evening came and morning came: the first day.

God said, "Let there be a vault through the middle of the waters to divide the waters in two." And so it was. God made the vault, and it divided the waters under the vault from the waters above the vault. God called the vault "heaven." Evening came and morning came: the second day.

God said, "Let the waters under heaven come together into a single mass, and let dry land appear." And so it was. God called the dry land "earth" and the mass of waters "seas," and God saw that it was good.

God said, "Let the earth produce vegetation: seed-bearing plants, and fruit trees on earth, bearing fruit with their seed inside, each corresponding to its own seed-bearing fruit with their seed inside, each corresponding to its own species." And so it was. . . . God saw that it was good. Evening came and morning came: the third day.

God said, "Let there be lights in the vault of heaven to divide day from night, and let them indicate festivals, days and years. Let them be lights in the vault of heaven to shine on the earth." And so it was. God made the two great lights, the greater light to govern the day, the smaller light to govern the night, and the stars. . . . God saw that it was good. Evening came and morning came: the fourth day.

God said, "Let the waters be alive with a swarm of living creatures, and let birds wing their way above the earth across the vault of heaven." And so it was. God created great sea-monsters and all the creatures that glide and teem in the waters in their own species, and winged birds in their own species. God saw that it was good. God blessed them, saying, "Be fruitful, multiply, and fill the waters of the seas; and let the birds multiply on land." Evening came and morning came: the fifth day.

God said, "Let the earth produce every kind of living creature in its own species: cattle, creeping things and wild animals of all kinds." And so it was. . . . God saw that it was good.

God said, "Let us make man in our own image, in the likeness of ourselves, and let them be masters of the fish of the sea, the birds of heaven, the cattle, all the wild animals, and all the creatures that creep along the ground."

God created man in the image of himself,
in the image of God he created him,
male and female he created them.

God blessed them, saying to them, "Be fruitful, multiply, fill the earth and subdue it. Be masters of the fish of the sea, the birds of heaven and all the living creatures that move on earth." God also said, "Look, to you I give all the seed-bearing plants everywhere on the surface of the earth, and all the trees with seed-bearing fruit; this will be your food. And to all the wild animals, all the birds of heaven and all the living creatures that creep along the ground, I give all the foliage of the plants as their food." And so it was. God saw all he had made, and indeed it was very good. Evening came and morning came: the sixth day.

Thus heaven and earth were completed with all their array. On the seventh day God had completed the work he had been doing. He rested on the seventh day after all the work he had undertaken. God blessed the seventh day and made it holy, because on that day he rested after all his work of creating.

Paradise and the Fall from Grace

At the time when Yahweh God made earth and heaven, there was as yet no wild bush on the earth nor had any wild plant yet sprung up, for Yahweh God had not sent rain on the earth, nor was there any man to till the soil. Instead, water flowed out of the ground and watered all the surface of the soil. Yahweh God shaped man from the soil of the ground and blew the breath of life into his nostrils, and man became a living being.

Yahweh God planted a garden in Eden, which is in the east, and there he put the man he had fashioned. From the soil, Yahweh God caused to grow every kind of tree, enticing to look at and good to eat, with the tree of life in the middle of the garden, and the tree of the knowledge of good and evil. . . .

Yahweh God took the man and settled him in the garden of Eden to cultivate and take care of it. Then Yahweh God gave the man this command, "You are free to eat of all the trees in the garden. But of the tree of the knowledge of good and evil you are not to eat; for, the day you eat of that, you are doomed to die."

Yahweh God said, "It is not right that the man should be alone. I shall make him a helper. . . ." Then Yahweh God made the man fall into a deep sleep. And, while he was asleep, he took one of his ribs and closed the flesh up again forthwith. Yahweh God fashioned the rib he had taken from the man into a woman, and brought her to the man. And the man said: "This one at last is bone of my bones and flesh of my flesh! She is to be called Woman, because she was taken from Man."

This is why a man leaves his father and mother and becomes attached to his wife, and they become one flesh. Now, both of them were naked, the man and his wife, but they felt no shame before each other.

Now the snake was the most subtle of all the wild animals that Yahweh God had made. It asked the woman, "Did God really say you were not to eat from any of the trees in the garden?" The woman answered the snake, "We may eat the fruit of the trees in the garden. But of the fruit of the tree in the middle of the garden God said, "You must not eat it, nor touch it, under pain of death." Then the snake said to the woman, "No! You will not die! God knows in fact that the day you eat it your eyes will be opened and you will be like gods, knowing good from evil." The woman saw that the tree was good to eat and pleasing to the eye and that it was enticing for the wisdom that it could give. So she took some of the fruit and ate it. She also gave some to her husband who was with her, and he ate it. Then the eyes of both of them were opened and they realized that they were naked. So they sewed fig-leaves to make themselves loin-cloths.

The man and his wife heard the sound of Yahweh God walking in the garden in the cool of the day, and they hid from Yahweh God among the trees of the garden. "Where are you?" he asked. . . . "Have you been eating from the tree I forbade you to eat?" The man replied, "It was the woman you put with me; she gave me some fruit from the tree, and I ate it." Then Yahweh God said to the woman, "Why did you do that?" The woman replied, "The snake tempted me and I ate." Then Yahweh God said to the snake,

"Because you have done this,
Accursed be you
of all animals wild and tame!
On your belly you will go
and on dust you will feed
as long as you live.
I shall put enmity
between you and the woman,
and between your offspring and hers;
it will bruise your head
and you will strike its heel."

To the woman he said:
"I shall give you intense pain in childbearing,
you will give birth to your children in pain.
Your yearning will be for your husband,
and he will dominate you."

To the man he said: "Because you listened to the voice
of your wife, and ate
from the tree of which I had forbidden you to eat,

Accursed be the soil because of you!
Painfully will you get your food from it
as long as you live. . . .
By the sweat of your face
will you earn your food,
until you return to the ground,
as you were taken from it.
For dust you are
and to dust you shall return."

The man named his wife "Eve" because she was
the mother of all those who live. Yahweh made tunics
of skins for the man and his wife and clothed them.
Then Yahweh God said, "Now that the man has
become like one of us in knowing good from evil, he
must not be allowed to reach out his hand and pick
from the tree of life too, and eat and live forever!" So
Yahweh God expelled him from the garden of Eden,
to till the soil from which he had been taken. He banished the man, and in front of the garden of Eden he
posted the great winged creatures and the fiery flashing sword to guard the way to the tree of life.

CONSIDER THIS:

1-13. After reading the selections from Genesis on the origin of the world, paradise, and the fall from grace,
analyze why these stories have been so influential in
Western Civilization. What do the Garden of Eden
and the Tree of Life represent? What are the two stories about the creation of woman? What is the relative
position of women to men at the biblical origin of
life? How have these passages from Genesis been used
to structure social attitudes and expectations throughout the centuries? Do they still have impact today?

The Hebrew Bondage

Then there came to power in Egypt a new king who
knew nothing of Joseph. "Look," he said to his subjects, "these people, the sons of Israel, have become so
numerous and strong that they are a threat to us. We
must be prudent and take steps against their increasing
any further, or if war should break out, they might add
to the number of our enemies. They might take arms
against us and so escape out of the country."
Accordingly they put slave-drivers over the Israelites to
wear them down under heavy loads. In this way they
built the store-cities of Pithom and Ramses for
Pharaoh. But the more they were crushed, the more
they increased and spread, and men came to dread the
sons of Israel. The Egyptians forced the sons of Israel
into slavery, and made their lives unbearable with hard
labor, work with clay and brick, all kinds of work in the
fields; they forced on them every kind of labor. . . .

The Burning Bush

During this long period the king of Egypt died. The
sons of Israel, groaning in their slavery, cried out for
help and from the depths of their slavery their cry
came up to God. God heard their groaning and he
called to mind his covenant with Abraham, Isaac and
Jacob. God looked down upon the sons of Israel, and
he knew. . . .

Moses was looking after the flock of Jethro, his
father-in-law, priest of Midian. He led his flock to the
far side of the wilderness and came to Horeb, the

mountain of God. There the angel of Yahweh appeared to him in the shape of a flame of fire, coming from the middle of a bush. Moses looked; there was the bush blazing, but it was not being burnt up. "I must go and look at this strange sight," Moses said, "and see why the bush is not burnt." Now Yahweh saw him go forward to look, and God called to him from the middle of the bush. "Moses, Moses!" He said. "Here I am," he answered. "Come no nearer," He said. "Take off your shoes, for the place on which you stand is holy ground. I am the God of your father," He said, "the God of Abraham, the god of Isaac and the God of Jacob." At this Moses covered his face, afraid to look at God. . . .

The Mission of Moses

God spoke to Moses and said to him, "I am Yahweh. To Abraham and Isaac and Jacob I appeared as El Shaddai; I did not make myself known to them by my name Yahweh. Also, I made my covenant with them to give them the land of Canaan, the land they lived in as strangers. And I have heard the groaning of the sons of Israel, enslaved by the Egyptians, and have remembered my covenant. Say this, then, to the sons of Israel, 'I am Yahweh. I will free you of the burdens which the Egyptians lay on you. I will release you from slavery to them, and with my arm outstretched and my strokes of power I will deliver you. I will adopt you as my own people, and I will be your God. Then you shall know that it is I, Yahweh your God, who have freed you from the Egyptians" burdens. Then I will bring you to the land I swore that I would give to Abraham, and Isaac, and Jacob, and will give it to you for your own; I, Yahweh, will do this!'" Moses told this to the sons of Israel, but they would not listen to him, so crushed was their spirit and so cruel their slavery.

Yahweh then said to Moses, "Go to Pharaoh, king of Egypt, and tell him to let the sons of Israel leave his land." But Moses answered to Yahweh's face: "Look," said he "since the sons of Israel have not listened to me, why should Pharaoh listen to me, a man slow of speech?" Yahweh spoke to Moses and Aaron and ordered them to both go to Pharaoh, king of Egypt, and to bring the sons of Israel out of the land of Egypt.

The Departure of the Israelites

When Pharaoh had let the people go, God did not let them take the road to the land of the Philistines, although that was the nearest way. God thought that the prospect of fighting would make the people lose heart and turn back to Egypt. Instead, God led the people by the roundabout way of the wilderness to the Sea of Reeds [Red Sea]. . . .

Yahweh went before them, by day in the form of a pillar of cloud to show them the way, and by night in the form of a pillar of fire to give them light: thus they could continue their march by day and by night. The pillar of cloud never failed to go before the people during the day, nor the pillar of fire during the night. . . .

When Pharaoh, king of Egypt, was told that the people had made their escape, he and his courtiers changed their minds about the people. "What have we done," they said, "allowing Israel to leave our service?" So Pharaoh had his chariot harnessed and gathered his troops about him, taking six hundred of the best chariots and all the other chariots in Egypt, each manned by a picked team. Yahweh made Pharaoh, king of Egypt, stubborn, and he gave chase to the sons of

Israel as they made their triumphant escape. So the Egyptians gave chase and came up with them where they lay encamped beside the sea—all the horses, the chariots of Pharaoh, his horsemen, his army—near Pi-hahiroth, facing Baalzephon. And as Pharaoh approached, the sons of Israel looked round—and there were the Egyptians in pursuit of them! The sons of Israel were terrified and cried out to Yahweh. To Moses they said, "Were there no graves in Egypt that you must lead us out to die in the wilderness? What good have you done us, bringing us out of Egypt? We spoke of this in Egypt, did we not? Leave us alone, we said, we would rather work for the Egyptians! Better to work of the Egyptians than die in the wilderness!" Moses answered the people, "Have no fear! Stand firm, and you will see what Yahweh will do to save you today: the Egyptians you see today, you will never see again. Yahweh will do the fighting for you: you have only to keep still."

Yahweh said to Moses, "Why do you cry to me so? Tell the sons of Israel to march on. For yourself, raise your staff and stretch out your hand over the sea and part it for the sons of Israel to walk through the sea on dry ground. I for my part will make the heart of the Egyptians so stubborn that they will follow them. So shall I win myself glory at the expense of Pharaoh, of all his army, his chariots, his horsemen. And when I have won glory for myself, at the expense of Pharaoh and his chariots and his army, the Egyptians will learn that I am Yahweh."

Then the angel of Yahweh, who marched at the front of the army of Israel, changed station and moved to their rear. The pillar of cloud changed station from the front to the rear of them, and remained there. It came between the camp of the Egyptians and the camp of Israel. The cloud was dark, and the night passed without the armies drawing any closer the whole night long. Moses stretched out his hand over the sea. Yahweh drove back the sea with a strong easterly wind all night, and he made dry land of the sea. The waters parted and the sons of Israel went on dry ground right into the sea, walls of water to right and to left of them. The Egyptians gave chase: after them they went, right into the sea, all Pharaoh"s horses, his chariots, and his horsemen. . . . Yahweh said to Moses "that the waters may flow back on the Egyptians and their chariots and their horsemen." Moses stretched out his hand over the sea and, as day broke, the sea returned to its bed. The fleeing Egyptians marched right into it, and Yahweh overthrew the Egyptians in the very middle of the sea. The returning waters overwhelmed the chariots and the horsemen of Pharaoh"s whole army, which had followed the Israelites into the sea; not a single one of them was left. But the sons of Israel had marched through the sea on dry ground, walls of water to right and to left of them. That day, Yahweh rescued Israel from the Egyptians, and Israel saw the Egyptians lying dead on the shore. Israel witnessed the great act that Yahweh had performed against the Egyptians, and the people venerated Yahweh; they put their faith in Yahweh and in Moses, his servant.

CONSIDER THIS:

1-14. What was Moses's mission as recorded in the Old Testament? Why is the Exodus from Egypt central to the Jewish experience? What does it say about Yahweh's relationship with the Hebrews?

Covenant and Commandments

After the Exodus of the Hebrews from Egypt, Yahweh established the nation of Israel and through Moses made a covenant with his chosen people that he would protect them in return for their obedience to his laws. The law code that God handed down to Moses on Mt. Sinai is called the Decalogue, or Ten Commandments, and is absolute in nature. Other laws that are less absolute and generally reflect the needs and values of Hebrew society are called the Covenant Code; they are included after the Ten Commandments and were probably written centuries later. Note the similarity between the Covenant Code and the laws of Hammurabi.

The Ten Commandments

Three months after they came out of the land of Egypt . . . on that day the sons of Israel came to the wilderness of Sinai. . . .

Moses then went up to God, and Yahweh called to him from the mountains, saying, "Say this to the House of Jacob, declare this to the sons of Israel, 'You yourselves have seen what I did with the Egyptians, how I carried you on eagle's wings and brought you to myself. From this you know that now, if you obey my voice and hold fast to my covenant, you of all the nations shall be my very own for all the earth is mine. I will count you a kingdom of priests, a consecrated nation.' Those are the words you are to speak to the sons of Israel.". . .

Yahweh said to Moses, "Go to the people and tell them to prepare themselves today and tomorrow. Let them wash their clothing and hold themselves in readiness for the third day, because on the third day Yahweh will descend on the mountain of Sinai in the sight of all the people. You will mark out the limits of the mountain and say, 'Take care not to go up the mountain or to touch the foot of it. Whoever touches the mountain will be put to death. No one must lay a hand on him: he must be stoned or shot down by arrow, whether man or beast; he must not remain alive.' When the ram's horn sounds a long blast, they are to go up the mountain.". . . .

Now at daybreak on the third day there were peals of thunder on the mountain and lightning flashes, a dense cloud, and a loud trumpet blast, and inside the camp all the people trembled. Then Moses led the people out of the camp to meet God; and they stood at the bottom of the mountain. The mountain of Sinai was entirely wrapped in smoke, because Yahweh had descended on it in the form of fire. Like smoke from a furnace the smoke went up, and the whole mountain shook violently. Louder and louder grew the sound of the trumpet, Moses spoke, and God answered him with peals of thunder. Yahweh came down on the mountain of Sinai, on the mountain top, and Yahweh called Moses to the top of the mountain; and Moses went up. . . .

Then God spoke all these words. He said, "I am Yahweh your God who brought you out of the land of Egypt, out of the house of slavery.

"You shall have no gods except me.

"You shall not make yourself a carved image or any likeness of anything in heaven or on earth beneath or in the waters under the earth; you shall not bow down to them or serve them. For I, Yahweh your God, am a jealous God and I punish the father"s fault in the sons, the grandsons, and the great-grandsons of those who hate me; but I show kindness to thousands of those who love me and keep my commandments.

"You shall not utter the name of Yahweh your God to misuse it, for Yahweh will not leave unpunished the man who utters his name to misuse it.

"Remember the sabbath day and keep it holy. For six days you shall labor and do all your work, but the seventh day is a sabbath for Yahweh your God. You shall do no work that day, neither you nor your son nor your daughter nor your servants, men or women, nor your animals nor the stranger who lives with you. For in six days Yahweh made the heavens and the earth and the sea and all that these hold, but on the seventh day he rested; that is why Yahweh has blessed the sabbath day and made it sacred.

"Honor your father and your mother so that you may have a long life in the land that Yahweh your God has given to you.

"You shall not kill.

"You shall not commit adultery.

"You shall not steal.

"You shall not bear false witness against your neighbor.

"You shall not covet your neighbor's house. You shall not covet your neighbor's wife, or his servant, man or woman, or his ox, or his donkey, or anything that is his."

The Covenant Code

'This is the ruling you [Moses] are to lay before them: . . .

"Anyone who strikes a man and so causes his death, must die. If he has not lain in wait for him but God has delivered him into his hands, then I will appoint you a place where he may seek refuge. But should a man dare to kill his fellow by treacherous intent, you must take him even from my altar to be put to death.

"Anyone who strikes his father or mother must die. Anyone who abducts a man—whether he has sold him or is found in possession of him—must die. Anyone who curses father or mother must die.

"If men quarrel and one strikes the other a blow with stone or fist so that the man, though he does not die, must keep his bed, the one who struck the blow shall not be liable provided the other gets up and can go about, even with a stick. He must compensate him, however, for his enforced inactivity, and care for him until he is completely cured.

"If a man beats his slave, male or female, and the slave dies at his hands, he must pay the penalty. But should the slave survive for one or two days, he shall pay no penalty because the slave is his by right of purchase.

"If, when men come to blows, they hurt a woman who is pregnant and she suffers a miscarriage, though she does not die of it, the man responsible must pay the compensation demanded of him by the woman's master; he shall hand it over, after arbitration. But should she die, you shall give life for life, eye for eye, tooth for tooth, hand for hand, foot for foot, burn for burn, wound for wound, stroke for stroke. . . .

"You must not molest the stranger or oppress him, for you lived as strangers in the land of Egypt. You must not be harsh with the widow, or with the orphan; if you are harsh with them, they will surely cry out to me, and be sure I shall hear their cry; my anger will flare and I shall kill you with the sword, your own wives will be widows, your own children orphans.

"If you lend money to any of my people, to any poor man among you, you must not play the usurer with him: you must not demand interest from him.

"If you take another's cloak as a pledge, you must give it back to him before sunset. It is all the covering he has; it is the cloak he wraps his body in; what else would he sleep in? If he cries to me, I will listen, for I am full of pity. . . ."

Moses went and told the people all the commands of Yahweh and all the ordinances. In answer, all the people said with one voice, 'We will observe all the commands that Yahweh has decreed.' Moses put all the commands of Yahweh into writing.

CONSIDER THIS:

1-15. Note the Hebrew concern for moral instructions and law. Compare the Covenant Code with the Code of Hammurabi on pages 4 and 28. In what ways are they similar? Were the Mesopotamians, Egyptians, and Hebrews all concerned with living a good, moral life? What values were most appreciated?

Wisdom and Psalms

When the Hebrews settled in the land of Canaan (now modern-day Israel) after the Exodus from Egypt in the early thirteenth century B.C.E., it soon became apparent that the loose confederacy of Hebrew tribes was ineffective when faced with enemies. Of special concern were the Philistines, who settled in the region about 1200 B.C.E., destroyed the Hebrew sanctuary at Shiloh about 1050 B.C.E., and carried off the Ark of the Covenant. In response to this, the Hebrew people demanded strong leadership and elected a king

"The Covenant Code" is from Exodus 21–22, 24, from Alexander Jones, ed., *The Jerusalem Bible*, pp. 104, 106, 108. Copyright © 1966 by Darton, Longman & Todd, Ltd., and Doubleday, a division of Random House, Inc. Used by permission of Doubleday, a division of Random House, Inc.

named Saul. He was not a particularly effective leader and died in battle with the Philistines. His successor was the famous David (1000–961 B.C.E.), whose personal defeat of the Philistine Goliath led to security and domestic reform. David established the Hebrew capital at Jerusalem and equipped it with a central administration. At last, a united Israel was born.

David's progressive spirit was continued by his son Solomon (961–922 B.C.E.), who strengthened centralized control of the state by the king. His construction of the Temple and palace complex required frequent taxes and even oppressive forced labor. Still, Solomon developed a reputation for wisdom and fairness. It was only later in his reign that he incurred the wrath of God.

Wisdom was of particular importance to the Hebrews. The Old Testament contains five Wisdom books: Job, Proverbs, Ecclesiastes, Ecclesiasticus, and Wisdom. Together with the Psalms, which also include much wisdom and the Song of Songs, reputedly written by Solomon the Wise himself, these books span nearly one thousand years.

Wisdom literature, however, was certainly not particular to the Hebrews, and the sages of Israel drew freely on Egyptian and Mesopotamian traditions. Hebrew wisdom focused on the practical side of life—commonsense advice, the foundations of good character and right action, as well as the realization that omnipotent Yahweh was the source of all wisdom and success.

The first selection is a masterpiece of poetry from the book of Job that meditates on the relationship between sin and suffering. The logical argument that the transgression of God's laws will result in suffering and retribution is called into question as Job, a good servant of God, is visited by disaster after disaster when his oxen are stolen, his servants and children killed, his body invaded by ulcers and wasted by disease. This had been a test of Job's faith in Yahweh, and throughout his ordeals he never questioned or reproached God's action even though he was not guilty of any sin, not even unknowingly. The message was clear: Although God's plan is unknowable, human destiny is dependent on complete submission and faith in the wisdom of Yahweh.

The following selections from Job and the Psalms seek to define faith, to acknowledge the omnipotence of Yahweh, and to celebrate the sublime wonders of nature, life, and love.

Job: "Clothed in Fearful Splendor"

Listen to this, Job, without flinching
    and reflect on the marvelous works of God.
Do you know how God controls them
    or how his clouds make the lightning flash?
Do you know how he balances the clouds—
    a miracle of consummate skill?
When your clothes are hot to your body
    and the earth lies still under the south wind,

can you, like him, stretch out the sky,
    tempered like a mirror of cast metal?
Teach me what we should say to him:
    but better discuss no further, since we are in the
    dark.
Does he take note when I speak?
    When human beings give orders, does he take
    it in?

There are times when the light vanishes,
    behind darkening clouds;
then comes the wind, sweeping them away.
    And brightness spreads from the north.
God is clothed in fearful splendor:
    he, Shaddai, is far beyond our reach.
Supreme in power, in equity,
    excelling in saving justice, yet no oppressor—
no wonder then that people fear him:
    everyone thoughtful holds him in awe!

CONSIDER THIS:

1-16. In this selection from Job, how is God's power defined? God is "clothed in fearful splendor," yet he is "no oppressor." How would you define the concept of fear in this passage?

1-17. How do you interpret the phrase, "but better discuss no further, since we are in the dark"? What is God's relationship with human beings?

Psalm 104: "All Creatures Depend on You"

Bless Yahweh, my soul.
Yahweh my God, how great you are!
Clothed in majesty and glory,
wrapped in a robe of light!

You stretch the heavens out like a tent,
you build your palace on the waters above;
using the clouds as your chariot,
you advance on the wings of the wind;
you use the winds as messengers
and fiery flames as servants.

You fixed the earth on its foundations,
unshakable for ever and ever;
you wrapped it with the deep as with a robe,
the waters overtopping the mountains.

At your reproof the waters took to flight,
they fled at the sound of your thunder,
cascading over the mountains, into the valleys,
down to the reservoir you made for them;
you imposed the limits they must never cross again,
or they would once more flood the land.

You set springs gushing in ravines,
running down between the mountains,
supplying water for wild animals,
attracting the thirsty wild donkeys;
near there the birds of the air make their nests
and sing among the branches.

From your high halls, you water the mountains,
satisfying the earth with the fruit of your works;
you make fresh grass grow for cattle
and those plants made use of by man,
for them to get food from the soil:
wine to make them cheerful,
oil to make them happy,
bread to make them strong.

The trees of Yahweh get rain enough,
those cedars of Lebanon he planted;
here the little birds build their nest
and, on the highest branches, the stork has its home.
For with the goats there are the mountains,
in the crags rock-badgers hide.

You made the moon to tell the seasons,
the sun knows when to set:
you bring darkness on, night falls,
all the forest animals come out:
savage lions, roaring for their prey,
claiming their food from God.

The sun rises, they retire,
going back to lie down in their lairs,
and man goes to work, and to labor until dusk.

Yahweh, what variety you have created,
arranging everything so wisely!

Earth is completely full of things you have made:
among them vast expanse of ocean,
teeming with countless creatures,
creatures large and small,
with the ships going to and from
and Leviathan whom you made to amuse you.

All creatures depend on you
to feed them throughout the year;
you provide the food they eat,
with generous hand you satisfy their hunger.

You turn your face away, they suffer,
you stop their breath, they die
and revert to dust.
You give breath, fresh life begins,
you keep renewing the world.

Glory for ever to Yahweh!
May Yahweh find joy in what he creates,
at whose glance the earth trembles,
at whose touch the mountains smoke!

I mean to sing to Yahweh all my life,
I mean to play for my God as long as I live.
May these reflections of mine give him pleasure,
as much as Yahweh gives me!
May sinners vanish from the earth
and the wicked exist no more!
Bless Yahweh, my soul.

CONSIDER THIS:

1-18. Compare Psalm 104 with the Egyptian *Hymn to the Aten*. Are the solar deity of Akhenaten and Yahweh similar in power and purpose? Compare the vocabulary and phrasing of the two hymns.

1-19. Both Aten and Yahweh were omnipotent and supreme in their respective societies. But the transition to one universal deity in Israel and Egypt was not without resistence. In fact, the worship of Aten did not long survive the death of the Pharaoh Akhenaten. Why was monotheism such a radical concept for the time? What dangers did it pose to the authority of the various priesthoods and to the stability of society?

Prophets: Amos, Isaiah, and Jeremiah

Solomon's oppressive policies split the Hebrew nation into two parts after his death: Israel became the northern kingdom and Judah formed in the south. Such division made the two kingdoms vulnerable to rising new empires. Israel fell to the Assyrians in 722 B.C.E. and Judah to the Chaldeans in 586 B.C.E., whereupon the Jews were removed from the land of Canaan in what was called the Babylonian Captivity. They were finally released when the Persian Cyrus the Great conquered the Chaldean empire and liberated Babylon in 539 B.C.E.

During the years 750–550 B.C.E., when the Hebrews were trying to survive in the face of foreign invasion, they were also struggling internally. A succession of prophets arose who claimed to speak for Yahweh and condemned social injustice and the people's general disregard for the covenant they had made with God under Moses. Amos was a sheep farmer from the desert of Judea who was called by Yahweh to preach to Israel. Rough and direct in his approach, Amos condemned corrupt city life, social abuses, and the insincerity that often accompanied ceremonial rituals. Isaiah was born about 765 B.C.E. and received his prophetic vision in 740 B.C.E. while associated with the Temple in Jerusalem. Isaiah was a brilliant poet whose concise yet majestic prose differentiated the sinfulness of humankind from the power and transcendent consolation of God. Yahweh insists on justice and sincerity among people. The words of Isaiah invoke the fathomless wisdom of God, confirm monotheism, and issue a clear first expression of religious universalism.

Amos: *"Let Justice Flow Like Water"*

I hate, I scorn your festivals,
I take no pleasure in your solemn assemblies.
When you bring me burnt offerings . . .
your oblations, I do not accept them
and I do not look at your communion sacrifices of fat
    cattle.

Spare me the din of your chanting,
let me hear none of your strumming on lyres,
but let justice flow like water,
and uprightness like a never failing stream!
Did you bring me sacrifices and oblation
those forty years in the desert, House of Israel?

Yahweh: *"There Is No God Except Me"*

Thus says Yahweh, Israel's king,
Yahweh Sabaoth, his redeemer:
I am the first and I am the last;
there is no God except me.
Who is like me? Let him call out,
let him affirm it and convince me it is so;
let him say what has been happening

since I instituted an eternal people,
and predict to them what will happen next!
Have no fear, do not be afraid:
have I not told you and revealed it long ago?
You are my witnesses.
Is there any God except me?
There is no Rock; I know of none.

Isaiah's Vision of Everlasting Peace

It will happen in the final days
that the mountain of Yahweh's house
will rise higher than the mountains
and tower above the heights.
Then all the nations will stream to it,
many peoples will come to it and say,
'Come, let us go up to the mountain of Yahweh,
to the house of the God of Jacob
that he may teach us his ways
so that we may walk in his paths.'
For the Law will issue from Zion
and the word of Yahweh from Jerusalem.

Then he will judge between the nations
and arbitrate between many peoples.
They will hammer their swords into ploughshares
and their spears into sickles.
Nation will not lift sword against nation,
no longer will they learn how to make war.

CONSIDER THIS:

1-20. In these two excerpts from Amos and Isaiah what are
the most important themes that define the vision and
values of Yahweh?

THEME: SOCIAL AND SPIRITUAL VALUES

The Reflection in the Mirror

The New Covenant of Jeremiah

"Deep within Them, I Shall Plant My Law"

The most influential of these several prophets was Jeremiah (626–586 B.C.E.). He not only decried the faithlessness of the people of Israel and warned of the wrath of God, but he also offered a solution to the problem: a new covenant. God destroys, but he also builds anew. Of utmost importance was a new covenant within each individual (rather than with the nation as a whole) that would renew moral and spiritual commitment.

Keep in Mind . . .

1-21. How would you characterize the "New Covenant" of Jeremiah?

The word that was addressed to Jeremiah by Yahweh, "Go and stand at the gate of the Temple of Yahweh and there proclaim this message. Say, 'Listen to the word of Yahweh, all you men of Judah who come in by these gates to worship Yahweh. Yahweh Sabaoth, the God of Israel, says this: Amend your behavior and your actions and I will stay with you here in this place. Put no trust in delusive words like these: This is the sanctuary of Yahweh, the sanctuary of Yahweh, the sanctuary of Yahweh! But if you do amend your behavior and your actions, if you treat each other fairly, if you do not exploit the stranger, the orphan and the widow (if you do not shed innocent blood in this place), and if you do not follow alien gods, to your own ruin, then here in this place I will stay with you, in the land that long ago I gave to your fathers for ever. Yet here you are, trusting delusive words, to no purpose! Steal, would you, murder, commit adultery, perjure yourselves, burn incense to Baal, follow alien gods that you do not know?—and then come presenting yourselves in this Temple that bears my name, saying: Now we are safe—safe to go on committing all these

abominations! Do you take this Temple that bears my name for a robbers' den? I, at any rate, am not blind—it is Yahweh who speaks. . . .

'And now, since you have committed all these sins—it is Yahweh who speaks—and have refused to listen when I spoke so urgently, so persistently, or to answer when I called you, I will treat this Temple that bears my name, and in which you put your trust, and the place I have given to you and your ancestors, just as I treated Shiloh. I will drive you out of my sight, as I drove all your kinsmen, the entire race of Ephraim.' . . . "See, the days are coming—it is Yahweh who speaks—when I am going to sow the seed of men and cattle on the House of Israel and on the House of Judah. And as I once watched them to tear up, to knock down, to overthrow, destroy and bring disaster, so now I shall watch over them to build and to plant. It is Yahweh who speaks. In those days people will no longer say: 'The fathers have eaten unripe grapes; the children's teeth are set on edge.' But each is to die for his own sin. Every man who eats unripe grapes is to have his own teeth set on edge.

"See, the days are coming—it is Yahweh who speaks—when I will make a new covenant with the House of Israel (and the House of Judah), but not a covenant like the one I made with their ancestors

---

on the day I took them by the hand to bring them out of the land of Egypt. They broke that covenant of mine, so I had to show them who was master. It is Yahweh who speaks. No, this is the covenant I will make with the House of Israel when those days arrive—it is Yahweh who speaks. Deep within them I will plant my Law, writing it on their hearts. Then I will be their God and they shall be my people. There will be no further need for neighbor to try to teach neighbor, or brother to say to brother, 'Learn to know Yahweh!' No, they will all know me, the least no less than the greatest—it is Yahweh who speaks—since I will forgive their inequity and never call their sin to mind."

> "There will be no further need for neighbor to try to teach neighbor, or brother to say to brother, 'Learn to know Yahweh!'"
>
> —JEREMIAH

CONSIDER THIS:

1-22. How does the "new covenant" of Jeremiah differ from the original (as embodied in the Ten Commandments) established by Yahweh with Moses? Why the need for a new covenant? Be specific in your use of the primary sources.

Chapter 2

Legend and History:
The World of Early Greece

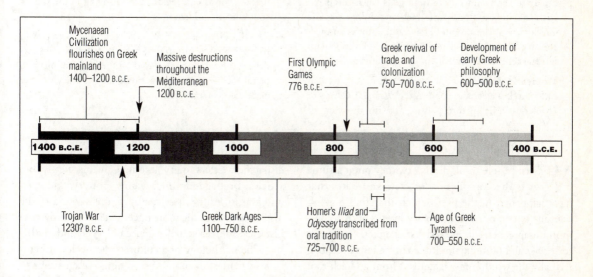

Zeus spoke, and nodded with his darkish brows, and immortal locks fell forward from the lord's deathless head, and he made great Olympus tremble.

—HOMER

Friendship between us is impossible, and there will be no truce of any kind till one of us has fallen and glutted the stubborn god of battles with his blood. So summon any courage you may have.

—HOMER

You could not step twice in the same river, for other and yet other waters are ever flowing on.

—HERACLITUS

Don't let a woman, wiggling her behind, and fluttering and coaxing take you in; she wants your barn: woman is just a cheat.

—HESIOD

Go and be happy, but remember whom you leave shackled by love.

—SAPPHO

- **The Power Structure:** What was the relationship between Homeric kings like Agamemnon and retainers like Achilles and Odysseus? Is aristocracy, or "rule by the best," a workable form of government?

- **Social and Spiritual Values:** What role did the gods play in the imagination of the early Greeks? How sophisticated was the pantheon of Greek gods when compared with the monotheism of the Hebrews? What was the Greek view of the afterlife? How do the stories and legends regarding the Greek gods and their interaction with humans reflect the creativity of Greek culture?

- **Women in History:** How were women portrayed in early Greek society as viewed in the *Iliad* and *Odyssey* of Homer? Is this picture consistent with the view of

women during the Golden Age of Greece in the fifth century B.C.E.? Did the Athenian democracy consider women political equals?

- **Revolution and Historical Transition:** What caused the destructions throughout the Mediterranean world around 1200 B.C.E.? How do historians develop theories that are consistent, logical, and satisfying in the face of contradictory evidence?

- **The Big Picture:** What roles do legend and myth play in history? Should historians accept or reject as valid evidence stories that have played on the imaginations of a people? How important is mythology to the character and success of a civilization?

When people think of history, they often assume it is the compilation of facts and dates that have happened in the past, which therefore play no relevant role in our contemporary lives. This is a common misapprehension fueled by sterile presentations in textbooks and numbing multiple-choice tests in school. Actually the word *history* is derived from a Greek root word meaning "inquiry." The task of the historian is not to compile "facts," but rather to inquire into the records of past societies in hopes of establishing what actually happened and, more importantly, why it happened. The historian has often been likened to a detective, searching for clues, analyzing and interpreting evidence. It is a profession that is immediately relevant. For in the discussion of past societies, historians deal primarily with human beings, their hopes and fears, their ideas, their hostilities, their successes and failures. Always at issue is the question "Why?" History, therefore, is about interpretation. What constitutes a "fact"? Because history is often written by the victors, they can interpret without defiance and create belief through propaganda. The so-called "truth" is often a casualty of such interpretation, and therein lies the value of assessment and reassessment of the past by professional historians.

In trying to establish just what happened in the past and why, historians focus on a wide variety of sources, most of which were not originally composed or constructed to serve as a window to the past: secret

dispatches, letters, diary accounts, poems, newspaper articles, propaganda fliers, coins, pottery, and even wall graffiti. All of these can open a new world to the historian. One of the more uncertain and controversial historical sources is the evidence of legend and myth.

The mythology of a culture—the stories of heroism, of deities, of moral instruction—often seems to reflect a fantasy world where reality is suspended and the pure joy of creativity is unleashed. But the legends of a culture not only tell us about the values of a people, they can also lead historians toward reconstruction of the past. This question of the appropriateness of legend in the reconstruction of the past is nowhere more evident than in the debate regarding the Trojan War and the Minoan and Mycenaean societies of Bronze Age Greece.

The evidence available to historians of Bronze Age Greece is mostly archeological. Pottery fragments, arrowheads, clay tablets, stone walls and shaft graves, bronze implements, and gold jewelry testify to civilizations that interacted with each other through trade and military combat. There are other unusual sources that we understand incompletely if at all: Mysterious scripts such as Linear A and Linear B offer an incomplete glimpse into a fascinating society. Their messages are obscure or unknown, and therefore historical interpretation is risky at best.

More relevant to our question of legend and history are the monumental narrative poems of the

Iliad and the *Odyssey*, which deal with the legendary Troy and its fight to the death with the forces from mainland Greece in about 1230 B.C.E. Can we accept these epics as valid historical sources, or must they be relegated to the world of fantasy? The skepticism is even more fundamental: Did their author, Homer, even exist? Was he one person or several, or simply the compiler of oral legends that had been handed down and amplified by several singers over the centuries?

The road toward Truth is a difficult path, obscured by time, conflicting evidence, or governments with ideological priorities. Every student must learn to evaluate the past and become his or her own historian. This is essential in creating the perspective necessary to evaluate one's own life and place in society.

KEY EVENTS IN EARLY GREEK HISTORY

1600–1400 B.C.E.   Minoan Greece
Bronze Age Minoan civilization flourishes on Crete. Palace at Knossos is complex and gives rise to the legend concerning King Minos and his labyrinth, which contains the half-man, half-bull Minotaur. Minoans are a peaceful people, but Cretan palaces destroyed about 1450 B.C.E. (except Knossos) by Mycenaean Greek invasion from the mainland. Minoan civilization excavated by British archeologist Sir Arthur Evans, who finds two mysterious pictographic and syllabic scripts, Linear A and Linear B.

1400–1200 B.C.E.   Mycenaean Greece
An aggressive culture based on the Greek mainland at Mycenae conquers the Minoans about 1400 B.C.E. Troy excavated by Heinrich Schliemann, who also found Linear B in Mycenae and believed that Homer's *Iliad* was not simply a myth.

1230–1220 B.C.E.   Trojan War
War fought between Mycenaean Greeks and Trojans recounted later (725 B.C.E.) by Homer in the epic poems the *Iliad* and the *Odyssey*. Trojan War perhaps weakened Mycenaean Greeks and made them vulnerable to invasions about 1200 B.C.E.

1200 B.C.E.   Widespread Mediterranean Destruction
Mycenaean settlements destroyed on mainland Greece (Athens excepted). Linear B tablets were burned and preserved in the fires that accompanied the destruction. Population flows east toward Asia Minor. The Hittite civilization is destroyed. Could this be the "Dorian invasion" of legend? Was this an internal revolution or a domestic civil war between rival cities?

1188 B.C.E.   Invasion of the "Sea Peoples"
Massive attack on Egypt repelled with great difficulty. Egyptian records on palace walls record invasion of "Sea Peoples" (Peleset). Could the "Sea Peoples" be Dorian invaders from north of Greece? Was the destruction of the Hittites and Egyptians the result of one invader who also destroyed the Mycenaean settlements, or of several peoples on the move?

1200–750 B.C.E.   Greek "Dark Ages"
During the Greek "Dark Ages" or Middle Ages, the population on the mainland is reduced, trade is curtailed, and Greeks forget how to write. They survive in small, geographically isolated communities that form the origins of the polis or city-state so important in fifth-century Greece.

776 B.C.E. First Olympic Games
Athletic competition develops between small developing Greek city-states. Greek chronology reckoned in four-year periods from this date are called "olympiads."

750–500 B.C.E. Archaic Greece
Greeks emerge from Dark Ages and begin process of trading and colonizing throughout the Mediterranean (west to Sicily and Italy). Greek alphabet, based on letters, not syllables, is adapted by Greeks, probably from the Phoenician example, and writing develops. The *Iliad* and the *Odyssey*, epic poems passed down through the Dark Ages by oral tradition, are compiled and composed, perhaps by a poet named Homer (ca. 725 B.C.E.).

The Trojan War: Homer's *Iliad*

The Trojan War stands as one of the most famous events in history. The poet Homer compiled the account of this epic confrontation between the Greeks (led by Agamemnon together with his greatest warrior, Achilles, and the "quick-witted" Odysseus) and the Trojans, whose warriors controlled the northwestern coast of modern Turkey. The Greeks had set out to avenge the abduction of the beautiful Helen, wife of the their overlord, Menelaus, by the wily Paris, prince of Troy. The Greek gods also assumed a prominence in the conflict. They had their favorites among the mortals and intervened as their "human personalities" demanded. The story of the *Iliad* and the destruction of Troy is a powerful classic of world literature.

The story begins with Achilles' anger at Agamemnon's claim of the beautiful woman Briseis, who had been granted to Achilles as a prize. The action moves to Achilles' friend, Patroclus, who fights and dies at the hands of Troy's greatest warrior, Hector, while Achilles sulks in his camp. The last passage recounts the vengeance of Achilles as he fights Hector to the death.

Rage—Goddess, sing the rage of Peleus' son Achilles,
murderous, doomed, that cost the Achaeans countless
  losses,
hurling down to the House of Death so many sturdy
  souls,
great fighters' souls, but made their bodies carrion,
feasts for the dogs and birds,
and the will of Zeus was moving toward its end.
Begin, Muse, when the two first broke and clashed.
Agamemnon lord of men and brilliant Achilles.
—Homer (Robert Fagels Translation)

The Wrath of Achilles

HOMER

King Agamemnon rose to the challenge: "Achilles, though you may be a great man, don't think that I will fall for that. I will not be outwitted or bullied by you. You think that I should give up the girl while you keep your own prize safe? Do you expect me to sit calmly while you rob me? Let the Greeks find me a suitable prize that I like in fair exchange, or I will simply take your own, or that of Ajax or of Odysseus—whomever I exploit will be an angry man! But we can worry about that later; for now, let's run a ship into the sea

"The Wrath of Achilles" is from Homer, *The Iliad*, translated by Samuel Butler (1900). Book 1.203–286. Translation modernized by the editor.

and outfit her with a special crew, include a few sacrificial animals, and send my prize, Chryseis, as well. And let one of our own act as commander—either Ajax, or Idomeneus, or yourself, son of Peleus, mighty warrior that you are, so that we may offer sacrifice and appease the anger of the gods."

Achilles scowled at him and answered, "You insolent bastard! Always filled with arrogance and greed! I can't imagine why the Greeks support you at all as they head into battle or on raiding parties. I didn't come here to fight because the Trojans did me any harm. I have no quarrel with them. They have not raided my cattle nor my horses, nor cut down my harvests on the rich plains of Pythia; for the roaring sea and a mountain range lie between us. The truth is that we joined the expedition to please you, you insufferable bastard, to fight the Trojans because of your shameless arrogance and for your idiot brother Menelaus. You just don't understand! And now you threaten to rob me of the prize for which I have fought, and which the sons of the Greeks have given me. Whenever the Greeks sack any rich city in this Trojan countryside, I never receive as great a prize as you do, though I am the one who makes every victory possible. When it comes time to share the spoils after I have fought valiantly, you always get the most and I must skulk back to my ships and take whatever I can get and be thankful. So now I am out of here, back to Pythia. It will be much better for me to return home with my ships, for I will not stay here and be insulted while I pile up gold and loot for you!"

Agamemnon answered, "So go ahead and take off! I won't try to stop you. I have others here who will respect me, and Zeus will be the first. Besides, of all the kings here, you are the most angry and disloyal. So what if you're brave? Who made you so but the gods? Go home, then, with your ships and comrades to lord it over your own subjects. I don't care about you or your anger and here's what I'm going to do: since Phoebus Apollo is taking Chryseis from me, I shall send her with my ship and my followers, but I shall come to your tent and take your own prize, the beautiful Briseis, so that you may realize how much more powerful I am than you. That will serve as a warning to others who may want to set themselves up as my equal."

This pushed Achilles over the edge. His heart was divided between two options: draw his sword, push the others aside, and kill Agamemnon—or restrain himself and check his anger. As he thought it through and began to draw his mighty sword from its scabbard, Athena appeared from Olympus and grabbed Achilles by his hair. She was visible to him alone and nobody else could see her. Achilles turned in amazement, and by the fire that flashed from her eyes, he at once knew that she was Athena. "Why are you here?" he said, "To see the arrogance of Agamemnon, son of Atreus? Let me tell you—and you know I will follow through on this—he shall pay for this insolence with his life."

And Athena replied, "I come from Olympus to bring you to your senses, if you'll only listen. . . . Stop this brawling and do not draw your sword. Go ahead and cut loose on him! Let him have it—with words. For I tell you that your restraint will be paid back when gifts three times as valuable as what you now have will be given to you in consolation for this outrage. Slow down, Achilles, and obey me."

Achilles checked his great hand on the silver hilt of his sword, and thrust it back into the scabbard as Athena told him. Not that Achilles was appeased . . . for the son of Peleus continued to rage at Agamemnon. "You drunken slob," he cried, "with the face of a dog and the heart of a lamb!" You never dare to go into battle and instead avoid all action, just as you avoid death itself. You'd much rather tip-toe around and rob the possessions of any man who contradicts you. You devour your people, a feeble folk who never stand up to you; they must be cowardly since you would never get away with insulting a real man to his face. Mark my words, for I am taking a solemn oath . . . : the day is coming when all the Greeks will miss Achilles on the field of battle. You will look and not find him, and you will be powerless, Agamemnon, to help your men as they fall by the hundreds, dying by the murderous sword of Hector. You won't know what to do and will tear out your heart in remorse for having insulted the best of the Greeks with such contempt."

CONSIDER THIS:

2-1. After reading the selections from Homer's *Iliad* on the Trojan War, what can you say about the relationships between Agamemnon, leader of the Greek expedition, and his warriors, such as Achilles? Was Agamemnon a strong king with absolute control over his men, or was he considered "first among equals"? What does this tell you about Mycenaean society?

2-2. What roles do the gods play in the selections from Homer's *Iliad*? What specific human characteristics do they exhibit, and how essential were they to the success or failure of each contesting army?

The Death of Hector

HOMER

[Priam, the old king,] reached out his arms towards his son and pleaded with him to come within the walls of Troy. "Hector," he cried, "I beg you not to face this man alone, or you will die at the hands of Achilles, for he is far stronger than you and a savage. . . . So come inside the walls to be the guardian of Trojan men and women or you will throw away your life, a victim of the son of Peleus. Have pity also on your wretched father while I am still alive and able to feel. Zeus has prepared a hideous fate for me in my old age, so much tragedy to witness before I die—the massacre of my sons, my daughters raped, their bedrooms pillaged, their babies murdered amid the rage of battle, and my sons' wives hauled away by the cruel hands of the Greeks. In the end, the fierce dogs of war will tear me to pieces at my own gates after someone has beaten the life out of my body with sword or spear. . . ."

Hector thought, "If I retreat within the safety of the city gates, Polydamas will be the first to criticize me, for it was he who urged me to lead the Trojans back to the city on that awful night when Achilles returned to the battlefield. I did not listen then, and I certainly should have. Now I can't look the Trojan men and women in the face knowing that my mistake destroyed our army. Someone would surely say, "Hector ruined us by his own arrogance." Of course it would be better for me to return after having fought Achilles and killed him, or to have died gloriously here before the walls of Troy. What if I were to promise to lay down my shield and helmet, lean my spear against the wall and go straight up to noble

Achilles? What if I were to promise to give up Helen, who was the cause of all this war, and all the treasure that we held from the Greeks? How about if I were to let the Greeks divide half of everything that the city contains among themselves? I could force the Trojans to take a solemn oath that they would hide nothing, but would divide everything in the city in two. . . .

As Hector thought things through, Achilles drew near to him as it were the god of War himself in his flashing helmet. Over his right shoulder he brandished his terrible ash spear, and the bronze gleamed around him like flashing fire or the rising sun. Hector looked up and began to tremble. . . .

Great Hector spoke first: "Though I have been chased three times around the mighty city of Priam, without daring to confront you, I shall no longer run for I am resolved to stand and fight—kill or be killed. But first, let us make a deal, you with your gods as witnesses, I with mine. If Zeus gives me strength and I kill you, I will not commit any atrocities to your body, but will only strip you of your armor and give up your body to the Greeks. Will you do the same for me?"

Achilles glared at him and answered, "Hector, are you mad? You must be insane to offer such a pact. There can be no terms between lions and men, just as the wolf will never see eye to eye with the lamb—it is the natural order, enemies to the end. There can be no understanding between you and me, no deal. We shall fight until one of us falls and gluts the god of war with his life's blood. So summon what strength you have

---

"The Death of Hector" is from Homer, *The Iliad*, translated by Samuel Butler (1900). Book 22. 44-50; 118-145; 156-162; 295-321; 363-388; 398-434; 465-484; 540-549; 566-573; 597-599; 607. Translation modernized by the editor.

and prepare to prove yourself the complete warrior. Little good it will do you, for you are about to die. No more chances, no deals. Pallas Athena is ready to help guide my spear and you shall now pay in full for all the pain and grief you have caused me when you slaughtered my friends on the field of battle . . . "

As he spoke, he drew the sharp blade that hung so great and strong by his side, and gathering himself together he sprang on Achilles like a soaring eagle that swoops down from the clouds to prey on some lamb or timid hare—that was Hector as he pulled his sword and sprang on Achilles. Achilles, mad with rage bolted towards him, eyeing Hector's armor that he had taken from Patroclus, looking for the small unprotected opening near the throat where the collar bone divides the neck from the shoulders—the easiest place to kill a man. As Hector charged him, Achilles drove the point of his spear home, right through the tender part of Hector's neck, though it did not sever his windpipe and left him able to speak. Hector fell headlong. . . .

As life ebbed out of him, Hector said to Achilles, "I am at your knees and beg you in the name of your parents, do not let the dogs devour my body near the Greek ships. My parents will give you gold and treasures, just send my body home so that the Trojans can hold funeral rites when I am dead."

Achilles glared at him and answered, "Dog, don't talk to me of knees or parents. If I could, I would cut your flesh into pieces and eat it raw, for all the pain you have caused me. Nothing will save you from the dogs. . . . Even if Priam should offer me your weight in gold, your mother shall never lay eyes on you again to lament the son she bore—the dogs and vultures will devour your body."

Hector with his dying breath then said, "I know what you are, and was sure that I could not change your mind, for your heart is as hard as iron. Nevertheless, think before you act in case you anger the gods and they remember how you treated me. Your turn will come and, though you are a great fighter, you will be brought down. . . ."

Hector was cut short by the shrouds of death that enfolded him as his soul flew for the House of Hades, lamenting its sad fate of one so young and strong. But Achilles turned to Hector's body, "Die!" he said,

"As for my own death, let it come whenever Zeus and the other gods see fit. . . ."

As he spoke, he pulled his spear from the body and threw it to one side. Next he stripped the blood-stained armor from Hector's shoulders. . . . Then Achilles abused Hector's body. He slit the tendons at the back of his feet from his heels to his ankles, then threaded through leather straps and so tied the body to his chariot with the head trailing on the ground. Achilles then lifted his famous armor on to the chariot and whipped his horses so they flew forward. Hector's body raised a cloud of dust as it dragged behind the chariot, his dark hair trailed on either side. His head, once so handsome, tumbled in the dust and became caked with grit—such was the spectacle that Zeus now allowed as Hector's body was outraged by his enemies in his own land.

[High atop the walls of Troy, Priam and his wife watched as Achilles dragged the body behind his chariot.] Hector's mother tore her hair and ripped off her veil with a cry. His father groaned in agony and the people of Troy began to wail in despair, as if all of Troy had just gone up in flames. . . .

Andromache, Hector's loving wife, heard the cries and flew from her house like a maniac straight to the walls with her servants tailing behind. As she looked out on the plain, she saw Achilles dragging her husband's body in front of the walls, the powerful horses hauling him at an easy trot over the ground toward the Greek ships.

Everything went dark before her eyes as Andromache fainted dead away and fell backward toward the ground. She lay there, supported by her husband's sisters and his brother's wives, who helped revive her. When she had recovered, she burst out in tears and sobbing uncontrollably started to lament to the women of Troy.

"Hector! Alas my darling, woe, woe to me," she cried. . . . "For you are now traveling to the House of Hades, so deep in the earth, leaving me a widow in your house. Your son, the son we conceived, we unhappy parents, is still an infant. And now that you are dead, Hector, you can do nothing to help him, nor can he bring joy to you. Though he may escape the horrors of this miserable war with the Greeks, his life will be one of hardship and sorrow. . . . And you, lying near the Greek ships far from your parents, will be eaten by the worms when the dogs have had their fill."

Andromache's voice rang out in tears, and the women joined in her lament.

CONSIDER THIS:

2-3. Focus on Hector's struggle. Was he a coward or a hero in his confrontation with death? What inspired him to fight Achilles? And how can Achilles, unforgiving to the last, be considered the supreme realist?

Homecoming: The *Odyssey* of Homer

The *Iliad* and the *Odyssey* were perhaps the most influential works in Greek history. Greek and Roman education was fundamentally concerned with the values expressed in these two works. Alexander the Great was even said to have slept with a copy of the *Iliad* under his pillow. And yet the *Odyssey* is very different in temperament and theme from the *Iliad*. The *Odyssey* speaks of homecoming, of love, longing, and revenge. It is the story of Odysseus, a great fighter for the Greeks at Troy whose inspired ploy of the Trojan horse resulted in the Greek victory over the Trojans. But in spite of his brilliance, or perhaps because of it, his homecoming was delayed for ten years as the gods conspired with monsters and witches to interrupt his life. His adventure with the one-eyed Cyclops and his visit to the underworld, where he meets the souls of Achilles and Agamemnon, are two of the most dramatic stories in literature. But Odysseus's return to his island of Ithaca, his introduction to his adult son, Telemachus, his vengeance on the suitors of his wife, Penelope, and their tearful recognition capture the brilliance of the poet history has called Homer.

I will drink life to the lees: all times I have enjoyed greatly, have suffered greatly, both with those that love me, and alone. . . . I am become a name; for always roaming with a hungry heart much have I seen and known; cities of men and manners, climates, councils, governments. . . . and drunk delight of battle, with my peers, far on the ringing plains of windy Troy. I am a part of all that I have met.

—Alfred Lord Tennyson ("Ulysses")

Sing to me of the man, Muse, the man of twists
    and turns
driven time and again off course, once he had plundered
the hallowed heights of Troy.
Many cities of men he saw and learned their minds,
many pains he suffered, heartsick on the open sea,
fighting to save his life and bring his comrades home. . . .
Launch out on his story, Muse, daughter of Zeus,
start from where you will—sing for our time too.

—Homer (Robert Fagels Translation)

The Adventure of the Cyclops

HOMER

"When the Cyclops had finished with all his work, he lit the fire, caught sight of us, and started asking questions:

"'Strangers, who are you? Where do come from? Are you traders, or do you cruise the sea as roving pirates, attacking every man, and taking on all rivals?'

"The Adventure of the Cyclops" is from Homer, *The Odyssey*, translated by Samuel Butler (1900), Book 9.280-335; 388-460; 515-562. Translation modernized by the editor.

"We were frightened out of our minds by his booming voice and the very sight of the monster, but I managed to say, 'We are Greeks on our way home from Troy, but by the will of Zeus, we have been driven far off course by angry winds and a violent sea. We are part of the army of Agamemnon, son of Atreus, who made himself famous throughout the whole world, by destroying so great a city and killing so many people. We therefore humbly ask you to take us in and show us some hospitality as any visitor might reasonably expect. For we are your suppliants and, as you know, this is in accordance with the will of the gods, for Zeus is the protector of travelers and guards their way by enforcing the rights of those in need.'

"To this, he scorned me with a pitiless answer, 'Stranger,' said he, 'you are a fool, or else you know nothing of this country. As if you would preach to me about fearing or respecting the gods! We Cyclopes don't care at all about Zeus or any of your blessed gods, since we are so much stronger than they. I will not spare you or your men out of any regard for Zeus, unless I feel like it. And now tell me where you moored your ship when you came on shore. Was it up the coast, or is she lying just off shore?'

"He was trying to gain an advantage over me, but I understood the world well enough to see through him, so I answered with a lie: 'Poseidon,' said I, 'hurtled my ship onto the rocks at the far end of your country, and wrecked it. We were thrown onto them from the open sea, but I and those who are with me escaped the jaws of death.'

"The cruel monster gave no reply, but he suddenly grabbed two of my men at once and dashed them down upon the ground as though they had been puppies. Their brains spilled out on the ground, and their blood drained into the earth. Then he tore them limb from limb and ate them for dinner. He gobbled them up like a lion in the wilderness, flesh, bones, marrow, and guts, without leaving anything. We could do nothing in reaction to this horrendous sight except cry and lift our hands up to Zeus. After the Cyclops had filled his huge belly and had washed it down with milk, he stretched himself out full on the ground and went to sleep. . . .

"'Look, Cyclops,' I said, you've been eating a lot of human flesh, so drink some of this excellent wine that we've stored on board our ship. I thought of offering it to you in the hope that you would have compassion and help me on my way home. But you are just a savage and I'm sick of it. You ought to be ashamed of yourself; how can you expect people to visit if you treat them in this way?'

"He then took the cup of wine and drank deeply. He was so delighted with the taste that he begged me for another bowl full. . . . I filled it up for him three more times, and he drained each bowl to the dregs. At last, when his head was swimming, I said to him cleverly: 'Cyclops, you ask my name and I will tell it you in return for the present you promised me. My name is Nobody. This is what my father and mother and all of my friends have always called me.'

"But the cruel monster replied, "Then I will eat all of Nobody's comrades before him, and will save Nobody for last. That shall be your gift.' As he spoke, he staggered around the room and fell in a drunken stupor, sprawling face upwards on the ground with his great neck twisted to one side. As he slept, he began to vomit and spewed out hunks of human flesh and a stream of wine. I immediately thrust a wooden pole deep into the ashes of the fire to heat it, and encouraged my men to make sure that none should turn coward and abandon me. Even though the wood was green, it was now glowing fiercely with heat, so I pulled the pole out of the fire just before it blazed, and gathered my men around me, for heaven had filled their hearts with courage. We drove the sharp end of the beam into the monster's eye, and pushing down on it with all my weight I kept turning it round and round as though I were boring a hole in a ship's plank with a drill. . . . So we twisted the red hot beam into his eye, until the blood boiled up around the wood and bubbled all over it as we worked it round and round. The fiery smoke from the burning eyeball scalded his eyelids and eyebrows, and the roots of the eye crackled in the fire, exactly the sound of a loud hiss that comes when a blacksmith plunges a great ax into cold water to strengthen it. . . . That was how the Cyclops' eye hissed around the stake of olive wood. He gave out a tremendous shriek and his hideous yells made the cave ring again and again. We backed away in terror, as he pulled the stake from his eye, streaming with blood and gore, and hurled it from him in a frenzy of rage and pain. He shouted to the other

Cyclopes who lived on the neighboring heights and so they gathered around his cave when they heard him crying and asked what was the matter with him.

"'What's wrong, Polyphemus,' they said, 'that you disturb our peace with your screaming and wake us up? Is somebody trying to rob you or kill you?'

"But Polyphemus shouted to them from inside the cave, 'It's Nobody's treachery! Nobody is killing me!'

"'Then,' they said, 'if nobody is attacking you, you must be sick. Sickness comes from Zeus and you can't do anything about it. All you can do is pray to your father, Poseidon. . . .'

[The next morning, Odysseus and his men escaped from the Cyclops's cave by holding on to the underside of Polyphemus's sheep. The blinded Cyclops felt the top of each sheep as they left the cave, but did not detect any of Odysseus's men.]

"As he spoke he drove the ram outside, but when we managed to get a little way outside of the cave and its courtyard, I first dropped from under the ram's belly, and then freed my men from theirs. Then we drove the sheep down to the ship, though the men were worried and kept looking backwards. . . . With a nod and a stern look, I focused their attention and told them to get all the sheep on board at once and put out to sea. So they went aboard, took their places, and plied the grey sea with their oars. Then, when I had got as far out as my voice would reach, I cut loose against Polyphemus.

"'Cyclops,' I yelled, 'you should have realized that the man you were taunting, whose friends you were eating in your own house, was no weakling. And now you are paying for all your vicious crimes. Now Zeus and all the gods have punished you!

"He got more and more furious as he heard me, so he tore off the top of a high mountain, and flung it just in front of our bow. As it plunged into the water, the sea rose and the backwash swept us toward the mainland, nearly onto the beach. . . . I signaled the men that they must row for their lives. 'Put your backs into it!' I yelled, and they responded with a will. When we had got twice as far as we were before, my spirit was up and in my rage, I yelled out to the Cyclops again, though the men begged me to shut up. 'Cyclops! If anyone asks you who put your eye out and condemned you to such deformed blindness, tell him that it was Odysseus, Sacker of Cities, son of Laertes, who lives in Ithaca!'"

CONSIDER THIS:

2-4. What human themes dominate the *Odyssey*? Note specific passages in the selections from the *Odyssey* that support your ideas. How are Odysseus's cleverness and wit demonstrated in the story of the Cyclops? What qualities in a warrior are most appreciated?

2-5. What values that were important to the Greeks were violated by the Cyclops?

Odysseus in the Underworld

HOMER

"I saw the soul of Agamemnon son of Atreus sadly approach me weeping bitterly as he stretched his arms out to embrace. But he had no strength, no substance any more and I also wept and pitied him as I searched his face with compassion. 'How did you die, Agamemnon, King of Men? Did Poseidon raise the winds and waves against you when you were at sea, or did your enemies destroy you on the mainland when you were stealing their cattle or sheep, or while you were fighting with them for their wives and cities?'

"'Odysseus,' he answered, 'noble son of Laertes, Poseidon did not wreck my ships in any storm, nor did my enemies kill me on land, but Aegisthus and my wicked wife, Clytemnestra, plotted my destruction and finished the job together. He opened his home to me and set out a feast, but then butchered me as a man fells an ox at slaughter. That was my miserable end. And all around me, my friends were murdered like sheep or pigs for the opulent banquet of some great nobleman. I know you have seen scores of men killed either in the thick of

"Odysseus in the Underworld" is from Homer, *The Odyssey*, translated by Samuel Butler (1900), Book 11.436-518; 528-558. Translation modernized by the editor.

battle, or in single combat, but you never saw anything so truly pitiable as the way in which we fell in that hall, with the mixing-bowl and the loaded tables strewn all around, and the ground running with our blood. I heard Priam's daughter, Cassandra, scream with horror as Clytemnestra [Agamemnon's wife] closed quickly and killed her right next to me. I lay dying upon the ground with his sword buried in my body, and raised my hands to kill that bitch, but she slipped away and wouldn't even close my lips or my eyes, though she knew that I was dying. Believe me, there is nothing in this world so cruel and so shameless as a woman who can contemplate such deeds. For who could imagine so hideous a crime as the deliberate butchery of her husband! Oh, I thought I was going to be welcomed home by my children and my servants, but the depth of her abominable crime has brought disgrace on herself and on all women, even the honest ones, who shall come ever after.'

"And I said, 'It's true that Zeus has hated the house of Atreus from the beginning through the deception and wickedness of women. See how many of us fell for Helen's sake, and now it seems that it was Clytemnestra who hatched the plot against you while you were away in Troy.'

"'Absolutely right,' continued Agamemnon, 'so don't be too gentle even with your own wife. Do not tell her all that you know perfectly well yourself. Tell her a part only, and keep the rest to yourself. Not that your wife, Odysseus, is likely to murder you, for Penelope is a remarkable woman with an excellent nature. We left her a young bride with an infant at her breast when we set out for Troy. This child no doubt has now grown to manhood, and he and his father will have a joyful reunion and embrace one another as is only natural. But my bitch of a wife, did not even allow me the happiness

of looking upon my son, but killed me before I could do so. So let me give you a word of advice that I hope you will take to heart: Do not sail directly into port when you get close to Ithaca, but move in carefully, secretly. Women, I tell you, are never to be trusted. . . .'

"As both of us sat crying and talking together, the spirit of Achilles came up to us together with Patroclus, Antilochus, and Ajax who was the finest and most honorable man of all the Greeks after Achilles, the son of Peleus. As Achilles moved in, he recognized me and spoke sadly, 'Odysseus, what next for you noble son of Laertes, that you would venture down to the house of Hades to mingle among the dead, who live on merely as disembodied spirits and are denied the labor that gives purpose to man?'

"And I answered, 'Achilles, son of Peleus, foremost champion among the Greeks, I came to consult Tiresias, and see if he could advise me about my return home to Ithaca, for I have not yet been able to get near Greece, nor to set foot in my own country, but have been dogged by misfortune at every turn. As for you, Achilles, no one was ever so fortunate as you have been, nor ever will be, for you were adored by all of us as long as you were alive, and now that you are here you are a great prince among the dead. Why are you still so bitter?'

"'Spare me your praise of Death,' he answered. I would rather be a slave on earth in the house of some poor man, than a king in hell among those who are done with life.'"

CONSIDER THIS:

2-7. What do we learn about the Greek view of death from Odysseus's visit to the underworld? How do you interpret Achilles' reply to Odysseus's question as to why he was still so bitter about death?

The Return of Odysseus

HOMER

As the Suitors bantered back and forth, Odysseus picked up the great bow, examined it all over, and then strung it effortlessly. . . . The suitors stood in shock as their faces turned pale. At that very moment, Zeus let

forth a loud thunderclap and the heart of Odysseus smiled at this sign of favor from the son of Cronos.

There was a single arrow lying on the table (for the rest that were about to serve death to the Suitors

"The Return of Odysseus" is from Homer, *The Odyssey*, translated by Samuel Butler (1900), Book 21.451-484; Book 22. 1-42; 186-245; 253-263; 269-272. Translation modernized by the editor.

were all inside the quiver) and Odysseus laid it on the bridge of the bow, and drew back the arrow and the string toward him. He aimed carefully and released. The arrow flew through the air, piercing each of the ax handles in turn. Odysseus didn't miss one. Then he turned to his son, Telemachus, and said:

"The stranger in your hall has not disgraced you. I had no problem stringing the bow and did not miss my target. These Suitors underestimated me, for I am strong and my powers are undiminished. . . . As he spoke he gave a nod and Telemachus pulled his sword from its scabbard, grabbed his spear, and stood armed beside his father.

The Destruction of the Suitors

Then Odysseus tore off his rags, and sprang to the floor with his bow and his quiver full of arrows. He spilled the arrows onto the ground at his feet and said, "The first contest is at an end. Let's continue the sport and with Apollo's help, I will hit another target which no man has yet taken on!"

And with that, he aimed his deadly arrow right at Antinous (the dominant Suitor), who had just reached for a gold cup to drink his wine. He wasn't thinking of death at that moment—indeed, who among the crowd would have thought that one man, however brave, could stand alone among so many and kill him? The arrow struck Antinous in the throat, and the point went clean through his neck, so that he fell over and the cup dropped from his hand, while a thick stream of blood gushed from his nostrils. As he fell, he kicked the table from him and all the food was dumped to the ground where it sopped up the blood and gore.

The unconquerable Odysseus glared at them and yelled: "Dogs, did you think that I wouldn't come back from Troy? You have eaten me out of house and home, raped the women of my household, and have put the make on my wife while I was still alive. You feared neither the gods, nor any man. I tell you one and all, your doom is sealed. Prepare to die."

[Odysseus and his son Telemachus then killed all of the suitors who were trapped in the Great Hall. After the battle, Odysseus met his wife, Penelope, for the first time in nineteen years. Penelope, who had resisted all overtures from the suitors, decided to confirm Odysseus's identity by subjecting him to a test.]

Penelope and Odysseus

"Penelope," he said, "the gods may have made you what you are, but for sheer obstinacy, you put all other women to shame. No other woman could bear to keep away from her husband when he had returned to her after twenty years of difficult misfortune. Well, nurse, I suppose you had better get a bed ready for one, for my wife has a heart of iron and I apparently will be sleeping alone." "My dear," answered Penelope, "I'm not being arrogant or indifferent to you, or even surprised, but I have a clear picture of you in my mind when you set sail from Ithaca so long ago. Nevertheless, Eurycleia, place the bed for him outside the bedroom that he himself built so well, and make it up with blankets and clean sheets."

This was Penelope's way of testing her husband. But Odysseus grew enraged and bellowed, "Wife, I am furious at what you have just said! Who could have taken my bed from the place in which I left it? He must have found it hard work, no matter how skilled a workman he was, unless some god came and helped him to move it. There is no man living, however strong and in his prime, who could move it from its place, for it is a magnificent bed that I made with my very own hands. There was a strong, young olive tree growing within the courtyard of the house, which had grown to full height with a stem as thick as a heavy post. I built my room round this with stone walls covered by a roof, and I made the double doors strong and secure. Then I cut off the top boughs of the olive tree and left the stump standing. Next I trimmed the stem and carefully rounded it with my ax, straightening my work by drawing a line on the wood, and making it into a bed post. I then bored a hole down the middle, and made it the center post of my bed. I worked hard until I had finished it by inlaying it with gold and silver. After this, I stretched a hide of red leather from one side of it to the other. So you see, I know all about it, and I want to find out whether it is still there, or whether anyone has removed it by cutting down the olive tree at its roots."

Penelope's knees began to tremble when she realized that his description was true and genuine. He knew their secret. Bursting with tears, she rushed to Odysseus and threw her arms around his neck, kissing and holding him. "Do not be angry with me Odysseus," she cried, "you, who are the wisest of men. We have suffered, both of us. The gods did not allow us to share the joys of our youth, and to grow old together. But don't be angry or hurt that I didn't rush to embrace you as soon as I laid eyes upon you. I have been hesitant and afraid that someone would come to deceive and take advantage of me with his lies, for there were many such men around this house over the years. But now, all is well. You have convinced me by knowing all about our bed, something that no one has ever seen but you and I. . . . You have won me completely." Then Odysseus broke down and cried as his heart melted. He held his dear and faithful wife close in his arms. And it was a sweet moment for her as well, sweet as the sight of land to desperate men swimming toward the safety of shore. . . . If that is happiness, what happiness it was for her to gaze upon her husband again. For she stood in his embrace, arms round his neck, never quite willing to let go. Dawn with her roses caught them at their tears.

CONSIDER THIS:

2-8. In the excerpt in which Odysseus returns to Ithaca, why does he decide to kill all the suitors of Penelope? What informal law in Greek society have the suitors violated? How did the Cyclops, Polyphemus, violate this same law? How did Penelope "test" Odysseus before she would accept him as her true husband? Why is Homer's *Odyssey* considered a classic of Western literature?

2-9. How are women portrayed in Homer's *Iliad* and *Odyssey*? Compare the homecoming experience of Agamemnon and his wife Clytemnestra with that of Odysseus and Penelope. Note also the sorrows of Hector's wife Andromache as she saw the body of her husband dragged around the city of Troy by the victor Achilles. What messages about war and suffering is Homer trying to convey? Compare these scenes with the agony of Andromache after the Greeks enter Troy victoriously as portrayed by Euripides in the selection entitled *The Trojan Women*, in Chapter 3.

Early Greek Literature (700–500 B.C.E.)

About 750 B.C.E., the Greeks had recovered from the destruction of 1200 B.C.E. and erupted upon the Mediterranean world not only with the great epics of Homer but also with goods to trade throughout the Mediterranean and colonies to found in Italy and southern France. This was an expansive time and serves as a prelude to the great political and literary achievements of fifth-century Athens. The following selections from poets of the eighth through sixth centuries B.C.E. are brilliant gems. From the conservative and stolid advice of Hesiod (ca. 700 B.C.E.) in his *Works and Days*, to the sensitive love lyrics of the female poet Sappho (ca. 600 B.C.E.), to the heroic celebrations of athletic achievement in Pindar (ca. 500 B.C.E.), Greek values and a special spirit of life emerge.

Pandora's Box of Evil

HESIOD

For the gods keep hidden from us the material of life. If they didn't, you would easily do enough in a day to satisfy your needs for a whole year without even working. Soon you would pack away your rudder and the fields worked by oxen and mules would go to waste.

But Zeus, in the anger of his heart at being tricked by Prometheus, hid the secret. Therefore, he planned sorrow and mischief against mankind. First he hid fire, but Prometheus stole it back from wise Zeus and concealed the flame in a hollow fennel-stalk, so that Zeus

"Pandora's Box of Evil" is from Hesiod, *Works and Days*, trans. H.G. Evelyn White in *The Homeric Hymns, Epic Cycle, Homerica* (Cambridge: Harvard University Press, 1914), lines 42-82, 90-105. Translation modernized by the editor.

the Thunderer did not see it. Afterwards, Zeus the Cloud Gatherer raged forth:

"Prometheus, most cunning of all, you are proud that you have outwitted me and stolen fire. So, a great plague on you and all men! Humankind will now pay for its fire! Here's another gift—something evil for their delight, and all will embrace their own destruction.

So spoke the father of men and gods, as he laughed aloud. And he told Hephaestus to hurry and mix earth with water and put in it a voice and the human power to move, and then fashion a face like an immortal goddess, sweet, lovely, a beautiful virgin. And then he directed bright-eyed Athena to teach the girl to weave, and golden Aphrodite to grace her with charm, cruel longing, and painful cares that weary the body. And he charged Hermes the Messenger, the Slayer of Argos, to mix in the essence of deceit and the morals of a bitch.

So Zeus ordered and they obeyed him. The Lame God (Hephaestus) molded the earth into a modest girl as directed. The goddess Athena clothed her, and the Graces and Divine Seduction adorned her with gold necklaces, while the Seasons crowned her head with spring flowers. Hermes worked into her a deceitful, yet beguiling nature, her crafty words always sprinkled with lies. And he called this woman, Pandora, because all who lived on Olympus had each given her a gift, this plague to all mankind. The trap was now complete. . . .

Before this time, all men lived on earth apart and free from sorrow, hard work, and heavy sickness that bring death to all men as they grow old quickly and in misery. But now this woman took off the great lid of the box with her hands and scattered all these evils that plague humankind. Only Hope remained secure within and under the rim of the great box—she did not fly out the door. The lid of the box stopped her, but all the other troubles, thousands of troubles, flew from the box, wandering among men. For the earth and the sea are full of evils, diseases attacking men day and night, bringing pain silently, for they were deprived of speech by Zeus the Wise. Thus, there is no way to avoid the will of Zeus.

Works and Days: Advice for the Wise

HESIOD

Invite your friend to dine with you, but not your enemy. Be especially friendly to your neighbor, for if any trouble occurs, he is there, close at hand while kinsmen take time to arm themselves. A bad neighbor is as great a plague as a good one is a great blessing. He who has a good neighbor has a precious possession. You'll never lose an ox if you have a vigilant neighbor. So appreciate him and pay him back equally or in greater measure, if you can, so that if you need him in the future, he'll be there.

Avoid evil profit, for it is as bad as failure itself. Love your friends, and visit whoever visits you. Give to those who also give, but not to those who will not give. A man should give to those who are generous, but not to those who are close-fisted and stingy. Give is a pleasant girl, but Take is bad and she brings death. For the one who gives willingly rejoices in his gift and is glad in his heart. But whoever is shameless and takes for himself, though it is something small, stiffens his heart and it grows cold.

Add to your stores in order to keep Famine from your door. For if you regularly add a bit at a time, it soon becomes substantial. You should be more confident of holding your wealth at home because business abroad is always risky. Think about this carefully: draw on what you have, but to need and not have is truly depressing. Take your fill when the cask is first opened, but at midpoint, be sparing and preserve as you go. When you get to the end, the dregs are not worth saving.

When you promise to pay a friend, always let the wages be fixed at the outset. Your brother may smile and all seem friendly, but you still need to have a witness. Ruin comes equally to those who are too trustful . . . or too distrustful.

Don't let a woman, flaunting herself and wagging her behind, coax and deceive you—she wants your barn! Women are just a bunch of cheats.

"*Works and Days*: Advice for the Wise" is from Hesiod, *Works and Days*, trans. H.G. Evelyn White in *The Homeric Hymns, Epic Cycle, Homerica* (Cambridge: Harvard University Press, 1914), lines 342–381, 405–410. Translation modernized by the editor.

If you only have one son, he will preserve his father's name and keeps his wealth growing. But if you have two sons, then you'll need to live longer and have more money. Yet Zeus can easily enrich a larger family. More children result in more hands, more work, and more profit. If your heart desires more wealth, then you need to do this: work, work, and more work. . . .

First of all, get a house, and a woman and an ox for the plough. The woman should be an unmarried slave, who can help you in the fields and get your house ready so that you will not have to borrow anything and be refused or do without. The seasons come and go quickly and all your work may be lost. So don't put off work until tomorrow or another day. Lazy men who put things off don't fill their barns. Work hard and enjoy the advantage, for idlers wrestle with ruin their entire lives.

Greek Love Poetry

SAPPHO

Let's toast your health,
Lucky bridegroom!
Now the wedding you
sought is over

And the girl you desired
is now your wife,
a bride who is beautiful

to the glance,
with eyes as soft as
honey, and a face

that Love has illumined
with its own special beauty.
Aphrodite has certainly
favored you!

✳✳✳

I haven't heard from her—not one word,
and now I wish I were dead.
When she left, she cried

constantly, and said to
me, "Sappho, we must endure
though I leave unwillingly."

I replied, "Go, and be happy,
but remember me, for you know well
how you have imprisoned me with love.
"Lest you forget, recall
our commitment to Aphrodite
and all the wonders that we shared,

"all the purple crowns,
roses, dill, and crocus
that braided your delicate neck

"with myrrh sprinkled on your head
and girls lingering on soft mats,
satisfied, all they needed close beside,

"all silent,
voiceless,
no blooming woods in the spring,
without song."

"Greek Love Poetry" is from *Songs of Sappho*, trans. Marion Mills Miller (New York: Frank-Maurice, 1925). Translation modernized by the editor

The Celebration of Athletic Glory

PINDAR

PYTHIAN X: For Hippokleas of Thessaly, Winner in the Boys' Double Foot-Race (498 B.C.E.)

For he is trying the Games.
And the people who live around
The valley in Parnassos
Have proclaimed him the greatest of the boys

In the double foot-race.
Sweet is the accomplishment of your goal,
Sweet too its beginning
When a god like Apollo

Inspires such a performance,
And a son steps into the shoes of his father,
Who was twice an Olympic victor,
In the armor of Ares, which knows war.
And the Games in that deep meadow
Under the rocks of Krisa, granted
Victory to Phrikias in the race.
May their luck hold in the future
So that their nobility will blossom!

They have received so great
A share of the Delights of Greece,
May the gods not envy them
And alter their luck.

Though the gods alone never taste pain,
Yet that man is happy and the
Wise poets sing his praises,
If he conquers with his hands or swift feet
And wins the greatest of prizes
Through perseverance and strength,
And lives to see
His young son, in turn, gather Pythian garlands.

"The Celebration of Athletic Glory" is from Pindar, *Selected Odes of Pindar*, trans. Thomas D. Seymour (Boston: Ginn & Co., 1882), *Pythian 10*, lines 7–25; *Isthmian 5*, lines 7–20. Translation modernized by the editor.

ISTHMIAN V: For Phylakidas of Aegina, Winner in the Trial of Strength (478 B.C.E.)

In the competition of the Games,
He has achieved glory,
Whose hair is tied back and wreathed with
    garlands,
As the victor with his hands
Or the swiftness of his feet.
Men's valor is judged by the gods,
And there are only two things that
Cultivate the sweetest bloom of life
Among the blossoms of prosperity:
To have good luck and a noble reputation.
Do not seek to become Zeus!
You have everything, if a share
Of these beautiful things comes to you.
Mortal goals befit mortal men.
But for you Phylakidas, a double victory awaits
At the Isthmian Games,
And at Nemea for you and your brother Pytheas
In the strength events. My heart sings.

CONSIDER THIS:

2-10. What advice does Hesiod offer regarding hope, evil, and profit in the excerpts from *Works and Days*? What does he think of women and "lazy men?" Note especially the passage that presents the world as "free from disease" until Pandora opened up the box and "scattered all the evils that plague humankind."

2-11. In contrast to Hesiod, what values and emotions are expressed by Sappho? Which is your favorite stanza from her poetry and why?

2-12. What qualities does Pindar admire in his celebration of athletic glory? How are these reflective of some of the values you found in excerpts from Homer's *Iliad* and *Odyssey*? How would you interpret Pindar's advice, "Do not seek to become Zeus!"? Can you apply this to Achilles or Odysseus?

Chapter 3

Democracy and Empire:
The Golden Age of Athens

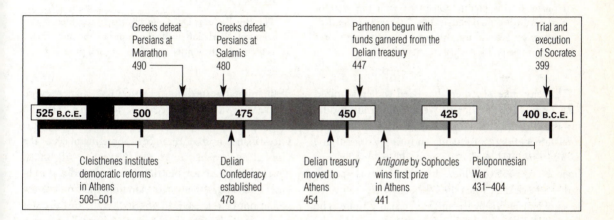

Greeks defeat Persians at Marathon 490

Greeks defeat Persians at Salamis 480

Parthenon begun with funds garnered from the Delian treasury 447

Trial and execution of Socrates 399

525 B.C.E. | 500 | 475 | 450 | 425 | 400 B.C.E.

Cleisthenes institutes democratic reforms in Athens 508–501

Delian Confederacy established 478

Delian treasury moved to Athens 454

Antigone by Sophocles wins first prize in Athens 441

Peloponnesian War 431–404

Of all the wondrous things on earth, the greatest of these is man.

—SOPHOCLES

Democracy is based on the conviction that man has the moral and intellectual capacity, as well as the inalienable right, to govern himself with reason and justice.

—HARRY S TRUMAN

Excessive freedom leads to anarchy, which in turn results in despotism, the most burdensome and most brutal slavery.

—PLATO

In the strict sense of the term, a true democracy has never existed and never will exist.

—JEAN-JACQUES ROUSSEAU

When the Athenians finally wanted not to give to society, but for society to give to them, when the freedom they wished for was freedom from responsibility, then Athens ceased to be free.

—EDWARD GIBBON

CHAPTER THEMES

- **The Power Structure:** How would you define democracy in the classical sense of the term? Was Athens a democracy? Is democracy the best and most natural form of government for people?

- **Imperialism:** How did Athens gain and maintain its empire? Can a democracy possess an empire, or is this a moral contradiction?

- **Women in History:** How were women portrayed in early Greek society as viewed in the *Iliad* and *Odyssey* of Homer? Is this picture consistent with the view of women during the Golden Age of Greece in the fifth century B.C.E.? Did the Athenian democracy consider women to be political equals to men?

- **Revolution and Historical Transition:** The history of fifth-century Greece has generally been viewed as a great success story. Is success in war or government a necessary foundation for success in the arts? How essential is arrogance to the progress of civilization? Was Athens created and then destroyed by its hubris?

- **The Varieties of Truth:** How do historians determine what is true? Does every historian have biases that result in a subjective interpretation of history? Is all truth, therefore, relative?

- **The Big Picture:** Do the great artistic and literary creations of civilization justify the means of obtaining them? Is there a political price to pay for cultural progress?

The city-state of Athens has been widely admired for its contributions to Western civilization during the fifth century B.C.E. This was a time of great intellectual energy, producing enduring works of art, architecture, philosophy, drama, and history. The confidence necessary to achieve such heights was granted early in the century when the Greek city-states united to repel two invasions by the mighty Persian Empire. The Spartan military machine had proved its worth at the battle of Thermopylae, and the Athenian reputation for cleverness was established by Themistocles at the battle of Salamis in 480 B.C.E. On this note of triumph, the Golden Age of Athens began.

During the period from 480 to 430 B.C.E., leaders such as Pericles extolled the superiority of Athenian democratic government and the freedom essential to Athenian greatness. Yet critics of the time pointed out the shortcomings of the democracy and of its leadership. At root, it might be argued that the greatness of Athenian civilization depended on its "allies," or fellow members of the Delian Confederacy. This Confederacy was established in 478 B.C.E., after the Persian wars, to ensure that the Greeks would not be attacked by Persia again. Furthermore, Greek cities on the coast of Asia Minor were to be freed and booty obtained from Persia to offset the costs of confederate expeditions and past losses. Theoretically, Athens had no greater vote than any of its confederates, but almost from the outset it held the keys to power, contributing both the administrators of the treasury on the island of Delos and the commanders

of the military expeditions. By 466 B.C.E., after several confederate victories, it became evident that Persia no longer posed a threat to the city-states of Greece or the Greek islands in the Aegean Sea. Some members of the Confederacy wished to secede (Naxos in 469 B.C.E., Thasos in 465 B.C.E.), but they were opposed and militarily crushed by Athens. Secession from the Confederacy would not be tolerated. In 454 B.C.E., the treasury was moved from the island of Delos to Athens. The patron goddess, Athena, supervised the protection of all tribute that came into Athens (called the "first fruits"). The great Athenian orator Pericles maintained the Athenian Empire (as the Delian Confederacy came to be called) partly to counter Spartan land power, and he managed it efficiently so as to produce revenues essential to the glorification of Athens. By 447 B.C.E., work on the Parthenon had begun, and several other building projects, artists, and sculptors would be financed by funds contributed by Athenian "allies."

Athens controlled its empire rigidly, maintaining order by imposing its own laws and customs on subject cities. Every four years subjects of the empire came to Athens to participate in the Panatheneia, a celebration honoring the patron goddess Athena. There they gathered to learn what their tax assessments would be for the next four years. The Athenians inscribed these assessments on a great monolith, located on the Acropolis, called the Tribute Lists. Such a blatant reminder of their subservience must have been difficult for the Athenian allies to bear.

From 431 to 404 B.C.E., the Spartans and Athenians entered into a great conflict that came to be called the Peloponnesian War. This war was born of Spartan distrust for the growing Athenian power and trade influence in areas previously controlled by Sparta and its allies. The two city-states, so different in outlook and political orientation, fought, as the historian Thucydides noted, the greatest war "in Greek history, affecting a large part of the non-Greek world, and . . . the whole of mankind."

In the end, Athens lost not only the physical struggle and its empire, but also the edge of confidence that had propelled its democracy and inspired its poets and statesmen. Perhaps the greatest indication of this loss was the execution of the philosopher Socrates. His penetrating questions demanded reflection on Athenian values and ideals. He considered himself a gadfly whose job it was to prod Athenians to self-awareness by challenging the very foundation of their beliefs. Socrates was condemned to death in 399 B.C.E. on rather nebulous charges. His death was symbolic of the rigid defensiveness of a decaying democracy.

The historical problem at issue here involves the compatibility of democracy and empire. From a moral standpoint, should a state that espouses freedom for all of its citizens control an empire that is maintained by fear and force? Is it even possible for a democratic government to rule an empire effectively? Finally, do the beauty and cultural worth of the monuments of a civilization justify the means of obtaining them? In other words, what price civilization?

FIGURE 3.1 The rocky plateau of the ancient Acropolis overlooks the city of Athens. The Parthenon (center), temple of the patron goddess Athena, was built with funds garnered from the Athenian Empire. What price civilization? (*Tourist Organization of Greece*)

KEY EVENTS IN THE DEVELOPMENT OF THE GREEK POLIS

650–500 B.C.E. Development of Sparta

Sparta quells a rebellion of helots (Messenian slaves) and defeats Argos in a long war (650 B.C.E.). Reforms transform Sparta into a military academy and camp, establishing rigid social, legal, and military system under founder Lycurgus and lawgiver Draco (621 B.C.E.). Development of hoplite phalanx (close order military formation).

600–550 B.C.E. Age of Tyrants

Because of difficult economic conditions, factional divisions within the ruling Greek aristocracies often resulted in the establishment of tyrants, strongmen who restructured society and oversaw public works and security within the polis.

600–500 B.C.E. Development of Early Greek Philosophy

Thales of Miletus (ca. 600 B.C.E.) and Pythagoras (ca. 550 B.C.E.) search for the primary elements around which life revolves and the numerical relationships and harmonies within the universe.

594 B.C.E. Reforms of Solon

Athens emerges from debt slavery through economic and social reforms and a revised constitution under the direction of Solon, the "sole archon." He establishes precedents for democracy.

546–510 B.C.E. Tyranny of Pisistratus

Pisistratus is a tyrant in Athens who rules beyond the authority of the laws, but is generally stable and progressive until his sons succeed him, become authoritarian, and are assassinated.

508 B.C.E. Reforms of Cleisthenes

Cleisthenes follows precedents established by Solon and creates a complex democratic system in Athens.

The Greek Polis: Two Ways of Life

"Man Is a Political Animal"

ARISTOTLE

The city-state, or polis, evolved during the period from 1200 to 500 B.C.E. and offered a unique organization for the Greeks. Each polis was independent in its particular form of government, provided for its own defensive arrangements, and conducted its own foreign policy. Thus one city-state might be a monarchy, another a democracy, and a third an oligarchy. Although there was great diversity among city-states, the polis provided a basic foundation for all social and political organization. The great philosopher Aristotle analyzed the origins of the polis in his treatise on *Politics*. He believed that human beings as social creatures could not live apart from the civilizing confines of the polis without degenerating into animal brutishness. Human beings needed to live within a community that actually controlled and improved their human nature, thus allowing them to think, create, and interact progressively.

"Man Is a Political Animal" is from Aristotle, *Politics*, trans. Benjamin Jowett, 1.1-2 (Oxford: The Clarendon Press, 1905). Translation modernized by the editor.

Every state is a community of some kind, and every community is established with a view to some good; for humankind always acts in order to obtain that which it thinks good. But, if all communities aim at some good, the state or political community, which is the highest of all, and which embraces all the rest, aims at good in a greater degree than any other, and at the highest good. . . .

When several villages are united in a single complete community, large enough to be nearly or quite self-sufficient, the state comes into existence, originating in the bare needs of life, and continuing to exist for the sake of a good life. And therefore, if the earlier forms of society [a household, a village] are natural, so is the state, for it is a natural evolution, and the nature of a thing is its final form. For whatever exists when fully developed, we call its nature, whether we are speaking of a man, a horse, or a family. Besides, the final, most perfected, and self-sufficient form of anything is the best. Therefore, it is evident that the state is a creation of nature, and that man is by nature a political animal. And he who by nature and not by mere accident is without a state, is either a bad man or a god; he is like the "tribeless, lawless, hearthless one," whom Homer denounces—this natural outcast from the state is a lover of war, who is on his own, isolated from all civilized society.

Now, that a human being is more of a political animal than bees or any other gregarious animals is evident. Nature, as we often say, makes nothing without purpose, and man is the only animal whom she has endowed with the gift of speech. And whereas mere voice is but an indication of pleasure or pain, and is therefore found in other animals, the power of speech allows discernment between that which is expedient and that which contradicts personal benefit, discernment between the just and the unjust. And it is a human characteristic that they alone have any sense of good and evil, of justice and injustice, and the association of living beings who have this sense makes a family and a state. . . .

The proof that the state is a creation of nature and exists for the benefit of the individual is that the individual, when isolated, is not self-sufficient, but only a part in relation to the whole. But he who is unable to live in society, or who has no need because he is sufficient for himself, must be, as I said, either a beast or a god: he is no part of a state. A social instinct is implanted in all humans by nature, and yet he who first founded the state was the greatest of benefactors. For human beings, when perfected, are the best of animals, but when separated from law and justice, they are the worst of all. Although humans have been equipped at birth with arms that are meant to be used with intelligence and for the sake of virtue, nevertheless they may be used for the worst ends to perpetrate armed injustice. Therefore, if a man is not virtuous, then he is the most degraded, most savage of animals, filled with lust and gluttony. But justice provides the bond between men in states, and the administration of law, which determines what is just, is the principle of order in political society.

Consider This:

3-1. Aristotle describes human beings as "political animals." What does he mean by this?

3-2. According to Aristotle's analysis, what is the purpose of the Greek polis? Without association within a political community, what happens to the individual? Do you agree with Aristotle?

The City-State of Sparta: The Reforms of Lycurgus

PLUTARCH

One of the most fascinating city-states was Sparta. In the eighth century B.C.E., it had prospered in a rather open political and economic environment. But in the late seventh century B.C.E., Sparta, under the leadership of Lycurgus, adopted a rigid military system that produced one of the most efficient and feared armies in antiquity. The Spartans enslaved some of the surrounding population (calling them *helots*) and used them to work the land while

"The City-State of Sparta" is from Plutarch, "Lycurgus," 9–12, in William S. Davis, ed., *Readings in Ancient History*, vol. 1 (New York: Allyn and Bacon, 1912), pp. 104–105. Translation modernized by the editor.

Spartan warriors honed their military skills. The following accounts describe the reforms of Lycurgus and the Spartan way of life. Although they never produced great literature or ideas, the Spartans were admired because they prevented chaos in their society.

Lycurgus commanded that all gold and silver coin should be called in, and that only a kind of money made of iron should be used. Because a great amount of iron was worth so very little, to lay up twenty or thirty pounds required a pretty large storage area, and to remove it, nothing less than a yoke of oxen! With the distribution of this money, at once a number of vices were banished from Sparta; for who would rob such a coin? Who would unjustly detain or take by force, or accept as a bribe, a thing which it was not easy to hide, nor indeed of any use if it were cut into pieces?

In the next place, he abolished all needless and superfluous arts. Merchants sent no shiploads into Spartan ports; no rhetoric master, no itinerant fortune teller, or gold or silversmith, engraver, or jeweler, set foot in a country that had no money; so that luxury, deprived little by little of the ingredients that fueled it, wasted to nothing, and died away of itself. For the rich had no advantage here over the poor, as their wealth and abundance had no foreign outlets, but were shut up at home doing nothing. And in this way they became excellent artists in common necessary things; bedsteads, chairs, and tables, and other family staples, were admirably well made there.

The third and most masterly stroke of this great lawgiver, by which he struck an even more effectual blow against luxury and the desire of riches, was the rule he made, that Spartans should all eat in common, of the same bread and same meat, and should not spend their lives at home, lying on costly couches at splendid tables, asking their tradesmen and cooks to fatten them up like greedy slobs, and to ruin not only their minds, but their very bodies, which, enfeebled by indulgence and excess, would stand in need of long sleep, warm baths, freedom from work, and care and attendance as if they were continually sick. . . . For the rich were obligated to go to the same table with the poor, could not use or enjoy their abundance, nor so much as please their vanity by looking at or displaying it. Nor were they allowed to eat at home first, and then attend the public tables, for every one had an eye upon those who did not eat and drink like the rest, and criticized them for being haughty and effeminate. . . .

Spartan Discipline

PLUTARCH

Child Rearing in Sparta

Nor was it in the power of the father to rear his child as he thought fit. The child belonged first to the state and the father was obliged to carry it before certain officials at a place called Lesche where some of the elders carefully inspected the infant, and if they found it strong and well formed, gave the order to raise it and allocated to it one of the nine thousand shares of land above mentioned for its maintenance. But if they found the child puny and ill-shaped, they ordered it to be taken to . . . a sort of chasm [and exposed to the elements], thinking it neither for the good of the child itself, nor for the public interest, that it should be brought up, if it did not from the very outset, appear healthy and vigorous. The nurses provided excellent care, for they did not bind children in blankets, but encouraged them to grow up free and unconstrained. Nor were the children picky eaters, or afraid of the dark or of being left alone and crying. Because they were so good at raising children, Spartan nurses were often hired by people of other countries.

"Spartan Discipline" is from Plutarch, "Lycurgus," 16–19, in William S. Davis, ed., *Readings in Ancient History*, vol. 1, (New York: Allyn and Bacon, 1912), pp. 107–111. Translation modernized by the editor.

Lycurgus did not allow fathers to hire tutors for their sons, nor could he raise his own children as he wished. Rather, as soon as they were seven years old they were to be enrolled in certain companies and classes, where they lived under the same order and discipline, doing their exercises and playing together. Whoever showed the most ability and courage was made captain and the other children always watched him and obeyed his orders, enduring patiently whatever punishment he inflicted; so that the whole course of a Spartan education was one continued exercise of a ready and perfect obedience. The old men were also spectators of their performances, and often raised quarrels and disputes among them, to have a good opportunity of finding out their different characters, and of seeing which would be valiant, which a coward, when they should come to more dangerous encounters. They taught the children to read and write just enough to serve their basic needs. Their primary purpose was to make them good subjects, and to teach them to endure pain and to conquer in battle. To this end, as they grew older, their discipline was proportionably intensified. Their hair was cut short and they went barefoot and played naked for the most part.

The Second Stage of the Spartan Education

After they were twelve years old, they were no longer allowed to wear any undergarment. They had one coat to serve them a year and their bodies were hard and dry, with little attention to baths and lotions. They were allowed these human indulgences on only a few days of the year. They lodged together in small groups on beds made of the reeds which grew by the banks of the river, and which they broke off with their hands without a knife. During the winter, they mingled some thistledown with their reeds, which helped them stay warm. . . . [Spartan youths were required to steal wood and herbs], which they did by creeping into the gardens, or sneaking into the eating houses: if they were caught in the act, they were whipped without mercy, for thieving so poorly and awkwardly. They also stole all other meat they could lay their hands on, observing every opportunity when people were asleep or more careless than usual. If they were caught, they were not only punished with whipping, but hunger too, because their already meager food ration was cut. Food rations, by the way, were designed to be minimal since this would force Spartan children to exercise their ingenuity and resourcefulness just to get by each day.

So seriously did the Spartan children go about their stealing, that a youth, who had stolen a young fox and hid it under his coat, allowed it to tear out his very guts with its teeth and claws, and died where he stood, rather than let it be seen. What is practiced to this very day in Sparta is enough to give credit to this story, for I myself have seen several of the youths beaten to death. . . .

They also taught them to speak in a natural and graceful manner, and to express much in few words . . . . Children in Sparta, by a habit of long silence, came to give just and wise answers. When some Athenian laughed at their short swords, King Agis answered him, "We find them long enough to reach our enemies." Just as their swords were short and sharp, so it seems to me, were their statements. They make the point and grab the attention of the listeners better than any other kind.

CONSIDER THIS:

3-3. According to these accounts, what were the qualities of character that were most admired in Spartan society? Describe the Spartan educational system. What did Spartan youth learn "in school"?

"Happiness Depends on Being Free, and Freedom Depends on Courage": The Funeral Oration of Pericles (430 B.C.E.)

THUCYDIDES

The Athenian polis was, in most respects, the opposite of Sparta. In 510 B.C.E., under the leadership of Cleisthenes, Athens adopted a democratic system in which all citizens were

"The Funeral Oration of Pericles" is from Thucydides, *The Peloponnesian War*, 2.35–2.45, in George W. Botsford, *A Sourcebook of Ancient History* (New York: The Macmillan Co., 1912), pp. 206–209. Translation modernized by the editor.

expected to vote, serve in public office, and offer themselves as jurors. Active participation in political affairs was demanded, and one who shunned such responsibility was called *idiotes*, or "private person"; the word has come down to us as *idiot*, with all its pejorative connotations.

The leader of the Athenian democracy in the middle of the fifth century B.C.E. was the great orator Pericles. After the first year of the Peloponnesian War (430 B.C.E.), Pericles spoke to the wives and parents of those who had died in the fighting in an attempt to justify their loss. The "Funeral Oration" that follows was recorded by the Athenian historian Thucydides; it is the quintessential expression of the structure and values of the Athenian democracy.

"I do not wish to make a long speech about the valor and military achievements of our ancestors who built our empire, or stemmed the tide of foreign aggression, or fended off attacks upon us by other Greek states. Rather, I would like to talk about the road we traveled to achieve our position of preeminence, our form of government, and the character through which we became a great city; these are the questions that concern me now before I speak of the dead, and will profitably instruct all of us, whether citizens or foreigners alike.

"Our constitution does not copy the laws of neighboring states; we are rather an example to them. It is true that we are called a democracy, for the administration of the state is in the hands of the many and not of the few. But the law assures equal justice when settling private disputes, and no social standing or other class considerations interferes with merit as the foundation for advancement in public life. Neither does poverty bar the way, for if a man is willing to serve the state, he is not hindered by the obscurity of his condition. We are free and tolerant in our private lives and obey the laws and the dictates of those we place in public office. And just as our political life is free, so too is our personal life. Far from being envious of our neighbors, we do not become angry with them for doing what each enjoys, nor do we cast a scornful glance at them which cannot fail to offend. But all this ease in our private relations does not make us lawless as citizens. We fear political chaos and this instructs us to obey the magistrates and the laws, particularly those that protect the weak, as well as unwritten laws that cannot be broken without disgrace.

"And we make it a point to refresh our spirits after we have finished work. We celebrate games and sacrifices throughout the year. In our own homes, we find an elegant refuge that helps daily to drive away our cares. Because of the dynamism of our city, the fruits of the whole earth flow into our harbors, so we enjoy the goods of other countries as freely as our own.

"Then again, our military expertise is in so many ways superior to that of our enemies. We throw open our city to the world, and we never expel a foreigner or prevent him from seeing or learning anything of which our enemies might profit. We don't rely on secret weapons or deceit to trick our enemies, but are confident of our own strength and patriotic spirit. There's also a difference in our educational system; the Spartans from their earliest youth undergo the most punishing training in courage, but we live at ease, yet are equally ready to face the same dangers as they. . . .

"If then we prefer to meet danger without dread, but also without laborious training, and with a courage which has been gained by habit and not enforced by law, is that not to our advantage? Although we do not court unnecessary pain, when the dark hour comes, we can still be as brave as those Spartans who never allow themselves to rest. Therefore, our city is equally admirable in peace and war.

"And that is not all. For we are also lovers of the beautiful—but without extravagance. Simple in our tastes, we cultivate the mind without loss of masculinity. We employ wealth, not for gossip and ostentation, but only when it has real purpose. Poverty is no disgrace. The true disgrace is doing nothing to avoid it. An Athenian citizen does not neglect the state while enhancing his own household. And even those of us who work in private business have a solid understanding of the political issues. We alone regard a man who refuses to participate in public affairs, not as harmless—but as useless. And even if most of us are not originators of political ideas, we are certainly sound judges of public policy. The worst thing is to rush to action without

FIGURE 3.2 The Parthenon was dedicated to Athena, the patron goddess of Athens: "Realize the greatness of Athens by fixing your eyes on her every day till your hearts are filled with love for her. And then, when all her glory breaks upon you, reflect that it was men of courage, men with a sense of duty and honor, men who were ashamed to fall below an elevated standard, who achieved all this."—Pericles (*Perry M. Rogers*)

first discussing the options extensively. For we Athenians have a particular ability to think before we act, rather than to hesitate and second-guess our decisions. And those are surely the bravest who, although they understand both the pains and pleasures of life, nevertheless do not hesitate in the face of danger.

"Another unique thing about our generous nature is that we cultivate friendships by conferring, not receiving favors. . . . And it is only the Athenians who benefit others without a cold, expedient calculation. Instead, we offer our commitment in the full confidence of freedom and a fearless spirit.

"In short, I say that Athens is the school of Greece! And I doubt if the world can produce a citizen like the Athenian who can handle so many emergencies with such expansiveness and versatility. This is no idle boast, but a matter of plain fact. Our strength of character has secured our preeminence among all states. For when her back is against the wall, Athens

alone of her contemporaries has proved greater than her reputation, and alone gives her rivals no embarrassment when they have been defeated, or her subjects any doubt of Athenian fitness to rule. In fact, there are mighty monuments of our power that will serve as witnesses to our glory throughout the ages. We will not need a Homer, whose poetry may please for the moment. . . . No, it is evident that we have compelled every land and every sea to open a path for our valor, and everywhere have planted eternal memorials of our friendship—or memorials to the suffering inflicted on our enemies. This, then, is the Athens for which each of these men, so determined not to lose her, fought and nobly gave their lives. Each of their survivors should be equally willing to lay down theirs.

"And if I have spoken at length about our city, it has been to demonstrate that we have more at stake in this war than others who have no such blessings to lose. I also wanted my words for the dead to mean something through the evidence of their sacrifice. My tribute is almost complete. The Athens that I have here celebrated owes its greatness to the courage and valor of these men, and others like them. Unlike most of the other Greeks, words cannot do justice to their deeds.

"And if you want a test of their worth, the proof can be found not only in this final seal of death, but for some, in this first demonstration of courage. No doubt these men had their faults, but we should focus on their gallantry against the enemy in defense of their homeland; this steadfast conduct as Athenian citizens will serve as a veil for their personal shortcomings. . . .

"So died these men, who were worthy of Athens. You, their survivors, must possess the same determination to sacrifice your lives on the field of battle, though you may pray to be spared their fate. And don't be contented with abstract words about the benefits of defending your country, though you know as well as I that these provide a valuable topic for an ambitious orator. Rather, I prefer that you realize the greatness of Athens by fixing your eyes on her every day till your hearts are filled with love for her. And then, when all her glory breaks upon you, reflect that it was men of courage, men with a sense of duty and honor, men who were ashamed to fall below an elevated standard, who achieved all this. No personal failure could ever have made them deprive their country of their courage; for they laid down their lives at her feet as the most glorious contribution they could give. And for that sacrifice, each of them receives our praise that will never die and a tomb that houses not simply their bodies, but that noblest of shrines, where their glory remains eternally remembered and is offered up on occasion to inspire others to action. For heroes have the whole earth as their memorial; and even in foreign lands where there is no visible shrine with their names inscribed, they will still be remembered in every heart. You must try to be like them. Know that happiness depends on being free, and freedom depends on courage. Never shrink from the dangers of war.

"Those who have the greatest reason to hate death are not the miserable and unfortunate, who have nothing to hope for; rather, they are those who by living run the risk of a complete reversal of fortune, and would feel it most intensely if things were to go badly for them. And surely, for any rational man, cowardice would be more painful to bear than death, especially when it comes unperceived in the midst of battle, while fighting with the full confidence of his patriotism. I therefore offer comfort, not condolence to the parents of the dead we remember here today."

Consider This:

3-4. How were the city-states of Athens and Sparta diametrically opposed? According to Pericles in his "Funeral Oration," what qualities made Athens great? What was the basis of Spartan achievement?

3-5. In his "Funeral Oration," how does Pericles justify Athenian imperialism? What benefits does Athens give its allies and what does it get in return? Is this equitable? Are there any weaknesses or defects in Pericles's arguments?

THEME: SOCIAL AND SPIRITUAL VALUES

The Historian at Work—Herodotus

"As Rich as Croesus": The Happiest of Men?

The Greek concept of the polis was not confined to the mainland of Greece or even to the islands of the Aegean Sea. The Greeks in the years after 750 B.C.E. spread their culture and values by establishing colonies in southern France, Italy, and Sicily in the west and along the eastern coast of Asia Minor (called Ionia) that fell under the control of the Persian Empire after 540 B.C.E. These Ionian Greeks established several city-states and lived in a kind of benign defiance of Persian authority. The great story of the clash between Persian might and Greek

"As Rich as Croesus" is from Herodotus, *The Histories*, 1.30–1.46, in George Rawlinson, trans., *The History of* Herodotus (New York: E. P. Dutton, 1910). Translation condensed and modernized by the editor.

independence that would consume the first half of the fifth century B.C.E. therefore begins on the Ionian coast and is told by one of the great historians of antiquity—Herodotus.

We know little about Herodotus's life except that he was born in Halicarnassus (now modern Bodrum in western Turkey) perhaps around 480 B.C.E. and spent much of his life in exile, traveling through the Mediterranean, spending time on the island of Samos, in Athens, and eventually ending up in southern Italy. His *Histories* provide evidence of his extensive travels, from Egypt and Phoenicia to Asia Minor and the Black Sea region. He was an active researcher and writer from the 450s to the 420s B.C.E.

Herodotus has been called the "Father of History" because he was the first western writer to go beyond a chronological narration of what happened to inquire why it happened. This is what separates mere narration from critical analysis. The question "why" is subjective and based on an analysis of particular facts in order to establish an interpretation of events. Herodotus waded into this murky water with a grand purpose as he set out in the first sentence of his history:

> "These are the investigations of Herodotus of Halicarnassus which he publishes in the hope of preserving from the decay of memory, the great and impressive acts of the Greeks and Persians, and to put on record the reasons for their conflict."
>
> —HERODOTUS

Herodotus wants to define great deeds and tell the story of East versus West, of the culture and civilization of Persia in opposition to the values and heroism of the Greeks, and to record the foundation of this clash. Herodotus writes a narrative history with the first elements of analysis regarding the origins and nature of the Persian wars.

Writing around 440 B.C.E. about events that occurred in 490 and 480 B.C.E., Herodotus was in a position to get a variety of perspectives in forming his narrative. But to tell the story of the war between the Persians and the Greeks, Herodotus spends nearly half of his history explaining the political and institutional organization of the Persian Empire, the character of its kings, and its control over different peoples and cultures throughout the far reaches of Persian influence. Along the way, Herodotus digresses with purposeful stories that reveal the interaction between the mighty and the weak, the brave and heroic with the brutal and corrupt. We learn all sorts of interesting asides about history, some of which provide our only information on the process of Egyptian mummification, Scythian burial customs, or the workings of the Persian postal system.

Herodotus is a comfortable guide, the type of story teller with a broad purpose and narrative skill who could fascinate his listeners for hours at the fireside. But it is through these personal stories that we ascertain character and appreciate Greek values that speak to the larger concerns of human nature and the human condition. Herodotus guides us now as he tells the famous story of Croesus, the powerful King of Lydia, himself a great conqueror who was eventually defeated by the Persians. His wealth and success were legendary, with many envious and aspiring to be "as rich as Croesus." When Croesus encounters the wise Athenian statesman, Solon, he asks him a simple question: Who is the happiest of men? Herodotus begins the tale . . .

When all these conquests had been added to the Lydian empire, and the prosperity of Sardis (the capital) was now at its height, there appeared, one after another, all the wise men of Greece living at the time, and among them Solon, the famous Athenian statesman and lawgiver. Solon had set out to see the world and had already visited the court of Amasis in Egypt and now came to visit Croesus at Sardis. Croesus received him as his guest, and lodged him in the royal palace. On the third or fourth day after he arrived, Solon was given a tour of the palace and the royal treasuries that were overflowing with their magnificent bounty. When Solon finished the inspection, Croesus sidled up to him and posed a question: "My Athenian guest, we have all heard of your wisdom and many travels throughout the world. . . . I am curious, therefore, to ask you whom of all the men that you have known do you consider to be the happiest?" Croesus asked this because he simply wanted the wise Solon to confirm what he already suspected—that he himself was the happiest of mortals. But Solon answered him without flattery or pretense, "Tellus of Athens, sire." Croesus was astonished at what he heard and demanded sharply, "And why do you think Tellus is the happiest of men?" To which Solon replied, "Well, first of all his country flourished under his direction, and he had sons who were handsome and good men, and he lived to see grandchildren born to each of them who grew up healthy and strong. And finally, after a long life of comfort and prosperity, his death was honorable and glorious. In a battle between the Athenians and their neighbors near Eleusis, he saved his countrymen by destroying the enemy and dying gallantly on the field of victory. The Athenians gave him a public funeral on the spot where he fell, and paid him the highest honors."

Croesus seemed a bit unnerved at the justifiable happiness of Tellus, but asked Solon who after Tellus seemed to him the happiest of men, expecting that Solon would certainly award him the second place. "Cleobis and Biton," Solon answered. "They hailed from the city-state of Argos and were satisfied with their lives, having never lived beyond their simple needs, and they were so strong physically that they had both gained prizes at the Olympic games. . . ."

When Solon had granted these youths second place, Croesus broke in angrily, "What? Do you disrespect my happiness to such an extent that you don't even put me on a level with these simple men?" "Croesus," replied Solon, "you asked a question concerning the condition of men, of one who knows that the gods are full of jealousy and fond of interfering in the lives of humans. A long life allows a man to witness and experience much, and most of this cannot be predicted or controlled. . . . Therefore, a man's life is pure chance. As for myself, I see that you are incredibly rich, Croesus, and the lord of many lands, but I cannot call you fortunate until I hear that you have ended your life happily. For it is certainly true that he who possesses great wealth is no nearer happiness than he who struggles to meet his daily needs . . . Many of the wealthiest people I have known were ultimately unlucky, and many of moderate means have had excellent luck. . . . If a man is healthy, without injury or pain, proud of his children, and in addition, ends his life well, then he may rightly be called happy. But until that time, he is not happy but simply lucky. . . . Mark well the end, Croesus, for the gods often give men a glimpse of happiness only to plunge them into despair and ruin."

> "Mark well the end, Croesus, for the gods often give men a glimpse of happiness only to plunge them into despair and ruin."
> —SOLON

The king saw Solon depart and thought the man must be a fool because he took no account of present circumstances, but would force all to withhold judgment until the very end of life. But soon after Solon had gone, the gods sent a dreadful vengeance upon Croesus to punish him for the arrogance of considering himself the happiest and most prosperous of men. First, he had a dream that foreshadowed the evils that were about to befall him where his son, Atys, would die by the blow of an iron weapon. When Croesus awoke, . . . he ordered that all weapons of war, the spears and javelins, be removed from the men's hall and piled on the floor of the bedrooms. He simply took precautions against the possibility that one of the weapons that hung on the walls might fall and strike his son.

Now it chanced that while Croesus was making arrangements for his son's wedding, there came to Sardis a man from Phrygia named Adrastos who hailed from the royal house, yet was stalked by misfortune because he had committed a blood crime. He had come to Croesus' court to ask for purification according to the Lydian customs. . . . Croesus granted his request and asked him what man or woman he had killed. "Oh great king," replied Adrastos, "the man I unintentionally killed was my own brother. For this my father drove me from my homeland and I lost everything." Croesus welcomed him and replied, "As long as you live within my lands, you shall not want for anything. Bear your misfortune as best you can, so you may recover." From then on, Adrastos lived in the palace of the king.

Now at this very same time in the mountain country of the Mysians near Olympus, a huge monster of a boar was destroying the local corn fields and none could hunt him down. . . . Finally, they decided to approach Croesus and asked him to send a hunting party under the command of his son in order to destroy the boar. But Croesus remembered his dream and answered, "Forget about having my son lead the expedition. He is about to be married and is busy enough with that. I will send along my huntsmen and hounds to rid your country of this animal."

The Mysians were fine with this solution, but the king's son suddenly entered the room and addressed Croesus: "Father, you used to allow me to participate in battles and hunting expeditions as an opportunity for me to demonstrate my ability and win glory. But now you pull me back and I cannot endure the shame. What must our citizens and my young bride think of me? Either let me go to destroy this boar, or give me a reason why it is best for me to obey you."

Then Croesus answered, "My son, you have not displeased me nor do I think you a coward. But I hesitate because of a vision that came to me in a dream that you were doomed to die young, pierced by an iron weapon. . . . You are my one and only son."

"Ah father," answered Atys, "I don't blame you for wanting to protect me from such a terrible vision. But perhaps you are mistaken in your interpretation. . . . Now you said yourself that the dream foretold that I would die impaled by an iron weapon. But the boar has no hands to strike me! I could understand had the dream said that I will die pierced by a tusk, but that was not the case for I go to fight a wild animal, not men. I beg you to let me go with them."

"There you have me, my son," said Croesus. Your interpretation is more logical than mine. All right, I'll let you go." Then the king sent for his Phrygian retainer, Adrastos, and said to him: "When you needed purification from your crime, I took you in, purified you, and gave you my friendship, and access to my wealth. It is time to pay back this kindness by accompanying my son on this hunting expedition. Watch over him, and see to it that no harm comes to him. Protect him should he be attacked by robbers on the road and thus prove your worth and reputation."

Adrastos answered, "Great king, I shall certainly do as you wish and will take your son under my wing and return him to you safe and sound so far as I am able." Thus assured, Croesus let them depart together with the hunting party. When they reached Olympus, the hunters scattered in pursuit of the boar. He was soon found and the hunters tightened a circle around him, hurling their weapons. Then Adrastos threw his spear, but missed the boar and hit Atys square. So the son of Croesus was indeed killed on the point of an iron weapon, and the warning of the vision came true.

It was a heavy blow to Croesus to learn that his child was dead and that the very man he had sent to ensure his safety was responsible for his death. When the Lydians arrived at court bearing the body of Atys, Adrastos reached out his hands to Croesus asking him to take his life as justice for his failure. He could not bear to live. "Enough my friend," replied Croesus. "You have taken this terrible burden upon yourself when you are simply the vehicle of fate. Some god is responsible for my misfortune, and I was forewarned of it a long time ago." Croesus buried the body of his son and Adrastos, who had earlier killed his brother unintentionally and now the son of his purifier and benefactor, thought himself the most unfortunate of wretches and killed himself upon the tomb of Atys. Croesus, now deprived of his son, suffering, miserable and alone, gave himself up to mourning for the next two years.

Consider This:

3-6. According to Herodotus, what are the particular elements of happiness? What is the difference between being fortunate or lucky and being happy?

3-7. Analyze the character of Croesus. Was he a good man? What was his flaw? What Greek values emerge from this story?

3-8. What point was Herodotus trying to impress on his readers with the story of Croesus?

Key Events in Fifth-Century Greek History

490 B.C.E. Battle of Marathon
Greek cities on the Ionian coast in Persian territory rebel (499–494 B.C.E.) and are aided by Athens. Athenians led by Miltiades defeat Persian forces sent on a revenge mission by Darius on the plains of Marathon.

480 B.C.E. Battle of Salamis
Persian forces under Xerxes invade Greece, overcome Spartan resistance at Thermopylae, and burn Athens before being defeated under the command of Themistocles at the Battle of Salamis.

478 B.C.E. Foundation of the Delian Confederacy
This confederacy is established among Aegean islands and Greek city-states in order to protect against future Persian attacks. Athens supplies the commanders and administers the treasury on the island of Delos.

454–431 B.C.E. Consolidation of the Athenian Empire
Treasury of the Delian Confederacy moved from Delos to Athens in 454 B.C.E. Parthenon begun in 447 B.C.E. with funds garnered from the Delian Confederacy's treasury in Athens. Transformation of the Delian Confederacy into the Athenian Empire. Tribute lists installed on the Acropolis to remind "allies" of their required payments to Athens. Cities or islands who refuse payment and seek to leave the Confederacy are crushed militarily (Naxos in 469 B.C.E., Thasos in 465 B.C.E.).

441 B.C.E. Antigone by Sophocles
Brilliant play recounts fate of Antigone, the daughter of the condemned Oedipus Rex. Performed in the theater of Dionysus at Athens, it wins first prize in the competition. Climax of Athenian tragic drama.

431–404 B.C.E. The Peloponnesian War
Brutal war pits Athens against Sparta for leadership of the Greek world. Pericles expounds on Athenian greatness in his funeral oration (430 B.C.E.). "The Mytilenian Debate" (427 B.C.E.) and

"The Melian Dialogue" (416 B.C.E.) by Thucydides and *The Trojan Women* (415 B.C.E.) by Euripides emphasize the hypocrisy between the ideals of Athenian democracy and the brutalities of imperial rule. Athens loses its empire and freedom in defeat.

399 B.C.E.   Death of Socrates

Trial and execution of Socrates, whose role as "gadfly" forced self-reflection on the Athenian democracy.

The Persian Wars and the Defense of Greece (490–480 B.C.E.)

In 499 B.C.E., the Ionian city-state of Miletus rebelled against Persian rule and asked the Athenians for support. Athens not only aided the rebels, but marched inland and burned one of the Persian capitals at Sardis. Such impulsive aggression could not go unpunished, and Persia's King Darius launched an invasion against Athens in 490 B.C.E., which the Greeks heroically repulsed on the plains of Marathon. The Persian defeat at Marathon served only to anger and frustrate an empire now bent on revenge. The new king, Xerxes, decided to take no chances and formed a massive army of about 250,000 men; this force made its way by land and sea north across the Dardanelles and down into Greece itself. In the face of such power, many Greek city-states surrendered to the Persian horde.

Xerxes grew confident as his massive army moved down from northern Greece toward Athens and the Peloponnesus where the Spartans lived. He summoned one of his advisors, Demaratos, a former Spartan king who had been exiled from his homeland for corruption and found asylum in Persia. Herodotus is once again our source here as Xerxes demands a true assessment of the Spartan reputation for bravery and ability in battle. Xerxes wants to know his enemy.

"The Spartans Will Fight"

HERODOTUS

"So tell me, Demaratos, will the Greeks stand their ground and oppose me? For I can't believe that even if all of them were assembled together that they could match me in battle. But, I would like to hear your opinion." Demaratos replied, "Sire, would you like to hear the truth or should I tell you what you want to hear?" Xerxes ordered him to tell the truth, saying that it would please him to know.

Demaratos then said, "Sire, since you insist, I shall speak the truth and nothing else that you might later regard as a lie. . . . Now, while I admire the Greeks in general, what I will tell you only applies to the Spartans. First of all, there is no way they will accept your intent to enslave Greece; and even if all of the other Greeks gave in to your power, the Spartans would certainly oppose you in battle. And don't even ask about numbers, because if there are 1,000 Spartans marching out, they will fight you; if there are more or less than that, it doesn't matter because they will fight you no matter what."

When Xerxes heard this he laughed: "Demaratos, how can you make such a wild statement—imagine, 1,000 men against all my troops! . . . Look at the situation rationally. How could 1,000 or even 10,000 or 50,000 men, all free, but without a unified command, stand up to an army such as mine? Even if there are 5,000 Greeks, we will outnumber them by more than 1,000 to one. I suppose that if they were all under the

"The Spartans Will Fight" is from Herodotus, *The Histories*, 7.101–7.104, in George Rawlinson, trans., *The History of* Herodotus (New York: E. P. Dutton, 1910). Translation modernized by the editor.

rule of a single king, as is our system, they might be better able to resist because they would be beaten and compelled to fight. But they would never respond to such a threat if they were free men!

To that Demaratos replied, "Sire, from the outset of our discussion, I knew that if I told you the truth, you would not like it. But since you forced me to speak the absolute truth, there it is. That is how matters stand with the Spartans. . . . The Spartans can certainly compete with other soldiers when they fight individually, but when they fight together, they are the best of all warriors. For although they are free, they are ruled by a powerful master—the law. It is the law that they fear and respect deeply from within and that law forbids them to flee from battle, no matter how many soldiers oppose them. The law demands that they emerge victorious—or die on the field."

The 300 Spartans at Thermopylae (480 B.C.E.)

The Persian threat to Greece was real and immediate. The Greeks sent small contingents of soldiers to delay the Persians in a narrow pass named Thermopylae. The Spartans finally arrived with only 300 hand-picked warriors under the command of Leonidas, one of their two kings. As the Persians drew near the pass at Thermopylae, the Greeks were terrified and discussed the wisdom of retreat. Leonidas would have none of it. He dismissed all of the other Greeks as the Spartan warriors prepared to resist the massive Persian force on their own. Meanwhile, Xerxes had sent a scout to assess the strength of the Greek forces. When he reported to the king, Xerxes could not believe his ears and called once again for Demaratos to explain.

Demaratos answered Xerxes, "Do you remember what I said about these Spartans when we were just setting out against Greece? You laughed at me then when you heard my assessment. . . . So listen to me now and believe: these Spartan warriors have come to fight you for control of this pass and that is just what they are preparing to do. But if you can beat these men and the rest who are protecting their homes, then all Greece will fall before you. For you are about to attack the proudest and most formidable army in Greece and truly the best of men."

For the next few days, as the Athenians evacuated the elderly, women, and children from their city to the safety of the island of Salamis, the Persians attacked the pass in waves, beaten back by the valor and tenacity of the Spartan force. Finally, a disgruntled Greek shepherd named Ephialtes told Xerxes of a way around the pass.

The Persians under Xerxes began to draw near; and the Greeks under Leonidas, as they now went forth determined to die, advanced much farther than on previous days, until they reached the more open portion of the pass. Before this, they had held their station within the wall, and from this had gone forth to fight at the point where the pass was the narrowest. Now they joined battle and slaughtered the Persians, who fell in heaps. Behind [the Persians] the captains of the squadrons, armed with whips, urged their men forward with continual blows. Many were thrust into the sea, and died there, while an even greater number were trampled to death by their own soldiers—no one helped the dying. For the Spartans, reckless of their own safety and desperate, since they knew that, as the mountain had been crossed, their destruction was near at hand, exerted themselves with the most furious valor against the Persians.

By this time the spears of the Spartans were all shattered, so with their swords they mowed down the ranks of the Persians. And here, as they thrust into the Persian ranks, Leonidas [the Spartan king] fell fighting bravely, together with many other famous Spartans, whose names I have learned on account of their great heroism, as indeed I have those of all the three hundred.

"The 300 Spartans at Thermopylae" is from Herodotus, *The Histories*, 7.209; 7.223–7.228, in George Rawlinson, trans., *The History of Herodotus* (New York: E. P. Dutton, 1910), pp. 207–209. Translation modernized by the editor.

FIGURE 3.3 The Temple of Nike was constructed in about 420 B.C.E. atop the Acropolis in Athens and dedicated to Athena as provider of victory. (*Perry M. Rogers*)

There fell too at the same time very many famous Persians, among them two brothers of Xerxes. . . .

And now there arose a fierce struggle between the Persians and the Spartans over the body of Leonidas, in which the Greeks four times drove back the enemy, and at last by their great bravery succeeded in bearing off the body. This combat had just ended when the Persians with Ephialtes approached from the rear, and the Greeks, when they realized this, changed their tactics. Drawing back into the narrowest part of the pass, and retreating even behind the cross wall, they gathered themselves on a small hill, where they stood all drawn up together in one close body. The hill is at the entrance of the pass, where the stone lion now stands which was set up in honor of Leonidas. Here they defended themselves to the last using swords if they still had them, and others resisting with their hands and teeth. Some of the Persians, who had pulled down the wall now attacked them in front, while others went round and now encircled them on every side, overwhelming and burying the rest of the Spartans beneath a shower of arrows and spears.

Thus the whole body of Spartans died nobly, but nevertheless one man is said to have distinguished himself above all the rest—Dieneces the Spartan. A speech that he made before the Greeks engaged the Persians remains on record. One of the Trachinians told him, "There are so many Persians, that when they shoot their arrows the sun will be darkened by their multitude." Dieneces, not at all frightened at these words, but making light of the Persian numbers answered, "Our Trachinian friend brings us excellent news. If the Persians darken the sun, then we shall fight in the shade."

The dead were buried where they fell. In their honor, not less in honor of those who died before Leonidas sent the allies away, an inscription was set up, which said:

Go, stranger, and to Sparta tell
That here, obedient to her laws, we fell.

After the massacre of the Spartans at Thermopylae, the Persians overran Athens and burned the city in revenge for the earlier destruction of their capital, Sardis. The Greek defense was led by an Athenian, Themistocles, who by a clever trick lured the Persians into the narrow straits between the Greek shore and the island of Salamis. There, they were crushed in a surprise attack by the Athenian fleet. Xerxes, the Persian king, watched impotently from a nearby hill. As the remaining Spartan king, Pausanias, was organizing the rest of the Greek force, Xerxes returned to Persia. His army would be cut to pieces, and Persia never threatened Greece again.

CONSIDER THIS:

3-9. Aristotle, in his discussion of the polis, argued that all things tend toward perfection in their final form and that therefore the mature structure of each city-state demonstrated this perfection. How did all Spartan discipline and education find its perfection in the stand of the Spartan warriors at Thermopylae? And how are the values of Athens, as recounted in Pericles' funeral oration, found in the victory of the Greeks over the Persians?

3-10. The Persian wars, as recounted by Herodotus, confirmed Greek values of independence and freedom that were inherent in the organization of the polis. How are these values reflected specifically in Herodotus's dialogue between Xerxes and Demaratos even before the battle itself? Xerxes doubted that free men would ever respond to such a crisis without being whipped by the lash. What was Demaratos's response?

Greek Tragedy (480–430 B.C.E.)

Oedipus the King (430 B.C.E.)

SOPHOCLES

The greatness of Athenian civilization in the fifth century B.C.E. was evident in many ways. Not only was the city decorated with temples such as the Parthenon and other monuments on the Acropolis, but Athens was also glorified by the splendor of its intellectual accomplishments. During the century, three dramatists emerged who are comparable in quality to Shakespeare: Aeschylus, Sophocles, and Euripides. Aeschylus, a true patriot, wanted to be remembered only as having fought at the battle of Marathon. Sophocles, a commander in the Athenian navy, won first place in dramatic competition for his play about Oedipus, an unfortunate king of Thebes who unwittingly killed his father (Laius) and married his mother. Such sin, even if unintended and unperceived, cannot go unpunished by the gods: When the truth is revealed, Jocasta (Oedipus's mother/wife) commits suicide and Oedipus blinds himself. The Athenians loved the "no-win" situation, both for the problems it presented and for the moral choices it demanded. In the following selection, note the importance of self-discovery and truth, no matter the outcome.

Attendant: O you most honourable lords of the city
of Thebes,
Weep for the things you shall hear, the things you
must see,
If you are true sons and loyal to the house of
Labdacus.
Not all the water of Ister, the waters of Phasis, Can
wash this dwelling clean of the foulness within, Clean
of the deliberate acts that soon shall be known,
Of all horrible acts most horrible, wilfully chosen.

Chorus: Already we have wept enough for the things
we have known,
The things we have seen. What more will your
story add?

Attendant: First, and in brief—Her Majesty is dead.

Chorus: Alas, poor soul: what brought her to this end?

Attendant: Her own hand did it. You that have not seen,
And shall not see, this worst, shall suffer the less.

But I that saw, will remember, and will tell what I
remember
Of her last agony.
You saw her cross the threshold
In desperate passion. Straight to her bridal-bed
She hurried, fastening her fingers in her hair.
There in her chamber, the doors flung sharply to,
She cried aloud to Laius long since dead,
Remembering the son she bore long since, the son
By whom the sire was slain, the son to whom
The mother bore yet other children, fruit
Of luckless misbegetting, there she bewailed
The twice confounded issue of her wifehood—
Husband begotten of husband, child of child.
So much we heard. Her death was hidden from us.
Before we could set out her tragedy,
The King broke in with piercing cries, and all
Had eyes only for him. This way and that
He strode among us. 'A sword, a sword!' he cried;
'Where is that wife, no wife of mine—that soil
Where I was sown, and whence I reaped my harvest!'
While thus he raved, some demon guided him—
For none of us dare to speak—to where she was.
As if in answer to some leader's call
With wild hallooing cries he hurled himself

Upon the locked doors, bending by main force
The bolts out of their sockets—and stumbled in.
We saw a knotted pendulum, a noose,
A strangled woman swinging before our eyes.
The King saw too, and with heart rending groans
Untied the rope, and laid her on the ground.
But worse was yet to see. Her dress was pinned
With golden brooches, which the King snatched out
And thrust, from full arm's length, into his eyes—
Eyes that should see no longer his shame, his guilt,
No longer see those they should never have seen,
Nor see, unseeing, those he had longed to see,
Henceforth seeing nothing but night. . . . To this
wild tune
He pierced his eyeballs time and time again,
Till bloody tears ran down his beard—not drops
But in full spate a whole cascade descending
In drenching cataracts of scarlet rain.
Thus two have sinned; and on two heads, not
one—
On man and wife—falls mingled punishment.
Their old long happiness of former times
Was happiness earned with justice; but to-day
Calamity, death, ruin, tears, and shame,
All ills that there are name for—all are here.

Antigone (441 B.C.E.)

SOPHOCLES

Sophocles continued the story of Oedipus in *Antigone*, a play about Oedipus's tainted children. The play won first prize in the dramatic competition and again demonstrates the tragedy of those who are not guilty but who are condemned by the misdeeds of others. In the following excerpt, Antigone and her sister Ismene must decide whether to bury the body of their brother, thus satisfying the laws of the gods, or to leave it unburied as the king (Creon) has decreed.

Scene: Before the Palace at Thebes

Enter Ismene from the central door of the Palace. Antigone follows, anxious and urgent; she closes the door carefully, and comes to join her sister.

Antigone: O sister! Ismene dear, dear sister Ismene!
  You know how heavy the hand of God is upon us;

How we who are left must suffer for our father,
Oedipus.
There is no pain, no sorrow, no suffering, no
dishonour
We have not shared together, you and I.
And now there is something more. Have you
heard this order,

"*Antigone*" is from Sophocles, *Antigone*, in *The Theban Plays*, trans. E. F. Watling (Baltimore and Harmondsworth, Middlesex: Penguin Books, 1947), pp. 126–129, 135–136 (lines 1–112, 339–370, 1262–1353). Copyright © E. F. Watling, 1947. Reprinted by permission of Penguin Books, Ltd.

This latest order that the King has proclaimed to the city?
Have you heard how our dearest are being treated like enemies?

Ismene: I have heard nothing about any of those we love,
Neither good nor evil—not, I mean, since the death
Of our two brothers, both fallen in a day.
The Argive army, I hear, was withdrawn last night.
I know no more to make me sad or glad.

Antigone: I thought you did not. That's why I brought you out here,
Where we shan't be heard, to tell you something alone.

Ismene: What is it, Antigone? Black news, I can see already.

Antigone: O Ismene, what do you think? Our two dear brothers. . . .
Creon has given funeral honours to one,
And not to the other; nothing but shame and ignominy.
Eteocles has been buried, they tell me, in state,
With all honourable observances due to the dead.
But Polynices, just as unhappily fallen—the order
Says he is not to be buried, not to be mourned;
To be left unburied, unwept, a feast of flesh
For keen-eyed carrion birds. The noble Creon!
It is against you and me he has made this order.
Yes, against me. And soon he will be here himself
To make it plain to those that have not heard it,
And to enforce it. This is not idle threat;
The punishment for disobedience is death by stoning.
So now you know. And now is the time to show
Whether or not you are worthy of your high blood.

Ismene: My poor Antigone, if this is really true,
What more can I do, or undo, to help you?

Antigone: Will you help me? Will you do something with me? Will you?

Ismene: Help you do what, Antigone? What do you mean?

Antigone: Would you help me lift the body . . . you and me?

Ismene: You cannot mean . . . to bury him? Against the order?

Antigone: Is he not my brother, and yours, whether you like it Or not? I shall never desert him, never.

Ismene: How could you dare, when Creon has expressly forbidden it?

Antigone: He has no right to keep me from my own.

Ismene: O sister, sister, do you forget how our father
Perished in shame and misery, his awful sin
Self-proved, blinded by his own self-mutilation?
And then his mother, his wife—for she was both—
Destroyed herself in a noose of her own making.
And now our brothers, both in a single day
Fallen in an awful exaction of death for death.
Blood for blood, each slain by the other's hand.
Now we two left; and what will be the end of us,
If we transgress the law and defy our king?
O think, Antigone; we are women; it is not for us
To fight against men; our rulers are stronger than we,
And we must obey in this, or in worse than this.
May the dead forgive me, I can do no other
But as I am commanded; to do more is madness.

Antigone: No; then I will not ask for your help.
Nor would I thank you for it, if you gave it.
Go your own way; I will bury my brother;
And if I die for it, what happiness!
Convicted of reverence—I shall be content
To lie beside a brother whom I love.
We have only a little time to please the living,
But all eternity to love the dead.
There I shall lie for ever. Live, if you will;
Live, and defy the holiest laws of heaven.

Ismene: I do not defy them; but I cannot act
Against the State. I am not strong enough.

Antigone: Let that be your excuse, then. I will go
And heap a mound of earth over my brother.

Ismene: I fear for you, Antigone; I fear—

Antigone: You need not fear for me. Fear for yourself.

Ismene: At least be secret. Do not breathe a word.
I'll not betray your secret.

Antigone: Publish it
To all world! Else I shall hate you more.

Ismene: Your heart burns! Mine is frozen at the
thought.

Antigone: I know my duty, where true duty lies.

Ismene: If you can do it; but you're bound to fail.

Antigone: When I have tried and failed, I shall have
failed.

Ismene: No sense in starting on a hopeless task.

Antigone: Oh, I shall hate you if you talk like that!
And he will hate you, rightly. Leave me alone
With my own madness. There is no punishment
Can rob me of my honourable death.

Ismene: Go then, if you are determined, to your folly.
But remember that those who love you . . . love
you still.

*[Condemned to death for defying the king and burying
her brother, Antigone explains her actions]*

Antigone: So to my grave,
My bridal-bower, my everlasting prison,
I go, to join those many of my kinsmen
Who dwell in the mansions of Persephone,
Last and unhappiest, before my time.
Yet I believe my father will be there
To welcome me, my mother greet me gladly,
And you, my brother, gladly see me come.
Each one of you my hands have laid to rest,
Pouring the due libations on your graves.
It was by this service to your dear body, Polynices,
I earned the punishment which now I suffer,
Though all good people know it was for your
honour.
O but I would not have done the forbidden thing
For any husband or for any son.
For why? I could have had another husband

And by him other sons, if one were lost;
But, father and mother lost, where would I get
Another brother? For thus preferring you,
My brother, Creon condemns me and hales me
away,
Never a bride, never a mother, unfriended,
Condemned alive to solitary death.
What law of heaven have I transgressed? What god
Can save me now? What help or hope have I,
In whom devotion is deemed sacrilege?
If this is God's will, I shall learn my lesson
In death; but if my enemies are wrong,
I wish them no worse punishment than mine. . . .

*[Antigone, thus condemned by Creon, commits suicide as
does her intended husband, Haemon, son of Creon. In
this passage, Creon realizes that he was blind to wisdom
and that his laws have defied the gods and cost him the
lives of his son and also his wife.]*

Enter Creon with the body of Haemon

Creon: The sin, the sin of the erring soul
Drives hard unto death.
Behold the slayer, the slain,
The father, the son.
O the curse of my stubborn will!
Son, newly cut off in the newness of youth,
Dead for my fault, not yours.

Chorus: Alas, too late you have seen the truth.

Creon: I learn in sorrow. Upon my head
God has delivered this heavy punishment,
Has struck me down in the ways of wickedness,
And trod my gladness under foot.
Such is the bitter affliction of mortal man.
Enter the Messenger from the palace.

Messenger: Sir, you have this and more than this to
bear.
Within there's more to know, more to your pain.

Creon: What more? What pain can overtop this
pain?

Messenger: She is dead—your wife, the mother of
him that is dead—

The death-wound fresh in her heart. Alas, poor
lady!

Creon: Insatiable Death, wilt thou destroy me yet?
What say you, teller of evil?
I am already dead,
And there is more?
Blood upon blood?
More death? My wife?

The central doors open, revealing the body of Eurydice.

Chorus: Look then, and see; nothing is hidden now.

Creon: O second horror!
What fate awaits me now?
My child here in my arms . . . and there, the
other. . . .
The son . . . the mother. . . .

Messenger: There at the altar with the whetted
knife
She stood, and as the darkness dimmed her eyes
Called on the dead, her elder son and this,
And with her dying breath cursed you, their
slayer.

Creon: O horrible. . . .
Is there no sword for me,
To end this misery?

Messenger: Indeed you bear the burden of two
deaths.
It was her dying word.

Creon: And her last act?

Messenger: Hearing her son was dead, with her own
hand she drove the sharp sword home into her
heart.

Creon: There is no man can bear this guilt but I.
It is true, I killed him.
Lead me away, away. I live no longer.

Chorus: 'Twere best, if anything is best in evil times.
What's soonest done, is best, when all is ill.

Creon: Come, my last hour and fairest,
My only happiness . . . come soon.
Let me not see another day.
Away . . . away. . . .

Chorus: The future is not to be known; our present
care
Is with the present; the rest is in other hands.

Creon: I ask no more than I have asked.

Chorus: Ask nothing.
What is to be, no mortal can escape.

Creon: I am nothing. I have no life.
Lead me away . . . .
That have killed unwittingly
My son, my wife.
I know not where I should turn,
Where look for help.
My hands have done amiss, my head is bowed
With fate too heavy for me.

Chorus: Of happiness the crown
And chiefest part
Is wisdom, and to hold
The gods in awe
This is the law
That, seeing the stricken heart
Of pride brought down,
We learn when we are old.

*[The last excerpt from Antigone is the famous choral
passage that expresses the Greek view of man.]*

Chorus: Wonders are many on earth, and the
greatest of these
Is man, who rides the ocean and takes his way
Through the deeps, through wind-swept valleys of
perilous seas
That surge and sway.
He is master of ageless Earth, to his own will
bending
The immortal mother of gods by the sweat of his
brow,
As year succeeds year, with toil unending
Of mule and plough.
He is lord of all things living; birds of the air,
Beasts of the field, all creatures of sea and land
He taketh, cunning to capture and ensnare
With sleight of hand;
Hunting the savage beast from the upland rocks,
Taming the mountain monarch in his lair,
Teaching the wild horse and the roaming ox

His yoke to bear.
The use of language, the wind-swift motion of brain
He learnt; found out the laws of living together
In cities, building him shelter against the rain
And wintry weather.
There is nothing beyond his power. His subtlety
Meeteth all chance, all danger conquereth.
For every ill he hath found its remedy,
Save only death.
O wondrous subtlety of man, that draws
To good or evil ways! Great honour is given
And power to him who upholdeth his country's laws
And the justice of heaven.
But he that, too rashly daring, walks in sin
In solitary pride to his life's end.
At door of mine shall never enter in
To call me friend.

CONSIDER THIS:

3-11. In addition to the entertainment of comedies and satyr plays, fifth-century Athenian drama also confronted the political dilemmas of the time and engaged the Athenian conscience with works by Aeschylus, Sophocles, and Euripides on the nature of the gods, justice and retribution, hubris, and the moral parameters of society. The Athenians enjoyed being painted into an ethical corner where they could not escape the ultimate wisdom that closed in around them as the story progressed. These topics reflect a prosperous and stable civilization that enjoyed artistic creativity and political freedom. What are some of Sophocles' main ideas about justice, responsibility, and law? How do these ideas reflect a prosperous and stable civilization?

The Athenian Empire, War, and Decline (480–404 B.C.E.)

By 479 B.C.E., the combined Greek armies defeated the Persian forces, who returned home never to invade Greece again. Still, many of the Greek city-states thought it wise to establish an organization intended to protect against any future Persian invasion, to gain booty, and to liberate Greek city-states on the coast of Ionia still under Persian control. Toward this end, many Greek islands pledged their eternal unity to the cause, formed the Delian Confederacy, and contributed money or ships for use against the Persians. Although all members had the same voting weight, the Athenians initially led the organization by supplying the generals and controlling the treasury. Gradually, however, the Athenian allies became Athenian subjects.

In 454 B.C.E. the Athenians moved the treasury of the Confederacy from the island of Delos to Athens itself. The patron goddess Athena was entrusted with protection of the funds and received an offering (1/60 of the tribute) for her services. Pericles used Athena's "commission" to rebuild and beautify Athens; the Parthenon, for example, was begun in 447 B.C.E. The Persian Empire was no longer a threat, and a peace treaty in 449 B.C.E. rendered the Confederacy obsolete. Still, Athens maintained allegiance and control of its empire by force.

From 450 B.C.E. to about 430 B.C.E., the tribute collected from Athenian subjects provided a consistent source of revenue to enhance Athenian glory. During this time, Athens managed its empire with an iron fist under the leadership of the great statesman Pericles. He not only commissioned the temples and public buildings on the Acropolis, but he also developed expansive trade relationships throughout the Aegean Sea. Gradually, Athenian ambition fostered by dominant sea power encroached on the security of the greatest land power of the age—Sparta. The Peloponnesian War (431–404 B.C.E.) was fought primarily over the threat that Athens posed to the security and economic well-being of Sparta and her allies.

THEME: REVOLUTION AND HISTORICAL TRANSITION

THE HISTORIAN AT WORK—THUCYDIDES
Bloodbath at Corcyra

Thucydides was the greatest historian of antiquity and established the foundations for an objective, critical approach to the discipline that, some have argued, was imitated, but never equaled by other historians until the nineteenth century C.E. Thucydides reveals glimpses of his life as he recounts the struggle between Athens and Sparta during the Peloponnesian War from 431 B.C.E. to 411 B.C.E., when his history breaks off.

Thucydides was an Athenian, the son of Olorus, which may have indicated a royal heritage from Thrace and a wealthy pedigree. Writing in the third person, Thucydides notes that he fought during the war as an Athenian general and was exiled for twenty years for his failure to secure the town of Amphipolis from the control of the Spartan general Brasidas. "Because of my exile," says Thucydides, "I had the leisure and flexibility to observe affairs more closely."

His access as he traveled to various locations and battle sites of the war gave him a unique insight and opportunities to question witnesses, investigate the material remains of buildings and inscriptions, consult other authors and poets, and even analyze the contents of graves. Thucydides himself said that his research "took some time and labor," and he worried that such disciplined investigations would "detract somewhat from the interest" of the public who were used to a gentler, more romantic-story approach to great events.

This approach was the great preserve of his older contemporary Herodotus, who was less critical of his sources, feeling no systematic need to test the accuracy of the stories he related. Herodotus's purpose was to explain the foundations and course of the Greek war with the Persians from 490–480 B.C.E. He provided the raw data and emphasized the moral superiority of the Greeks without the intrusion of his own personal interpretation.

Not so with Thucydides. Instead, he believed that he had to establish the truth through his own critical assessment and interpretation of the events. Thucydides worked hard to choose military events carefully, to establish an accurate chronology, and to reveal cause and effect mostly through political speeches and by injecting his own commentary on the horrors of revolution in Corcyra in 427 B.C.E. or the poorly conceived and misdirected Athenian disaster in Sicily in 415 B.C.E.

In each case, Thucydides probes the more profound and general truths about human nature and experience. He is no sunny cheerleader for Greek superiority, but rather a careful observer of life, who articulates with powerful language and a razor-sharp focus the realities of political necessity, imperialism, and human beings in crisis. The Peloponnesian War was his war—no noble defense of Greek homeland against foreign intrusion, but a brutal civil contest to the death. Thucydides watched as the glories and ideals of Athenian civilization died hard on the battlefield and were laid to rest in the graveyard of the soul. For Thucydides human conflict was inevitable, a swirling miasma of lust and power, a brutal universe of uncontrollable passion beyond all reason. In the first excerpt, Thucydides explains his vision and method of scientific inquiry.

"Bloodbath at Corcyra" is from Thucydides, *History of the Peloponnesian War*, 1.1; 1.21–1.22. 3.81–3.83., trans. Richard Crawley (Oxford: The Clarendon Press, 1903). Translation modernized by the editor.

"A Possession for All Time"

Thucydides, an Athenian, wrote the history of the war between the Peloponnesians and the Athenians, beginning at the moment that it broke out, and believing that it would be a great war and more worthy of remembrance than any that had preceded it. For he argued that both states were at the height of their military power, and he could see the rest of the Greeks taking sides in the quarrel. Those who delayed doing so immediately were at least thinking about it. Indeed, this was the greatest movement yet known in history, not only for the Greeks, but also for a large part of the non-Greek world—I had almost said of mankind. For though the events of remote antiquity, and even those that more immediately preceded the war, could not over the years, be clearly ascertained, nevertheless, my critical research points to the conclusion that there was nothing on so great a scale, either in war or in other matters. . . .

On the whole, however, the conclusions I have drawn from the evidence cited are legitimate. Assuredly they will not be challenged either by the lines of some poet displaying the exaggeration of his craft, or by the compositions of the chroniclers that are popular at the expense of the truth. Their accounts cannot be substantiated by evidence, and time has robbed most of them of historical value by transforming them into legend. Rejecting these, I'm satisfied with being guided by the clearest evidence, and having arrived at conclusions as exact as can be expected in matters of such antiquity. Speaking of this war, despite the natural desire of the participants to overrate its importance and then return to their admiration of the past when it is over, yet an examination of the facts will show that it was certainly the greatest war ever known.

As to the speeches in this history, some were delivered before the war began, others while it was going on; some I heard myself, others I got from various quarters; it was in all cases difficult to remember them word for word, so my process has been to make the speakers say what was in my opinion demanded of them by the various occasions, of course adhering as closely as possible to the general sense of what they actually said. And with reference to the narrative of events, I never depended on the first source that I encountered, and did not even trust my own impressions, but based my analysis on what I saw myself, or on other eyewitnesses whose accuracy I questioned relentlessly and by the most severe and detailed tests possible. I have worked hard to sift through conflicting accounts of different eye witnesses because of faulty memory or prejudice for one side or the other. And it is very likely that the historical character of my narrative may be disappointing to the ear and therefore limit its popularity, but I shall be satisfied if those who want an exact knowledge of the past as an aid to the interpretation of the future (since the future will resemble the past if not reflect it given the continuity of human nature), will judge it useful. Finally, I have written my work, not as an essay that seeks to win the applause of the moment, but as a possession for all time. . . .

CONSIDER THIS:

3-12. Why did Thucydides decide to write his history of the Peloponnesian War? Do you think he exaggerated when he called it "the greatest war ever known"? What evidence does he cite to support this conclusion?

3-13. Thucydides has been called the first "scientific historian" based on his process of critically assessing his sources for legitimacy. How specifically did he select his sources and avoid the problems of faulty memory and prejudice?

3-14. Thucydides is a daunting historian partly because of the difficulty of his language, but perhaps more due to the depth and complexity of his ideas. He intended his history to be "a possession for all time." What did he mean by that? What does it tell you about his personal standards and seriousness of purpose?

The Revolution in Corcyra: "Lust for Power Arising from Greed and Ambition"

We see Thucydides at his critical best in recounting the Corcyrean revolution of 427 B.C.E. The Peloponnesian War was fought throughout the Greek world on the Ionian coast of Asia Minor, on the Aegean islands of Melos and Thasos, and in the Sicilian harbor of Syracuse. Corcyra was a city-state located on the northwest coast of Greece. It was officially an Athenian ally, but the town was rife with political factions of oligarchs loyal to Sparta and common agitators supportive of Athens. They clashed in brutal and prolonged combat throughout the city. Thucydides is starkly analytical in his assessment of one of the first popular revolutions of the war, where domestic bitterness bottled up for years under the veneer of law spilled forth into the streets, activated and legitimized by the war. The passions of greed and revenge undermined public order as neighbors, friends, and family fed off the political rivalries that tore their ordered society apart. Thucydides need not have feared that his history would degenerate into a dry chronicle of events. This is dramatic analytical writing of the highest order as Thucydides states his observations and then draws his conclusions about the passions of human nature unleashed and out of control.

[Over the span of seven days], . . . the Corcyraeans were engaged in butchering those of their fellow citizens whom they regarded as their enemies: and although the ostensible crime was that of attempting to overthrow the democracy, some were killed also for private hatred, others by their debtors because of the money owed to them. Death raged in every form, and as usually happens at such times, there was no length to which violence did not go; sons were killed by their fathers, and those seeking shelter in the temples were dragged from the altar or slain upon it; while some were even walled up in the temple of Dionysus and died there.

> "Revolution has always produced such horrific sufferings and will always do so, as long as the nature of mankind remains the same."
>
> —THUCYDIDES

So bloody was the march of the revolution, that the impression made was all the greater because it was one of the first to occur. Later on, one may say, the whole Greek world was torn apart by those popular leaders who supported the Athenians, and by the oligarchs who looked to the Spartans for help. In a time of peace, there would have been neither reason nor desire to invite foreign interference, but in war, with an alliance always at the command of either faction to crush their adversaries and thereby gain their own corresponding advantage, each revolutionary faction supported foreign intervention. Revolution has always produced such horrific sufferings and will always do so, as long as the nature of mankind remains the same, though in a more severe or mild form, and varying in their development, according to the nature of the circumstances. In peace and prosperity, states and individuals generally get along better because they do not find themselves suddenly confronted with the necessities of empire; but war makes it impossible to satisfy the most basic needs of people, and so proves a rough master. War forces most men's characters down to a level consistent with their circumstances. Revolution thus ran its course from city to city, and the places where it finally arrived, the citizens having heard the news about prior cruelties, carried to a still greater excess the refinement of their inventions, as demonstrated in the creativity of their barbarism and the atrocity of their reprisals. Words changed their ordinary meaning and were redefined by those in control. Reckless audacity was now defined as "loyal courage"; prudent hesitation became "overt cowardice"; moderation was held to be "a cover for unmanly weakness"; the ability to see all sides of a question, as "indecision to act on any." Frantic violence became the true quality of a man; cautious plotting, a justifiable means of self-defense. He who advocated violence was always considered trustworthy; his opponent, a man to be suspected. To succeed in a plot was to have a clever mind; to figure out and stop a plot was even more ingenious; but whoever tried to prevent such plots through moderate negotiation was accused of weakening and destroying their party and was called a coward who was afraid of the enemy. In short, he who could outdo others in destructive acts was applauded and so was he who infected people with evil, people who never before would have thought in those terms. The tie to one's party became stronger than any tie of blood and family. And those who were blindly devoted to their party were ready to dare anything without reservation. For such party devotion was never based on established law or public benefit, but was formed in defiance of the laws from pure self-interest. The seal of good faith was not divine law, but complicity in crime. The fair proposals of a political rival were met with jealous precautions by the stronger of the two, and not with a generous confidence. Revenge was also of greater importance than even self-preservation. Either side offered to reconcile only to gain a clear advantage in the negotiation, and this "state of grace" only held good so long as no other pathway was available; but when political advantage reared its ugly head, he who first seized the opportunity to take his enemy off-guard thought this faithless vengeance sweeter than anything else—because he cared less about his own safety than the fact that success through treachery gained him a reputation for superior intelligence. Indeed, it is generally true that men are readier to call scoundrels clever than simple men honest, and are as ashamed of being the second as they are proud of being the first.

The cause of all these evils was the lust for power arising from greed and ambition; and from these passions flowed the violence of competitive parties. The leaders in the cities professed the most positive ideas, on the one side with the cry of political equality for the people, on the other of a moderate and stable aristocracy. They sought political advantage for themselves in those public interests

which they pretended to cherish. And they used any means necessary to ascend the ladder of power. In their acts of vengeance they went to even greater lengths, not stopping at what justice or the good of the state demanded, but making the party's whim of the moment their only standard, and invoking with equal readiness the condemnation of an unjust verdict or the authority of force to stoke the fire of the animosities of the hour. Neither party honored religion, but used fine phrases and positive messages to accomplish some dreadful purpose. Meanwhile, moderate citizens fell prey to both factions, either because they were disliked for not joining the quarrel, or because men were envious of their survival.

Thus revolution give birth to every form of wickedness in Greece. The simplicity that is such a foundation of a noble nature was laughed down and disappeared, and society was divided into camps where no one trusted another. It was impossible to put an end to this because there was no man's word with enough credibility to reconcile enemies. Each man was strong only in the conviction that nothing was secure—he had to look only to his own safety and could not afford to trust others. . . .

> **"Envy had exercised its fatal power and revenge had been set above piety, personal gain over justice."**
> —THUCYDIDES

Meanwhile, Corcyra gave the first example of most of the crimes noted, especially the revenge of the people against their rulers who had never given them equitable treatment or anything except the back of their hand for insolence—and now the people had their oppressors at their mercy. There were also those who sought to relieve themselves of a grinding poverty by confiscating their neighbor's goods. And lastly, there were crimes committed not because of class antagonisms, but because of the hatred of political equals who were carried away into savage and pitiless excesses by their blind rage. In the confusion into which life was now thrown in the cities, human nature, always rebelling against the law and having now trampled them under foot, gladly showed itself ungoverned in passion, above respect for justice, and the enemy of all authority. Envy had exercised its fatal power and revenge had been set above piety, personal gain over justice. Indeed, men are reckless with their future and too often prosecute their own revenge and in doing so eliminate those common laws of humanity to which all alike can look for salvation in adversity. They forget that in their own hour of need, they will look for those very laws—and not find them.

CONSIDER THIS:

3-15. Thucydides, in analyzing the Corcyrean revolution, focuses specifically on how words change their meaning during times of crisis and how they are "redefined" by those in control of the state. Choose a few of his examples and explain the change. Do you agree with him that words are ephemeral and often do not represent absolute concepts, but reflect political necessities of the moment that are always subject to changing circumstances? Can you give examples from the contemporary political scene?

3-16. Thucydides argues that the cause of the vicious bloodbath in Corcyra was "lust for power arising from greed and ambition." When political parties polarize on the left and the right, what happens to the moderate center? What did Thucydides mean when he argued that "men are reckless with their future and too often prosecute their own revenge"? Why is this dangerous?

3-17. What was Thucydides' vision of human nature? What causes the "blind rage," envy, and revenge that leads to the degeneration of the state? What did he mean by his observation that "War forces most men's characters down to a level consistent with their circumstances"? What, according to Thucydides, is necessary for the stability and security of society?

3-18. What makes Thucydides a great historian? How does he differ from Herodotus in his purpose and in the process of finding truth in the past?

The Mytilenian Debate (427 B.C.E.)

THUCYDIDES

After the first two years of the Peloponnesian War, Pericles died from a plague then raging in Athens. With the loss of this far-sighted statesman, the democracy fell prey to more demagogic leaders who influenced people with effective oratory but whose policies were often extreme. The prime example of this extremist leadership was a man named Cleon, who succeeded Pericles in influence.

In 428 B.C.E., the city of Mytilene, located on the island of Lesbos and a subject of the Athenian empire, rebelled against its master. After the revolt was quelled, Cleon convinced the Athenian people to execute all the men of Mytilene and to sell the women and children into slavery. A ship was sent out immediately to implement the sentence of the democracy. The next day, says the historian Thucydides, there was a sudden change of feeling, and the Athenians reflected on the implications of their decision. The debate that ensued says much about the nature of Athenian democracy and imperialism. The first speaker is Cleon, who had originally proposed the harsh punishment.

Cleon's Argument

"I have remarked again and again that a democracy cannot manage an empire, but never more than now, when I see you regretting your condemnation of the Mytilenians. Having no fear or suspicion of one another in daily life, you deal with your allies on the same principle, and you do not consider that whenever you yield to them out of pity or are misled by

"The Mytilenian Debate" is from Thucydides, *History of the Peloponnesian War*, 3.39–3.40; 3.46–3.49, trans. Benjamin Jowett vol. 1, 2nd ed. (Oxford: The Clarendon Press, 1900), pp. 207, 210–212, 216–219. Translation modernized by the editor.

their lies, you are guilty of a weakness dangerous to yourselves, and receive no thanks from them. You should remember that your empire is a despotism exercised over unwilling subjects, who are always conspiring against you. They do not obey in return for any kindness which you do them to your own disadvantage, but obey only in so far as you are their masters. They do not love and respect you—they respect and are controlled by force alone. Besides, what can be more detestable than to be perpetually changing your minds? . . . We should from the first have made no difference between the Mytilenians and the rest of our allies, and then their insolence would never have risen to such a height; for men naturally despise those who fawn over them, but respect those who do not give way to them. . . . Consider this: if you impose the same penalty upon those of your allies who wilfully rebel and upon those who are [forced to rebellion] by the enemy, which of them will not revolt upon any pretext however trivial, seeing that, if they succeed, they will be free, and, if they fail, no irreparable consequences will follow? We in the meantime shall have to risk our lives and our fortunes against one state after another. When we conquer in the future, we shall recover only a ruined city, and the revenues that define our strength will be lost to us. But if we fail in conquering others, the number of our adversaries will be increased. And when we ought to be focused on repelling our enemies, . . . we shall be wasting time in fighting against our own allies.

Don't hold out any hope, which the eloquent rhetoric of the Mytilenians may inspire, or their money can buy, that they should be excused and that their error should seem to be simple human weakness. Their attack on our authority was deliberate and malicious—they knew what they were doing. This was my original contention, and I still maintain that you should abide by your former decision, and not be misled either by pity, or by the charm of words, or by a too forgiving attitude. There are no three things more destructive to your imperial power. Mercy should be reserved for the merciful, and not thrown away on those who would never have compassion on us, and who must by the force of circumstances always be our enemies. . . . Be true then to yourselves, and recall as vividly as you can what you felt at the time; think how you would have given the world to crush your enemies, and now take your revenge. Do not be soft-hearted at the sight of their distress, but remember the danger which was once hanging over your heads. Punish them as they deserve, and prove by an example to your other allies that rebellion will be punished with death. If this is made quite clear to them, your attention will no longer be diverted from your enemies by wars against your own allies."

Diodotus's Response

Such were the words of Cleon; and after him Diodotus the son of Eucrates, who in the previous assembly had been the chief opponent of the decree which condemned the Mytilenians, came forward again and spoke as follows: . . .

"We ought not to act hastily out of a mistaken reliance on the security which the penalty of death affords. Nor should we drive our rebellious subjects to despair; they must think that there is always a place for repentance, or that they may at any moment give up their mistaken policy. Consider: at present, although a city may actually have revolted, when she becomes conscious of her weakness she will capitulate while still able to defray the cost of the war and to pay tribute for the future; but if we are too severe, won't the citizens make better preparations, and when besieged, resist to the last, knowing that it is all the same whether they come to terms early or late? Shall not we ourselves suffer? For we shall waste our money by sitting down before a city which refuses to surrender; when the place is taken it will be a mere wreck, and we shall in the future lose the revenues derived from it; and in these revenues lies our military strength. Do not then weigh offences with the severity of a judge, when you will only be injuring yourselves, but have an eye to the future; let the penalties which you impose on rebellious cities be moderate, and then their wealth will be undiminished and at your disposal. Do not hope to find a safeguard in the severity of your laws, but only in the vigilance of your administration. At present we do just the opposite; a free people under a strong government will always revolt in the hope of independence; and when we have put them down we think that they cannot be punished too severely. But instead of inflicting extreme penalties on free men who revolt, we should practice extreme vigilance before they revolt, and never allow such a thought to enter their minds. When however they have been once put down we ought to reduce their crimes as much as possible. . . .

Be assured then that what I advise is for the best, and doesn't give in to pity nor to leniency, for, like Cleon, I do not think that you should be influenced by any such motives. Simply weigh the arguments which I have urged, and accept my proposal: Pass sentence on the [ringleaders of the rebellion], but leave the rest of the inhabitants where they are. This will be good policy for the future, and will strike terror into your enemies for the present. For wise policy against an enemy is more effective than blind and irrational violence.

Thus spoke Diodotus, and such were the proposals on either side which most nearly represented the opposing parties. The citizens struggled with these two arguments, and though the vote by a show of hands was very close, the motion of Diodotus prevailed. The Athenians instantly sent out another trireme, hoping that, if the second could overtake the first, which had a start of about twenty-four hours, it might be in time to save the city. The Mytilenian envoys provided wine and barley for the crew, and promised great rewards if they arrived first. And such was their energy that they continued rowing while they ate their barley ... and slept and rowed by turns. Fortunately, no wind rose to oppose and slow them, and because the first of the two ships was not sailing in any great hurry on her distasteful mission, the second one did arrive after the first— but not much later. [The commander] had already read the decree and was about to put it into execution, when the second ship appeared and prevented the massacre.

So near was Mytilene to destruction. . . .

CONSIDER THIS:

3-19. What are the main issues argued by Cleon and Diodotus in "The Mytilenian Debate"? Is mercy an issue? What argument seems more persuasive if one wants to maintain an empire? Why?

3-20. How does Thucydides use speeches from various statesmen to provide interest and perspective? Is this a legitimate technique for a "scientific historian"? Does it reduce his credibility or enhance the impact of his writing?

The Melian Dialogue (416 B.C.E.)

THUCYDIDES

Although Mytilene escaped Athenian wrath after reevaluation by the democracy, the island of Melos was not so lucky. Melos, located off the southern tip of the Peloponnesus, was a Spartan colony. Even so, the Melians maintained strict neutrality during the Peloponnesian War. Thucydides, the Athenian historian, wrote this contrived dialogue to demonstrate the brutal force used by Athens in maintaining its empire. The ideals expounded by Pericles in the "Funeral Oration" are thus balanced by power politics in which logic is no defense and might makes right. Melos was conquered by Athens in 416 B.C.E.

The next summer the Athenians made an expedition against the isle of Melos. The Melians are a colony of Sparta that would not submit to the Athenians like the other islanders, and at first remained neutral and took no part in the struggle, but afterwards, when the Athenians plundered their territory with great violence,

"The Melian Dialogue" is from Thucydides, *The History of the Peloponnesian War*, 5.84–5.116, trans. and ed. R. W. Livingstone (Oxford: The Clarendon Press, 1943), pp. 266–274. Reprinted by permission of Oxford University Press.

the Melians assumed an attitude of open hostility. The Athenian generals encamped in their territory with their army, and before doing any harm to their land sent envoys to negotiate. . . . The Athenian envoys then said:

Athenians: If you have met us in order to make predictions about the future, or for any other purpose than to look existing facts in the face and to discuss the safety of your city on this basis, we will break off the conversations; otherwise, we are ready to speak.

Melians: In our position it is natural and excusable to explore many ideas and arguments. But the problem that has brought us here is our security, so, if you like, let's discuss your ideas on your own terms.

Athenians: Then we will not make a long and unconvincing speech, full of fine phrases, to prove that our victory over Persia justifies our empire, or that we are now attacking you because you have wronged us, and we ask you not to expect to convince us by saying that you have not injured us, or that, though a colony of Sparta, you did not join her. . . .

Melians: As you ignore justice and have made self-interest the basis of discussion, we must take the same ground, and we say that in our opinion it is in your interest to maintain a principle which is for the good of all—that anyone in danger should have just and equitable treatment and any advantage, even if not strictly his due, which he can secure by persuasion. This is your interest as much as ours, for your fall would involve you in a crushing punishment that would be a lesson to the world.

Athenians: We have no apprehensions about the fate of our empire, if it did fall; those who rule other peoples, like the Spartans, are not formidable to a defeated enemy. Nor is it the Spartans with whom we are now contending: the danger is from subjects who of themselves may attack and conquer their rulers. But leave that danger for us to face. At the moment, we shall say that we are looking out for the safety of your state; for we wish you to become our subjects with least trouble to ourselves, and we would like you to survive in our interests as well as your own.

Melians: It may be your interest to be our masters: how can it be ours to be your slaves?

Athenians: By submitting you would avoid a terrible fate, and we should gain by not destroying you.

Melians: Would you not agree to an arrangement under which we should keep out of the war, and be your friends instead of your enemies, but neutral?

Athenians: No: your hostility injures us less than your friendship. Your friendship, to our subjects, is an illusion of our weakness, while your hatred exhibits our power.

Melians: Is this the interpretation that your subjects put on it? Do they not distinguish between states in which you have no concern, and peoples who are most of them your colonies, and some conquered rebels?

Athenians: They think that one nation has as good rights as another, but that some survive because they are strong and we are afraid to attack them. So, apart from the addition of our empire, your subjection would give us security: the fact that you are islanders (and weaker than others) makes it more important that you should not get the better of Athens, who is mistress of the sea.

Melians: But do you see no safety in our neutrality? Will you not make enemies of all neutral powers when they see your conduct and reflect that some day you will attack them? Will not your action strengthen your existing opponents, and induce those who would otherwise never be your enemies to become so against their will?

Athenians: No. The mainland states, secure in their freedom, will be slow to take defensive measures against us, and we do not consider them so formidable as independent island powers like yourselves, or subjects already smarting under our control. These are most likely to take a thoughtless step and bring themselves and us into obvious danger.

Melians: Surely, then, if you are ready to risk so much to maintain your empire, and the enslaved peoples so much to escape from it, it would be criminal cowardice in us, who are still free, not to take any and every measure before submitting to slavery?

Athenians: No, if you reflect calmly: for this is not a competition in heroism between equals, where your honor is at stake, but a question of self-preservation to save you from a struggle with a far stronger power.

Melians: Still, we know that in war fortune is more impartial than the disproportion in numbers might lead one to expect. If we submit at once, our position is desperate; if we fight, there is still a hope that we shall stand secure.

Athenians: Hope encourages men to take risks; men in a strong position may follow her without ruin, if not without loss. But when they stake all that they have to the last coin (for Hope is a spendthrift), she reveals her real self in the hour of failure, and when her nature is known she leaves them without means of self-protection. You are weak, your future hangs on a turn of the scales; avoid the mistake most men make, who might save themselves by rational policy, and then, when visible hopes desert them, in this extreme situation they turn to the invisible—prophecies and oracles and all those things which delude men with hopes, and result in their destruction.

Melians: We too, you can be sure, realize the difficulty of struggling against your power and against Fortune if she is not impartial. Still we trust that the gods will not allow us to be worsted by Fortune, for in this quarrel we are right and you are wrong. Besides, we expect the support of Sparta to reinforce us, for she is bound to help us as her colony, if for no other reason, and from a sense of honor. So our confidence is not entirely unreasonable.

Athenians: As for divine favor, we think that we can count on it as much as you, for neither our claims nor our actions are inconsistent with what men believe about the gods or desire for themselves. We believe that the gods, and we know that men, by natural law always rule where they are stronger. We did not make the law nor were we the first to act on it; we found it existing, and it will exist forever, long after we are gone; and we know that you and anyone else as strong as we are would do as we do. As to your expectations from Sparta and your belief that she will help you from a sense of honor, we congratulate you on your innocence but we do not admire your folly. So far as they themselves and their natural traditions are concerned, the Spartans are a highly virtuous people; as for their behavior to others, much might be said, but we can put it briefly by saying that, most obviously of all people we know, they identify their interests with justice and the best course with honor. Such principles do not favor your present irrational hopes of deliverance.

Melians: That is the chief reason why we have confidence in them now; in their own interest they will not wish to betray their own colonists and so help their enemies and destroy the confidence that their friends in Greece feel in them.

Athenians: Apparently you do not realize that safety and self-interest go together, while the path of justice and honor is dangerous; and danger is a risk which the Spartans are little inclined to run. . . . Here experience may teach you like others, and you will learn that Athens has never abandoned a siege from fear of another foe. You said that you proposed to discuss the safety of your city, but we observe that in all your speeches you have never said a word on which any reasonable expectation of it could be founded. Your strength lies in hope for the future; in comparison with the forces now arrayed against you, your resources are too small for any hope of success. You will show a great lack of judgment if you do not come to a more reasonable decision after we have withdrawn. Surely you will not fall back on the idea of honor, which has been the ruin of so many when danger and disgrace were staring them in the face. How often, when men have seen the fate to which they were tending, have they been enslaved by a phrase and drawn by the power of this seductive word to fall of their own free will into irreparable disaster, bringing on themselves by their folly a greater dishonor than fortune could inflict! If you are wise, you will avoid that fate. The greatest of cities makes you a fair offer, to keep your own land and become her tributary ally: there is no dishonor in that. The choice between war and safety is given you; do not obstinately take the worse alternative. The most successful people are those who stand up to their equals, behave properly to their superiors, and treat their inferiors fairly. Think it over when we withdraw, and reflect once again that you will have only one country, and that its prosperity or ruin depends on one decision.

The Athenians then withdrew from the conference; and the Melians, left to themselves, came to a decision corresponding with what they had maintained in the discussion, and answered, "Our resolution, Athenians, is unaltered. We will not in a moment deprive our city of the freedom by which the gods have preserved it until now, nor will we give up our expectation for Spartan help. So, we will try to save ourselves. Meanwhile we invite you to allow us to be friends to you and enemies of neither party, and to retire from our country after making such a treaty as shall seem fit to us both."

Such was the answer of the Melians. The Athenians broke up the conference saying, "To judge from your decision, you are unique in regarding the future as more certain than the present and in allowing your wishes to convert unseen disaster into reality. Since you have staked your fortune and all your hopes for survival on the Spartans, so will you be most completely deceived."

The Athenian envoys now returned to the army, and as the Melians showed no signs of yielding the generals at once began hostilities, and drew up a line around the Melians and began to siege the city. . . .

Summer was now over . . . and the siege was pressed ever more vigorously; there was some treachery in the town, and the Melians surrendered at discretion to the Athenians, who put to death all the grown men whom they took, and sold the women and children for slaves. . . .

CONSIDER THIS:

3-21. In "The Melian Dialogue," what is the basic argument of the Athenians? of the Melians? Choose the most effective phrases from this source and explain why they are important and what they reveal about the nature of power and democracy. Is Thucydides a moralist? What is his view of human nature?

3-22. Do you think it is possible for a democracy to rule an empire, or is this a moral contradiction? Can you apply this question the British Empire in the nineteenth century, or to the United States in a contemporary setting?

THEME: WOMEN IN HISTORY

THE REFLECTION IN THE MIRROR

Hubris: The Conceit of Power

The Trojan Women (415 B.C.E.)

EURIPIDES

One year after the destruction of Melos, the great Athenian dramatist Euripides reacted to the incident by composing *The Trojan Women*. The subject of his play is the fate of the women of Troy after their husbands had been killed and their city destroyed by the Greek

---

"*The Trojan Women*" is from Euripides, *The Women of Troy*, in *The Bacchae and Other Plays*, trans. Philip Vellacott (Baltimore and Harmondsworth, Middlesex: Penguin Books, 1954), pp. 105–107 (lines 704–778). Copyright © Philip Vellacott, 1954. Reprinted by permission of Penguin Books, Ltd.

force in 1230 B.C.E. In the following passage, Andromache, widow of the valiant Trojan leader Hector, is informed of the fate proscribed for her young son. Note how her argument parallels that of "The Melian Dialogue." *The Trojan Women* failed to win a prize in the dramatic competition that year.

KEEP IN MIND . . .

3-23. What are the dominant themes in *The Trojan Women*?

Talthybius: Andromache, widow of the bravest of the Trojans: do not hate me. It is with great reluctance that I have to convey to you the decision unanimously reached by the Greeks and their two generals, the sons of Pelops.
Andromache: What is this? Your words hint at the worst.
Talthybius: It was decided that your son—how can I say it?
Andromache: He is to have a different master from mine?
Talthybius: No Greek will ever be his master.
Andromache: What? Is he to be the one Trojan left behind in Troy?
Talthybius: My news is bad. It is hard to find words.
Andromache: Thank you for your sympathy. What have you to say?
Talthybius: You must know the worst: they mean to kill your son.
Andromache: Oh, gods! His sentence is worse than mine.
Talthybius: In a speech delivered before the whole assembly Odysseus carried his point—
Andromache [sobbing passionately]: Oh, Oh! This is more than I can bear.
Talthybius: —that the son of so distinguished a father must not be allowed to attain manhood—
Andromache: May he hear the same sentence passed on his own son!
Talthybius: —but should be thrown down from the battlements of Troy. Now show yourself a sensible woman, and accept this decision. Don't cling to him, or imagine you have any chance of resisting: you have none. Bear what must be like a queen. There is no one who can help. You can see

for yourself: your city and your husband are gone; you are in our hands. Shall we match our strength against one woman? We can. So I hope that you won't feel inclined to struggle, or to call down curses on the Greeks, or do anything that might lead to violent measures or resentment. If you say anything to anger the army, this child will die without rites of pity, without burial. If you are quiet, and accept the inevitable in a proper spirit, you will be allowed to lay your child in his grave, and you will find the Greeks more considerate to yourself.
Andromache: Darling child, precious beyond all price! You will die, killed by our enemies, leaving your mother to mourn. Your noble father's courage, which saved others, has condemned you; his spirit was a fatal inheritance. I thought, on that day when I entered Hector's house as a bride, on that ill-fated night, that my son would rule the teeming multitudes of the East—not die by a Greek ritual of murder.

Are you crying, little one? Do you understand? Why do you tug my hand, cling to my dress, nestling like a bird under its mother's wing? No Hector will rise from the grave and step forth to save you, gripping his glorious spear; none of your father's brothers, no army of Phrygians. You must leap from that horrible height, and fall, and break your neck, and give up your life, and be pitied by no one.

> "You must leap from that horrible height, and fall, and break your neck, and give up your life, and be pitied by no one."
>
> —ANDROMACHE

My baby, so young in my arms, and so dear! O the sweet smell of your skin! When you were newly born, how I wrapped you up and gave you my breast, and tended you day and night, and was worn out with weariness—all for nothing, for nothing! Now say good-bye to me for the last time; come close to your mother, wind your arms round my neck, and put your lips to mine.

O men of Hellas, inventors of cruelty unworthy of you! Why will you kill him? What has he done?—Helen, child of Hyndareus, you are no daughter of divine Majesty! You had many fathers, and I can name them: the Avenging Curse was one, Hate was the next, then Murder and Death and every evil that lives on earth! I will swear that Zeus never fathered you to ruin men's lives by tens of thousands through Asia and Hellas! My curse on you! With the shining glance of your beauty you have brought this rich and noble country to a shameful end.

Take him! Carry him away, throw him down, if your edict says 'Throw!' Feast on his flesh! God is destroying us! I have no power to save my child from death. Hide my miserable body, throw me on board! I go to my princely marriage, and leave behind me my dear child.

CONSIDER THIS:

3-24. In what ways does this excerpt from *The Trojan Women* by Euripides parallel the arguments of "The Melian Dialogue"?

3-25. Why is this passage so impressive? What was Euripides trying to say about power and innocence? What does the mere production of a play critical of Athenian foreign policy say about the nature of freedom in Athens? Why do you think the play failed to win a prize that year in the competition?

THE BROADER PERSPECTIVE:

3-26. The Greeks believed that hubris, or the conceit of violating the limits of human action imposed by the gods, would always be punished. Eleven years after the production of this play, Athens lost the Peloponnesian War, was deprived of its empire, and lost its cultural dominance. Was this defeat retribution for the Athenian conceit of power? Had divine justice delivered the punishment for Athenian hubris?

The Sicilian Disaster (413 B.C.E.)

In 415 B.C.E., the Athenians embarked on a grand plan to capture the city of Syracuse on the island of Sicily; Athens intended to use it as a base against Sparta and her allies. The Spartans, therefore, aided Syracuse, and eventually the Athenian fleet was bottled up in the harbor and destroyed (413 B.C.E.). In this selection, Thucydides reflects on the fate of the Athenians and the meaning of the disaster.

Those who were imprisoned in the quarries were at the beginning of their captivity harshly treated by the Syracusans. There were great numbers of them, and they were crowded in a deep and narrow place. At first the sun by day was still scorching and suffocating, for they had no roof over their heads, while the autumn nights were cold, and the extreme of temperature engendered violent disorders. Being cramped for room they had to do everything on the same spot. The corpses of those who died from their wounds, exposure to heat and cold, and the like, lay heaped one upon another. The smells were intolerable; and they were at the same time afflicted by hunger and thirst. During eight months they were allowed only about

"The Sicilian Disaster" is from Thucydides, *The History of the Peloponnesian War*, 7.87–8.1, trans. Benjamin Jowett, vol. 2, 2nd ed. (Oxford: The Clarendon Press, 1900), pp. 333–336. Translation modernized by the editor.

half a pint of water and a pint of food a day. Every kind of misery which could befall a man in such a place befell them. This was the condition of all the captives for about ten weeks. At length the Syracusans sold them, with the exception of the Athenians and of any Sicilian or Italian Greeks who sided with them in the war. The whole number of the public prisoners is not accurately known, but they were not less than seven thousand.

Of all the Hellenic actions which took place in this war, or indeed, as I think, of all Hellenic actions which are on record, this was the greatest—the most glorious to the victors, the most ruinous to the vanquished; for they were utterly and at all points defeated, and their sufferings were prodigious. Fleet and army perished from the face of the earth; nothing was saved, and of the many who went forth few returned home.

Thus ended the Sicilian expedition.

The news was brought to Athens, but the Athenians could not believe that the armament had been so completely annihilated, although they had the positive assurances of the very soldiers who had escaped from the scene of action. At last they knew the truth; and then they were furious with the orators who had joined in promoting the expedition—as if they had not voted it themselves—and with the soothsayers, and prophets, and all who by the influence of religion had at the time inspired them with the belief that they would conquer Sicily. Whichever way they looked there was trouble; they were overwhelmed by their calamity, and were in fear and consternation unutterable. The citizens and the city were alike distressed; they had lost a host of cavalry and hoplites and the flower of their youth, and there were none to replace them. And when they saw an insufficient number of ships in their docks, and no crews to man them, nor money in the treasury, they despaired of survival. . . . Their enemies in Greece, whose resources were now doubled, would . . . set upon them with all their might both by sea and land, and would be assisted by their own rebellious allies. Still they determined, so far as their situation allowed, not to give way. . . . After the manner of a democracy, they were very disciplined while their fright lasted. . . .

CONSIDER THIS:

3-27. Thucydides, the historian, maintained that one of the reasons Athens lost the Peloponnesian War was that it was guilty of "hubris," or going beyond the limits imposed by the gods. How does "The Sicilian Disaster" reflect this? Does this belief appear in Sophocles' plays as well? Be specific in your answer.

Women and War: Lysistrata (411 B.C.E.)

ARISTOPHANES

Athens not only produced great tragedians such as Sophocles and Euripides, but great comic dramatists as well. The brilliant playwright Aristophanes poked fun at the major personalities of the day (Socrates included) and influenced public opinion about the most divisive political issues. Aristophanes was born about 447 B.C.E. at a time when Athens was at the height of its power and influence. He was often critical of the democracy and especially the prosecution of the Peloponnesian War. After the tragic destruction of Athenian forces at Syracuse in 413 B.C.E., and the impotent leadership in the years that followed, Aristophanes contrived his own solution for the end of the war, which he presented in 411 B.C.E. in the play Lysistrata: The women of both Sparta and Athens would take the initiative in stopping the war by withholding sex while their husbands were on leave until the men came to their senses!

Of special note here is the presentation of women in Athenian society. Although it is debated whether women were allowed to attend the theater (Plato gives evidence that they did), in other ways their lives were extremely restricted. They were not allowed to leave their homes unescorted and could not vote, hold public office, own property, or even attend social gatherings in their own homes. They were essentially bound to the will and decisions of their husbands or fathers. Perhaps the biggest joke in Athens after the presentation of *Lysistrata* was that women could have conceived and organized such a bold and effective plan for ending the Peloponnesian War. In this scene, the leader of the Athenian women, Lysistrata, and her compatriot, Stratyllis, confront the male Athenian leadership.

Magistrate: Anyway, what business are war and peace of yours?

Lysistrata: I'll tell you.

Magistrate: [restraining himself with difficulty]: You'd better or else.

Lysistrata: I will if you'll listen and keep those hands of yours under control.

Magistrate: I can't—I'm too livid. . . . Say what you have to say.

Lysistrata: In the last war we were too modest to object to anything you men did—and in any case you wouldn't let us say a word. But don't think we approved! We knew everything that was going on. Many times we'd hear at home about some major blunder of yours, and then when you came home we'd be burning inside but we'd have to put on a smile and ask what it was you'd decided to inscribe in the pillar underneath the Peace Treaty. And what did my husband always say?—"Shut up and mind your own business!" And I did.

Stratyllis: I wouldn't have done!

Magistrate: He'd have given you one if you hadn't.

Lysistrata: Exactly—so I kept quiet. But sure enough, next thing we knew you'd make an even sillier decision. And if I so much as said, "Darling, why are you carrying on with this silly policy?" he would glare at me and say, "Back to your weaving, woman, or you'll have a headache for a month. Go and attend to your work; let war be the care of the menfolk."

Magistrate: Quite right too, by Zeus.

Lysistrata: Right? That we should not be allowed to make the least little suggestion to you, no matter how much you mismanage the City's affairs? And now, look, every time two people meet in the street, what do they say? "Isn't there a man in the country?" and the answer comes, "Not one." That's why we women got together and decided we were going to save Greece. What was the point of waiting any longer, we asked ourselves. Well now, we'll make a deal. You listen to us—and we'll talk sense, not like you used to—listen to us and keep quiet, as we've had to do up to now, and we'll clear up the mess you've made.

Magistrate: Insufferable effrontery! I will not stand for it!

Lysistrata [magisterially]: Silence!

Magistrate: You, confound you, a woman with your face veiled, dare to order me to be silent! Gods, let me die! . . .

Leader: Disgraceful!—women venturing to prate
In public so about affairs of State!
They even (men could not be so naive)
The blandishments of Sparta's wolves believe!
The truth the veriest child could surely see:
This is a Monarchist Conspiracy.
I'll fight autocracy until the end:
My freedom I'll unswervingly defend. . . .
And from this place
I'll give this female one upon the face!

[He slaps Stratyllis hard on the cheek.]

Stratyllis [giving him a blow in return that sends him reeling]:
Don't trifle with us, rascals, or we'll show you
Such fisticuffs, your mothers will not know you!

Chorus of Women: My debt of love today
To the City I will pay,
And I'll pay it in the form of good advice;
For the City gave me honour
(Pallas blessing be upon her!),
And the things I've had from her deserve their price. . . .

Stratyllis: See why I think I have a debt to pay?
'But women can't talk politics,' you say.
Why not? What is it you insinuate?
That we contribute nothing to the State?
Why, we give more than you! See if I lie:
We cause men to be born, you make them die.
What's more, you've squandered all the gains of old;
And now, the taxes you yourselves assess
You do not pay. Who's got us in this mess?
Do you complain? Another grunt from you,
And you will feel the impact of this shoe! . . .

Leader: If once we let these women get the semblance of a start,
Before we know, they'll be adept at every manly art!

Consider This:

3-28. What can you discern from Aristophanes' *Lysistrata* about the treatment of women in Greek society? Note how critical the women are about how the war has been conducted. What was Aristophanes trying to do—criticize the state, or make light of the impotent status of women? Do you regard satire as a legitimate vehicle for reform?

THEME: THE INSTITUTION AND THE INDIVIDUAL

AGAINST THE GRAIN

The Trial of Socrates

"You Will Not Easily Find Another Like Me"

PLATO

The Peloponnesian War came to an end in 404 B.C.E. The Athenians suffered a humiliating defeat and were divested of their empire, military forces, and dignity. A Spartan occupation force assumed control of the city and replaced Athenian democracy with the reactionary rule of the Thirty Tyrants, vindictive Athenian citizens who used the months from 404 B.C.E. to 403 B.C.E. to settle scores with their former political enemies. Although a democracy was reinstituted, it no longer espoused the tolerance of ideas and freedom of speech that had been such a part of former Athenian glory. A true indicator of this decline was the trial of Socrates.

Socrates, a stonecutter by trade, had dutifully served the Athenian state in a political capacity and as a soldier in war. He disliked the advances of popular teachers called "sophists" who claimed to be able to teach anything for a fee. Socrates instead claimed that he knew nothing and set about informally teaching people to question in the hope that they would find wisdom for themselves. He considered himself a gadfly whose responsibility it was to prod the democracy continually in hopes that self-reflection might produce wise policy. His so-called "services" were free of charge, and he became quite influential among the youth of Athens. In 399 B.C.E. he was accused by various Athenian leaders of not believing in the gods of the state and of corrupting the youth. His most famous pupil, Plato, watched the proceedings in the court and wrote an account of Socrates' defense called the *Apology*; an excerpt is presented below. In the end, Socrates was condemned to death and actually insisted on drinking the poisonous hemlock. In his martyrdom lay the destruction of Athenian ideals.

Keep in Mind ...

3-29. How did Socrates answer the specific charges leveled against him by the Athenian government?

This inquisition has led to my having many enemies of the worst and most dangerous kind, and has given occasion also to many injuries. . . .

"The Trial of Socrates" is from Plato, *Apology*, in *The Dialogues of Plato*, trans. Benjamin Jowett, 3rd ed. (Oxford: The Clarendon Press, 1875). Translation modernized by the editor.

There is another thing: young men of the richer classes, who have not much to do, come about me of their own accord; they like to hear the pretenders examined, and they often imitate me, and proceed to examine others; there are plenty of persons, as they quickly discover, who think they know something, but really know little or nothing; and then those who are examined by them instead of being angry with themselves are angry with me: This confounded Socrates, they say; this villainous misleader of youth!—and then if somebody asks them, Why, what evil does he practice or teach? they do not know, and cannot tell; but in order that they may not appear to be at a loss, they repeat the ready-made charges which are used against all philosophers about teaching things up in the clouds and under the earth, and having no gods, and making the worse appear the better cause; for they do not like to confess that their pretense of knowledge has been detected—which is the truth: and as they are numerous and ambitious and energetic, and are drawn up in battle array and have persuasive tongues, they have filled your ears with their loud and inveterate slanders. And this is the reason why my three accusers, Meletus and Anytus and Lycon, have set upon me. . . .

Some one will say: And are you not ashamed, Socrates, of a course of life which is likely to bring you to an untimely end? To him I may fairly answer: There you are mistaken: a man who is good for anything ought not to calculate the chance of living or dying; he ought only to consider whether in doing anything he is doing right or wrong— acting the part of a good man or of a bad. . . . And therefore if you let me go now, . . . if you say to me, Socrates, this time we will not mind Anytus, and you shall be let off, but upon one condition, that you are not to enquire and speculate in this way any more, and that if you are caught doing so again you shall die; if this was the condition on which you let me go, I should reply: Men of Athens, I honor and love you; but I shall obey God rather than you, and while I have life and strength I shall never cease from the practice and teaching of philosophy, exhorting anyone whom I meet and saying to him after my manner: You, my friend—a citizen of the great and mighty and wise city of Athens—are you not ashamed of heaping up the greatest amount of money and honor and reputation, and caring so little about wisdom and truth and the greatest improvements of the soul, which you never regard or heed at all? And if the person with whom I am arguing, says: Yes, but I do care; then I do not leave him or let him go at once; but I proceed to interrogate and examine and cross-examine him, and if I think that he has no virtue in him, but only says that he has, I reproach him with undervaluing the greater, and overvaluing the less. . . . This is my teaching, and if this is the doctrine which corrupts youth, I am a mischievous person.

> "I am that gadfly . . . and all day long and in all places am always fastening upon you, arousing and persuading and reproaching you. . . . I would advise you to spare me."
>
> —SOCRATES

And now, Athenians, I am not going to argue for my own sake, as you may think, but for yours, that you may not sin against God by condemning me, who am his gift to you. For if you kill me you will not easily find a successor to me, who, if I may use such a ludicrous figure of speech, am a sort of gadfly, given to the state by God; and the state is a great and noble steed who is tardy in his motions owing to his very size, and requires to be stirred into life. I am that gadfly which God has attached to the state, and all day long and in all places am always fastening upon you, arousing and persuading and reproaching you. You will not easily find another like me, and therefore I would advise you to spare me. I dare say that you may feel out of temper (like a person who is suddenly awakened from sleep), and you think that you might easily strike me dead as Anytus advises, and then you would sleep on for the remainder of your lives, unless God in his care of you sent you another gadfly. . . .

FIGURE 3.4 *The Trial of Socrates* by Jacques-Louis David (*Corbis/Bettmann*)

And now, O men who have condemned me, I would give prophecy to you; for I am about to die, and in the hour of death men are gifted with prophetic power. And I prophecy to you who are my murderers, that immediately after my departure punishment far heavier than you have inflicted on me will surely await you. Me you have killed because you wanted to escape the accuser, and not to give an account of your lives. But that will not be as you suppose: far otherwise. For I say that there will be more accusers of you than there are now; accusers whom hitherto I have restrained: and as they are younger they will be more inconsiderate with you, and you will be more offended at them. If you think that by killing me you can prevent someone from censuring your evil lives, you are mistaken; that is not a way of escape which is either possible or honorable; the easiest and noblest way is not to be disabling others, but to be improving yourselves. This is the prophecy which I utter before my departure to the judges who have condemned me. . . .

Still I have a favor to ask of them. When my sons are grown up, I would ask you, O my friends, to punish them; and I would have you trouble them, as I have troubled you if they seem to care about riches, or anything, more than about virtue; or if they pretend to be something when they are really nothing—then cut them short, as I have held you accountable, for not caring about that for which they ought to care, and for thinking that they are something when they are really nothing. And if you do this, both I and my sons will have received justice at your hands.

The hour of departure has arrived, and we go on our ways—I to die, and you to live. Which is better God only knows.

CONSIDER THIS:

3-30. How is Socrates critical of the Athenian leaders in his *Apology*? What does he say in particular about freedom and virtue? Why is the condemnation of Socrates symbolic of the failure of Athenian civilization?

Chapter 4

The Age of Alexander the Great

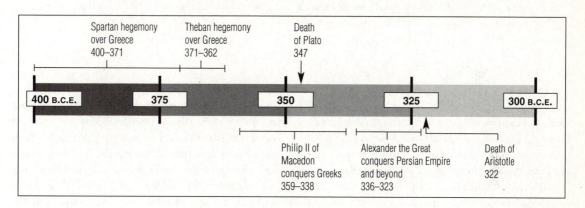

Spartan hegemony over Greece 400–371

Theban hegemony over Greece 371–362

Death of Plato 347

400 B.C.E. | 375 | 350 | 325 | 300 B.C.E.

Philip II of Macedon conquers Greeks 359–338

Alexander the Great conquers Persian Empire and beyond 336–323

Death of Aristotle 322

Liberty doesn't work as well in practice as it does in speeches.

—WILL ROGERS

There is no conflict between liberty and safety. We will have both or neither.

—RAMSEY CLARK

The best government is a benevolent tyranny tempered by an occasional assassination.

—VOLTAIRE

Greatness lies not in being strong, but in the right use of strength.

—HENRY WARD BEECHER

The great are great only because we are on our knees.

—PIERRE-JOSEPH PROUDHON

CHAPTER THEMES

- **The Power Structure:** After the death of Alexander the Great, his empire broke down into smaller regions ruled by lesser kings who fought among themselves. Can a government that is based on a cult of personality endure once that personality dies? Do "power vacuums" result in desperate and inherently unstable governments? Is the transfer of power therefore the most crucial and dangerous phase of politics?

- **Imperialism:** Alexander the Great expanded his empire beyond the known limits of the Greek world. By bringing Greek culture to the East, was Alexander a force for progress? Can imperialism be progressive?

- **The Varieties of Truth:** Who was Alexander the Great? To what extent were his exploits the stuff of legend, with little foundation in reality? How do we separate the myth from the man? Is the so-called hero in history simply a myth?

- **Women in History:** What were Plato's ideas regarding an ideal society ruled by "philosopher-kings"? What role was assigned to women in this ideal society, and how would children be reared in Plato's Republic? What does this say about the role of women in Greek society?

- **Revolution and Historical Transition:** Had Alexander not lived, would history have been different? What if Alexander had turned west instead of east in his search for empire—how would history have been changed? How important is the influence of the individual on historical events? In what ways did civilization progress in spite of Alexander? Can we call the fourth century B.C.E. and the Hellenistic period an age of decline?

- **The Big Picture:** Should Alexander be called "the Great," or does greatness lie not in conquering but in consolidating and maintaining society? Were the Romans better role models in this regard than the Greeks?

In the fifth century B.C.E., the Greek city-state of Athens developed a society imbued with democratic ideals and creative inspiration. The century has become known as the Golden Age because Athenian contributions in art, philosophy, drama, and literature have been recognized as fundamental in the advancement of Western civilization. The century closed, however, on a pessimistic note. The vast political and economic differences between Athens and Sparta drove the two city-states into the long and costly Peloponnesian War. At the war's conclusion in 404 B.C.E., Athenian power had been destroyed and with it the confidence and energy necessary for cultural leadership.

Sparta, as the victor in the war, was now thrust into a position of leadership over the Greeks. Yet it too had been weakened in the struggle and, in any event, was an insular polis whose citizens did not enjoy spending time away from the domestic affairs in their own territory. Spartan leadership (or "hegemony," as it was called) over the Greeks did not last long and was replaced in 371 B.C.E. by the dominant city-state of Thebes. Under the innovative military direction of a general named Epaminondas, the Thebans were able to assume hegemony until his death in 362 B.C.E. Although one polis wielded the greatest influence, others attempted to compete, asserting their own power and influence. In this spirit, Athens reestablished its democracy and even tried to regain its empire through alliance and conquest. Eventually, internal problems restricted its conduct of foreign affairs.

During the first half of the fourth century B.C.E., Greece in general and Athens in particular were in a state of domestic chaos. Nearly continuous warfare and political strife interfered with trade and thus contributed to economic dislocation and depression. A widening gulf developed between rich and poor, and this was reflected in political dissension and indecision. There was a genuine desire to return to the days of glory and honor when Athens commanded the respect of the world, yet debate ensued on how to regain such a position. Many eyes turned toward the Persians, whose defeat in 480 B.C.E. by Greek tenacity and ingenuity had ushered in the Golden Age. The Athenian orator Isocrates strongly advocated foreign conquest as the panacea for economic depression and political turmoil, but he also knew that the Greeks had to be unified to defeat Persian power. His solution was to support the leadership of the King of Macedon, Philip II. In this, Isocrates was opposed by perhaps the greatest orator of all, Demosthenes, who firmly believed that accepting the leadership of Philip in such a cause was in fact accepting the end of Greek freedom. His speeches against Philip (called the "Philippics") are models of persuasive argument. Demosthenes influenced the democracy to resist the advances of Philip, but in 338 B.C.E. Athens was militarily defeated and forced to join the League of Corinth in support of Macedon.

With Greece securely under his control, Philip could now afford to move ahead with his plans to invade Persia. But in 336 B.C.E. he was assassinated during a wedding feast. His twenty-year-old son Alexander, who had inherited his ambition for the conquest of Persia, assumed his position as King of Macedon. Alexander certainly capitalized on his father's plans and preparations, and his conquest of the Persian Empire became the stuff of legends. It is difficult to decide which of his adventures are fact and which are fiction. His influence on the world around him and on the course of history has also been hotly debated. It is easy to degenerate into historical "what-ifs"? What if Alexander had not decided to conquer Persia, but had turned west instead toward the infant

Roman civilization? What would have happened to Greece if Alexander had died early in the Persian campaign? Had he lived longer, would he still be called "the Great"? These questions are unanswerable, but his conquest of the world was a feat of amazing endurance and determination. It is important to ask the right questions in order to obtain meaningful answers.

The period after Alexander's death in 323 B.C.E. is called Hellenistic, or "Greek-like." The age of Greek political domination was past, and soon the Romans would conquer and control the region. Still, the Greeks of the fourth and third centuries B.C.E. continued to

influence Western civilization with the philosophies of Plato, Aristotle, and various schools of Stoics, Epicureans, and Cynics. The Greeks continued to dominate artistic style, education, and scholarship, providing tutors and oratorical instruction for the Mediterranean world. Scientific inquiry was one of the great advancements of the age, and urban planning can largely be traced to the Greeks of this period. In all, we see transition from the dying ideals of the Greeks to the more realistic and practical foundations of Roman civilization. This chapter focuses on the highlights of this important period.

KEY EVENTS IN THE AGE OF ALEXANDER

347 B.C.E.   Death of Plato
Plato's philosophy reflects a disillusionment with democracy and instead advocates the rule of enlightened philosopher-kings in his famous work, *The Republic*.

359–338 B.C.E.   The Rise of Macedon
Philip II becomes King of Macedon (359 B.C.E.) and seeks involvement in Greek affairs. Debate in Athens between supporters who want Philip's leadership (Isocrates) and those who believe him dangerous to Greek freedom (Demosthenes). League of Corinth established (338 B.C.E.) after Greek defeat at Chaeronea.

336–323 B.C.E.   Reign of Alexander III, the Great
Alexander accedes to power after assassination of his father, Philip II. Alexander invades Persia (334 B.C.E.), controls Egypt, defeats King Darius III, and reaches the Indus Valley (327 B.C.E.). He dies of fever, and his generals carve up the parts of his empire that did not fall away immediately. Transition to Hellenistic ("Greek-like") era.

322 B.C.E.   Death of Aristotle
A student of Plato and teacher of Alexander, Aristotle's mind inquired into political philosophy, ethics, the sciences, and literary criticism. After Aristotle, philosophies such as Epicureanism and Stoicism will focus on helping individuals cope in a world of constant change.

The Rise of Macedon and the Fall of Greece (350–330 B.C.E.)

The First Philippic (351 B.C.E.)

DEMOSTHENES

In 359 B.C.E., Philip II became king of Macedon, an area just to the north of Greece. It had always been a backward and disunited region, but within two years Philip succeeded in organizing and training an aggressive and competent army. His intentions,

"The First Philippic" is from Demosthenes, *First Philippic*, 2–12, 38, 45, 50, in *Orations of Demosthenes*, trans. Charles R. Kennedy (New York: D. Appleton & Co., 1912).

however, were unknown to the Greeks. The great Athenian orator Demosthenes saw Philip's increasing participation in Greek affairs as alarming and dangerous. In the following speech against Philip, Demosthenes tried to rouse the democracy to action against a threat that few realized.

Men of Athens, nothing, if you are on your guard, is to be feared, nothing, if you are negligent, goes as you desire. . . . For all men will side with and respect those whom they see prepared and willing to take action. . . . If you will adopt this principle now . . . and if each citizen who can and ought to give his service to the state is ready to give it without excuse, the rich to contribute, the able-bodied to enlist; if, put bluntly, you will become your own masters and each cease expecting to do nothing himself while his neighbor does everything for him, then, God willing, you will recover your own, get back what has been frittered away, and turn the tables on Philip. Do not imagine that his power is everlasting like that of a god. There are those who hate and fear and envy him, men of Athens, even among those who now seem most friendly. We can assume that all the feelings that are in other men belong also to his adherents. But now they are all afraid, having no refuge because of your apathy and indolence, which I urge you to abandon at once. For you see, men of Athens, to what pitch of arrogance the man has advanced: he leaves you not even the choice of action or inaction, he threatens and uses outrageous language, he cannot rest content in possession of his conquests but continually widens their circle, and while we dally and delay, he throws this net around us.

When then, Athenians, when will you act as becomes you? What are you waiting for? When it is necessary? I suppose. And how should we regard what is happening now? Surely to free men the strongest necessity is the disgrace of their condition. Or tell me, do you like wailing about and asking one another, "Is there any news?" Could there be more startling news than that a Macedonian is subduing Athenians and directing the affairs of Greece? "Is Philip dead?" you ask. "No, but he is sick." What difference does it make? Should anything happen to this man, you will soon create a second Philip if that is the way you attend to affairs. For this Philip has grown great not so much by his own strength as by our negligence. . . . Shameful it is, men of Athens, to delude ourselves, and by putting off everything unpleasant to miss the time of action and be unable even to understand that skillful makers of war should not follow circumstances, but be in advance of them; for just as a general may be expected to lead his armies, so statesmen must guide circumstances if they are to carry out their policies and not be forced to follow at the heels of events. Yet you, men of Athens, with greater resources than any people—ships, infantry, cavalry, revenue—have never up to this day made proper use of them. . . .

One thing is clear: he will not stop, unless someone stops him. Are we to wait for this? Do you think all is well if you dispatch empty ships and the vague hope of some deliverer? Shall we not man the fleet? Shall we not sail with at least a part of our troops, now if never before? Shall we not make a landing on his coast? "Where, then, shall we land?" someone asks. The war itself, men of Athens, will uncover the weak parts of his empire, if we make the effort; but if we sit at home listening to the orators accuse and malign one another, no good can ever be achieved. I believe that wherever you send a force of our own citizens—or even partly ours—there Heaven will bless us and Fortune will aid our struggle. . . . Remember only that Philip is our enemy, that he has long been robbing and insulting us, that wherever we have expected aid from others we have found hostility, that the future depends on ourselves, and that unless we are willing to fight him there we shall perhaps be forced to fight here. . . . You need not speculate about the future except to assure yourselves that it will be disastrous unless you face the facts and are willing to do your duty.

CONSIDER THIS:

4-1. What was Demosthenes' main message to the Athenians in "The First Philippic"? How did he view Philip, and what did he want the Athenians to do about him? Be specific in your citation of evidence.

"They Speak of Nothing but Your Power" (346 B.C.E.)

ISOCRATES

Although Philip had his enemies in Greece, he also had his supporters. Many viewed him as a positive force, as a pathway to greater Greek glory. Philip, it was argued, would finally unite the Greek city-states and lead them in the conquest of Persia. The most vocal advocate of this position was the orator Isocrates. The following excerpt from his "Address to Philip" sets forth his views that a strong man was necessary to stop domestic disputes and provide the leadership necessary to fulfill Greece's destiny.

I chose to address my discourse to you Philip, [because] you were the possessor to a greater degree than any man in Hellas of wealth and power, the only two things in existence which can both persuade and compel—things which I think will also be required by the enterprise which I am going to propose. For my intention is to advise you to take the lead both in securing the harmony of Hellas and in conducting a campaign against the barbarians; and as persuasion is expedient in dealing with the Greeks, so force is useful in dealing with the barbarians. Such, then, is the general scope of discourse. . . .

I will now direct my remarks to the subject at hand. I say that, while neglecting none of your own interests, you ought to try to reconcile Argos, Sparta, Thebes, and our state; for if you are able to bring these together you will have no difficulty in uniting the others as well. . . . And you have a good opportunity, for . . . it is a good thing to appear as the benefactor of the leading states and at the same time to be furthering your own interests no less than theirs. . . . It is also beyond question that there is nothing which all men remember so well as benefits received in times of trouble. And you can see how they have been reduced to distress by war. . . .

While I admit that there is no one else who could reconcile these states, to you such an undertaking is not difficult. For I see that you have accomplished many things which others considered hopeless and beyond expectations, and that therefore it would not be strange if you alone should be able to effect this union. In fact, men of high aspirations and eminent position should not attempt enterprises which any ordinary man could carry out, but should confine themselves to those which no one could attempt except men of abilities and power like yours. . . .

I should be satisfied with what I have already said on this subject had I not omitted one point, not from forgetfulness, but from a certain unwillingness to mention it. However, I think I ought to disclose it now, for I am of the opinion that it is as much to your advantage to hear what I have to say concerning it as it is becoming to me to speak with an accustomed freedom.

I perceive that you are being slandered by those who are jealous of you and are accustomed to throw their own cities into confusion—men who regard the peace which is for the good of all as a war against their own selfish interests. Unconcerned about everything else, they speak of nothing but your power, asserting that its growth is not for the interests of Hellas but against them, and that you have been already for a long time plotting against us all, and that, while you pretend to be anxious to assist, you are in reality endeavoring to get the Peloponnesus into your power. . . . By talking such nonsense and pretending that they possess an accurate knowledge of affairs, and by predicting a speedy overthrow of the whole world, they persuade many. . . .

On these points no sensible man would venture to contradict me. And I think that it would occur to any others who should propose to advise in favor of the expedition to Asia to point out that all whose lot it has been to undertake war against the Persian kings have risen from obscurity to renown, from poverty to wealth, and from low estate to the ownership of many lands and cities. . . . When Fortune honorably leads the way, it is a disgrace to lag behind and show yourself unready to advance in whatever direction she wishes.

CONSIDER THIS:

4-2. What did Isocrates advocate in his "Address to Philip"? Are his arguments persuasive? Do you regard him as a traitor to Athens or as a far-sighted statesman?

"'They Speak of Nothing but Your Power'" is from Isocrates, *Philip*, 16, 30–31, 42, 72–75, 89, 152, in *Orations of Isocrates*, trans. J. H. Freese, vol. I (London: G. Bell & Sons, 1894).

On the Crown (330 B.C.E.)

DEMOSTHENES

By 338 B.C.E., it was apparent that Philip intended to conquer Greece whether for good or ill. Demosthenes managed to whip up an Athenian defense, but his efforts were too little and too late to compete with the military power of Macedon. The Greeks were defeated in the battle of Chaeronea (338 B.C.E.), and Philip then called representatives of the various city-states of Greece to a meeting at Corinth. Sparta alone refused to come, and Philip wisely did not demand its presence. The League of Corinth was founded to unite Greece and free all Greek states under the control of Persia. The League thus became the legal basis of Philip and Alexander's invasion of Persia. Philip forged Greek unity by eliminating Greek independence. Macedonian garrisons maintained the loyalty of the Greeks.

Eight years after Philip defeated the Greeks and enrolled them as members of the League of Corinth, the great Athenian orator Demosthenes delivered a speech defending his policy of resistance to the Macedonians. The speech, "On the Crown," has been viewed as a funeral oration on Greek freedom.

[If the defeat of the Greeks at the hands of Philip could have been foreseen,] not even then should the city have abandoned her policy [of opposition] if she had any regard for glory, or ancestry, or the future. As it is, she appears to have failed, a thing to which all men are liable if the gods so decide. But if Athens, claiming to be the leader of Greece, had abandoned her claim, she would have incurred the charge of betraying all to Philip. Why, had we resigned without a struggle that which our ancestors had encountered every danger to win, who would not have spit upon you. . . . But it seems that to the Athenians of that day [fifth century] such conduct would not have been national, or natural, or endurable; no one could at any period of time persuade the city to attain herself to the security of slavery to the powerful and unjust: through every age has she persevered in a perilous struggle for first place in honor and glory. And this you esteem so noble and consistent with your character that among your ancestors you honor most those who acted in such a spirit. . . . The Athenians of that day looked not for an orator or a general who would lead them to a pleasant servitude; they scorned to live if it could not be in freedom. Each of them considered that he was not born to his father or mother only, but also to his country. What is the difference? He who thinks himself born for his parents only is satisfied to wait for his fated and natural end; he who thinks himself born for his country as well will sooner die than see her in slavery, and he will regard the insults and indignities which must be borne in a city enslaved as more to be feared than death itself. . . . But never, never can you have done wrong, men of Athens, in undertaking the battle for the freedom and safety of all! I swear it by your ancestors—those who met the peril at Marathon, those who took the field at Plataea, those in the sea battles at Salamis and Artemisium, and many other brave men who repose in the public monuments, all of whom alike, as being worthy of the same honor, the country buried, not the successful and victorious alone! For the duty of brave men has been done by all; their fortune has been such as heaven assigned to each.

CONSIDER THIS:

4-3. What specifically did the loyalty oath for the League of Corinth require of the Greek city-states? Was it abusive in its demands? In the final analysis, why did Athens lose its freedom? Was it inevitable? Who gave better advice for the welfare of Greece, Isocrates or Demosthenes?

"On the Crown" is from Demosthenes, *On the Crown*, 198–200, 203–205, 208, in *Orations of Demosthenes*, trans. Charles R. Kennedy (New York: D. Appleton & Co., 1912).

Alexander the Great?

"Carve Out a Kingdom Worthy of Yourself!"

PLUTARCH

One of the most fascinating and controversial figures of history was Alexander III of Macedon. After Philip's assassination in 336 B.C.E., Alexander was elected to the kingship and continued with his father's plans to invade and conquer Persia. His exploits became legendary, and in this regard it is difficult to separate fact from fiction. The following selection recounts an early indication of Alexander's special abilities when he tamed a horse too wild for others to control.

Philonicus the Thessalian brought the horse Bucephalus to Philip, offering to sell him for thirteen talents; but when they went into the field to try him, they found him so very vicious and unmanageable, that he reared up when they tried to mount him, and would not so much as endure the voice of any of Philip's attendants. And as they were leading him away as wholly useless and intractable, Alexander, who stood by said, "What an excellent horse are they going to lose because they cannot manage him with any skill or boldness!" Philip at first took no notice of what he said, but when he heard Alexander repeat the same thing several times, and saw how frustrated he was that the horse was being sent away, "Do you criticize," said Philip, "those who are older than yourself, as if you knew more, and were better able to manage him then they?" "I could manage this horse," replied Alexander, "better than others do." "And if you do not," said Philip, "what will you forfeit for your rashness?" "I will pay," answered Alexander, "the whole price of the horse." At this the whole company fell laughing; and as soon as the wager was settled among them, he immediately ran to the horse, and, taking hold of the bridle, turned him directly towards the sun, having, it seems, observed that he was disturbed at and afraid of the motion of his own shadow; then letting him go forward a little, still keeping the reins in his hand, and stroking him gently when he began to grow eager and fiery, . . . with one nimble leap, Alexander securely mounted him, and when he was seated, little by little drew in the bridle, and curbed him without either striking or spurring him. Presently, when he found him free from all rebelliousness, and only impatient to run, he let him go at full speed, inciting him now with a commanding voice, and urging him also with his heel. Philip and his friends looked on at first in silence and anxiety for the result, [but when Alexander came] back rejoicing and triumphing for what he had performed, they all burst out into acclamations of applause; and his father, shedding tears, it is said, for joy, kissed him as he came down from his horse, and in his transport said, "O my son, carve out a kingdom equal to and worthy of yourself, for Macedonia is too small for you."

The Destruction of Persepolis

DIODORUS SICULUS

When Alexander left for Persia, he took with him a potent military force, but also naturalists and historians to study the Persian environment and record his exploits. Alexander, like most of his compatriots, drank heavily and preferred his wine undiluted (as opposed to the Greek custom). The following account describes the destruction of the magnificent Persian capital at Persepolis after Alexander had routed enemy troops. The next morning he woke up and regretted having burned to the ground one of the greatest libraries of the ancient world.

"'Carve Out a Kingdom Worthy of Yourself'" is from Plutarch, *Life of Alexander*, 5, in *Readings in Ancient History*, ed. William S. Davis, vol. 1 (Boston: Allyn and Bacon, 1912), pp. 301–302.

"The Destruction of Persepolis" is from Diodorus Siculus, *Bibliotheca Historica*, 7.70–7.72, in George W. Botsford, *A Sourcebook of Ancient History* (New York: The Macmillan Co., 1912), pp. 277–280. Translation modernized by the editor.

The Macedonians forced their way into Persepolis, put all the men to the sword, and rifled through all the possessions and estates in the city. They looted here and there vast quantities of gold and silver, clothes (some of the finest purple), and furniture, all of which became the prizes of the victors. And the great royal throne of the Persian king, once famous throughout the world, was now scorned and mocked. For though the Macedonians spent days and days looting, their thirst for greed was insatiable. And they were so vicious in their plundering that they fought one another with drawn swords and many were killed in quarrel. Some things that were of extraordinary value they divided with their swords, and each took a share; others in rage cut off the hands of those who grabbed hold of a thing that was in dispute. To the extent that Persepolis excelled all other cities in glory and sophistication, to the same extent did it now become the standard of misery and abject destruction.

Then Alexander seized all the treasures in the citadel, a vast quantity of gold and silver from the royal treasuries that had been collected and laid up since the time of Cyrus, the first king of Persia. Part of the treasure Alexander took to pay for the war and ordered a separate part of it to be kept at Susa, another Persian capital. For this, he ordered thousands of mules and camels to convey all the treasure to the many places he had ordered. Because he hated the inhabitants of Persepolis with a passion, he resolved not to trust them with anything—Persepolis was to be utterly destroyed.

Then, Alexander made a sumptuous feast for the entertainment of his friends in commemoration of his victory and offered magnificent sacrifices to the gods. And when his military officers and other companions were feasting and carousing, madness seized upon the souls of the men. Many were young and made little use of reason when they were staggering around drunk.

FIGURE 4.1 A mosaic of Alexander the Great leading his Macedonian troops into battle. Alexander conquered but never consolidated his vast empire. (*Art Resource, NY*)

"Come on! Bring out the torches!" they cried as they wanted to light fire to the citadel to avenge the destruction of Greek temples by the Persians. Another shouted, "So brave an exploit belongs only to Alexander to perform!" Stirred by these words, Alexander jumped up on the table and his entire group followed. The king grabbed a torch and threw it into the palace. Others followed and soon the violence of the fire consumed the entire city.

The Character and Leadership of Alexander

ARRIAN

Alexander's military abilities are beyond question, but it takes more than tactical knowledge to inspire and encourage a force of men to move thousands of miles away from their homeland in pursuit of the unknown. Finally, deep in India, Alexander's troops forced him to forget the "ends of the earth" and to return to Macedon. The journey home was difficult, and Alexander lost many men to the hardship of the desert. His leadership, as the following account reveals, was never in doubt.

Alexander was very handsome, had an active, searching mind, and a great love of physical exertion. He cared deeply about his honor and courted danger in order to demonstrate his heroic courage. He was arrogant, but maintained a cool, self-control in the midst of action. His fame was enhanced by his ability to inspire courage in his soldiers, to fill them with hopes of success, and to dispel fear through his own calm. He often got the jump on his enemies, outmaneuvering them before they even knew what was going on.

Alexander was also exceedingly clever and acted decisively when others hesitated. He could anticipate success and intuitively knew how to cope with each situation. He took risks and when the outcome was in doubt, defied uncertainty, and managed each situation with boldness. . . .

At this point in my story I must tell you one of the finest things Alexander ever did. . . . The army was crossing a desert of sand with the sun blazing down upon them. They were dying of thirst but struggled on to find water though it was still far away. Alexander, like everyone else, was tormented by thirst, but continued to march on foot at the head of his men. He could barely continue, but understood that each of the men would be better able to endure their misery if all knew that the pain was truly shared by Alexander. As they dragged on, some soldiers who had gone ahead to look for water actually found a small trickle that had collected in a shallow gully. They bent down and laboriously scooped up whatever they could and hurried back with their priceless treasure. As they approached Alexander, they poured the water into a helmet and gave it to him. Alexander carefully thanked them for the extraordinary gift, took the helmet, and, in full view of his troops, poured the water on the ground. The men were stunned. Whatever water was wasted by Alexander through this act was like giving a drink to every man in the army. I cannot praise this act enough. It was clear proof not only of Alexander's endurance, but also of his genius for leadership.

"Making Humankind a Single People"

PLUTARCH

Over the centuries the debate has raged as to why Alexander conquered the Persian Empire and beyond. Was he a megalomaniac whose sole purpose was to gratify himself by conquering others? Was he propelled by insatiable curiosity or lust for wealth? Or did Alexander have

"The Character and Leadership of Alexander" is from Arrian, *Anabasis*, 6.26 and 7.28, in George W. Botsford, *A Sourcebook of Ancient History* (New York: The Macmillan Co., 1912), pp. 280–281. Translation modernized by the editor.

"Making Humankind a Single People" is from Plutarch, *DeAlexandri Magni Fortuna est Virtute, Oratio I,* in George W. Botsford, *A Sourcebook of Ancient History* (New York: The Macmillan Co., 1912), p. 282. Translation modernized by the editor.

larger concerns? When he had his soldiers take Persian brides, was he trying, by intermingling blood and customs, to break the intellectual and physical confines of the Greek city-states and thus unite East and West? Or was the creation of his empire the result of impulse and chance? The following account by Plutarch addresses some of these questions.

Alexander did not follow Aristotle's advice to lead the Greeks and enslave all non-Greeks by cultivating the former as friends and kinsmen, and treating the latter as animals. Had he done so his kingdom would have been filled with conflict, exiles, and treachery; but he believed that the gods had sent him to mediate and govern the world. And those men whom he could not persuade, he dominated through force of arms. He brought these diverse people together from every land and combined their lives, customs, marriages, and manner of living within a great melting pot. He argued that the entire inhabited world should become their native land, his military power their common protection, his soldiers their brothers, their enemies his enemies. Nor should Greeks be distinguished from all other peoples and given special treatment just because they were Greeks. For everything—from food and clothing, to marriages and manners—would be blended together and united through common blood and children.

Alexander did not cross Asia like some common thief, nor did he want to ravage, pillage, and destroy other cultures simply for the loot that could be obtained. . . . Instead, he always had a larger vision to bring together many races under one ruler and under one form of government. His goal was to make

humankind a single people. Had not the gods taken his soul from us too soon, there would have been a singe law watching over all humankind. And everyone would have looked to a single form of justice as a common source of light. But now, that part of the world that never knew Alexander has been derived of the sun forever.

TAKING SIDES: THE ENIGMA OF ALEXANDER

4-4. After reading the sources on Alexander the Great, what kind of man was he? Do Alexander's accomplishments warrant the epithet "the Great"? Does "greatness" imply more than conquest? Is it more difficult to conquer than it is to consolidate and rule territory?

4-5. Assess the motives of Alexander the Great. Did he conquer for personal glory, for the glory of Macedon and Greece, for vengeance against the Persians, or to better his father?

4-6. What do you think of the "Brotherhood of Man" argument advocated by Plutarch? Was Alexander really trying to tie East and West together? Compare this idealistic vision with Alexander's destruction of Persepolis. Was Alexander more of a progressive or a destructive force?

4-7. To what extent can an individual change the course of history?

The Thought of the Age

The Philosophy of Plato

Plato's influence on Western philosophy has been so decisive that one scholar remarked that all subsequent thought is but a series of footnotes to Plato. He had grown into manhood during the Peloponnesian War in the late fifth century B.C.E. In the chaos and political dissension that accompanied the Athenian defeat, Plato watched as his mentor Socrates was falsely accused and then executed in 399 B.C.E. on charges of atheism and corrupting the youth of Athens. His disillusionment with democracy is reflected in the following passage from one of his dialogues. Plato distrusted the wisdom of majority rule and advocated instead the leadership of enlightened "philosopher-kings" who would control rather than consult the masses.

The Unenlightened Majority

PLATO

Socrates: And now, my friend, as you are already beginning to be a public character, and are admonishing and reproaching me for not being one, suppose that we ask a few questions of one another. Tell me, then Callicles, how about making any of the citizens better? Was there ever a man who was once vicious, or unjust, or intemperate, or foolish, and became by the help of Callicles good and noble? Was there ever such a man, whether citizen or stranger, slave or freeman? Tell me, Callicles, if a person were to ask these questions of you, what would you answer? Whom would you say that you had improved by your conversation? May there not be good deeds of this sort which were done by you as a private person, before you came forward in public? If you have any, will you mention them?

Callicles: You are pugnacious, Socrates.

Socrates: No, I ask you, not out of pugnacity, but because I really want to know in what way you think that affairs should be administered among us—whether, when you come to the administration of them, you have any other aim but the improvement of the citizens? Have we not already admitted many times over that this is the duty of a public man? No, we have surely agreed to that, for if you will not answer for yourself I must answer for you. But if this is what the good man ought to effect for the benefit of his own State, allow me to recall to you the names of those whom you were just now mentioning, Pericles, and Cimon, and Miltiades, and Themistocles [all leaders of Athens in the fifth century B.C.E.], and ask whether you still think that they were good citizens.

Callicles: I do.

Socrates: But if they were good, then clearly each of them must have made the citizens better instead of worse?

Callicles: Yes.

Socrates: And, therefore, when Pericles first began to speak in the assembly, the Athenians were not so good as when he spoke last?

Callicles: Very likely.

Socrates: No, my friend, "likely" is not the word; for if he was a good citizen, the inference is certain.

Callicles: And what difference does that make?

Socrates: None; only I should like further to know whether the Athenians are said to have been made better by Pericles, or, on the contrary, to have been corrupted by him; for I hear that he was the first who gave the people pay, and made them idle and cowardly, and encouraged them in the love of talk and of money.

Callicles: You heard that, Socrates, from [Spartan sympathizers].

Socrates: But what I am going to tell you now is not mere hearsay, but well known both to you and me: that at first, Pericles was glorious and his character unimpeached by any verdict of the Athenians—this was during the time when they were not so good—yet afterwards, when they had been made good and gentle by him, at the very end of his life, they convicted him of theft, and almost put him to death, clearly under the notion that he was a malefactor.

Callicles: Well, but how does that prove Pericles' badness?

Socrates: Why, surely you would say that he was but a bad manager of asses or horses or oxen, who had received them originally neither kicking nor butting nor biting him, and imparted to them all these savage tricks? Would he not be a bad manager of any animals who received them gentle, and made them fiercer than they were when he received them? What do you say to that?

Callicles: I will do you the favor of saying "yes."

Socrates: And will you also do me the favor of saying whether man is an animal?

Callicles: Certainly he is.

Socrates: And was not Pericles a shepherd of men?

Callicles: Yes.

Socrates: And if he was a good political shepherd, ought not the animals who were under him, as we were just now acknowledging, to have become more just, and not more unjust?

Callicles: Quite right.

"The Unenlightened Majority" is from Plato, *Gorgias*, in *The Dialogues of Plato*, trans. Benjamin Jowett, vol. III (New York: Charles Scribner's Sons, 1911), pp. 106–108.

Socrates: And are not just men gentle, as Homer says?—or are you of another mind?

Callicles: I agree.

Socrates: And yet he really did make them more savage than he received them, and their savageness was shown towards himself; and this was the last thing which he would have desired.

Callicles: Do you want me to agree with you?

Socrates: Yes, if I seem to you to speak the truth.

Callicles: I will admit what you say.

Socrates: And if they were more savage, must they not have been more unjust and inferior?

Callicles: Granted.

Socrates: Then upon this view, Pericles was not a good statesman?

Callicles: That is, upon your view.

Socrates: No, the view is yours, after what you have admitted. What do you say about Cimon again? Did not the very persons whom he was serving ostracize him, in order that they might not hear his voice for ten years? And they did just the same to Themistocles, adding the penalty of exile; and they voted that Miltiades, the hero of Marathon, should be thrown into the pit of death, and he was only saved by the chief Prytanis [public official]. And yet, if they had been really good men as you say, this would never have happened to them. For the good charioteers are not those who at first keep their place, and then, when they have broken-in their horses, and themselves become better charioteers, are thrown out—that is not the way either in charioteering or in any other sort of occupation. What do you think?

Callicles: I should think not.

Socrates: Well, and that proves the original assertion that no one has ever shown himself a good statesman in this State; and you admitted that this was true of our present statesmen, but not true of former ones, and you preferred them to the others; but they have turned out to be no better than our present ones. . . .

CONSIDER THIS:

4-8. What were some of Plato's ideas about democracy? Why did he feel this way? Do you think his assessment is correct?

Allegory of the Cave

PLATO

As a student of Socrates, Plato shared his view that universal truths exist and can be discovered. Plato went further by developing a system called the "Theory of Ideas," which defies simple explanation but rather requires a kind of immersion in thought to understand its tenets. Plato's doctrine is founded on the belief that there are two worlds, one we can readily see and experience with our senses and the other unseen and eternal. All objects in the sensory world are imperfect and transitory; the only true and perfect things, the eternal Ideas, exist in the abstract realm. Man's task in life is to struggle toward the ideal realm, the world of thought and spirit, by pursuing reason and logic. In this way, Plato hoped to address the concerns of his day. For Plato, democracy had failed, misdirecting society into constant turmoil, war, doubt, and depression. He saw a need to look to a higher ideal, a realm that was secure and that offered answers and organization in a chaotic world. As Plato noted in his work The Republic, "Until philosophers are kings or the kings and rulers of this world have the spirit of philosophy, until political power and wisdom are united . . . states will never have rest from their evils, nor . . . will the human race."

The following passage from *The Republic* explains Plato's Theory of Ideas. In the "Allegory of the Cave," he stresses the need to move away from the "shadows" that exist in the everyday realm of the senses into the lighted world of eternal truth and spiritual reality. Notice that Plato also believes those who see the light, move toward it, and are thus freed from the captivity of the shadows need to return to enlighten others; this is how civilization will progress.

"Allegory of the Cave" is from Plato, *The Republic*, 7.514–7.521, in *The Dialogues of Plato*, trans. Benjamin Jowett, vol. II (Boston: The Aldine Publishing Company, 1911), pp. 265–274. Translation modernized by the editor.

Behold! Human beings living in an underground den, which has a mouth open toward the light and reaching all along the den; here they have been from their childhood, and have their legs and necks chained so that they cannot move, and can only see before them, being prevented by the chains from turning round their heads. Above and behind them a fire is blazing at a distance, and between the fire and the prisoners there is a raised way; and you will see, if you look, a low wall built along the way, like the screen which marionette players have in front of them, over which they show the puppets. And do you see men passing along the wall carrying all sorts of vessels, and statues and figures of animals made of wood and stone and various materials, which appear over the wall? Some of them are talking, others silent.

You have shown me a strange image, and they are strange prisoners.

Like ourselves, I replied; and they see only their own shadows, or the shadows of one another, which the fire throws on the opposite wall of the cave?

True, he said; how could they see anything but the shadows if they were never allowed to move their heads?

And of the objects which are being carried in like manner they would only see the shadows. And if they were able to converse with one another, would they not suppose that they were naming what was actually before them?

Very true.

And suppose further that the prison had an echo which came from the other side, would they not be sure to notice when one of the passersby spoke that the voice which they heard came from the passing shadows? To them the truth would be literally nothing but the shadows of the images.

And now look again, and see what will naturally follow if the prisoners are released and exonerated of their error. At first, when any of them is liberated and compelled suddenly to stand up and turn his neck around and walk and look toward the light, he will suffer sharp pains; the glare will distress him, and he will be unable to see the realities of which in his former state he had seen the shadows; and then conceive someone saying to him, that what he saw before was an illusion, but that now, when he is approaching nearer to being and his eye is turned toward more real existence, he has a clearer vision—what will be his reply? And you may further imagine that his instructor

is pointing to the objects as they pass and requiring him to name them—will he not be perplexed? Will he not think that the shadows which he formerly saw are truer than the objects which are now shown him?

And if he is compelled to look straight at the light, will he not have a pain in his eyes which will make him turn away to take refuge in the objects of vision which he can see, and which he will conceive to be in reality clearer than the things which are now being shown to him?

And suppose once more, that he is reluctantly dragged up a steep and rugged ascent, and held fast until he is forced into the presence of the sun himself, is he not likely to be pained and irritated? When he approaches the light his eyes will be dazzled, and he will not be able to see anything at all of what are now called realities. He will require to grow accustomed to the sight of the upper world. And first he will see the shadows best, next the reflection of men and other objects in the water, and then the objects themselves; then he will gaze upon the light of the moon and the stars and the spangled heaven; and he will see the sky and the stars by night better than the sun or the light of the sun by day. Last of all he will be able to see the sun, and not mere reflections of him in the water, but he will see him in his own proper place, and not in another; and he will contemplate him as he is. He will then proceed to argue that this is he who gives the seasons and the years, and is the guardian of all that is in the visible world, and in a certain way the cause of all things which he and his fellows have accustomed to behold.

And when he remembered his old habitation, and the wisdom of the den and his fellow prisoners, do you not suppose that he would be happy about the change, and pity them? And if they were in the habit of conferring honors among themselves on those who were quickest to observe the passing shadows and to remark which of them went before, and which followed after, and which were together; and who were therefore best able to draw conclusions as to the future, do you think that he would care for such honors and glories or envy the possessors of them? Would he not say with Homer, "Better to be the poor servant of a poor master," and to endure anything, rather than think as they do and live after their manner?

Imagine once more such a one coming suddenly out of the sun to be replaced in his old situation; would he not be certain to have his eyes full of darkness? And if there were a contest, and he had to compete in measuring the shadows with the prisoners who had never moved out of the den, while his sight was still weak, and before his eyes had become steady (and the time which he needed to acquire this new habit of sight might be very considerable), would he not be ridiculous? Men would say of him that up he went and down he came without his eyes; and that it was better not even to think of ascending; and if anyone tried to loose another and lead him up to the light, let them only catch the offender, and they would put him to death.

This entire allegory, you may now append, dear Glaucon, to the previous argument; the prison-house is the world of sight, the light of the fire is the sun, and you will not misunderstand me if you interpret the journey upwards to be the ascent of the soul into the intellectual world according to my poor belief, which, at your desire, I have expressed—whether rightly or wrongly God knows. But, whether true or false, my opinion is that in the world of knowledge the idea of good appears last of all, and is seen only with an effort: and, when seen, is also inferred to the universal author of all things beautiful and right, parent of light, and of the lord of light in this visible world, and the immediate source of reason and truth in the intellectual; and that this is the power upon which he who would act rationally either in public or private life must have his eye fixed.

I agree, he said, as far as I am able to understand you.

Moreover, you must not wonder that those who attain to this beatific vision are unwilling to descend to human affairs; for their souls are ever hastening into the upper world where they desire to dwell; which desire of theirs is very natural, if our allegory may be trusted.

Yes, very natural. . . .

Then the business of us who are the founder of the State will be to compel the best minds to attain that knowledge which has been already declared by us to be the greatest of all—they must continue to ascend until they arrive at the good; but when they have ascended and seen enough we must not allow them to do as they do now.

What do you mean?

I mean that they remain in the upper world: but this must not be allowed; they must be made to descend again among the prisoners in the den, and

partake of their labors and honors, whether they are worth having or not.

But is not this unjust? he said; ought we to give them an inferior life, when they might have a superior one?

You have forgotten, my friend, the intention of the legislator, who did not aim at making any one class in the State happy above the rest; the happiness was to be in the whole State, and he held the citizens together by persuasion and necessity, making them benefactors of the State, and therefore benefactors of one another; to this end he created them, not that they should please themselves, but they were to be his instruments in binding up the State.

True, he said, I had forgotten.

Observe, Glaucon, that there will be no injustice in compelling our philosophers to have a care and providence of others; we shall explain to them that in other States, men of their class are not obliged to share in the toils of politics: and this is reasonable, for they grow up at their own sweet will, and the government would rather not have them. Now the wild plant which owes culture to nobody, has nothing to pay for culture. But we have brought you into the world to be rulers of the hive, kings of yourselves and of the other citizens, and have educated you far better and more perfectly than they have been educated, and you are better able to share in the double duty. Wherefore each of you, when his turn comes, must go down to the general underground abode, and get the habit of seeing in the dark; for all is habit; and by accustoming yourselves you will see ten thousand times better than the dwellers in the den, and you will know what the images are, and of what they are images, because you have seen the beautiful and just and good in their truth. And thus the order of our State, and of yours, will be a reality, and not a dream only, as the order of States too often is, for in most of them men are fighting with one another about shadows and are distracted in the struggle for power, which in their eyes is a great good. Whereas the truth is that the State in which the rulers are most reluctant to govern is best and most quietly governed, and the State in which they are most willing, the worst.

Quite true, he replied.

And will our pupils, when they hear this, refuse to share in turn the toils of State, when they are allowed to spend the greater part of their time with one another in the heaven of ideas?

Impossible, he answered; for they are just men, and the commands which we impose upon them are just; there can be no doubt that every one of them will take office as a stern necessity, and not like our present ministers of State.

Yes, my friend, and there lies the point. You must contrive for your future rulers another and a better life than that of a ruler, and then you may have a well-ordered State; for only in the State which offers this, will they rule who are truly rich, not in silver and gold, but in virtue and wisdom, which are the true blessings of life. Whereas if they go to the administration of public affairs, poor and hungering after their own private advantage, thinking that hence they are to snatch the good of life, order there can never be; for they will be fighting about office, and the civil and domestic broils which thus arise will be the ruin of the rulers themselves and of the whole State.

Most true, he replied.

CONSIDER THIS:

4-9. In Plato's "Allegory of the Cave," how do you interpret the fire, shadows, and prisoners? How does Plato express his Theory of Ideas in this allegory?

The Equality of Women in the State

PLATO

This passage presents Plato's thoughts concerning the role of women in his idealized Republic. In it, he denounces some of the laws and traditions of Greek society that restricted the political rights and social access of females to such an extent that Greek women were mere trustees of their husbands and fathers. In Plato's Republic, however, women would not only vote but would have access to positions of authority and responsibility, as magistrates and priests. The training of Guardians, who because of their character and intellect ruled the State, and the fitness of women for that position are at issue in the following passage from *The Republic*. The questions that Plato addresses reflect our modern concern for equality of opportunity between men and women. But note how Plato extends the argument at the end to a problematical level. At what point does true equality become socially unacceptable?

Socrates: Can you mention any pursuit of man in which the male sex does not have all qualities in a far higher degree than the female? Need I waste time in speaking of the art of weaving, and the management of pancakes and preserves, in which womankind does really appear to be great, and in which the superiority of the other sex is the most laughable thing in the world?

Glaucon: You are quite right, in maintaining the general inferiority of the female sex; at the same time many women are in many things superior to many men, though, speaking generally, what you say is true.

Socrates: And so, my friend, in the administration of a State neither a woman as a woman, nor a man as a man has any special function, but the gifts of nature are equally diffused in both sexes; all the pursuits of men are the pursuits of women also, and in all of them a woman is inferior to a man?

Glaucon: Very true.

Socrates: Then are we to impose all our enactments on men and none of them on women?

Glaucon: That will never do.

Socrates: One woman has a gift of healing, another not; one is a musician and another is not musician?

Glaucon: Very true.

Socrates: And one woman has ability in gymnastics and military exercises, while another is unwarlike and hates gymnastics?

"The Equality of Women in the State" is from Plato, *The Republic*, in *The Dialogues of Plato*, trans. Benjamin Jowett, vol. II (New York: Scribner, Armstrong, and Co., 1874), pp. 280–283. Translation modernized by the editor.

Glaucon: Beyond question.

Socrates: And one woman is a philosopher, and another is an enemy of philosophy; one has spirit, and another is without spirit?

Glaucon: That is also true.

Socrates: Then one woman will have the temper of a guardian, and another not; for was not the selection of the male guardians determined by these sort of differences?

Glaucon: That is true.

Socrates: Then the woman has equally with the man the qualities which make a guardian; she differs only in degrees of strength?

Glaucon: That is obvious.

Socrates: And those who have such qualities are the women who are to be selected as the companions and colleagues of our guardians, and who will resemble them in ability and character?

Glaucon: Clearly.

Socrates: And being of the same nature with them, ought they not to have the same pursuits?

Glaucon: They ought.

Socrates: Then, as we were saying before, there is nothing unnatural in assigning music and gymnastics to the wives of the guardians. To that we come round again.

Glaucon: Yes, Socrates.

Socrates: The law which enacted this instead of being an impossibility or mere aspiration was agreeable to nature, and the contrary practice, which prevails at present, is in reality a violation of nature.

Glaucon: That appears to be true.

Socrates: There was, first, the possibility, and secondly, the advantage of such an arrangement, which has to be considered?

Glaucon: Yes.

Socrates: And the possibility has been allowed?

Glaucon: Yes.

Socrates: And the advantage has next to be acknowledged?

Glaucon: That is the next question.

Socrates: You would admit that the same education which makes a man a good guardian will make a woman a good guardian; for their original nature is the same?

Glaucon: Yes, Socrates. . . . .

Socrates: Well, and may we not further say that the guardians are the best of our citizens?

Glaucon: By far the best.

Socrates: And will not these be the best women?

Glaucon: Yes, again I say the very best.

Socrates: And can there be anything better for the interests of the State than that the men and women of a State should be as good as possible?

Glaucon: There can be nothing better.

Socrates: And our course of music and gymnastics will accomplish this?

Glaucon: Certainly.

Socrates: Then we have made an enactment not only possible but in the highest degree advantageous to the State?

Glaucon: True.

Socrates: Then let the wives of our guardians strip, having virtue for their robes, and share in the toils of war and the defense of their country; only in the distribution of labor are the lighter tasks to be assigned to the women, as being the weaker vessels, but in other respects their duties are to be the same. And as for the man who laughs at naked women exercising in gymnastics for the sake of the highest good, his laughter is a fruit of unripe wisdom, which he gathers, and he himself is ignorant of what he is laughing at, or what he is about; for this is, and ever will be, the best of sayings, that the useful is virtuous and the hurtful is bad.

Glaucon: Very true.

Socrates: Here, then, is one difficulty in our law about women which we have escaped; the wave has not swallowed us up alive for enacting that the guardians of either sex should have all their pursuits in common; to the utility and possibility of this the argument is its own witness.

Glaucon: Yes, Socrates, that was a mighty wave which you have escaped.

Socrates: Yes, but a much greater wave is coming; you will not think much of this when you see the next.

Glaucon: Go on, let me see.

Socrates: The law, which is the sequel of this and of all that has preceded, is to this effect: "that the wives of these guardians are to be common, and their children also common, and no parent is to know his own child, nor any child his parent."

Glaucon: Yes, Socrates, that is a much greater wave than the other; and the utility as well as the possibility of such a law is far more doubtful.

Socrates: I do not think, Glaucon, that there can be any dispute about the very great utility of having wives and children in common—the possibility is quite another matter, and will be very much disputed.

Glaucon: Both would be disputed, hot and strong!

CONSIDER THIS:

4-10. In what specific ways can Plato's view of women in his ideal Republic be considered progressive? Compare his proposal with the restricted status of women in Greek society. How does Plato extend the argument for equality at the end of the dialogue? Is true equality socially unacceptable?

The Thought of Aristotle

Aristotle (384–322 B.C.E.) was another of the great philosophers of this era who would greatly influence thinkers in the Middle Ages. A student of Plato and tutor to Alexander the Great, Aristotle believed that ideal forms and truths existed but were not found in some abstract world apart from everyday life. In fact, one could discover Truth by observing sensory objects and then logically (through the process of induction) discerning their universal characteristics. Thus Aristotle was very practical and believed that all theories must be abandoned if they could not be observed to be true. Aristotle wrote widely on politics and ethics and is very contemporary in application. Note how many of the following ideas can be applied to our own world.

Virtue and Moderation: The Doctrine of the Mean

ARISTOTLE

Aristotle's principle concern in his *Ethics* is moral virtue, which might best be described as "good character." One obtains a good character by continually doing right acts until they become second nature. In defining "right action," Aristotle offers his Doctrine of the Mean, which serves as a guide toward achieving moral virtue and happiness. Right acts are those that lie between two extremes: courage, therefore, is the mean between the extremes of cowardice and rashness. Aristotle explains this in the following passage.

It is not enough to merely define virtue as a quality of character. We must also say what kind of quality it is. Now we can accept that the effect of all virtue or excellence is not only to render the object to which it belongs perfect in itself, but also to cause it to function perfectly: for example, excellence in the eye renders perfect both the structure of the eye, and its function—having good eyes causes us to see well; and similarly, excellence in a horse produces not merely a fine animal, but a good racer or charger in battle. If then this holds good in all cases, human virtue will mean the quality that produces a good man and that will also cause him to perform his own function well. . . . In the case of every whole that is divisible into parts, it is possible to take a larger or a smaller share of it, or an equal share; and those amounts may be measured either in relation to the thing itself or in relation to us. I mean that whereas the middle of an object is the point equally distant from each of its extremities, which is one and the same for everybody, the medium quantity in its relation to us is the amount that is not excessive and not deficient, and this is not the same for everybody. . . . For instance, supposing that for

"Virtue and Moderation: The Doctrine of the Mean" is from Aristotle, *Nichomachean Ethics*, 2.6, trans. H. Rackham, (Oxford: B. Blackwell, 1915), pp. 36–38. Translation modernized by the editor.

an athlete in training ten pounds of food is too large a ration and two pounds too small, the trainer will not necessarily advise six pounds, as possibly that will be too large or too small an allowance for the particular person—a small ration for Milo, the great wrestler, but a large one for a novice in athletics; and the same applies to the amount of running or wrestling prescribed in training. This is how every expert avoids excess and deficiency and adopts the middle amount—not the exact half of the object he is dealing with, but a medium quantity in relation to the person concerned.

Such then is the manner in which every kind of skill operates successfully, by looking to the middle point and making its work conform with it. This accounts for the remark commonly made about successful productions, that you cannot take anything away from them or add anything to them. The implication is that excess and deficiency impair excellence, and a median quantity secures it. If then we are right in saying that good craftsmen when at work keep their eyes fixed on a middle point, and if virtue, no less than nature herself, surpasses all the arts and crafts in accuracy and excellence, it follows that excellence will be the faculty of hitting a middle point. I refer to moral excellence or virtue; and this is concerned with emotions and actions,

in which it is possible to have excess, or deficiency, or a medium amount. For instance, you can feel either more or less than a moderate amount of fear and boldness, and of desire and anger and pity, and of pleasant or painful emotions generally; and in both cases the feelings will be wrong. But to feel these emotions at the right time and on the right occasion and towards the right people and for the right motives and in the right manner is a middle course, and the best course; and this is the mark of goodness.

And similarly, there is excess and deficiency or a middle amount in the case of actions. Now virtue is concerned with emotions and actions; excess and deficiency in them are wrong, and a middle amount receives praise and achieves success, both of which are marks of virtue. . . . We may thus conclude that virtue or excellence is a characteristic involving choice, consisting essentially in a middle state—middle in relation to ourselves, and as determined by principle, by the standard that a man of practical wisdom would apply. And it is a middle state between two vices, one of excess and one of deficiency; and this in view of the fact that vices either exceed or fall short of the right amount in emotions or actions, whereas virtue finds and chooses the mean.

The Status of Women

ARISTOTLE

He who thus considers things in their first growth and origin, whether a state or anything else, will obtain the clearest view of them. In the first place (1) there must be a union of those who cannot exist without each other; for example, of male and female, that the race may continue; and this is a union which is formed, not of deliberate purpose, but because, in common with other animals and with plants, mankind have a natural desire to leave behind them an image of themselves. And (2) there must be a union of natural ruler and subject, that both may be preserved. For he who can foresee with his mind is by nature intended to be lord and master, and he who can work with his body is a subject, and by nature a slave; hence master and slave have the same interest. . . .

Of household management we have seen that there are three parts—one is the rule of a master over slaves, which has been discussed already, another of a father, and the third of a husband. A husband and father rules over wife and children, both free, but the rule differs, the rule over his children being a royal, over his wife a constitutional rule. For although there may be exceptions to the order of nature, the male is by nature fitter for command than the female, just as the elder and full-grown is superior to the younger and more immature. . . .

Now it is obvious that the same principle applies generally, and therefore almost all things rule and are ruled according to nature. But the kind of rule differs; the freeman rules over the slave after another manner

"The Status of Women" is from Aristotle, *Politics*, Bk. I, trans. Benjamin Jowett (Oxford: Clarendon Press, 1885), pp. 49–54.

from that in which the male rules over the female, or the man over the child; although the parts of the soul are present in all of them, they are present in different degrees. For the slave has no deliberative faculty at all; the woman has, but it is without authority, and the child has, but it is immature. So it must necessarily be with the moral virtues also; all may be supposed to partake of them, but only in such manner and degree as is required by each for the fulfillment of his duty. . . . The courage of a man is shown in commanding, of a woman in obeying. . . . All classes must be deemed to have their special attributes; as the poet says of women, "Silence is a woman's glory," but this is not equally the glory of man. . . .

CONSIDER THIS:

4-11. How does Aristotle's philosophy differ from that of Plato? What is Aristotle's view of the function and status of women? Compare this with Plato's ideas about the equality of women in society. Define the "Doctrine of the Mean." Why is Aristotle called a "practical philosopher"?

THE BROADER PERSPECTIVE:

4-12. After Alexander's death in 323 B.C.E., many things changed throughout the Greek world. Gone was a dominant Greek vision as Alexander's empire broke apart into smaller kingdoms led by lesser rulers. This Hellenistic or "Greek-like" world produced art that was, in many cases, brutally realistic rather than the idealistic statuary of the fifth century B.C.E. And Hellenistic philosophy was concerned with surviving in an insecure world where political and social chaos was fast becoming a norm of life. Many people found consolation in the Stoic philosophy, which was fatalistic and advocated adherence to duty and responsibility, or that of Epicurus (342–270 B.C.E.). The Epicureans denied that there was any interference of gods in human affairs or any life after death. All things were composed of atoms, which eventually returned to the "void." For an Epicurean, pleasure was the key to life. And finally, Pyrrhro of Elis developed another important Hellenistic philosophy called Skepticism. The Skeptics delighted in pointing out the inadequacies of the various competing philosophies of the day. They thought that nothing could really be known because reality was distorted by appearances. Because nothing could be known, they consoled themselves by insisting that nothing mattered. Life thus consisted of adaptation and acceptance of the world as it was. How, therefore, did this Hellenistic outlook on life differ from that of the Hellenic vision of the fifth century B.C.E. when Athens was the dominant cultural power? In what ways did Plato and Aristotle provide the intellectual transition between the eras?

Chapter 5

The Roman Republic: Origins, Breakdown, and Rebirth

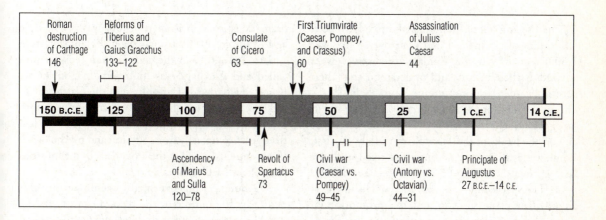

Men are much more attracted by immediate than by remote events; when they find things going well in the present, they are pleased, and think of nothing else.

—Niccolò Machiavelli

Idealism is the noble toga that political gentlemen drape over their will to power.

—Aldous Huxley

No one with absolute power can be trusted to give it up even in part.

—Justice Louis D. Brandeis

CHAPTER THEMES

- **The Power Structure:** How would you define the concept of a republic, and how does it differ from a democracy? Is a republic a more practical and workable form of government than a democracy? Why did the Roman Republic fail?

- **The Institution and the Individual:** How did the Gracchan revolution in economic and social reforms contribute to changes in Roman society? Did those changes ultimately result in the disintegration of the Roman Republic under the weight of military competition?

- **Imperialism:** How did success in the establishment of an empire by military force contribute to the prestige of generals and the decline of the Roman Republic? Does success in conquering territory give greater credence to the voices of extremism?

- **The Varieties of Truth:** Some historians have maintained that Augustus's rule was based less on his control of the military machine than on his patronage of poets in the realm. How was his image enhanced by various forms of propaganda? In this regard, could you compare

111

Augustus to Alexander the Great, or to Adolf Hitler or Joseph Stalin?

- **Revolution and Historical Transition:** How did Augustus fill the power vacuum left by the Roman civil war and maintain stability throughout the Roman world? Does history move in a cycle between chaos and stability? Why are some societies able to maintain stability longer than others? What are the sources of societal instability and chaos? Do these forces lead to repressive regimes that maintain domestic control at the expense of personal freedom?

- **The Big Picture:** Do all societies pass through a critical period of change that results in renewal or destruction? Must societies be challenged in order to survive and progress? Is this "challenge and response" theory of civilization applicable to one's personal life? Is a civilization, like a human being, a biological entity?

The rise and fall of the Roman Empire have been topics of fascination and controversy for over 1,500 years. Even the Romans themselves were amazed at their history and understood that their accomplishments were unique and their legacy imposing. The story of Rome began, as legend has it, on April 21, 753 B.C.E., with the foundation of the city on the banks of the Tiber River in Italy. At first, Rome was a monarchy; various kings ruled until the last was overthrown and a republic created in 509 B.C.E. The succeeding years saw the establishment of an unwritten constitution and the promotion of domestic reforms to assure political equality for all citizens—a condition the Romans proudly achieved without violence.

Besides solving domestic concerns, the Romans came into contact with neighboring tribes. Primarily because of their military superiority, achieved by discipline and organization, the Romans were able to defeat adversaries and thus extend the boundaries of their city. By 270 B.C.E., Rome had expanded to the southern tip of Italy and had succeeded in establishing contractual alliances with the peoples it had defeated. The Romans were liberal in their settlements, allowing cities to keep their own governments, traditions, and laws, demanding only tribute and military support in return. The Italian alliance was strong and proved essential in the succeeding years.

The challenge to Roman authority, however, was not long in coming. In 264 B.C.E., the Carthaginians, who had established a commercial hegemony of sorts over the western Mediterranean, believed that the ascendant Rome threatened their control of the region. A series of Carthaginian (Punic) wars began that not only challenged the authority of Rome but also threatened its very existence. Perhaps the most dramatic episode in Roman history was the struggle against the great Carthaginian general Hannibal, from 218 to 202 B.C.E. In the end, Roman tenacity prevailed and Carthage was humbled. In 146 B.C.E., Rome finally decided to obliterate the Carthaginian presence altogether. The walls of Carthage were torn down and curses pronounced over the area. Rome had freed itself completely from physical and psychological threat and now stood at the crossroads of the future as ruler of the Mediterranean.

Although Rome seemed preeminent in this region by the middle of the second century B.C.E., other domestic problems were fast arising to threaten the state from within. The Romans had destroyed the Carthaginian menace largely by depending on an army composed of free farmers who had exchanged their hoes for swords. After the victory over Hannibal, many returned to their farms to find that Hannibal's fifteen-year presence in Italy had destroyed their land. Rather than rebuild, which was expensive and a gamble in any event, many decided to sell their property to members of the senatorial aristocracy. The nobility thus increased their land holdings and created plantations called *latifundia*, which were farmed by the cheap slave labor abundant after the Punic wars. Because one had to own property to be in the army, many of the displaced veterans went to the city of Rome, hoping to find employment. A gulf widened between rich and poor that threatened the unity of the state.

In response to this, a tribune named Tiberius Gracchus proposed redistributing the senatorial estates. His murder by the nobility in 133 B.C.E. established a precedent for violence, which had never before played a role in Roman domestic politics. As violence and intimidation became acceptable tools of change, the state balanced on the brink of chaos. Soon generals such as Marius and Sulla, promising glory, booty, and land after service, offered men entrance into the army without the customary property qualification. In this way, a new army became the focal point of power, an army composed of professional soldiers who owed their loyalty to their general rather than to the state. Under the direction of men such as Marcus Crassus, Pompey the Great, and Julius Caesar, the army became a tool for the achievement of glory and the defense of one's dignity. The Republic degenerated into civil war and finally into dictatorship. With the death of the Republic, the ideals and character that had established equality among Roman citizens and defeated the likes of Hannibal also died. When Rome emerged from the throes of civil war, the victor Augustus established peace and prosperity. Still, his promotion of republican forms of government could not belie the autocracy that formed the basis of his rule. Citizens were made to feel free, however, and most were thus willing to trade the true liberty of a republic for the benefits of peace and security offered by Augustus's new "principate."

This chapter explores the development of the Roman Republic, its destruction, and its transformation into the principate of Augustus. Of particular importance is the topic of freedom. What was the basis of Roman strength and achievement, and why did the state collapse under the weight of generals who fought in defense of their traditional ideas of dignity and liberty? What is the importance of recognizing appearance and reality in any government? If one feels free in a controlled state, is one truly free? The problem of appearance versus reality is of great concern in modern democracies, where leaders are often elected or their policies implemented not on the basis of what is said but on how it is said. Media manipulation was as alive in Augustan Rome as it is in twenty-first-century America. Perhaps the true genius of the Romans was their capacity for adaptation and transformation. Survival is often the result of such compromises.

Roman Virtues in the Early and Middle Republic (753–150 B.C.E.)

The Romans viewed their rise to dominance throughout the Mediterranean region and beyond as the fulfillment of their destiny. From their origins in 753 B.C.E. as one of many small tribes occupying the seven hills surrounding a marshy center, it was the Roman people who solved each problem, conquered each tribe, established each alliance, and met each test they faced. This success was no accident of history in their minds, but rather the realization of their moral superiority and dominant will that then created the most powerful war machine in antiquity and enabled their administration to hold effective sway over a formidable empire for hundreds of years.

It was this story of challenge and response that the emperor Augustus (who reigned from 27 B.C.E. to 14 C.E.) wanted to recount for posterity when he encouraged the historian Titus Livy to write the history of Rome starting with the foundation of the city. This work of over 142 books occupied Livy for forty years, until his death in 17 C.E. Augustus, who had emerged victorious in the civil war against Mark Antony after the death of Julius Caesar in 44 B.C.E., was in the midst of "refounding" Rome and "restoring the Republic" that had been so brutally torn asunder by the greed and lust for power of its generals. Augustus needed to refashion Roman morality and reestablish Roman gravity and dignity. Livy's contribution lay in recounting the fabled stories from Rome's glorious past and to exalt the virtues of courage, honor, discipline, and sacrifice that had generated fear and respect among Rome's enemies and loyalty and stability from its citizens. In the Preface to his monumental work, Livy set forth his vision.

THE HISTORIAN AT WORK—TITUS LIVY

The Power of the Past

Whether the task I have undertaken of writing a complete history of the Roman people from the very beginning of their existence will reward me for the labor spent on it, I neither know for certain, nor even if I did know would I comment. For I see that this is a time-honored and common practice, that each new writer believes invariably that he will either demonstrate greater accuracy in his historical narrative, or surpass all the ancients in the excellence of his style. However this may be, it will still be a great satisfaction to me to have taken part as best I can by investing the history of the foremost nation in the world with a deeper interest; and if my own reputation withers amid the competition of rival historians, I would console myself with their greatness. The subject of the history of Rome, moreover, is one that demands immense labor. It goes back beyond 700 years and, after starting from small and humble beginnings, has grown to such dimensions that it begins to be overburdened by its own greatness. I have very little doubt, too, that for the majority of my readers the earliest times and those immediately succeeding, will bore them; they will hurry on to these modern days in which Roman might, so long in the making, is now wasting away through internal decay. I, on the other hand, shall gain a reward for all my hard work by closing my eyes to the evils which our generation has witnessed for so many years. As long as I am devoting all my thoughts to recounting the glorious past, I can avoid the disturbing anxieties of the present, even if I understand their truths.

The traditions of what happened prior to the foundation of the City or while it was being built, are more appropriate for the creativity of the poet than for the authentic assessment of the historian, and I have no intention of establishing either their truth or their falsehood. For the ancients require a certain license where the intermingling of human actions with those of the gods confer a greater dignity on the origins of states. Now, if any nation ought to be allowed to claim a sacred origin and point back to divine parenthood, that nation is Rome. . . . But whatever opinions or criticisms others may hold of our traditions, I regard them as of small importance. The subjects which I consider essential are these—the life and morals of the community, and the men and the qualities by which they accumulated and expanded the empire through domestic policy and foreign war. Then, as the standard of morality gradually lowered, the reader must follow the decay of our national character, observing how at first it slowly sank, then slipped downward more and more rapidly, until it finally began to plunge into headlong ruin and we reach these days, where we can bear neither our diseases nor their remedies.

> There is such an exceptional and relevant advantage from the study of the past, that you can see, set in the clear light of historical truth, examples of every possible type.
> —TITUS LIVY

There is such an exceptional and relevant advantage from the study of the past, that you can see, set in the clear light of historical truth, examples of every possible type. From this research, you may select for yourself and your country what to imitate, and also what measures, as being inappropriate at the beginning and disastrous in its results, you must avoid. Unless, however, I have gotten it completely wrong in trying to assess the Rome I love, there has never existed any nation greater in

"The Power of the Past" is from Livy, *The History of Rome from Its Foundation*, trans. Rev. Canon Roberts, Vol. 1, Preface (New York: E. P. Dutton and Co., 1912). Translation modernized by the editor

power, with a purer morality, or more productive in good examples; or any state in which avarice and luxury have been so late in making their inroads, or poverty and frugality so highly and continuously honored, showing so clearly that the less wealth men possess the less they covet. In our own century, wealth brought greed in its train, and the unlimited desire for pleasure created in men a passion for ruining themselves and everything else through self-indulgence and unrestrained perversion. We should not, however, begin this monumental work with criticism, but should start with favorable omens, and prayers to gods and goddesses that they might give us success in the great task before us.

CONSIDER THIS:

5-1. Livy seems to love and admire Rome, yet refers time and again to the "decay of national character." According to Livy, what qualities of character and performance made Rome great and why did Rome's glory degenerate over time?

5-2. Livy has reasons for focusing on the stories and legends of early Rome, even though he concedes that they are "more appropriate for the creativity of the poet than for the authentic assessment of the historian." He acknowledges that he has "no intention of establishing either their truth or their falsehood." Why then does he emphasize these stories? What was important to Livy?

THE BROADER PERSPECTIVE:

5-3. What was Livy's purpose in writing his history of Rome? Should an historian be unbiased in his or her approach to a subject, or is this even possible? Does critical thinking encourage a balanced perspective in order to obtain a moderate assessment? Or does historical writing require passion to give it a moral purpose? What is the job of the historian?

5-4. Note that the Greek historian, Thucydides, rejected the more popular "lines of the poet displaying the exaggerations of his craft . . . at the expense of the truth." Thucydides argued that history must be "guided by the clearest evidence" in reconstructing the past and establishing truth. Do you agree with Thucydides on this? If so, does this mean that Livy is an inferior historian?

The Oath of the Horatii: "One of the Great Stories of Ancient Times"

LIVY

The following stories as compiled by Livy emphasize the foundation of Roman greatness and the expectations for Augustus's new glory. The first story recounts the struggle in about 670 B.C.E. between the Alban tribe and the Romans for local control. The hero, Horatius, defined the concepts of Roman discipline and valor. In the second excerpt, the Roman matron, Lucretia, provided the model of sacrifice after Sextus Tarquinius, the son of the Roman king, raped her. Lucretia demonstrated that her honor was more important than her life. Her sacrifice furnished the spark that toppled the Roman kingship and paved the way for the establishment of the Republic in 509 B.C.E. It is interesting to note that this effort was headed by Marcus Junius Brutus, the ancestor of the more famous tyrannicide, who in 44 B.C.E sought to free Rome from the clutches of the dictator Julius Caesar.

"The Oath of the Horatii" is from Livy, *The History of Rome from Its Foundation*, trans. B. O. Foster, Vol. 1: 1.24–1.25 (Cambridge, MA: Harvard University Press, 1919), pp. 83, 85, 87, 91. Translation modernized by the editor

This story is truly one of the greatest in ancient times. . . . It so happened that in each army, there were three bothers who were triplets—all the same age and equally strong—who belonged to the families of the Horatii and Curiatii. The rival commanders proposed that these two pairs of triplets should fight against each other as champions of their respective countries. Whoever emerged victorious would hold sway over the vanquished. No one objected to the challenge and a time and place was arranged. Before proceeding with the battle, a solemn treaty was made between the Romans and the Albans, providing that the nation whose champions triumphed would hold undisputed power over the other.

Eager for combat, the six brothers advanced into the space between the two lines of battle. . . . The stakes were high—either empire or slavery would be determined by the luck or valor of three men. The crowd was tormented by the suspense. The signal was given, and with drawn steel, like advancing battle-lines, the six young men rushed to the charge, breathing the courage of great armies.

There was a mighty clash of shields and a flash of glittering blades, while a deep shudder ran through the crowd that, so long as there was no advantage to either side, was powerless to speak or breathe. Hand to hand they fought, their bodies struggling, their blades flashing, cutting, as the blood from their wounds began to

FIGURE 5.1 *The Oath of the Horatii:* "The stakes were high—either empire or slavery would be determined by the luck or valor of three men."—Livy [Jacques-Louis David, French, 1748–1825. *The Oath of the Horatii,* 1784, oil on canvas, 14' × 11'. Louvre Museum, Paris, France. Bridgeman-Giraudon/*Art Resource*

flow. Alba's three brothers had all been cut, but then one Roman, then another fell to the ground nearly dead from their wounds. A great cheer burst from the Alban army, while the Roman soldiers on the other side lost hope; their remaining warrior, though unhurt, was now surrounded by the three Curiatii.

The young man, though no match for his three opponents together, was ready to fight them one at a time. So, to divide their attack, he fled, thinking that each of them would pursue him with what speed their individual wounds would allow. Horatius had run just a short distance when he turned around and noticed that two of his opponents were strung out at wide intervals, but that one was nearly upon him. The Roman turned and attacked. While the Alban army was calling out to the other Curiatii to help their brother, Horatius cut him down and, flushed with victory, was already looking for his next victim. After he killed the second Alban brother, the Roman army then let out a cheer that steeled Horatius and encouraged him to finish the job.

Now they faced each other, one against one. But they were anything but evenly matched. Horatius remained unhurt and elated by his victory over the two Curatii brothers. His opponent dragged himself along, faint from loss of blood and exhausted with running. He had seen his brothers slaughtered before his eyes and was a beaten man facing a triumphant foe. What followed was no combat. "I have killed two already," the Roman shouted, "to avenge my dead brothers. The third I will offer up to settle this quarrel that Rome may rule Alba." His enemy could barely hold up his shield. With a downward thrust, Horatius buried his sword in the Alban's throat, cut him down and stripped him of his armor where he lay.

The Romans welcomed their hero with cheers and celebration, their joy all the greater for their narrow escape from disaster. The two armies then buried their dead with widely different feelings. Alba was subject now to her Roman mistress.

CONSIDER THIS:

5-5. What were the virtues demonstrated by the Horatii in this struggle to the death? Note the pressure placed on the shoulders of the last Roman brother, as success or failure became a personal responsibility. What message was being given to each Roman soldier?

The Rape of Lucretia

LIVY

Lucretia, though it was late at night, was busily spinning wool, while her maidens worked around her in the lamplight as she sat in the hall of her house. The prize of this contest in womanly virtues fell to Lucretia. As her husband, Collatinus, and the young Tarquin princes approached, they were graciously received, and the victorious husband courteously invited the young men to have dinner at his table. It was there that Sextus Tarquinius, inflamed by Lucretia's beauty and proven chastity, was seized with a wicked lust and determined to rape her. But nothing happened that night and the young men returned to camp.

But a few days later Sextus, without informing Collatinus, returned with one companion. Since Lucretia did not suspect his intent, he was hospitably welcomed, given dinner and then, as an honored visitor, escorted to the guest-chamber for the night. Sextus Tarquinius waited until all was quiet and everyone fast asleep. He then drew his sword and made his way to Lucretia's room where she was sleeping. Holding her down with his left hand on her breast, "Be still, Lucretia," he whispered. "I am Sextus Tarquinius. My sword is in my hand. Utter a sound, and you die!" Lucretia opened her eyes in terror. No help in sight–only imminent death. Then Tarquin began to tell her of his love, to plead, to threaten—anything that might conquer her heart. But she was strong and would not relent. Not even the fear of death could move her.

"The Rape of Lucretia" is from Livy, *The History of Rome from Its Foundation*, trans. B. O. Foster, Vol. 1: 1.57–1.59 (Cambridge, MA: Harvard University Press, 1919), pp. 83, 85, 87, 91. Translation modernized by the editor

But when he threatened to disgrace her by killing his slave and then stripping Lucretia naked and laying her dead body by his side so that all might think that she had been executed after her adultery with a servant had been discovered—well, even the most perfect chastity could not stand up to that dire threat. Tarquin then raped her and departed, exulting in his conquest of such an honorable woman.

Poor Lucretia wrote to her father in Rome and to her husband in Ardea, urging them both to come immediately with a trusted friend, for something dreadful had happened... . They found Lucretia sitting in her room deep in her tears. Her husband asked, "Is everything all right?"and she answered, "Far from it, for what can be right with a woman who has lost her honor? Another man has left his mark in your bed, Collatinus. But only my body has been violated, not my heart, as death shall be my witness. Promise me that this adulterer, this scum shall be punished. Sextus Tarquinius raped me. He came last night disguised as my guest, but entered my bedchamber and took his pleasure. He ruined me and ruined himself—if you are men."

They promised her, every man in his turn. They tried to comfort her, told her she was helpless, innocent. He alone was the guilty one and only her mind had sinned, not her body. Since she had not intended to sin, there could never be any guilt.

"It is for you to determine," Lucretia answered, "what is due to *him*. As for me, although I am innocent of any blame, I shall still take my punishment. Lucretia will never set a precedent for unchaste women to deny their responsibilities." Taking a knife which she had concealed beneath her dress, she plunged it into her heart, fell forward, and died.

Her father and husband were beside themselves with grief. While they stood crying helplessly, Brutus drew the bloody knife from Lucretia's body, and holding it before him cried: "By this blood, from a girl of perfect chastity until a tyrant wronged her, I swear—and I call upon the gods to witness!—that with sword, with fire, and what other means I can, I will hunt down Lucius Tarquinius the Proud, his wicked wife, and all his children, and never again will I let them or any other man be King in Rome."

CONSIDER THIS:

5-6. In this story, how did Livy define purity and guilt? What made Lucretia a good Roman?

5-7. Note the pressure placed on her father and husband to avenge her death "if you are men." In this instance, virtue and action were closely linked. It was not enough merely to agree with ideals—one had to live them, or die in their defense.

The Courage of Mucius Scaevola

LIVY

As we have seen, the Romans respected moral vision, but also demanded action in support of ideals. Horatius and Lucretia both were willing to live or die in support of an absolute morality. The Romans admired individuals who put something valuable on the line that they could not personally afford to lose, but were willing nonetheless. Livy spoke directly to Roman youth about disgrace and courage with the story of Gaius Mucius Scaevola.

After the Romans had successfully thrown off the rule of the Etruscan kings and had established their republic in 509 B.C.E., they still had to defend and maintain their liberty by repelling Etruscan attacks. In this story, Rome was under siege by Lars Porsenna, an aggressive Etruscan king who sought once again to enslave its inhabitants. Mucius Scaevola decided to put something on the line.

"The Courage of Mucius Scaevola" is from Livy, *The History of Rome from Its Foundation*, trans. Rev. Canon Roberts, Vol. 1, 2.12–2.13 (New York: E. P. Dutton and Co., 1912). Translation modernized by the editor

There once was a young noble, Gaius Mucius, who regarded it as a disgrace that while Rome in the days of servitude under her kings had never been blockaded in any war or by any enemy, she should now, in the day of her freedom, tolerate a siege by those very Etruscans whose armies she had often defeated. So he thought that he would avenge this disgrace through his own personal valor by penetrating the enemy's camp. But on second thought, he worried that if he did so, unknown by anyone and without orders from the consuls, that were he arrested by Roman guards on the outposts, then he might be brought back as a deserter... . So he went to the senate and said, "Fathers, I would like to swim across the Tiber and enter the enemy's camp, not simply to pillage or inflict retaliation for their aggression, but I propose, with heaven's help, an even greater deed." The senate gave their approval. Mucius grabbed a sword, hid it in his robe and started out. He slipped into the enemy camp and made his way within a dense crowd toward the royal tribunal. The Etruscans at that time were distributing pay to the soldiers and the paymaster, who was sitting by the king and dressed almost exactly like him, was very busy, as the soldiers kept coming to him incessantly. Afraid to ask which of the two was the king, lest his ignorance should betray him, Mucius struck as fortune directed the blow and killed the paymaster instead of the king. He tried to force his way back with his blood-stained dagger through the shocked crowd, but he was seized and dragged back to the royal tribunal by the king's bodyguard. Here, alone and helpless, and in the greatest danger, he bellowed at the king: "I am a citizen of Rome. Men call me Gaius Mucius. As your enemy, I will destroy you and have as much courage to meet death as I have to inflict it. It is in our Roman nature to act bravely and to suffer bravely. Know that I am not alone in seeking your death, for I am but the first wave of a long line of Roman soldiers who are committed to the same end and desire personal honor for themselves. You had better get prepared to fight for your life every hour of every day, for this is the war which we the youth of

Rome declare against you. You won't have to worry about a pitched battle, a clash of massed armies, for the matter will be settled between you alone and each one of us individually." The king, furious with anger, and at the same time terrified at such an ominous future, threatened that if Mucius did not quickly explain the details of this vague plot, the king would roast him alive. "Look," Mucius shouted, "and learn how little your physical threats mean to someone committed to an honorable and glorious death." Then he plunged his right hand into a fire burning on the altar and held it there, roasting slowly, with no hint of pain. The king, astounded at this defiance to all natural fear, sprang from his seat and ordered the youth to be removed from the altar. "Go," he said, "you have been a worse enemy to yourself than to me. I would honor your courage if it were displayed on behalf of my country, but as it is, I send you away alive out of respect." Then Mucius, reciprocating this generosity replied, "Since you honor courage, know that with Romans, you can never gain by threats what you can obtain by kindness. Three hundred of us, the strongest of our Roman youth, have sworn to attack you in this way. The lot simply fell to me first. The rest, in their turn, will come until we succeed and you die."

Mucius was then set free and later received the name "Scaevola," from the loss of his right hand. Envoys from the Etruscan king followed him to Rome. The king's narrow escape from the first of many attempts (which he owed only to the mistake of his assailant), and the prospect of having to meet as many attacks as there were conspirators, so unnerved him that he made proposals of peace to Rome. In recognition of his courage, the senate gave Gaius Mucius Scaevola a piece of land across the river, which was afterwards known as the Mucian Meadows.

CONSIDER THIS:

5-8. What were the traditional Roman values embodied by Mucius Scaevola? Compare him to Horatius and Lucretia. What composite of Roman character emerges?

KEY EVENTS IN THE EARLY AND MIDDLE ROMAN REPUBLIC

753–509 B.C.E.   The Period of the Kings
Rome is founded in 753 B.C.E. and led by kings until they are expelled and the Republic is created in 509 B.C.E.

509–285 B.C.E.   The Struggle of the Orders
Plebeians struggle for full rights in the state against patrician interests. Plebeians obtain social, political, and economic equality without violence by 285 B.C.E. and Italy is consolidated under Roman rule.

264–202 B.C.E.   The Punic Wars
The rising Roman land power confronts Carthaginian interests in Sicily and in the western Mediterranean and wins the First Punic War (264–242 B.C.E.). Carthaginian general Hannibal seeks revenge and the destruction of Rome in the Second Punic War (218–202 B.C.E.). Rome is victorious under the leadership of Scipio Africanus.

149–146 B.C.E.   The Third Punic War
Persuaded by Cato the Elder, Rome declares war on Carthage and destroys the city along with Corinth in 146 B.C.E. Rome extends its control over the Mediterranean world:

133–121 B.C.E.   The Agrarian Reforms of the Gracchi
The tribune, Tiberius Gracchus, proposes redistributing senatorial estates among Roman people. He is killed during an ensuing riot (133 B.C.E.). His brother Gaius is murdered in 121 B.C.E. Breakdown of Roman unity begins.

"Hannibal at the Gates!"

LIVY

When the great Carthaginian general Hannibal was but nine years old, his illustrious father Hamilcar Barca took him to an altar and made him swear that he would hate the Romans and make them his enemies. Hamilcar was expressing his anger at having been "sold out" by the Carthaginian government when it surrendered to Rome prematurely in concluding the First Punic War in 241 B.C.E. Hannibal took the oath seriously and at age twenty-four assumed control of Carthaginian forces with a bold plan of attack. He violated the terms of the peace with Rome in 219 B.C.E. and began the Second Punic War by unexpectedly heading over the Alps and descending upon northern Italy.

Hannibal was unbeatable as Roman forces fell time and again to his complex tactics and staggering ingenuity. The Romans and their allies lost tens of thousands of men in his onslaught and were only successful in deflecting Hannibal's entrance into Rome. But such tactics of hit and run could never result in victory and were considered cowardly and "un-Roman." In 216 B.C.E., the Roman commanders again offered battle. The armies met at Cannae, where the Carthaginians destroyed over 70,000 Romans, who charged into a clever enveloping trap set by Hannibal. Rome's allies now began to desert and the cry went up: "Hannibal is at the gates!"

"Hannibal Is at the Gates" is from Livy, *The History of Rome from Its Foundation*, trans. F. G. Moore, Vol. 6: 22.51–22.53 (Cambridge, MA: Harvard University Press, 1919), pp. 352, 354, 356, 358. Translation modernized by the editor

The historian Livy now recounts the fear and desperation just after the battle as all seemed lost. It was at this critical juncture that a young savior arose in the figure of Lucius Cornelius Scipio. Only eighteen years old in this scene, he embodied the ancient Roman virtues of courage and discipline, which allowed him eventually to defeat Hannibal by taking the war to Hannibal's homeland in North Africa. Scipio afterwards assumed the title "Africanus," and his valor was recounted time and again as Romans looked back to this moment of destiny and decried the absence of such virtues after 100 B.C.E. as the Republic was destroyed by competing generals amid civil war.

At dawn next morning, the Carthaginians looked over the carnage of the battlefield, shocking even to an enemy, and collected their spoils. All over the field, thousands of Roman soldiers lay dead, mingled among their horses, thrust together by the shifting tide of the battle. Here and there, the wounded whose bodies were covered with blood, struggled to rise up from among the corpses. The morning cold had roused them briefly, but they were quickly killed. Others were found alive, but immobilized because tendons in their thighs and behind their knees had been cut through; they craned their necks and begged the Carthaginian soldiers to cut their throats. Some had tried to smother themselves by digging holes and burying their faces within, choking on the soil. Strangest of all was a Numidian soldier who was found still alive with horribly lacerated nose and ears, under the body of a Roman soldier; this soldier, unable to grasp his sword any longer, had died while tearing his enemy apart with his teeth. The remaining Romans, those who had the strength and heart—a total of about 4,000 infantry together with 200 cavalry—escaped to Canusium; some marched there in a column, others struggled as best they could individually over the countryside. Among these fugitives were four military tribunes who were discussing the situation with a few friends. Philus, the son of an ex-consul, interrupted them with startling news: all was lost and any hope was useless—the future would be filled only with misery and despair. Several high-ranking men led by Lucius Caecilius Metellus were planning to abandon Italy and live in exile with some foreign prince across the sea. This news had a dreadful effect on the morale of the remnants of the army. It came as a new kind of horror on top of everything else and shocked the men into a stupor of disbelief. Those who had been listening to the tribunes' discussion decided to call a general conference, but young Scipio—the man who was destined to command the Roman armies in this war—said that crisis was upon them and that what was needed

was bold action, not indecisive words. "Come with me immediately," he cried, "and bring your sword, if you wish to save our country. The enemy's camp is truly wherever such thoughts can rise!" With a few followers, he went directly to where Metellus was staying. Scipio burst into the house, and found them making their plans to abandon Italy. Holding his bared sword over their heads, Scipio cried: "I swear with all the passion of my heart that I shall never desert our country, or permit any other citizen of Rome to leave her in peril. If I break my oath, may Jupiter, Greatest and Best, strike me down in shame, along with my house, my family and all I possess! Swear the same oath, Caecilius—and the rest of you swear as well. If anyone refuses, this sword is drawn against him." They could not have been more frightened had they been staring into the face of Hannibal himself. Every man took the oath, and committed himself to Scipio's authority.

CONSIDER THIS:

5-9.   Hannibal's brilliant victories inspired a crisis in morale as Rome faced its most difficult and desperate struggle to survive. Note the resolve of the young Scipio in the face of fear and doubt. He made it clear at the crucial moment that the "enemy's camp," that is their true power, lay in the defeatist thoughts of his fellow Romans.

5-10.   What role did shame play in the reaction to Scipio's stand and what does this say about the Romans? In Scipio, we find the historical embodiment of the Roman values set forth in the mythological stories of Horatius, Lucretia, and Mucius Scaevola. Does every great nation have foundation myths to which their citizens turn during times of uncertainty to remind them of their values? George Washington and the cherry tree? George Washington throws a silver dollar across the Potomac? Abraham Lincoln walks miles to return a book that he had borrowed? Character is king.

"Cracks in the Wall": The Breakdown Begins (150–100 B.C.E.)

After the defeat of Hannibal by Scipio Africanus at the battle of Zama in 202 B.C.E., the Romans turned their attention to the East. They were hesitant to inject themselves into Greek affairs, but the constant internal bickering between city-states tested Roman patience. Finally, in 146 B.C.E., the Roman commander leveled Corinth to the ground as a warning that Rome would not tolerate domestic chaos and dissent.

In the same year, the Romans also settled affairs in North Africa. Though Carthage was no longer a military threat and had adhered faithfully to the terms of its treaty with Rome, Carthage nevertheless loomed as the eternal enemy in the Roman mind. The influential senator Cato the Elder ended each speech with the words "And Carthage must be destroyed. . . ." The Third Punic War was fought from 149–146 B.C.E. out of misplaced Roman fears. When it was over, the Romans tore down the walls of Carthage, pronounced curses over the area, and sowed salt into the ground so that nothing would ever grow there again. The historian Appian of Alexandria (95?–165 C.E.) provides this vivid description of the destruction of Carthage under the command of Scipio Aemilienus, a descendant of the great Africanus.

The Destruction of Carthage (146 B.C.E.)

APPIAN

Now Scipio moved quickly to attack Byrsa, the strongest part of Carthage, where most of the inhabitants had taken refuge. There were three streets ascending from the forum to this fortress, along which, on either side, were houses built closely together and six stories high, from which the Romans were attacked by spears and arrows. The Romans, therefore, took control of the lower houses and then made a bridge by throwing timbers from one rooftop to another in order to cross and take on the defenders. While this fight was raging on the roofs, another was going on in the streets below. There were the horrific sounds of groans, shrieks, shouts, and every kind of agony. Some were stabbed, others were hurled alive from the roofs to the pavement, falling and impaled on the heads of spears or swords. No one dared to set fire to the houses because of those who were still on the roofs—until Scipio reached Byrsa. Then he set fire to the three streets all together, and gave orders to keep the passageways clear of burning material so that the army might move back and forth freely.

Then came new scenes of horror. As the fire spread and carried everything down, the soldiers did not wait to destroy the buildings a bit at a time, but all at once. So the crashing grew louder, and many corpses fell with the stones into the center. Others were seen still living, especially old men, women, and young children who had hidden in the innermost nooks of the houses, some of them wounded, some burned, and crying pitifully. Still others, who were thrown off the highest roofs and fell together with the stones, timbers, and fire, were torn apart in all shapes of horror, crushed and mangled. Nor was this the end of their miseries, for those who were removing the rubbish from the streets with axes and pitchforks, and making the roads passable, tossed the dead and the living together into trenches in the ground, dragging them along like sticks and stones, and turning them over with their iron tools. Some, who were thrown in head first, with their legs sticking out of the ground, writhed a long time. Others fell with their feet down, and their heads above ground. Horses ran over them, crushing their faces and skulls, not purposely on the part of the riders, but in their mad rush to get away. Nor did those who were clearing the street do these things on purpose; but the tug of war, the glory of

"The Destruction of Carthage" is from Appian, *The Civil Wars*, trans. Horace White (New York: The Macmillan Company, 1899), pp. 229–232. Translation modernized by the editor

approaching victory, the rush of the soldiers, the orders of the officers, the blast of the trumpets, tribunes and centurions marching their cohorts here and there—all together made everybody frantic and nearly disconnected from the horrors happening all around them.

The massacre went on for six days and nights. The soldiers had to be rotated regularly so that they would not be exhausted by the work, the slaughter, and all those horrific sights. . . .

Scipio looked out upon this famous city that had flourished for 700 years after its foundation and had ruled over so many lands, islands, and seas, rich with armies and fleets, elephants and money, equal to the mightiest monarchies, but far surpassing them in bravery and spirit (since without ships or arms, and in the face of famine, it had sustained continuous war for three years). Carthage now lay prostrate before him—totally destroyed. Scipio, beholding this spectacle, is said to have shed tears and publicly lamented the fate of the enemy. After thinking by himself for a long time and reflecting on the rise and fall of cities, nations, and empires, as well as of individuals, and especially on the fate of Troy, that once proud city, on that of the Assyrians, the Medes, and the Persians, greatest of all, and later the splendid Macedonian empire, the words of the poet Homer escaped his lips:

> "For in my heart and soul, I also know this well:
> the day will come when sacred Troy must die.
> King Priam must die and all his people with him."
> (*Iliad*, 6.530–6.533)

When asked what he meant by this, Scipio said that he did not hesitate frankly to include his own country in this vision. He feared for Rome when he considered the changing and ironic nature of human affairs.

CONSIDER THIS:

5-11. According to Appian, the Roman commander Scipio Aemilienus wept as he watched the annihilation of Carthage. Why? Why was he not joyful at the victory?

5-12. How do you interpret Scipio's quote from Homer's *Iliad*? What did he see for the future of Rome?

THE BROADER PERSPECTIVE:

5-13. In 146 B.C.E., Rome destroyed both Carthage and the Greek city of Corinth. Some historians have seen this rather extreme policy as an indication that Rome no longer was the vibrant and confident power that had defeated Hannibal, but was lost and in search of a vision for ruling its expanding empire. By substituting destruction for the patient demands of diplomacy and negotiation, how did Rome limit its options in the international arena? Does violence close doors and diplomacy keep them open—or does diplomacy simply postpone the inevitable? What role do patience and violence play in international relations? Is it prudent to "speak softly and carry a big stick?"

5-14. Must a great nation have a great enemy in order to define itself? And when a nation no longer faces its traditional enemy, is there often a period of soul-searching and even policy drift before a defining moment gives new relevance to the nation? After the Soviet Union collapsed in 1991, the United States had difficulty defining its mission in the world until it was given new purpose after 9/11 by launching the "War on Terror." Keep your eyes on Rome—the period from 146 to 30 B.C.E. will be a time of internal conflict and dissension as the Republic falls prey to the very generals who granted success and security in establishing the Roman empire.

The Growth of the Latifundia

APPIAN

After the Punic wars, the influx of cheap slave labor had undermined the livelihood of the Roman soldier, who often returned home to find his farmland neglected or destroyed and hence unworkable. There was then a great resentment of the *latifundia* system that had absorbed the farms of Roman soldiers, as the following selection notes.

"The Growth of the Latifundia" is from Appian, *The Civil Wars*, 1.7–9, in *Readings in Ancient History*, ed. William S. Davis, vol. 2, (Boston: Allyn and Bacon, 1913), pp. 104–105. Translation modernized by the editor

The wealthy, getting hold of the greater part of the undistributed lands, growing bold by lapse of time and thinking they would never be ousted, added to their original holdings the small farms of their poor neighbors. This they did partly by purchase, yet partly by force: and so they cultivated the vast tracts of land in lieu of mere private estates. To work them they used slaves as farm hands and herdsmen, lest free laborers should be forced to quit farm work for the army. The ownership of slaves brought huge profit from the multitude of the children of the slaves, who increased because they were exempt from army service. Thus the magnates became marvelously rich, and the race of slaves multiplied through the land, while the free folk of Italy dwindled alike in numbers and power, ground down as they were by poverty, taxation, and constant service in the army. If any relaxation from these evils came, they passed their time in sheer idleness, for the land was in the clutches of the rich, who employed slaves as farmhands, not freemen.

The Murder of Tiberius Gracchus (133 B.C.E.)

PLUTARCH

In 133 B.C.E., a tribune named Tiberius Gracchus proposed a land redistribution plan designed to limit the amount of acreage any individual could hold. In this way, he hoped to salvage the free farmer. Members of the senatorial oligarchy were the first to resort to violence in the murder of Tiberius, thus ending a Roman tradition of peaceful domestic reform through compromise. Tiberius's brother, Gaius, who proposed further reforms ten years later, was also killed. This breakdown in political unity is noted by the critic Sallust in the selection that follows this account by Plutarch.

[Nasica, a senatorial leader, urged strong measures:] "Let every one who will defend the laws follow me." [Nasica,] then, casting the edge of his toga over his head, hastened to the Capitol; those who accompanied him also wrapped their togas also about their arms and forced their way after him. And as they were persons of the greatest authority in the city the common people did not venture to obstruct their passing, but were so eager to clear the way for them that they tumbled over one another in haste. The attendants they brought with them had furnished themselves with clubs and wooden rods from their houses, and they themselves picked up the feet and other fragments of stools and chairs, which were broken by the hasty flight of the common people.

Thus armed, they moved toward Tiberius, knocking down and pushing away all of those who were in front of him, and killing many. Tiberius tried to save himself by flight. As he was running, he was stopped by one who caught hold of him by the toga; but he threw it off, and fled in his undergarments only. And stumbling over those who before had been knocked down, as he was trying to get up again, Publius Satureius, a tribune, and one of his colleagues, gave him the first fatal stroke, by hitting him upon the head with a foot of a stool. The second blow was delivered by Lucius Rufus, as though it were a point of pride. The massacre continued as over three hundred were killed by clubs and wooden rods, none by an iron weapon.

This, we are told, was the first act of violence that ended in the spilling of blood among the Romans, since the rejection of the monarchy [in 509 B.C.E.]. All former quarrels which were neither small nor about trivial matters, were always settled peacefully by mutual concessions on either side, the Senate yielding for fear of the common people, and the commons out of respect to the Senate. . . . But it is evident that this conspiracy was led against Tiberius, more out of the hatred and malice of rich men, than for the reasons which they commonly pretended against him. They abused his dead body with unworthy insults and would not even allow his own brother, though he earnestly pleaded, to bury Tiberius in the night, but threw him, together with the other corpses, into the river.

"The Murder of Tiberius Gracchus" is from Plutarch, *Life of Tiberius Gracchus*, 16–20, in *Readings in Ancient History*, ed. William S. Davis, vol. 2 (Boston: Allyn and Bacon, 1913), pp. 108–109. Translation modernized by the editor

"Vengeance with Excessive Cruelty"

SALLUST

Now political parties and factions, with all their attendant evils, originated at Rome a few years before this as the result of peace and of an abundance of everything that mortals prize most highly. For before the destruction of Carthage, the people and senate of Rome together governed the Republic peacefully and with moderation. There was not strife among the citizens either for glory or for power; fear of the enemy preserved the good morals of the state. But when the minds of the people were relieved of that fear, they naturally became arrogant and corrupt, vices which are always fostered by prosperity. Thus the peace for which they had longed in time of adversity, after they gained it proved to be more cruel and bitter than adversity itself. For the nobles began to abuse their position and the people their liberty, and every man for himself robbed, pillaged, and plundered. Thus the community was split into two parties, and between these the state was torn to pieces. . . .

For example, when Tiberius and Gaius Gracchus, whose forefathers had added greatly to the power of the Republic in the Punic and other wars, began to assert the freedom of the common people and expose the crimes of the corrupt, the nobility, who were guilty, were therefore panic stricken. They accordingly opposed the reforms of the Gracchi. . . . And first Tiberius, then a few years later Gaius, who had followed in his brother's footsteps, were slain with the sword, although one was a tribune and the other a commissioner for founding colonies. . . . It must be admitted that the Gracchi were so eager for victory that they had not shown a sufficiently moderate spirit. . . .

The nobles then abused their victory to gratify their passions; they put many men out of the way by the sword or by banishment, and thus became dreaded rather than influential in the future. It is this spirit which has commonly ruined great nations, when one party desires to triumph over another by any and every means and to avenge itself on the vanquished with excessive cruelty.

CONSIDER THIS:

5-15. Violence seems to be a key to understanding the fall of the Roman Republic and the establishment of the Augustan principate. Use this "key" to analyze the primary sources. How and why was violence employed? When you consider all the primary sources, why did the Romans, who had a long tradition of moderation, succumb to violence? Is violence symptomatic of the decline of a civilization?

KEY EVENTS IN THE LATE ROMAN REPUBLIC

120–78 B.C.E. Ascendancy of the Generals
Marius begins conversion of Roman armies into professional and personal forces that become more loyal to individual generals than to the state. Fights Sulla for supremacy, who responds with bloody retribution and proscriptions in 78 B.C.E.

73 B.C.E. The Revolt of Spartacus
Spartacus, a Thracian gladiator, terrorizes the Italian countryside, encouraging a serious slave revolt. Crassus crushes him and crucifies rebels along the Appian Way into Rome.

"'Vengeance with Excessive Cruelty'" is from Sallust, *The War with Jugurtha*, 41–42, trans. J. C. Rolfe (Cambridge, MA: Harvard University Press, 1921), pp. 223, 225, 227. Translation modernized by the editor

67–66 B.C.E. The Rise of Pompey the Great

Pompey is the greatest general of the era as he defeats Mediterranean pirates in 67 B.C.E. and gains command against Mithradates of Pontus in 66 B.C.E.. Competition for position and influence continues among Pompey, Crassus, and Julius Caesar.

63 B.C.E. The Catilinarian Conspiracy

Cicero becomes consul and thwarts conspiracy by the disgruntled and unsuccessful senator named Catiline. Cicero gains influence through great oratory.

60 B.C.E. The First Triumvirate

Political alliance known as the First Triumvirate established between Caesar, Pompey, and Crassus in a bid to control the Roman Republic. Caesar gains command in Gaul (59 B.C.E.).

49–45 B.C.E. Civil War

Unity of First Triumvirate degenerates and civil war breaks out between senatorial supporters under Pompey and Caesar's popular faction. Pompey is murdered in Egypt; Caesar defeats Pompey's supporters and controls Roman world.

44 B.C.E.–31 B.C.E. Civil War Again

Julius Caesar assassinated by Brutus, Cassius, and other Republicans, who decry Caesar's despotism (44 B.C.E.). Competition for power between Octavian, Caesar's heir, and Mark Antony, Caesar's friend and general. Cicero murdered by Antony's men. Octavian destroys Cleopatra's fleet at Actium, and Mark Antony commits suicide (31 B.C.E.). Octavian in control of the Roman world by 27 B.C.E..

27 B.C.E.–14 C.E. The Augustan Principate

Octavian "restores" the Roman Republic and assumes the title of Princeps (First Citizen) and later that of Augustus. This is a "sham government," a republic in form, but despotism in fact.

The Fall of the Roman Republic (100–31 B.C.E.)

By the opening of the first century B.C.E., Roman armies were no longer recruited from the free land-holding farmers, but rather from those displaced veterans and unemployed men who had migrated to Rome. A successful general named Marius offered them employment in the army without the requirement of property ownership. Marius thus created a professional army of soldiers who were promised land, booty, and glory; in return, they gave loyalty to their general. Competition for commands against important foreign enemies became intense and sometimes resulted in civil war. Blood-letting by Marius and his chief rival Sulla became epidemic in its proportions as the competition for power intensified in the 80s and 70s B.C.E.

But the old guard was changing and the future from 75–50 B.C.E. belonged to talented and audacious young commanders who used their success and popularity with the troops to accumulate wealth and establish new political alliances to further their careers. Among the most important personalities of the age were Marcus Licinius Crassus, Gnaus Pompey Magnus, Marcus Tullius Cicero, and Gaius Julius Caesar.

One of Sulla's commanders, Marcus Licinius Crassus, became known in antiquity as the richest man in Rome. He argued that one could not be considered wealthy unless one could maintain an army at personal expense. Wealth became a major factor in achieving political influence in the late Republic, and Crassus was a master at bribery and extortion.

A major figure of the first century B.C.E., Pompey was considered by many to be the greatest general of his age. He earned a reputation for efficiency: When given the two-year assignment to rid the Mediterranean of pirates, a problem that had gone unsolved for decades, Pompey accomplished the feat in three months. He then left for the East and was accorded a magnificent triumph over Rome's persistent enemy Mithradates in 61 B.C.E.

Another major figure of the late Republic was Marcus Tullius Cicero. Cicero came from a family of little social distinction, and his rise to the consulship in 63 B.C.E. was the result of his oratorical skill. Cicero's greatest moment occurred when he discovered a plot to overthrow the government, led by a dissolute politician named Catiline.

All of these politicians coveted and achieved power through wealth, military glory, or oratorical ability. Rome was not big enough to contain their ambitions, and from about 75 to 50 B.C.E. they competed for glory and political control as Rome moved closer to civil war. We see a glimpse of this intense rivalry early in 73 B.C.E. when a Thracian slave named Spartacus, who had been condemned to the mines, was sold as a gladiator to die in the arena. He organized a revolt and swept through southern Italy, defeating all Roman forces sent against him until he met his match in Crassus. Our historian for this famous event is Appian of Alexandria.

THEME: REVOLUTION AND HISTORICAL TRANSITION

THE HISTORIAN AT WORK—APPIAN

The Revolt of Spartacus

Our knowledge of ancient history often depends on whether material has survived intact, in pieces, or at all throughout the centuries. Certainly the archeological evidence of buildings, pottery, and inscriptions is essential in reconstructing ancient societies, but modern historians often long for articulate, detailed, and accurate written information that offers a credible chronology and insight into events, rather than a reconstruction based on myth, rumor, and innuendo, on a simple moral vision, or on a condescending political approach.

The historians we have already encountered, like Herodotus, Thucydides, and Livy, are among the best in the ancient world. They were curious and disciplined, for the most part, and all possessed narrative ability and critical insight, though each had limitations that modern historians must scrutinize before accepting their accounts as evidence of truth.

But Appian of Alexandria is perhaps more typical of the problems modern scholars of the ancient world face in recounting the past. In reconstructing Roman history, we are confronted with major gaps in historical time periods. One big hole occurs after the Second Punic war in 202 B.C.E. to about 120 B.C.E. Livy's account of this period has been lost, and there are major gaps in the history of Polybius, a secondary historian who wrote much later. Appian is our only source for the Third Punic War and the destruction of Carthage in 146 B.C.E. and for the very important agrarian crisis that resulted in the deaths of Tiberius Gracchus in 133 B.C.E. and his brother Gaius in 121 B.C.E. So, who was Appian and to what extent can we depend on the accuracy of his history?

All that we know about Appian must be gleaned from his own writings and from the writings of his friend Fronto, the tutor of the emperor Marcus Aurelius in the second century C.E. Appian was a native of Alexandria, Egypt, and lived from about 95 to 165 C.E. He served as an advocate in the imperial law courts in Rome and later became a procurator, or

---

"The Revolt of Spartacus" is from Appian, *The Civil Wars*, trans. Horace White, vol. 3: 1.116–1.120 (New York: The Macmillan Company, 1913). Translation modernized by the editor

financial officer. Appian's history is unusual because it is not organized chronologically, but ethnographically in detached segments corresponding to Roman wars against various peoples and among themselves. So, out of twenty-four books, eleven have come down to us complete or nearly so, including accounts of the Spanish wars; Punic wars; Illyrian, Syrian, and Mithradatic wars; and five books regarding the civil wars of the late Roman Republic until 35 B.C.E.

But Appian is writing long after these events occurred, and he quotes from secondary accounts and sometimes from the rather self-serving writings of Julius Caesar and Augustus. Appian, therefore, was a narrator of events rather than a first-rate philosophic or "scientific" historian. His accuracy has often been questioned as well. Appian's style is direct rather than complex, yet he can be animated, forceful, and even eloquent in his presentation of events. His dramatic version of the destruction of Carthage is compelling, as is his account of the rebellion of Spatacus in 73 B.C.E. We have a few other versions of the famous revolt of this Thracian gladiator and his army of slaves, but Appian's is generally the most reliable. This is a thrilling story of desperate men trying to survive against all odds.

In Italy about this same time, Spartacus, a Thracian by birth, who had once served as a soldier in the Roman army but had since become a prisoner and sent to train as a gladiator in Capua, persuaded about seventy of his fellow gladiators to break for their own freedom rather than to be used simply for the entertainment of spectators. They knocked off the guards, armed themselves with clubs and daggers that they confiscated from people on the roads and took refuge on Mount Vesuvius. They were joined there by many fugitive slaves and even some freemen from the fields. Spartacus, together with two gladiators named Oenomaus and Crixus who served as subordinate officers, led the force in plundering the countryside. Since Spartacus divided all the spoils equally, men flocked to his camp. The Romans quickly pulled together a force, not of seasoned legionaries, but of random conscripts from the countryside first under the command of Varinius Glaber and then Publius Valerius, because they really did not consider this a serious war, but something like a minimal disturbance led by local raiders. This rag-tag force attacked Spartacus, who beat them decisively. Spartacus even took the horse of Varinius, so narrowly did the Roman general escape capture by a gladiator!

After this initial victory, more and more people flocked to Spartacus until his army numbered 70,000 men, and he began to arm himself in earnest by manufacturing weapons and collecting equipment for all his men. Rome now sent out both consuls with two legions and one of them defeated Crixus near Mount Garganus and killed him together with two-thirds of his force. Spartacus tried to escape through the Apennine Mountains to the Alps and Gaul, but one of the consuls anticipated him and blocked his retreat while the other consul hung on his rear. Spartacus turned and destroyed each of these armies, one after the other. The Romans retreated in confusion, the force scattered in different directions. Spartacus then took 300 Roman prisoners and sacrificed them to the memory of Crixus. He then burned all useless equipment, killed the rest of his prisoners, and butchered his pack-animals in order to move more quickly. Spartacus had decided to march on Rome, and would not be hindered even by many Roman deserters who wanted to join him. The Roman consuls made a second stand in Picenum and once again, Spartacus defeated them in another great battle.

It was at this point that Spartacus changed his mind and decided against marching on Rome because he was not yet ready for that kind of a fight. His entire force could not match the Romans in arms and equipment, and no city had as yet joined him; besides, his force was composed only of slaves, deserters, and human riff-raff. So he seized the mountains around Thurii and took the city itself. . . . He then purchased iron and brass from local merchants and his men outfitted themselves with plenty of weapons that they used to raid the countryside for supplies. When they met the Romans again, they defeated them and returned to camp laden with spoils.

This war had now lasted three years and the Romans, who had ridiculed it at the beginning as merely the work of gladiators and slaves, now took it as a formidable challenge to their authority. When it came time to elect the new generals, none came forth as candidates because all were afraid that they would have to face Spartacus. But one man, Licinius Crassus, who was a wealthy member of the aristocracy, assumed the command and marched forth against Spartacus with six legions and then added the two defeated consular legions when he reached the front. Crassus decided to punish these legions for their failure by forcing them to draw lots and killing every tenth man, thus destroying about 4,000 of them as examples. Once he demonstrated to the troops that he meant business and was more dangerous to them than the enemy, he came upon a detachment of Spartacus' men who were in a separate camp and killed over two-thirds of them, about 10,000 in all. He then drew up his forces and met Spartacus himself and beat him in a brilliant engagement. Crassus followed up his victory by pursuing Spartacus' broken army as they made their way to the sea where they were trying to sail across to Sicily. He caught up with them and encircled the entire army of slaves with a network of ditches and walls. Trapped, Spartacus tried to break through and make his way to the hills of the Samnite country, but Crassus killed about 6,000 of his men in the morning and about the same number by evening at the cost of only three Roman dead and seven wounded. The punishment doled out by Crassus to the Roman army had inspired their will to win, and Spartacus, who had expected reinforcements, now decided to change tactics. He no longer met the Roman forces head on, but harassed them by random attacks at different times, and by setting fire to bundles of wood and then throwing them into the ditches that surrounded them. Spartacus made the work of containing him difficult for the Romans. He also crucified a Roman soldier in the space between the two armies in order to show his men what fate awaited them if they did not win in battle.

When the senate in Rome heard about the siege, they decided to take no chances of a defeat in a protracted war against the gladiators, so they appointed the rising general Pompey, who had just returned from Spain, to an additional command on the field. The Roman senators believed that the threat from Spartacus was immediate and substantial. Crassus reacted to this interference by pressing the confrontation with Spartacus even more emphatically since he certainly did not want Pompey to steal his thunder by defeating Spartacus on his own. Spartacus exploited this situation by offering to negotiate with Crassus, but the latter would have none of it. So Spartacus decided to risk a battle and broke through the lines of the sieging force, pushing his way clear toward Brundisium on the Adriatic coast with Crassus in hot pursuit. When Spartacus learned that the Roman general Lucullus had just arrived at Brundisium with his army after his victory over Mithradates in the East, he nearly despaired of everything, and decided to draw his army up and fight Crassus to the death. The battle was long and bloody, as might have been expected with so many tens of thousands of desperate men contending for life.

> The battle was long and bloody, as might have been expected with so many tens of thousands of desperate men contending for life.
>
> —APPIAN

Spartacus was wounded in the thigh with a spear and sank down on his knee, holding his shield in front of him and resisting the great mass of men that was flooding toward him. Soon he was surrounded and killed. The remainder of his army was thrown into confusion and butchered in huge numbers. So great was the slaughter that it was impossible to count the slain as they fell. The Roman loss was about 1,000. The body of Spartacus was never found. A large number of his men fled from the battle into the mountains and Crassus followed on their heels. They formed themselves into four groups and kept fighting until there were only 6,000 survivors. These were taken prisoner by the Romans and crucified all along the Appian Way from Capua to Rome.

CONSIDER THIS:

5-16. What does the revolt of Spartacus tell you about Roman military might around 73 B.C.E.? Why was it so difficult to defeat Spartacus? Why were Roman commanders afraid to take him on? Did the risk of loss against slaves outweigh the benefits of victory? Why was the quality of the opponent so important to the Romans? Why was it better to defeat Hannibal or Mithradates than to destroy Spartacus?

5-17. Why did the Romans crucify thousands of Spartacus's defeated slaves along the Appian Way? Does this demonstration of Roman power indicate

strength or a weakened, rather paranoid Rome struggling to cope with the great influx of slaves after the Punic wars?

5-18. What do you think of Appian as an historian? Compare him to Livy or Thucydides. What does Appian do well?

THE BROADER PERSPECTIVE:

5-19. The tale of Spartacus, a Thracian slave condemned to the brutal life of a gladiator who challenged the overwhelming might of Rome, is a story simply perfect for Hollywood. This historical event also served as a propaganda opportunity for the creation of a revolutionary ballet in the Soviet Union during the 1950s. Spartacus was depicted as the embodiment of the furious defiance of proletarian will against the evils of capitalist repression. Do you see any of this drama and moral relevance in Appian's account? Does Appian seem anti-Roman? Does he seem to admire Spartacus, or is Crassus the hero of this episode?

The Civil War (49–45 B.C.E.)

The most famous Roman of them all, Julius Caesar, had a difficult time achieving the kind of military glory or wealth needed to compete with Pompey and Crassus. When he finally got a major command in Gaul (58 B.C.E.), he conquered and consolidated the area, gaining wealth and the loyalty of his troops. After first cooperating with Pompey and Crassus, Caesar realized he would have to fight a senatorial aristocracy that distrusted him and championed Pompey. The first selection by the biographer Suetonius recounts Caesar's famous decision to cross the Rubicon River, thus beginning the civil war. Cicero, a supporter of Pompey and the senate, also gives his perspective in letters written in the midst of this crisis.

"The Die Is Cast": Caesar Crosses the Rubicon

SUETONIUS

When the news came to Ravenna, where Caesar was staying that [his compromise plan] had been utterly rejected, . . . he immediately sent forward some troops, yet secretly, to prevent any suspicion of his plan. . . . Coming up with his troops on the banks of the Rubicon, which was the frontier of his province, he halted for a while, and turning over in his mind the importance of his next step, he turned to those about

---

"'The Die Is Cast': Caesar Crosses the Rubicon" is from Suetonius, *Life of Caesar*, 31–33, in *Readings in Ancient History*, ed. William S. Davis, vol. 2 (Boston: Allyn and Bacon, 1913), pp. 149–150. Translation modernized by the editor.

him, saying: "We can still retreat! But once we pass this little bridge—nothing is left but to fight it out with arms!" Caesar cried out, "Let us go when the omens of the gods and the crimes of our enemies summon us! THE DIE IS NOW CAST!" Accordingly he marched his army over the river.

"We Must Trust to the Mercy of the Storm"

CICERO

Menturnea, January 22, 49 B.C.E.

It is civil war, though it has not sprung from division among our citizens but from the daring of one abandoned citizen. He is strong in military forces, he attracts adherents by hopes and promises, he covets the whole universe. Rome is delivered to him stripped of defenders, stocked with supplies: one may fear anything from one who regards her temples and her homes not as his native land but as his loot. What he will do, and how he will do it, in the absence of senate and magistrates, I do not know. He will be unable even to pretend constitutional methods. But where can our party raise its head, or when? ... We depend entirely upon two legions that were kept here by a trick and are practically disloyal. For so far the draft has found unwilling recruits, disinclined to fight. But the time of compromise is past. The future is obscure. We, or our leaders, have brought things to such a pass that, having put to sea without a rudder, we must trust to the mercy of the storm.

Formiae, February 8 or 9, 49 B.C.E.

I see there is not a foot of ground in Italy which is not in Caesar's power. I have no news of Pompey, and I imagine he will be captured unless he has taken to the sea. . . . . What can I do? In what land or on what sea can I follow a man when I don't know where he is? Shall I then surrender to Caesar? Suppose I could surrender with safety, as many advise, could I do so with honor? By no means. . . . The problem is insoluble.

Formiae, March 1, 49 B.C.E.

I depend entirely on news from Brundisium. If Caesar has caught up with our friend Pompey, there is some slight hope of peace: but if Pompey has crossed the sea, we must look for war and massacre. Do you see the kind of man into whose hands the state has fallen? What foresight, what energy, what readiness! Upon my word, if he refrains from murder and rapine he will be the darling of those who dreaded him most. The people of the country towns and the farmers talk to me a great deal. They care for nothing at all but their lands, their little homesteads, and their tiny fortunes. And see how public opinion has changed: they fear the man they once trusted [Pompey] and adore the man they once dreaded [Caesar]. It pains me to think of the mistakes and wrongs of ours that are responsible for this reaction.

Julius Caesar: The Colossus That Bestrode the World?

Julius Caesar looms large in the annals of Western civilization. A master politician, he was also an efficient and inspiring military leader, known especially for his tactical ability and for resourcefulness under pressure. Caesar managed to defeat Pompey in a major battle at Pharsalus in 48 B.C.E. Pompey fled to Egypt, where he was murdered on orders of the young pharaoh who hoped thereby to ingratiate himself with Caesar. When Caesar arrived in Egypt, he mourned Pompey as a noble warrior and former son-in-law. Caesar was able, in the next years, to defeat the rest of Pompey's supporters, and he arrived in Rome amidst joyous acclamations from the people. But a faction of about sixty senators saw in Caesar's reforms and imperial manner the makings of a king. They planned his murder and assassinated him on March 15, 44 B.C.E.

"'We Must Trust to the Mercy of the Storm'" is from Cicero, *Letter to Atticus*, 7.13, 7.22, 8.13, trans. E. O. Winstead (Cambridge, MA: Harvard University Press, 1913), pp. 61, 63, 89, 161, 163

Caesar was a complex individual, a man of vaunting ambition, an intellectual, a supporter of popular causes, a military commander who garnered the respect and loyalty of soldiers whose very lives depended on his cool assessment of risk and reward. In death, he was even more controversial. Historians throughout the centuries have had difficulty evaluating his intent. Did Caesar intend to stabilize society by eliminating the Republic and imposing a popular and benign dictatorship that would renew the greatness of Rome? Did he want to become king? Did the conspirators save Roman liberty or condemn it? The following selections from the biographers Suetonius and Plutarch provide us with accounts of Caesar's contradictory nature.

Caesar's Reforms

SUETONIUS

Turning his attention to the reorganization of the state, [Caesar] reformed the calendar, which the pontiffs had ago messed up by neglecting to order the necessary intercalations, so that the harvest festivals did not come in summer nor those of the vintage in the autumn. He adjusted the year to the sun's course by making it consist of 365 days, abolishing the intercalary month and adding one day every fourth year. . . .

He filled the vacancies in the senate, enrolled additional patricians, and increased the number of praetors, aediles, and quaestors as well as of minor officials. . . . He shared the elections with the people on this basis: that except in the case of the consulship, half of the magistrates should be appointed by the people's choice while the rest should be those whom he personally had nominated. . . . He then reduced the number of those who received grain at public expense from 320,000 to 150,000. He conferred citizenship on all who practiced medicine at Rome, and on all teachers of the liberal arts, to make them more desirous of living in the city and to induce others to resort to it.

As to debts, he disappointed those who looked for their cancellation, which was often agitated, but finally decreed that the debtors should satisfy their creditors according to a valuation of their possessions at the price which they paid for them before the Civil War—an arrangement which wiped out about a fourth part of their indebtedness. He dissolved all associations, except those on ancient foundation. He increased the penalties for crimes. . . .

He administered justice with the utmost conscientiousness and strictness. Those convicted of extortion he even expelled from the senatorial order. . . . In particular, he enforced the law against extravagance. . . .

For the beautification and convenience of the city, as well as for guarding and extending the bounds of the empire, he formed more projects and more extensive ones every day: first of all, to raise a temple to Mars, greater than any in existence, filling up and leveling the pool in which he had exhibited the sea fight, and to build a theater of vast size over by the Tarpeian Rock; to reduce the civil law to fixed limits, and of the vast mass of statutes to include only the best and most essential in a limited number of volumes; to open to the public the greatest possible libraries of Greek and Latin books, assigning to Marcus Varro the charge of procuring and classifying them; to drain the Pomptine Marshes; to let out the water from Lake Fucinus; to make a highway from the Adriatic across the summit of the Apennines to the Tiber; to cut a canal through the Isthmus of Corinth; to check the Dacians, who had poured into Pontus and Thrace; then to make war on the Parthians by way of Lesser Armenia, but not to risk a battle with them until he had first tested their mettle. All these enterprises and plans were cut short by his death.

"Caesar's Reforms" is from Suetonius, *Life of Caesar*, trans. J. C. Rolfe, vol. 1, 37–38, 40–44 (Cambridge, MA: Harvard University Press, 1913), pp. 55, 57, 59, 61, 63

Abuse of Power

SUETONIUS

After weighing Caesar's actions and words, many thought that he abused his power and was justly killed. For not only did he accept excessive honors, such as an uninterrupted consulship, the dictatorship for life, and the censorship of public morals, as well as the forename Imperator, the surname of Father of his Country, a statue among those of the kings, and a raised couch in the orchestra; but he also allowed honors to be bestowed on him which were too great for mortal man: a golden throne in the Senate house and on the judgment seat; a chariot and litter in the procession at the circus; temples, altars, and statues beside those of the gods; a special priest, and the calling of one of the months by his name. In fact, there were no honors which he did not receive or confer at pleasure. . . .

No less arrogant were his public utterances . . . that the Republic was nothing, a mere name without body or form; that Sulla did not know his ABC's when he laid down his dictatorship; that men ought now to be more careful in addressing him, and to regard his word as law. . . .

But it was the following action that roused deadly hatred against him. When the Senate approached him in a body with many highly honorary decrees, he received them before the temple of Venus Genetrix without rising. Some think that when he attempted to get up, he was held back by Cornelius Balbus; others, that he made no such move at all, but on the contrary frowned angrily on Gaius Trebatius when he suggested that he should rise. And this action of his seemed the more intolerable, because when he himself in one of his triumphal processions rode past the benches of the tribunes, he was so incensed because a member of the college, Pontius Aquila by name, did not rise, that he cried: "Come then, Aquila, take back the Republic from me, you mighty tribune"; and for several days he would not make a promise to anyone without adding, "That is, if Pontius Aquila will allow me."

The Assassination of Julius Caesar (44 B.C.E.)

PLUTARCH

Antony, Caesar's faithful friend and a man of great physical strength, was detained outside the building by Brutus Albinus, who deliberately engaged him in a long conversation. When Caesar entered, the senate rose in his honor. Some of Brutus's accomplices stood behind his chair while others went to meet him, pretending to support the petition of Tullius Cimber for the recall of his brother from exile. They kept up their entreaties until he came to his chair. When he was seated he rejected their request, but they continued more and more urgently until he began to grow angry. Cimber then grasped his toga with both hands and pulled it off his neck, which was the signal for the attack. Casca struck the first blow, stabbing Caesar in the neck with his dagger. But the wound was not mortal or even dangerous, probably because at the beginning of so bold an action he was very nervous. Caesar therefore was able to turn around and grasp the dagger and hold on to it. At the same time they both cried out, Caesar in Latin, "Casca, you villain! What does this mean!" and Casca in Greek to his brother, "Brother, help!"

After such a beginning, those who were unaware of the conspiracy were so astonished and horrified that they could neither run away or assist Caesar, nor could they even utter a word. But all the conspirators now drew their daggers and hemmed Caesar in on every side. Whichever way he turned he met with blows and saw nothing but cold steel gleaming in his face. Like

"Abuse of Power" is from Suetonius, *Life of Caesar*, trans. J. C. Rolfe, vol. 1, 76–78 (Cambridge, MA: Harvard University Press, 1913), pp. 99, 101, 103.

"The Assassination of Julius Caesar" is from Plutarch, *Life of Caesar*, 66, trans. John and William Langhorne (New York: Harper and Brothers, 1872).

FIGURE 5.2 A contemporary view of the ruins of the Roman Forum from the Temple of Saturn: "As yourselves, your empires fall. And every kingdom hath a grave."—William Hobbington. (*Perry M. Rogers*)

some wild beast attacked by hunters, he found every hand lifted against him, for they had agreed that all must share in this sacrifice and flesh themselves with his blood. For this reason, Brutus also stabbed him in the gut. Some say that Caesar resisted all the others, shifting his body to escape the blows and calling for help, but when he saw Brutus's drawn dagger he covered his head with his toga and sank to the ground. Either by chance or because he was pushed by his murderers, he fell against the pedestal of Pompey's statue and drenched it with his blood. So Pompey himself seemed to preside over this act of vengeance, treading his enemy under his feet and enjoying his agonies. Those agonies were great, for they say he received twenty-three wounds. And many of the conspirators wounded each other as they aimed their blows at him.

TAKING SIDES: JULIUS CAESAR—THE COLOSSUS THAT BESTRODE THE WORLD?

5-20. How would you characterize the reforms of Julius Caesar? Which, in your opinion, were the most important and necessary? Did Caesar seem committed

to stabilizing and improving conditions within the state? Or did these reforms benefit him personally?

5-21. Now compare Suetonius's account of Caesar's abuse of power. How did Caesar violate traditions and demonstrate arrogance? Why was he assassinated? Were his actions in fact tyrannical, or was Caesar in the process of transforming the state from a chaotic republic to an efficient dictatorship? Did Caesar offer the Romans a new opportunity to achieve political stability through his absolute leadership, a model for government based on early traditions of kingship?

5-22. This question goes right to intent: Caesar in his political rise catered to the interests of the common people and had beaten his rivals, like Pompey and Crassus, through tenacity and strategic brilliance. But once he had all the components in place and the Roman world was his, do you think his intent was to stabilize Rome and build for the future? Or to insulate himself from the masses and achieve a personal rule as had Sulla before him? What do the sources indicate about his intent?

5-23. Aldous Huxley noted that "idealism is the noble toga that political gentlemen drape over their will to power." According to the sources, did Caesar promote any ideals that could justify his accession to power? Or had he simply been forced to fight during the civil war in order to survive? Perhaps the problem is that Caesar did not have enough time to fashion and develop his own personal rule. We can't tell whether he would have been a benign monarch or a brutal tyrant. But did Rome need such heavy guidance at this particular point in its history? Can absolute rule ever be justified? Do you think that Caesar's murder protected Roman freedom or condemned Romans to more civil war and death?

5-24. After Caesar's assassination, his murderers made no plans, thinking that the Republic, once freed of the dictator, would be restored automatically. Why is this considered a naïve idea? Should the conspirators also have killed Mark Antony? Why or why not?

The Power Vacuum (44–31 B.C.E.)

Whether Caesar intended to establish a monarchy will remain a subject of controversy among historians. But his death unleashed the forces of violence and chaos as the state once again endured civil wars, first against Caesar's assassins, then between Caesar's trusted commander Mark Antony and his nephew and heir Gaius Octavian. Cicero, ever the republican, harshly criticized Antony in several orations and paid for it with his life.

"A Public Prostitute": The Philippic against Mark Antony

CICERO

Shall we then examine your conduct from the time when you were a boy? I think so. Let's begin at the beginning. Do you remember when you were just an adolescent that you went bankrupt? Your father's fault you will say. Okay, I admit that. But then you became a man and graduated to men's clothing—actually, you wore women's clothing, didn't you? Indeed, at first you were just a public prostitute with a set price, and not a cheap one at that! But very soon your friend, Curio, stepped in and took you off the streets, made you more respectable, made you a real wife, made a steady, married woman of you. No little boy bought only for sexual gratification was ever so completely under the power of his master as you were under Curio's. How many times did his father throw you out of his house? How often did he post guards to prevent you from entering? While you, hungering for your boy, eager to collect your promised fee, climbed in through the roof under cover of night—that house simply couldn't hold your raging lust. . . .

But let's say no more of your debauchery and sex-crimes. They are things I just can't mention in decent company. Instead, let's delve, Senators, into the rest of Antony's life. I really want to focus on the things Antony did during the time of the Civil War, amid the greatest miseries of the Republic—and what he does every day. . . .

Just as seeds are the origins of trees and plants, so it is certain that he is the seed of this horrific war. Senators, do you grieve at the loss of three Roman armies? It is Antony who annihilated them. Do you mourn the spirits and regret the loss of so many of our illustrious citizens? It is Antony who killed them. The authority of your own senatorial order has been destroyed. Antony destroyed it. Every evil that has visited us since that time—and what evils haven't we seen?—can be laid at the feet of Antony. He is responsible. There can be no other conclusion. He has been our Helen of Troy—the cause of war in this Republic, the cause of pestilence, the cause of ruin. . . .

So, you wicked criminal, you alone advised Julius Caesar to become king; you wanted to transform him from your fellow-consul to your lord and master. You

---

"The Philippic Against Mark Antony" is from Cicero, *The Second Philippic Against Mark Antony*, trans. C. D. Yonge, in *The Orations of Marcus Tullius Cicero*, 18, 19, 22, 46 (London: George Bell & Sons, 1894), pp. 37–39, 42, 54, 67–68. Translation modernized by the editor

inflicted this test on the Roman people—the ultimate test of their capacity to suffer and endure.

Antony, think at long last of your country. Think of the people from whom you originate, not those with whom you now associate. Reconcile yourself to the Republic. . . . When I was a young man, I defended it and will not abandon it now that I am old. I stood up to the swords of Catiline and I shall not tremble before yours. No—I would gladly sacrifice myself, if my death could restore the freedom of Rome... . In fact, after all the honors I have gained, Senators, after all of my accomplishments, I now wish for death. I only pray for two things: first, that in my death, I leave the Roman

people free—the immortal gods could grant me no greater gift. My other prayer is that each man's fate be tied directly to his conduct in the service of Rome!

CONSIDER THIS:

5-25. Note how Cicero peppers this speech with insinuations about Antony's sexuality and personal life, calling him a "public prostitute," a spendthrift, and a betrayer of Republican ideals. Analyze this speech carefully and note the specific passages where Cicero digs at Antony. Can you understand, if not justify, Antony's wrath?

The Murder of Cicero: "Antony's Greatest and Bitterest Enemy"

APPIAN

Cicero, who had held supreme power after Caesar's death as much as a public speaker could, was proscribed together with his son, his brother, his brother's son and all his household, faction, and friends. He fled in a small boat, but as he could not endure the seasickness he landed and went to a country place of his own . . . near Caieta, a town of Italy, and here he remained quiet. . . . Many soldiers were hurrying around in squads, inquiring if Cicero had been seen anywhere. Some people, moved by good will and pity, said that he had already put to sea. But a shoemaker . . . who had been a most bitter enemy of Cicero, pointed out the path to Laena, the centurion, who was pursuing with a small force.

Thereupon the slaves, thinking that more soldiers were coming, were terror-stricken and Laena, although he had once been saved by Cicero when under trial, drew [Cicero's] head out of the litter and cut it off, striking it three times, or rather sawing it off because of his inexperience. He also cut off the hand with which Cicero had written the speeches against Antony as tyrant, which he had entitled Philippics in imitation of Demosthenes. Then some of the soldiers hastened on horseback and others by ship to bring the good news quickly to Antony. The latter was sitting in front of the tribunal in the Forum when Laena, a long distance off,

showed him the head and hand by lifting them up and shaking them. Antony was delighted beyond measure. He crowned the centurion and gave him 25,000 Attic drachmas in addition to the stipulated reward, for killing the man who had been his greatest and bitterest enemy. The head and hand of Cicero were suspended for a long time from the Rostra in the Forum where formerly he had been accustomed to make public speeches, and more people came together to behold this spectacle than had previously come to listen to him. It is said that even at his meals Antony placed Cicero's head before his table, until he became satiated with the horrible sight. Thus was Cicero, a man famous for his eloquence and one who had rendered the greatest service to his country when he held the office of consul, violently murdered and insulted after his death.

CONSIDER THIS:

5-26. Cicero seems like such an unusual individual during this period. How did he differ from his rivals, such as Pompey, Crassus, and Mark Antony? How did Cicero achieve power, and why was he killed? What do his career and death tell you about the nature of power in the late Republic?

"The Murder of Cicero" is from Appian, *The Civil Wars*, trans. Horace White, vol. 4, 4.4.19–20 (Cambridge, MA: Harvard University Press, 1913), pp. 171, 173, 175

AGAINST THE GRAIN

Cleopatra: Queen of the Nile

PLUTARCH

"The Attraction Was Something Bewitching"

One of the most fascinating personalities of this period was Cleopatra, Queen of Egypt. She had bewitched Caesar when he arrived in Egypt on the trail of Pompey, and he brought her back to Rome. Mark Antony saw her there and, after Caesar's assassination, became romantically involved with her. As the first excerpt indicates, her beauty and ability were renowned; Antony fell under her spell. She fought with him at Actium in 31 B.C.E. against the forces of Octavian, and after their defeat, both committed suicide in Egypt. Years later, the poet Horace, writing in support of Octavian, gave an assessment of her, as recounted in the second excerpt.

KEEP IN MIND . . .

5-27. In the following selections, what specific words do Plutarch and Horace use to describe Cleopatra?

On her arrival, Antony sent to invite her to supper. She thought it fitter he should come to her; so, willing to show his good humor and courtesy, he complied, and went. He found the preparations to receive him magnificent beyond expression. . . .

For her actual beauty, it is said, was not in itself so remarkable that none could be compared with her, or that no one could see her without being struck by it, but the contact of her presence, if you lived with her, was irresistible; the attraction of her person, joining with the charm of her conversation, and the character that attended all she said or did, was something bewitching. It was a pleasure merely to hear the sound of her voice, with which, like an instrument of many strings, she could pass from one language to another; so that there were few of the barbarian nations that she answered by an interpreter; to most of them she spoke herself.

"She Was No Weak-Kneed Woman"

HORACE

Now for a drinking spree, now for a loose-footed
light fantastic, now is the time to pay
our debt to the gods, my friends,
and spread a spectacular banquet.

Before today, to bring the Caecuban from
family storerooms was wrong, while the crazy
queen was still scheming with her
sickly eunuchs, her pack of perverts,

"'The Attraction Was Something Bewitching'" is from Plutarch, *Life of Antony*, 15–19, in *Readings in Ancient History*, ed. William S. Davis, vol. 2 (Boston: Allyn and Bacon, 1913), pp. 163–164

"'She Was No Weak-Kneed Woman'" is from Horace, *Odes*, 1.37, in *The Odes and Epodes of Horace*, trans. Joseph P. Clancy (Chicago: University of Chicago Press, 1960), pp. 70–71. Copyright © 1960 by the University of Chicago. Reprinted by permission of the publisher

to send the Capitol crashing and bury
the empire: wild were her dreams of doing
whatever she wished, the best
luck was her liquor. She sobered up
when her ships caught fire, scarcely one unscathed,
and delusions of mind nursed on Egypt's wine
were cured by Caesar [Octavian] with the facts
of fear, his navy close as she fled
from Italy, like a hawk going after
a gentle dove, or a swift hunter tracking
a hare over snow-covered fields
in Thessaly: chains awaited this
damnable monster. But a heroine's death
was her goal: she showed no female shivers
at the sight of a sword, and her
fast-sailing fleet sought no secret harbors.
Her courage was great: she looked on her fallen
palace, a smile still on her face, and boldly
played with venomous serpents,
her flesh drinking their bitter poison,
so highly she dared, her mind set on her death.
Not for her the enemy ship, the crownless
voyage, her role in the grand
parade: she was no weak-kneed woman.

CONSIDER THIS:

5-28. Plutarch described Cleopatra as "irresistible" and "bewitching." What was the attraction? Why was she so impressive? Do you detect any Roman biases against women in these accounts? Why was Cleopatra so different?

5-29. Horace, writing for Cleopatra's victorious rival, Octavian, described her as a "damnable monster," both dangerous and scheming, but also "crazy" and courageous. In what ways did Cleopatra embody Roman virtues? How important was it for Horace to present Cleopatra as a "suitable" enemy of Rome—a foe worthy of respect and yet fated to be vanquished by the righteous power of Octavian?

THE BROADER PERSPECTIVE:

5-30. Note how poets and writers employed by the victors often create the historical image of a particular enemy. It is essential to fight against a formidable foe who can be characterized as evil. Was it easier for the United States, for example, to fight Hitler in World War II, or Saddam Hussein in the Iraq war, than it was to fight the abstract evil of Communism in Vietnam or terrorism throughout the world?

The Establishment of the Augustan Principate

By 27 B.C.E., Antony was dead and Octavian, by virtue of his military support, controlled the entire Roman Empire. At this point, he went to the senate and proclaimed that he had restored the Republic. On request of the senators, he decided to assume the advisory position of princeps, or "first citizen," and the honorary title of "Augustus." The Republic was to function as it had in the past, with voting in the assemblies, election of magistrates, and traditional freedoms. But as long as Augustus controlled the army, his "advice" could not be safely ignored. His system of government, called the principate, lasted in the same basic form until 180 C.E. The following accounts describe the powers of the princeps (or emperor, as he was also called). Note especially the cynicism of the historian Tacitus, who saw through the facade of republicanism and decried the loss of liberty.

The Powers and Authority of the Emperor

DIO CASSIUS

In this way the power of both people and senate passed entirely into the hands of Augustus, and from this time there was, strictly speaking, a monarchy; for monarchy would be the truest name for it. Now, the Romans so

"The Powers and Authority of the Emperor" is reprinted by permission of the publishers and the Loeb Classical Library from Dio Cassius, *Roman History*, trans. Earnest Cary, Vol. 6, 53.17.1–53.18, 53.3.21 (Cambridge, MA: Harvard University Press, 1917), pp. 235, 237, 241, 243, 249, 251

detested the title "monarch" that they called their emperors neither dictators nor kings nor anything of this sort. But the final authority for government ultimately rests with them. In order to preserve the appearance of having this authority (not through their power but by virtue of the laws), the emperors have taken for themselves all the offices (including the titles) which under the Republic possessed great power with the consent of the people. . . . Thus, they very often become consuls instead of the "king" or "dictator." These latter titles they have never assumed since they fell out of use in the constitution but the actuality of those offices is secured to them. . . . By virtue of the titles named, they secure the right to raise troops, collect funds, declare war, make peace, and rule foreigners and citizens alike everywhere and always. . . .

Thus by virtue of these Republican titles they have clothed themselves with all the powers of the government, so that they actually possess all the prerogatives of kings without the usual title. For the appellation "Caesar" or "Augustus" confers upon them no actual power but merely shows in the one case that they are the successors of their family line, and in the other the splendor of their rank. The name "Father" perhaps gives them a certain authority over us all—the authority which fathers once had over their children; yet it did not signify this at first, but betokened honor and served as an admonition both to them to love their subjects as they would their children, and to their subjects to revere them as they would their fathers. . . .

Augustus did not enact all laws on his sole responsibility, but some of them he brought before the popular assembly in advance, in order that, if any features caused displeasure, he might learn it in time and correct them; for he encouraged everybody whatsoever to give him advice, in case anyone could think of any improvement in them, and he accorded them great freedom of speech; and he actually changed some provisions. Most important of all, he took the consuls as his advisors, one of each of the other kinds of officials, and fifteen men chosen by lot from the remainder of the senatorial body, so that it was his custom to communicate proposed legislation after a fashion through these to all the other senators. For although he brought some matters before the whole senate, he generally followed this course, considering it better to take under preliminary advisement in a leisurely fashion most matters, and especially the most important ones, in consultation with a few; and sometimes he even sat with these men in trials. The senate as a body, it is true, continued to sit in judgment as before, and in certain cases transacted business with embassies and envoys from both peoples and kings; and the people and the plebs, moreover, continued to come together for the election; but nothing was actually done that did not please the emperor. At any rate, in the case of those who were to hold office, he himself selected and nominated some; and though he left the election of others in the hands of the people and the plebs, in accordance with the ancient practice, yet he took care that no persons should hold office who were unfit or elected as the result of factious combinations or bribery.

CONSIDER THIS:

5-31. What were the specific rights of an emperor? Do they sound reasonable and necessary for efficient rule? Or were they arbitrary and prone to abuse? Was the emperor truly a "first citizen," or was he an autocratic monarch?

The Transition from Republic to Principate

TACITUS

Augustus won over the soldiers with gifts, the populace with cheap grain, and all men with the sweetness of peace, and so grew greater by degrees, while he concentrated in himself the functions of the Senate, the magistrates, and the laws. He was wholly unopposed, for the boldest spirits had fallen in battle, or in the proscription, while the remaining nobles, the readier they were to be slaves, were raised the higher by wealth and

---

"The Transition from Republic to Principate" is from Tacitus, *Annals*, 1.2–4, trans. Alfred Church and William Brodribb (New York: Macmillan and Co., 1891).

promotion, so that, aggrandized by revolution, they preferred the safety of the present to the dangerous past. Nor did the provinces dislike that condition of affairs, for they distrusted the government of the Senate and the people, because of the rivalries between the leading men and the rapacity of the officials. . . . At home all was tranquil, and there were magistrates with the same titles; there was a younger generation, sprung up since the victory of Actium, and even many of the older men had been born during the civil wars. How few were left who had seen the Republic.

Thus the State had been revolutionized, and there was not a vestige left of the old sound morality. Stripped of equality, all looked up to the commands of a sovereign without the least apprehension for the present, while Augustus in the vigor of life, could maintain his own position, that of his house, and the general tranquility.

CONSIDER THIS:

5-32. What options for ruling the state did Octavian have after he defeated Antony? What was his political solution to the collapse of the Roman Republic? What are Tacitus's specific criticisms of the Augustan system?

THE BROADER PERSPECTIVE:

5-33. The Augustan system of government has often been regarded as a "sham," a deception that made the people feel they had control of their government when in fact they did not. Is freedom most importantly a thing of the mind? If the institutions of government are controlled yet *appear* to be free, and if you *feel* that you are free, are you free? How important is it to be truly free? Can you comment on this question using contemporary examples from the world around you?

FIGURE 5.3 This depiction of Augustus and his family is from the Altar of Peace, constructed in 9 B.C.E. to commemorate his new secure world order. The presentation of family as a stabilizing element was a primary topic of Augustan propaganda. His own family caused him no end of concern and difficulty. (*Perry M. Rogers*)

Res Gestae: The Accomplishments of Augustus

AUGUSTUS

The following document was written by Augustus himself in 14 C.E., the year of his death. Although it is largely factual and therefore important as a historical source, it is nevertheless a subjective political document that summarizes his career as he wanted it remembered.

Below is a copy of the accomplishments of the deified Augustus by which he subjugated the entire world under the control of the Roman people, and of the great sums of money spent by him on the state and the Roman people, as engraved on two bronze pillars set up in Rome.

1. At the age of nineteen, on my own initiative and at my own expense, I raised an army by means of which I liberated the Republic, which was oppressed by the tyranny of a faction. Because of this the Senate admitted me to its order with honorific titles in the consulship of Gaius Pansa and Aulus Hirtius. At the same time, the granted me consular rank in voting, and *imperium* [the right of military command]. It ordered me as propraetor, along with the consuls, to see to it that the state suffered no harm. . . .

2. I drove the men who killed my father, Julius Caesar, into exile, thereby avenging their crime by due process of law. Then, when they again tried to destroy the Republic, I defeated them twice in battle.

3. I waged many wars throughout our empire by land and by sea, both civil and foreign, and when victorious I showed mercy to all Roman citizens who sought pardon. Foreign peoples who could safely be pardoned I preferred to spare rather than to execute. About 500,000 Roman citizens were under military oath to me. Of these, when their terms of service were ended, I settled in colonies or sent back to their own towns a little more than 300,000, and to all these I allotted lands or granted money as rewards for military service. . . .

5. I refused to accept the dictatorship that was offered to me in the consulship of Marcus Marcellus and Lucius Arruntius by the people and by the senate. When there was a dangerous shortage of grain, I accepted responsibility for the empire's safety and administered the grain supply, so that within a few days I freed all of our people from the imminent panic and danger by my expenditures and efforts. The consulship, too, which was also offered to me at that time as an annual office for life, I refused to accept. . . . I refused to accept any office offered me which was contrary to the traditions of our ancestors.

13. The temple of Janus Quirinus, which our ancestors wanted closed whenever peace with victory was secured by sea and by land throughout the entire empire of the Roman people, and which before I was born [was] closed only twice since the founding of the city, was during my principate three times ordered by the senate to be closed.

22. Three times in my own name, and five times in the names of my sons or grandsons, I gave gladiatorial shows in which about 10,000 fought . . . . Twenty-six times in my own name or in the names of my sons or grandsons, I provided for the pleasure of the people hunting spectacles of African wild beasts in the circus or in the Forum or in the amphitheaters; in these exhibitions about 3,500 animals were killed.

26. I expanded the boundaries of all the provinces [and] . . . added Egypt to the empire of the Roman people.

34. In my sixth and seventh consulships, after I had put an end to the civil wars, having attained supreme power by universal consent, I transferred the state from my own power to the control of the Roman Senate and people. For this service of mine I received the title of Augustus by decree of the Senate. . . . After that time I excelled all in authority, but I possessed no more power than the others who were my colleagues in each magistracy.

"*Res Gestae:* The Accomplishments of Augustus" is from *Res Gestae Divi Augusti*, in *Readings in Ancient History*, ed. William S. Davis, vol. 2 (Boston: Allyn and Bacon, 1913), pp. 180–182. Translation modernized by the editor

35. When I held my thirteenth consulship, the Senate, the equestrian order, and the entire Roman people gave me the title of "father of the country" and decreed that this title should be inscribed in the vestibule of my house, in the Julian senate house, and in the Augustan Forum on the pedestal of the chariot which was set up in my honor by decree of the senate. At the time I wrote this document I was in my seventy-sixth year.

CONSIDER THIS:

5-34. Analyze "The Accomplishments of Augustus." Note the specific vocabulary in section 1. Which words have the greatest impact and why? What is Augustus trying to tell you in this document? Are there any phrases throughout that are designed to show Augustus in a good light but mask the truth?

THE BROADER PERSPECTIVE:

5-35. In section 34 of "The Accomplishments of Augustus," Augustus says, "I excelled all in authority, but I possessed no more power than others who were my colleagues in each magistracy." The authority of the emperor was the basis for the success of the Augustan principate. What is the difference between "power" and "authority"? Can you relate this concept to the presidency of the United States? Does the success of our president depend on his power or his authority?

5-36. How important is it for a leader to promote "efficient" policies in the establishment of power? Does *efficient* mean "repressive?" Note that the absolute monarchies of seventeenth-century Europe, as well as fascist and totalitarian regimes of the twentieth century, promoted efficiency and stability as virtues of a stable society. Can a government become "too efficient" and provoke popular resentment of its policies?

The Mission: "To Spare the Conquered and Crush the Proud"

VIRGIL

Propaganda is an important component of the success of any new government or regime. It has been asserted that if people are told things often enough, they will believe them. One of the great accomplishments of the Augustan principate was the establishment and maintenance of a period of peace and stability that lasted for over 200 years. It was during the Pax Romana, or the Roman Peace as it was called, that Roman roads, aqueducts, and baths were built, the provinces of the empire flourished, the Roman legal system developed, and Christianity grew. Augustus cultivated his poets well; in turn, they celebrated the new order. He is remembered particularly through the efforts of Horace and the great lyric poet Virgil, as the following selection indicates.

There will be future glory for the Trojans in their Italian descendants, whose destiny awaits. . . . Under the auspices of Romulus, Rome will extend her empire to the ends of the earth and her glory to heaven, encircling her seven hills with a wall to hold her brood of heroes. Here is Caesar and the entire Julian clan. And there he is, the man promised to you so often, Augustus Caesar, son of a god, who will once again establish the Golden Age. . . .

Others will no doubt cast bronze with greater delicacy, will win greater likenesses from marble, will plead cases in the law courts with greater authority, chart the motions of the sky and stars with greater accuracy. You, O Roman, remember to rule the nations with might. This will be your genius—to demand peace, to spare the conquered and crush the proud!

CONSIDER THIS:

5-37. What role does propaganda have in the success of a new government? In what ways is the previous selection a good example of propaganda?

5-38. Virgil has been considered by many classical historians to be the greatest of Latin poets, the finest example of the best Rome had to offer. But some critics have argued that this is great propaganda masquerading as great literature. What do you think? Must great literature speak to the ages and be free of the taint of propaganda?

"'To Spare the Conquered and Crush the Proud'" is from Virgil, *The Aeneid*, 6.756–6.853.

Chapter 6

Caesar and Christ

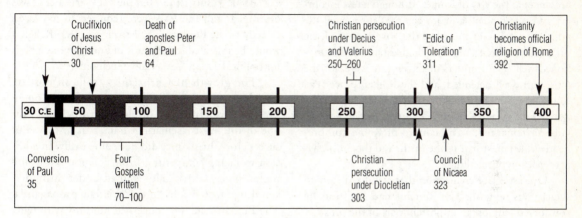

Christianity, above all, has given a clear-cut answer to the demands of the human soul.

—ALEXIS CARREL

The blood of martyrs is the seed of the Church.

—TERTULLIAN

The tyrant dies and his rule ends, the martyr dies and his rule begins.

—SØREN KIERKEGAARD

So urgent . . . is the necessity of believing, that the fall of any system of mythology will probably be succeeded by the introduction of some other mode of superstition.

—EDWARD GIBBON

CHAPTER THEMES

- **Social and Spiritual Values:** What are the basic tenets of the Christian religion? How did they differ from the values and beliefs of Roman state religion, other mystery cults, and paganism in general?

- **The Power Structure:** Why did the Romans, who easily tolerated so many other religious cults, find the Christian religious movement so dangerous? Why were Christians persecuted? Can one serve both Caesar and Christ at the same time with equal devotion?

- **Revolution and Historical Transition:** How did Christianity survive persecution and become the official religion of the Roman Empire by the fourth century C.E.? Was persecution essential to the victory of Christianity? In what ways did Christianity change the civilization of Rome? How did Christianity provide the foundation for medieval civilization?

- **The Big Picture:** To what extent does any society depend on a religious base? Does religion contribute to political and social stability or instability? How important is mythology to the character and success of a civilization?

The Roman Empire in the first and second centuries C.E. was a model of administrative excellence. Aqueducts, sewers, and public baths contributed to the cleanliness and convenience of city dwellers, and a vast highway network linked the provinces to the city of Rome. Although a few incompetent emperors and a major civil war threatened the political stability of the state, the government of the principate, which Augustus had established, functioned well. The frontiers of the empire were, for the most part, well defended, and the Roman peace (Pax Romana) ensured the maintenance of Western civilization. As the great eighteenth-century historian Edward Gibbon remarked, "The empire of Rome comprehended the fairest part of the earth, and the most civilized portion of mankind."

One aspect of civilization that stabilized Roman society was religion. The Romans had traditionally considered religion an important part of the prosperity of the state. They had established an intricate system of worship that employed nature gods and pagan deities syncretized from the Greeks, and a priesthood that ensured the state enjoyed a close relationship with the gods by divining the future through the reading of animal entrails and the interpretation of omens. The state religion during the first century C.E. also came to include the worship of the emperor. Sacrifices to his health, however, were primarily patriotic and did not demand or even encourage the emotional involvement of the people. For such satisfaction, many turned to the consoling logic of philosophy or the emotional excitement of Eastern mystery cults.

During the period of the Republic, the Roman state had come into contact with several religious cults, such as those worshiping Isis, Cybele, Mithras, and Dionysus, and it had tolerated them so long as they did not disturb the peace or break Roman law. In fact, the cults provided an emotional outlet that the Roman state religion did not supply. Roman toleration of foreign customs and religions had helped maintain the empire. The Jews, for example, were respected by the Romans and even accorded special protection and tax exemption. This toleration ended when the Jews, objecting to the Roman presence in their land, revolted in 66 C.E. The Romans methodically crushed the rebellion four years later, by overrunning the Jewish fortification at Masada.

As a result, the Temple at Jerusalem was destroyed, and the Jews were required to pay taxes directly to the Romans. The lesson was clear: Religion would be tolerated so long as it did not serve as a basis for political action—especially rebellion.

The growth of Christianity from an obscure Jewish sect to the official religion of the Roman Empire during the first through fourth centuries is one of the most fascinating dramas in history. But success for Christianity did not come easily. In addition to facing competition from religious cults and philosophies, Christianity labored under misunderstandings fostered by anti-Christian propaganda. The Roman state was concerned not only with what was described as a morally dissolute religion, but perhaps most of all with the threat Christianity posed to the political stability of the state. Christians refused to worship the emperor (merely a token of political allegiance), and their talk of a "messiah" and a "kingdom" connoted political unrest and agitation. Rome tried to punish and even eradicate the religion in sporadic persecutions (Nero in 64, Decius in 250, Diocletian and Galerius from 303 to 311), but Roman policy was often confused and ambivalent. By 311, Christianity was tolerated and later endorsed by the Emperor Constantine. By the end of the fourth century, Christianity had become the official religion of the Roman Empire.

In this chapter, we look closely at the relationship between Christianity and the Roman state. The theme of religious versus secular authority is fundamentally important in Western civilization. Which is more powerful? Which legacy is more enduring? To what extent does a society need a religious base, and how does religion contribute to political and social stability or instability? These issues are all essential to our understanding of civilization; they play a particularly important role in the history of Rome.

Roman State Religion and the Mystery Cults

The Roman government was very strict in its own adherence to the state religion. Certain priesthoods even offered formulaic prayers to the gods for the safety and security of the state. In some ways, this practice resembled a legal contract that provided a sacrifice in return for a service. Because the Romans did not worship living beings, a sacrifice for the health of the emperor did not demonstrate much more than political loyalty. Such practices were devoid of emotion or personal commitment, so many turned for solace to the Eastern mystery cults. As the following selections reveal, the popularity and frenzied ritual of the various cults demonstrated the need for such an outlet, and they alerted Rome to its responsibility for keeping an orderly society.

The Imperial Cult: The Deification of Augustus

DIO CASSIUS

[The senate] declared Augustus immortal, assigned to him a college of priests and sacred rites, and made Livia [his wife], who was already called Julia and Augusta, his priestess; . . . On her part, she bestowed a million sesterces upon a certain Numerius Atticus, a senator and ex-praetor, because he swore that he had seen Augustus ascending to heaven in the manner of the traditions concerning Proculus and Romulus. A shrine voted by the senate and built by Livia and Tiberius was erected to him in Rome, and others in many different places, some of the communities building them voluntarily and others unwillingly. Also the house at Nola where he passed away was made a precinct sacred to him. While his shrine in Rome was being erected, they placed a golden image of him on a couch in the temple of Mars and to this they paid all the honors that they were afterwards to give his statue. Other honors voted him were that his image should not be borne in anybody's funeral procession, that the consuls should celebrate his birthday with games like those in honor of Mars, and that the tribunes of the plebs, since they were sacrosanct, should manage these Augustan Games. These officials conducted everything in the customary manner. . . .

Invasion of the Eastern Cults

MINUCIUS FELIX

Hence it is that throughout wide empires, provinces, and towns, we see each people having its own individual rites and worshiping the local gods—the Eleusinians Ceres, the Phrygians the Great Mother, the Epidaurians Aesculapius, the Chaldaeans Baal, the Syrians Astarte, the Taurians Diana, the Gauls Mercury, the Romans one and all. Thus it is that their power and authority have embraced the circuit of the whole world, and have advanced the bounds of the Empire beyond the paths of the sun and the confines of ocean, while they practice in the field god-fearing valor, make strong their city with awe of sacred rites, with chaste virgins, with many a priestly dignity and title. . . . In captured fortresses, even in the first flush of victory, they reverence the conquered deities. Everywhere they entertain the gods and adopt them as their own; they raise altars even to the unknown deities, and to the spirits of the dead. Thus is it that they adopt the sacred rites of all nations, and as a result have earned dominion. . . .

"The Imperial Cult" is from Dio Cassius, *Roman History*, 56.46 in the Loeb Classical Library, trans. Earnest Cary, vol. 7 (Cambridge, MA: Harvard University Press, 1924), pp. 105–107.

"Invasion of the Eastern Cults" is from Minucius Felix, *Octavius*, 6, 23.1 in the Loeb Classical Library, trans. Gerold H. Rendall (Cambridge, MA: Harvard University Press, 1931), pp. 327, 329, 381, 383.

Consider the sacred rites of the mysteries; you will find tragic deaths, dooms, funerals, mourning and lamentations of woebegone gods. Isis, with her Dog-head and shaven priests, mourning, bewailing, and searching for her lost son; her miserable votaries beating their breasts and mimicking the sorrows of the unhappy mother; then, when the stripling is found, Isis rejoices, her priests jump for joy, the Dog-head glories in his discovery; and, year by year, they never stop losing what they find or to finding what they lose. Is it not absurd either to mourn your object of worship, or to worship your object of mourning? Yet these old Egyptian rites have now found their way to Rome, so that you may play the fool to the swallow and sistrum of Isis, the scattered limbs and the empty tomb of your Serapis or Osiris.

Orgiastic Frenzy

APULEIUS

They appeared clothed in a variety of colors, misshapen, their faces smeared with vile paint and their eyes daubed over with oil. They wore turbans and bright-orange robes made of fine linen and silk with yellow shoes. . . . Then with their arms uncovered up to their shoulders, they held huge swords and axes above their heads, all the while shouting and dancing about in a frenzy, so aroused were they by the sound of the pipes. After we had passed several little houses, we came to the villa of a certain rich property owner, where they entered and immediately began their wailing and frenzied dancing. And they kept bending their heads low, twisting their necks and whirling their long hair around in a circle. They started to bite their own flesh and finally each one cut his arms with the two-edged sword he was carrying. One of them started panting heavily, as if he were filled with the spirit of some god, and seemed to go insane. . . . He began to speak as if in a trance, inventing some weird prophecy, and confessing that he had broken the rules of the holy religion. Demanding just punishment at his own hands for the horrific crime, he seized a whip, a special accessory of these effeminate men, and started lashing himself as the ground became wet and defiled with blood. . . . But when they finally tired, or at least were satisfied with lacerating themselves, they put a stop to this bloody business. . . .

CONSIDER THIS:

6-1. Characterize the Roman state religion. What are the advantages of such a structured approach to religion? Why were the mystery cults so popular, and why did Rome tolerate them?

6-2. Note the deification of the emperor Augustus. Why was it important for the emperors to promote the imperial cult?

KEY EVENTS IN EARLY CHRISTIANITY

4 B.C.E.–30 C.E.   Life span of Jesus of Nazareth

According to the New Testament, Jesus preached a message of love, charity, and humility. He was crucified in Judea by the Roman procurator, Pontius Pilate, after incurring the enmity of Jewish religious leaders.

35   Conversion of the Apostle Paul

Born Saul, a Hellenized Jew, Paul of Tarsus was a Roman citizen who persecuted Christians until his own conversion. He was instrumental in spreading Christianity throughout the eastern Mediterranean.

"Orgiastic Frenzy" is from Apuleius, *The Golden Ass*, 8.27–8.28, based on the 1566 translation by William Adlington. Translation modernized by the editor.

64–65 First Christian Persecution
The emperor Nero blames a destructive fire in Rome on the Christians in order to deflect suspicion from himself. Both Paul and the apostle Peter were killed in the succeeding persecution.

70–100 The Gospels
Four Gospel accounts of Jesus's early life written (Matthew, Mark, Luke, John).

The Message of Jesus

The New Testament of the Bible records the life of Jesus in four Gospels (Matthew, Mark, Luke, and John), the Acts of the Apostles, twenty-one epistles (didactic letters), and the Book of Revelation. The New Testament is the primary source for the teaching of Jesus, who was crucified by the Romans about 30 C.E. The following excerpts relate some of the more pacifistic Christian beliefs regarding love, sympathy, forgiveness, and the nature of the Kingdom of God.

The Baptism of Jesus

At that time Jesus went from Galilee to the Jordan, and came to John to be baptized by him. But John tried to make him change his mind. "I ought to be baptized by you," John said, "yet you come to me!" But Jesus answered him, "Let it be this way for now. For in this way we shall do all that God requires." So John agreed.

As soon as Jesus was baptized, he came up out of the water. Then heaven was opened to him, and he saw the Spirit of God coming down like a dove and lighting on him. And then a voice said from heaven, "This is my own dear Son, with whom I am well pleased." . . .

From that time Jesus began to preach his message: "Turn away from your sins! The Kingdom of heaven is near!"

The Sermon on the Mount

Jesus went all over Galilee, teaching in their meeting houses, preaching the Good News of the Kingdom, and healing people from every kind of disease and sickness. The news about him spread through the whole country of Syria, so that people brought him all those who were sick with all kinds of diseases, and afflicted with all sorts of troubles: people with demons, and epileptics and paralytics—Jesus healed them all. Great crowds followed him from Galilee and the Ten Towns, from Jerusalem, Judea, and the land on the other side of the Jordan.

Jesus saw the crowds and went up a hill, where he sat down. His disciples gathered around him, and he began to teach them:

"Happy are those who know they are spiritually poor:
　　the Kingdom of heaven belongs to them!
"Happy are those who mourn:
　　God will comfort them!
"Happy are the meek:
　　they will receive what God has promised!

"The Baptism of Jesus" is from Matthew 3:13–17, 4:17, from the *Good News New Testament, The New Testament in Today's English Version*, 4th ed. (1976). Copyright © American Bible Society 1966, 1971, 1976. Reprinted by permission. All subsequent references to the New Testament are reprinted from this translation.

"The Sermon on the Mount" is from Matthew 4:23–25; 5:1–25, 5:38–48, 6:5–15.

"Happy are those whose greatest desire is to do what
    God requires:
    God will satisfy them fully!
"Happy are those who show mercy to others:
    God will show mercy to them!
"Happy are the pure in heart:
    they will see God!
"Happy are those who work for peace among men:
    God will call them his sons!
"Happy are those who will suffer persecution because
    they
    do what God requires:
    the Kingdom of heaven belongs to them!

"Happy are you when men insult you and mis-treat you and tell all kinds of evil lies against you because you are my followers. Rejoice and be glad, because a great reward is kept for you in heaven. This is how men mistreated the prophets who lived before you.

"You are like salt for the earth. If the salt loses its taste, there is no way to make it salty again. It has become worthless, and so it is thrown away where people walk on it.

"You are like the light for the world. A city built on a high hill cannot be hid. Nobody lights a lamp to put it under a bowl; instead he puts it on the lamp-stand, where it gives light for everyone in the house. In the same way your light must shine before people, so that they will see the good things you do and give praise to your Father in heaven.

"Do not think that I have come to do away with the Law of Moses and the teaching of the prophets. I have not come to do away with them, but to give them real meaning. Remember this! As long as heaven and earth last, the least point or the smallest detail of the Law will not be done away with—not until the end of all things. Therefore, whoever breaks even the small-est of the commandments, and teaches others to do the same, will be least in the Kingdom of heaven. On the other hand, whoever obeys the Law, and teaches others to do the same, will be great in the Kingdom of heaven. I tell you, then, you will be able to enter the Kingdom of heaven only if your standard of life is far above the standard of the teachers of the Law and the Pharisees.

"You have heard that men were told in the past, 'Do not murder; anyone who commits murder will be brought before the judge.' But now I tell you: whoever is angry with his brother will be brought before the judge; whoever calls his brother 'You good-for-nothing!' will be brought before the Council; and whoever calls his brother a worthless fool will be in danger of going to the fire of hell. So if you are about to offer your gift to God at the altar and there you remember that your brother has something against you, leave your gift there in front of the altar and go at once to make peace with your brother; then come back and offer your gift to God. . . .

"You have heard that it was said, 'An eye for an eye, and a tooth for a tooth.' But now I tell you: do not take revenge on someone who does you wrong. If anyone slaps you on the right cheek, let him slap your left cheek too. And if someone takes you to court to sue you for your shirt, let him have your coat as well. And if one of the occupation troops forces you to carry his pack one mile, carry it another mile. When someone asks you for something, give it to him; when someone wants to borrow something, lend it to him.

"You have heard that it was said, 'Love your friends, hate your enemies.' But now I tell you: love your enemies, and pray for those who mistreat you, so that you will become the sons of your Father in heaven. For he makes his sun to shine on bad and good people alike, and gives rain to those who do right and those who do wrong. Why should you expect God to reward you, if you love only the people who love you? Even the tax collectors do that! And if you speak only to your friends, have you done any-thing out of the ordinary? Even the pagans do that! You must be perfect—just as your Father in heaven is perfect. . . .

"And when you pray, do not be like the hyp-ocrites! They love to stand up and pray in the meeting houses and on the street corners so that everybody will see them. Remember this! They have already been paid in full. But when you pray, go to your room and close the door, and pray to your Father who is unseen. And your Father, who sees what you do in private, will reward you.

"In your prayers do not use a lot of words, as the pagans do, who think that God will hear them because of their long prayers. Do not be like them; God is your Father and he already knows what you need before you ask him. This is the way you should pray:

Our Father in heaven:
May your name be kept holy,

May your Kingdom come,
May your will be done on earth as it is in heaven.

Give us today the food we need;
Forgive us what we owe you as we forgive what others owe us;
Do not bring us to hard testing, but keep us safe from Evil. . . .

"For if you forgive others the wrongs they have done you, your Father in heaven will forgive you. But if you do not forgive others, then your Father in heaven will not forgive the wrongs you have done."

The Good Samaritan

Then a certain teacher of the Law came up and tried to trap him. "Teacher," he asked, "what must I do to receive eternal life?" Jesus answered him, "What do the scriptures say? How do you interpret them?" The man answered: "You must love the Lord your God with all your heart, and with all your soul, and with all your strength, and with all your mind"; and, "You must love your neighbor as yourself." "Your answer is correct," replied Jesus; "do this and you will live."

But the teacher of the Law wanted to put himself in the right, so he asked Jesus, "Who is my neighbor?" Jesus answered: "A certain man was going down from Jerusalem to Jericho, when robbers attacked him, stripped him and beat him up, leaving him half dead. It so happened that a priest was going down that road; when he saw the man he walked on by, on the other side. In the same way a Levite also came there, went over and looked at the man, and then walked on by, on the other side. But a certain Samaritan who was traveling that way came upon him, and when he saw the man his heart was filled with pity. He went over to him, poured oil and wine on his wounds and bandaged them; then he put the man on his own animal and took him to an inn, where he took care of him. The next day he took out two silver coins and gave them to the innkeeper. "Take care of him," he told the innkeeper, "and when I come back this way I will pay you back whatever you spend on him." And Jesus concluded, "Which one of these three seems to you to have been a neighbor to the man attacked by the robbers?" The teacher of the Law answered, "The one who was kind to him." Jesus replied, "You go, then, and do the same."

The Mission of Jesus

One of the more difficult regions of the empire for the Roman government to manage was the province of Judea. Encompassing the Jewish homeland, it was a continual hotbed of disagreement and dissatisfaction. The career of a Roman administrator might easily be placed in jeopardy if he failed to maintain peace. Although much of this dissent was in response to Roman occupation of the area, various Jewish sects also competed among themselves for influence in the region. Thus, the appearance of a young, popular leader

"The Good Samaritan" is from Luke 10:25–37.

who was proclaimed by some as "King of the Jews" and who himself claimed to be the long-awaited Messiah gave pause to both the Jewish hierarchy and Roman authorities. The following selections from Matthew reveal Jesus' own conception of his mission.

Instructions to the Twelve Disciples

Jesus called his twelve disciples together and gave them power to drive out the evil spirits and to heal every disease and every sickness. These are the names of the twelve apostles: first, Simon (called Peter) and his brother Andrew; James and his brother John, the sons of Zebedee; Philip and Bartholomew; Thomas and Matthew, the tax collector; James, the son of Alphaeus, and Thaddaeus; Simon the patriot, and Judas Iscariot, who betrayed Jesus.

Jesus sent these twelve men out with the following instructions: "Do not go to any Gentile territory or any Samaritan towns. Go, instead, to the lost sheep of the people of Israel. Go and preach, 'The Kingdom of heaven is near!' Heal the sick, raise the dead, make the lepers clean, drive out demons. You have received without paying, so give without being paid; do not carry a beggar's bag for the trip, or an extra shirt, or shoes, or a walking stick. A worker should be given what he needs.

"When you come to a town or village, go in and look for someone who is willing to welcome you, and stay with him until you leave that place. When you go into a house say, 'Peace be with you.' If the people in that house welcome you, let your greeting of peace remain; but if they do not welcome you, then take back your greeting. And if some home or town will not welcome you or listen to you, then leave that place and shake the dust off your feet. Remember this! On the Judgment Day God will show more mercy to the people of Sodom and Gomorrah than to the people of that town!

"Listen! I am sending you just like sheep to a pack of wolves. You must be as cautious as snakes and as gentle as doves. Watch out, for there will be men who will arrest you and take you to court, and they will whip you in their meeting houses. You will be brought to trial before rulers and kings for my sake, to tell the Good News to them and to the Gentiles.

When they bring you to trial, do not worry about what you are going to say or how you will say it; when the time comes, you will be given what you will say. For the words you speak will not be yours; they will come from the Spirit of your Father speaking in you.

"Men will hand over their own brothers to be put to death, and fathers will do the same to their children; children will turn against their parents and have them put to death. Everyone will hate you, because of me. But the person who holds out to the end will be saved. And when they persecute you in one town, run away to another one. I tell you, you will not finish your work in all the towns of Israel before the Son of Man comes. . . .

"Do not think that I have come to bring peace to the world; no, I did not come to bring peace, but a sword. I came to set sons against their fathers, daughters against their mothers, daughters-in-law against their mothers-in-law; a man's worst enemies will be the members of his own family.

"Whoever loves his father or mother more than me is not worthy of me; whoever loves his son or daughter more than me is not worthy of me. Whoever does not take up his cross and follow in my steps is not worthy of me. Whoever tries to gain his own life will lose it: whoever loses his life for my sake will gain it.

"Whoever welcomes you, welcomes me; and whoever welcomes me, welcomes the one who sent me. Whoever welcomes God's messenger because he is God's messenger will share in his reward; and whoever welcomes a truly good man, because he is that, will share in his reward. And remember this! Whoever gives even a drink of cold water to one of the least of these my followers, because he is my follower, will certainly receive his reward." . . .

"Instructions to the Twelve Disciples" is from Matthew 10:1–42.

Peter: The Rock

Jesus went to the territory near the town of Caesarea Phillipi, where he asked his disciples, "Who do men say the Son of Man is?" "Some say John the Baptist," they answered. "Others say Elijah, while others say Jeremiah or some other prophet." "What about you?" he asked them. "Who do you say I am?" Simon Peter answered, "You are the Messiah, the Son of the living God." "Simon, son of John, you are happy indeed!" answered Jesus. "For this truth did not come to you from any human being, it was given to you directly by my Father in heaven. And so I tell you: you are a rock, Peter, and on this rock I will build my church. Not even death will ever be able to overcome it. I will give you the keys of the Kingdom of heaven: what you prohibit on earth will be prohibited in heaven; what you permit on earth will be permitted in heaven." Then Jesus ordered his disciples that they were not to tell anyone that he was the Messiah.

Suffering, Persecution, and the Son of Man

From that time on Jesus began to say plainly to his disciples: "I must go to Jerusalem and suffer much from the elders, the chief priests, and the teachers of the Law. I will be put to death, and on the third day I will be raised to life." Peter took him aside and began to rebuke him. "God forbid it, Lord!" he said. "This must never happen to you!" Jesus turned around and said to Peter: "Get away from me, Satan! You are an obstacle in my way, for these thoughts of yours are men's thoughts, not God's!"

Then Jesus said to his disciples: "If anyone wants to come with me, he must forget himself, carry his cross, and follow me. For the man who wants to save his own life will lose it; but the man who loses his life for my sake will find it. Will a man gain anything if he wins the whole world but loses his life? Of course not! There is nothing a man can give to regain his life. For the Son of Man is about to come in the glory of his Father with his angels, and then he will repay everyone according to his deeds. Remember this! There are some here who will not die until they have seen the Son of Man come as King." . . .

As Jesus sat on the Mount of Olives, the disciples came to him in private. "Tell us when all this will be," they asked, "and what will happen to show that it is the time for your coming and the end of the age."

Jesus answered: "Watch out, and do not let anyone fool you. Because many men will come in my name, saying, 'I am the Messiah!' and fool many people. You are going to hear the noise of battles close by and the news of battles far away; but, listen, do not be troubled. Such things must happen, but they do not mean that the end has come. One country will fight another country, one kingdom will attack another kingdom. There will be famines and earthquakes, everywhere. All these things are like the first pains of childbirth.

"Then men will arrest you and hand you over to be punished, and you will be put to death. All mankind will hate you because of me. Many will give up their faith at that time; they will betray each other and hate each other. Then many false prophets will appear and fool many people. Such will be the spread of evil that many people's love will grow cold. But the person who holds out to the end will be saved. And this Good News about the Kingdom will be preached throughout all the world, for a witness to all mankind—and then will come the end. . . .

"Soon after the trouble of those days the sun will grow dark, the moon will no longer shine, the stars will fall from heaven, and the powers in space will be driven from their course. Then the sign of the Son of Man will appear in the sky; then all the tribes of earth will weep, and they will see the Son of Man coming on the clouds of heaven with power and great glory. The great trumpet will sound, and he will send out his angels to the four corners of the earth, and they will gather his chosen people from one end of the world to the other. . . ."

"Peter: The Rock" is from Matthew 16:13–18.

"Suffering, Persecution, and the Son of Man" is from Matthew 16:21–28, 24:3–14, 29.

The Final Judgment

"When the Son of Man comes as King, and all the angels with him, he will sit on his royal throne, and all the earth's people will be gathered before him. Then he will divide them into two groups, just as a shepherd separates the sheep from the goats: he will put the sheep at his right and the goats at his left. Then the King will say to the people on his right: 'You who are blessed by my Father: come! Come and receive the kingdom which has been prepared for you ever since the creation of the world. I was hungry and you fed me, thirsty and you gave me drink; I was a stranger and you received me in your homes, naked and you clothed me; I was sick and you took care of me, in prison and you visited me.' The righteous will then answer him: 'When, Lord, did we ever see you hungry and feed you, or thirsty and give you drink? When did we ever see you a stranger and welcome you in our home, or naked and clothe you? When do we ever see you sick or in prison, and visit you?' The King will answer back, 'I tell you, indeed, whenever you did this for one of these poorest brothers of mine, you did it for me!'

"Then he will say to those on his left: 'Away from me, you who are under God's curse! Away to the eternal fire which has been prepared for the Devil and his angels! I was hungry but you would not feed me, thirsty but you would not give me drink; I was a stranger but you would not welcome me in your homes, naked but you would not clothe me; I was sick and in prison but you would not take care of me.' Then they will answer him: 'When, Lord, did we ever see you hungry, or thirsty, or a stranger, or naked, or sick, or in prison, and we would not help you?' The King will answer them back, 'I tell you, indeed, whenever you refused to help one of these poor ones, you refused to help me.' These, then, will be sent off to eternal punishment; the righteous will go to eternal life."

CONSIDER THIS:

6-3. What was Jesus' basic message and mission? Discuss this with specific examples. Do you see anything in his message that might be considered politically threatening to the Roman state? Consider, in particular, the vocabulary.

The Work of Paul

Paul of Tarsus (ca. 10–65 C.E.) was a Hellenized Jew who had once persecuted Christians before his conversion. He was instrumental in establishing fundamental doctrines and in spreading the teachings of Jesus throughout the Roman Empire, seeking converts among Jews and Gentiles alike on faith, love, and the Resurrection of Christ.

Paul's Answer to the Intellectuals

Christ did not send me to baptize. He sent me to tell the Good News, and to tell it without using the language of men's wisdom, for that would rob Christ's death on the cross of all its power.

For the message about Christ's death on the cross is nonsense to those who are being lost; but for us who are being saved, it is God's power. For the scripture says,

I will destroy the wisdom of the wise,
I will set aside the understanding of the scholars.

So then, where does that leave the wise men? Or the scholars? Or the skillful debaters of this world? God has shown that this world's wisdom is foolishness!

For God in his wisdom made it impossible for men to know him by means of their own wisdom. Instead, God decided to save those who believe, by means of the "foolish" message we preach. Jews want miracles for proof, and Greeks look for wisdom. As for us, we proclaim Christ on the cross, a message that is offensive to the Jews and nonsense to the Gentiles, but for those whom God has called, both Jews and

"The Final Judgment" is from Matthew 25:31–46.

"Paul's Answer to the Intellectuals" is from 1 Corinthians 1:17–2:8.

Gentiles, this message is Christ, who is the power of God and the wisdom of God. For what seems to be God's foolishness is wiser than men's wisdom, and what seems to be God's weakness is stronger than men's strength.

Now remember what you were, brothers, when God called you. Few of you were wise, or powerful, or of high social status, from the human point of view. God purposely chose what the world considers nonsense in order to put wise men to shame, and what the world considers weak in order to put powerful men to shame. He chose what the world looks down on, and despises, and thinks is nothing, in order to destroy what the world thinks is important. . . .

When I came to you, my brothers, to preach God's secret truth to you, I did not use long words and great learning. For I made up my mind to forget everything while I was with you except Jesus Christ, and especially his death on the cross. So when I came to you I was weak and trembled all over with fear, and my speech and message were not delivered with skillful words of human wisdom, but with convincing proof of the power of God's Spirit. Your faith, then, does not rest on man's wisdom, but on God's power.

Yet I do speak wisdom to those who are spiritually mature. But it is not the wisdom that belongs to this world, or to the powers that rule this world—powers which are losing their power. The wisdom I speak is God's secret wisdom, hidden from men, which God had already chosen for our glory, even before the world was made. None of the rulers of this world knew this wisdom. If they had known it, they would not have nailed the Lord of glory to the cross.

"Neither Jew Nor Greek, Male Nor Female"

But before faith came, we were kept under guard by the Law [of the Jews], locked up to wait for the faith which would eventually be revealed to us. So the Law was serving as a slave to look after us, to lead us to Christ, so that we could be justified by faith. But now that faith has come, we are no longer under a slave looking after us; for all of you are the children of God, through faith in Christ Jesus, since every one of you that has been baptized has been clothed in Christ. There can be neither Jew nor Greek, there can be neither slave nor freeman, there can be neither male nor female—for you are all one in Christ Jesus. And simply by being Christ's, you are the decedents of Abraham, the heirs named in the promise.

The Resurrection of Christ

And now I want to remind you, brother, of the Good News which I preached to you, which you received, and on which your faith stands firm. That is the gospel, the message that I preached to you. You are saved by the gospel if you hold firmly to it—unless it was for nothing that you believed.

I passed on to you what I received, which is of the greatest importance: that Christ died for our sins, as written in the Scriptures; that he was buried and raised to life on the third day, as written in the Scriptures; that he appeared to Peter, and then to all twelve apostles. Then he appeared to more than five hundred of his followers at once, most of whom are still alive, although some have died. Then he appeared to James, and then to all the apostles.

Last of all he appeared also to me—even though I am like one who was born in a most unusual way. For I am the least of all the apostles—I do not even deserve to be called an apostle, because I persecuted God's church. But by God's grace I am what I am, and the grace that he gave me was not without effect. On the contrary, I have worked harder than all the other apostles, although it was not really my own doing, but God's grace working with me. So then, whether it came from me or from them, this is what we all preach, this is what you believe.

"'Neither Jew Nor Greek, Male Nor Female'" is from Galatians 3:23–29.

"The Resurrection of Christ" is from 1 Corinthians 15:1–22, 31–32, 35–39, 42–55.

Now, since our message is that Christ has been raised from death, how can some of you say that the dead will not be raised to life? If that is true, it means that Christ was not raised; and if Christ has not been raised from death, then we have nothing to preach, and you have nothing to believe. More than that, we are shown to be lying against God, because we said of him that he raised Christ from death—but if the dead are not raised, neither has Christ been raised. And if Christ has not been raised, then your faith is a delusion and you are still lost in your sins. It would also mean that the believers in Christ who have died are lost. If our hope in Christ is good for this life only, and no more, then we deserve more pity than anyone else in all the world.

But the truth is that Christ has been raised from death, as the guarantee that those who sleep in death will also be raised. For just as death came by means of a man, in the same way the rising from death comes by means of a man. For just as all men die because of their union to Adam, in the same way all will be raised to life because of their union to Christ. . . .

Brothers, I face death every day! The pride I have in you in our life in Christ Jesus our Lord makes me declare this. If I have fought "wild beasts" here in Ephesus, as it were, simply from human motives, what have I gained? As the saying goes, "Let us eat and drink, for tomorrow we will die"—if the dead are not raised to life. . . .

Someone will ask, "How can the dead be raised to life? What kind of body will they have?" You fool! When you plant a seed in the ground it does not sprout to life unless it dies. And what you plant in the ground is a bare seed, perhaps a grain of wheat, or of some other kind, not the full-bodied plant that will grow up. God provided that seed with the body he wishes; he gives each seed its own proper body. . . .

This is how it will be when the dead are raised to life. When the body is buried it is mortal; when raised, it will be immortal. When buried, it is ugly and weak; when raised, it will be beautiful and strong. When buried, it is a physical body; when raised, it will be a spiritual body. There is, of course, a physical body, so there is bound to be a spiritual body. For the scripture says: "The first man, Adam, was created a living being"; but the last Adam is the life-giving Spirit. It is not the spiritual that comes first, but the physical, and then the spiritual. The first Adam was made of the dust of the earth; the second Adam came from heaven. Those who belong to the earth are like the one who was made of earth; those who are of heaven are like the one who came from heaven. Just as we wear the likeness of the men made of earth, so we will wear the likeness of the Man from heaven.

This is what I mean, brothers: what is made of flesh and blood cannot share in God's Kingdom, and what is mortal cannot possess immortality.

Listen to this secret: we shall not all die, but in an instant we shall all be changed, as quickly as the blinking of an eye, when the last trumpet sounds. For when it sounds, the dead will be raised immortal beings, and we shall all be changed. For what is mortal must clothe itself with what is immortal: what will die must clothe itself with what cannot die. So when what is mortal has been clothed with what is immortal, and when what will die has been clothed with what cannot die, then the scripture will come true:

"Death is destroyed: victory is complete!"
"Where, O Death, is your victory?
Where, O Death, is your power to hurt?"

CONSIDER THIS:

6-4. What were Paul's contributions to the message of Jesus? How did the Pax Romana contribute to the success of missionaries like Paul who were spreading the word of Christ?

Conflict and the Development of the Christian Church

Roman Imperial Policy Regarding Jews and Christians

Because Christianity emerged from Jewish religious traditions and cultural identity, we must look to Rome's relationship with the Jews in order to understand the developing Christian church. As we have noted, Rome was generally tolerant of foreign religions, and this was especially true of Judaism. Romans respected historical continuity and especially a culture that was far older than theirs. In fact, the Jews were generally allowed to practice their religion in the region of Galilee within the province of Judea (modern day Israel and Palestine) with a minimum of regulation or restriction. Rome allowed them to worship Yahweh, and they were even allowed to collect their own tax to be paid directly to the Temple in Jerusalem. This was a benefit that other peoples did not enjoy.

It was also true, however, that the Jews did not want to be assimilated into Roman society, but rather wanted to remain independent religiously and politically. This proved difficult for the Romans to understand. In their administration of empire, they had consistently demanded political loyalty and taxes in return for social and cultural freedom. This arrangement lay at the heart of the Pax Romana—stability and security within the empire and protection from external invasion. Deviation from this governing principle led to drastic action like the destruction of Corinth in 146 B.C.E. by a Roman administration fed up with petty Greek bickering.

The Jews refused to separate religious freedom from political independence. They were the chosen people of God and resisted Roman presence in their homeland. The Romans tried to find an accommodation by installing Jewish kings in the region like Herod the Great (died 4 B.C.E.) and his son, Herod Antipas (died 39 C.E.), who could control the Jewish population, if not conciliate it. Jewish religious leaders regarded them as Roman puppets, and tensions increased with constant disturbances during the time of Christ in about 30 C.E. Jews suffered expulsions from Rome under Caligula in 40 and great suspicion under Nero (who wanted to blame the fire of 64 on the Jews before he settled on the Christians). Roman patience finally wore thin when the Jews rose in rebellion, and Rome in response launched a military campaign from 67 to 71 under the command of the general Vespasian and his son Titus. They were methodical in the prosecution of this war, and the Jewish rebellion was put down with devastating results. Jerusalem was burned and the Temple destroyed with its contents hauled back to Rome in triumph. Jews lost their tax privileges as the Romans established a special "Jewish Account" that applied Jewish taxes for the benefit of the Temple of Jupiter on the Capitoline Hill in Rome. The Jews would continue to fight against the might of Rome with subsequent rebellions from 115 to 117 under the emperor Trajan and from 132 to 135 under Hadrian. After 135, the Jews were effectively controlled and all privileges were cancelled, including observance of the Sabbath, the right to hold meetings, and any protection under Roman law. Rome was efficient and consistent: Political rebellion would not be tolerated.

THEME: SOCIAL AND SPIRITUAL VALUES

THE HISTORIAN AT WORK—FLAVIUS JOSEPHUS

Mass Suicide at Masada

Our primary historian of the war against the Jews from 67–71 C.E. is Flavius Josephus. He was a Jew, born Joseph ben Matthias in 37 C.E. into a prosperous and influential family, a descendant of kings. In the year 64 (the same year that Nero watched the burning of Rome), Josephus visited that city on a diplomatic mission to the imperial government. He impressed Roman officials in spite of his youth and was appointed governor of Galilee. Although he was taken prisoner by Vespasian at the outbreak of the Jewish war the next year, he was treated with respect and became a true believer in the efficiency, military power, and moral vision of

Rome. He served Vespasian and Titus with unyielding devotion, finally becoming a Roman citizen and taking the family name of his benefactors—Flavius. Many historians through the years have had difficulty with his crossed loyalties, referring to him as "The Traitor of Jerusalem." Supported by the revenue from land that had been confiscated from fellow Jews in the region as the spoils of war, Josephus settled down to write, and produced works on Jewish antiquities and, most importantly, on the Jewish War. His primary motive was to prove that the Romans were right in settling the province of Judea with practical efficiency and that he was not only justified in supporting them, but was a loyal Jew after all.

It is therefore interesting to read Josephus's account of the horrific siege of Masada. This fortress was the last regional holdout against Roman might and the scene of the mass sacrifice of the Jews in defense of their freedom.

After Bassus died in Judea, Flavius Silva succeeded him as procurator there. Silva realized that although the entire country of Judea had been subdued in this war, there was but one strong hold that was still in rebellion. Therefore, he pulled his army together from many corners of the country, and made an expedition against it. This fortress was called Masada. The resistance there was commanded by a man named Eleazar, a resourceful and powerful leader, who also controlled the local brigands called the Sicarii. . . .

Silva wasted no time in stamping out resistance in the area around Masada and established garrisons to control the region. At this point, the Roman general decided to lead his army against Eleazar and those Sicarii who held the fortress of Masada. First, he built a wall around the entire fortress, so that none of the besieged might easily escape. Then he pitched his camp on favorable terrain for a siege where the table top rock of Masada is closest to the neighboring mountain. But this location was difficult to provision, for not only food had to be painstakingly brought in from a great distance, but also water that was essential for the Roman camp, since there was no water source nearby. When all was methodically in place, Silva started sieging the place. . . .

Masada had been established long before by a high priest named Jonathan, who had built a fortress atop a high tabletop mountain. There were only a few paths winding for several miles up to the top and they were narrow and very dangerous, as people and animals often lost footing and fell to their deaths. At the top was a rock fortress with 90-foot walls. This citadel was a difficult obstacle to control since it had been designed to frustrate the attacks of enemies.

Within this fortress, the Jews had stored grain in large quantities and also wine, oil, and dates in abundance, so that many people could subsist for a long time. . . . Also stored there was a large quantity of all sorts of weapons of war, which had been established by King Herod and could supply ten thousand men. . . . The Romans knew that Herod had prepared this fortress for his own use, as a refuge in case his own people should depose him and install another king to rule them. . . .

Since the Roman commander Silva had built a wall around the outside of the mountain, as we have already noted, and was therefore able to prevent any of the Jews from escaping, he undertook the siege itself. . . . The siege machines had been developed by the emperor Vespasian and his son Titus and there was also a 90 foot siege tower that was plated with iron, out of which the Romans threw javelins and stones from the engines. Soon, those Jews who were defending the lower walls below the fortress had to pull back lest they be killed when they lifted up their

"Mass Suicide at Masada" is from *The Works of Flavius Josephus*, trans. William Whiston (Hartford, CT: S. S. Scranton, 1905), Books 8.1–8.7; 9.1–9.2. Translation condensed and modernized by the editor.

heads. At the same time Silva ordered that great battering ram to be brought to the front and bashed against the walls repeatedly so that with some difficulty, they broke down the first defensive wall that offered the Jews protection at the lower levels of Masada. However, the Sicarii moved quickly and built another wall within that, which did not allow the Romans to take advantage of the height of the siege towers. When Silva saw this, he thought it best to burn the wall down by tossing a great number of torches all along the exterior. Since it was made of wood, the wall went up in a great conflagration. . . . So the Romans, with assistance from God, returned to their camp with joy, and resolved to attack their enemies the very next day. They set their guards more carefully that night, lest any of the Jews should escape without being discovered.

But the Jewish leader, Eleazar, did not once think of running, nor would he permit any one else to do so. But when he saw that their wall had been burned down by the fire, and could devise no other way of escaping, he knew that it was inevitable that the Romans would make their way to the top. He also knew what they would do to the rebels, to their children and wives. So he decided that the Jews would all commit suicide rather than surrender to Rome. Eleazar gathered the most courageous of his companions together, and encouraged them to do so in a speech: "Since we, long ago, my generous friends, resolved never to be servants to the Romans, nor to any other than to God himself, who alone is the true and just Lord of mankind, the time has now come to stand behind that resolution in practice. . . . We were the very first to revolt against the Romans, and we are the last to fight against them. God has granted us a favor that it is still in our power to die bravely, and in a state of freedom, which has not been the case with the other Jews, who were conquered unexpectedly. It is very plain that we shall be taken within a day's time, but it is still a wonderful thing to die in glory, together with our dearest friends. This is what our enemies themselves cannot prevent, though they would love to take us alive. We simply cannot beat them and it is evident that God must be displeased with us for he

has overlooked the destruction of so many men and allowed the holy city of Jerusalem to be burned and demolished by our enemies. . . . Consider how God has not allowed us to prevail and live in freedom, and still has not delivered us, even while we still have great stores of food and arms. We have been deprived by God himself of all hope of deliverance. This was the result of God's anger against us for our manifold sins, our insolence and extravagance. Let us receive our punishments not from the Romans, but from God himself as executed by our own hands. Let our wives die before they are abused, and our children before they have tasted slavery. And after we have killed them, let us confer this honor upon each other. We will thus preserve ourselves in freedom and that will be an excellent funeral monument. But first, let us destroy our money and the fortress by fire, for the Romans will be frustrated that they will neither be able to seize our wealth or our bodies. Only our provisions will remain so that they will know when we are dead that we were not subdued for lack of food and water, but because we preferred death to slavery. . . ."

Now as Eleazar was finishing this exhortation, they all cut him off short, and hurried to complete the arrangements. . . . They were indeed miserable men whose distress forced them to kill their wives and children with their own hands, as the least offensive option before them. Because they were not able to bear their grief any longer, they immediately laid all they had in a pile, and set fire to it. They then chose ten men by lot from their number to kill all the rest. Each man lay down by his wife and children on the ground, and threw his arms around them, offering their necks to those who had been chosen by lot to do the cutting. And when these ten had fearlessly killed them all, they once again cast lots for themselves. The man selected would kill the other nine and after all were dead, should kill himself. The nine stepped up willingly and offered their necks to the executioner. The last man looked at the other bodies to make sure that all were dead, then set fire to the citadel and with the great force of his hand ran his sword right through himself. He fell dead next to his relatives.

FIGURE 6.1 Spoils from the destruction of the Temple of Jerusalem. Roman troops ended the stubborn resistance of the Jews in 70 C.E. and brought back many of the Jewish artifacts to be displayed in Titus's great triumphal march through the city of Rome. Submission and safety were the other alternatives for provincials. (*Perry M. Rogers*)

So these people died with the intention that they would not leave so much as one soul among them all alive to be subject to the Romans. Yet was there an old woman, and another who was a relative of Eleazar with five children, who had hidden themselves in caverns under ground . . . when the rest, some nine hundred and sixty in number, decided to commit mass suicide. . . .

Now the Romans expected that they would finish the siege operation in the morning and made an assault on the fortress. But they saw no enemy and simply felt a terrible solitude everywhere as they watched the fire burn on the top of Masada. They had no idea what had happened. At last, they made a shout to bring out anyone who was within and the women heard this noise and came out of their underground cavern. They told the Romans what had happened and how it had been done. It was difficult for the Romans to believe their story, but as they put the fire out they came upon the mass of Jewish dead. The Romans were shocked and took no pleasure in the sight although these were their enemies. They simply wondered at the courage of Jewish resolution. So many dead, so much destruction and sacrifice. . . .

6-5. Why were the Jews willing to commit mass suicide at Masada? What was the justification given by their leader, Eleazar?

6-6. What does this siege operation tell you about the Roman army? Historians often refer to the "Roman military machine." What do they mean?

6-7. Do you sense any bias in Josephus's account of the destruction of Masada? He was a Jew who believed in the efficient administration and values of the Romans. Was Josephus a traitor to his people or a loyal Roman? Could he have been both a loyal Jew and a loyal Roman?

6-8. From Josephus's description of the dramatic scene at Masada, do you get a sense of Jewish nationalism? Why did a small group of Jews make a stand at Masada? Were the Romans abusive in their administration of Judea? Or were the Jews simply unwilling to live under the control of any political authority but their own?

6-9. In our modern world, the Israeli nation has had to fight several wars against Arab countries over the years in order to protect its homeland. All Israelis are required to serve in the military forces. Does it surprise you that the induction ceremony always takes place on top of Masada? What is the point that the Israeli government is trying to make?

KEY EVENTS IN THE DEVELOPMENT OF CHRISTIANITY

250–260   Major Persecution of Christians
Under the emperors Decius (249–251) and Valerius (253–260), persecutions seek to limit popular spread of Christianity. This is a reversal of Roman policy in the second century under the emperor Trajan (117) who advised, "Do not seek the Christians out."

303   The Persecution of Diocletian
Empire-wide persecution of Christians under the emperor Diocletian begins. The emperor Galerius issues the "Edict of Toleration" (311).

325   The Council of Nicaea
After victory against his rivals at the Battle of the Milvian Bridge (312), the emperor Constantine supports Christianity and works to resolve divisive theological issues concerning the nature of Christ at the Council of Nicaea, which declares Arianism a heresy. Orthodox position contained in the Nicene Creed: Jesus is both fully human and fully divine.

361–363   Julian the Apostate
Roman emperor tries unsuccessfully to revive paganism.

392   Theodosian Code
Christianity becomes the official religion of the Roman Empire. Pagan worship prohibited.

430   Death of Saint Augustine
Augustine becomes Bishop of Hippo (396) and writes his autobiography (*Confessions*) and his monumental defense of Christianity, *The City of God* (413–426).

440–461   Reign of Pope Leo I
Leo promulgated the Petrine theory: Rome was the center of Christianity and he was the successor to Saint Peter, the Vicar of Christ, and the direct authority for the will of God.

The Persecution of Christians under Nero (64 C.E.)

TACITUS

At the beginning of their movement, Christians had difficulty achieving an identity distinct from the Jews. But by the middle of the first century C.E., they had begun to spread Jesus' beliefs into the provinces. Christianity was not immediately popular, and many despised the missionaries for their zealous conversion methods. Paul himself had difficulty appealing to the Athenians in 51 C.E. The first recorded persecution of Christians took place in 64 C.E. when the emperor Nero blamed a destructive fire in Rome on them to deflect suspicion from himself. It was in this persecution, confined to the city of Rome, that Saint Peter and Saint Paul were killed.

All human efforts, all the lavish gifts of the emperor, and the propitiations of the gods, did not banish the sinister belief that the fire was the result of an order. Consequently, to get rid of the report, Nero fastened the guilt and inflicted the most exquisite tortures on a class hated for their abominations, called Christians by the populace. Christus, from whom the name had its origin, suffered the death penalty during the reign of Tiberius at the hands of one of our procurators, Pontius Pilate, and a most mischievous superstition, thus checked for the moment, again broke out not only in Judea, the first source of the evil, but even in Rome, where all things hideous and shameful from every part of the world find their center and become popular. Accordingly, an arrest was first made of all who pleaded guilty; then, upon their information, an immense multitude was convicted, not so much of the crime of firing the city, as of "hatred against mankind." The Christians were mocked as they were killed. Covered with the skins of beasts, they were torn by dogs and perished, or were nailed to crosses, or were doomed to the flames and burnt, to serve as a nightly illumination, when daylight had expired. . . . Even for criminals who deserved extreme and exemplary punishment, there arose a feeling of compassion. For it was not, as it seemed, for the public good, but to glut one man's cruelty that they were being destroyed.

"The Infection of This Superstition Has Spread"

PLINY THE YOUNGER

The emperor Trajan (d. 117) enjoyed a reputation as a strong leader whose military conquests added to the empire and whose administrative talents helped secure it. The following selection is a letter from the Roman governor of Bithynia, Pliny the Younger. A friend of Trajan's, Pliny was anxious about maintaining the peace in his province and confused about official policy toward the Christians. Trajan's famous reply is also included.

Letter of Pliny the Younger to Trajan

It is my custom, my Lord, to refer to you all things concerning which I am in doubt. For who can better guide my indecision or enlighten my ignorance?

I have never taken part in the trials of Christians. Therefore, I do not know for what crime or to what extent it is customary to punish or investigate. I have been worried about whether any consideration should be given to age, or whether the treatment of the young differs from that of the old. If they repent, should I pardon them, or should someone who had been a Christian gain nothing if he ceases to be one? Should I punish those who confess to being Christians, even if there is no proof that they have committed specific crimes that are

"The Persecution under Nero" is from Tacitus, *Annals*, 15.44, trans. Alfred Church and William Brodribb (New York: Macmillan, 1891).

"The Infection of This Superstition Has Spread" is from Pliny the Younger, *Letters*, 10.96–10.97, in *Translations and Reprints from the Original Sources of European History*, ed. D. C. Munro and Edith Bramhall, vol. 4, no. 1 (Philadelphia, 1898).

generally associated with the religion? Until I get more specific instructions from you, I will continue to follow this procedure in the case of those who have been brought before me as Christians. I ask them whether they are Christians. Those who have confessed I question a second and a third time, threatening them with punishment, if they do not recant their association. Those who persist in claiming their identity as Christians, I order executed. For I have not doubted that, whatever it was that they had confessed, their stubbornness and inflexible obstinacy ought certainly to be punished. There were others of similar madness, but because they were Roman citizens, I signed an order sending them to Rome.

Because of the attention we focused on this process, the crimes quickly spread and more cases arose. And then anonymous accusations against many people began arriving in the court. Those who denied that they were or had been Christian, ought, I thought, to be dismissed since they repeated after me a prayer to your image. Besides, they cursed Christ, one of which things they say those who are really Christians cannot be compelled to do. Others, accused by the informer, said that they were Christians and afterwards denied it; in fact, they had been but had ceased to be, some many years ago, some even twenty years before. They all worshiped your image and the statues of the gods and cursed Christ. They maintained that the substance of their fault or error had been that on a fixed day they were accustomed to come together before daylight and sing by turns a hymn to Christ as though he were a god, and to bind themselves through prayer, not for some crime, nor to commit robbery, theft, or adultery, nor to betray a trust. . . . After this, it was customary to disperse and to come together again to partake of food of an ordinary and harmless kind. Even this they ceased to do after the publication of my edict in which, according to your orders, I had forbidden associations. Therefore, I decided it the more necessary to examine two female slaves, who were called deaconesses, in order to find out what was true, and to do it by torture. I found nothing but a vicious, extravagant superstition.

Consequently, I postponed the examination and decided to consult you. For it seemed to me that the subject would justify consultation, especially on account of the number of those involved. For many of all ages, of every rank, and even of both sexes are and will be endangered. The infection of this superstition has not only spread to the cities, but also to the villages and country districts. But it seems possible to check it and cure it. It is plain enough that the temples, which had been almost deserted, have begun to be frequented again, that the sacred rites, which had been neglected for a long time, have begun to be restored, and that food for sacrifice, for which until now there was scarcely a purchaser, is sold. From this, it is easy to imagine that a multitude of people can be reclaimed if repentance is permitted.

Trajan's Reply

You have followed the correct procedure, my dear Pliny, in conducting the cases of those who were accused before you as Christians, for no general rule can be laid down as a set form. They are not to be sought out; if they are brought before you and convicted, they ought to be punished, with the proviso that whoever denies that he is a Christian and proves it by worshiping our gods, even though he may have been under suspicion in the past, shall obtain pardon on repentance. In no case should attention be paid to anonymous charges, for they afford a bad precedent and are not worthy of our age.

The Persecution under Diocletian (305 C.E.)

LACTANTIUS

Diocletian was an important emperor who in 285 C.E. instituted reforms that were crucial to the survival of the empire. Still, he persecuted Christians with a zeal not seen since that of the emperor Decius in 250 C.E. This was the last empire-wide persecution, but also the severest and most sustained, lasting from 303 to 311.

"The Persecution under Diocletian" is from Lactantius, *On the Deaths of the Persecutors*, 12–14, trans. Gilbert Burnet, 1767. Translation modernized by the editor.

The next day an edict was published that deprived Christian men of all honors and rank and decreed that they should be tortured and prosecuted without having the right to sue for any wrong. . . . Finally, the edict decreed at they should be deprived of their freedom and not be allowed to defend themselves. One man, though it was wrong, had the courage to rip down this edict and tear it up. . . . Immediately, he was arrested and not only tortured, but was legally burned, all the while demonstrating admirable endurance until he was at last consumed by the flames.

But Galerius [Diocletian's colleague] was not satisfied with the harsh terms of the edict and sought other ways to influence Diocletian. Galerius was determined to elicit an excessively cruel reaction from Diocletian, so he employed private agents to set the palace on fire; and when part of it had gone up in flames, the Christians were accused as public enemies. As the palace burned, so too did public prejudice flare against the very name of Christian. Rumors were rampant that the Christians had plotted in conspiracy with the court eunuchs to destroy the princes, and that the two emperors had almost been burned alive in their own palace. But Diocletian, who always wanted to seem clever and intelligent, suspected nothing of the deception. Inflamed with anger, he began immediately to torture all his servants.

CONSIDER THIS:

6-10. What was Roman policy on Christianity? Why was Rome concerned about the Christians? How did Christians threaten the Roman state, and why were they persecuted? Why were Christians finally tolerated by Constantine and Theodosius?

"A Religion of Lust": Anti-Christian Propaganda

MINUCIUS FELIX

In the confusion surrounding the Christian movement, many pagans were willing to believe whatever they heard about the religion. The following selection is by a Roman lawyer named Minucius Felix around 250 C.E. Note the emphasis on threatening political terms such as *faction* and *conspiracy*.

Isn't it deplorable that a faction . . . of wild, hopeless outlaws attacks the gods? They gather together ignorant people from the lowest dregs of humanity, and simple-minded women, easily deceived as their sex is, and thereby organize a rabble of unholy conspirators, leagued together only at night by ritual fasts and barbarous foods not for the purpose of something sacred and proper, but for sacrilege—a clandestine tribe that shuns the light, silent in public but always plotting in secret. They despise our temples as unworthy, they spit upon the gods, they ridicule our sacred rites. And although they are themselves pitiful scum, they pity . . . our priests; although they run around half-naked, they despise our offices and official robes. What amazing stupidity! What incredible arrogance!

They don't seem to mind being tortured, but dread pain in some afterlife. And while they fear to die after death, they don't fear it in the meantime, since hope deceptively soothes away their terror with the promise of a life to come.

A decay of morality spreads daily throughout the entire world, and the degenerate shrines of this impious conspiracy multiply relentlessly. This plot must be completely rooted out and destroyed. These Christians recognize one another by secret signs and signals; they love one another before they are even acquainted. They promote a kind of religion of lust and call themselves promiscuously brothers and sisters, so that ordinary fornication . . .becomes incest. Indeed, this self-centered, mad superstition glories in crimes. There

"'A Religion of Lust': Anti-Christian Propaganda" is from Minucius Felix, *Octavius*, 8.3–12.6, trans. Gerald H. Rendall, based on the unfinished version by W. C. A. Kerr (New York: G. P. Putnam's Sons, 1931). Translation modernized by the editor.

must be some truth to the rumors we hear because you could not make up tales of such gross abominations! I hear that they absurdly consecrate and worship the head of an ass, the most repulsive of beasts—this is so typical of the degenerate morality that lies at the foundation of this religion. Others say that they revere the private parts of their director and high priest, and adore them as if belonging to a parent. I can't confirm whether this is true, but you know that suspicion naturally attaches itself to secret and nocturnal rites. Imagine! They venerate a criminal who was put to death on a wooden cross! Well, that's a suitable altar for such a group of abandoned and impious men and truly characterizes the kind of worship they deserve.

What we hear of Christian initiation rites is as detestable as it is notorious. They take a baby and cover it with a blanket in order to deceive the initiate. Then they encourage the neophyte Christian to hit the blanket again and again and without his knowing it, the infant is killed by his random blows. They greedily lap up its blood—how shocking!—and eagerly distribute its limbs to the congregation. Then they pledge themselves to mutual silence and therefore link themselves in crime. . . .

Their form of banqueting is notorious—everywhere people are talking about it. On an appointed day they assemble at a dinner with all their children, sisters, and mothers, people of both sexes and every age. There, after much feasting, when the banquet has gotten out of control and intoxication has inflamed the drunken passions of incestuous lust, the telltale light is upset and extinguished, and in the shameless dark they exchange embraces indiscriminately, and all, if not actually, yet by complicity are equally involved in incest. . . .

Consider This:

6-11. Analyze the Roman propaganda directed against the Christians. In your opinion, what makes it effective or ineffective propaganda?

THEME: SOCIAL AND SPIRITUAL VALUES

The Reflection in the Mirror

"Christians to the Lions!"

A Christian Defense

TERTULLIAN

In response to pagan misconception, Christian apologists like Tertullian (160–230 c.e.) sought to clarify and defend the Christian position.

Keep in Mind . . .

6-12. According to Tertullian, what are the main reasons for persecution of the Christians?

Magistrates of the Roman Empire, seated as you are before the eyes of all, in almost the highest position in the state to pronounce judgment: if you are not to conduct an open and public examination and inquiry as to what the real truth is with regard to the Christians; if, in this case alone your authority fears or blushes to conduct a public investigation with the diligence demanded by justice; if, finally—as happened lately in the private courts—hatred of this group has been aroused to the extent that it actually blocks their defense, then let the truth reach your ears by the private and quiet avenue of literature. . . .

"A Christian Defense" is from *Tertullian: Apologetical Works, and Minucius Felix, Octavius*, trans. Sister Emily Joseph Daly, C.S.J. (New York: Fathers of the Church, 1950), vol. X: *Fathers of the Church* (Washington, D.C.: The Catholic University of America Press), pp. 7–8, 10–12, 15–16, 25, 35, 85–86, 88, 102. Reprinted by permission of the Catholic University of American Press, Washington D.C.

This, then, is the first grievance we lodge against you, the injustice of the hatred you have for the name of Christian. The motive which appears to excuse this injustice is precisely that which both aggravates and convicts it; namely, ignorance. For, what is more unjust than that men should hate what they do not know, even though the matter itself deserves hatred? Only when one knows whether a thing deserves hatred does it deserve it. But, when there is no knowledge of what is deserved, how is the justice of hatred defensible? Men remain in ignorance as long as they hate, and they hate unjustly as long as they remain in ignorance.

> "Men remain in ignorance as long as they hate, and they hate unjustly as long as they remain in ignorance."
> —TERTULLIAN

The proof of their ignorance, which condemns while it excuses their injustice, is this: In the case of all who formerly indulged in hatred [of Christianity] because of their ignorance of the nature of what they hated, their hatred comes to an end as soon as their ignorance ceases. . . .

If then, it is decided that we are the most wicked of men, why do you treat us so differently from those who are on a par with us, that is, from all other criminals? . . . Christians alone are permitted to say nothing that would clear their name, vindicate the truth, and aid the judge to come to a fair decision. One thing only is what they wait for; this is the only thing necessary to arouse public hatred: the confession of the name of Christian, not an investigation of the charge. Yet, suppose you are trying any other criminal. If he confesses to the crime of murder, sacrilege, incest, or treason—to particularize the indictments hurled against us—you are not satisfied to pass sentence immediately; you weigh the attendant circumstances, the character of the deed, the number of times it was committed, the time, the place, the witnesses, and the partners-in-crime. In our case

there is nothing of this sort. No matter what false charge is made against us, we must be made to confess it; for example, how many murdered babies one has devoured, how many deeds of incest one has committed under cover of darkness, what cooks and what dogs were on hand. Oh, what glory for that governor who should have discovered someone who had already consumed a hundred infants! . . .

Now that I have set down these remarks as a preface, as it were, to stigmatize the injustice of the public hatred against us, I shall take the stand to defend our innocence. Not only shall I refute the charges which are brought against us, but I shall even hurl them back upon those who make them. . . . We shall reply to each charge individually; to those which we are said to commit in secret and to those which we are found to be committing before the eyes of all—charges on the basis of which we are held to be criminals, deceivers, reprobates, and objects of ridicule. . . .

We are spoken of as utter reprobates and are accused of having sworn to murder babies and to eat them and of committing adulterous acts after the repast. Dogs, you say, the pimps of darkness, overturn candles and procure license for our impious lusts. We are always spoken of in this way, yet you take no pains to bring into the light the charges which for so long a time have been made against us. Now, either bring them into the light, if you believe them, or stop believing them, inasmuch as you have not brought them to the light! . . .

"You do not worship the gods," you say, "and you do not offer sacrifice for the emperors." It follows that we do not offer sacrifices for others for the same reason that we do not do it even for ourselves—it follows immediately from our not worshiping the gods. Consequently, we are considered guilty of sacrilege and treason. This is the chief accusation against us—in fact, it is the whole case—and it certainly deserves investigation, unless presumption and injustice dictate the decision, the one despairing of the truth, the other refusing it. We cease worshiping your gods when we find out that they are nonexistent.

FIGURE 6.2 The Coliseum in Rome, where hundreds of Christians were sporadically sacrificed to the lions as condemned reprobates during the imperial era in the first through fourth centuries C.E. "If the weather will not change, if there is an earthquake, a famine, a plague—straightway the cry is heard: 'Toss the Christians to the lions!'"—Tertullian (*Perry M. Rogers*)

For, in our case, we pray for the welfare of the emperors to the eternal God, the true God, the living God, whom even the emperors themselves prefer to have propitious to them before all other gods. They know who has given them power; they know— for they are men—who has given them life; they feel that He is the only God in whose power alone they are, commencing with whom they are second, after whom they stand first, who is before all and above all gods. . . . Looking up to Him, we Christians—with hands extended, because they are harmless, with head bare because we are not ashamed, without a prayer leader because we pray from the heart—constantly beseech Him on behalf of all emperors. We ask for them long life, undisturbed power, security at home, brave armies, a faithful Senate, an upright people, a peaceful world, and everything for which a man or a Caesar prays. . . .

There is also another, even greater obligation for us to pray for the emperors; yes, even for the continuance of the empire in general and for Roman interests. We realize that the tremendous force which is hanging over the whole world, and the very end of the world with its threat of dreadful afflictions, is arrested for a time by the continued existence of the Roman Empire. This event we have no desire to experience, and, in praying that it may be deferred, we favor the continuance of Rome. . . . On the other hand, those men deserve the name of a secret society who band together in hatred of good and virtuous men, who cry out for the blood of the innocent, at the same time offering as a justification of their hatred the idle plea that they consider that the Christians are the cause of every public calamity and every misfortune of the people. If the Tiber rises as high as the city walls, if the Nile does not rise to the fields, if the weather will not change, if there is an earthquake, a famine, a plague—straightway the cry is heard: "Toss the Christians to the lion!" So many of them for just one beast?

CONSIDER THIS:

6-13. Is Tertullian fair in his assessment of the Roman position and actions? Does he do a good job of defending the Christian position against such misstatements?

The Early Church Fathers

The defense of Christianity in the face of anti-Christian propaganda and persecution by Roman officials during the second century was an important component in defining Christian doctrine. But the process of selecting or rejecting ideas that were competing within a fluid intellectual environment became an even more crucial mission for the eventual success of Christianity.

The main struggle of early Christian apologists was against Gnosticism, a religious movement that existed before Christianity and that sought to dissolve distinctions among competing religions and fuse them into a broad abstract vision of God as Spirit. Because Jesus, in the Christian conception of the Trinity, was viewed at once as pure God, pure man, and pure Spirit, the early Christian fathers focused on defending this Trinitarian relationship. In addition, they sought to preserve the unity of Christianity by deciding just how a Christian lived within the world and by defining the nature of an ecumenical church that served as the authority for the teaching of Christian doctrine.

The next selection is by Origen (ca. 185–254), who was a brilliant visionary of the unity of Christian theology. He was an original thinker and a great teacher whose allegorical and subjective interpretation of Scripture was both controversial and influential in the development of Christian thought.

First Principles of the Early Church (225 C.E.)

ORIGEN

All who believe and are convinced that grace and truth came by Jesus Christ, and who know Christ to be the truth, . . . derive the knowledge which calls men to lead a good and blessed life from no other source but the very words and teachings of Christ. . . .

Many of those, however, who profess to believe in Christ, hold conflicting opinions not only on small and trivial questions, but also on some that are great and important; on the nature, for instance, of God or of the Lord Jesus Christ or of the Holy Spirit, and in addition on the natures of those created beings, the dominions and the holy powers. In view of this it seems necessary first to lay down a definite line and unmistakable rule in regard to each of these, and to postpone the inquiry into other matters until afterwards. . . .

The kinds of doctrines which are believed in plain terms through the apostolic teaching are the following:

First, that God is one, who created and set in order all things, and who, when nothing existed, caused the universe to be. He is God from the first creation and foundation of the world, the God of all righteous men. . . .

"First Principles of the Early Church" is from Origen, *First Principles*, trans. G.W. Butterworth (London: Society for Promoting Christian Knowledge, 1916), pp. 1–6.

Then again: Christ Jesus, he who came to earth, was begotten of the Father before every created thing. And after he had ministered to the Father in the foundation of all things, for "all things were made through him," in these last times he emptied himself and was made man, was made flesh, although he was God: and being made man, he still remained what he was, namely God. He took to himself a body like our body, differing in this alone that it was born of a virgin and of the Holy Spirit. And this Jesus Christ was born and suffered in truth and not merely in appearance, and truly died our common death. Moreover, he truly rose from the dead, and after the resurrection companied with his disciples and was then taken up into heaven.

Then again, the apostles delivered this doctrine, that the Holy Spirit united in honor and dignity with the Father and Son. In regard to him it is not yet clearly known whether he is to be thought of as begotten or unbegotten, or as being himself also a son of God or not; but these are matters which we must investigate to the best of our power from holy scripture, inquiring with wisdom and diligence. . . .

Next after this the apostles taught that the soul, having a substance and life of its own, will be rewarded according to its deserts after its departure from this world; for it will either obtain an inheritance of eternal life and blessedness, if its deeds shall warrant this, or it must be given over to eternal fire and torments, if the guilt of its crimes shall so determine. . . .

Further, in regard to the devil and his angels and the opposing spiritual powers, the Church teaching lays it down that these beings exist, but what they are or how they exist it has not explained very clearly. Among most Christians, however, the following opinion is held, that this devil was formerly an angel, but became an apostate and persuaded as many angels as he could to fall away with him; and these are even now called his angels.

The Church teaching also included the doctrine that this world was made and began to exist at a definite time and that by reason of its corruptible nature it must suffer dissolution. But what existed before this world, or what will exist after it, has not yet been made known openly to the many, for no clear statement on the point is set forth in the Church teaching. . . .

This also is contained in the Church teaching, that there exist certain angels of God and good powers, who minister to him in bringing about the salvation of men; but when these were created, and what they are like, or how they exist, is not very clearly defined. And as for the sun, moon and stars, the tradition does not clearly say whether they are living beings or without life.

Everyone therefore who is desirous of constructing out of the foregoing a connected body of doctrine must use points like these as elementary and foundation principles, in accordance with the commandment which says, "Enlighten yourselves with the light of knowledge." Thus by clear and cogent argument he will discover the truth about each particular point and so will produce, as we have said, a single body of doctrine, with the aid of such illustrations and declarations as he shall find in the Holy Scriptures and of such conclusions as he shall ascertain to follow logically from them when rightly understood.

CONSIDER THIS:

6-14. In the selection, "First Principles of the Early Church," Origen seems concerned that the Holy Scriptures be "rightly understood." In this early statement of doctrine, which issues are clarified by Origen and which issues are unclear in the church teaching?

6-15. Origen seeks the "light of Knowledge" in producing a "single body of doctrine." Why was it important for the early church to do this?

The City of God

SAINT AUGUSTINE

One of the most important voices of early Christianity was that of Saint Augustine. He was born in North Africa in 354 C.E. and lived, by his own admission, a rather dissolute life until his conversion to Christianity in 386 at age thirty-two. He became a priest in 391 and

"*The City of God*" is from Augustine, *The City of God*, trans. M. Dods (Buffalo, NY: The Christian Literature Co., 1887), pp. 412–413.

Bishop of Hippo in 396. His greatest work, *The City of God*, was written as a consequence of the sack of Rome in 410 by Alaric the Visigoth. In it, Augustine answered pagan charges that this catastrophe was the result of the anger of the old gods against Christianity.

In the following excerpt, Augustine explores the relationship between the City of Man and the City of God. His towering intellect maintained a close connection with classical intellectual traditions and provided continuity for Western and Eastern Christianity during a difficult and chaotic time.

But the families which do not live by faith seek their peace in the earthly advantages of this life; while the families which live by faith look for those eternal blessings which are promised, and use as pilgrims such advantages of time and of earth as do not fascinate and divert them from God. . . . The earthly city, which does not live by faith, seeks an earthly peace, and the end it proposes, in the well-ordered concord of civic obedience and rule, is the combination of men's wills to attain the things which are helpful to this life. The heavenly city, or rather the part of it which sojourns on earth and lives by faith, makes use of this peace only because it must, until this mortal condition which necessitates it shall pass away. Consequently, so long as it lives like a captive and a stranger in the earthly city, though it has already received the promise of redemption, . . . [it has no difficulty obeying] the laws of the earthly city, whereby the things necessary for the maintenance of this mortal life are administered; and thus, as this life is common to both cities, so there is a harmony between them in regard to what belongs to it. . . .

This heavenly city, then, while it exists on earth, calls citizens out of all nations, and gathers together a society of pilgrims of all languages, not caring about diversities in the manners, laws, and institutions whereby earthly peace is secured and maintained, but recognizing that, however various these are, they all tend to one and the same end of earthly peace. It therefore is so far from rescinding and abolishing these diversities, that it even preserves and adopts them, so long only as no hindrance to the worship of the one supreme and true God is thus introduced. Even the heavenly city, therefore, while in its state of pilgrimage, avails itself of the peace of earth, and, so far as it can without injuring faith and godliness, desires and maintains a common agreement among men regarding the acquisition of the necessities of life, and makes this earthly peace bear upon the peace of the reasonable creatures, consisting as it does in the perfectly ordered and harmonious enjoyment of God and of one another in God. When we shall have reached that peace, this mortal life shall give place to one that is eternal, and our body shall be no more this animal body which by its corruption weights down the soul, but a spiritual body feeling no want.

THEME: SOCIAL AND SPIRITUAL VALUES

AGAINST THE GRAIN

Augustine: From Sinner to Saint

The Confessions

SAINT AUGUSTINE

In 399, Augustine wrote the *Confessions*, an account of his life and conversion to Christianity. In the following excerpt, Augustine records his personal struggle to trade the pleasures of the world for the glory of God.

"*The Confessions*"is from Saint Augustine, *The Confessions*, trans. R. S. Pine-Coffin, Book 8.11–8.12 (New York and Harmondsworth, Middlesex: Penguin Books, 1961), pp.156;158-159. Copyright © 1961 R.S. Pine-Coffin. Reprinted by permission of Penguin Books, Ltd.

KEEP IN MIND . . .

6-16. Why did Augustine doubt his commitment to Christ? When he was "on the brink of resolution," what pushed him over the edge?

This was the nature of my sickness. I was in torment, reproaching myself more bitterly than ever as I twisted and turned in my chain. I hoped that my chain might be broken once and for all, because it was only a small thing that held me now. All the same it held me. And you, O Lord, never ceased to watch over my secret heart. In your stern mercy, you lashed me with the twin scourge of fear and shame in case I should give way once more and the worn and slender remnant of my chain should not be broken but gain new strength and bind me all the faster. In my heart I kept saying, "Let it be now, let it be now!", and merely by saying this I was on the point of making it, but I did not succeed. Yet I did not fall back into my old state. I stood on the brink of resolution, waiting to take fresh breath. I tried again and came a little nearer to my goal, and then a little nearer still, so that I could almost reach out and grasp it. But I did not reach it. I could not reach out to it or grasp it because I held back from the step by which I should die to death and become alive to life. My lower instincts, which had taken firm hold of me, were stronger than the higher, which were untried. And the closer I came to the moment which was to mark the great change in me, the more I shrank from its horror. But it did not drive me back or turn me from my purpose: it merely left me hanging in suspense. . . .

> "I probed the hidden depths of my soul and wrung its pitiful secrets from it."
>
> —SAINT AUGUSTINE

I probed the hidden depths of my soul and wrung its pitiful secrets from it, and when I mustered them all before the eyes of my heart, a great storm broke within me, bringing with it a great deluge of tears. . . . Somehow, I flung myself down beneath a fig tree and gave way to the tears which now streamed from my eyes, the sacrifice that is acceptable to you. . . . For I felt that I was still the captive of my sins, and in my misery I kept crying, "How long shall I go on saying 'tomorrow, tomorrow?' Why not now? Why not make an end of my ugly sins at this moment?" . . .

So I hurried back to the place where I had put down the book containing Paul's Epistles. I seized it and opened it and in silence I read the first passage on which my eyes fell: *Not in reveling and drunkenness, not in lust and wantonness, not in quarrels and rivalries. Rather, arm yourselves with the Lord Jesus Christ; spend no more thought on nature and nature's appetites.* I had no wish to read more and no need to do so. For in an instant, as I came to the end of the sentence, it was as though the light of confidence flooded into my heart and all the darkness of doubt was dispelled.

CONSIDER THIS:

6-17. Why did Augustine have such difficulty in committing himself to God? What did this commitment mean?

6-18. In Augustine's process of conversion to Christianity, Paul's *Epistles* were of great importance. What did Paul mean when he said "arm yourselves with the Lord Jesus Christ; spend no more thought on nature and nature's appetites"? Why did Augustine have to reject "nature's appetites"? Does this seem "unnatural"? Why must there be a higher standard of commitment and even sacrifice to do God's work?

The Triumph of Christianity

On decree of the emperor Galerius in 311 C.E., Christianity proceeded from a persecuted to a tolerated sect. The emperor Constantine next raised Christianity to a favored position but still continued to erect pagan temples and was not formally baptized until he was on his deathbed in 337. After an unsuccessful attempt to revive paganism under the emperor Julian the Apostate in 360, Christianity finally became the official religion of the Roman Empire under Theodosius the Great in 392.

In the Early Middle Ages from about 500 to 1000, the church struggled to maintain unity and purity of doctrine against the threat of heresy and the contending authority of the Byzantine emperor, who exercised secular control over the Christian church in the East. The authority of the pope (technically, the bishop of Rome) as universal leader of Christianity was established in the Western church by Matthew 16:18: "And I say to you, that you are Peter, and upon this rock I will build my church; and the gates of hell shall not prevail against it. And I will give to you the keys to the Kingdom of Heaven." According to the pope's interpretation of this verse, which was disputed by the patriarchs of the East, Rome was the center of Christianity, and he was the successor to Saint Peter, the Vicar of Christ and the direct authority for the will of God. The Petrine theory is explained in the first selection by Pope Leo I (440–461).

The second reading is an oath from an English bishop named Boniface. His commitment to the doctrine of papal supremacy expresses the ideal of devotion.

The Petrine Theory

POPE LEO I

Col. 628: Our Lord Jesus Christ, the Savior of the world, caused his truth to be promulgated through the apostles. And while this duty was placed on all the apostles, the Lord made Saint Peter the head of them all, that from him as from their head his gifts should flow out into all the body. So that if anyone separates himself from Saint Peter he should know that he has no share in the divine blessing.

Col. 995: Constantinople has its own glory and by the mercy of God has become the seat of the empire. But secular matters are based on one thing, ecclesiastical matters on another. For nothing will stand which is not built on the rock [Peter] which the Lord laid in the foundation. . . .

Col. 1031: You will learn with what reverence the bishop of Rome treats the rules and canons of the church if you read my letters by which I resisted the ambition of the patriarch of Constantinople, and you will see also that I am the guardian of the catholic faith and of the decrees of the church fathers.

Col. 615: We have the care of all the churches, and the Lord, who made Peter the prince of the apostles, holds us responsible for it.

Col. 881: It is reasonable and just that the holy Roman church, through Saint Peter, the prince of the apostles, is the head of all the churches of the whole world.

Col. 147: In my humble person he [Peter] should be seen and honored who has the care over all the shepherds and the sheep committed to him, and whose dignity is not lacking in me, his heir, although I am unworthy.

"The Petrine Theory" is from Oliver Thatcher and Edgar McNeal, eds., *A Source Book of Medieval History* (New York: Charles Scribner's Sons, 1905), pp. 85–86.

Loyalty to the Pope: Oath to Gregory II (723 C.E.)

BISHOP BONIFACE

I, Boniface, by the grace of God bishop, promise thee, Saint Peter, prince of the apostles, and thy vicar, blessed pope Gregory, and his successors, through the Father, Son, and Holy Spirit, the inseparable Trinity, . . . that I will hold the holy Catholic faith in all its purity, and by the help of God I will remain in unity with it, without which there is no salvation. I will in no way consent to anyone who acts against the unity of the church, but, as I have said, I will preserve the purity of my faith and give my support to thee [Saint Peter] and to thy church, to which God has given the power of binding and loosing, and to thy vicar, and to his successors. And if I find out that any bishops are acting contrary to the ancient rules of the holy fathers, I will have no communion or association with them, but I will restrain them as far as I can. But if I cannot restrain them I will report it at once to my lord the pope. And if I shall ever in any way, by any deceit, or under any pretext, act contrary to this my promise, I shall be found guilty in the day of judgment, and shall suffer the punishment. . . . This text of my oath, I, Boniface, unworthy bishop, have written with my own hand, and have placed it over the most holy body of Saint Peter; before God as my witness and judge, I have taken this oath, which also I promise to keep.

COMPARE AND CONTRAST:

6-19. Explain the Petrine Theory and analyze its purpose. In the excerpt by Leo I, the pope is viewed as the shepherd and the Christian community as the sheep committed to him. Compare this with Saint Cyprian's view that Christians should "rival lambs and sheep in their meekness and gentleness." Why was the image of this relationship important to the structure of early Christianity?

6-20. How does Bishop Boniface in his oath to Pope Gregory II exemplify Christian obedience and humility?

"Loyalty to the Pope: Oath to Gregory II" is from Oliver Thatcher and Edgar McNeal, eds., *A Source Book of Medieval History* (New York: Charles Scribner's Sons, 1905), pp. 93–95.

Chapter 7

The Pax Romana and the Decline of Rome

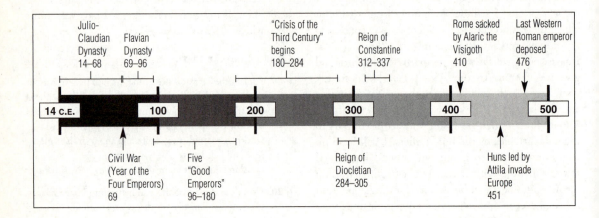

But you, Roman, must remember that you have to guide nations by your authority, for this is to be your skill, to graft tradition onto peace, to show mercy to the conquered, and to wage war until the arrogant are brought low.

—VIRGIL, THE AENEID

As yourselves, your empires fall. And every kingdom hath a grave.

—WILLIAM HOBBINGTON

We can destroy ourselves by cynicism and disillusionment just as effectively as by bombs.

—KENNETH CLARK

Civilization is a stream with banks. The stream is sometimes filled with blood from people killing, stealing, shouting and doing things historians usually record, while on the banks, unnoticed, people build homes, make love, raise children, sing songs, [and] write poetry. . . . The history of civilization is the story of what happened on the banks.

—WILL AND ARIEL DURANT

CHAPTER THEMES

- **The Power Structure:** The system of government instituted by Augustus, called the "principate," functioned as a complex blend of power and authority. How well did his successors as emperors of Rome maintain his system of rule? Is freedom most importantly a thing of the mind? If the institutions of government are controlled, yet *appear* to be free, and if you *feel* that you are free, are you free?

- **Imperialism:** How did the Romans control their empire? Were they efficient rulers who were respected by their subjects? Is imperialism that results in political and social stability necessarily a bad thing?

- **Revolution and Historical Transition:** What were the components of Roman decline? Did the Romans make specific mistakes, or is decline a natural and inevitable fate of each society? How much can a society change and adapt before it loses the elements that initially gave it purpose and success?

- **The Big Picture:** Is each civilization biological in nature, and does it have a "life span" like human beings? What are the most important remnants of one civilization that form the seeds of the succeeding civilization?

The Roman Republic had once been hailed as a progressive society of balance and restraint, where freedom was guaranteed by law and defended with the blood of those committed to such ideals. Yet during the first century B.C.E., the Republic was destroyed, a victim of extremist political factions, domestic dissension, and violence. Roman armies, which had once silenced foreign foes, became the preserve of generals who were committed more to their personal advancement than to the security of the state. The Republic died amid the clash of civil war, and in its place flourished a "restored Republic," the principate of Augustus.

The Augustan principate was designed to establish and maintain peace and harmony in the state. The institutions of the Republic were retained; people voted in the assemblies, senators vied for office and discussed issues in much the same way as they had done for years. Augustus, in his role as princeps (first citizen), merely advised the senate on issues that he thought were important for the welfare of the empire. But because the army was loyal to him and represented the true power in the state, Augustus's opinions and suggestions assumed the greatest importance. Yet Augustus maintained a political equilibrium by stressing his authority, not his blatant military power. He respected the dignity of the senators and their need to feel as if they actually controlled the government; in return, they generally supported his political solutions to deal with the chaos of the Roman Republic. And although some senators grumbled and decried this facade of freedom, the system nevertheless worked for over 200 years. Those succeeding emperors who played the game well, respected the dignity of the senate, and maintained control of the army usually survived and prospered. Those who did not, such as the emperors Caligula and Domitian, were assassinated.

Because the Augustan system of government brought political security to the state, the Roman Empire flourished in peace, a universal peace known as the Pax Romana. It was during this time that the city of Rome served as the emporium of the world. All roads indeed ended sooner or later in the center of the magnificent city, whose population swelled to a million inhabitants. To hail from the provinces of the empire and to see Rome for the first time must have been a numbing experience. The theaters, baths, sewers, aqueducts, and monuments provided services and entertainment on a magnificent scale. And the spectacle was even more impressive in the Coliseum, where gladiators fought, or in the Circus Maximus, where over 250,000 people could thrill to the chariot races.

Outside the city, a road system was built that connected the provinces of the empire and unified Europe as never before. The provincials were allowed to retain their own customs, languages, and religions; all Rome demanded in return were taxes and peace. It is testament to the loyalty and satisfaction of provincial subjects that Rome maintained the security of its enormous empire with only about 350,000 soldiers.

Still, perhaps the greatest failure in Western civilization was Rome's inability to sustain its hegemony. Confronted with political, social, and economic dislocation in the third century C.E., Rome struggled to survive. External pressures by Germanic tribes also took their toll on an increasingly overburdened army that no longer reflected the efficiency and tenacity of the famous Roman legions. The Roman Empire declined gradually, losing its unity and organization by the fifth century C.E. The eternal question is, why?

This chapter evaluates the Roman Empire during its era of strength and its period of decline. This is a particularly relevant chapter because many have compared Roman society to American society. Some have thus viewed Roman civilization as a laboratory in which we might see the seeds of our own destruction. But what are the components of greatness and decline? And can we ascertain our position along the way? Rome has many lessons to offer that continue to make its history important and meaningful.

FIGURE 7.1 This contemporary view of the Roman Forum from the Palatine Hill, which contained the palaces of the emperors, can now only hint at the majesty of the great capital of the Roman Empire and the busy "emporium of the world." (*Perry M. Rogers*)

KEY EVENTS DURING THE EARLY ROMAN EMPIRE

27 B.C.E.–14 C.E.   The Principate of Augustus

Augustus "restores" the Roman Republic yet controls it as emperor through his authority and military power.

14–68 C.E.   The Julio-Claudian Dynasty

Augustus's vision of the principate is maintained in spite of problems within this dysfunctional family (Tiberius, Caligula, Claudius, Nero).

66–70   The Jewish War

Jewish rebellion crushed by Titus after the siege of the fortress at Masada. Temple destroyed in Jerusalem, and the Arch of Titus commemorating the victory erected in the Roman forum. A final Jewish rebellion is led by Simon Bar-Kochba and brutally suppressed in 135.

68–69 Year of the Four Emperors

Civil war results in suicide of Nero and power struggle eventually won by Vespasian, who establishes the Flavian dynasty.

69–96 Flavian Dynasty

Generally progressive dynasty emerges from the civil war of 69. Vespasian and his sons, Titus and Domitian, are competent rulers, though Domitian will be assassinated in 96. The Coliseum is erected in Rome. Eruption of Mt. Vesuvius destroys Pompeii and Herculaneum (79).

96–180 The Five Adoptive Emperors

Also called the "Good Emperors" (Nerva, Trajan, Hadrian, Antoninus Pius, Marcus Aurelius), these rulers expand the Roman Empire and preside over the Pax Romana. Succession is based on an adoptive principle of choosing a leader who will maintain the efficiency and stability of the state. Breaks down with accession of Commodus, son of Marcus Aurelius (180–193).

Strength and Success (14–180 C.E.)

Political and Military Control

The Augustan system of government generally functioned well during the first century C.E., outlasting bad emperors and a brief civil war, and prospering especially during the reigns of Tiberius, Claudius, and Vespasian. Rome's greatest achievement during this period was the establishment of peace throughout the empire, which was maintained by an efficient and dedicated army.

The Imperial Army

FLAVIUS JOSEPHUS

If one goes on to study the organization of [the Roman] army as a whole, it will be seen that this vast empire of theirs has come to them as the prize of valor, and not as a gift of fortune. For they do not wait for the outbreak of war, nor do they sit with folded hands in peacetime only to put them in motion in the hour of need. On the contrary, as though they had been born with weapons in hand, they never have a truce from training, never wait for the emergencies to arise. Moreover, their peacetime maneuvers are no less strenuous than veritable warfare; each soldier daily throws all his energy into his drill, as though he were in action. Hence that perfect ease with which they sustain the shock of battle. . . .

The Romans never lay themselves open to a surprise attack. That is because no matter what hostile territory they may invade, they never engage in battle until they have fortified their camp. . . . Thus, an improvised city, as it were, springs up, with its market place, its artisan quarter, its judgment seats, where officers adjudicate any differences which may arise. The outer wall and all the installations within are completed more quickly than thought, so numerous and skilled are the workmen. . . .

Once entrenched, the soldiers take up their quarters in their tents by companies, quietly and in good order. All their fatigue duties are performed with the same discipline, the same regard for security: the procuring of wood, of food supplies, and water, as

"The Imperial Army" is from Josephus, *The Jewish War*, trans. H. St. J. Thackery, 3.5.71–107, in the Loeb Classical Library (Cambridge, MA: Harvard University Press, 1927), pp. 597, 599, 601, 603, 605.

required—each company having its allotted task. The hour for supper and breakfast is not left to individual discretion; all take their meals together. The hours for sleep, sentinel duty, and rising are announced by the sound of trumpets; nothing is done without a word of command. At daybreak the rank and file report to their respective centurions, the centurions go to salute the tribunes, the tribunes with all the officers then wait on the commander-in-chief, and he gives them according to custom the watchword and other orders to be communicated to the lower ranks. The same precision is maintained on the battlefield; the troops wheel smartly round in the requisite direction, and, whether advancing to the attack or retreating, all move as a unit.

When it is time to break camp, the trumpet sounds a first call and men instantly go to work by striking the tents and making all ready for departure. The trumpets sound a second call to prepare the march; at once they pile their baggage on the mules and other beasts of burden, and stand ready to start. . . . They then set fire to the encampment, both because they can easily construct another . . . and to prevent the enemy from ever making use of it. A third time the trumpets give a similar signal for departure, to hasten the movements of stragglers, whatever the reason for their delay, and to ensure that none is out of his place in the ranks. Then the herald, standing on the right of the commander, inquires in their native tongue whether they are ready for war. Three times they loudly and lustily shout in reply, "We are ready," some even anticipating the question; and worked up to a kind of martial frenzy, they raise their right arms in the air along with the shout. . . .

The infantry are armed with cuirasses and helmets and carry a sword on either side; that on the left is far the longer of the two, the dagger on the right being no longer than the span of the forearm. The picked infantry, forming the general's guard, carry a spear and round shield, the regiments of the line a javelin and oblong shield; the equipment of the latter includes, further, a saw, a basket, a pick, and an axe, not to mention a strap, a bill-hook, a chain, and three days' rations, so that an infantry man is almost as heavily laden as a pack mule. . . .

By their military exercises the Romans instill into their soldiers fortitude not only of body but also of soul; fear, too, plays its part in their training. For they have laws which punish with death not merely desertion but even a slight neglect of duty. And their generals are held in even greater awe than the laws. For the high honors with which they reward the brave prevent the offenders whom they punish from regarding themselves as treated cruelly.

This perfect discipline with regard to their generals makes the army an ornament of peacetime, and in battle welds the whole into a single body; so compact are their ranks, so alert their movements in turning, so quick their ears for orders, their eyes for signals, their hands for tasks. Prompt as they consequently ever are in action, none are slower than they in succumbing to suffering, and never have they been known in any predicament to be beaten by numbers, by ruses, by difficulties of terrain, or even by fortune—for victory is more certain for them than fortune.

A Roman Triumph

ZONARAS

Now the celebration of a military victory which they call a triumph was somewhat as follows. When any great success worthy of a triumph had been gained, the general was immediately saluted as imperator by the soldiers. . . . On arriving home he would assemble the senate and ask to have the triumph voted him.

And if he obtained a vote from the senate and from the people, his title of imperator was confirmed. . . .

Arrayed in the triumphal dress and wearing armlets, with a laurel crown upon his head, and holding a branch in his right hand, he called together the people. After praising collectively the troops who had served

"A Roman Triumph" is from Zonaras, Dio Cassius, *Roman History*, trans. Earnest Cary, vol. 1, 7.21, in the Loeb Classical Library (Cambridge, MA: Harvard University Press, 1914), pp. 193, 195, 197, 199, 201.

with him, and some of them individually, he presented them with money and honored them also with decorations. Upon some he bestowed armlets and spears without the iron; to others he gave crowns, sometimes of gold, sometimes of silver, bearing the name of each man and the representation of his particular feat. . . . And these rewards were not only given to men singly, as the result of individual deeds of prowess, but were also bestowed upon whole companies and legions. A large part of the spoils also was assigned to the soldiers who had taken part in the campaign; but some victors have distributed the spoils even among the entire populace and have devoted them toward the expenses of the festival or turned them over to the treasury. . . .

After these ceremonies the triumphant general would mount his chariot. Now this chariot did not resemble one used in games or in war, but was fashioned in the shape of a round tower. And he would not be alone in the chariot, but if he had children or relatives, he would make the girls and the infant male children get up beside him in it and place the older ones upon the horses. . . . If there were many of them, they would accompany the procession on chargers, riding along beside the victor. . . . Thus arrayed, they entered the city, having at the head of the procession the spoils and trophies and figures representing the captured forts, cities, mountains, rivers, lakes, and seas—everything, in fact, that they had taken. If one day did not suffice for the exhibition of these things in procession, the celebration was held during a second and a third day. When these adjuncts had gone on their way, the victorious general arrived at the Roman Forum, and after commanding that some of the captives be led to prison and put to death, he rode up to the Capitol. There he performed certain rites and made offerings and dined in the porticoes up there, after which he departed homeward towards evenings, accompanied by flutes and pipes. Such were the triumphs in [Republican] times.

CONSIDER THIS:

7-1. According to Josephus and Zonaras, why was the Roman military successful in maintaining the Pax Romana? What benefits could troops expect from the state and their generals?

Imperial Patronage

PLINY THE YOUNGER

Essential to the welfare of provincial communities was imperial support from Rome itself. We have a rare opportunity to view the affairs of one province in particular. The governor of Bithynia (near the Black Sea) was a man named Pliny the Younger. His letters to the emperor Trajan, in about 112 C.E., depict a close relationship that resulted in improvements for the province. Note, however, Trajan's reluctance to support an organized group of firemen. The emperor was wary of the potential force for organized rebellion masked by such a seemingly innocent facade.

Pliny to Trajan: The people of Prusa, Sire, have a public bath in a neglected and dilapidated state. They wish—with your kind permission—to restore it; but I think a new one ought to be built, and I reckon you can safely comply with their wishes.

Trajan to Pliny: If the building of a new bath will not cripple the finances of Prusa, we can indulge their

wishes; only it must be understood that no new taxes are to be raised to meet the cost, and that their contributions for necessary expenses shall not show any falling off.

Pliny to Trajan: A desolating fire broke out in Nicomedia, and destroyed a number of private houses, and two public buildings—the almshouse and the temple of Isis—although a road ran

"Imperial Patronage" is from Pliny the Younger, *Letters*, 10.25 ff., in *Readings in Ancient History*, ed. William S. Davis, vol. 2 (Boston: Allyn and Bacon, 1913), pp. 215–217.

between them. The fire was allowed to spread farther than necessary, first owing to the violent wind, and second, to the laziness of the citizens—they stood by without moving and simply watched the conflagration. Besides, there was not a single public fire engine or bucket in the place, and not one solitary appliance for mastering a fire. However, these will be provided upon orders I have already given. But, Sire, I would have you consider whether you think a fire company of about 150 men ought not to be formed? I will take care that no one who is not a genuine fireman shall be admitted. Again, there would be no trouble in keeping an eye on so small a body.

Trajan to Pliny: You have formed the idea of a possible fire company at Nicomedia on the model of various others already existing; but remember that the province of Bithynia, and especially city states like Nicomedia, are the prey of factions. Give them whatever name we want, and however good are the reasons for organization, such associations will soon degenerate into [dangerous] secret societies. It is better policy to provide fire apparatus, and to encourage property holders to make use of them, and if need comes, press the crowd which collects into the same service.

Pliny to Trajan: Sire, the people of Nicomedia spent 3,229,000 sesterces upon an aqueduct, which was left in an unfinished state, and I may say in ruin, and they also levied taxes to the extent of 2,000,000 sesterces for a second one. This, too, has been abandoned, and to get a water supply those who have wasted these vast sums must go to a new expense. I have visited a splendid clear spring, from which it seems to me the supply ought to be brought to the town [and have formed a scheme that seems practicable].

Trajan to Pliny: Steps must certainly be taken to provide Nicomedia with a water supply; and I have full confidence you will undertake the duty with all due care. But I profess it is also part of your diligent duty to find out who is to blame for the waste of such sums of money by the people of Nicomedia on their aqueducts, and whether or not there has been any serving of private interests in this beginning and then abandoning of [public] works. See that you bring to my knowledge whatever you find out.

Techniques of Roman Control

TACITUS

Imperial patronage and good will depended on the maintenance of peace in the provinces. The Roman army was an efficient fighting machine that had the responsibility not only to protect the empire from external invasion but also to quell any internal disturbance. Successful governors were not heavy-handed when they brought stability to a region, but sought ways to win the loyalty of the inhabitants, as the following selection indicates. Agricola, a successful general, has just assumed his responsibilities as governor of Britain in 78 C.E.

Agricola, by the repression of abuses in his very first year of office, restored to peace its good name. When summer came and he assembled his forces, he continually showed himself in the ranks, praised good discipline, and kept the stragglers in order. He would himself choose the position of the camp, himself explore the estuaries and forests. Meanwhile he would allow the enemy no rest, laying waste his territory with sudden incursions, and, having sufficiently alarmed him, would then by [clemency] display the allurements of peace. In consequence, many states, which up to that time had been independent, gave hostages, and laid

---

"Techniques of Roman Control" is from Tacitus, *Agricola*, 20–21, trans. Alfred Church and William Brodribb (New York: Macmillan, 1877).

aside their animosities; garrisons and forts were established among them with a skill and diligence with which no newly-acquired part of Britain had before been treated.

The following winter passed without disturbance. . . . Agricola gave private encouragement and public aid to the building of temples, courts of justice and dwelling-houses, praising the energetic, and reproving the indolent. Thus honorable rivalry took the place of compulsion. He likewise provided a liberal education for the sons of the chiefs. . . . Hence, too, a liking

sprang up for our style of dress, and the "toga" became fashionable. Step by step [the Britons] were led to things which dispose to vice: the lounge, the bath, the elegant banquet. All this in their ignorance, they called civilization, when it was but a part of their servitude.

CONSIDER THIS:

7-2. Was the relationship of Rome to its provinces generally a good one? If so, what made the Romans good rulers? On balance, what were the benefits of living in the provinces under Roman control?

THEME: THE POWER STRUCTURE

THE HISTORIAN AT WORK—TACITUS

The Murder of Agrippina

Cornelius Tacitus (56?–117 C.E.) was one of the greatest historians in antiquity. Just as Titus Livy was the dominant historian of Rome's early and middle Republic, Tacitus is our most important source for the history of the Roman Empire under the Julio-Claudian emperors in the first century C.E.

Little is known about Tacitus's life and career. He was probably born into an aristocratic Roman family in southern France, studied rhetoric in Rome, and excelled at oratory. He married into a distinguished Roman family and became a member of the senate. His father-in-law was the great general, Agricola, and this marriage gave Tacitus access to important sources of information and to a class of people who defended and administered the Roman Empire under the Flavian dynasty from 68–96 and the Adoptive Emperors from 98 until his death in 117. Tacitus wrote a famous biographical tribute to Agricola in 98, followed by his important ethnographic study of the Germanic tribes entitled *Germania*. His *Histories* cover the period of the civil wars after the death of Nero in 68 until the emergence of the Flavian dynasty under Vespasian in 69.

But he saved his most important and concentrated effort for last. His *Annals*, published in the year of his death, is a history of the Julio-Claudian dynasty from Augustus's death in 14 C.E. through the reigns of Tiberius, Caligula, Claudius, and Nero. Originally comprised of sixteen books, a large portion was lost over the years, and we have had to rely on other, lesser historians and biographers to fill in the many gaps.

Nevertheless, Tacitus proves his worth through a cogent analysis of events at the Julio-Claudian court. This was a dysfunctional family that intermarried for political gain and fought among themselves for power and ultimate supremacy. It is a story of deceit, greed, ruthless ambition, madness, and immorality, set amid a background of imperial stability as the Pax Romana spread throughout the Mediterranean world. Augustus may have fashioned the survival of the Roman state by guiding it from a failed republic to new heights

"The Murder of Agrippina" is from Tacitus, *Annals*, 14.1–14.10, 14.13, trans. Alfred Church and William Brodribb (New York: Macmillan, 1877). Translation modernized by the editor.

through the creation and management of the principate, but Tacitus saw right through the deceit of a "sham republic" and alerted his readers to the despotic and authoritarian foundations of Roman power. True freedom ultimately was sacrificed to a new vision of "perceived freedom," and Tacitus lamented the destruction of the values that made Rome great.

The following excerpt from the *Annals* goes right to this issue as the emperor Nero, tired of his controlling and scheming mother, Agrippina, decides to have her murdered. Tacitus's prose style is measured and complex, and his narrative power remains unsurpassed.

The historian Cluvius tells us that Agrippina in her eagerness to control her son Nero went so far as to adorn herself suggestively and at midday, when Nero was already drunk with wine and feasting, sidled up to her son and offered him her body. Agrippina's relatives had earlier observed her wanton kisses and caresses with great concern. They saw the handwriting on the wall, but it was Nero's tutor and advisor, Seneca, who decided to turn to the freedwoman, Acte, for a solution. Seneca hurried her into the room and at her own peril she let loose at Nero, telling him that incest was forbidden, and though his mother might boast of it, the soldiers would never approve of such an impious ruler.

The historian Fabius Rusticus tells us that it was not Agrippina, but Nero who lusted for the crime that was interrupted by the fast-thinking Acte. Cluvius's account, however, is accepted by most other historians and people generally believe it. That Agrippina really conceived of such forbidden wickedness in her heart or not is hard to ascertain, but remember that such strange passion seemed rather credible in a woman who when young allowed herself to be seduced by Lepidus in the hope of achieving power. She had demonstrated her remarkable ambition once again by giving herself to the influential freedman, Pallas, who ran the emperor Claudius' court administration. Agrippina had trained herself for power by using all her infamous wiles, especially in arranging a marriage to her own uncle Claudius.

Nero accordingly avoided any private discussions with her and when Agrippina withdrew to her estates at Tusculum or Antium, praised her for taking time to relax. At last, Nero became convinced that she was too powerful a threat no matter

where she lived. So he set out to destroy her, merely deliberating whether the murder should be accomplished by poison, the sword, or some other violent method. Poison at first seemed the best option, but . . . Agrippina had prepared herself for that threat through the accumulation of antidotes. . . .

One of Nero's trusted advisors by the name of Anicetus, who was also commander of the fleet at Misenum and had been Nero's boyhood tutor, had always hated Agrippina as much as she hated him. Well, he had a great idea that they could build a ship with a device that, once it set out to sea, could be activated to collapse the ship and kill Agrippina in the process. "Nothing," he said, "is more natural than an accident at sea. That she should die of a shipwreck caused by the wind and the waves would never be considered suspicious. Then you as emperor could honor your deceased mother with the construction of temples and shrines and every other display of your filial affection."

Nero liked this idea. Especially so because he was currently celebrating a five-day festival for Minerva at Baiae. So Nero asked his mother to attend the festival noting that children ought to be more tolerant and respectful of their parents, thus demonstrating his desire to reconcile with her. Agrippina bought it. As she approached, Nero welcomed her with outstretched hands and a close embrace and he took her to his country house that was located right on the bay at Baiae. . . .

Here the "collapsible ship" remained docked, ready to return Agrippina back home after a banquet that night. All this was set up to conceal the crime. Now it appears that Agrippina had gotten wind of the plot, and as she was conveyed to the banquet in her litter was not sure what to believe.

Once there, Nero's soothing words and gracious reception allayed her fears. Agrippina sat in an honored position near the emperor. Nero prolonged the banquet with stimulating conversation, both serious at times, and light with an air of youthful familiarity. After an enjoyable evening, Nero escorted his mother as she departed the banquet, clinging to her with kisses to her eyes and breasts, either to crown his hypocrisy or because the last sight of his mother on the eve of her destruction caused some hesitation even in that brutal heart.

The stars were brilliant that night and the gods granted the calm of a tranquil sea as if to condone the crime. Agrippina was enjoying the company of two of her favorite attendants, Crepereius Ballus, who stood near the helm and Acceronia, who was reclining at Agrippina's feet. Nero's mother spoke joyfully of her son's repentance and his new attitude that signaled her recovered influence. The ship had not gone far when the signal was given to activate the device. The ceiling immediately gave way under the load of a large quantity of lead bars and Crepereius was crushed and killed right away. Agrippina and Acceronia were protected by the projecting sides of the couch and nobody knew what was happening, not even the conspirators who expected the vessel to break up and sink. The conspirators among the crew then rushed to one side in order to sink it, but this was counteracted by the majority of the crew who weren't in the plot and then worked to stabilize the ship. The result was that instead of a violent collapse, both Agrippina and Acceronia were dumped into the water. Acceronia, apparently unable to swim, started yelling that she was Agrippina and desperately asked the crew to save the emperor's mother. She was immediately beaten to death by the crew with poles and oars. Agrippina watched everything silently and in the confusion wasn't recognized. She had received a wound to her shoulder, but was able to swim to some small boats that took her to shore where she then made it to her house.

Agrippina now understood everything. She reflected on the deceitful invitation to the banquet with its pretended honor as a lure, how close she had been to shore, too close for a shipwreck by

dangerous winds or unseen rocks, how the vessel had collapsed from the top down as if a mechanism had been tripped intentionally rather than by any unforeseen nautical problem. She also pondered the death of Acceronia. . . . Then she sent her freedman Agerinus to tell Nero how by the grace of the gods and his good fortune, she had escaped a terrible disaster. She begged him, alarmed by his mother's close brush with death as any son would be, not to come to her now as she needed rest. . . .

> Acceronia . . . started yelling that she was Agrippina and desperately asked the crew to save the emperor's mother. She was immediately beaten to death. . . .
>
> —TACITUS

Nero, meanwhile, was waiting for news of her death and when he was told that she escaped with only a slight wound, he knew there would be no question in Agrippina's mind of his guilt. Paralyzed with terror that she would hunt him down for her vengeance by arming the slaves or stirring up the soldiers, or even going to the senate and the people to charge him with attempted murder and the destruction of her friends, Nero went berserk and pleaded for advice. He at once summoned his trusted tutors and advisors, Seneca and Burrus, who was also Praetorian Guard commander. . . . Burrus argued that the Guard would support Agrippina, since she was the daughter of their famous favorite, Germanicus. It was left to the fleet commander, Anicetus, who had devised the scheme, to make good on his promise of Agrippina's death. Anicetus said he was up to the task. "Go," Nero said, "as fast as you can and take as many men as you need to execute her. . . ."

Once Agrippina's danger was known to the people of Baiae, they walked down to the beach with torches, praying, crying, and hoping. When all knew that she was safe, they prepared to wish her joy, but were frightened and sent away by the force of armed soldiers just arriving. Anicetus then surrounded Agrippina's house, burst open the gates and brushed away the slaves who met them until he came to the door of her bedchamber. . . .

Anicetus, together with a century of his marines, confronted Agrippina. "If," she said, "you have come to check up on me, tell the emperor that I have recovered. But, if you are here to commit a crime, then it can't be on the orders of my son, for he would not sanction his own mother's murder." The assassins closed in round her and a captain smashed her head with a club. Then, as the centurion bared his sword for the kill, Agrippina turned square and exclaimed, "Cut my womb open," and was killed with a rain of blows.

> Agrippina turned square and exclaimed, "Cut my womb open," and was killed with a rain of blows.
> —TACITUS

So far, our accounts agree. Some have said at this point that Nero gazed on his mother after her death and praised her beauty, while others deny it. Her body was cremated that same night without any attention. . . . Many years before, Agrippina had anticipated this death herself and had denied the possibility. For when she consulted the astrologers about Nero, they replied that he would kill his mother. "Let him kill me," she said, "provided he is emperor!"

CONSIDER THIS:

7-3. Tacitus's account of Agrippina's murder is a focused and tightly constructed story that demonstrates his narrative skill. But it also has a moral purpose. What does he think of Agrippina and Nero? A normal family is bound together by the ties of love—what divides Nero and his mother? What motivates both characters?

7-4. Is Tacitus a discerning historian who critically assesses his sources and seeks the truth methodically? Or does he seem to enjoy wallowing in the details of illicit and scandalous rumors? Give specific examples from the text to support your ideas. Is Tacitus a responsible historian?

7-5. What is Tacitus's point in writing his history of the Julio-Claudian emperors? What does this excerpt tell us about enlightened imperial rule during the early Roman Empire? Was the efficiency of Roman government dependent on imperial leadership or on the strength of the institutional organization established under Augustus? How can governments survive such myopic and paranoid leadership?

"All Roads Lead to Rome"

The city of Rome was the vibrant center of this extensive empire. It provided services and entertainment to a teeming population of about a million inhabitants from all over the world. The following excerpts reveal the advantages and disadvantages of city life.

The Glory of the City

STRABO

[The Romans] paved the roads, cut through hills, and filled up valleys, so that the merchandise may be conveyed by carriage from the ports. The sewers, arched over with hewn stones, are large enough in parts for actual hay wagons to pass through, while so plentiful is the supply of water from the aqueducts, that rivers may be said to flow through the city and the sewers, and almost every house is furnished with water pipes and copious fountains.

"The Glory of the City" is from Strabo, *Geography*, 5.3.8, in *Readings in Ancient History*, ed. William S. Davis, vol. 2 (Boston: Allyn and Bacon, 1913), pp. 179–181.

We may remark that the ancients [of Republican times] bestowed little attention upon the beautifying of Rome. But their successors, and especially those of our own day, have at the same time embellished the city with numerous and splendid objects. Pompey, the Divine Caesar [i.e., Julius Caesar], and Augustus, with his children, friends, wife, and sister have surpassed all others in their zeal and munificence in these decorations. The greater number of these may be seen in the Campus Martius which to the beauties of nature adds those of art. The size of the plain is remarkable, allowing chariot races and the equestrian sports without hindrance, and multitudes [here] exercise themselves with ball games, in the Circus, and on the wrestling grounds. . . . The summit of the hills beyond the Tiber, extending from its banks with panoramic effect, presents a spectacle which the eye abandons with regret.

Near to this plain is another surrounded with columns, sacred groves, three theaters, an amphitheater, and superb temples, each close to the other, and so splendid that it would seem idle to describe the rest of the city after it. Because of this, the Romans have esteemed it the most sacred place, and have erected funeral monuments there to the illustrious persons of either sex. The most remarkable of these is that called the "Mausoleum" [the tomb of Augustus] which consists of a mound of earth raised upon a high foundation of white marble, situated near the river, and covered on the top with evergreen shrubs. Upon the summit is a bronze statue of Augustus Caesar, and beneath the mound are the funeral urns of himself, his relatives, and his friends. Behind is a large grove containing charming promenades. . . . If then you proceed to visit the ancient Forum, which is equally filled with basilicas, porticoes, and temples, you will there behold the Capitol, the Palatine, and the noble works that adorn them, and the piazza of Livia [Augustus's Empress],— each successive work causing you speedily to forget that which you have seen before. Such then is Rome!

FIGURE 7.2 A view of the Arch of Titus and the magnificent Roman Coliseum beyond. Each successive building "caused you speedily to forget that which you have seen before. Such then is Rome!"— Strabo. (*Perry M. Rogers*)

The Artistic Vision

The Roman Aqueduct Pont du Gard

The magnificence of Rome and its reputation as "emporium to the world" showed through its impressive architecture. The imposing majesty of the Coliseum and the Circus Maximus, the Pantheon, law courts, and triumphal arches—all testified to the consolidation of Roman power. This massive architecture was designed to dazzle, even as the buildings provided practical services for the people of Rome.

But Roman architecture was most importantly based on a Roman engineering genius. Roads, some of which are still used today, linked the empire from the misty forests of Germany in the north to Pontus on the Black Sea and to Alexandria at the mouth of the Nile in Egypt. Just as trade and the defense of Rome relied on this network of roads, so too did the health of the urban population depend on the infrastructure of sewer systems that eliminated waste and reduced disease.

But the most impressive demonstration of Roman engineering genius, the perfect union of form and function, can be found in the magnificent system of aqueducts that transported water for hundreds of miles throughout the Roman Empire. The most famous of these, and perhaps the most majestic of all Roman ruins, was the Pont du Gard in southern France. It was constructed beginning about 20 B.C.E. by Marcus Agrippa, a general and close friend of the emperor Augustus, to transport water down a carefully calculated grade

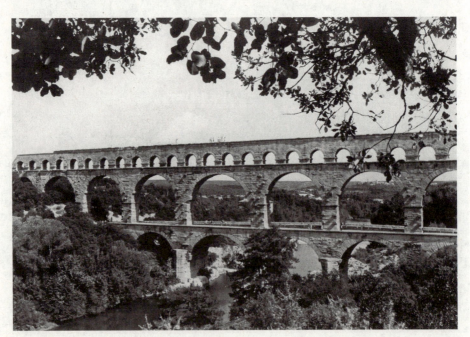

FIGURE 7.3 The Pont du Gard, perhaps the most majestic of all Roman ruins, was an aqueduct that carried water through southern France. The provinces were thus served by Roman engineering genius. (*Perry M. Rogers*)

FIGURE 7.4 Pont du Gard detail. (*Perry M. Rogers*)

to the city of Nimes across the river Gard from a natural spring almost fifty kilometers to the north. Rome itself was supplied by several aqueducts that brought water directly into the emperor's apartments on the Palatine Hill and to the imposing Baths of Caracalla.

CONSIDER THIS:

7-6. What was the function of a Roman aqueduct? What are the most evident architectural components of the Pont du Gard?

7-7. Why might the Pont du Gard be considered a perfect union of form and function in Roman architecture? In what ways was it both a necessary part of the infrastructure serving the needs of the public and an artistic expression of Roman stability and power?

The Magnificence of the Baths

LUCIAN

The following descriptions by the philosopher Seneca and the satirist and rhetorician Lucian about 150 C.E. help us appreciate what an integral part the baths played in the social life of Rome and its provinces—all made possible by great aqueducts like the Pont du Gard.

On entering [the baths], one is received into a public hall of good size, with ample accommodation for servants and attendants. On the left are the lounging rooms, also of just the right sort for a bath, attractive, brightly lighted retreats. Then, beside them, a hall, larger than need be for the purposes of a bath, but necessary for the reception of richer persons. Next, . . . locker rooms to undress in, on each side, with a very high and brilliantly lighted hall between them, in which are three swimming pools of cold water; it is finished in Laconian marble, and has two statues of white marble in the ancient style. . . .

On leaving this hall, you come into another which is slightly warmed instead of meeting you at once with fierce heat; it is oblong, and has an apse on each side. Next to it, on the right, is a very bright hall, nicely fitted up for massage, which has on each side an entrance decorated with Phrygian marble, and receives those who come in from the exercising floor. Then near this is another hall, the most beautiful in the world, in which one can stand or sit with comfort, linger without danger, and stroll about with profit. It also is resplendent with Phrygian marble clear to the roof. Next comes the hot corridor, faced with Numidian marble. The hall beyond it is very beautiful, full of abundant light and aglow with color like that of purple hangings. It contains three hot tubs.

When you have bathed, you need not go back through the same rooms, but can go directly to the cold room through a slightly warmed chamber. Everywhere there is copious illumination and full indoor daylight. . . . Why should I go on to tell you of the exercising floor and of the cloak rooms? . . . Moreover, it is beautified with all other marks of thoughtfulness—with two toilets, many exits, and two devices for telling time, a water clock that makes a bellowing sound and a sundial.

The Bath House

SENECA

I live over a bath house. Now picture in your mind such an assortment of voices that the sound is enough to make you sick. When the stronger guys are exercising and swinging heavy leaden weights in their hands, when they are working hard or at least pretending, I hear their groans; and whenever they exhale, I hear their hissing and labored breathing. Whenever I have to put up with some lazy bastard who is happy to get a cheap rubdown, I also have to listen to the changing sounds of the slave's hands (whether the hand is flat or curved) as it beats on his shoulders. If some professional ball player enters and starts keeping score, it's all over for me. Add to this, the arrest of some thug or thief, not to mention the guy who loves to sing in the bath, and those who can't help barreling headlong into the water with a big splash, and you get the idea. And think about those who produce unnatural wailing as they pluck hair while gossiping in a thin and strident voice in order to attract more business. They are never silent except when plucking armpits and make the customer yell instead of themselves. It is disgusting for me to

"The Magnificence of the Baths" is from Lucian, *Hippias*, trans. A. M. Harmon, vol. 1, in the Loeb Classical Library (Cambridge, MA: Harvard University Press, 1913), pp. 39, 41, 43.

"The Bath House" is from Seneca, *Moral Epistles*, 56.1–56.2, trans. Richard Gummere, vol. 1, in the Loeb Classical Library (Cambridge, MA: Harvard University Press, 1917). Translation modernized by the author.

recount the varied cries of the sausage seller, the candy confectioner, and of all the peddlers of the cook shops, who hawk their wares each with his own peculiar intonation.

CONSIDER THIS:

7-8. In what ways did the public bath serve both the hygienic and social needs of the Romans? How important was the aqueduct to the continuity and progress of Roman civilization?

The Dark Side of Rome

JUVENAL

I cannot bear, Romans, a Greek Rome; and yet, how small a portion of our dregs is from Greece! Long since, Syrian Orontes [a river] has flowed into the Tiber, and has brought with it its language and manners. . . . The coming of the Greek has brought us a Jack-of-all-trades—grammarian, rhetorician, geometrician, painter, wrestling manager, prophet, rope-walker, physician, magician—he knows everything. Bid the hungry Greekling go to heaven, he will go. . . . The poor among the Romans ought to have emigrated in a body long ago. Not easily do those emerge from obscurity whose noble qualities are cramped by domestic poverty. But at Rome the attempt is still harder for them; a great price must be paid for a wretched lodging, a great price for slaves' keep, a great price for a modest little dinner. A man is ashamed to dine off earthenware. . . . Here splendor of dress is carried beyond people's means; here something more than is enough is occasionally borrowed from another man's strongbox. This vice is common to all of us; here all of us live in a state of pretentious poverty. In a word, in Rome everything costs money. . . .

Many a sick man dies here from want of sleep, the sickness itself having been produced by undigested food clinging to the fevered stomach. For what rented lodgings allow of sleep? It takes great wealth to sleep in the city. Hence the origin of the disease. The passage of carriages in the narrow winding streets, and the abuse of the drivers of the blocked teams would rob even [the heaviest sleepers] of sleep.

If a social duty calls him, the rich man will be carried through the yielding crowd and will speed over their heads on his huge Liburnian litter bearers; he will read on his way, or write, or even sleep inside, for a litter with closed windows induces sleep. Yet he will arrive before us. We in our hurry are impeded by the wave in front, while the multitude which follows us presses on our back in dense array; one strikes me with his elbow, another with a hard pole, one knocks a beam against my head, another a wine jar. My legs are sticky with mud; before long I am trodden on all sides by large feet, and the hobnails of a soldier stick into my toe. . . .

Observe now the different and varied dangers of the night. What a height it is to the lofty roofs, from which a tile brains you, and how often cracked and broken utensils fall from windows—with what a weight they mark and damage the pavement when they strike it! You are foolish if you go out to supper without making a will. There are just so many fatal chances as there are wakeful windows open at night when you are passing by. Hope, then, and carry this pitiable prayer about with you, that they may be content merely to empty broad wash basins over you.

"Bread and Circuses"

FRONTO

The emperors were very careful not to neglect the basic needs of the inhabitants of Rome. Since an unemployed population was bored and therefore prone to rioting, the emperors promoted building programs that not only enhanced the glory of the city, but also employed the masses. A great number of citizens who could not afford food received free grain from a government welfare program. It was therefore important

"The Dark Side of Rome" is from Juvenal, *Satires*, 3, trans. J. D. Lewis (London: Trubner, 1873). Translation modernized by the editor.

" 'Bread and Circuses' " is from Fronto, *Elements of History*, 17.

that grain ships arrived regularly from Egypt, for a hungry populace was also restless and prone to disturbance. Finally, the people demanded entertainment, and the Roman government responded with gladiatorial games in the Coliseum and chariot races in the Circus Maximus. The Circus was especially popular and could hold 250,000 people at one time—a quarter of the population of Rome! "Bread and Circuses," therefore, produced a balanced harmony in the great city.

It was politically wise for the emperor never to neglect even actors and others who performed on the stage, in the circus and the arena, since he knew that the stability of the Roman people depended on two elements above everything else: the grain supply and the shows. Therefore, the success of the government depends on entertainment as much as on serious things. Even distributions of money directly to the people are less popular than the shows because they appease only the poorest people on the grain dole individually, while the shows keep the entire population of Rome distracted and happy.

"The Give and Take of Death": Gladiatorial Combat

SENECA

By chance I attended a mid-day exhibition, expecting some fun, wit, and relaxation—an exhibition at which men's eyes have a rest from the slaughter of their fellowmen. But it was quite the reverse. The previous combats were the essence of compassion; but now all the trifling is put aside and it is pure murder. The men have no defensive armor. They are exposed to blows at all points, and no one ever strikes in vain. . . . In the morning they throw men to the lions and the bears; at noon, they throw them to the spectators. The spectators demand that the killer shall face the man who is to kill him in his turn; and they always reserve the "winner" for a later butchering. The outcome of every fight is death, and the means are fire and sword. This sort of thing goes on while the arena is empty. You may respond: "But he was a highway robber; he killed a man!" And what of it? Granted that, as a murderer, he deserved this punishment, what crime have you committed, poor fellow, that you should deserve to sit and see this show? In the morning they cried "Kill him! Lash him! Burn him! Why does he shrink in fear from the sword? Why does he strike so feebly? Why doesn't he die like a man? Whip him to meet his wounds! Let them receive blow for blow, with chests bare and exposed to the stroke!" And when the games stop for the intermission, they announce: "A little throat-cutting in the meantime, so that there may still be something going on!"

CONSIDER THIS:

7-9. Discuss some of the benefits and drawbacks of life in imperial Rome. Do you consider the Romans barbaric because they often enjoyed such sports as chariot racing or gladiatorial combat? Can you think of any modern parallels to such activity in our own society?

"Charming Privacy": The Rural Aristocrat

PLINY THE YOUNGER

City life had its excitement and advantages, but many of the rich preferred the seclusion of their country estates, especially during the summer months. Pliny the Younger, a Roman aristocrat, offered the following glimpse into life in the country.

In the morning Spurinna keeps his couch; at the second hour he calls for his shoes and walks three miles, exercising mind as well as body. If he has friends with him, the time is passed in conversation on the noblest

"'The Give and Take of Death'" is from Seneca, *Moral Epistles*, 7.3–7.5, trans. Richard Gummere, vol. 1, in the Loeb Classical Library (Cambridge, MA: Harvard University Press, 1917). Translation modernized by the editor.

"'Charming Privacy'" is from Pliny the Younger, *Letters*, 3.1, in *Readings in Ancient History*, ed. William S. Davis, vol. 2 (Boston: Allyn and Bacon, 1913), pp. 241–242.

themes, otherwise a book is read aloud, and sometimes this is done even when his friends are present, but never in such a way as to bore them. Then he sits down, and there is more talk for preference; afterward he enters his carriage, taking with him either his wife . . . or one of his friends, a distinction I recently enjoyed. How delightful, how charming that privacy is! What glimpses of old times one gets! What noble deeds and noble men he tells you of! What lessons you drink in! Yet at the same time, he blends his learning with modesty, that he never seems to be playing the schoolmaster.

After riding seven miles he walks another mile, then resumes his seat, or betakes himself to his room and his pen; for he composes, both in Latin and Greek, the most scholarly lyrics. They have a wonderful grace, wonderful sweetness and wonderful humor, and the chastity of the writer enhances its charm. When he is told that the bathing hour has come, . . . he takes a walk naked in the sun, if there is no wind. Then he plays at ball for a long spell, throwing himself heartily into the game, for it is by means of this kind of active exercise that he battles with old age.

After his bath, he lies down and waits a little while before taking food, listening in the meantime to the reading of some light and pleasant book. All this time his friends are at perfect liberty to imitate his example or do anything else they prefer. Then dinner is served, the table being as bright as it is modest, and the silver plain and old-fashioned: he has also some Corinthian vases in use, for which he has a taste but not a mania. The dinner is often relieved by actors of comedy, so that the pleasures of the table may have a seasoning of letters. Even in the summer, the meal lasts well into the night, but no one finds it long, for it has kept up with such good humor and charm. The consequence is that, though he has passed his seventy-seventh year, his hearing and eyesight are as good as ever, his body is still active and alert, and the only symptom of his age is his wisdom.

This is the sort of life that I [Pliny] have vowed and am determined to have. I shall begin with great enthusiasm, as soon as my age justifies my beating a retreat from the cares of the world.

Social and Intellectual Aspects of the Pax Romana

The Roman Woman

From the early years of the Roman Republic in the sixth and fifth centuries B.C., the legal status of women was based on demands for social stability that were carefully tied to the traditional Roman virtues of honor and duty. Early laws obligated women, having no refuge outside of matrimony, to conform themselves entirely to the will of their husbands, who ruled their wives as necessary and inseparable possessions. Accordingly, if a wife was virtuous and obedient to her husband, she was mistress of the house to the same degree that he was master. She controlled the daily functioning of the household, managed the servants, raised the children, and in all respects was expected to reflect and enhance the social status of her family. After the death of her husband, the Roman matron was heir to his property and shared equally with her children.

If she committed any wrong, however, the law allowed the husband to mete out punishment. In early Roman society, the power of the father over his family was absolute. He could arrange the marriages of his daughters, imprison his wife or children, beat them, put them in chains, keep them restricted to the house or at work in the fields, or even put them to death for insubordination. Adultery on the part of a wife was the gravest of offenses and punishable by death. This was an act of reckless folly that dishonored the household and sullied the good name of the husband. Even drunkenness could be punished by death as a potential contributor to adultery.

But women of good family were often prized in the marriage market because they served as the cement for political alliances and therefore became conduits to power and wealth. By the first century B.C.E. and in the early imperial period, women of the upper classes had achieved a position of almost complete emancipation. Women such as Cornelia, the daughter of Scipio Africanus, the conqueror of Hannibal, or Clodia, the mistress of the poet Catullus, exerted a powerful influence on the politics of the time. Indeed, Livia, the wife of Augustus, or Agrippina, the wife of the emperor Claudius and the mother of the emperor Nero, were dangerous players at the imperial court.

The following sources testify to the variety of relationships between Roman men and women. The first underscores the restricted status and traditional expectations of women in the early Republic. The second is a funeral eulogy delivered by Quintus Lucretius Vespillo about 8 B.C.E. in honor of his wife, Turia—truly an admired and valued life companion.

"Subordinate Beauty"

VALERIUS MAXIMUS

Then there is the blunt marital sternness of Gaius Sulpicius Gallus. He repudiated his wife with an abrupt yet somewhat justified decision because he had detected her out of doors with her head uncovered. "The law," he said, "prescribes my eyes only as the ones to which you may prove your beauty; it is for these eyes that you should adorn yourself with embellishments of beauty, for these eyes be good-looking and entrust yourself. If any one else looks upon you, because you have attracted him by a needless provocation, there must be suspicious and wrongful intent connected with it."

This was also the view of Quintus Antistius Vetus when he divorced his wife because he had seen her talking privately in public with some common freedwoman. For he was not so much disturbed by the fault itself as that he sought to avoid potential wrongdoing [from such an association] rather than to punish it.

There should be added to these cases Publius Sempronius Sophus, who inflicted upon his wife the ignominy of divorce for no other reason than that she had dared to be a spectator at the games without his knowledge. And so, when in the past such action was taken against women, their minds were far from transgressions.

The Funeral Eulogy of Turia

QUINTUS LUCRETIUS VESPILLO

Marriages of such long duration, not dissolved by divorce, but terminated by death alone, are indeed rare. For our union was prolonged in unclouded happiness for forty-one years. Would that our long marriage had come to its final end by *my* death, and that I as the older, which was more just, had yielded to fate.

Why recall your natural qualities, your modesty, deference, affability, your amiable disposition, your faithful attendance to household duties, your enlightened religion, your unassuming elegance, the modest simplicity of your attire? Need I speak of your attachment to your kindred, your affection for your family—when you cherished my mother as you did your own parents—you who share countless other virtues with Roman matrons who cherish their fair name? These qualities which I claim for you are your own; few have possessed the like and been able to hold on to and maintain them; the experience of men teaches us how rare they are. . . .

You gave proof of your generosity not only towards very many of your kin, but especially in your filial devotion. . . . You brought up in our home . . .

"Subordinate Beauty" is from Valerius Maximus, *Memorable Deeds and Sayings*, 6.3.9–12, in D. C. Munro, *A Source Book of Roman History* (Boston, 1904).

"The Funeral Eulogy of Turia" is from *Corpus Inscriptionum Latinarum*, Vol. 6, Nos. 1527 and 31670.

some worthy young girls of your kinship. And that these might attain to a station in life worthy of your family, you provided them with dowries. . . .

When all the world was again at peace and the Republic reestablished, peaceful and happy days followed for us. We longed for children, which an envious fate denied us. Had Fortune permitted herself to smile on us in the ordinary fashion, our happiness would have been complete. But advancing age put an end to our hopes. Despairing of your fertility and disconsolate to see me without children, you spoke of divorce because of my unhappiness on this account, offering to yield our home to another spouse more fertile. . . . I must admit that I was so angry that I was deprived of my mind, and that I was so horrified at your proposal that I scarcely regained control of myself. That you should have spoken of divorce between us before the decree of fate had been given;

that you should have conceived of any reason why you, while you were still alive, should cease to be my wife, you who when I was almost an exile from life remained most faithful. . . .

Would that our time of life had permitted our union to endure until I, the older, had passed away. . . . By fate's decree, your course was run before mine. You left me the grief, the longing for you, the sad fate to live alone.

CONSIDER THIS:

7-10. How would you describe the status of women in Roman society? How did this status change from the early Republic to the early Empire?

7-11. What were the expectations placed on Roman matrons? What particular virtues did Turia's husband admire? To what extent were women social equals of their husbands within and outside of the home?

Slavery in the Roman Empire

Rome was a slave-holding society; it had obtained thousands of slaves during the Republic as spoils of conquest. Despite the decrease in war captives during the Pax Romana, there was still a thriving slave trade. The philosopher and politician Seneca commented, "On one occasion, a proposal was made by the senate to distinguish slaves from freemen by their dress; it then became apparent how great would be the impending danger if our slaves began to count our number." Slaves generally led a life of toil without many benefits; a slave in the mines might last a couple of years. Still, domestic service was often pleasant, and educated slaves from Greece became trusted tutors or accountants. Although the Romans feared slave rebellions, they passed legislation designed to regulate the treatment of slaves. In fact, Romans generally respected their slaves and often granted manumission. When a slave became a freedman, he gained in social stature and, with knowledge of a trade, could even make a fortune (as did Trimalchio in the selection below) or control the strings of political power; the emperors were often supported (or dominated in the case of the emperor Claudius) by their freedmen. The following excerpts discuss the nature of slavery in the Roman Empire.

A Slave Rebellion

PLINY THE YOUNGER

Gaius Plinius to his dear Acilius, greeting:

Here is the terrible story, which really deserves more than just a letter, about how Larcius Macedo, a man of praetorian rank, was treated by his slaves. It's true that he was an arrogant and cruel master who had forgotten,

or perhaps remembered all too well, that his own father was once a slave.

He was bathing at his villa near Formiae when suddenly he was surrounded by his slaves. One seized him by the throat, another struck him in the

"A Slave Rebellion" is from Pliny the Younger, *Letters*, 3.14, trans. by William Melmoth, in *The Epistles of Pliny*, ed. by Clifford H. Moore (Boston: The Bibliophile Society, 1925). Translation modernized by the editor.

face, another beat him on the chest, the stomach, and even—this is hard to talk about—kicked him repeatedly in the balls. Macedo went limp so they threw him on the hot floor to see if he was still alive. He didn't move a muscle, either because he was unconscious or at least pretended to be. The slaves thought he was dead and carried him out where his faithful slaves received him with great wailing and concern. Refreshed by the cool air and stirred by their shrieking, Macedo opened his eyes and moved his body to show that he was still alive. The guilty slaves had taken off in all directions, but most were apprehended, though the search is ongoing. Macedo was kept alive with great difficulty for a few days, just enough time for him to get his revenge before he died.

The Proper Treatment of Slaves

SENECA

The proverb is current: "As many enemies as you have slaves." They are not enemies when we acquire them; we make them enemies. I shall pass over the other cruel and inhuman conduct toward them; for we mistreat them, not as if they were men, but as if they were beasts of burden. When we recline at a banquet, one slave mops up the disgorged food, another crouches beneath the table and gathers up the leftovers of the tipsy guests. Another carves the priceless game birds; with unerring strokes and skilled hand he cuts choice morsels along the breast and rump. . . . Another, who serves the wine, must dress like a woman and wrestle with his advancing years; he cannot get away from his boyhood, but is dragged back to it; and though he has already acquired a soldier's figure, he is kept beardless by having his hair smoothed away or plucked out by the roots, and he must remain awake throughout the night, dividing his time between his master's drunkenness and his lust—in the bedchamber he must be a man, at the feast a boy. Another, whose duty it is to put a valuation on the guests, must stick to his task, poor fellow, and watch to see whose flattery and whose immodesty, whether of appetite or of language, is to get them an invitation for tomorrow. . . .

Kindly remember that he whom you call your slave sprang from the same stock, is smiled upon by the same skies, and like yourself breathes, lives, and dies. It is just as possible for you to see in him a freeborn man as for him to see in you a slave. . . . I do not wish to involve myself in too large a question and discuss the treatment of slaves, toward whom we Romans are excessively haughty, cruel, and insulting. But this is my advice in a nutshell: Treat those below you as you would be treated by those above you. And as often as you reflect how much power you have over a slave, remember that your master has just as much power over you. "But I have no master," you say. You are still young, perhaps you will have one. . . .

You should therefore not be deterred by these finicky persons from showing yourself to your slave as an affable person and not proudly superior to them. They ought to respect you rather than fear you. . . . He who respects also loves, and love and fear do not mix.

Social Mobility: "Once a Mere Worm, Now a King"

PETRONIUS

Come, my friends, make yourselves at home. I too was once just like you, but by my ability I've reached my present position. What makes man is the heart, the rest is all trash. "I buy well, and I sell well"—others have different ideas. I am ready to burst with good luck. . . . My good management brought me to my present good fortune.

"The Proper Treatment of Slaves" is from Seneca, *Moral Epistles*, 47, trans. Richard M. Gummere, vol. 1, in the Loeb Classical Library (Cambridge, MA: Harvard University Press, 1917). Translation modernized by the editor.

"Social Mobility" is from Petronius, *Satyricon*, 65.8–67.6, in *Petronii Cena Trimanchionis*, trans. W. D. Lowe (Cambridge: Cambridge University Press, 1905).

I was only as big as the candlestick here when I came from Asia, in fact I used to measure myself by it every day and I smeared my lips with the lamp oil to get a hairy face quicker. Still for fourteen years I was my master's favorite. And where's the disgrace in doing what one's master tells one? All the same I managed to get into my mistress's good graces, too (you know what I mean: I hold my tongue, as I am not one to boast).

But by heaven's help I became master in the house, and then I took in my fool of a lord. To be brief, he made me co-heir with the emperor to his property, and I got a senator's fortune. But no one is ever satisfied, and I wanted to go into business. To cut it short, I built five ships, I loaded them with a cargo of wine—it was worth its weight in gold at that time—and I sent it to Rome. You would have thought I had ordered my bad luck: every ship was wrecked; it's a fact, no story. . . . Do you think I failed? No, I swear the loss only whetted my appetite as if nothing had happened. I built more ships, larger, better, and luckier ones, and everybody called me a courageous man—you know, a great ship shows great strength. I loaded them with wine again, bacon fat, beans, perfume, and slaves. . . . On one voyage I cleared around 10,000,000 sesterces. I immediately bought back all the estates that had belonged to my patron. I built a mansion, I bought up young slaves to sell, and beasts of burden: everything I touched grew like a honeycomb.

Once I was worth more than my whole native town put together, I quit the game: I retired from business and started lending money, financing freedmen. . . . I'll have done well enough in my lifetime. Meantime, with Mercury watching over me, I built this residence. As you know, it was a cottage; now it's fit for a god. It's got four dining rooms, twenty bedrooms, two marble colonnades, and the upstairs apartments, my own bedroom where I sleep, . . . an excellent porter's lodge, and enough guest rooms for all my friends. . . . And there are lots of other things, which I'll show you presently. Believe me, have a penny, you're worth a penny; have something, you'll be treated like something. And so your friend, once a mere worm, is now a king.

CONSIDER THIS:

7-12. Why do you think that Romans held slaves? Did they treat their slaves well? Was there any social mobility in the Roman Empire? What does this say about the relative freedom of Roman society?

The Stoic Philosophy

The Romans were never known for their contributions to abstract thought and did not produce a unique philosophy. Still, they borrowed well and adapted ideas that complemented their values. For the Roman, duty and organization were particularly important; consequently, the Stoic philosophy, which had originated in Greece in the third century B.C.E., was especially popular among the aristocracy. According to Stoic tenets, a divine plan ordered the universe, so whatever lot or occupation fell to one in life should be accepted and coped with appropriately. Restraint and moderation characterized the ideal Stoic, and he advocated tolerance as an essential component of the "brotherhood of man." To a Stoic who felt that his honor was somehow compromised, suicide was an acceptable and dutiful way of preserving his dignity. The following selections come from the writings of two Stoics of diverse backgrounds. Seneca was tutor to the emperor Nero and finally committed suicide at his command in 66 C.E.; Marcus Aurelius became emperor in 161 C.E., an occupation he did not seek but dutifully executed.

"What Is the Principal Thing in Life?"

SENECA

What is the principal thing in human life? . . . To raise the soul above the threats and promises of fortune; to consider nothing as worth hoping for. For what does fortune possess worth setting your heart upon? . . . What is the principal thing? To be able to endure adversity with a joyful heart; to bear whatever

"What Is the Principal Thing in Life?" is from Seneca, *Natural Questions*, 3. Preface, 10–17, trans. J. Clarke (London, 1910). Translation modernized by the editor.

occurs just as if it were the very thing you desired to have happen to you. For you would have felt it your duty to desire it, had you known that all things happen by divine decree. Tears, complaints, lamentations are rebellion [against divine order]. . . .

What is the principal thing? To have life on the very lips, ready to issue when summoned. This makes a man free, not by right of Roman citizenship, but by right of nature. He is, moreover, the true freeman who has escaped from bondage to self; that slavery is constant and unavoidable—it presses us day and night alike, without pause, without respite. To be a slave to self is the most grievous kind of slavery; yet its chains may easily be broken, if you cease making large demands on yourself, if you stop seeking a personal reward for your services, and if you have perspective and really understand your nature and your age, even if you are young. Finally, if you ask yourself, "Why do I rave, and pant, and sweat? Why do I work so hard? Why do I haunt the Forum? Man needs but little, and that not for long."

Meditations

MARCUS AURELIUS

1. He who acts unjustly acts impiously. For since the universal nature has made rational animals for the sake of one another to help one another according to what they deserve, but in no way to injure one another. He who transgresses the will of nature is clearly guilty of impiety towards the highest divinity. And whoever lies is guilty of impiety to the same divinity; for there is a universal nature of things that are; and things that are have a relation to all things that come into existence.

2. It would be a man's happiest lot to depart from mankind without having had any taste of lying and hypocrisy and luxury and pride. However, to breathe out one's life when a man has had enough of these things is the next best voyage, as the saying goes. . . .

3. Do not despise death, but be well content with it, since this too is one of those things that nature wills. For to be young and to grow old, to gain experience and to reach maturity, to cut your teeth, grow a beard and watch it turn grey, to beget, and to become pregnant and to bring forth, and all the other natural operations that the seasons of your life bring, so death is also a part of the process of life. This, then, is consistent with the character of a thoughtful man, to be neither careless nor impatient nor contemptuous of death, but to wait for it as ordered and natural. . . .

4. Wipe out imagination, check desire, extinguish appetite. Keep your mind in control.

5. Soon you will have forgotten the world, and soon the world will have forgotten you.

CONSIDER THIS:

7-13. Pick out specific passages from the selections on Stoicism that reflect the tenets of that philosophy as described in the section introduction. Why can this be considered a philosophy compatible with Roman values?

KEY EVENTS DURING THE LATE ROMAN EMPIRE

180–284   "Crisis of the Third Century"

The decline of Roman leadership evident as a series of myopic emperors emerge from the military ranks ("barrack emperors") and cannot sustain political stability in the face of economic crisis and Germanic invasions. There are twenty-six emperors in a fifty-year period (235–285), and only one died a natural death.

Meditations is from Marcus Aurelius, *Meditations*, trans. George Long (London: The Chesterfield Library, 1862), pp. 241–242, 253. Translation modernized by the editor.

284–305   Reign of Diocletian
Diocletian becomes emperor and disposes with the pretense of the Principate. The emperor now becomes "dominus," or lord, and rules absolutely in a government called the Dominate. Diocletian develops a succession plan called the Tetrarchy designed to provide a secure succession by dividing the Roman Empire among four rulers, but ultimately proves unsuccessful.

312–337   Rule of Constantine
Economic reforms postpone Roman collapse. Dedication of Constantinople as new capital of the empire (330). Constantine presides over the Council of Nicaea (325) and sets precedent for Caesaro-Papism: secular dominance of state over church in Byzantine Empire.

379–395   Rule of Theodosius
He is the last emperor to control both the eastern and western halves of the Roman Empire. Christianity becomes the official state religion (392).

410   Alaric the Visigoth
Rome invaded and burned by one of its own confederate generals. Last time Rome was invaded by hostile forces was by the Gauls in the fourth century B.C.E. Trouble brewing . . . St. Augustine writes *The City of God* (413–426).

450–476   The Germanic Invasions
Roman defense breaks down in a series of external invasions by Germanic tribes: Anglo-Saxon invasion of Britain (450); Huns invade Europe led by Attila, "Scourge of God" (451–453), but defeated by Roman and Frankish forces; Vandals overrun Rome (455) then move toward Spain and North Africa; Odoacer deposes last Western Roman emperor, Romulus Augustulus (476).

489–493   Theodoric the Ostrogoth
Theodoric establishes Ostrogothic Kingdom in Italy. Rome ceases to exist as a singular entity. Transition to the Middle Ages.

Failure and Decline (180–500 C.E.)

"Empire for Sale" (193 C.E.)

DIO CASSIUS

The Roman Empire generally prospered during the first and second centuries C.E. During the third century, however, the empire gradually fell prey to problems that had existed to some extent in preceding years but had never reached crisis proportions. One of the main problems was a lack of leadership. Rome had survived bad emperors before, but during the fifty years from 235 to 285 C.E., there were twenty-two emperors, and only one died a natural death in his bed. The rest fell victim to assassination or violent death on the battlefield. The following excerpt describes the political chaos upon the death of the emperor Pertinax in 193 C.E. The empire was sold to the highest bidder by the emperor's personal troops, the Praetorian Guard. The so-called "winner," Didius Julianus, ruled for three months before he himself was killed by these same Praetorian guardsmen.

"'Empire for Sale'" is from Dio Cassius, *Roman History*, 74.11.2–6, trans. Earnest Cary, vol. 9, in the Loeb Classical Library (Cambridge, MA: Harvard University Press, 1927), pp. 143, 145.

Didius Julianus, at once an insatiate money getter and a wanton spendthrift, who was always eager for revolution, and hence had been exiled by Commodus to his native city of Milan, now, when he heard of the death of Pertinax, hastily made his way to the [Praetorian] camp and, standing at the gates of the enclosure, made bids to the soldiers for the rule over the Romans. Then ensued a most disgraceful business and one unworthy of Rome. For, just as if it had been in some market or auction room, both the city and its entire Empire were auctioned off. The sellers were the ones who had murdered their emperor, and the would-be buyers were Sulpicianus and Julianus, who vied to outbid each other, one from the inside, the other from outside. They gradually raised their bids up to 20,000 sesterces per soldier. Some of the soldiers would carry word to Julianus, "Sulpicianus offers so much; how much more do you bid?" And to Sulpicianus in turn, "Julianus promises so much; how much do you raise him?" Sulpicianus would have won the day, being inside and being prefect of the city and also the first to name the figure of 20,000, had not Julianus raised his bid no longer by a small amount but by 5,000 at one time, shouting it in a loud voice and also indicating the amount with his fingers. So the soldiers, captivated by this extravagant bid . . . brought Julianus inside and declared him emperor.

News of the Attacks

JEROME

In addition to a lack of consistently strong and effective leadership, there were also significant economic problems throughout the empire. Gold and silver mines in the West were no longer very productive, and yet Romans still hungered for the oils and spices of the East so that these precious metals drained away in return for disposable luxury items. The currency was debased again and again. As the content of silver and gold coins was reduced dramatically, so too was confidence in the value of money itself. Many areas were reduced to a simple barter economy as frightened people hoarded coins and even buried them in the ground as a hedge against an uncertain future.

But perhaps the most distressing and ultimately ruinous cause for the fall of the empire was the constant influx of Germanic invaders. Rome had been able to cope with Germanic incursions during the first and second centuries either by defeating them militarily or by allowing them to fight with Roman troops as confederates. In the latter circumstance, Germans were often "Romanized," as it were, learning the Latin language and respecting Roman traditions. Perhaps because of perceptions of Roman weakness, or in response to pressures from other nomadic eastern peoples (such as the Huns), in the mid-second and third centuries the Germanic tribes moved more aggressively into the empire, often overwhelming Roman armies that were hampered by a lack of political and military direction. By the fifth century, the empire had been overrun. Jerome, a Christian writer in the East, described the scene in the western provinces.

Innumerable and most ferocious people have overrun the whole of Gaul. The entire area bounded by the Alps, the Pyrenees, the ocean and the Rhine is occupied by the Quadi, Vandals, Carmatians, Alanni, Gepides, Saxons, Burgundians, Alammani—oh weep for the empire—and the hostile Pannonians. . . . Mainz, once a noble city, is captured and razed, and thousands have been massacred in the church. Worms has succumbed to a long siege. Rheims, the impregnable, Amiens, Artois, Tours, Nimes and Strasburg are in the hands of the Germans. The provinces of Aquitaine, . . . of Lyons and Narbonne are completely occupied and devastated either by the sword from without or famine within. I cannot mention Toulouse without tears, for until now it has been spared, due to the merits of its saintly bishop Exuperus. The Spaniards tremble, expecting daily the invasion and recalling the horrors Spaniards suffer in continual anticipation.

Who would believe that Rome, victor over all the world, would fall, that she would be to her people both the womb and the tomb. Once all the East, Egypt, and Africa acknowledged her sway and were counted among her men servants and her maid servants. Who would believe that holy Bethlehem would receive as beggars, those nobles, both men and women, who once abounded in riches? Where we cannot help, we mourn and mingle our tears with theirs. . . . There is not an hour, not even a moment, when we are not occupied with crowds of refugees, when the peace of the monastery is not invaded by a horde of guests so that we shall either have to shut the gates or neglect the Scriptures for which the gates were opened. Consequently, I have to snatch furtively the hours of the night, which now with winter approaching are growing longer, and try to dictate by candle light and thus . . . relieve a mind distraught. I am not boasting of our hospitality, as some may suspect, but simply explaining to you the delay.

CONSIDER THIS:

7-14. What were some of the main reasons for the decline of the Roman Empire? In your opinion, which is the most important factor for the decline of a civilization and why?

THEME: REVOLUTION AND HISTORICAL TRANSITION

THE REFLECTION IN THE MIRROR

The Decline of the West

Decline and Christianity

EDWARD GIBBON

One of the most famous theories for the decline of the Roman Empire belongs to Edward Gibbon, the celebrated eighteenth-century historian. His work *The Decline and Fall of the Roman Empire* (1776) has proved an authoritative analysis of the end. But his emphasis on the importance of Christianity as a source of Roman decline still inspires controversy.

KEEP IN MIND . . .

7-15. According to Edward Gibbon, why was Christianity an important factor in the decline of the Roman Empire?

As the happiness of a future life is the great object of religion, we may hear, without surprise or scandal, that the introduction, or at least the abuse, of Christianity had some influence on the decline and fall of the Roman empire. The clergy successfully preached the doctrines of patience and pusillanimity; the active virtues of society were discouraged; and the last remains of the military spirit were buried in the cloister; a large portion of public and private wealth was consecrated to the specious demands of charity and devotion; and the soldiers' pay was lavished on the useless multitudes of both sexes, who could only plead the merits of abstinence and chastity. Faith, zeal, curiosity, and the more earthly passions of malice and ambition kindled the flame of theological discord; the church, and even the state, were distracted by religious factions, whose conflicts were sometimes bloody, and always implacable; the attention of the emperors was diverted from camps to [church] synods; the

"Decline and Christianity" is from Edward Gibbon, *The History of the Decline and Fall of the Roman Empire*, ed. J. B. Bury, vol. 4 (London, 1901), pp. 162–163.

FIGURE 7.5 Ruins of the Temple of Castor and Pollux in the Roman forum: "If the decline of the Roman Empire was hastened by the conversion of [the Emperor] Constantine, his victorious religion broke the violence of the fall, and mollified the ferocious temper of the conquerors."—Edward Gibbon (*Perry M. Rogers*)

Roman world was oppressed by a new species of tyranny; and the persecuted sects became the secret enemies of their country. Yet party-spirit, however pernicious or absurd, is a principle of union as well as of dissension. The bishops, from eighteen hundred pulpits, inculcated the duty of passive obedience to a lawful and orthodox sovereign; their communion of distant churches; and the benevolent temper of the gospel was strengthened, though confined by the spiritual alliance of the Catholics. The sacred indolence of the monks was devoutly embraced by a servile and effeminate age; but, if

> "The introduction, or at least the abuse, of Christianity had some influence on the decline and fall of the Roman empire."
>
> —EDWARD GIBBON

superstition had not afforded a decent retreat, the same vices would have tempted the unworthy Romans to desert, from baser motives, the standard of the republic. Religious precepts are easily obeyed, which indulge and sanctify the natural inclinations of their votaries; but the pure and genuine influence of Christianity may be traced in its beneficial though imperfect, effects on the Barbarian proselytes of the North. If the decline of the Roman Empire was hastened by the conversion of [the Emperor] Constantine, his victorious religion broke the violence of the fall, and mollified the ferocious temper of the conquerors.

CONSIDER THIS:

7-16. Do you find Gibbon's theory of Roman decline to be valid? Why or why not? Note his use of the phrases *passive obedience* and *sacred indolence*. Did Christianity end the warrior spirit that had made Rome great and replace it with a Christian emphasis on "loving one's neighbor" and "turning the other cheek"?

The Barbarization of Civilization

M. I. ROSTOVTZEFF

The decline of Roman civilization presents an appropriate occasion for reflection on the lessons that can be learned from the experience. The following modern historian offers his perspective.

None of the existing theories fully explains the problem of the decay of ancient civilization, if we can apply the word "decay" to the complex phenomenon which I have endeavored to describe. Each of them, however, has contributed much to the clearing of the ground, and has helped us to perceive that the main phenomenon, which underlies the process of decline, is the gradual absorption of the educated classes by the masses and the consequent simplification of all the functions of political, social, economic, and intellectual life, which we call the barbarization of the ancient world.

The evolution of the ancient world has a lesson and a warning for us. Our civilization will not last unless it be a civilization not of one class, but of the masses. The Oriental civilizations were more stable and lasting than the Greco-Roman, because, being chiefly based on religion, they were nearer to the masses. Another lesson is that violent attempts at leveling have never helped to uplift the masses. They have destroyed the upper classes, and resulted in accelerating the process of barbarization. But the ultimate problem remains like a ghost, ever present and unlaid: Is it possible to extend a higher civilization to the lower classes without debasing its standard and diluting its quality to the vanishing point? Is not every civilization bound to decay as soon as it begins to penetrate the masses?

THE BROADER PERSPECTIVE:

7-17. Do you agree or disagree with Rostovtzeff that the decline of an organized and well-integrated

"The Barbarization of Civilization" is from M. I. Rostovtzeff, *The Social and Economic History of the Roman Empire*, vol. 1, 2nd ed., revised by P. M. Fraser (Oxford: The Clarendon Press, 1957), p. 541. Reprinted by permission of Oxford University Press.

civilization is tied to a barbarization of social classes? Develop and comment on his specific argument. Is decline primarily an economic and social problem? Or does it necessarily stem from political and military failure?

7-18. The process of decline has fascinated humanity for centuries. Are civilizations biological in nature? Are they born and do they grow, mature, age, and die, as do other living entities? Did Rome ultimately fail because it was no longer Rome? Does each civilization progress and transfer its benefits to the developing successor civilization?

7-19. Are there any warning signs for decline, and can a civilization reverse the process once it has started? Does technology have anything to do with decline? As we advance technologically, does this speed up the process of decline? Compare Roman and American societies in this regard.

Chapter 8

Icon, Scimitar, and Cross:
Early Medieval Civilization (500–1100)

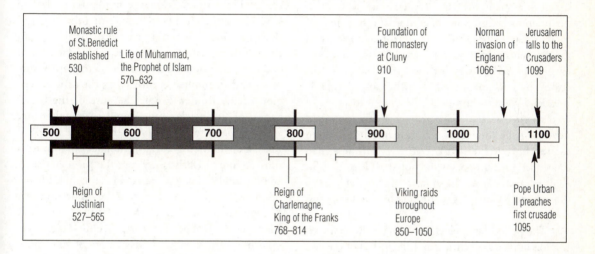

Monastic rule of St.Benedict established 530

Life of Muhammad, the Prophet of Islam 570–632

Foundation of the monastery at Cluny 910

Norman invasion of England 1066

Jerusalem falls to the Crusaders 1099

500   600   700   800   900   1000   1100

Reign of Justinian 527–565

Reign of Charlemagne, King of the Franks 768–814

Viking raids throughout Europe 850–1050

Pope Urban II preaches first crusade 1095

Understanding is the reward of faith. Therefore, do not seek to understand that you may believe, but believe that you may understand.

—Saint Augustine

If the work of God could be comprehended by reason, it would no longer be wonderful.

—Pope Gregory I

There are two ways to slide through life: to believe everything or to doubt everything; both ways save us from thinking.

—Alfred Korzybski

CHAPTER THEMES

- **Social and Spiritual Values:** How did the establishment of the Christian church and the development of the papacy structure Christian beliefs, thus providing a spiritual foundation for the Middle Ages? How was devotion, whether Christian or Islamic, an encompassing theme for the period?

- **The Power Structure:** What conditions contributed to the establishment of feudalism? How did feudalism provide political and social solutions for the disruptions of the Early Middle Ages?

- **Imperialism:** Both Justinian and Charlemagne tried to reconquer and reestablish the Roman Empire. Why did they fail? Why were Muslim armies so successful in gaining territory in the Middle East and North Africa?

- **Revolution and Historical Transition:** In what ways did medieval civilization represent a change from the civilizations of the ancient world and the Renaissance yet to come? Can we speak of progress in the Middle Ages, or was the entire period a "Dark Age"?

- **The Big Picture:** To what extent can religion serve as a progressive and stabilizing force in society? How did Christianity give energy and direction to medieval civilization?

Some historians have argued that one of the greatest disasters in history was the failure of Rome to maintain its civilization. The internal economic and social decay of the third and fourth centuries, and the weakened military and political structure of the empire, paved the way for the barbarization of the realm by an uncontrolled influx of Germanic invaders. Western Europe was subjected to an era of chaos and disaster, marked by brutish force and devoid of the moderation that maintains civilized existence; by the fifth century, darkness had descended on Europe. As the noted art historian Sir Kenneth Clark said, "In so far as we are the heirs of Greece and Rome, we got through by the skin of our teeth."

The period between the collapse of Roman civilization in the fifth century and the revival of classical learning in the Renaissance of the fifteenth century is called the Middle Ages or the medieval world. People of the Renaissance viewed their era as one of light and progress, of renewed hope, where the emphasis centered no longer on God but on humanity. It was a secular era that condemned the chanting of prayers as mindless and viewed the collection of holy relics as absurd; it saw these practices as contradictory to the freedom of a new society focused on creativity. The Middle Ages were viewed with regret and scorn. Petrarch, a poet of the fourteenth century, lamented that "the Muse of History has been dead for a thousand years." When Rome fell, the "Dark Ages" settled over western Europe and civilization retreated—and then remained static.

This view of the Middle Ages was accepted and remained popular until perhaps the nineteenth century, when a more detached and less advocative scholarship began to assess critically the contributions and limitations of the medieval world. Perhaps the Middle Ages seemed so foreign because it was generally an age of faith, in contrast to the secular and rational emphasis of the modern world. The Christian church had been born during the height of Roman civilization and developed by drawing from Roman organization, making accommodation and enduring occasional persecution. Christianity survived and triumphed eventually as the official religion of the Roman Empire because of the broad appeal of its doctrine, its committed membership, and its superior organization. Although the facade of Roman civilization gradually crumbled, the spiritual substructure of Christianity kept the Latin language, architectural styles, and other Roman cultural benefits alive. This was not easy given the dislocation that Europe experienced from about 500 to 1000 C.E. This period (called the Early Middle Ages) was indeed a difficult time. It was an era of transition, when leaders such as Charlemagne in Europe and Justinian in the eastern Byzantine Empire were reestablishing political control. Waves of Viking invasions, starting around 850, led to major changes in social and political organization as peasants sought protection and nobles raised armies. Feudalism, which originated in late Roman times, became a complex yet workable system of establishing authority and ordering society.

This period of disruption ended by 1100 as the Viking invasions dwindled in intensity and frequency. No longer was European civilization struggling to survive; anxiety gave way to confidence and confirmation that God held sway over the world. This confidence would soon be tested when the Pope, as the vicar of Christ, summoned knights from throughout Europe to reclaim the Holy Land from the control of the infidel Muslims. While Europe had been defending itself from Viking attacks, a new religion had established itself in the desert sands of North Africa and the Middle East. The Crusades now brought two developing civilizations, each on the edge of political and religious consolidation, into a conflict that focused their energies and gave purpose and direction to their respective missions in the Greek East, in the Roman West, and in the Islamic heartlands.

KEY EVENTS IN THE EARLY MIDDLE AGES

527–565 Reign of Justinian
Progressive leader rules Byzantine Empire from Constantinople. Justinian attempts to reconquer North Africa and Italy, codifies Roman law, and builds the church Hagia Sophia. Infamous wife Theodora refuses to abandon throne during Nika Riots in 532.

530 Benedictine Monastic Rule
Saint Benedict establishes strict standards and regulations in the West that emphasize a common experience among monks, rather than the hermitic emphasis in the eastern Mediterranean.

570–632 Life of Muhammad
According to the *Qur'an* (650), Muhammad received revelations from the angel Gabriel, attacked idolatry in Mecca, was driven out in 622 (*Hegira*), and established himself at Medina, where he founded Islam as a missionary, fervently monotheistic religion that quickly expands throughout North Africa, Spain, and into southeastern Asia.

732–768 The Foundation of the Carolingian Empire
Charles Martel ("The Hammer") defeats the Muslims at Poitiers. His relative, Pepin the Short, formerly Mayor of the Palace under the Merovingian Dynasty, becomes King of the Franks (751). Establishes Carolingian Dynasty and serves as papal protector.

768–814 Reign of Charlemagne
Defeats Lombards in northern Italy (774) and establishes empire throughout modern-day France, parts of Germany and eastern Europe, Italy, and northern Spain. Charlemagne crowned emperor by Pope Leo III (800). Establishment of Carolingian Renaissance with palace schools under the direction of Alcuin of York. Frankish empire maintained by son Louis the Pious (814–840), who succeeds Charlemagne as emperor. Treaty of Verdun (843) partitions Carolingian Empire among sons of Louis the Pious. Disagreement and chaos follow.

910 Monastery of Cluny Founded
With its strict emphasis on the rule of Saint Benedict, Cluny provides foundation for a general reform of the church.

962–987 Establishment of Ottonian and Capetian Rule
Saxons under Otto II succeed Carolingians in Germany (962), and Hugh Capet succeeds Carolingians in France by establishing Capetian Dynasty (987).

1066 Norman Invasion of Britain
Led by William the Conqueror, the Norman invasion across the English channel results in victory over the Anglo-Saxon king Harold Godwinson at the Battle of Hastings (1066).

Byzantine Civilization

The Emperor Justinian (527–565)

As the Western Roman Empire succumbed to Germanic invaders in the fourth and fifth centuries C.E., power shifted from Rome, which was at constant risk, to the city of Byzantium. The emperor Constantine the Great began the rebuilding of Byzantium in 324 and renamed the city Constantinople in 330. Its well-defended and critical location on the lucrative eastern trade routes at the entrance to the Black Sea augured a dynamic future. Greek culture dominated the region, and this eastern successor to the glory of Rome became known as the Byzantine Empire. Between 324 and its demise in 1453, the Byzantine Empire provided an important link between the Eastern and Western cultures of the former Roman Empire.

One of the most famous and arguably the most influential rulers of this empire was Justinian. He and Theodora, his brilliant but dissolute wife, ruled from 527 to 565 with the official policy of "one God, one empire, one religion." To this end Justinian sought to reestablish Byzantine control over the former Roman Empire in the West through an ambitious and partially successful policy of conquest and consolidation. Justinian also collated and revised or codified Roman law, which was perhaps the most enduring legacy of his reign.

The first selections are from the "poison pen" of Procopius, Justinian's court historian. In his *Secret History*, Procopius paints a tabloid view of the degenerate characters of Justinian and his infamous wife, Theodora. She, in fact, was the daughter of a bear trainer in the circus, who through her forceful will and sexual talents was able to rise to the heights of power. Whether one believes the portrait of Procopius or not, Theodora must have been a remarkable woman whose influence and character shone through when Justinian was faced with the Nika riots in 532.

The Secret History of Justinian and Theodora

PROCOPIUS

The Depravity of Theodora

[On her rise to power], Theodora joined the actors in all the business of the theater and played a regular part in their stage performances, making herself the butt of their ribald buffoonery. She was extremely clever and had a biting wit, and quickly became popular as a result. There was not a particle of modesty in the little hussy, and no one ever saw her taken aback; she complied with the most outrageous demands without the slightest hesitation, and she was the sort of girl who if somebody walloped her . . . would make a jest of it and roar with laughter; and she would throw off her clothes and exhibit naked to all and sundry those regions, both in front and behind, which the rules of decency require to be kept veiled and hidden from masculine eyes.

She used to tease her lovers by keeping them waiting, and by constantly playing about with novel methods of intercourse she could always bring the lascivious to her feet; so far from waiting to be invited by anyone

---

she encountered, she herself by cracking dirty jokes and wiggling her hips suggestively would invite all who came her way, especially if they were still in their teens. Never was anyone so completely given up to unlimited self-indulgence. Often she would go to a bring-your-own-food dinner-party with ten young men or more, all at the peak of their physical powers and with fornication as their chief object in life, and would lie with all her fellow-diners in turn the whole night long: when she had reduced them all to a state of exhaustion she would go to their menials, as many as thirty on occasions, and copulate with every one of them; but not even so could she satisfy her lust . . . .

Such then was the birth and upbringing of this woman, the subject of common talk among women of the streets and among people of every kind. But when she arrived back in Byzantium Justinian conceived an overpowering passion for her. At first he consorted with her only as a mistress, though he did promote her to Patrician rank. This at once enabled Theodora to possess herself of immense influence and of very considerable wealth. For as so often happens to men consumed with passion, it seemed in Justinian's eyes the most delightful thing in the world to lavish all his favors and all his wealth upon the object of his passion. And the whole State became fuel for this passion. With Theodora to help him he impoverished the people far more than before, not only in the capital but in every part of the Empire. As both had long been supporters of the Blue Faction [chariot race fans in the Hippodrome],

they gave the members of this faction immense powers over State affairs. It was a very long time before the evil was mitigated to any great extent . . . .

The Demon Justinian

Some of those who were in the Emperor's company late at night, conversing with him (evidently in the Palace)—men of the highest possible character—thought that they saw a strange demonic form in his place. One of them declared that he more than once rose suddenly from the imperial throne and walked round and round the room; for he was not in the habit of remaining seated for long. And Justinian's head would momentarily disappear, while the rest of his body seemed to continue making these long circuits. The watcher himself, thinking that something had gone seriously wrong with his eyesight, stood for a long time distressed and quite at a loss. But later the head returned to the body, and he thought that what a moment before had been lacking was, contrary to expectation, filling out again. A second man said that he stood by the Emperor's side as he sat, and saw his face suddenly transformed to a shapeless lump of flesh: neither eyebrows nor eyes were in their normal position, and it showed no other distinguishing feature at all; gradually, however, he saw the face return to its usual shape. I did not myself witness the events I am describing, but I heard about them from men who insist that they saw them at the time.

The Nika Riot (532)

PROCOPIUS

An insurrection broke out unexpectedly in Byzantium among the populace, and, contrary to expectation, it proved to be a very serious affair, and ended in great harm to the people and to the senate. . . . In every city the population has been divided for a long time past into the Blue and the Green factions; but within comparatively recent times it has come about that, for the sake of these names and the seats which the rival

factions occupy in watching the games, they spend their money and abandon their bodies to the most cruel tortures, and even do not think it unworthy to die a most shameful death. And they fight against their opponents knowing not for what end they imperil themselves, but knowing well that, even if they overcome their enemy in the fight, the conclusion of the matter for them will be to be carried off straightway to

"The Nika Riot" is from Procopius, *History of the Wars*, trans. H. B. Dewing, in the Loeb Classical Library (Cambridge, MA: Harvard University Press, 1914), pp. 219–239. Translation modernized by the editor.

the prison, and finally, after suffering extreme torture, to be killed. So as they grow up, they cultivate an inexplicable hostility against their fellow men—it's always there and will never disappear.

At this time the officers of the city administration in Byzantium were carrying away some of the rioters to their death. But .the members of the two factions, conspiring together and declaring a truce with each other, seized the prisoners and then straightway entered the prison and released all those who were in confinement there, whether they had been condemned on a charge of stirring up sedition, or for any other unlawful act. And all the officials of the city government were killed indiscriminately. Meanwhile, all sane citizens were fleeing to the opposite mainland amidst a conflagration as the city burned like it had fallen to an enemy. . . . During this time the emperor and his consort with a few members of the senate shut themselves up in the palace and remained quietly there. The watchword that the populace passed around to one another was Nika [Victory], and the insurrection has been called by this name up to the present time. . . .

Now the emperor Justinian and his court were deliberating as to whether it would be better for them if they remained or to flee in ships. As opinions flew around the room, the Empress Theodora held forth: "As to the belief that a woman ought not to be daring among men or to assert herself boldly among those who are holding back from fear, I consider that the present crisis most certainly [demands that we] settle the issue immediately. . . . My opinion then is that we cannot flee especially now though it might save us. For just as it is impossible for a man who has seen the Christian light to die, so it is unendurable for someone who has been an emperor to become a fugitive. May I never be separated from this purple [the color of royalty], and may I not live that day on which those who meet me shall not address me as empress. If, now, it is your wish to save yourself, O Emperor, there is no difficulty. For we have much money, and there is the sea, here the boats. However, consider whether it will not come about after you have been saved that you would gladly exchange that safety for death. As for myself, I agree with an ancient saying that royalty is a good burial-shroud." When the queen had spoken this, all were filled with boldness, and, turning their thoughts towards resistance, they began to consider how they might be able to defend themselves if any hostile force could come against them.

CONSIDER THIS:

8-1. After reading the selections on the Byzantine rulers Justinian and Theodora, what kind of people do you think they were? Why has Procopius's portrait of them become the dominant, popular characterization? What insights into their characters and reign does the selection on the Nika riots offer?

The Wonders of Saint Sophia

PAUL THE SILENTIARY

Byzantine art has a stylized, religious emphasis that is distinguished by its naturalism, attention to intricate detail, and ornamented finery. The greatest monument of Byzantine architecture is Hagia Sophia, or the Church of the Divine Wisdom, in modern Istanbul. Built in a mere five years from 532 to 537, the emperor Justinian intended it as the keystone of a vast architectural campaign.

The interior of Hagia Sophia (also called Saint Sophia) rejects any hint of homogeneity. There are columns of granite from Egypt, porphyry from Turkey, and green marble from Greece. The sunlight plays against beautiful mosaics and creates a mystical aura. Even more engaging are the minarets and other Islamic additions made after

"The Wonders of Saint Sophia" is from Paul the Silentiary, *Descriptio S. Sophiae*, in *The Church of St. Sophia Constantinople*, trans. W. Lethaby and H. Swainson (New York, 1894), pp. 42–52. Translation modernized by the editor.

Constantinople fell to the Ottoman Turks in 1453. Hagia Sophia today celebrates its eclectic artistic heritage.

The following description of Hagia Sophia is from a lengthy poem in praise of the church by Paul the Silentiary written after 562, about 30 years after construction was completed.

The great helmet of the dome rises above all into the immeasurable air and bends over, like the radiant heavens, to embraces the church. And at the highest part, at the crown, was depicted the cross, the protector of the city. And it is wondrous to see how the dome gradually rises, upwards to a sharp point, but is like the firmament that rests on air, though the dome is fixed on the strong backs of the arches . . . . Everywhere the walls, built with stone from the quarries of Proconnesus, glitter with wondrous designs. The marbles are cut and joined like painted patterns, formed into squares or eight-sided figures, and the stones also show the forms of living creatures . . . .

A thousand lamps within the temple, hanging aloft by winding chains, show their gleaming light. Some are placed in the aisles, others in the center or to east and west, or on the crowning walls, shedding the brightness of flame. Thus the night seems to flout the light of day, and be itself as rosy as the dawn . . . .

So through the spaces of the great church come rays of light, expelling clouds of care, and filling the mind with joy. The sacred light cheers all. Even the sailor gliding his bark on the waves, leaves behind him the unfriendly winds of the raging Pontus [Black Sea], and is guided in his course by the divine light of the church itself. Yet not only does it guide the merchant at night, like the rays from the Pharos [lighthouse] on the coast of Africa, but it also shows the way to the living God.

FIGURE 8.1 Exterior Photo of Hagia Sophia (*Turkish Tourism and Information Office*)

CONSIDER THIS:

8-2. In the following passage from Paul the Silentiary, note the central role that Saint Sophia played in the unity of the Byzantine community.

8-3. The architectural historian Marvin Trachtenberg noted that Hagia Sophia realized the "ideal Byzantine model" of architecture. How would you define Byzantine artistic style, and how does Hagia Sophia reflect it?

Byzantine Spiritual Foundations

The religious history of the Byzantine Empire is particularly interesting, owing to the relatively unrestricted and speculative intellectual heritage of the Greek East. A free flow of ideas had always been a feature of Greek philosophy, and the Christian churches in the eastern Mediterranean had been absorbed in this tradition. The patriarchs of Constantinople, Alexandria, Antioch, and Jerusalem were especially influential and competitive. Many doctrinal differences arose between the pope in Rome and these eastern patriarchs over such issues as the nature of the Trinity and the worship of religious icons (representation of saints and other religious artifacts), not to mention whether papal authority held primacy for Byzantine Christians. Eventually these matters led to a split in the Christian church in 1054, with the establishment of Eastern Orthodox Christianity and Roman Catholic Christianity. The churches still remain split, though Pope John Paul II renewed the call for unity in the twenty-first century.

Byzantine emperors had a long tradition of involvement with religious affairs. In fact, the term Caesaro-papism describes this melding of political power and religious authority in the person of the emperor. The first selection discusses the concern over the appearance of a dangerous heresy in the late third century, which threatened the unity of the early Christian church. Arius was an Egyptian priest who argued that Jesus was the Son of God and since sons always existed after fathers, then Jesus could not be both the Son of God and God at the same time. Jesus was a created being and therefore not eternal, nor made of the same substance (*homousion*) as the Father. Arius believed that Jesus was made of similar substance (*homoiousion*), but was primarily human. Constantine himself called the Council of Nicaea in 325 to settle the dispute, and therein was formed the Nicene Creed, which settled the matter and provided a precedent for secular influence within the Eastern churches.

Heresy: The Threat of Arianism

EUSEBIUS

In this manner the emperor [Constantine], like a powerful herald of God, [wrote] to all the provinces, at the same time warning his subjects against superstitious error, and encouraging them in the pursuit of true godliness. But in the midst of his joyful anticipations of the success of this measure, he received tidings of a most serious disturbance which had invaded the peace of the Church. This intelligence he heard with deep concern, and at once tried to devise a remedy for the evil. The origin of this disturbance may be thus described.

"Heresy: The Threat of Arianism" is from Eusebius, *The Life of the Blessed Emperor Constantine*, in *A Select Library of Nicene and Post-Nicene Fathers of the Christian Church*, trans. Ernest C. Richardson, vol. I (New York: The Christian Literature Company, 1890), pp. 515–516.

The people of God were in a truly flourishing state, and abounding in the practice of good works. No terror from without assailed them, but a bright and most profound peace, through the favor of God, encompassed his Church on every side. Meantime, however, the spirit of envy was watching to destroy our blessings, which at first crept in unperceived, but soon reveled in the midst of the assemblies of the saints. At length it reached the bishops themselves, and arrayed them in angry hostility against each other, on pretense of a jealous regard for the doctrines of Divine truth. Hence it was that a mighty fire was kindled as it were from a little spark, and which, originating in the first instance in the Alexandrian church, overspread the whole of Egypt and Libya, . . . and eventually extended its ravages to the other provinces and cities of the empire; so that not only the prelates of the churches might be seen encountering each other in the strife of words, but the people themselves were completely divided, some adhering to one faction and others to another. So notorious did the scandal of these proceedings become, that the sacred matters of inspired teaching were exposed to the most shameful ridicule in the very theaters of the unbelievers . . . .

The Nicene Creed (325)

EUSEBIUS

[In accordance with the Emperor Constantine's instructions,] the bishops drew up this formula of faith:

We believe in one God, the Father Almighty, Maker of all things visible and invisible: and in one Lord Jesus Christ, the Son of God, the only-begotten of the Father, that is of the substance of the Father; God of God, Light of light, true God of true God; begotten not made, consubstantial with the Father; by whom all things were made both which are in heaven and on earth; who for the sake of us men, and on account of our salvation, descended, became incarnate, was made man, suffered and rose again on the third day; he ascended into the heavens and will come to judge the living and the dead. We believe also in the Holy Spirit. But those who say "There was a time when he was not," or "He did not exist before he was begotten," or "He was made of nothing," or assert that "He is of other substance or essence than the Father," or that the Son of God is created, or mutable, or susceptible of change, the Catholic and apostolic Church of God rejects . . . .

Consequently [Christ] is no creature like those which were made by him, but is of a substance far excelling any creature; which substance the Divine Oracles teach was begotten of the Father by such a mode of generation as cannot be explained nor even conceived by any creature. Thus also the declaration that "the Son is consubstantial [*homoousios*] with the Father" having been discussed, it was agreed that this must not be understood in a corporeal sense, or in any way analogous to mortal creatures; inasmuch as it is neither by division of substance, nor by any change of the Father's substance and power, since the underived nature of the Father is inconsistent with all these things. That he is consubstantial with the Father then simply implies, that the Son of God has no resemblance to created things, but is in every respect like the Father only who begat him; and that he is of no other substance or essence but of the Father . . . . Accordingly, since no divinely inspired Scripture contains the expression, "of things which do not exist" and "there was a time when he was not," and such other phrases as are therein subjoined, it seemed unwarrantable to utter and teach them.

"The Nicene Creed" is from Eusebius, *The Life of the Blessed Emperor Constantine*, in *A Select Library of Nicene and Post-Nicene Fathers of the Christian Church*, trans. Ernest C. Richardson, vol. I (New York: The Christian Literature Company, 1890), pp. 515–518.

Iconoclasm and Orthodoxy: The Second Council of Nicaea (787)

Another primary religious dispute within Eastern Christianity was the tradition of worshiping images of Christ, the Virgin, and the saints. Although this was acceptable practice in Western churches, in 726 the Byzantine emperor Leo IV abolished the cult of images by imperial edict. This was called iconoclasm, and it is a primary example of Caesaro-papism. In 787, however, the empress Irene, who served as regent to her young son, reestablished the veneration of images at the Second Council of Nicaea, as the following source indicates. This policy remained under dispute for centuries.

We, therefore, following the royal pathway and the divinely inspired authority of our holy Fathers and the traditions of the Catholic Church for, as we all know, the Holy Spirit dwells in her, define with all certitude and accuracy, that just as the figure of the precious and life-giving cross, so also the venerable and holy images, as well in painting and mosaic, as of other fit materials, should be set forth in the holy churches of God . . . . For by so much the more frequently as they are seen in artistic representation, by so much the more readily are men lifted up to the memory of their prototypes, and to a longing after them; and to these should be given due salutation and honorable reverence, not indeed that true worship which pertains alone to the divine nature; but to these, as to the figure of the precious and life-giving cross, and to the book of the Gospels and to other holy objects, incense and lights may be offered according to ancient pious custom. For the honor which is paid to the image passes on to that which the image represents, and he who shows reverence to the image shows reverence to the subject represented in it.

Those, therefore, who dare to think or teach otherwise, or as wicked heretics dare to spurn the traditions of the Church and to invent some novelty, or else to reject some of those things which the Church hath received, to wit, the book of the Gospels, or the image of the cross, or the pictorial icons, or the holy relics of a martyr, or to devise anything subversive of the lawful traditions of the Catholic Church, or to turn to common uses the sacred vessels and the venerable monasteries, if they be bishops or clerics we command that they be deposed [and] be cut off from communion.

CONSIDER THIS:

8-4. Why was the Arian heresy such a threat to the religious unity of Christianity? How did the Nicene Creed solve the controversy? How would you interpret the statement that Jesus was "begotten not made"?

8-5. What was the emperor Constantine's role in the Council of Nicaea, and how does this reflect the principles of Caesaro-papism?

A Western Attitude toward the Byzantine Greeks (1147)

ODO OF DEUIL

One of the primary obstacles to the eventual success of the Crusades was the lack of trust and cooperation between the Roman Catholic Church in the West and the Greek Orthodox Church in the East. These two Christian churches had separated in 1054 over doctrinal differences, and this rift fueled a political and economic competition between Western forces and those of the Byzantine emperor. The following selection notes Western disgust for the Byzantine Greeks at the beginning of the Second Crusade.

"Iconoclasm and Orthodoxy" is from Joseph G. Ayer Jr., ed., *A Source Book for Ancient Church History* (New York: Charles Scribner's Sons, 1913), pp. 696–697.

"A Western Attitude toward the Byzantine Greeks" is from Odo of Deuil, *De Profectione Ludovici VII*, ed. and trans. Virginia G. Berry, p. 57. Copyright © 1948 by Columbia University Press. Reprinted by permission of Columbia University Press.

We know other heresies of theirs, both concerning their treatment of the Eucharist and concerning the procession of the Holy Ghost, but none of these matters would mar our page if not pertinent to our subject. Actually, it was for these reasons that the Greeks had incurred the hatred of our men, for their error had become known even among the lay people. Because of this they were judged not to be Christians, and the Franks considered killing them a matter of no importance and hence could with more difficulty be restrained from pillage and plundering.

And then the Greeks degenerated entirely . . . putting aside all manly vigor, both of words and of spirit, they lightly swore whatever they thought would please us, but they neither kept faith with us nor maintained respect for themselves. In general they really have the opinion that anything which is done for the holy empire [that is, Byzantium] cannot be considered perjury.

Islamic Civilization

The Religious Tenets of the Qur'an

The rise of Islamic civilization is a story of faith and confrontation amidst societies in political and cultural transition. The basic ideas of the Islamic worldview derived from a single prophetic revelation of the prophet Muhammad in the Qur'an: "There is but one God and his prophet is Muhammad." It is a simple revelation that has formed the basis of one of the world's most influential religions.

Muhammad (ca. 570–632) was an orphan who had worked on a caravan before marrying a wealthy widow. He was a man of great spiritual depth who had become troubled about the idolatry, worldliness, and lack of social conscience that plagued his society. Muhammad's discontent with this moral status quo and his searching nature positioned him to found a new religion that would address the needs of his particular Arabic community. On repeated occasions, he felt himself called by God (*Allah*) to "rise and warn" his fellow Arabs about their moral vacuousness. God's word had been delivered through other prophets prior to Muhammad, including Abraham, Moses, and Jesus. But the final revelation of God's work, the recitation (*qur'an*), was given to Muhammad by the messenger angel Gabriel. The message was clear: The Prophet Muhammad was to warn Arabs of God's displeasure with idolatrous worship and injustices to the weak and sick, the poor, widows, orphans, and women. God spoke of a judgment day when believers would enjoy the pleasures of paradise and nonbelievers would be cast into eternal hellfire, to be damned forever. God forgives the penitent and rewards those who respect his law and offer proper gratitude. Through submission (*islam*) to God's will, one becomes submissive (*muslim*) in worship and morality. A fervent monotheism is essential to the acceptance of the religion of Islam. Only humans have been given the choice either to obey or to reject the one true God.

At first Muhammad's revelations and strict demands invited opposition and even persecution in the city of Mecca, but his reputation as a moral leader increased and he was accepted in the city of Medina. This emigration (*hegira*) from Mecca to Medina in 622 became the starting point for year one of the Islamic calendar, signifying the creation of the Islamic community (*umma*).

Devotion to Islam is based on five basic principles or "pillars": (1) the acceptance of one God, Allah, and Muhammad as his prophet; (2) recitation of prayers five times a day toward Mecca after ritual purification before worship; (3) daytime fasting and abstinence from sexual relations from sunrise to sunset for one month a year; (4) payment of a tithe to support poor and unfortunate Muslims; and (5) a pilgrimage to Mecca at least once in a lifetime (hajj), if one is able. The moral codes of Islam help define the religion: allegiance to the Islamic community, abstention from alcohol and pork, and modesty in personal affairs.

After Muhammad's death in 632, the Islamic community struggled to maintain its unity because Muhammad had not named a successor. The success of Islam in organizing itself and in promoting the religion not only throughout Arab lands but beyond to Europe and the East is one of the great dramas of history. The influence of Islam on our contemporary world is formidable indeed, and it is important to understand the spiritual foundations of this impressive religion. The following excerpts are primarily from the Qur'an and provide insight into some of the most important aspects of Islam.

The Heritage of Islam

In the Name of Allah, the Compassionate, the Merciful

This Book is not to be doubted. It is a guide for the righteous, who have faith in what they cannot see and are devout in prayer; those who give to charity a portion of what We have given to them and who believe in the revelations of God, those that were offered to you and to others before you. It is a guide for those who are rightly led by the Lord and devoutly believe in a life to come. These believers shall certainly triumph.

As for the unbelievers, it does not matter whether you forewarn them—they will not have faith. God has sealed their hearts and ears and their sight is shallow and faint. A grave punishment awaits them . . . .

We gave the Scriptures to Moses and after him We sent other apostles. We gave Jesus, son of Mary, true signs and strengthened him with the Holy Spirit. Will you then deny each apostle whose message does not sit well with you by calling some imposters and by killing others? They say: "Our hearts are sealed," but God has cursed them for their unbelief, they who have but little faith.

And now a Book has come to them from God, a Book that confirms their faith and contains the truth, but they deny it. They know that it contains the truth, and have long prayed for help against the unbelievers, but they still deny it. God's curse be upon these infidels! Truly they have gambled away their souls for evil. To deny the truth of God's own revelation, even when

they admit that God can reveal His bounty to whomsoever He chooses from among His servants! They have incurred God's dire wrath. A disgraceful punishment awaits the unbelievers . . . .

Many People of the Book [Jews and Christians] want to lead you back to unbelief, even though you have embraced the Faith, and though they plainly know the truth. They are envious. Forgive them and tolerate them until God makes known His will. God has power over all things.

Be diligent in your prayers and give money to the poor. Whatever good you do shall be rewarded by God. God watches all your actions.

They declare: "None shall enter Paradise but Jews and Christians." These are but wishful fantasies. Say: "Give us your proof, if what you say is true." Indeed, those who give themselves completely to God and do good works shall be rewarded and shall have nothing to fear or to regret.

The Jews say the Christians are mistaken, and the Christians say it is the Jews who are misguided. Yet they both read the Scriptures. The ignorant reject them both. God will sort things out on the Day of Resurrection . . . .

They say: "Accept the Jewish or the Christian faith and you shall find direction and truth."

Say: "Of course not! We believe in the faith of Abraham, who was virtuous and just. He was no idolater."

"The Heritage of Islam" is from *The Qur'an*, in *Sacred Books of the East*, trans. J. Palmer, Vol. 6 (1880), 2.1; 2.87–2.88; 2.109–2.113; 2.135; 2.172–2.173; 2.177; 2.190–2.196; 82.1; 82.19. Translation modernized by the editor.

Say: "We believe in God and all that was revealed to Abraham, Ishmael, Isaac, Jacob, and the tribes, all that was revealed to Moses and Jesus and the other prophets by their Lord. We do not distinguish among any of them, but have surrendered ourselves to God."

If they accept your faith, then they shall find correct guidance; but if they reject it, they shall surely be set apart from the Lord. God is all the defense you need—he alone knows all and bears all . . . .

Believers, eat the healthy food that We have provided for you and give thanks to God, if you truly worship Him.

He has forbidden you carrion, blood, and pork or any flesh that has been consecrated other than in the name of God. But if you must eat these foods out of necessity and did not intend to sin or to transgress God's will, then you shall not incur guilt. God is forgiving and merciful . . . .

Righteousness does not consist in whether you face towards the East or the West. The righteous man believes in God and the Last Day, in the angels and the Book and the prophets. The righteous man gives his money away to his relatives, to orphans and the poor. Though he may love his wealth, nevertheless, he shares it with the traveler in need, with destitute beggars, and spends it for the redemption of those held captive. The righteous man concentrates on his prayers and gives alms to the community; he follows through on his promises and is steadfast during adversity and in times of war. Such are the true believers, such are those who respect God . . . .

For the sake of God, fight against those who fight against you, but do not attack them first. God does not love aggressors.

Kill them wherever you find them. Drive them out of the lands from which they drove you. Idolatry is more distressing than bloodshed. But do not fight them within the precincts of the holy Mosque unless they attack you there. But if they attack you, put them to the sword. This is how the unbelievers will be rewarded. But if they repent, know that God is forgiving and merciful.

Fight against the unbelievers until idolatry no longer exists and the religion of God reigns supreme. But if they stop fighting and desist, do not fight anyone except those who commit evil . . . .

Give generously for the sake of God and do not commit suicide. Be charitable—God loves the charitable.

Travel on pilgrimage and visit the Sacred House [in Mecca] for His sake. If you cannot travel there, then send whatever offerings that you can afford and do not shave your heads until the offerings have reached their destination. But if you are ill or are mentally unbalanced, you must make up for this by fasting or by giving alms or by sacrificing something of importance . . . . When the sky breaks apart, the stars scatter, the oceans roll together, and graves are thrust open, each soul shall know judgment—what it has done and what it has failed to do.

O man! What evil has taken you from your God who created you, who allowed you to walk upright and gave you proportion? He could have molded you in whatever shape He chose. Yet you do not believe in the Last Judgment. Guardians of the Lord are certainly watching you and recording all of your deeds.

The righteous shall surely dwell in paradise. But the wicked shall burn in Hell when the Day of Judgment arrives—there is no escape from it.

Would that you knew when the Day of Judgment will arrive! Oh, would that you knew when the Day of Judgment will arrive! It is the day when every soul will stand alone and God will reign supreme.

The Qur'an on Women

In the Name of Allah, the Compassionate, the Merciful

Men, fear your Lord, who created you from one soul and from that soul your mate. Through them, he populated the earth with many men and women.

Fear God, in whose name you work with one another, and honor the mothers who bore you. God is always watching you.

"The Qur'an on Women" is from is from *The Qur'an*, in *Sacred Books of the East*, translated by J. Palmer, Vol. 6 (1880), 4.1–4.2; 4.10–4.14; 4.34–4.35. Translation modernized by the editor.

Inheritance

And give orphans their property, but do not exchange their valuables for things that are worthless. And do not cheat them of their possessions, for that would certainly be a great sin. If you fear that you cannot do justice to orphan [girls] fairly, then marry women who seem good to you—two, three, or four of them. But if you do not think that you can treat them equitably, then marry only one of them or any slave girls you might own. This will make it easier for you to be just.

Give women their dowries freely and if they are good enough to give any of it to you as a free gift, then take it as a lawful possession. . . .

God instructs you with regard to your children to give your son twice the inheritance of your daughter. If there are more than two girls, then let them have two-thirds of the inheritance. But if there is only one, then give her half. As to parents, each of them should receive a sixth, if the deceased has a child. But if he has no sons or daughters and his parents inherit, then let his mother have a third. If he has brothers, his mother should have a sixth after he has paid any legacy or debt he may have owed.

You may not know whether your parents or your children are more beneficial to you. But this is a law of God and He is omniscient and wise. . . .

On the Authority of Men over Women

If any of your women commit adultery, call four witnesses from among yourselves and if these testify to their guilt, then keep the women in their houses until they die or until God finds another way. . . .

Men have authority over women because God has preferred them over women and also because they spend their wealth to maintain them. Good women are obedient, devoted, and guard their modesty and private parts in the absence of their husbands, because God has cared for them. But if you fear disobedience from some, admonish them and send them to their bedrooms and beat them. Then, if they submit and are obedient, take no more action against them. God is high and great. . . .

If a woman is afraid that she will be treated badly or deserted by her husband, then she should seek an agreement to separate through mutual consent. . . . No matter how you try, you cannot treat all your wives impartially. Do not neglect any of them and leave them in suspense as to your intent. If you do what is right and guard yourselves against evil, God will be forgiving and merciful. If the couple should separate, God will take care of both out of His own abundance: God is munificent and wise.

CONSIDER THIS:

8-6. What are the basic tenets of Islam as noted in the selections from the Qur'an? Was Muhammad, like Jesus, considered to be divine in nature?

8-7. How do you interpret the phrase "For the sake of God, fight against those who fight against you, but do not attack them first. God does not love aggressors"? The next statement reads, "Kill them wherever you find them. Drive them out of the lands from which they drove you." Do you find these ideas to be contradictory? Why or why not?

8-8. How are women viewed by the Qur'an? Do women have legal rights? Do they assume equal status with men?

THEME: SOCIAL AND SPIRITUAL VALUES

THE REFLECTION IN THE MIRROR

The Love of Allah

"The Love of Allah Should Conquer a Man's Heart"

AL-GHAZZALI

Abu Hamid Muhammad al-Ghazzali (1058–1111) was an important Muslim scholar and theologian whose writings and influence gave credibility to the mystical devotions of Sufism,

"The Love of Allah" is from Al-Ghazzali, *The Alchemy of Happiness*, trans. Claud Field, The Wisdom of the East Series (London: John Murray Publishers Ltd., 1910), pp. 51–54. Translation modernized by the editor.

thereby integrating it within orthodox Islam. For years, al-Ghazzali lectured on philosophy and jurisprudence at Nizamiyah college in Baghdad before suddenly disposing of his worldly goods and adopting the simple poverty of a Sufi, or mystic. Living a communal monastic existence, al-Ghazzali attracted many followers who found his emphasis on simplicity and complete spiritual devotion to be transformational. The following passage from a work entitled The Alchemy of Happiness testifies to his expansive and influential vision of Islam.

KEEP IN MIND . . .

8-9. How is the quest for human perfection related to the love of God?

The love of God is the highest of all topics, and is the final aim to which we have been tending hitherto. We have spoken of spiritual dangers as they hinder the love of God in a man's heart, and we have spoken of various good qualities as being the necessary preliminaries to it. Human perfection resides in this, that the love of God should conquer a man's heart and possess it wholly, and even if it does not possess it wholly it should predominate in the heart over the love of all other things. Nevertheless, rightly to understand the love of God is so difficult a matter that one sect of theologians have altogether denied that man can love a Being who is not of his own species, and they have defined the love of God as consisting merely in obedience. Those who hold such views do not know what real religion is.

All Muslims are agreed that the love of God is a duty. God says concerning the believers, "He loves them and they love Him," and the Prophet [Muhammad] said, "Till a man loves God and His Prophet more than anything else he has not the right faith . . . ."

When we apply this principle to the love of God we shall find that He alone is really worthy of our love, and that, if any one does not love Him, it is because he does not know Him. Whatever we love in any one we love because it is a reflection of Him. It is for this reason that we love Muhammad, because he is the Prophet and the Beloved of God, and the love of learned and pious men is really the love of God. We shall see this more clearly if we consider the causes which excite love.

The first cause is this, that man loves himself and the perfection of his own nature. This leads him directly to the love of God, for man's very existence and man's attributes are nothing else but the gift of God, but for whose grace and kindness man would never have emerged from behind the curtain of non-existence into the visible world. Man's preservation and eventual attainment to perfection are also entirely dependent upon the grace of God. It would indeed be a wonder, if one should take refuge from the heat of the sun under the shadow of a tree and not be grateful to the tree, without which there would be no shadow at all. Precisely in the same way, were it not for God, man would have no existence nor attributes at all. Why, then, should he not love God, unless he is ignorant of Him? Doubtless fools cannot love Him, for the love of Him springs directly from the knowledge of Him, and where should a fool acquire knowledge?

> "[Some theologians] have defined the love of God as consisting merely in obedience. Those who hold such views do not know what real religion is."
>
> —AL-GHAZZALI

CONSIDER THIS:

8-10. According to al-Ghazzali, why should Muslims love God?

8-11. Al-Ghazzali argues that if one does not love God, one does not know Him. Therefore, ignorance alone results in the rejection of God. So, why is the love of God a logical necessity? Is this the same as saying that "the love of God is a duty"?

Islamic Science and Mathematics

The Islamic community during the Middle Ages and beyond was not simply concerned with matters of faith and obedience to doctrine. As Muslim armies covered North Africa and the Middle East, even venturing into Europe, they carried with them some of the great advancements of Islamic civilization. Muslim learning was embraced in such academic centers as Córdoba, Spain, where Jewish scholars were central in establishing a conduit of knowledge to the West by translating Arabic science and medical texts into Spanish and Latin. Many of these ideas in astronomy, medicine, advanced mathematics, law, literature, poetry, philosophy, and history fell on deaf ears in the West because of the fear of doctrinal contamination. Indeed, for Western Christians, the followers of Allah were the "Infidel," to be feared and opposed through Crusades to recapture the Holy Land for the glory of a Christian God.

The following selections attest to the framework of learning and inquiry that was an impressive benefit of Islamic civilization.

On the Separation of Mathematics and Religion
AL-GHAZZALI

Mathematics comprises the knowledge of calculation, geometry, and cosmography: it has no connection with the religious sciences, and proves nothing for or against religion; it rests on a foundation of proofs which, once known and understood, cannot be refuted. Mathematics tend, however, to produce two bad results.

The first is this: Whoever studies this science admires the subtlety and clearness of its proofs. His confidence in philosophy increases, and he thinks that all its departments are capable of the same clearness and solidity of proof as mathematics. But when he hears people speak on the unbelief and impiety of mathematicians, of their professed disregard for the Divine Law, which is notorious, it is true that, out of regard for authority, he echoes these accusations, but he says to himself at the same time that, if there was truth in religion, it would not have escaped those who have displayed so much keenness of intellect in the study of mathematics.

Next, when he becomes aware of the unbelief and rejection of religion on the part of these learned men, he concludes that to reject religion is reasonable. How many of such men gone astray I have met whose sole argument was that just mentioned. . . .

It is therefore a great injury to religion to suppose that the defense of Islam involves the condemnation of the exact sciences. The religious law contains nothing which approves them or condemns them, and in their turn they make no attack on religion. The words of the Prophet, "The sun and the moon are two signs of the power of God; they are not eclipsed for the birth or the death of any one; when you see these signs take refuge in prayer and invoke the name of God"—these words, I say, do not in any way condemn the astronomical calculations which define the orbits of these two bodies, their conjunction and opposition according to particular laws.

On the Causes of Small-Pox
AL-RAZI

Although [scholars] have certainly made some mention of the treatment of Small-Pox (but without much accuracy and distinctness), yet there is not one of them who

has mentioned the cause of the existence of the disease, and how it comes to pass that hardly any one escapes it, or who has disposed the modes of treatment in their

"On the Separation of Mathematics and Religion" is from Al-Ghazzali, *The Confession of Al-Ghazzali*, trans. Claud Field, The Wisdom of the East Series (London: John Murray Publishers Ltd., 1908), pp. 33–34.

"On the Causes of Small-Pox" is from Abu Bekr Muhammad Ibn Zacariya Al-Razi, *A Treatise on Small-Pox and Measles*, trans. William A. Greenhill (London, 1848), pp. 28–31.

right places. And for this reason I . . . have mentioned whatever is necessary for the treatment of this disease, and have arranged and carefully disposed everything in its right place, by GOD's permission. . . .

I say then that every man, from the time of his birth until he arrives at old age, is continually tending to dryness; and for this reason the blood of children and infants is much moister than the blood of young men, and still more so than that of old men. . . . Now the Small-Pox arises when the blood putrefies and ferments, so that the superfluous vapors are thrown out of it, and it is changed from the blood of infants, which is like must, into the blood of young men, which is like wine perfectly ripened: and Small-Pox itself may be compared to the fermentation and the hissing noise which takes place in must at that time. And this is the reason why children, especially males, rarely escape being seized with this disease, because it is impossible to prevent the blood's changing from this state into its second state. . . .

As to young men, whereas their blood is already passed into the second state, its maturation is established, and the superfluous particles of moisture which necessarily cause putrefaction are now exhaled; hence it follows that this disease only happens to a few individuals among them, that is, to those whose vascular system abounds with too much moisture, or is corrupt in quality with a violent inflammation. . . .

And as for old men, Small-Pox seldom happens to them, except in pestilential, putrid, and malignant constitutions of the air, in which this disease is chiefly prevalent. For a putrid air, which has an undue proportion of heat and moisture, and also an inflamed air, promotes the eruption of this disease. . . .

CONSIDER THIS:

8-12. What do the selections on mathematics and the scientific description of smallpox tell you about Islamic values? According to Al-Ghazzali, should mathematics and religion be separated? Why or why not?

The Dawn of the European Middle Ages

Beowulf: The Germanic Hero

Epic poetry has been used throughout history to transmit cultural traditions from one generation to another, initially without the aid of writing. Oral narratives like the Sumerian epic of Gilgamesh or Homer's Iliad and Odyssey tell of legends and the glorious deeds of national ancestors. Because many of these heroic stories were at some time written down, they allow historians to understand the values and motivation of past societies.

Beginning in the third century, Germanic tribes wandered throughout the Western Roman Empire, contributing to its political disintegration and establishing new traditions on the Roman foundation. Out of these Germanic wanderings came a rich oral tradition that included the great epic adventures of Beowulf, written in Old English in the eighth century.

In the following excerpt, the Anglo-Saxon king Beowulf (Lord of the Geats) fights to the death with a fire-breathing dragon, who guards a great treasure trove.

The king of the Geats roared a furious challenge. He shouted until his voice penetrated the cavern and his battle-cry thundered under the grey rock. The guardian of the treasure-hoard [Grendel] bristled with rage when it recognized the voice of a man. There was no time for appeasement. The monster's scorching breath spurted ahead of it, out of the rock, while earth reverberated. The

hero, facing the barrow, swung his shield to meet the enemy; upon which the reptile was spurred to take the offensive. Already the king had drawn his sharp ancestral sword. But each of the adversaries was in awe of the other. The prince resolutely stood his ground in the shelter of his great shield while the Worm gathered its coils together. Bent like a bow, the flaming monster hurtled

"Beowulf: The Germanic Hero" is from *Beowulf*, trans. David Wright (New York and Harmondsworth, Middlesex: Penguin Books, 1957), pp. 87–91, 101. Copyright © 1957 by David Wright. Reprinted by permission of Vicki Beatson, literary executor and trustee to David Wright.

towards him and rushed upon its fate. But the king's shield gave protection to life and limb for a shorter time than he had hoped. For the first time Beowulf had to fight without success, because fate refused to grant it to him. Raising his hand, the lord of the Geats struck the glittering monster with his sword, but the blade bounded off the scales and scarcely bit, just when the king had most need. The blow infuriated the guardian of the barrow. It spat a blast of glistering fire which leapt here and there. The king could boast of no advantage now that his naked blade had failed him in battle, as no good sword should do. It was no easy thing for Beowulf to make up his mind to quit this world and take up his lodging in some other whether he liked it or not. But this is the way in which everyone has to die.

Soon the antagonists joined battle once more. The Dragon had taken fresh heart and found its second wind, while the king, hedged round with fire, suffered agony. His comrades-in-arms, who were sons of princes, utterly failed to support him in strength like good fighting-men, but fled into a wood to save their lives. Yet one among them was pricked by conscience. To a right-thinking man, blood must always be thicker than water.

His name was Wiglaf son of Weohstan, a well-liked Swedish prince of the house of Aelfhere. Wiglaf could see that the king, in spite of his armor, was in distress from the flames . . . . In bitterness of heart Wiglaf reminded his comrades of their duty. "I can remember a time when we used to accept to whom we swore that if ever he fell into straits like these we would make some return for our fighting-gear—these swords and helmets. That is why he gave me valuable gifts, and you as well. He thought that we were brave spearmen and daring soldiers . . . . Let us go forward to our king's assistance . . . ." Then he dived into the perilous smoke, bearing arms to the king's help and crying ...: "Brave prince, renowned for feats of arms, defend your life with all your might—I am coming to your help!"

At these words the Worm angrily emerged once more in swirls of sparkling flame, to take the field against its enemies, the human beings which it hated. Wiglaf's shield was burnt to the boss by a cataract of fire, while his corselet gave him no protection. The lad slipped quickly behind his kinsman's shield as soon as the flames had burnt his own to cinders.

But the king was still mindful of his fame and struck so hard with his sword that, driven by the impetus, it struck square in the Dragon's head. Yet Beowulf's patterned sword, Naegling, failed him. It shattered to splinters. Never had it been his luck that a sword should be of use to him during a fight. His hand, they say, was so strong that the force of his blows overtaxed any weapon. Even when he carried one which was hardened in battle he was no better off.

The flame-spitting Dragon screwed up its courage for a third attack. When it saw its chance it set savagely upon the hero, catching him around the neck with lacerating fangs. A torrent of gore gushed out, and Beowulf was spattered with his own life-blood. . . .

Collecting his wits, the king pulled out a razor-sharp dagger which he wore at his corselet, and ripped open the belly of the Worm. Together the kinsmen killed their adversary. That is how a man should act in a right corner! It was Beowulf's crowning hour of triumph, his last feat of arms, and the end of his life's work.

For the wound which the Dragon had just inflicted upon him began to burn and swell. Beowulf soon discovered that mortal poison was working in his breast and had bitten deep into his entrails . . . . In spite of his pitiful wound, Beowulf began to speak. He knew well enough that his span of life and term of happiness on earth was over, his sum of days wholly spent, and death very close.

"I now would wish to hand over my armor to a son of mine, were it my luck to have had an heir of my body to come after me. I have reigned over this people for half a century, and there was not a king of any neighboring nation who dared to attack me with an army or to threaten me with war. The destiny allotted to me on earth I endured; what was mine I defended well. I did not pick quarrels nor swear false oaths. Though wounded to death, I can rejoice in all these things; because when the life quits my body God cannot accuse me of the murder of my kin . . . ."

The people of the Geats prepared for Beowulf, as he had asked of them, a splendid pyre hung about with helmets, shields, and shining corselets. Then, mourning, the soldiers laid their loved and illustrious prince in the midst. Upon the hill the men-at-arms lit a gigantic funeral fire . . . . Then twelve chieftains, all sons of princes, rode round the barrow lamenting their loss, speaking of their king, reciting an elegy, and acclaiming the hero. They praised his manhood and extolled his heroic deeds. It is right that men should pay homage to their king with words, and cherish him in their hearts, when he has taken leave of the body. So the Geats who had shared his hall mourned the death of their lord, and said that of all kings he was the gentlest and most gracious of men, the kindest to his people and the most desirous of renown.

CONSIDER THIS:

8-13. In the Anglo-Saxon epic *Beowulf*, what values are important to this society as represented by the hero Beowulf? Apart from his ability in combat, why was he considered a great king? Why did Beowulf have to die? How would you describe his burial?

Charlemagne: The Moderate and Progressive King

EINHARD

Biographical writing constitutes a considerable part of medieval literature, but much of it cannot be relied on for accuracy. Medieval biographers who wrote about the lives of saints or kings often exaggerated their accomplishments for the sake of providing solid examples of moral living. A major exception to this practice was Einhard, a secretary and public works administrator at Charlemagne's court. Although his biography has some inaccuracies, nevertheless it is regarded as a trustworthy account of the life and deeds of Charlemagne, ruler of the Frankish empire from 768 to 814.

Charles was large and strong, and of lofty stature, though not excessively tall. The upper part of his head was round, his eyes very large and animated, nose a little long, hair auburn, and face laughing and merry. His appearance was always stately and dignified, whether he was standing or sitting, although his neck was thick and somewhat short and his abdomen rather prominent. The symmetry of the rest of his body concealed these defects. His gait was firm, his whole carriage manly, and his voice clear, but not so strong as his size led one to expect. His health was excellent, except during the four years preceding his death, when he was subject to frequent fevers; toward the end of his life he limped a little with one foot. Even in his later years he lived rather according to his own inclinations than the advice of physicians; the latter indeed he very much disliked, because they wanted him to give up roasts, to which he was accustomed, and to eat boiled meat instead. In accordance with national custom, he took frequent exercise on horseback and in the chase, in which sports scarcely any people in the world can equal the Franks. He enjoyed the vapors from natural warm springs, and often indulged in swimming, in which he was so skillful that none could surpass him; and hence it was that he built his palace at Aix-la-Chapelle, and lived there constantly during his later years. . . .

Charles was moderate in eating, and especially so in drinking, for he abhorred drunkenness in anybody, much more in himself and those of his household; but he could not easily abstain from food, and often complained that fasts injured his health. He rarely gave entertainments, only on great feast-days, and then to large numbers of people. His meals consisted ordinarily of four courses not counting the roast, which his huntsmen were accustomed to bring in on the spit; he was more fond of this than of any other dish. While at table, he listened to reading or music. The subjects of the readings were the stories and deeds of olden time. He was fond, too, of Saint Augustine's books, and especially of the one entitled *The City of God*. He was so moderate in the use of wine and all sorts of drink that he rarely allowed himself more than three cups in the course of a meal. . . .

Charles had the gift of ready and fluent speech, and could express whatever he had to say with the

"Charlemagne: The Moderate and Progressive King" is from Frederick Ogg, ed., *A Source Book of Medieval History* (New York: American Book Company, 1907), pp. 109–114.

FIGURE 8.2 Charlemagne's simple yet impressive throne in Aachen: "Charles was large and strong, and of lofty stature, though not excessively tall. His appearance was always stately and dignified, whether he was standing or sitting. (*Perry M. Rogers*)

utmost clearness. He was not satisfied with ability to use his native language merely, but gave attention to the study of foreign ones, and in particular was such a master of Latin that he could speak it as well as his native tongue; but he could understand Greek better than he could speak it. He was so eloquent, indeed, that he might have been taken for a teacher of oratory. He most zealously cherished the liberal arts, held those who taught them in great esteem, and conferred great honors upon them. He took lessons in grammar of the deacon Peter of Pisa, at that time an aged man. Another deacon, Albin of Britain, surnamed Alcuin, a man of Saxon birth, who was the greatest scholar of the day, was his teacher in other branches of learning. The king spent much time and labor with him studying rhetoric, dialectic, and especially astronomy. He learned to make calculations, and used to investigate with much curiosity and intelligence the motions of the heavenly bodies. He also tried to write, and used to keep tablets and blanks in bed under his pillow, that at leisure hours he might accustom his hand to form the letters; however, as he began his efforts late in life, and not at the proper time, they met with little success.

He cherished with the greatest fervor and devotion the principles of the Christian religion, which had been instilled into him from infancy. Hence it was that he built the beautiful basilica at Aix-la-Chapelle, which he adorned with gold and silver and lamps, and with rails and doors of solid brass. He had the columns and marbles for this structure brought from Rome and Ravenna, for he could not find such as were suitable elsewhere. He was a constant worshiper at this church as long as his health permitted, going morning and evening, even after nightfall, besides attending mass. He took care that all the services there conducted should be held in the best possible manner, very often warning the sextons not to let any improper or unclean thing be brought into the building, or remain in it. He provided it with a number of sacred vessels of gold and silver, and with such a quantity of clerical robes that not even the door-keepers, who filled the humblest office in the church, were obliged to wear their everyday clothes when in the performance of their duties. He took great pains to improve the church reading and singing, for he was well skilled in both, although he neither read in public nor sang, except in a low tone and with others.

He was very active in aiding the poor, and in that open generosity which the Greeks call alms; so much so, indeed, that he not only made a point of giving in his own country and his own kingdom, but when he discovered that there were Christians living in poverty in Syria, Egypt, and Africa, at Jerusalem, Alexandria, and Carthage, he had compassion on their wants, and used to send money over the seas to them. The reason that he earnestly strove to make friends with the kings beyond seas was that he might get help and relief to the Christians living under their rule. He cared for the Church of Saint Peter the Apostle at Rome above all other holy and sacred places, and heaped high its treasury with a vast wealth of gold, silver, and precious stones. He sent great and countless gifts to the popes; and throughout his whole reign the wish that he had nearest his heart was to reestablish the ancient authority of the city of Rome under his care and by his influence, and to defend and protect the Church of Saint Peter, and to beautify and enrich it out of his own store above all other churches. Nevertheless, although he held it in such veneration, only four times did he repair to Rome to pay his vows and make his supplications during the whole forty-seven years that he reigned.

The Missi Dominici (802)

The greatness of a ruler has often been determined not just by how much territory he conquered but by how well he maintained it. The administration of an empire as vast as Charlemagne's depended on efficient servants of the king. The selections that follow testify to Charlemagne's organization and efficient rule. The *Missi Dominici* were members of the church and nobility who traveled throughout the realm administering justice by acting as an appellate court; it was an attempt to inject the presence of the king directly into the law and affairs of the realm.

Concerning the embassy sent out by the lord emperor. Therefore, the most serene and most Christian lord emperor Charles chose from his nobles the wisest and most prudent men, both archbishops and some of the other bishops also, and venerable abbots and pious laymen, and has sent them throughout his whole kingdom, and through them by all the following chapters has allowed men to live in accordance with the correct law. Moreover, where anything which is not right and just has been enacted in the law, he has ordered them to investigate this most diligently and to inform him of it; since he desires, God granting, to reform it. And let no one, through his cleverness or astuteness, dare to oppose or thwart the written law, as many would like to do, or the judicial sentence passed upon him, or to do injury to the churches of God or the poor or the widows or the wards or any Christian. But all shall live entirely in accordance with God's precept, justly and under a just rule, and each one shall be admonished to live in harmony with his fellows in his business or profession; the canonical clergy ought to observe in every respect a canonical life without seeking base gain, nuns ought to keep diligent watch over their lives, laymen and the secular clergy ought rightly to observe their laws without malicious fraud, and all ought to live in mutual charity and perfect peace.

CONSIDER THIS:

8-14. In what ways did Charlemagne's administration of his empire reflect authority and structure?

"The *Missi Dominici*" is from Dana Munro, ed., *Translations and Reprints from the Original Sources of European History*, vol. 6, part 5 (Philadelphia: University of Pennsylvania, 1899), p. 16.

AGAINST THE GRAIN

The Carolingian Renaissance

Education and the Scriptures

CHARLEMAGNE

Charlemagne's involvement in his empire went beyond its administrative regulation. He believed that learning was an essential aspect of life and established palace schools run by great scholars such as Alcuin of York. In these schools, members of the nobility were taught to read and write. In practical terms, this contributed to greater communication and a more efficient administration of the empire. In spiritual terms, the Bible and other Christian writings were now open to study and revision; accuracy was demanded by the emperor. The following selections are from letters written by Charlemagne to the clergy of his realm. They are clear statements of his educational policy.

KEEP IN MIND . . .

8-15. What was the Carolingian Renaissance, and what do these aspects of Charlemagne's rule say about life in the "Dark Ages"?

Charles, by the grace of God, King of the Franks and Lombards and Patrician of the Romans, to Abbot Baugulf and to all the congregation, also to the faithful committed to you, we have directed a loving greeting by our ambassadors in the name of omnipotent God.

We, together with our faithful, have considered it to be useful that the bishoprics and monasteries entrusted by the favor of Christ to our control, . . . ought to be zealous in teaching those who by the gift of God are able to learn, . . . so that those who desire to please God by living rightly should not neglect to please him by speaking correctly . . . . For although correct conduct may be better than knowledge, nevertheless knowledge precedes conduct. Therefore, each one ought to study what he desires to accomplish, so that so much the more fully the mind may know what ought to be done, as the tongue praises omnipotent God without the hindrances of errors . . . . For

when in the years just passed letters were often written to us from several monasteries in which it was stated that the brethren who lived there offered up in our behalf sacred and pious prayers, we have recognized in most of these letters both correct thoughts and uncouth expressions; because what pious devotion dictated faithfully to the mind, the tongue, uneducated on account of the neglect of study, was not able to express in the letter without error . . . . And we all know well that, although errors of speech are dangerous, far more dangerous are errors of the understanding. Therefore, we exhort you not only not to neglect the study of letters, but also with most humble mind, pleasing to God, to study earnestly in order that you may be able more easily and more correctly to penetrate the mysteries of the divine Scriptures . . . . And may this be done with a zeal as great as the earnestness

> "For we desire you to be . . . devout in mind, learned in discourse, chaste in conduct and eloquent in speech."
> —CHARLEMAGNE

"Education and the Scriptures" is from Dana Munro, ed., *Translations and Reprints from the Original Sources of European History,* vol. 6, pt. 5 (Philadelphia: University of Pennsylvania, 1899), pp. 12–14.

with which we command it. For we desire you to be, as it is fitting that soldiers of the church should be, devout in mind, learned in discourse, chaste in conduct and eloquent in speech, so that whosoever shall seek to see you out of reverence for God, or on account of your reputation for holy conduct, just as he is edified by your appearance, may also be instructed by your wisdom, which he has learned from your reading or singing, and may go away joyfully giving thanks to omnipotent God. Do not neglect, therefore, if you wish to have our favor, to send copies of this letter to all your fellow-bishops and to all the monasteries . . . farewell.

CONSIDER THIS:

8-16. In what ways did Charlemagne's administrative and educational regulation of his empire reflect his authority and foresight?

8-17. Why did Charlemagne demand attention to reading and writing? Was the church at risk when more people could read the Bible and other Christian literature? Why?

1066: The Norman Conquest of England

WILLIAM OF MALMESBURY

The year 1066 stands out as one of the most recognizable dates in world history. When the English king Edward the Confessor died childless on January 5, 1066, Harold Godwinson, a prominent English noble, was accepted by his fellow barons as king. Although Edward had settled on Harold as his successor, he had earlier negotiated with his cousin William the Bastard, Duke of Normandy. William, who had survived constant treachery and danger since boyhood, had developed into a ruthlessly efficient and aggressive warrior who now looked to English lands as his birthright. On September 27, 1066, William embarked with his army of 7,000 cavalry and infantry from the shores of Normandy to sail across the English Channel and landed on the southeast coast near the town of Hastings. Harold Godwinson was prepared to meet him, but had been deflected by a Norwegian attack in northern England led by King Harald Hardraade. After defeating the Norwegians at the battle of Stamford Bridge (near York) on September 25, Harold quickly marched his army to the south where William had already been able to consolidate his landing force. Harold's tired and physically depleted force nevertheless fought bravely at the Battle of Hastings on October 14, 1066, but to no avail. Harold took an arrow through the eye in the midst of the battle and the English force fell apart. On Christmas Day, 1066, William the Conqueror was formally crowned King of England, and the Normans began the long-term consolidation of the English countryside. The merging of Anglo-Saxon and Norman cultures remained difficult for generations, but William's leadership set the precedent for strong royal authority and efficient administration. William of Malmsbury provides the following account of one o f the most fateful battles in military history.

The courageous leaders mutually prepared for battle, each according to his national custom. The English, as we have heard, passed the night without sleep, in drinking and singing, and in the morning proceeded without delay against the enemy. All on foot, armed with battle-axes, and covering themselves in front by the juncture of their shields, they formed an impenetrable body which would assuredly have secured their safety that day had not the Normans, by a feigned flight, induced them to open their ranks, which till

"The Norman Conquest of England" is from James Harvey Robinson, ed., *Readings in European History,* 2 Vols. (Boston: Ginn & Co., 1904–06), pp. 224–229. Translation modernized by the editor.

that time, according to their custom, had been closely compacted. King Harold himself, on foot, stood with his brothers near the standard in order that, so long as all shared equal danger, none could think of retreating.

On the other hand, the Normans passed the whole night in confessing their sins, and received the communion of the Lord's body in the morning. Their infantry, with bows and arrows, formed the vanguard, while their cavalry, divided into wings, was placed in the rear. The duke, with serene countenance, declaring aloud that God would favor his as being the righteous side, called for his arms. . . . Then starting the Song of Roland, in order that the warlike example of that hero might stimulate the soldiers, and calling on God for assistance, the battle commenced on both sides, and was fought with great ardor, neither side giving ground during the greater part of the day . . . . This alternating victory, first of one side and then of the other, continued so long as Harold lived to check the retreat; but when he fell, his brain pierced by an arrow, the flight of the English ceased not until night.

In the battle both leaders distinguished themselves by their bravery. Harold, not content with the functions of a general and with exhorting others, eagerly assumed himself the duties of a common soldier. He was constantly striking down the enemy at close quarters, so that no one could approach him with impunity, for straightway both horse and rider

would be felled by a single blow. So it was at long range, as I have said, that the enemy's deadly arrow brought him to his death.

William, too, was equally ready to encourage his soldiers by his voice and by his presence, and to be the first to rush forward to attack the thickest of the foe. He was everywhere fierce and furious; he lost three choice horses, which were that day killed under him. The dauntless spirit and vigor of the intrepid general, however, still held out. Though often called back by the kind remonstrance of his bodyguard, he still persisted until approaching night crowned him with complete victory. And no doubt the hand of God so protected him that the enemy should draw no blood from his person, though they aimed so many javelins at him . . . . This was a fatal day to England, and melancholy havoc was wrought in our dear country during the change of its lords.

CONSIDER THIS:

8-18. Do you perceive any bias in William of Malmesbury's account of the Battle of Hastings? How did he describe the conduct of the English force the night before the battle? Compare this to his description of the Norman troops. When and where do you think William of Malmesbury wrote his history? Is truth often a casualty of victory? What is the job of an historian?

THE ARTISTIC VISION

The Bayeux Tapestry

The Norman Conquest and the Sisters of Bayeux

The story of the Norman conquest of England was stitched into a tapestry for posterity by an order of nuns in Bayeux, a small town near the coast of Normandy. The tapestry was probably commissioned by Odo of Bayeux, the half-brother of William the Conqueror, and it is remarkable as a work of art. But the tapestry also had a larger purpose. Through more than seventy scenes covering 231 feet in length, the tapestry argues William's legitimate

FIGURE 8.3 The death of the Anglo-Saxon king Harold during the Battle of Hastings in 1066. This scene from the Bayeux Tapestry testifies to the brutal realities of medieval warfare. The Norman invader William the Bastard with his victory at Hastings became William I, King of England. (*Perry M. Rogers*)

claim to the English throne and also demonstrates his courage and military efficiency that resulted in his glorious victory over Harold Godwinson. In this scene, Harold is struck down during the battle of Hastings by a blow that sealed his fate and that of England.

CONSIDER THIS:

8-19. To what extent is this a valuable historical source in addition to a remarkable work of art? Or is it most valuable as a work of propaganda? Do the victors always write the history?

THE BROADER PERSPECTIVE:

8-20. Having twice barely escaped destruction during the French Revolution of 1789 to 1798, the Bayeux Tapestry was exhibited in Paris from 1803–1804 during Napoleon's accession as French emperor. Such a work of art that demonstrated a heritage of French power and victory would naturally be appealing to a conqueror like Napoleon interested in promoting national unity. The tapestry today remains in the city of Bayeux near the coast of Normandy and has been removed only twice—once during the Franco-German war of 1871 and again during World War II from its beginning in September 1939 to the surrender of Germany in the spring of 1945. Although Paris fell to Germany in both wars, the French protected the Bayeux Tapestry as an important symbol of their national heritage and as a remembrance of the conquest of England by William of Normandy nearly a thousand years before.

Feudalism

The Viking Onslaught (850–1050)

One of the most haunting of medieval images is the prow of a Viking ship. As these ships glided down the rivers of Europe, people understood that death and destruction would follow in their wake. The word Viking means warrior; it is a general appellation for the Swedes, Danes, and Norwegians who left Scandinavia in the ninth century looking for booty and adventure. The sleek, open ships of the Northmen, as the Vikings were also called, hugged the coasts of Europe and Russia, sailed down the rivers, and survived passage across the open Atlantic to help the Vikings establish settlements in North America. The navigational techniques of the Vikings and their establishment of trade routes to the Black Sea are reminders that they were important contributors to positive aspects of Western civilization. But for the medieval family, their presence inspired fear and desperation. "The Annals of Xanten" that follow were originally the work of several ninth-century monks. These fragments chronicle the destruction brought by the Vikings and underscore the decline of the Carolingian dynasty; the successors to Charlemagne simply could not protect against the ravages of constant invasion. The second selection is by Abbo, a monk in Paris, who witnessed the siege of his city.

The Annals of Xanten (845–854)

According to their custom, the Northmen plundered Eastern and Western Frisia and burned the town of Dordrecht, with two other villages, before the eyes of Lothaire [Charlemagne's grandson], who was then in the castle of Nimwegen, but could not punish the crime. The Northmen, with their boats filled with immense booty, including both men and goods, returned to their own country.

At this same time, as no one can mention or hear without great sadness, the mother of all churches, the basilica of the apostle Peter, was taken and plundered by the Moors, or Saracens, who had already occupied the region of Beneventum. The Saracens, moreover, slaughtered all the Christians whom they found outside the walls of Rome, either within or without this church. They also carried men and women away as prisoners. They tore down, among many others, the altar of the blessed Peter, and their crimes from day to day bring sorrow to Christians. Pope Sergius departed life this year.

After the death of Sergius no mention of the apostolic see has come in any way to our ears. Rabanus [Maurus], master and abbot of Fulda, was solemnly chosen archbishop as the successor of Bishop Otger, who died. Moreover the Northmen here and there plundered the Christians and engaged in a battle with the counts Sigir and Liuthar. They continued up the Rhine as far as Dordrecht, and nine miles farther to Megingard, when they turned back, having taken their booty.

While King Louis [Charlemagne's son] was ill his army of Bavaria took its way against the Bohemians. Many of these were killed and the remainder withdrew, much humiliated, into their own country. The heathen from the North wrought havoc in Christendom as usual and grew greater in strength; but it is revolting to say more of this matter.

On January 1st of that season, . . . towards evening, a great deal of thunder was heard and a mighty flash of lightning seen; and an overflow of water afflicted the human race during this winter. In the following summer an all too great heat of the sun burned the earth. Leo, pope of the apostolic see, an extraordinary man, built a fortification round the

---

"The Annals of Xanten" is from J. H. Robinson, ed., *Readings in European History*, vol. 1 (Boston: Ginn and Company, 1904), pp. 158–162.

FIGURE 8.4 The Oseberg Ship. Graceful and flowing, nevertheless, the appearance of the prow of a Viking ship often signaled danger to the inhabitants of Europe. (*The Norwegian Information Service in the United States*)

church of Saint Peter the apostle. The Moors, however, devastated here and there the coast towns in Italy . . . .

The Normans inflicted much harm in Frisia and about the Rhine. A mighty army of them collected by the river Elbe against the Saxons, and some of the Saxon towns were besieged, others burned, and most terribly did they oppress the Christians. A meeting of our kings took place on the Maas. The steel of the heathen glistened; excessive heat; a famine followed. There was not fodder enough for the animals. . . .

The Siege of Paris (806)

ABBO

The Northmen came to Paris with 700 sailing ships, not counting those of smaller size which were commonly called barques. At one stretch the Seine was lined with the vessels for more than two leagues, so that one might ask in astonishment in what cavern the river had been swallowed up, since it was not to be seen. The second day after the fleet of the Northmen arrived under the walls of the city, Siegfried, who was . . . in command of the expedition, came to the dwelling of the illustrious bishop. He bowed his head and said: "Gauzelin, have compassion on yourself and on your flock. We beseech you to listen to us, in order that you may escape death. Allow us only the freedom of the city. We will do no harm and we will see to it that whatever belongs either to you or to Odo shall be strictly respected." Count Odo, who later became king, was then the defender of the city. The bishop replied to Siegfried, "Paris has been entrusted to us by the Emperor Charles, who, after God, king and lord of the powerful, rules over almost all the world. He has put it in our care, not at all that the kingdom may be ruined by our misconduct, but that he may keep it and be assured of its peace. If, like us, you had been given the duty of defending these walls, and if you should have done that which you ask us to do, what treatment do you think you would deserve?" Siegfried replied: "I should deserve that my head be cut off and thrown to the dogs. Nevertheless, if you do not listen to my demand, tomorrow our war machines will destroy you with poisoned arrows. You will be the prey of famine and of pestilence and these evils will renew themselves perpetually every year." So saying, he departed and gathered together his comrades.

In the morning the Northmen, boarding their ships, approached the tower and attacked it. They shook it with their engines and stormed it with arrows. The city resounded with clamor, the people were aroused, the bridges trembled. All came together to defend the tower. There Odo, his brother Robert, and the Count Ragenar distinguished themselves for bravery; likewise the courageous Abbot Ebolus, the nephew of the bishop. A keen arrow wounded the prelate, while at his side the warrior Frederick was struck by a sword. Frederick died, but the old man, thanks to God, survived. There perished many Franks; after receiving wounds they were deprived of life. At last the enemy withdrew, carrying off their dead. . . . At sunrise the Danes once more . . . engaged the Christians in violent combat. On every side arrows sped and blood flowed. With the arrows mingled the stones hurled by slings and war-machines; the air was filled with them. The tower which had been rebuilt during the night groaned under the strokes of the darts, the city shook with the struggle, the people ran hither and thither, the bells jangled. The warriors rushed together to defend the tottering tower and to repel the fierce assault. . . . The redoubtable Odo who never experienced defeat continually revived the spirits of the worn-out defenders. He ran along the ramparts and hurled back the enemy. On those who were secreting themselves so as to undermine the tower he poured oil, wax, and pitch, which, being mixed and heated, burned the Danes and tore off their scalps. Some of them died; others threw themselves into the river to escape the awful substance . . . .

Now came the Emperor Charles, surrounded by soldiers of all nations, even as the sky is adorned with resplendent stars. A great throng, speaking many languages, accompanied him. He established his camp at the foot of the heights of Montmartre, near the tower. He allowed the Northmen to have the country of Sens to plunder; and in the spring he gave them 700 pounds of silver on condition that by the month of March they leave France for their own kingdom. Then Charles returned, destined to an early death.

CONSIDER THIS:

8-21. How was Paris saved from the devastation of the Northmen? Would you call this a victory for the Franks? What does this accommodation say about the strength of the Franks and the security of western Europe?

"The Siege of Paris" is from Frederick Ogg, ed., *A Source Book of Medieval History* (New York: American Book Company, 1907), pp. 168–171.

The Feudal Relationship

Feudalism in its more refined form was born of the chaos caused by the Viking invasions, internal disputes, and poor leadership, which together contributed to the destruction of Charlemagne's empire. As central authority (in the person of the king) collapsed, there evolved rather naturally a system of decentralized rule in which the most important nobles of the realm (lords) protected their own regional holdings by contracting with lesser nobles (vassals) who fought for them. This involved an expression of homage, in which the vassal promised fealty (loyalty) to the lord. In return, the vassal was usually granted a fief (parcel of land) from which he derived an income and, depending on the size of his land holdings, some measure of prestige. The vassal, in turn, might have other vassals pledged to himself in a hierarchy of support. This process was called subinfeudation and became quite complex since vassals could contract with several lords at once. In that case, one's ultimate fealty belonged to the original or most important noble, called the liege lord.

Feudalism, then, is the political, military, and legal relationship between a lord and a vassal. It had existed rather informally since the later Roman Empire, but became more sophisticated and widespread during the ninth century as the Viking invasions demanded some form of defense. The lords provided the leadership, the vassals composed the army, and the people sought the protection of such regional strong-men. In return for this protection, the free peasant often gave up his land and labored on the fief of a noble for a specified amount of time. The peasant thus became a serf and was responsible for the production and upkeep of the lord's manor. The social, economic, and legal relationship between a serf and a member of the fighting nobility for whom he worked is called manorialism. The following selections represent various aspects of medieval feudalism.

Legal Rules for Military Service

KING LOUIS IX

The baron and all vassals of the king are bound to appear before him when he shall summon them, and to serve him at their own expense for forty days and forty nights, with as many knights as each one owes; and he is able to extract from them these services when he wishes and when he has need of them. And if the king wishes to keep them more than forty days at their own expense, they are not bound to remain if they do not wish it. And if the king wishes to keep them at his expense for the defense of the realm, they are bound to remain. And if the king wishes to lead them outside of the kingdom, they need not go unless they wish to, for they have already served their forty days and forty nights.

Liege Homage

I, John of Toul, make known that I am the liege man of the lady Beatrice, countess of Troyes, and of her son, Theobald, count of Champagne, against every creature, living or dead, save my allegiance to lord Enjorand of Coucy, lord John of Arcis, and the count of Grandpre. If it should happen that the count of Grandpre should be at war with the countess and count of Champagne on his own quarrel, I will aid the

"Legal Rules for Military Service" is from Edward P. Cheyney, ed., *Translations and Reprints from the Original Sources of European History*, vol. 4, pt. 3 (Philadelphia: University of Pennsylvania, 1897), p. 30.

"Liege Homage" is from Oliver Thatcher and Edgar McNeal, eds., *A Source Book of Medieval History* (New York: Charles Scribner's Sons, 1905), pp. 364–365.

count of Grandpre in my own person, and will send to the count and countess of Champagne the knights whose service I owe to them for the fief which I hold of them. But if the count of Grandpre shall make war on the countess and the count of Champagne on behalf of his friends and not in his own quarrel, I will aid in my own person the countess and count of Champagne, and will send one knight to the count of Grandpre for the service which I owe him for the fief which I hold of him, but I will not go myself into the territory of the count of Grandpre to make war on him.

CONSIDER THIS:

8-22. Define feudalism. What conditions contributed to the rise of this system? Be specific in citing appropriate sources. How does homage differ from liege homage? What were some of the obligations of a vassal to his lord?

THE BROADER PERSPECTIVE:

8-23. Construct a sequence of contemporary events in the United States that could result in the imposition of feudal government. How realistic a proposal is this? Could it happen?

Restraint of Feudal Violence: The Truce of God (1063)

Feudalism was a system of governance that dealt well with crisis and chaos. When invaders approached, the lord called his vassals into service (levy), and the enemy was engaged. Feudalism and manorialism regularized life and afforded security in an otherwise insecure age. Therefore, these systems were maintained even during times of peace. But vassals were trained to fight and became restless when they were not "employed." Disputes between lords broke out frequently and often resulted in bloodshed and the destruction of property. Tournaments, where knights (vassals) could display their manly prowess in a somewhat controlled atmosphere, were developed to channel the destructive energy of these nobles. In this respect, the laws of chivalry and the Crusades kept regional peace and directed hostility away from Europe and toward the infidel Muslims in the Holy Land. The church went further, attacking the problem of aggression by establishing laws of conduct since called the "Truce of God." Note the church's acceptance of trial by ordeal and what it entailed.

Drogo, bishop of Terouanne, and count Baldwin [of Hainault] have established this peace with the cooperation of the clergy and people of the land.

Dearest brothers in the Lord, these are the conditions which you must observe during the time of the peace which is commonly called the truce of God, and which begins with sunset on Wednesday and lasts until sunrise on Monday.

1. During those four days and five nights no man or woman shall assault, wound, or slay another, or attack, seize, or destroy a castle, burg, or villa, by craft or by violence.
2. If anyone violates this peace and disobeys these commands of ours, he shall be exiled for thirty years as a penance, and before he leaves the bishopric he shall make compensation for the injury which he committed. Otherwise he shall be excommunicated by the Lord God and excluded from all Christian fellowship.
3. All who associate with him in any way, who give him advice or aid, or converse with him, unless it be to advise him to do penance and to leave the bishopric, shall be under excommunication until they have made satisfaction.
4. If any violator of the peace shall fall sick and die before he completes his penance, no Christian shall visit him or move his body from the place where it lay, or receive any of his possessions.

"Restraint of Feudal Violence: The Truce of God" is from Oliver Thatcher and Edgar McNeal, eds., *A Source Book of Medieval History* (New York: Charles Scribner's Sons, 1905), pp. 417–418.

5. In addition, brethren, you should observe the peace in regard to lands and animals and all things that can be possessed. If anyone takes from another an animal, a coin, or a garment, during the days of the truce, he shall be excommunicated unless he makes satisfaction . . . .

6. During the days of the peace, no one shall make a hostile expedition on horseback, except when summoned by the count; and all who go with the count shall take for their support only as much as is necessary for themselves and their horses.

7. All merchants and other men who pass through your territory from other lands shall have peace from you.

8. You shall also keep this peace every day of the week from the beginning of Advent to the octave of Epiphany and from the beginning of Lent to the octave of Easter, and from the feast of Rogations [the Monday before Ascension Day] to the octave of Pentecost.

9. We command all priests on feast days and Sundays to pray for all who keep the peace, and to curse all who violate it or support its violators.

10. If anyone has been accused of violating the peace and denies the charge, he shall take the communion and undergo the ordeal of hot iron. If he is found guilty, he shall do penance within the bishopric for seven years.

Ordeal of Hot Iron

After the accusation has been lawfully made, and three days have been passed in fasting and prayer, the priest, clad in his sacred vestments with the exception of his outside garment, shall take with a tongs the iron placed before the altar; and, singing the hymn of three youths, namely, "Bless him all his works," he shall bear it to the fire, and shall say this prayer over the place where fire is to carry out the judgment: "Bless, O Lord God, this place, that there may be for us in it sanctity, chastity, virtue and victory, and sanctimony, humility, goodness, gentleness and plenitude of law, and obedience to God the Father and the Son and the Holy Ghost." After this, the iron shall be placed in the fire and shall be sprinkled with holy water; and while it is heating, he shall celebrate mass. But when the priest shall have taken the Eucharist, he shall adjure the man who is to be tried . . . and shall cause him to take the communion. Then the priest shall sprinkle holy water above the iron and shall say: "The blessing of God the Father, the Son, and the Holy Ghost descend upon this iron for the discerning of the right judgment of God." And straightway the accused shall carry the iron to a distance of nine feet. Finally his hand shall be covered under seal for three days, and if festering blood be found in the track of the iron, he shall be judged guilty. But if, however, he shall go forth uninjured, praise shall be rendered to God.

CONSIDER THIS:

8-24. What was the purpose of the Truce of God? What in particular were some of the penalties for breaking the peace? Describe the "ordeal of hot iron." Why did the church sanction such a trial?

"Ordeal of Hot Iron" is from Ernest F. Henderson, ed., *Select Historical Documents of the Middle Ages* (London: George Bell and Sons, 1896), pp. 314–315.

Chapter 9

The Sword of Faith:
The High Middle Ages (1100–1300)

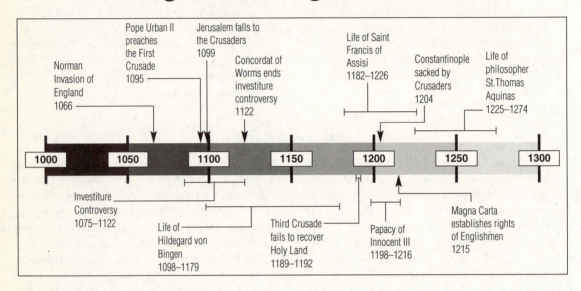

Norman Invasion of England 1066

Pope Urban II preaches the First Crusade 1095

Jerusalem falls to the Crusaders 1099

Concordat of Worms ends investiture controversy 1122

Life of Saint Francis of Assisi 1182–1226

Constantinople sacked by Crusaders 1204

Life of philosopher St. Thomas Aquinas 1225–1274

1000 1050 1100 1150 1200 1250 1300

Investiture Controversy 1075–1122

Life of Hildegard von Bingen 1098–1179

Third Crusade fails to recover Holy Land 1189–1192

Papacy of Innocent III 1198–1216

Magna Carta establishes rights of Englishmen 1215

To believe in God is impossible—not to believe in Him is absurd.

—VOLTAIRE

To raise society to a higher level is the chief business of the Church. To overcome evil with good is the genius of Christianity.

—A. P. GOUTHREY

Man is great only when he is kneeling.

—POPE PIUS XII

The tyrant dies and his rule ends, the martyr dies and his rule begins.

—SØREN KIERKEGAARD

CHAPTER THEMES

- **Social and Spiritual Values:** Was medieval society primarily spiritual or secular? In the confrontation between church and state, which authority was dominant, and which legacy more enduring? How did the papacy decline and lose influence in the face of royal control?

- **Imperialism:** Some historians have considered the Crusades to be examples of a great "religious enterprise." To what extent were the Crusades about religion and to what extent were they about the assertion of blatant military imperialism and lust for conquest?

- **Women in History:** What were the social and political positions of women during the Middle Ages? Were the Middle Ages a period of relative freedom for women, and to what extent was the position of women based on the popular worship of the Virgin Mary? Were women figuratively "placed on pedestals," and did the medieval concept of chivalry enhance their social positions? How did the Islamic view of women differ?

- **The Big Picture:** Why do people need religion? How can it be manipulated by the state to control a population? Are popes, in essence, the same as kings?

The years from about 1100 to 1300 (called the High Middle Ages) represent the acme of medieval civilization. During this era, universities were established and the great cathedrals were built as testaments of faith and devotion to God. This Christian devotion bordered on fanaticism as thousands marched off to the glory of the Crusades, hoping to achieve divine victory against the Muslims. The issue of authority was also brought more fully into question as popes and kings contended for ultimate supremacy in the earthly realm.

The conflict between religious and secular authority is one of the fundamental themes of Western civilization. Because of the diversity of human needs ranging from physical security to emotional support, establishing and maintaining order and harmony in a city or state is a complex and difficult task. It might be argued that two basic spheres of leadership exist in human affairs: the secular sphere, including matters of government, law, and domestic harmony, as well as defense and foreign affairs; and the spiritual sphere, generally, but not exclusively, attending to less tangible and more abstract human concerns. Questions of deity, creation, ethics, life, death, and afterlife are the concerns of religious leadership. For one person or a small group of people to rule effectively, they not only must control the apparatus of physical coercion in the state (military, police, etc.), but must also be recognized as head, or at least protector, of the people's religion. Thus the pharaohs of Egypt were revered as divine beings; in ancient Rome, the emperors bore the title Pontifex Maximus and served as head of the state religion, often to be deified after death. In modern totalitarian autocracies, control of party and state must be balanced by control of the state church or suppression of religion. Such is the essence of despotic authority.

We should therefore not be surprised to find that in the Middle Ages many kings and popes aspired to both secular and religious power. Both claimed supremacy over the other and based their positions on the evidence of scripture and logical argument. On one hand, a king might well argue that the very survival of the church depended on his military strength; as defender of the faith, his will should prevail. On the other hand, the pope's position as successor to Saint Peter and representative of God on earth commanded the respect of all. For he was entrusted with the "Keys of Heaven," and there could be no exception to the ultimate authority of God.

It is difficult to assess the Middle Ages as a whole because there are so many different aspects to consider. However, one dominant theme is religious devotion. Devotion to God was a foundation of the medieval world; the ascetic principles and dutiful prayers of the monks had great purpose in maintaining a proper relationship with the Creator. Popular devotion was also evident in the construction of magnificent cathedrals like Notre Dame, Chartres, and Canterbury. Generations of construction workers labored to make their local cathedral impressive in the eyes of God. They were followed by generations of pilgrims who journeyed long distances simply to pray and offer gifts to an enshrined saint. The devotion of a vassal to his lord also proved to be the foundation of political organization, and the abstract devotion of a knight to chivalric ideals provided purpose and direction in life. The relationship of chaos and unity is another major theme. Much of the history of this period involves attempts to achieve unity by restraining the forces that contributed to chaos. In this respect, the conflicts between the representatives of church and state, as well as the Viking invasions and the Black Death of the Late Middle Ages, were

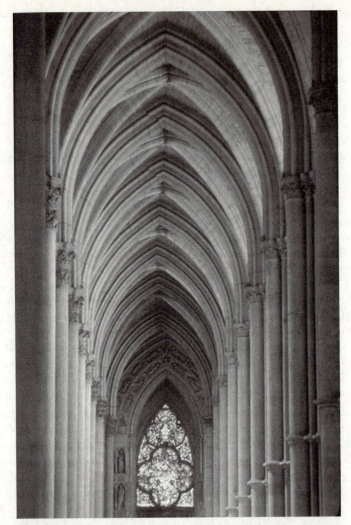

FIGURE 9.1 The impressive nave of Rheims cathedral. Medieval civilization flowed from a spiritual base. *(Perry M. Rogers)*

primary threats to the unity of medieval civilization. They were countered by movements that organized and directed energy, such as the Crusades or the cult of the Virgin Mary (to whom so many cathedrals were dedicated), or by the security of the feudal relationship. In so many other ways, the Middle Ages was an era of economic and technological progress—progress that flowed from a spiritual base.

The historical sources contained in this chapter reflect the problems and pressures of the medieval world and offer insight into the conditions and ideas that are truly representative of this important era.

KEY EVENTS IN THE HIGH MIDDLE AGES

1075–1122   The Investiture Controversy
Pope Gregory VII and Holy Roman Emperor Henry IV struggle for supremacy between church and state. Eventually resolved by their successors with the Concordat of Worms (1122): Church would elect prelates and invest them with spiritual authority; the emperor then invests them with secular lands, goods, and privileges.

1091–1153   Life of Saint Bernard
A visionary leader and talented organizer, Bernard founds monastery at Clairvaux (1115) and leads monastic reform movement throughout Europe.

1095–1099   The First Crusade
At the Council of Clermont, Pope Urban II calls for a crusade to free the Holy Land from Muslim control (1095). Jerusalem falls to the Crusaders in 1099, beginning forty-five years of Western rule in the Holy Land.

1154–1189   Reign of King Henry II of England
Henry's friend, chancellor, and Archbishop of Canterbury, Thomas Becket, murdered on Henry's orders (1170) and subsequently canonized. Dysfunctional family led by Henry's brilliant and powerful wife, Eleanor of Aquitaine, and joined by sons Richard, Geoffrey, and John foments several rebellions against Henry.

1182–1226   Life of Saint Francis of Assisi
Founder of the Franciscan order of friars, Saint Francis is one of the most influential Christian leaders during the Middle Ages.

1189–1192   The Third Crusade
Attended by King Richard III of England, King Philip Augustus of France, and Holy Roman Emperor Frederick Barbarossa, this famous crusade fails to recover Holy Land from Muslims because of the active resistance of Saladin.

1198–1216   Papacy of Innocent III
The foremost medieval pope, Innocent dominated secular kings and controlled England as a feudal fief. His papacy represents height of spiritual power and influence during the Middle Ages.

1215   Magna Carta
The English barons force King John of England to sign the Great Charter that establishes basic rights of Englishmen and functions as a repository of precedent for civil liberties.

1225–1274   Life of Saint Thomas Aquinas
Generally regarded as the most insightful and important medieval philosopher.

The Medieval Church in Ascendancy

The Crusading Movement

Launching the Crusades: "It Is the Will of God!" (1095)

ROBERT THE MONK

The first expedition to free the Holy Land from the control of the Infidel Muslim was launched in 1095 at the Council of Clermont. Pope Urban II presided and in a rousing speech excited the crowd with this impassioned plea for action. Although we are not sure about the accuracy of the text (we have five contemporary versions), the following account by Robert the Monk is credible and clearly illustrates Urban's justification for the First Crusade as well as his popular appeal.

In 1095 a great council was held in Auvergne, in the city of Clermont. Pope Urban II, accompanied by cardinals and bishops, presided over it. It was made famous by the presence of many bishops and princes from France and Germany. After the council had attended to ecclesiastical matters, the pope went out into a public square, because no house was able to hold the people, and addressed them in a very persuasive speech, as follows: "O race of the Franks, O people who live beyond the mountains [the Alps], O people loved and chosen of God, as is clear from your many deeds, distinguished over all other nations by the situation of your land, your catholic faith, and your regard for the holy church, we have a special message and exhortation for you. For we wish you to know what a grave matter has brought us to your country. The sad news has come from Jerusalem and Constantinople that the people of Persia, an accursed and foreign race, enemies of God, a generation that set not their heart aright, and whose spirit was not steadfast with God [*Ps. 78:8*], have invaded the lands of those Christians and devastated them with the sword, rapine, and fire. Some of the Christians they have carried away as slaves, others they have put to death. The churches they have either destroyed or turned into mosques. They desecrate and overthrow the altars. They circumcise the Christians and pour the blood from the circumcision on the altars or in the baptismal fonts. Some they kill in a horrible way by cutting open the abdomen, taking out a part of the entrails and tying them to a stake; they then beat them and compel them to walk until all their entrails are drawn out and they fall to the ground. Some they use as targets for their arrows. They compel some to stretch out their necks and then they try to see whether they can cut off their heads with one stroke of the sword. It is better to say nothing of their horrible treatment of the women. They have taken from the Greek empire a tract of land so large that it takes more than two months to walk through it. Whose duty is it to avenge this and recover that land, if not yours? For to you more than to other nations the Lord has given the military spirit, courage, agile bodies, and the bravery to strike down those who resist you. Let your minds be stirred to bravery by the deeds of your forefathers, and by the efficiency and greatness of [Charlemagne], and of Ludwig his son, and of the other kings who have destroyed Turkish kingdoms, and established Christianity in their lands. You should be moved especially by the holy grave of our Lord and Savior which is now held by unclean peoples, and by the holy places which are treated with dishonor and irreverently desecrated with their uncleanness.

"Launching the Crusades" is from Oliver Thatcher and Edgar McNeal, eds., *A Source Book of Medieval History* (New York: Charles Scribner's Sons, 1905), pp. 518–520.

"O bravest of knights, descendants of unconquered ancestors, do not be weaker than they, but remember their courage. If you are kept back by your love for your children, relatives and wives, remember what the Lord says in the Gospel: 'He that loveth father or mother more than me is not worthy of me' [*Matt. 10:37*]; 'and everyone that hath forsaken houses, or brothers, or sisters, or father, or mother, or wife, or children, or lands for my name's sake, shall receive a hundredfold and shall inherit everlasting life' [*Matt. 19:29*]. Let no possessions keep you back, no concern for your property. Your land is shut in on all sides by the sea and mountains, and is too thickly populated. There is not much wealth here, and the soil scarcely yields enough to support you. On this account you kill and devour each other, and carry on war and mutually destroy each other. Let your hatred and quarrels cease, your civil wars come to an end, and all your dissensions stop. Set out on the road to the holy sepulcher, take the land from that wicked people, and make it your own. . . . This land our Savior made illustrious by his birth, beautiful with his life, and sacred with his suffering; he redeemed it with his death and glorified it with his tomb. This royal city is now held captive by her enemies, and made pagan by those who know not God. She asks and longs to be liberated and does not cease to beg you to come to her aid. She asks aid especially from you because, as I have said, God has given more of the military spirit to you than to other nations. Set out on this journey and you will obtain the remission of your sins and be sure of the incorrigible glory of the kingdom of heaven."

When Pope Urban had said this and much more of the same sort, all who were present were moved to cry out with one accord, "It is the will of God, it is the will of God!" When the pope heard this he raised his eyes to heaven and gave thanks to God, and, commanding silence with a gesture of his hand, he said: "My dear brethren, today there is fulfilled in you that which the Lord says in the Gospel, 'Where two or three are gathered in my name, there am I in the midst' [*Matt. 18:20*]. For unless the Lord God had been in your minds you would not all have said the same thing. For although you spoke with many voices, nevertheless it was one and the same thing that made you speak. So I say unto you, God, who put those words into your hearts, has caused you to utter them. Therefore let these words be your battle cry, because God caused you to speak them. Whenever you meet the enemy in battle, you shall all cry out, 'It is the will of God! It is the will of God!'"

CONSIDER THIS:

9-1. In the Clermont speech of Pope Urban II, what specific reasons are given for the necessity of a Crusade to the Holy Land? How does he justify a military expedition in which bloodshed could be expected?

Out of Control: The Fall of Jerusalem (1099)

The Crusaders who set out at the behest of Pope Urban II in 1096 were quite successful in defeating Muslim armies, capturing territory along the pilgrimage route into Syria, and maintaining it with defensive castles established at Edessa and Antioch. Their ultimate goal, however, was Jerusalem, a city sacred to Christian, Jew, and Muslim alike. Its bloody fall to the Christian forces in 1099 is described in the following account known as the *Gesta Francorum*.

During this siege, we suffered so badly from thirst that we sewed up the skins of oxen and buffaloes, and we used to carry water in them for the distance of nearly six miles. We drank the water from these

"Out of Control: The Fall of Jerusalem" is from Rosalind Hill, ed., *Gesta Francorum* (London: Oxford University Press, 1962), pp. 89–92. Reprinted by permission of Oxford University Press.

vessels, although it stank, and what with foul water and barley bread we suffered great distress and affliction every day, for the Saracens used to lie in wait for our men by every spring and pool, where they killed them and cut them to pieces; moreover they used to carry off the beasts into their caves and secret places in the rocks.

Our leaders then decided to attack the city with engines, so that we might enter it and worship at our Savior's Sepulcher. They made two wooden siege-towers and various other mechanical devices. Duke Godfrey filled his siege-tower with machines, and so did Count Raymond, but they had to get the timber from far afield. When the Saracens saw our men making these machines, they built up the city wall and its towers by night, so they were exceedingly strong. When, however, our leaders saw which was the weakest spot in the city's defenses, they had a machine and a siege-tower transported round to the eastern side one Saturday night. They set up these engines at dawn, and spent Sunday, Monday and Tuesday in preparing the siege-tower and fitting it out, while the count of St. Gilles was getting his engine ready on the southern side. All this time we were suffering so badly from the shortage of water that for one penny a man could not buy anything sufficient to quench his thirst.

On Wednesday and Thursday we launched a fierce attack upon the city, both by day and by night, from all sides, but before we attacked, our bishops and priests preached to us, and told us to go in procession round Jerusalem to the Glory of God, and to pray and give alms and fast, as faithful men should do. On Friday at dawn we attacked the city from all sides but could achieve nothing, so that we were all astounded and very much afraid, yet, when that hour came when our Lord Jesus Christ deigned to suffer for us upon the cross, our Knights were fighting bravely on the siege-tower, led by Duke Godfrey and Count Eustace his brother. At that moment one of our knights, called Lethold, succeeded in getting on to the wall. As soon as he reached it, all the defenders fled along the walls and through the city, and our men went after them, killing them and cutting them down

as far as Solomon's Temple, where there was such a massacre that our men were wading up to their ankles in enemy blood.

Count Raymond was bringing up his army and a siege-tower from the south to the neighborhood of the wall, but when he heard that the Franks were in the city he said to his men, Why are you so slow? Look! All the other Franks are in the city already! Then the amir who held David's Tower surrendered to the count, and opened for him the gate where the pilgrims used to pay their taxes, so our men entered the city, chasing the Saracens and killing them up to Solomon's Temple, where they took refuge and fought hard against our men for the whole day, so that all the temple was streaming with their blood. At last, when the pagans were defeated, our men took many prisoners, both men and women, in the temple. They killed whom they chose, and whom they chose they saved alive. On the roof of the Temple of Solomon were crowded great numbers of pagans of both sexes. . . .

After this our men rushed round the whole city, seizing gold and silver, horses and mules, and houses full of all sorts of goods, and they all came rejoicing and weeping from excess of gladness to worship at the Sepulcher of our Savior Jesus, and there they fulfilled their vows to him. Next morning they went cautiously up on to the Temple roof and attacked the Saracens, both men and women, cutting off their heads with drawn swords. Some of the Saracens threw themselves down headlong from the temple. . . . Our leaders then took counsel and ordered that every man should give alms and pray that God would choose for himself whomsoever he wished, to rule over the other and to govern the city. They also commanded that all the Saracen corpses should be thrown outside the city because of the fearful stench, for almost the whole city was full of their dead bodies. So the surviving Saracens dragged the dead ones out in front of the gates, and piled them up in mounds as big as houses. No-one has ever seen or heard of such a slaughter of pagans, for they were burned on pyres like pyramids, and no-one save God alone knows how many there were. . . .

THE HISTORIAN AT WORK—USAMAH IBN-MUNQIDH

Infidel: A Muslim Perspective

It has been said that history is often written through the eyes of the conquerors. And although one cannot speak of a "winner" or "loser" in the Crusades because of the complexities of the issues, it is true that there were distinct Christian and Islamic perspectives. Usamah Ibn-Munqidh (1095–1188) remains one of our most important Arab sources for the Crusades. A diplomat, politician, and historian, Usamah was born into an aristocratic family in the small, independent emirate of Shalzar and was the nephew of its emir. He received an excellent education and was raised in a sophisticated and highly regulated Islamic society that carefully respected social boundaries.

As a diplomat, he had entry into the highest administrative levels of the various political authorities in the region. He traveled extensively from Damascus to Jerusalem and on to the courts of Fatimid Egypt. He was a respected negotiator and often worked to secure alliances between one emirate and another, or even between Arabs and Europeans like the enemy Franks during the Third Crusade. He was a devout Muslim, but enjoyed his discussions with various Christian kings and military leaders, establishing significant friendships along the way. Curious and observant, Usamah was fascinated with the Christian practice of trial by ordeal and was often shocked by Frankish ignorance regarding medicine. However, he never doubted their courage in battle. The following accounts give a particularly interesting view of the Christians, their customs, and Muslim confidence in the protection of Allah.

KEEP IN MIND . . .

9-2. What is Usamah's opinion of Frankish warriors during the Third Crusade?

The Protection of Allah

I saw a proof of the goodness of Allah and of his splendid protection when the Franks (the curse of Allah upon them!) encamped against us with knights and foot-soldiers. We were separated from one another by the Orontes River, whose waters were so swollen that the Franks could not reach us and we were prevented from reaching them. They pitched their tents on the mountain, while some took up their position in the gardens in their neighborhood, set their horses free in the meadows and went to sleep. Some young foot-soldiers from Schaizar took off their clothes, took their swords, swam towards these sleepers and killed several of them. Then a number of our enemies rushed at our companions, who took to the water and returned, while the Frankish army rushed down the mountain on horseback like a flood. Near them there was a mosque, the mosque of Abou'l-Madjd ibn Soumayya, in which there was a man named Hasan az-Zahid (the ascetic), who lived on a flat roof and used to retire to the mosque to pray. He was dressed in black woolen clothes. We saw him, but we had no means of reaching him. The Franks came, got down at the gate of the mosque and went towards him, while we said, "Power and might belong to Allah alone! The Franks will kill him." But he, by Allah, neither stopped praying nor moved from his position. The Franks stopped, turned away, remounted their horses and rode off, while he remained motionless in the same place,

"The Protection of Allah" is from G. R. Potter, trans., *The Autobiography of Ousama (1095–1188)* (London: George Routledge and Sons, 1929), pp. 123–124. Translation modernized by the editor.

continuing to pray. We did not doubt that Allah (glory be to him!) had blinded the Franks with regard to him and had hidden him from their sight. Glory to the Almighty, the Merciful!

The Franks: "Superior in Courage, but Nothing Else"

Glory be to Allah, the creator and author of all things! Anyone who is acquainted with what concerns the Franks can only glorify and sanctify Allah the All-Powerful; for he has seen in them animals who are superior in courage and in zeal for fighting but in nothing else, just as beasts are superior in strength and aggressiveness.

I will report some Frankish characteristics and my surprise as to their intelligence. . . . Among the curiosities of medicine among the Franks, I will tell how the governor of Al-Mounaitira wrote to my uncle to ask him to send him a doctor who would look after some urgent cases. My uncle chose a Christian doctor named Thabit (?). He remained absent only ten days and then returned to us. There was a general exclamation: "How rapidly you have cured your patients!" Thabit replied: "They brought before me a knight with an abscess which had formed in his leg and a woman who was wasting away with a consumptive fever. I applied a little plaster to the knight; his abscess opened and took a turn for the better; the woman I forbade certain food and improved her condition." It was at this point that a Frankish doctor came up and said: "This man is incapable of curing them." Then, turning to the knight, he asked, "Which do you prefer, to live with one leg or die with two?" "I would rather live with one leg," the knight answered. "Bring a stalwart knight," said the Frankish doctor, "and a sharp hatchet." Knight and hatchet soon appeared. I was present at the scene. The doctor stretched the patient's leg on a block of wood and then said to the knight, "Strike off his leg with the hatchet; take it off at one blow." Under my eyes the knight aimed a violent blow at it without cutting through the leg. He aimed another blow at the unfortunate man, as a result of which his marrow came from his leg and the knight died instantly. As for the woman, the doctor examined her and said,

"She is a woman in whose head there is a devil who has taken possession of her. Shave off her hair!" His prescription was carried out, and like her fellows, she began once again to eat garlic and mustard. Her consumption became worse. The doctor then said, "It is because the devil has entered her head." Taking a razor, the doctor cut open her head in the shape of a cross and scraped away the skin in the center so deeply that her very bones were showing. He then rubbed the head with salt. In her turn, the woman died instantly. After having asked them whether my services were still required and obtained an answer in the negative, I came back, having learned about their woefully brutal medicine.

At Neapolis, I was once present at a curious sight. They brought in two men for trial by battle, the cause being the following. Some Muslim brigands had raided some property in the neighborhood of Neapolis. A farmer was suspected of having guided the brigands to this spot. The farmer fled but soon returned, because the king had imprisoned his children. "Treat me with equity," said the accursed man, "and allow me to fight the one who accused me of bringing the brigands into the village." The king then told the lord who had received the village as a fief: "Send for his opponent." The lord returned to his village, picked out a blacksmith who was working there, and said to him, "You must go and fight a duel." For the owner of the fief wanted to make sure that none of his field workers got himself killed because then his crops would suffer.

I saw this blacksmith. He was a strong young man, but one who, walking or sitting, always wanted something to drink. As for the other, the challenger to single combat, he was an old man of great courage, who snapped his fingers as a token of defiance and prepared for the fight without disruption. The sheriff [and] governor of the town appeared,

---

"The Infidel: 'Superior in Courage, but Nothing Else'" is from G. R. Potter, trans., *The Autobiography of Ousama (1095–1188)* (London: George Routledge and Sons, 1929), pp. 172–175, 181–182. Translation modernized by the editor.

gave each of the two fighters a cudgel and shield and made the crowd form a ring round them.

The fight started. The old man forced the blacksmith backwards, throwing him on to the edge of the crowd, and then returned to the middle of the ring. The exchange of blows was so violent that the rivals, who remained standing, seemed to make up one pillar of blood.

The fight continued, while the sheriff urged them to force a conclusion. "Quicker," he shouted to them. The blacksmith had experience at wielding a hammer. When the old man was exhausted, the blacksmith aimed a blow at him, but lost control of the hammer which sailed over the old man and fell behind him. The blacksmith then crouched over the old man in order to put his fingers into eyes, but he could not easily find them because of the streams of blood which were flowing from them. So he got up, reached for the hammer, and struck the man's head so violently that he finished him off.

At once they put a rope round the neck of the corpse, which they took away and hung on a gallows.

The lord who had chosen the blacksmith gave him a considerable piece of property, put him on a horse with his followers, and sent him away. See from this example what law and judicial proceedings mean among the Franks (the curse of Allah upon them!).

CONSIDER THIS:

9-3. What are the overriding themes in Usamah Ibn-Munqidh's accounts of Muslim contact with the Franks? How does he characterize these Europeans?

9-4. In contrast, what are the inherent qualities of Muslim soldiers and society?

9-5. Usamah's stories appear credible because they are based on eyewitness accounts that he has seen himself or finds reliable. Do you believe him? What was his purpose as a diplomat and historian?

THE BROADER PERSPECTIVE:

9-6. Note how Usamah barely contains his contempt for Frankish medicine and the evident lack of respect for human suffering, justice, and life itself. In offering these eyewitness accounts of European brutality, how does he define enemy culture and place himself in the position of an ethical arbiter? In so doing, does Usamah actually define the progressive elements of Islamic civilization by contrasting them with the Franks who represent Christian values? So, in this view, why should the Muslim warriors oppose Christian invasion of their land? What higher goals justify their opposition? Is this an effective technique for writing history?

9-7. Most historians have found Usamah's perspective and observations of the clash of cultures during the Third Crusade to be balanced and fair for the most part. He praises courage and condemns ignorance and shortsighted action when he sees it. And Usamah makes no direct statements in these accounts regarding the relative truth or merits of Islam and Christianity as religions, except to give rather formulaic praise of Allah or condemnation of the Franks ("May Allah curse them!"). Do you perceive any political purpose to his history? Yet is there an implication of the ethical superiority of one religion or one culture over the other? Does this subtlety make him an effective historian or a deceptive and biased apologist?

The Investiture Controversy (1075–1122)

From about 1050 to 1300, a series of German popes, who had been influenced by the monastic reform movements of the tenth and early eleventh centuries, sought to purge the church of major abuses. Two of the most important abuses that had led to moral debasement of the clergy and the withdrawal of laymen from the organized church were simony (the purchase of church offices through money or illicit obligations) and the marriage or concubinage of clergy. The particular issue, however, that touched off a period of strained church-and-state relations was that of investiture.

A long-established practice allowed lay magnates such as feudal lords, kings, and, most importantly, Holy Roman emperors to govern their territory with the help of bishops and archbishops, known as prelates. The prelates were generally educated, loyal, able administrators who provided a necessary link between the noble or king and his dependents. The kings chose and rewarded the prelates, and by the eleventh century also "invested" them with ring and staff, the symbols of episcopal power, sometimes with the words "receive thy church." The recent reform movement of the internal affairs of the church naturally lent itself to a redefinition of the church's position on lay magnates. The reformers came to challenge this practice of "lay investiture," arguing that the choice and investment of prelates was rightly a spiritual matter. In so doing, they challenged the basis of effective rule and royal authority.

The controversy came to a head when a young monk named Hildebrand succeeded to the papacy amid popular acclamation. He had established a reputation as an ardent and respected reformer and took the name Gregory VII (1073–1085). His main antagonist was the aggressive Holy Roman emperor, Henry IV (1056–1106). The two soon quarreled over the issue of investiture, and Gregory did not hesitate to use his "spiritual sword," which included the extreme penalty of excommunication from the sacraments of the church and, as a result, eternal damnation in Hell. In the succeeding test of wills, the supremacy of church or state was hotly disputed.

In a spiritual age, does the abstract control over one's soul demand more respect and allegiance than the tangible military power of the secular leader? The investiture dispute was but one incident among several between church and state that were vigorously pursued at the time. The contest for primacy continued until the fourteenth century, when events like the transfer of the papacy from Rome to Avignon (the Babylonian Captivity) and the division of the church (the Great Schism) led to a crisis in spiritual leadership. And yet, this basic controversy continues in the modern world whenever prayer in school is discussed and the concept of separation between church and state is debated. The investiture controversy makes us aware of the historical roots of this problem.

The Excommunication of Emperor Henry IV (February 1076)

POPE GREGORY VII

Pope Gregory VII's decrees against lay investiture were in effect a declaration of papal primacy over the secular power of the Holy Roman emperor. However, they did not deter Henry from supporting his own candidate for the bishopric of Milan against the pope's choice. This led to a brisk and inflammatory correspondence between the two. Henry deposed Gregory as pope, and Gregory countered by deposing Henry as Holy Roman emperor. In addition, Gregory excommunicated Henry from the church, which had political as well as religious implications: Henry's nobles were thereby freed from their oaths of allegiance to him.

Saint Peter, prince of the apostles, incline your ear to me, I beseech thee, and hear me, thy servant, whom you have nourished from my infancy and have delivered from my enemies that hate me for my fidelity to thee. . . . It is not by my efforts, but by thy grace, that I am set to rule over the Christian world which was specially entrusted to thee by Christ. It is by thy grace and as thy representative

---

"The Excommunication of Emperor Henry IV" is from Oliver Thatcher and Edgar McNeal, eds., *A Source Book of Medieval History* (New York: Charles Scribner's Sons, 1905), pp. 155–156.

that God had given to me the power to bind and to loose in heaven and earth. Confident of my integrity and authority, I now declare in the name of omnipotent god, the Father, Son, and Holy spirit, that Henry, son of the emperor Henry, is deprived of his kingdom of Germany and Italy; I do this by thy authority and in defense of the honor of thy church, because he has rebelled against it. He who attempts to destroy the honor of the church should be deprived of such honor as he may have held. He has refused to obey as a Christian should, he has not returned to God from whom he had wandered, he has had dealings with excommunicated persons, he has done many iniquities, he has despised the warnings which I sent to him for his salvation, he has cut himself off from thy church, and has attempted to rend it asunder; therefore, by thy authority, I place him under the curse. It is in thy name that I curse him, that all people may know that thou art Peter, and upon thy rock the son of the living God has built his church, and the gates of hell shall not prevail against it.

"Go to Canossa!" Henry's Penance (January 28, 1077)

POPE GREGORY VII

In joining battle with Gregory, Henry had misjudged his opponent. Although most of the German bishops (whom Henry had appointed) supported him, his nobles, already restless, took the opportunity to rebel against their excommunicated king. Under such pressure, Henry promised to respect the pope and finally humbled himself before Gregory at the papal retreat high in the mountains at Canossa. There, Gregory granted him absolution, as recorded in a letter to the German nobles dated January 28, 1077. Henry's oath at Canossa follows.

In the meantime we learned that the king was approaching. Now before he entered Italy he had sent to us and had offered to make complete satisfaction for his fault, promising to reform and henceforth to obey us in all things, provided we would give him our absolution and blessing. We hesitated for some time, taking occasion in the course of the negotiations to reprove him sharply for his former sins. Finally, he came in person to Canossa, where we were staying, bringing with him only a small retinue and manifesting no hostile intentions. Once arrived, he presented himself at the gate of the castle, barefoot and clad only in wretched woolen garments, beseeching us with tears to grant him absolution and forgiveness. This he continued to do for three days, until all those about us were moved to compassion at his plight and interceded for him with tears and prayers. Indeed, they marveled at our hardness of heart, some even complaining that our action savored rather of heartless tyranny than of chastening severity. At length his persistent declarations of repentance and the supplications of all who were there with us overcame our reluctance, and we removed the excommunication from him and received him again into the bosom of the holy mother church. . . . Now that this arrangement has been reached to the common advantage of the church and the empire, we purpose coming to visit you in your own land [Germany] as soon as possible. For, as you will perceive from the conditions stated in the oath, the matter is not to be regarded as settled until we have held consultation with you. Therefore we urge your action. We have not bound our self to anything, except that we assured the king that he might depend upon us to aid him in everything that looked to his salvation and honor.

"'Go To Canossa!': Henry's Penance" is from Oliver Thatcher and Edgar McNeal, eds., *A Source Book of Medieval History* (New York: Charles Scribner's Sons, 1905), pp. 158–159.

Oath at Canossa (January 1077)

EMPEROR HENRY IV

I, Henry, king, promise to satisfy the grievances which my archbishops, bishops, dukes, counts, and other princes of Germany or their followers may have against me, within the time set by Pope Gregory and in accordance with his conditions. If I am prevented by any sufficient cause from doing this within that time, I will do it as soon after that as I may. Further, if Pope Gregory shall desire to visit Germany or any other land, on his journey to that place, his sojourn there, and his return afterwards, he shall not be molested or placed in danger of captivity by me or by anyone whom I can control. This shall apply to his escort and retinue and to all who come and go in his service. Moreover, I will never enter into any plan for hindering or molesting him, but will aid him in good faith and to the best of my ability if anyone else opposes him.

After Henry's oath of allegiance to the pope in 1077, he attempted to reestablish authority among his nobles in Germany who had in the meantime supported a rival named Rudolf. After three years of civil war, Gregory finally decided to support Rudolf and for a second time deposed and excommunicated Henry. Gregory's attempt at "king-making" was badly timed. Henry's influence was growing, and in December 1080 he defeated and killed Rudolf. Henry's momentum could not be halted, and he soon denounced Gregory and invaded Italy, finally occupying Rome in 1084 and besieging the pope in the fortress of Saint Angelo. Although Gregory was rescued by his allies, he died in 1085, convinced that he had failed in all his endeavors. For the rest of his reign, Henry was harassed by rebellious German nobles. He never succeeded in establishing the strong, stable monarchy that his father had enjoyed. His own son was leading a rebellion against him when Henry died in 1106.

A solution to the lay investiture problem was not to be found between Gregory VII and Henry IV. Not until 1122 in the Concordat of Worms did Pope Calixtus II and Henry V arrive at a compromise: The church would nominate and elect prelates and then invest them with the ring and staff, symbols of spiritual authority. The emperor thus formally renounced his power to so invest prelates. In exchange, the pope recognized the emperor's right to be present during the election of prelates, and in a disputed election the emperor's decision was to be final. The emperor was also allowed to invest a prelate with the "regalia" of his office (lands, worldly goods, and privileges).

With the Concordat of Worms, the investiture struggle ended in a workable compromise, though it did not satisfy extremists in either camp. The dispute may have been resolved, but the struggle between church and state, empire and papacy was to be renewed with even greater violence in the thirteenth and fourteenth centuries.

CONSIDER THIS:

9-8. Both Emperor Henry IV and Pope Gregory VII opposed each other with actions as well as with words. What weapons did the pope have at his disposal to combat the emperor, and in turn, how could the emperor combat the pope? What were the weaknesses and strengths of each arsenal?

9-9. From the evidence at hand, analyze the personalities of Gregory and Henry. Were these men similar in temperament? Why were Henry and Gregory unable to reach an agreement along the lines of the later Concordat of Worms?

9-10. From your study of the investiture controversy, which is the stronger power—the church or the state? By their very nature, must they oppose each other? Is complete separation of church and state a solution to the problem of supremacy? Do you see any modern ramifications to this problem?

"Oath at Canossa" is from Oliver Thatcher and Edgar McNeal, eds., *A Source Book of Medieval History* (New York: Charles Scribner's Sons, 1905), p. 160.

THEME: THE VARIETIES OF TRUTH

THE ARTISTIC VISION

The Art of Stained Glass

The Gothic cathedral was perhaps the quintessential testament to the power of faith and the institutional stability of the High Middle Ages. Pilgrims viewed the spires of these magnificent cathedrals looming in the distance as they made their way to pray at altars dedicated to the Virgin Mary or to offer gifts at the shrines of martyred saints. But cathedrals were not impersonal monoliths or mere depositories of Christian relics, for within their walls was contained the abstract presence of God. The imposing verticality of the central nave that inspired awe in the faithful was tempered by the warmth of light that filtered into the cathedral through immense and intricate panels of stained glass.

There is a mystery to stained glass. It captures the light and transforms it into a living expression of doctrine. These decorated windows express the transcendental concepts of devotion and salvation, of power and permanence through a kaleidoscope of color.

Since most of the devout could not read and did not have access to the Bible, they relied on clergy to interpret the Gospels and sustain their faith. In many ways, stained glass served as a medium for communicating the life of Christ in a wondrous way. As one medieval monk put it, stained glass showed "simple people unfamiliar with the Scriptures what they should believe." But in another sense, the faithful experienced a window more than read it. Here was the artistic expression of a local community of glaziers who conceived of an infinite variety of shapes and combinations arranged to fashion the mystery of Christian faith.

Stained glass, therefore, had very specific purposes, whether as artistic expressions of pride or faith from a community of believers or as a conveyance of doctrine. As such, stained glass expressed spiritual truth, but often had larger political and social ramifications as well. Kings and nobles, for example, would demonstrate their piety and status by funding Rose windows or the glass in dedicated chapels within a cathedral. On a larger stage, stained glass sometimes provided an eternal expression of the relationship between church and state, as it still does today in England's Canterbury Cathedral.

A Martyrdom in Glass: The Murder of Saint Thomas Becket

EDWARD GRIM

The conflict between spiritual and secular authority was one of the fundamental themes of medieval civilization. Both king and pope claimed supremacy over the other and based their positions on the evidence of scripture and logic. A king might well argue that the very survival of the church depended on his military strength; as defender of the faith, his will should prevail. On the other hand, the pope's position as successor to Saint Peter and representative of God on earth commanded the respect of all. For he was entrusted with the "Keys of Heaven," and there could be no exception to the ultimate authority of God.

This confrontation was played out most intensely during the reign of the English king Henry II (1154–1189). Upon the death of Theobald, Archbishop of Canterbury, in 1161, Henry was faced with the dilemma of appointing a new Primate of England. Hopeful of

---

"A Martyrdom in Glass" is from Edward Grim, *Vita S. Thomae, Cantuariensis Archepiscopi et Martyris*, in James Robertson, ed., *Materials for the Life of Thomas Becket*, vol. 2 (London: Rolls Series, 1875–1885).

gaining an upper hand on the pope, he decided to appoint his friend and chancellor, Thomas Becket. By having "his man" installed as leader of the English church, Henry hoped to impose his royal will on religious affairs.

Becket was immediately invested as a priest and then ordained a bishop the next day. Later that afternoon on June 2, 1162, Thomas Becket became Archbishop of Canterbury, serving Henry both as chancellor and Primate of England.

But Becket could not reconcile his divided loyalty between God and king. He shifted his allegiance, born apparently of a new and sincere spiritual devotion, to the church. And in the ensuing confrontation with Henry concerning the issue of secular control over religious tribunals, Becket stood in opposition to the encroachment of the state over spiritual jurisdiction.

Frustrated with Becket's commitment to the "honor of God," Henry was purported to have raged to his knights: "What sluggards, what cowards have I brought up in my court, who care nothing for their allegiance to their lord. Who will rid me of this meddlesome priest?"

In the late afternoon of December 29, 1170, five knights arrived at Canterbury Cathedral and found Becket at the altar. They drew their swords and split him in two. The following account of the murder comes from Becket's biographer, Edward Grim, a monk who was present at the execution and was himself wounded in the attack. Henry hunted down the guilty knights and did penance at Becket's tomb. In 1173, Pope Alexander III hailed Becket as a Christian martyr and elevated him to sainthood. Becket's shrine at Canterbury became one of the most celebrated pilgrimage sites in western Europe and the destination of Geoffrey Chaucer's pilgrims in The Canterbury Tales.

Keep in Mind . . .

9-11. How are the stained glass panels of the martyrdom of Thomas Becket and the penance of Henry II reflected in this eyewitness account of Becket's murder by Edward Grim?

When the holy archbishop entered the cathedral, the monks who were glorifying God abandoned vespers, which they had begun to celebrate, and ran to their father whom they had heard was dead but they saw alive and unharmed. They hastened to close the doors of the church in order to bar the enemies from slaughtering the bishop, but [Becket] turned toward them and ordered that the doors be opened. "It is not proper," he said, "that a house of prayer, a church of Christ, be made a fortress since although it is not shut up, it serves as a fortification for his people; we will triumph over the enemy through suffering rather than by fighting—and we come to suffer, not to resist." Without delay the sacrilegious men entered the house of peace and reconciliation with swords drawn; indeed, the sight alone as well as the rattle of arms inflicted not a small amount of horror on those who watched. And those knights who approached the

confused and disordered people who had been observing vespers . . . exclaimed in a rage: "Where is Thomas Becket, traitor to the king and kingdom?" No one responded and instantly they cried out more loudly, "Where is the archbishop?" Unshaken, Becket replied to this voice as it is written: "The righteous will be like a bold lion and free from fear." He descended from the steps to which he had been taken by the monks who were fearful of the knights and said in an adequately audible voice, "Here I am, not a traitor of the king but a priest; why do you seek me?" . . .

With rapid motion they laid sacrilegious hands on him, [attempting to drag] him roughly outside of the walls of the church so that there they would slay him or carry him from there as a prisoner, as they later confessed. But when it was not possible to easily move him from the column, he bravely pushed one of the knights who was pursuing and drawing near to him; he called him a panderer saying, "Don't touch me, Rainaldus, you who owe me faith and obedience, you who foolishly follow your accomplices." On account of the rebuff, the knight was suddenly set on fire with a terrible rage and, wielding a sword against

FIGURE 9.2 Canterbury Cathedral: The Martyrdom of Thomas Becket. (*Perry M. Rogers*)

the [Archbishop] said, "I don't owe faith or obedience to you that is in opposition to the fealty I owe my lord king." The invincible martyr, seeing that the hour which could bring the end to his miserable mortal life was at hand and already promised by God to be the next to receive the crown of immortality, with his neck bent as if he were in prayer and with his joined hands elevated above, commended himself and the cause of the Church to God, Saint Mary, and the blessed martyr Saint Denis.

He had barely finished speaking when the impious knight, fearing that Thomas would be saved by the people and escape alive, suddenly set upon him and shaved off the very top of his head. . . . Then, with another blow received on the head, Becket remained firm. But with the third, the stricken martyr bent his knees and elbows, offering himself as a living sacrifice, saying in a low voice, "For the name of Jesus and the protection of the church, I am ready to embrace death." The third knight inflicted a grave wound on the fallen one; with this blow he shattered the sword on the stone, and Becket's crown, which was large, separated from his head so that the blood turned white from the brain yet not less did the brain turn red from the blood. . . . The fourth knight drove away those who were gathering so that the others could finish the murder more freely and boldly. The fifth . . . placed his foot on the neck of the holy priest and precious martyr and (it is horrible to say) scattered the brains with the blood across the floor, exclaiming to the rest, "We can leave this place, knights—he will not get up again."

CONSIDER THIS:

9-12. After Thomas Becket's elevation to sainthood, his shrine at Canterbury became a popular pilgrimage destination and a lucrative source of

FIGURE 9.3 Canterbury Cathedral: Henry II doing penance at Becket's tomb. *(Perry M. Rogers)*

income for the church. Analyze the stained glass in this segment depicting Becket's martyrdom. How do these images cultivate not just the story of Becket's sacrifice, but also the concept of spiritual primacy over the secular power of the state? In this case, how did the stained glass serve both a spiritual and political cause?

THE BROADER PERSPECTIVE:

9-13. If stained glass was a wondrous art form that expressed the devotion of medieval communities, to what extent was it also a kind of propaganda for the indoctrination of "simple minds" in support of the spiritual and political authority of the church?

Medieval Monasticism

Monasticism arose in Egypt and western Asia and was practiced by monks who were true hermits. Their life was one of ascetic denial and personal devotion to God. As the movement spread to the West in the middle of the fourth century and became more popular, the monks began to live together in houses. Although they preserved as much of their personal isolation as possible, it became necessary to formulate rules of conduct. These rules, however, were not severe or even binding in most cases; monks did not even have to take a vow to remain in the monastery. The reforms of Saint Benedict were designed to remedy this problem and other abuses that permeated the monastic life. Benedict moved away from the hermetic emphasis of the East in favor of a common experience among the brothers in the order. His strict rule was popularized by Pope Gregory I (himself a Benedictine) and became the basis for all reforms in monasticism for several centuries. The following excerpts provide a glimpse into this structured life of contemplation and isolation from the world.

The Rule of Saint Benedict (530)

Ch. 1. The kinds of monks: There are four kinds of monks. The first kind is that of the cenobites, those who live in a monastery according to a rule, and under the government of an abbot. The second is that of the anchorites, or hermits, who have learned how to conduct the war against the devil by their long service in the monastery and their association with many brothers, and so, being well trained, have separated themselves from the troop, in order to wage single combat, being able with the aid of God to carry on the fight alone against the sins of the flesh. The third kind (and a most abominable kind it is) is that of the sarabites, who have not been tested and proved by obedience to the rule and by the teaching of experience, as gold is tried in the furnace, and so are soft and pliable like a base metal; who in assuming the tonsure are false to God, because they still serve the world in their lives. They do not congregate in the master's fold, but dwell apart without a shepherd, by twos and threes, or even alone. Their law is their own desires, since they call that holy which they like, and that unlawful which they do not like. The fourth kind is composed of those who are called gyrovagi (wanderers), who spend their whole lives wandering about through different regions and living three or four days at a time in the cells of different monks. They are always wandering about and never remain long in one place, and they are governed by their own appetites and desires. They are in every way worse than the sarabites. But it is better to pass over in silence than to mention their manner of life. Let us, therefore, leaving these aside, proceed, with the aid of God, to the consideration of the cenobites, the highest type of monks.

Ch. 6. Silence: . . . It is the business of the master to speak and instruct, and that of the disciples to hearken and be silent. And if the disciple must ask anything of his superior, let him ask it reverently and humbly, lest he seem to speak more than is becoming. Filthy and foolish talking and jesting we condemn utterly, and forbid the disciple ever to open his mouth to utter such words.

Ch. 7. Humility: . . . The sixth step of humility is this, that the monk should be contented with any lowly or hard condition in which he may be placed, and should always look upon himself as an unworthy laborer, not fitted to do what is entrusted to him. . . . The seventh step of humility is this, that he should not only say, but should really believe in his heart that he is the lowest and most worthless of all men. . . . The eighth step of humility is this, that the monk should follow in everything the common rule of the monastery and the examples of his superiors. . . .

The twelfth step of humility is this, that the monk should always be humble and lowly, not only in his heart, but in his bearing as well. Wherever he may be, in divine service, in the oratory, in the garden, on the road, in the fields, whether sitting, walking, or standing, he should always keep his head bowed and his eyes upon the ground. He should always be meditating upon his sins and thinking of the dread day of judgment, saying to himself as did that publican of whom the gospel speaks: "Lord, I am not worthy, I a sinner, so much as to lift mine eyes up to heaven" *[Luke 18:13]*; and again with the prophet: "I am bowed down and humbled everywhere" *[Ps. 119:107]*. . . .

Ch. 22. How the monks should sleep: The monks shall sleep separately in individual beds, and the abbot shall assign them their beds according to their conduct. If possible all the monks shall sleep in the same dormitory, but if their number is too large to admit of this, they are to be divided into tens or twenties and placed under the control of some of the older monks. A candle shall be kept burning in the dormitory all night until daybreak. The monks shall go to bed clothed and girt with girdles and cords, but shall not have their knives at their sides, lest in their dreams they injure one of the sleepers. They should be always in readiness, rising immediately upon the signal and hastening to the service, but appearing there gravely and modestly. The beds of the younger brothers should not be placed together, but should be scattered

"The Rule of Saint Benedict" is from Oliver Thatcher and Edgar McNeal, eds., *A Source Book of Medieval History* (New York: Charles Scribner's Sons, 1905), pp. 434–438, 445–447, 457, 459, 461–462, 467–468, 471–474.

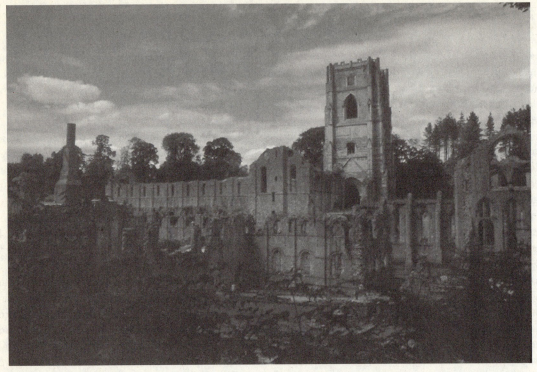

FIGURE 9.4 Fountains Abbey was an impressive cloister for the Cistercian order of monks in northern England. *(Perry M. Rogers)*

among those of the older monks. When the brothers arise they should gently exhort one another to hasten to the service, so that the sleepy ones may have no excuse for coming late. . . .

Ch. 33. Monks should not have personal property:
The sin of owning private property should be entirely eradicated from the monastery. No one shall presume to give or receive anything except by the order of the abbot; no one shall possess anything of his own, books, paper, pens, or anything else; for monks are not to own even their own bodies and wills to be used at their own desire, but are to look to the father [abbot] of the monastery for everything. So they shall have nothing that has not been given or allowed to them by the abbot; all things are to be had in common according to the command of the Scriptures, and no one shall consider anything as his own property. If anyone has been found guilty of this most grievous sin, he shall be admonished for the first and second offence, and then if he does not mend his ways he shall be punished.

Ch. 38. The weekly reader:
There should always be reading during the common meal, but it shall not be left to chance, so that anyone may take up the book and read. On Sunday one of the brothers shall be appointed to read during the following week. . . . At the common meal, the strictest silence shall be kept, that no whispering or speaking may be heard except the voice of the reader. The brethren shall mutually wait upon one another by passing the articles of food and drink, so that no one shall have to ask for anything; but if this is necessary, it shall be done by a sign rather than by words, if possible. In order to avoid too much talking no one shall interrupt the reader with a question about the reading or in any other way, unless perchance the prior may wish to say something in the way of explanation. . . .

Ch. 39. The amount of food:
Two cooked dishes, served either at the sixth or the ninth hour, should be sufficient for the daily sustenance. We allow two because of differences in taste, so that those who do

not eat one may satisfy their hunger with the other, but two shall suffice for all the brothers, unless it is possible to obtain fruit or fresh vegetables, which may be served as a third. . . . In the case of those who engage in heavy labor, the abbot may at his discretion increase the allowance of food, but he should not allow the monks to indulge their appetites by eating or drinking too much. For no vice is more inconsistent with the Christian character. . . .

Ch. 48. The daily labor of the monks: Idleness is the great enemy of the soul, therefore the monks should always be occupied, either in manual labor or in holy reading. . . . When the ninth hour sounds they shall cease from labor and be ready for the service at the second bell. After dinner they shall spend the time in reading the lessons and the psalms. During Lent the time from daybreak to the third hour shall be devoted to reading, and then they shall work at their appointed tasks until the tenth hour. At the beginning of Lent each of the monks shall be given a book from the library of the monastery which he shall read entirely through. One or two of the older monks shall be appointed to go about through the monastery during the hours set apart for reading, to see that none of the monks are idling away the time, instead of reading, and so not only wasting their own time but perhaps disturbing others as well. . . . Sunday is to be spent by all the brothers in holy reading, except by such as have regular duties assigned to them for that day. And if any brother is negligent or lazy, refusing or being unable profitably to read or meditate at the time assigned for that, let him be made to work, so that he shall at any rate not be idle. . . .

Ch. 58. The way in which new members are to be received: Entrance into the monastery should not be made too easy. . . . So when anyone applies at the monastery, asking to be accepted as a monk, he should first be proved by every test. He shall be made to wait outside four or five days, continually knocking at the door and begging to be admitted; and then he shall be taken in as a guest and allowed to stay in the guest chamber a few days. If he satisfies these preliminary tests, he shall then be made to serve a novitiate of at least one year, during which he shall be placed under the charge of one of the older and wiser brothers, who shall examine him and prove, by every possible means, his sincerity, his zeal, his obedience, and his ability to endure shame. And he shall be told in the plainest manner all the hardships and difficulties of the life which he has chosen. If he promises never to leave the monastery the rule shall be read to him after the first two months of his novitiate, and again at the end of six more months, and finally, four months later, at the end of his year. Each time he shall be told that this is the guide which he must follow as a monk, the reader saying to him at the end of the reading: "This is the law under which you have expressed a desire to live; if you are able to obey it, enter; if not, depart in peace." Thus he shall have been given every chance for mature deliberation and every opportunity to refuse the yoke of service. But if he still persists in asserting his eagerness to enter and his willingness to obey the rule and the commands of his superior, he shall then be received into the congregation, with the understanding that from that day forth he shall never be permitted to draw back from the service or to leave the monastery. . . .

The Vow of a Monk

I hereby renounce my parents, my brothers and relatives, my friends, my possessions and my property, and the vain and empty glory and pleasure of this world. I also renounce my own will, for the will of God. I accept all the hardships of the monastic life, and take the vows of purity, chastity, and poverty, in the hope of heaven; and I promise to remain a monk in this monastery all the days of my life.

CONSIDER THIS:

9-14. What is monasticism and what medieval values does it represent? Why was the monastic movement so popular? Which of the rules of Saint Benedict impress you most and why? Compared to other lifestyles in the Middle Ages, was it hard being a monk?

"The Vow of a Monk" is from Oliver Thatcher and Edgar McNeal, eds., *A Source Book of Medieval History* (New York: Charles Scribner's Sons, 1905), p. 486.

Visions of Ecstasy

HILDEGARD OF BINGEN

Hildegard of Bingen (1098–1179) has emerged through recent scholarship as one of the most creative and accomplished voices from the Middle Ages. A religious visionary and head of a convent near Bingen, Germany, Hildegard also wrote hymns and chants in honor of saints and the Virgin Mary. Her noble family dedicated her at birth to the Church and she received a rudimentary religious education near a Benedictine monastery. Throughout her life, starting at age three, Hildegard had visions of luminous objects that grew more detailed and complex as she aged. When Hildegard was forty-two-years old, she had a vision in which "the heavens were opened and a blinding light of exceptional brilliance flowed through my entire brain." This gave her an instant understanding of the meaning of the religious texts, and she was commanded to write down her visionary observations. Modern-day physicians who have analyzed the descriptions of her visual hallucinations have regarded them as symptomatic of classic migraines.

With the blessing of Pope Eugenius, Hildegard finished her first visionary work, Scivias ("Know the Ways of the Lord"). In the following excerpt, Hildegard discusses the omnipotence and indivisibility of God. She believed that human beings were the most glorious expression of God's work and the vehicle through which the dimensions of God's macrocosm might be understood. Hildegard's story is an inspirational account of a vibrant intellect that transcended the cultural and gender barriers of the medieval world.

And I heard the voice saying to me from the living fire: "O you who are wretched earth and, as a woman, untaught in all learning of earthly teachers and unable to read literature with philosophical understanding, you are nonetheless touched by My light, which kindles in you an inner fire like a burning sun; cry out and relate and write these My mysteries that you see and hear in mystical visions. So do not be timid, but say those things you understand in the Spirit as I speak them through you. . . . Therefore, O uncertain mind, who are taught inwardly by mystical inspiration, though because of Eve's transgression you are trodden on by the masculine sex, speak of that fiery work this sure vision has shown you."

The Living God, then, Who created all things through His Word, by the Word's Incarnation brought back the miserable human who had sunk himself in darkness to certain salvation. What does this mean?

On God's Omnipotence

This *blazing fire* that you see symbolizes the Omnipotent and Living God, Who in His most glorious serenity was never darkened by an evil; *incomprehensible*, because He cannot be divided by any division; *inextinguishable*, because He is that Fullness that no limit ever touched; *wholly living*, for there is nothing that is hidden from Him or that He does not know; and *wholly Life*, for everything that lives takes its life from Him, as Job shows, inspired by Me, when he says: "Who is ignorant that the hand of the Lord has made all these things? In His hand is the soul of every living thing and the spirit of all human flesh" [*Job 12:9–10*]. What does this mean? No creature is so dull of nature as not to know what changes in the things that make it fruitful cause it to attain its full growth. The sky holds light, light air, and air the birds; the earth nourishes plants, plants fruit and fruit animals; which all testify that they were put there by a strong hand, the supreme power of the Ruler of All, Who in His strength has provided so for them all that nothing is lacking to them for their use. And in the omnipotence of the same Maker is the motion of all living things that seek the earth for earthly things like the animals which are not inspired by God with reason, as well as the awakening of those who dwell in human flesh and have reason, discernment, and wisdom. How?

The Discernment of the Soul

The soul goes about in earthly affairs, laboring through many changes as fleshly behavior demands. But the spirit raises itself in two ways: sighing, groaning and desiring God; and choosing among options in various matters as if by some rule, for the soul has discernment in reason. Hence Man contains in himself the likeness of heaven and earth. In what way? He has a circle, which contains his clarity, breath and reason, as the sky has its lights, air and birds; and he has a receptacle containing humidity, germination, and birth, as the earth contains fertility, fruition and animals. What is this? O human, you are wholly in every creature, and you forget your Creator; you are subject to Him as was ordained, and you go against His commands?

CONSIDER THIS:

9-15. What evidence does Hildegard offer as examples of God's omnipotence? What does Hildegard mean when she says "O human, you are wholly in every creature"?

9-16. In this passage, how does Hildegard represent herself? What limitations did she impose on herself simply by virtue of her sex? How were women generally perceived at this time?

The Canticle of Brother Sun (1225)

SAINT FRANCIS OF ASSISI

One of the most remarkable figures in the world of the medieval church was Saint Francis. Born in 1181 to a wealthy merchant in the little town of Assisi, Saint Francis eventually rejected his prescribed role as heir to the family business, gave his belongings to the poor, and became a barefoot preacher. He quickly gained adherents by advocating a simple rule of poverty and complete service to God. His order received the approval of Pope Innocent III in 1209. He died in 1226 and was canonized in 1228. He was buried in the impressive basilica San Francesco in Assisi, an ironic turn, because Saint Francis had always preached the virtues of poverty and simplicity.

The Franciscans were not a monastic order, but rather considered their business to be within the world. They were called friars, or brothers, and combined the asceticism and simplicity of a regular order of monks with the popular contact that was the preserve of the secular order of priests. With a foot in both worlds of the church and with a dedication to poverty and simplicity, the Franciscans were a kind of hybrid, both reviled and admired by competing forces within the church.

Saint Francis's great love of nature and the purity of his devotion to God are distilled in perhaps the most articulate and sensitive of his poems, "The Canticle of Brother Sun." He began it in 1225, during his last illness amid intense physical suffering, and added the final verses about Sister Death shortly before his own death. The "Canticle," for all the depth of feeling it evokes about nature and the creatures he cared so much about, is an earnest prayer and hymn of praise to God.

Most high, all-powerful, all good, Lord!
All praise is yours, all glory, all honor
And all blessing.
To you, alone, Most High, do they belong.
No mortal lips are worthy
To pronounce your name.
All praise be yours, my Lord, through all that you
    have made,
And first my lord Brother Sun,

Who brings the day; and light you give to us
through him.
How beautiful is he, how radiant in all his splendor!
Of you, Most High, he bears the likeness.
All praise be yours, my Lord, through Sister Moon
and Stars;
In the heavens you have made them, bright
And precious and fair.
All praise be yours, my Lord, through Brothers Wind
and Air,
And fair and stormy, all the weather's moods,
By which you cherish all that you have made.
All praise be yours, my Lord, through Sister Water,
So useful, lowly, precious and pure.
All praise be yours, my Lord, through Brother Fire,
Through whom you brighten up the night.
How beautiful is he, how gay! Full of power and
strength.

All praise be yours, my Lord, through Sister Earth,
our mother,
Who feeds us in her sovereignty and produces
Various fruits with colored flowers and herbs.
All praise be yours, my Lord, through those who
grant pardon
For love of you; through those who endure
Sickness and trial.
Happy those who endure in peace,
By you, Most High, they will be crowned.
All praise be yours, my Lord, through Sister Death,
From whom no mortal can escape.
Woe to those who die in mortal sin!
Happy those She finds doing your will!
The second death can do no harm to them.
Praise and bless my Lord, and give him thanks,
And serve him with great humility.

THEME: THE POWER STRUCTURE

Against the Grain

Papal Supremacy and Magna Carta

"The Rights of Englishmen": Magna Carta (1215)

The figure of Pope Innocent III (1198–1216) dominated the medieval papacy. He firmly believed that his position as the Vicar of Christ and successor to the apostle Peter accorded him primacy in spiritual and secular affairs. In the eleventh century, Pope Gregory VII had also exercised his authority by excommunicating the Holy Roman Emperor, who was in defiance of Gregory's sanctions regarding lay investiture. But in the end, Gregory had conceded to the threats of blatant military force. The power of God, and especially the penalties that God might impose through his representative, the pope, were not of this earth and could not compete with the immediate terror a king might inflict. Still, this did not deter Innocent, who defied and dominated the kings of Europe.

In 1207, King John of England refused to accept Innocent's choice for Archbishop of Canterbury and defied the pope by selecting his own candidate and extorting money from the church. Innocent responded by excommunicating John and placing all of England under interdict. Finally, when it appeared that the king of France was preparing an invasion of England under Innocent's direction, John gave way—in style. Not only did he have to repay the money he had taken from the church, but he was forced to surrender his realm to the pope, who returned it as a fief. In essence, John was now a vassal of his feudal lord, the

---

"Magna Carta" is from E.G. Henderson, ed., *Select Historical Documents of the Middle Ages* (London: George Bell and Sons, 1896), pp. 358–361. Translation modernized by the editor.

pope. This was a major humiliation for the secular power of the king that encouraged the competing authority of his nobility.

John's difficulties with Pope Innocent III were just the tip of the iceberg. For several years, John had taxed the church and the nobility to maintain fiscal stability in his quarrels with the pope while protecting his lands in Normandy. John had also imprisoned or detained many of those who had resisted his exactions. It is therefore not surprising that after 1213, the Archbishop of Canterbury, Stephen Langton, organized the barons against John by demanding that the king formally grant specific liberties. Previous monarchs had often made promises or issued concessions to their barons, but these had been granted by, not exacted from the king. Matters had come to a head for John, and he signed the Magna Carta on the fields of Runnymede in June, 1215. In subsequent years, the Magna Carta became a symbol against oppression by arbitrary power and influenced both the national and state constitutions of the United States. Herewith are the "basic rights of Englishmen":

JOHN, by the grace of God, King of England, Lord of Ireland, Duke of Normandy and Aquitaine, and Count of Anjou, to his archbishops, bishops, abbots, earls, barons, justices, foresters, sheriffs, stewards, servants, and to all his officials and loyal subjects, Greeting.

KNOW THAT BEFORE GOD, for the health of our soul and those of our ancestors and heirs, to the honor of God, the exaltation of the holy Church, and the better ordering of our kingdom . . . [let it be declared]:

1. FIRST, THAT WE HAVE GRANTED TO GOD, and by this present charter have confirmed for us and our heirs in perpetuity, that the English Church shall be free, and shall have its rights undiminished, and its liberties unimpaired. That we wish this so to be observed, appears from the fact that by our own free will, before the outbreak of the present dispute between us and our barons, we granted and confirmed by charter the freedom of the Church's elections—a right reckoned to be of the greatest necessity and importance to it—and caused this to be confirmed by Pope Innocent III. This freedom we shall observe ourselves, and desire to be observed in good faith by our heirs in perpetuity.

12. No [tax] may be levied in our kingdom without its general consent, unless it is for the ransom of our person, to make our eldest son a knight, and (once) to marry our eldest daughter. For these purposes only a reasonable tax may be levied. Taxes from the city of London are to be treated similarly.

13. The city of London shall enjoy all its ancient liberties and free customs, both by land and by water. We also will and grant that all other cities, boroughs, towns, and ports shall enjoy their liberties and free customs.

14. To obtain the general consent of the realm for the assessment of a tax—except in the three cases specified above—we will cause the archbishops, bishops, abbots, earls, and greater barons to be summoned individually by letter. To those who hold lands directly of us we will cause a general summons to be issued, through the sheriffs and other officials, to come together on a fixed day (of which at least forty days notice shall be given) and at a fixed place. . . .

20. For a trivial offence, a free man shall be fined only in proportion to the degree of his offence, and for a serious offence correspondingly, but not so heavily as to deprive him of his livelihood. . . . None of these fines shall be imposed except by the assessment on oath of reputable men of the neighborhood.

21. Earls and barons shall be fined only by their equals, and in proportion to the gravity of their offence.

28. No constable or other royal official shall take corn or other movable goods from any man

without immediate payment, unless the seller voluntarily offers postponement of this.

30. No sheriff, royal official, or other person shall take horses or carts for transport from any free man without his consent.

31. Neither we nor any royal official will take wood for our castle, or for any other purpose, without the consent of the owner.

32. We will not keep the lands of people convicted of felony in [royal control] for longer than a year and a day, after which they shall be returned to the lords of the fiefs concerned.

38. In the future, no official shall place a man on trial upon his own unsupported statement without producing credible witnesses to the truth of the charge.

39. No free man shall be seized or imprisoned, or stripped of his rights or possessions, or outlawed or exiled, or deprived of his standing in any other way, nor will we proceed with force against him, or send others to do so, except by the lawful judgment of his equals or by the law of the land.

40. To no one will we sell, to no one deny or delay right or justice.

42. In the future, it shall be lawful for any man to leave and return to our kingdom unharmed and without fear by land or water, [in order to conduct affairs] for the common benefit of the realm . . . [as long as he preserves his allegiance to us].

52. To any man whom we have deprived or dispossessed of lands, castles, liberties, or rights, without the lawful judgment of his equals, we will at once restore these. In cases of dispute, the matter shall be resolved by the judgment of [a council of] twenty-five barons. . . .

55. All fines that have been given to us unjustly and against the law of the land, and all fines that we have exacted unjustly, shall be entirely remitted or the matter decided by a majority judgment of [a council of] twenty-five barons.

60. All these customs and liberties that we have granted shall be observed in our kingdom in so far as concerns our own relations with our subjects. Let all men of our kingdom, whether clergy or laymen, observe them similarly in their relations with their own men.

61. SINCE WE HAVE GRANTED ALL THESE THINGS for God, for the better ordering of our kingdom, and to allay the discord that has arisen between us and our barons, and since we desire that they shall be enjoyed in their entirety with lasting strength, forever, we grant to the barons the following security:

   • The barons shall elect twenty-five of their number to keep, and cause to be observed with all their might, the peace and liberties granted and confirmed to them by this charter.

   • If we, our chief justice, our officials, or any of our servants offend in any respect against any man . . . and the offence is made known to four of the said twenty-five barons, they shall come to us . . . to declare it and claim immediate redress. . . .

62. We have remitted and pardoned fully to all men any ill-will, hurt, or grudges that have arisen between us and our subjects, whether clergy or laymen, since the beginning of the dispute. . . .

63. IT IS ACCORDINGLY OUR WISH AND COMMAND that the English Church shall be free, and that men in our kingdom shall have and keep all these liberties, rights, and concessions well and peaceably in their fullness and entirety for themselves and their heirs, of us and our heirs, in all things and all places forever.

Both we and the barons have sworn that all this shall be observed in good faith and without deceit. Given by our hand in the meadow that is called Runnymede, between Windsor and Staines, on the fifteenth day of June in the seventeenth year of our reign (1215).

CONSIDER THIS:

9-17. What are the most important rights that the barons and the English church exacted from King John? How do they limit the arbitrary power of the king?

Innocent Protects His Investment (1216)

POPE INNOCENT III

This selection shows Innocent protecting his feudal interests as lord of his English fief by supporting John against his barons. This rebuke came after the barons had forced John to sign the Magna Carta in 1215.

Innocent, etc., to his beloved sons, the magnates and barons of England, greeting and apostolic benediction.

We are gravely troubled to learn that a quarrel has arisen between our most beloved son, John, King of England, and some of you, about certain questions that have recently been raised. Unless wise counsel prevails and diligent measures are taken to end this quarrel, it will cause injury. It is currently reported that you have rashly made conspiracies and confederacies against him, and that you have insolently, rebelliously, presumptuously, and with arms in your hands, said things to him, which, if they had to be said, should have been said humbly and submissively. We utterly condemn your conduct in these matters. You must no longer try, by such means, to hinder the king in his good plans. By our apostolic authority we hereby dissolve all conspiracies and confederacies that have been made since the quarrel between the crown and the church began, and forbid them under threat of excommunication. We order you to endeavor by clear proofs of humility and devotion to placate your king and to win his favor by rendering him those customary services which you and your ancestors have paid to him and his predecessors. And in the future, if you wish to make a request of him, you shall do it, not insolently, but humbly and reverently, without offending his royal honor; and thus you will more readily obtain what you wish. We ask and beseech the king in the Lord and command him, in order to obtain forgiveness of his sins, to treat you leniently, and graciously to grant you just petitions. And thus you yourselves may rejoice to know that he has changed for the better, and on this account you and your heirs may serve him and his successors more promptly and devotedly. We ask, and, by this apostolic writing, command you to bear yourselves in such a way that England may obtain the peace she so earnestly longs for, and that you may deserve our aid and support in your times of trouble.

CONSIDER THIS:

9-18. Note Pope Innocent III's response to the Magna Carta. How did he specifically protect his interests as the feudal lord of England? Did the barons simply exchange one arbitrary ruler for another? What does this say about the secular authority of Innocent III's papacy?

THE BROADER PERSPECTIVE:

9-19. The Magna Carta of 1215 was only in force for a few months before John violated its tenets with the blessing of the pope and went to war against his barons. The Great Charter, therefore, was unsuccessful in resolving the issues between the king and his nobility. It was reissued with revisions in 1217, after John's death, and again in 1225, after John's son, Henry III, came of age. The Charter gradually became less a statement of current law than a source for legal principles. How did the Magna Carta influence the Constitution of the United States?

"Innocent Protects His Investment" is from Oliver Thatcher and Edgar McNeal, eds., *A Source Book for Medieval History* (New York: Charles Scribner's Sons, 1905), pp. 219–220.

Mind and Society in the Middle Ages

The World of Thought

Political Theory: The Responsibilities of Kingship (1159)

JOHN OF SALISBURY

John of Salisbury was a trained logician who served as advisor to the Archbishop of Canterbury, Thomas Becket. Becket became famous for his defiance of King Henry II—defiance that resulted in his murder and subsequent martyrdom. John dedicated his *Statesman's Book* to Becket in 1159; it was a compendium of political theory that he had acquired from the Bible, classical texts, and his own observation of political affairs. Note the emphasis on the respective responsibilities of the secular and spiritual spheres.

The prince stands on a pinnacle which is exalted and made splendid with all the great and high privileges which he deems necessary for himself. And rightly so, because nothing is more advantageous to the people than that the needs of the prince should be fully satisfied; since it is impossible that his will should be found opposed to justice. Therefore, according to the usual definition, the prince is the public power, and a kind of likeness on earth of the divine majesty. Beyond doubt a large share of the divine power is shown to be in princes by the fact that at their nod men bow their necks and for the most part offer up their heads to the axe to be struck off, and, as by a divine impulse, the prince is feared by each of those over whom he is set as an object of fear. And this I do not think could be, except as a result of the will of God. For all power is from the Lord God, and has been with Him always, and is from everlasting. The power which the prince has is therefore from God, for the power of God is never lost, nor severed from Him, but He merely exercises it through a subordinate hand, making all things teach His mercy or justice. "Who, therefore, resists the ruling power, resists the ordinance of God," in Whose hand is the authority of conferring that power, and when He so desires, or withdrawing it again, or diminishing it. . . .

Princes should not think that it detracts from their princely dignity to believe that their own decisions regarding justice should be less preferred to the justice of God, whose justice is an everlasting justice,

and His law is equity. . . . No prince accordingly is the minister of the common interest and the loyal servant of equity, but he represents the public in the sense that he punishes the wrongs and injuries of all, and all crimes, with even-handed equity. His rod and staff also, administered with wise moderation, restore irregularities and false departures to the straight path of equity, so that deservedly may the Spirit congratulate the power of the prince with the words, "Thy rod and thy staff, they have comforted me." His shield, too, is strong, but it is a shield for the protection of the weak, and one which wards off powerfully the darts of the wicked from the innocent. Those who derive the greatest advantage from his performance of the duties of his office are those who can do least for themselves, and his power is chiefly exercised against those who desire to do harm. Therefore he brandishes a sword, with which he sheds blood without blame, without becoming thereby a man of blood, and frequently puts men to death without incurring the guilt of homicide. . . .

The prince, therefore, receives the sword from the hand of the Church, although she herself has no sword of blood at all. Nevertheless she has this sword, but she uses it through the hand of the prince, upon whom she confers compulsive physical power, retaining to herself authority over spiritual things in the person of the pontiffs. The prince is, then, as it were, a minister of the priestly power, and one who exercises that side

"Political Theory: The Responsibilities of Kingship" is from John Dickinson, trans., *The Statesman's Book of John of Salisbury* (New York: Alfred A. Knopf, 1927), pp. 3–4, 6–9, 65.

of the sacred offices which seems unworthy of the hands of the priesthood. For every office existing under, and concerned with the execution of the sacred laws is really a religious office, but is inferior when it punishes crimes, which is more typical in the person of the hangman. . . .

The place of the head in the body of the commonwealth is filled by the prince, who is subject only to God and to those who exercise His office and represent Him on earth, even as in the human body the head is guided and governed by the soul. . . .

CONSIDER THIS:

9-20. According to John of Salisbury, what are the responsibilities of a king? From whom does he derive his power, and why should he be respected? What is his relationship to the church? How can the king serve both the public interest and God?

The Existence of God

SAINT THOMAS AQUINAS

The twelfth century was truly remarkable for its intellectual focus and development of thought. The new commitment to learning was reflected in a system of argument and study called Scholasticism. Scholars edited and commented on ancient writers, methodically arguing for the acceptance or rejection of such philosophers as Aristotle and Plato. No longer was it enough simply to accept the existence of God without a rational argument of proof. Saint Thomas Aquinas (1225–1274) is generally regarded as the most insightful and important philosopher of the Middle Ages. The following excerpts from his *Summa Theologica* demonstrate the structure of Scholastic argument and relate his conclusions on the existence of God. Saint Bernard's passage on the love of God reflects the argument of faith.

Third Article: Whether God exists?

Objection 1: It seems that God does not exist; because if one of two contraries be infinite, the other would be altogether destroyed. But the name God means that He is infinite goodness. If, therefore, God existed, there would be no evil discoverable; but there is evil in the world. Therefore God does not exist.

Objection 2: Further, it is superfluous to suppose that what can be accounted for by a few principles has been produced by many. But it seems that everything we see in the world can be accounted for by other principles, supposing God did not exist. For all natural things can be reduced to one principle, which is human reason, or will. Therefore there is no need to suppose God's existence.

I Answer That: The existence of God can be proved in five ways: The first and more manifest way is the argument from motion. It is certain, and evident to our senses, that in the world some things are in motion. . . . [Now], whatever is moved must be moved by another. If that by which it is moved be itself moved, then this also must needs be moved by another, and that by another again. But this cannot go on to infinity, because then there would be no first mover, and, consequently, no other mover, seeing that subsequent movers move only inasmuch as they are moved by the first mover; as the staff moves only because it is moved by the hand. Therefore it is necessary to arrive at a first mover, moved by no other; and this everyone understands to be God.

The second way is from the nature of efficient cause. In the world of sensible things we find there is an order of efficient causes. There is no case known (neither is it, indeed, possible) in which a thing is found to be the efficient cause of itself; for so it would be prior to itself, which is impossible. Now in efficient causes it is not possible to go on to infinity, because in all efficient causes following in order, the first is the

"The Existence of God" is from *Summa Theologica*, trans. A. C. Pegis, in *Basic Writings of Saint Thomas Aquinas*, vol. 1 (New York: Random House, 1945), pp. 21–24. Reprinted by permission of the Estate of Anton Pegis.

cause of the intermediate cause and the intermediate is the cause of the ultimate cause, whether the intermediate cause be several, or one only. Now to take away the cause is to take away the effect. Therefore, if there be no first cause among efficient causes, there will be no ultimate, nor any intermediate, cause. . . . Therefore it is necessary to admit a first efficient cause, to which everyone gives the name of God.

The third way is taken from possibility and necessity, and runs thus. We find in nature things that are possible to be and not to be, since they are found to be born, and to die, and consequently they are possible to be and not to be. But it is impossible for these always to exist, for that which is possible not to be at some time is not. Therefore, if everything is possible not to be, then at one time there could have been nothing in existence. Now, if this were true, even now there would be nothing in existence, because that which does not exist only begins to exist by something already existing. Therefore, if at one time nothing was in existence, it would have been impossible for anything to have begun to exist; and thus even now nothing would be in existence—which is clearly false. Therefore, not all beings are merely possible, but there must exist something the existence of which is necessary. But every necessary thing either has its necessity caused by another, or not. Now, it is impossible to go on to infinity in necessary things which have their necessity caused by another, as has been already proved in regard to efficient causes. Therefore, we must admit the existence of some being having of itself its own necessity, and not receiving it from another, but rather causing in others their necessity. This all men speak of as God.

The fourth way is taken from the gradation to be found in things. Among beings there are some more and some less good, true, noble, and the like. But "more" and "less" are predicated on different things,

according as they resemble in their different ways something which is the maximum, as a thing is said to be hotter according as it more nearly resembles that which is hottest. There is then something which is truest, something best, something noblest, and, consequently, something which is most being; for those things that are greatest in truth are greatest in being . . . . Therefore, there must also be something which is to all beings the cause of their being, goodness, and every other perfection. And this we call God.

The fifth way is taken from the governance of the world. We see that things which lack knowledge, such as natural bodies, act for an end, and this is evident from their acting always, or nearly always, in the same way, so as to obtain the best result. Hence it is plain that they achieve their end, not fortuitously, but designedly. Now whatever lacks knowledge cannot move towards an end, unless it be directed by some being endowed with knowledge and intelligence; as the arrow is directed by the archer. Therefore some intelligent being exists by whom all natural things are directed to their end; and this being we call God.

Reply to Objection 1: As Augustine says: "Since God is the highest good, He would not allow any evil to exist in His works, unless His omnipotence and goodness were such as to bring good even out of evil." This is part of the infinite goodness of God; that He should allow evil to exist, and out of it produce good.

Reply to Objection 2: Since nature works for a determinate end under the direction of a higher agent, whatever is done by nature must be traced back to God, as to its first cause. . . . For all things that are changeable and capable of defect must be traced back to an immovable and self-necessary first principle, as was shown in the body of this Article.

The Love of God

SAINT BERNARD OF CLAIRVAUX

You would hear from me, then, why and how God is to be loved? I answer: The cause of loving God is God; the manner is to love without measure. Is this enough?

Yes, perhaps, for the wise. But I am debtor to the unwise as well; where enough is said for the wise, we must comply with the others also. Therefore I will not

"The Love of God" is from E. G. Gardner, trans., *On the Love of God* (London: J. M. Dent and Sons, 1916), p. 27.

refuse to repeat it, more fully rather than more deeply, for the sake of the slower in apprehension. I may say that God is to be loved for His own sake for a double reason: because nothing can be loved more justly, nothing more fruitfully. . . . Assuredly I find no other worthy cause of loving Him, save Himself. . . .

CONSIDER THIS:

9-21. What is Saint Thomas Aquinas's essential argument for the existence of God? Does it sound logical to you? Is it persuasive, or can you find defects in the proof? Is Saint Bernard's argument more satisfying?

The Dialectical Method: Sic et Non

PETER ABELARD

One of the greatest minds of the Middle Ages belonged to Peter Abelard. He was a renowned scholar and teacher whose method of inquiring into spiritual issues often created formidable enemies (among them, Saint Bernard of Clairvaux). Abelard's method of apply-ing critical thought to the interpretation of sacred texts is best revealed in his famous work *Sic et Non* (*Yes and No*). Abelard would pose a problem and then cite arguments, sup-ported by the most revered church fathers, that the statement was true. He then produced another series of logical and well-supported arguments that proved it false. Abelard did not want to reconcile the conflicting views, but by this dialectical process he hoped to "sharpen the minds" of his students. The pathway to Truth had to be critically examined. The follow-ing excerpts demonstrate his method and are good examples of Scholastic argument.

Inasmuch as among the many words of the saints there are some which . . . not only [differ] but actually [con-tradict one another], we are not to judge lightly of these saints who themselves will judge the world. . . . If there are divine mysteries which we cannot understand in the spirit in which they were written, better to reserve judgment than to define rashly. We are not to rely on apocryphal writings and we must be sure that we have the correct text on the canonical. For example, Matthew and John say that Jesus was crucified at the sixth hour, but Mark at the third. This is an error of transcription in Mark. We are to observe because he carelessly incor-porated the work of someone else, as Augustine con-fessed he had done with reference to Origen. We must bear in mind the diversity of situation in which particu-lar sayings were uttered. In case of controversy between the saints, which cannot be resolved by reason, we should hold to that opinion which has the most ancient and powerful authority. And if sometimes the fathers were in error we should attribute this not to duplicity but ignorance, and if sometimes they were absurd, we are to assume that the text is faulty, the interpreter in error or simply that we do not understand.

Therefore it has seemed to us fitting to collect from the holy fathers apparently contradictory passages that tender readers may be incited to make inquiry after the truth. . . . By doubting we come to inquire, and by inquiry we arrive at the truth. . . . We are including nothing from the Apocrypha and nothing from the writings of Augustine which he later retracted.

Example XXXII. That God may do all things and that He may not

Chrysostom said that God is called almighty because it is impossible to find anything that is impossible for Him. Nevertheless He cannot lie, or be deceived, He cannot be ignorant. He cannot have a beginning or an end.

He cannot forget the past, be involved in the present or be ignorant of the future. Finally, He can-not deny Himself. Augustine said there are some things God can do as to His power, but not as to His justice. Being himself justice He cannot commit injustice. He is omnipotent in the sense that He can do what He wants. But He cannot die, He cannot change and He cannot be deceived.

"The Dialectical Method: *Sic et Non*" is from Roland Bainton, ed., *The Medieval Church* (Princeton, NJ: D. Van Nostrand, 1962), pp. 129–130. Reprinted by permission of Wadsworth Publishing Company.

Example XI. That the divine persons differ from each other and that they do not

Athanasius said there is one person of the Father, one of the Son and one of the Holy Spirit. The Father is not made, created, or begotten. The son comes solely from the Father. He is not made or created but He is begotten. The spirit proceeds from the Father and the Son. He is not begotten or created but proceeding. But Pope Leo I said, "In the divine Trinity nothing is dissimilar, nothing unequal."

Consider This:

9-22. Peter Abelard summed up his attitude in this way: "By doubting, we come to inquire, by inquiring, we come to the truth." Saint Anselm said, "I believe in order that I may understand." What is the essential difference between the two statements? Do you believe that Abelard was seeking to undermine faith in God? What is the "truth" he sought?

THEME: THE INSTITUTION AND THE INDIVIDUAL

THE REFLECTION IN THE MIRROR

The Tragedy of Abelard and Heloise

A Story of Calamities

PETER ABELARD

The great logician, teacher, and scholar Peter Abelard (*Sic et Non*) became legendary for his tragic love affair with a student named Heloise. He had attained an enviable yet controversial reputation among scholars and churchmen. But his life changed drastically when he met Heloise and the two fell passionately in love. Abelard relates the saga in his autobiography, *A Story of Calamities*.

Now there lived in the city of Paris at the time a young girl named Heloise, the niece of a canon called Fulbert. Her uncle's love for her was equaled only by his desire that she have the best education available. She was not bad looking, but stood out above all others in her knowledge of letters. This particular quality added greatly to her charm, since such knowledge is so rare in a woman that it had won her a high reputation throughout the kingdom. It was this girl that I decided to pursue and move to my bed, feeling confident that she would be an easy mark. After all, I was young, exceptionally handsome, and possessed a glowing reputation that allowed me to make practically any woman I wanted without fearing rejection. Knowing that she loved knowledge and letters, I thought she would be all the more ready to consent, and that

even if we were parted, we could still be together by exchanging written messages, thereby speaking more openly than in person. In that way, we could always live in a kind of joyous intimacy.

I was very hot for this girl and looked for an opportunity of meeting with her privately each day, thereby more easily winning her over. So I persuaded her uncle, with the help of some of his friends, to take me into his household, which was quite close to my school, in return for a small payment. My pretext for this was that I couldn't spare the time from my studies to take care of my own place and besides, I simply couldn't afford it. Fulbert was avaricious and hungered for money, and at the same time was also ambitious in wanting to further his niece's education in letters. So, for these two reasons, I easily won his consent to

"The Tragedy of Abelard and Heloise" is from Peter Abelard, *Historia Calamitatum or The Story of My Misfortunes*, trans. Henry Adams Bellows (New York, 1922), excerpts from Books 6 and 7. Translation modernized by the editor.

obtain entrance to the household. He wanted my money and his niece would profit from my teaching. Things on the romantic front opened up quickly, and far more than I ever expected, when he entrusted her completely to my guidance, begging me to give her instruction whenever I might be free from my academic duties, no matter the day or night, and if I found her to be lazy, then I could punish her severely. The man's simplicity was amazing! It was as if he were entrusting a tender lamb to the care of a ravenous wolf! I had a free range to plow. . . .

Need I say more? We were united, first in the house that sheltered our love, and then in our hearts that burned with it. With our lessons as a pretext, we abandoned ourselves entirely to love. Our talk was intimate and our kisses far outnumbered any scholarly words, so that the books lay open before us, decidedly mute. My hands strayed far more often to her breasts than to the pages, and love drew our eyes to gaze upon each other more often than words in the texts ever captured our attention. . . . In short, our passionate desires opened all doors and left no stage of love-making untried. And if love itself could imagine any new technique or possibility, we welcomed it. Our inexperience in the art of love made us all the more fervent in the pursuit of even greater delights, so that our thirst for one another was never quenched.

As this passion absorbed me more and more, I devoted ever less time to philosophy and to the work of the school. Indeed, it became a real burden to go to the school or linger there, since my nights were vigils of love and my days deserts of study. My lecturing became utterly careless and uninspired— mere repetitions of the same old things, all just a matter of prolonged routine. And when inspiration did come to me, it was for writing love poetry, not the secrets of philosophy. . . .

After several months had passed, Heloise's uncle found out about her affair with Abelard. He separated the lovers, but they continued to meet and Heloise became pregnant. Abelard secretly married her and arranged that she remain in a convent for safety after the baby was born. Abelard continues the story:

When her uncle and his friends and relatives heard of this, they were convinced that I had tricked them, and had found an easy way of ridding myself of Heloise forever by making her a nun. Violently incensed, they plotted against me, and one night while I slept peacefully in a secret room in my lodgings, they bribed one of my servants to allow them entry. Then they fell on me and took their cruel vengeance with an appalling barbarity so as to shock the entire world. For they cut me—cut off my genitals that had offended them so. Then they fled, but two of them were quickly caught. As punishment for their crime, they had their eyes gouged out and then were mutilated as I had been. One of them was the very servant whose greed had led him to betray me.

When morning came, the whole city assembled before my house. They were amazed and bewildered, some crying, others threatening me, still others grieving so that the scene is impossible to describe. In particular, the clerks and my own pupils so tortured me with their weeping and wailing that I suffered more intensely from their sympathy than from the pain of my wounds. I truly felt disgrace and abject humiliation. I kept thinking about my esteemed reputation, and how easily it had been trashed—no, completely blotted out—in one evil moment. I also saw too how God had punished me by striking me down in the parts of my body with which I had sinned. This was justice, indeed. . . . What road to take? How could I hold up my head in public, every finger pointing directly at me, every tongue deriding with shame, a monstrous spectacle to all I met? . . .

I must confess that it was an overwhelming sense of shame and remorse rather than any devout commitment to God that drove me to the seclusion of the monastic order—I wanted to disappear. Heloise had already agreed to take the veil at my suggestion and entered a convent. So we both put on the religious habit, I in the Abbey of St. Denis, and she in the Convent of Argenteuil. I remember very well that there were many people who tried to dissuade her from submitting her sweet youth to the yoke of monastic rule—this

was a penance too hard to bear. But all in vain, for sobbing and weeping, she replied in Cornelia's famous lament:

O noble husband, who never should have shared
    my bed,
Has fortune such power to bend that lofty head?
Why did I marry you and leave in disarray?
Now claim your due, and see me gladly pay. . . .

Though they never saw one another again, Abelard and Heloise continued to correspond for years. Some letters discussed academic and spiritual subjects, while others reflected on their tragic love. Through it all, the letters reveal that the couple overcame self-pity and found acceptance of a changed, but everlasting, relationship.

CONSIDER THIS:

9-23. Why was the love between Abelard and Heloise so tragic? It is interesting that both Abelard and

Heloise retreated to monastic orders after their crisis. Why do you think they did this? What does this action say about the medieval church?

The Medieval Woman

Whether Woman Was Fittingly Made from the Rib of Man?

SAINT THOMAS AQUINAS

Throughout most of the Middle Ages, women were portrayed in a negative light, completely subservient to men, as temptresses to the will of God, banished from the halls of government and the fields of battle, and confined to the bed and nursery. But the twelfth century saw a renaissance of sorts in the position of women. The popularity of the Virgin Mary soared, and cathedrals were dedicated in her name. Women such as Eleanor of Aquitaine, the empress Matilda, Blanche of Castile, and Marie de France assumed an unprecedented influence in the affairs of state. This resurgence did not continue much beyond the century, but important precedents had been set.

    The following selections are from the *Summa Theologica* of Saint Thomas Aquinas. Although he subscribed to the rigid Aristotelian concept of woman as the "misbegotten male," and thus reflected the church's conservatism, he was also willing to concede a certain dignity (albeit minor) regarding woman's creation and participation in baptism.

Objection 1: It would seem that woman should not have been formed from the rib of man. For the rib was much smaller than the woman's body. Now from a

smaller thing a larger thing can be made only, either by addition . . . or by [thinning out], because, as Augustine says: A body cannot increase in bulk

"Whether Woman Was Fittingly Made from the Rib of Man?" is from The Fathers of the English Dominican Province, trans., *The Summa Theologica of St. Thomas Aquinas* (London: Burns, Oates & Washbourne, 1920), Part 1, Question 92.

except by [thinning out]. But the woman's body is not [thinner] than man's, at least not in the proportion of a rib to Eve's body. Therefore Eve was not formed from a rib of Adam.

Objection 2: Further, in those things which were first created there was nothing superfluous. Therefore a rib of Adam belonged to the integrity of his body. So if a rib was removed, his body remained imperfect; which is unreasonable to suppose.

Objection 3: Further, a rib cannot be removed from man without pain. But there was no pain before sin. Therefore, it was not right for a rib to be taken from the man, that Eve might be made from it.

On the contrary, it is written (*Genesis, 2.22*): God built the rib, which He took from Adam, into a woman.

I Answer That: It was right for the woman to be made from a rib of man. First, to signify the social union of man and woman, for the woman should neither use authority over man, and so she was not made from his head; nor was it right for her to be subject to man's contempt as his slave, and so she was not made from his feet. [She was made from the rib of man by Divine Power], for the sacramental signification; for from the side of Christ sleeping on the Cross the Sacraments flowed—namely blood and water—on which the Church was established.

Whether a Woman Can Baptize?

SAINT THOMAS AQUINAS

Objection 1: It seems that a woman cannot baptize. For we read in the acts of the Council of Carthage: However learned and holy a woman may be, she must not presume to teach men in the church, or to baptize. But in no case is a woman allowed to teach in church, according to *I Cor. 14.35*: It is a shame for a woman to speak in the church. Therefore it seems that neither is a woman in any circumstances permitted to baptize.

Objection 2: Further, to baptize belongs to those having authority; wherefore baptism should be conferred by priests having charge of souls. But women are not qualified for this; according to *I Tim. 2.12*: I suffer not a woman to teach, nor to use authority over man, but to be subject to him. Therefore a woman cannot baptize.

On the contrary, Pope Urban II says: . . . baptism is valid when, in cases of necessity, a woman baptizes a child in the name of the Trinity. . . .

But since the head of the woman is the man, and the head of . . . man, is Christ (*I Cor. 11.3*), a

woman should not baptize if a man be available for the purpose; just as neither should a layman in the presence of a cleric, nor a cleric in the presence of a priest. . . .

In carnal generation male and female co-operate according to the power of their proper nature; wherefore the female cannot be the active, but only the passive, principle of generation. But in spiritual generation, they do not act, either of them, by their proper power, but only instrumentally by the power of Christ. Consequently, on the same grounds either man or woman can baptize in a case of urgency.

CONSIDER THIS:

9-24. According to the readings, how did Saint Thomas Aquinas view women? Is his logic regarding the creation of women and their participation in baptism impeccable? In what ways does he evince a conservative and rather typical medieval view of woman, and in what ways is he more liberal in his attitude?

"Whether a Woman Can Baptize?" is from The Fathers of the English Dominican Province, trans., *The Summa Theologica of St. Thomas Aquinas* (London: Burns, Oates & Washbourne, 1920), Part 3, Question 67.

Chivalric Ideals: The Function of Knighthood

JOHN OF SALISBURY

The High Middle Ages saw the transition from a rather crude and barbaric nobility to one controlled by ideals of right action and proper conduct. Knights were expected to comport themselves with dignity and spiritual devotion, especially in the presence of ladies. Knighthood became a rigorous trial, and tales of the quest for the Holy Grail or the mystical unicorn became popular. The following account of John of Salisbury presents the ideal of knighthood.

FIGURE 9.5 Noblewomen watching a tournament. This painting reflects chivalric ideals of the knight and his lady. In fact, these mock battles served a useful purpose in providing a semi-controlled outlet for the aggression of the nobility. (*Lebrecht Music and Arts Photo Library*)

"Chivalric Ideals: The Function of Knighthood" is from Frederick Ogg, ed., *A Source Book of Medieval History* (New York: American Book Company, 1907), p. 401.

But what is the office of the duly ordained soldiery? To defend the Church, to assail infidelity, to venerate the priesthood, to protect the poor from injuries, to pacify the province, to pour out their blood for their brothers (as the formula of their oath instructs them), and, if need be, to lay down their lives. The praises of God are in their throat, and two-edged swords are in their hands to execute punishment on the nations and rebuke upon the peoples, and to bind their kings in chains and their nobles in links of iron. But to what end? To the end that they may serve madness, vanity, avarice, or their own private self-will? By no means. Rather to the end that they may execute the judgment that is committed to them to execute; wherein each follows not his own will but the deliberate decision of God, the angels, and men, in accordance with equity and the public utility. . . . For soldiers that do these things are "saints," and are the more loyal to their prince in proportion as they more zealously keep the faith of God; and they advance the more successfully the honor of their own valor as they seek the more faithfully in all things the glory of their God.

CONSIDER THIS:

9-25. Explain the concept of chivalry. What were the most important functions of knighthood? Why was it important to provide an ideal for knights?

The Minds of Women: "Freer and Sharper"

CHRISTINE DE PIZAN

The chivalric ideal of the High Middle Ages generally enhanced the position of women in medieval society. With the popularity of the Virgin Mary in the twelfth and thirteenth centuries, women were viewed less as temptresses who encouraged sinful thoughts and acts and more as respected individuals, worthy of love and adoration. Knights fought for the honor of their Lady, whom they set on a pedestal and worshiped from afar. Yet some women were becoming less inhibited about their feelings and measured their worth less as objects of male desire and more as intellectual and social equals.

Christine de Pizan (1364–ca. 1430) was born of a Venetian father who served as an astrologer to the French court. Christine married a court secretary, but her status as an Italian in a French world marginalized her social status, especially after the death of her husband in 1389. Well-educated and independent of mind, Christine wrote *The Book of the City of Ladies* as a rebuttal against the misogynistic argument that women, because of the corruption initiated by Eve in the Garden of Eden, were temptresses and inherently inferior to men in ability and worth. Christine's answer to this attack assumed that women shared the goodness of God and that although weaker physically, they were certainly intellectually equal to men, if given the proper education and opportunities. This argument is decidedly contemporary as we still seek to find equity between men and women under law and in the marketplace.

The following excerpt is a conversation between Christine and "Lady Reason" concerning the ability and worth of the female mind. This was an extraordinary argument at the time, and it shifted the status of women from a dependence on chivalric notions of male protection to independent worth.

"The Minds of Women" is from Christine de Pizan, *The Book of the City of Ladies*, 1.27. Translation by the editor is based on the transcription of the French text (*Le Livre de la Cité des Dames*) by Marureen Cheney Cunow (1975).

After listening to her arguments, I replied to Lady Reason: "Truly my lady, God has demonstrated great wonders in the strength of these women whom you mention. But help me understand whether God, who has given so many favors to women, ever honored any of them with great intelligence and knowledge. Do they even have the capacity for learning? For I would really like to know why men regard women as intellectually weak."

Lady Reason replied, "My dear Christine, isn't it obvious from what I've already told you that the exact opposite is true? Indeed, let me prove it even more clearly with some conclusive examples. Let me say once again (and don't doubt me on this) that if it were customary to send little girls to school in order to teach them all variety of subjects like we teach little boys, then they would learn the subtleties of the arts and sciences just as easily and thoroughly as the boys. And indeed, this often happens because, as I said earlier, although women may be weaker and less agile than men physically, nevertheless their minds are freer and sharper, whenever they apply themselves."

"My lady, what are you saying? Can you expand on this point a bit? Surely, men would never accept this argument without proof, for they believe that, simply being men, they generally know much more than women."

She answered, "Do you know why women know less?"

"No, my lady, not unless you tell me."

"It's because women are focused on the house and are only involved with the limited demands of running a household. Nothing so expands the mind of any rational creature than a whole variety of rich and diverse experiences."

"Well, my lady, since women do have agile minds that can absorb and understand just like men, why don't they actually know more?"

"Because, my dear, the public good doesn't require them to do what men are expected to do. As I said before, it is simply enough for women to perform the duties for which they are best suited. As for the notion that women's intelligence is inferior to men's just because experience seems to indicate that they know less than men, one only has to find a few peasants living in the high mountains or farming the remote countryside who are so backward and ignorant that they seem like animals. And yet, Nature has no doubt provided them with the same qualities of body and mind that are found among the wisest and most learned men in our great cities and towns. But all this can be reduced to a basic proposition that some men and women are more naturally endowed intellectually than others. The female sex is just as clever as the male sex."

CONSIDER THIS:

9-26. Christine poses the question whether women have the "capacity for learning" that men possess. What is the proof she offers in the affirmative? Is this a strong argument?

THE BROADER PERSPECTIVE:

9-27. In the selection entitled "Visions of Ecstasy" on page 252, written about 1140, the visionary Hildegard of Bingen recounted the voice of God: "O you who are wretched earth and, as a woman, untaught in all learning of earthly teachers and unable to read literature with philosophical understanding, you nonetheless are touched by My light." Thus, in spite of Hildegard's limitations as an ignorant woman, God still offered His light to her. God went on to note that "because of Eve's transgression you [Hildegard] are trodden on by the masculine sex." How would Christine de Pizan have responded to these ideas? Had the conception of woman as transgressor, as limited and restricted, changed by 1405 when Christine wrote *The Book of the City of Ladies*?

Chapter 10

The Waning of the Middle Ages (1300–1450)

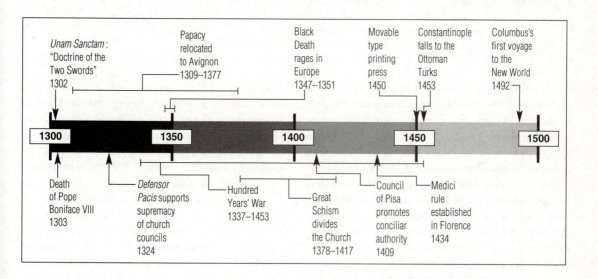

Unam Sanctam: "Doctrine of the Two Swords" 1302

Papacy relocated to Avignon 1309–1377

Black Death rages in Europe 1347–1351

Movable type printing press 1450

Constantinople falls to the Ottoman Turks 1453

Columbus's first voyage to the New World 1492

1300 1350 1400 1450 1500

Death of Pope Boniface VIII 1303

Defensor Pacis supports supremacy of church councils 1324

Hundred Years' War 1337–1453

Great Schism divides the Church 1378–1417

Council of Pisa promotes conciliar authority 1409

Medici rule established in Florence 1434

There is a Reaper whose name is Death,
And, with his sickle keen,
He reaps the bearded grain at a breath,
And the flowers that grow between.

—Henry Wadsworth Longfellow

We all labor against our own cure, for death is the cure of all diseases.

—Thomas Browne

Ring around the rosie,
Pocket full of posies,
Ashes, Ashes,
We all fall down.

—Children's rhyme

My guide said, "I am one who accompanies this living man; we go downward from level to level, and I mean to show him Hell."

—Dante Alighieri

- **Social and Spiritual Values:** How did the Black Death alter the spiritual commitment of medieval civilization? When faced with the specter of unrelenting catastrophe, do people become more committed to spiritual austerity or do they abandon these values for immediate gratifications?

- **The Power Structure:** Why did the secular power of monarchs overcome the spiritual authority of the Church during the Late Middle Ages? As nation-states began to mature and consolidate, was the secularization of society inevitable?

- **Revolution and Historical Transition:** What is the role of disease in history? How potent is disease as a force for historical change? How fatalistic are you? Must there be a plague or a war every so often for the world's population to remain in proper balance?

- **The Big Picture:** What were the political, social, and spiritual elements of decline that characterized late medieval civilization? Does every society commit suicide?

In October 1347, a Genoese fleet docked in Sicily at the port of Messina. The entire crew was either dead or dying, afflicted with a disease that clung, as the chronicler noted, "to their very bones." The ship had arrived from the Black Sea region and was filled with grain ready for distribution. Also aboard were the omnipresent rats, Black rats, infested with fleas that, in turn, harbored the *Yersinia pestis* bacillus. Before the fleet could be quarantined, the rats had run down the ropes and into the city. Over the next four years, the scene would be repeated again and again. The Black Death had arrived.

The mere words *Black Death* have an ominous ring about them. They dredge up images of rotting corpses, broken families, and despair. The people of Europe were devastated by a disease they did not understand and were not prepared to suffer. It was an epidemic of such magnitude that one third to one half of the population of Europe was killed. In a contemporary study by the Rand Corporation, the Black Death ranked as one of the three greatest catastrophes in the history of the world. It did much more than eliminate people; it altered the very foundation of medieval life and jeopardized the unity of Western civilization.

In addition to the Black Death, the calamitous fourteenth century endured the physical destruction of the bloody Hundred Years' War between France and England from 1337 to 1453. As bodies piled up with numbing regularity, all eyes focused on the spiritual center of medieval civilization for solace and guidance. But the unity of Christendom that had inspired devotion and the spiritual commitment from generations of faithful came under siege as the papacy abandoned Rome and centered itself in Avignon, France.

This so-called "Babylonian Captivity" from 1303 to 1377 produced a series of varied claimants to the papal throne that ultimately resulted in the Great Schism, the actual division of Western Christianity from 1378 to 1417. The spiritual leadership of Christendom lost credibility as power flowed to holy councils of cardinals and other prelates who sought to end the disastrous division by asserting their theoretical right to bind the wounds of the universal church through a series of decrees. Even after Christendom unified once again under a single pope in 1417, it was evident that the days of papal supremacy over secular forces were gone forever. Pope Innocent III (1198–1216) had earlier dominated kings and Holy Roman emperors with just the threat of excommunication. In contrast, Pope Boniface VIII (1294–1303) was captured by agents of the French king, Philip IV, beaten and left in a Roman gutter to die. Times had changed.

The Late Middle Ages spanned the years from about 1300 to 1450 and was a time of stress as the church declined in stature. The fourteenth century tottered between the chaos of the bloody Hundred Years' War and perhaps the most destructive force yet encountered in Western civilization—Black Death. In this chapter, we encounter evidence of great trauma— a desperate civilization in the grip of psychological terror and prolonged political and spiritual dislocation. The waning of the Middle Ages was often punctuated by dramatic horrors. It was this era of crisis that gave way to the ideals and attitudes of the Renaissance. The transition was made possible by a new human-centered energy, much as the transition from the ancient world was effected by energy sustained through devotion to God. But it should be remembered that the transition between the Middle Ages and the Renaissance was not abrupt, but gradual. We must resist the simplistic assumption that the medieval world was an "age of faith," rooted in mundane abstractions, and that the Renaissance was an "age of light," where people had thrown off the shackles of religion. In truth, such a gross distortion has little foundation in the historical evidence of the period.

KEY EVENTS IN THE LATE MIDDLE AGES

1294–1303   Papacy of Boniface VIII
Boniface boldly reasserts church's claim to temporal power in *Clericis Laicos* (1298) and *Unam Sanctam* (1302). Boniface attacked, captured, and beaten by agents of the French king, Philip IV (1303). Church losing battle for influence to secular kings.

1309–1377   "Babylonian Captivity"
Residency of popes transferred to Avignon, France. Removal of papacy from the traditional seat of Saint Peter in Rome hurts authority and credibility. One of the greatest critics of papal degeneration is Petrarch (1304–1374), who is considered to be the "Father of Humanism."

1337–1453   Hundred Years' War
Fought over disputed English claims to the French throne, this war rages intermittently for 116 years: Pivotal turning points: English victory at Crécy (1346); English victory at Agincourt under the leadership of King Henry V (1415); Joan of Arc leads French to victory at Orléans. She is executed as a heretic in 1431.

1347–1351   Black Death
The bubonic plague first strikes in Sicily and moves north throughout Europe, killing nearly half the population. Successive but less devastating plagues occur into the next century. Giovanni Boccaccio writes *The Decameron*.

1378–1417   The Great Schism
A division of Christianity develops between supporters of the popes in Rome and those who still reside in Avignon. Dispute has political ramifications as countries develop military alliances based on support of Rome or Avignon. Issue finally resolved by councils of the church (Conciliar Movement).

1381   The Peasant Revolt
John Ball and Wat Tyler lead the English Peasant Revolt in protest over new taxes, tolls, and reduced wages. Short-lived and brutally crushed by aristocrats, it leaves the country divided for years. Black Death returns.

1415   John Huss Burned at the Stake
Czech reformer John Huss is executed for heresy after having been granted safe conduct by the Church. After a decade of belligerent protests, the Hussites win significant religious reforms in Bohemia.

1453   Constantinople Falls to the Ottoman Turks
The Byzantine Empire ends with the fall of Constantinople. During the next two centuries, the Ottoman Turks will pressure the gates of Vienna and consolidate control of the Middle East. The Ottoman Empire will survive until 1918.

The Crisis of the Medieval Church

The Papacy under Siege

The struggle for supremacy between church and state, which had stirred such dissension in the eleventh and twelfth centuries, seemed to have been settled by the strong leadership of Pope Innocent III in the early thirteenth century. Innocent simply dominated the secular world without a moment of hesitation. But conditions had changed by the late thirteenth century. The forceful kings of England and France were constantly in need of money and began levying taxes against the clergy of their realms. Boniface VIII (1294–1303), in the papal bull (decree) *Clericis Laicos*, viewed this as an encroachment on the liberty of the church.

The second selection, *Unam Sanctam*, was another decree in which Boniface promulgated the famous "Doctrine of the Two Swords," designed to promote the unity of Christianity and the supremacy of the pope. This policy eventually failed: Boniface was attacked, captured, and humiliated by agents of the French king, Philip IV; Boniface died soon after. The days of papal supremacy were over.

Clericis Laicos (1298)

POPE BONIFACE VIII

It is said that in times past laymen practiced great violence against the clergy, and our experience clearly shows that they are doing so at present, since they are not content to keep within the limits prescribed for them, but strive to do that which is prohibited and illegal. And they pay no attention to the fact that they are forbidden to exercise authority over the clergy and ecclesiastical persons and their possessions. But they are laying heavy burdens on bishops, churches, and clergy, both regular and secular, by taxing them, levying contributions on them, and extorting the half, or the tenth, or the twentieth, or some other part of their income and possessions. They are striving in many ways to reduce the clergy to servitude and to subject them to their own sway. And we grieve to say it, but some bishops and clergy, fearing where they should not, and seeking a temporary peace, and fearing more to offend man than God, submit, improvidently rather than rashly, to these abuses [and pay the sums demanded], without receiving the papal permission. Wishing to prevent these evils . . . by our apostolic authority, we decree that if any bishops or clergy, regular or secular, of any grade, condition, or rank, shall pay, or promise, or consent to pay laymen any contributions, or taxes, or the tenth, or the twentieth, or the hundredth, or any other part of their income or of their possessions, or of their value, real or estimated, under the name of aid, or loan, or subvention, or subsidy, or gift, or under any other name or pretext, without the permission of the pope, they shall, by the very act, incur the sentence of excommunication. And we also decree that emperors, kings, princes, dukes, counts, barons, [etc.] who shall impose, demand, or receive such taxes, or shall seize the property of churches or of the taxes, or shall seize the property of churches or of the clergy, shall incur the sentence of excommunication. We also put under the interdict all communities which shall be culpable in such matters. And under the threat of deposition we strictly command all bishops and clergy, in accordance with their oath of obedience, not to submit to such taxes without the express permission of the pope. . . . From this sentence of excommunication and interdict no one can be absolved except in the moment of death, without the authority and special permission of the pope. . . .

Clericis Laicos is from Oliver Thatcher and Edgar McNeal, eds., *A Source Book of Medieval History* (New York: Charles Scribner's Sons, 1905), pp. 311–313.

Unam Sanctam (1302)

POPE BONIFACE VIII

The true faith compels us to believe that there is one holy catholic apostolic church, and this we firmly believe and plainly confess. And outside of her there is no salvation or remission of sins. . . . In this church there is "one Lord, one faith, one baptism" [*Eph. 4:5*]. . . . Therefore there is one body of the one and only church, and one head, not two heads, as if the church were a monster. And this head is Christ and his vicar, Peter and his successor. . . . If therefore Greeks or anyone else say that they are not subject to Peter and his successors, they thereby necessarily confess that they are not of the sheep of Christ. For the Lord says in the Gospel of John, that there is one fold and only one shepherd [*John 10:16*]. By the words of the gospel, we are taught that the two swords, namely, the spiritual authority and the temporal are in the power of the church. . . . The former is to be used by the church, the latter for the church; the one by the hand of the priest, the other by the hand of kings and knights, but at the command and permission of the priest. Moreover, it is necessary for one sword to be under the other, and the temporal authority to be subjected to the spiritual; for the apostle says, "For there is no power but of God: and the powers that are ordained of God" [*Rom. 13:1*]; but they would not be ordained [i.e., arranged or set in order] unless one were subjected to the other, and, as it were, the lower made the higher by the other. . . . And we must necessarily admit that the spiritual power surpasses any earthly power in dignity and honor, because spiritual things surpass temporal things. We clearly see that this is true from the paying of tithes, from the benediction, from the sanctification, from the receiving of the power, and from the governing of these things. For the truth itself declares that the spiritual power must establish the temporal power and pass judgment on it if it is not good. Thus the prophecy of Jeremiah concerning the church and the ecclesiastical power is fulfilled: "See, I have this day set thee over the nations and over the kingdoms, to root out, and to pull down, and to destroy, and to throw down, to build, and to plant" [*Jer. 1:10*]. Therefore if the temporal power errs, it will be judged by the spiritual power, and if the lower spiritual power errs, it will be judged by its superior. But if the highest spiritual power errs, it can not be judged by men, but by God alone. For the apostle says: "But he that is spiritual judgeth all things, yet he himself is judged of no man" [*1 Cor. 2:15*]. Now this authority, although it is given to man and exercised through man, is not human, but divine. For it was given by the word of the Lord to Peter, and the rock was made firm to him and his successors, in Christ himself, whom he had confessed. For the Lord said to Peter: "Whatsoever thou shalt bind on earth shall be bound in heaven: and whatsoever thou shalt loose on earth shall be loosed in heaven" [*Matt. 16:19*]. Therefore, whosoever resists this power thus ordained of God, resists the ordinance of God [*Rom. 13:2*]. . . . We therefore declare, say, and affirm that submission on the part of every man to the bishop of Rome is altogether necessary for his salvation.

CONSIDER THIS:

10-1. In the papal decrees *Clericis Laicos* and *Unam Sanctam*, what concepts was Boniface VIII trying to promote? Is he persuasive in the logic of his argument? What does the "Doctrine of the Two Swords" entail? What do those who defy the decrees risk? Why would a king be willing to risk such a penalty?

The Argument against Papal Supremacy: Defensor Pacis (1324)

MARSILIUS OF PADUA

Marsilius of Padua was a canon of the church in Padua; he wrote *Defensor Pacis* (Defender of the Peace) in 1324. It is a political treatise that was heavily influenced by the ideas of

Unam Sanctam is from Oliver Thatcher and Edgar McNeal, eds., *A Source Book of Medieval History* (New York: Charles Scribner's Sons, 1905), pp. 314–317.

Defensor Pacis is from Oliver Thatcher and Edgar McNeal, eds., *A Source Book of Medieval History* (New York: Charles Scribner's Sons, 1905), pp. 318–321.

Aristotle. Marsilius firmly believed that all authority was generated from the whole body of citizens. Contrary to the arguments of Boniface VIII, Marsilius believed that a council of Christian prelates had the right to control the church, which existed merely to serve the spiritual needs of citizenry. In this, he foreshadowed some of the arguments employed in the conciliar movement later in the century. The following selections are conclusions from this treatise.

2. The general council of Christians or its majority alone has the authority to define doubtful passages of the divine law, and to determine those that are to be regarded as articles of the Christian faith, belief in which is essential to salvation; and no partial council or single person of any position has the authority to decide these questions.

3. The gospels teach that no temporal punishment or penalty should be used to compel observance of divine commandments.

5. No mortal has the right to dispense with the commands or prohibitions of the [New Testament]. . . .

7. Decretals and decrees of the bishop of Rome, or of any other bishops or body of bishops, have no power to coerce anyone by secular penalties or punishments. . . .

10. The election of any prince or other official, especially one who has the coercive power, is determined solely by the expressed will of the [citizens].

11. There can be only one supreme ruling power in a state or kingdom.

14. No bishop or priest has coercive authority or jurisdiction over any layman or clergyman, even if he is a heretic.

16. No bishop or priest or body of bishops or priests has the authority to excommunicate anyone or to interdict the performance of divine services. . . .

17. All bishops derive their authority in equal measure immediately from Christ, and it cannot be proved from the divine law that one bishop should be over or under another, in temporal or spiritual matters.

22. The prince who rules by the authority of the laws of Christians, has the right to determine the number of churches and temples, and the number of priests, deacons, and other clergy who shall serve in them.

30. The prince alone, acting in accordance with the laws of the [people], has the authority to condemn heretics, delinquents, and all others who should endure temporal punishment, to inflict bodily punishment upon them, and to exact fines from them.

CONSIDER THIS:

10-2. Discuss the ideas of Marsilius of Padua. In what ways do they specifically threaten the authority of the pope? How do they run counter to the ideas of Boniface VIII in *Unam Sanctam*?

THEME: REVOLUTION AND HISTORICAL TRANSITION

THE ARTISTIC VISION

Giotto at the Creative Edge

Despite the ongoing clash between secular and spiritual authorities that threatened the continuity of medieval civilization, there were sophisticated and progressive artistic developments afoot that established precedents for the great achievements of the Italian Renaissance in the fifteenth and sixteenth centuries. Among the fundamental innovators of the Late Middle Ages was an artist named Giotto.

Giotto di Bondone (1267–1337) was born to a small landed farmer in a tiny village near Florence. He became apprenticed as a young boy to the workshop of Cimabue, a well-known Florentine painter, who recognized his extraordinary artistic abilities. An architect, sculptor, and painter, Giotto encountered a world that was grounded in devotion to the spiritual and artistic dictates of the medieval church. In this world, the creativity of the artist was often subordinated to the exposition of doctrine and the manifestation of God's glory. Artistic representations of the Passion of Christ were filled with reverence; the pictorial embodiment of the Word of God required a certain conformity of conception and presentation. In the Greek East, icons or "snapshot" depictions of the Holy Family and saints became important conduits for meditation and faith in a simple, yet specific framework.

But for Giotto, this framework became too confining. Like his friend Dante, Giotto was a transitional figure between the static conformity of medieval restraint and the human world of emotions and expressive devotion. Giotto's work broke free from the iconographic stylings of Byzantine art and introduced a naturalism in his background landscapes and in his depictions of human beings. Although he still dealt with traditional religious subjects, we nevertheless admire the human presence—the subtleties of anguish and faith that are expressed through the eyes, the parting of the lips, the glance that connotes fear or sorrow.

Nowhere is this more evident than in Giotto's *Lamentation over the Dead Christ* (1304–1306). This is a scene of sorrow and hope as Mary, the mother of God, holds Christ's lifeless head gently in her enveloping arms. There is a calm serenity in her intense gaze, an expression perhaps of inner certainty that the Passion of Christ was running its course and that salvation for humankind was at hand. Thus, the sense of despair and sorrow that is so personally registered on the faces of the mourners as they direct their eyes to the head of Christ is tempered with the sense of hope expressed in Mary's maternal adoration. The mourners on the left side of the painting are balanced with the startled intensity of the center as Saint John thrusts his arms back in wonder. The action flows to Mary Magdalene, who is carefully inspecting the wounds on Christ's feet, and ends in the calm detachment of Joseph of Arimathea and Nicodemus. The angels in the sky each reveal their sorrow in anguished contortions. The landscape of a barren rocky outcrop cuts diagonally across the scene from a leafless tree and directs the eye to Christ. These elements combine to impart a sense of sorrow and despair, all reconciled by the pathos of Mary's serene inspiration. The complexity of Giotto's conception and technique contrasts with other religious scenes of the time that are characterized by a remoteness and sense of awe.

Giotto was recognized by his own contemporaries as the first genius of the Italian Renaissance. The biographer Giorgio Vasari, an artist himself, discusses Giotto's influence in the following selection:

FIGURE 10.1 Giotto, *Lamentation over the Dead Christ* (1304–1306). (*Cappella Scrovegni/Arena Chapel/Padua– SuperStock, Inc.*)

Giotto di Bondone: "The Student of Nature Herself"

GIORGIO VASARI

KEEP IN MIND . . .

10-3. According to Vasari, what was Giotto's role in the transition to a more natural style of art?

The debt owed by painters to Nature, which serves them continually as an example, that from her they may select the best and finest parts for reproduction and imitation, is due also, in my opinion, to the Florentine painter Giotto; because when the methods and outlines of good painting had been buried for so many years under the ruins caused by war, he alone, although born in the midst of unskillful artists, through God's gift in him, revived what had fallen into such an evil plight and raised it to a condition which one might call good. Certainly it was nothing short of a miracle, in so gross and unskillful an age, that Giotto should have worked to such purpose that design, of which the men of the time had little or no conception, was revived to a vigorous life through him. . . .

Giotto proceeded to Assisi, a city of Umbria, where he was summoned by Fra Giovanni di Muro della Marca, at that time general of the friars of Saint Francis. In the upper church of this town he painted a series of thirty-two scenes in fresco of the life of Saint Francis, under the course which runs round the church, below the windows, sixteen on each side, with such perfection that he acquired the highest reputation. In truth the work exhibits great variety, not only in the gestures and postures of the different figures, but in the composition of each subject. . . .

One of the most beautiful of these represents a thirsty man, whose desire for water is represented in the most lively manner as he kneels on the ground to drink from a spring, with such wonderful reality that one might imagine him to be a real person. . . . Let it suffice to say that by these works,

Giotto acquired the highest reputation for the excellence of his figures, for his arrangement, sense of proportion, truth to Nature, and his innate facility that he had greatly increased by study, while he never failed to express his meaning clearly. Giotto indeed was not so much the student of any human master as of Nature herself. . . .

When San Francesco was at length finished, Giotto returned to Florence, where he painted with extraordinary care a picture of Saint Francis in the fearful desert of Vernia, to be sent to Pisa. Besides a landscape full of trees and rocks, a new thing in those days, the attitude of the saint, who is receiving the stigmata, on his knees, with great eagerness, exhibits an ardent desire to receive them and an infinite love towards Jesus Christ, who is in the air surrounded by angels granting them to him, the varied emotions being all represented in the most telling manner imaginable. . . . The work may now be seen in San Francesco at Pisa, on a pillar beside the high altar, where it is held in high veneration in memory of so great a man.

CONSIDER THIS:

10-4. Giotto painted a series of frescoes depicting the life of Christ. Note the intensity of Mary's gaze as she holds Jesus in the painting *Lamentation over the Dead Christ*. Do you see how this focal point almost freezes the action taking place around it? What makes Giotto an artist so revolutionary that he resides "on the creative edge" of his century?

10-5. Giotto painted another series of frescoes based on the life of Saint Francis of Assisi. Vasari describes two of them in his account of the life of Giotto. What is his assessment? Saint Francis impresses us as the embodiment of delicate love and regard for life. In this sense, how does Giotto's art complement Saint Francis's "Canticle of Brother Sun," located in Chapter 9?

"The Student of Nature Herself" is from Giorgio Vasari, *The Lives of the Painters, Sculptors, and Architects*, vol. 1 (New York: E. P. Dutton & Co., Inc., 1900), pp. 65–66, 68–70.

The Babylonian Captivity and the Conciliar Movement

One of the great spiritual crises of the Late Middle Ages was known as the "Babylonian Captivity." From 1309 to 1377, the popes resided not in Rome, but in southern France, in the town of Avignon. They established a papal palace there, and the city became the haunt of pleasure seekers who were indulged by the luxuriant and corrupt papacy. This period of self-imposed exile from the spiritual seat of the papal power in Rome irreparably damaged the church. One of the greatest critics of this situation was the humanist Petrarch, who grew up in Avignon and wrote this letter between 1340 and 1353, just before he moved to Rome.

On the Abuses of Avignon

PETRARCH

Now I am living in France, in the Babylon of the West. The sun in its travels sees nothing more hideous than this place on the shores of the wild Rhone, which suggests the hellish streams of Cocytus and Acheron. Here reign the successors of the poor fishermen of Galilee: they have strangely forgotten their origin. I am astounded as I recall their predecessors, to see these men loaded with gold and clad in purple, boasting of the spoils of princes and nations; to see luxurious palaces and heights crowned with fortifications, instead of a boat turned downwards for shelter.

We no longer find the simple nets which were once used to gain a frugal sustenance from the lake of Galilee, and with which, having labored all night and caught nothing, they took, at daybreak, a multitude of fishes, in the name of Jesus. One is stupefied nowadays to hear the lying tongues, and to see worthless parchments turned by a leaden seal into nets which are used, in Christ's name, but by the arts of [the Devil], to catch hordes of unwary Christians. These fish, too, are dressed and laid on the burning coals of anxiety before they fill the insatiable [mouth] of their captors.

Instead of holy solitude, we find a criminal host and crowds of the most infamous satellites; instead of soberness, licentious banquets; instead of pious pilgrimages, preternatural and foul sloth; instead of the bare feet of the apostle, the snowy coursers of brigands fly past us, the horses decked in gold and fed on gold, soon to be shod with gold, if the Lord does not check this slavish luxury. . . .

Here I am, at a more advanced age, back in the haunts of my childhood, dragged again by fate among the disagreeable surroundings of my early days, when I thought I was freed from them. I have been so depressed and overcome that the heaviness of my soul has passed into bodily afflictions, so that I am really ill and can only give voice to sighs and groans. . . . Sweet water cannot come from a bitter source. Nature has ordered that the sighs of an oppressed heart shall be distasteful, and the words of an injured soul harsh.

"The Wolf Is Carrying Away Your Sheep"

SAINT CATHERINE OF SIENA

As the Black Death raged through Europe in 1347, Catherine Benincasa was born in Siena to a prosperous wool dyer. As a child, she displayed a positive, but ascetic disposition and was enraptured by celestial visions. She dedicated herself to God in 1366 and spent the rest of her life tending to plague victims and condemned prisoners; she also served as an intermediary

"On the Abuses of Avignon" is from James H. Robinson, ed., *Readings in European History*, vol. 1 (Boston: Ginn and Company, 1904), pp. 502–504.

"The Wolf Is Carrying Away Your Sheep" is from Vida D. Scudder, trans. and ed., *Saint Catherine of Siena as Seen in Her Letters* (London: J.M. Dent & Sons, Ltd., 1906), pp. 125–126.

between contending political factions in Florence and Pisa. Perhaps because of her faith in the process of arbitration, she became a confidant to the papacy and a respected voice in advocating the unity of the church under the spiritual leadership of the pope. During the Babylonian Captivity and the Great Schism that followed, she worked tirelessly until her death in 1380, offering advice and direction, as her letters indicate, to a papacy under siege.

The following excerpt is from a letter written to Pope Gregory XI in 1375 in which she counseled leadership and action, tempered by moderation and piety. The work of Saint Catherine of Siena testifies to the positive influence in contemporary affairs of a dedicated medieval woman.

In the name of Jesus Christ crucified and of sweet Mary: Most holy and most reverend my father in Christ Jesus: I Catherine, your poor unworthy daughter, servant and slave of the servants of Christ, write to you in His precious blood with desire to see you a good shepherd. For I reflect, sweet father, that the wolf is carrying away your sheep, and there is no one found to help them. So I hasten to you, our father and our shepherd, begging you on behalf of Christ crucified, to learn from Him, who with such fire of love gave Himself to the shameful death of the most holy cross, how to rescue that lost sheep, the human race, from the hands of the demons. . . . Then comes the Infinite goodness of God, and sees the evil state and the loss and the ruin of these sheep, and sees that they cannot be won back to Him by wrath or war. . . .

God, therefore, seeing that man is so ready to love, throws the book of love straight at him, giving him the Word, His Only-Begotten Son, who takes our humanity to make a great peace. . . . This sweet Word jousted with His arms upon the wood of the most holy Cross, death fighting a tournament with life, and life with death, so that by His death He destroyed our death, and to give us life, He sacrificed the life of His body. So then with love He has drawn us to Him, and has overcome our malice with His kindness, in so much that every heart should be drawn to Him, since greater love one cannot show. . . .

Holiest sweet father of mine, I see no other way for us and no other aid to winning back your sheep, which have left the fold of Holy Church in rebellion, not obedient nor submissive to you, their father. I pray you therefore, in the name of Christ crucified, and I will that you do me this grace, to overcome their malice with your kindness. Yours we are, father! I know and realize that they all feel that they have done wrong; but although they have no excuse for their crimes, nevertheless it seemed to them that they could not do differently, because of the many sufferings and injustices and iniquitous things they have endured from bad shepherds and governors. . . . I ask you then, father, to show them mercy. Do not regard the ignorance and pride of your sons, but with the food of love and your kindness inflict such mild discipline and benign reproof as shall satisfy you, Holiness, and restore peace to us miserable children who have done wrong.

I tell you, sweet Christ on earth, on behalf of Christ in Heaven, that if you do this, without strife or tempest, they will all come grieving for the wrong they have done, and lay their heads on your bosom. Then you will rejoice, and we shall rejoice, because by love you have restored the sheep to the fold of Holy Church. . . .

On me then, your poor daughter, take out any vengeance that you will. Ah me, father, I die of grief and cannot die! Come, come, and resist no more the will of God that calls you; the hungry sheep await your coming to hold and possess the place of your predecessor and Champion, Apostle Peter. For you, as the Vicar of Christ, should abide in your own place. Come, then, come, and delay no more; do not fear anything that might happen, since God will be with you. I ask humbly your benediction for me and all my sins; and I beg you to pardon my presumption. I say no more. Remain in the holy and sweet grace of God-Sweet Jesus, Jesus Love.

CONSIDER THIS:

10-6. According to Catherine of Siena, why is the "wolf carrying away" the sheep entrusted to the Church? Whose fault was this? Is Catherine critical of this pope? What does she fear? And what is her solution to the situation?

The Great Schism: The Cardinals Revolt (1378)

In 1378, Pope Gregory XI died and the cardinals elected Bartholomew, Archbishop of Bari, to replace him as Urban VI. But when it became evident that the new pope was going to move the papal seat back to Rome, the French cardinals became upset and elected a second pope, Clement VII, who remained in Avignon. This was the beginning of the "Great Schism," or division, of the church. The unity of Christendom collapsed as each pope excommunicated the other and drew support from different European states. In the following manifesto, the French cardinals explain the reasoning behind their action.

After the apostolic seat was made vacant by the death of our lord, pope Gregory XI, who died in March, we assembled in conclave for the election of a pope, as is the law and custom, in the papal palace, in which Gregory had died. . . . Officials of the city with a great multitude of the people, for the most part armed and called together for this purpose by the ringing of bells, surrounded the palace in a threatening manner and even entered it and almost filled it. To the terror caused by their presence they added threats that unless we should at once elect a Roman or an Italian, they would kill us. They gave us no time to deliberate but compelled us unwillingly, through violence and fear, to elect an Italian without delay. In order to escape the danger which threatened us from such a mob, we elected Bartholomew, archbishop of Bari, thinking that he would have enough conscience not to accept the election, since every one knew that it was made under such wicked threats. But he was unmindful of his own salvation and burning with ambition, and so, to the great scandal of the clergy and of the Christian people, and contrary to the laws of the church, he accepted this election which was offered him although not all the cardinals were present at the election, and it was extorted from us by the threats and demands of the officials and people of the city. And although such an election is null and void, and the danger for the people still threatened us, he was enthroned and crowned, and called himself pope and apostolic. But according to the holy fathers and to the law of the church, he should be called apostate, anathema, Antichrist, and the mocker and destroyer of Christianity. . . .

The Council of Pisa (1409)

With the development of the Great Schism, the church found itself in an unprecedented and dangerous position. There was no legal machinery to end the schism, and the Holy Roman Emperor decided not to end it by force. Confronted with this stalemate, some church scholars suggested that a council of influential prelates be called to discuss the situation and recommend a solution. The conciliar movement, as it was called, presented several problems for the papacy. Since the fifth century, the pope, as heir to Saint Peter and as Vicar of Christ, had assumed authority for all theological and administrative decisions concerning the fate of the Christian church in the West. Must he now bend to the authority of a group of "overseers" who could issue decrees and dictate orders that the pope would have to obey? Indeed, many doubted that a council of the church could be called by anyone but the pope, or that such a council would have the authority to decide between two papal claimants. The council was finally called by the cardinals in 1409. Their statement is presented here.

"The Great Schism: The Cardinals Revolt" is from Oliver Thatcher and Edgar McNeal, eds., *A Source Book of Medieval History* (New York: Charles Scribner's Sons, 1905), pp. 325–326.

"The Council of Pisa" is from Oliver Thatcher and Edgar McNeal, eds., *A Source Book of Medieval History* (New York: Charles Scribner's Sons, 1905), pp. 327–328.

This holy and general council, representing the universal church, decrees and declares that the united college of cardinals was empowered to call the council, and that the power to call such a council belongs of right to the aforesaid holy college of cardinals, especially now when there is a detestable schism. The council further declared that this holy council, representing the universal church, caused both claimants of the papal throne to be cited in the gates and doors of the churches of Pisa to come and hear the final decision [in the matter of the schism] pronounced, or to give a good and sufficient reason why such sentence should not be rendered.

The Council of Constance (1417)

In its final decree, the Council of Pisa deposed both popes and elected a new one; however, neither of the existing popes accepted this decision, so for a time there were three claimants to the papal throne. Another church council was called at Constance (1414–1417) to rectify the situation. This council succeeded in establishing one head of the church, and the schism ended. The conciliar movement thus gained prestige and authority. Many wanted a regular convocation of councils, as the following excerpt indicates. Still, councils after Constance were not nearly as productive. Nationalistic rivalries among prelates condemned the conciliar movement to tortuous bickering and inaction. The popes successfully resisted attempts to change the administration of the church or to institute popular reforms. In 1459, Pope Pius II condemned all attempts at conciliar domination.

A good way to till the field of the Lord is to hold general councils frequently, because by them the briers, thorns, and thistles of heresies, errors, and schisms are rooted out, abuses reformed, and the way of the Lord made more fruitful. But if general councils are not held, all these evils spread and flourish. We therefore decree by this perpetual edict that general councils shall be held as follows: The first one shall be held five years after the close of this council, the second one seven years after the close of the first, and forever thereafter one shall be held every ten years. One month before the close of each council the pope, with the approval and consent of the council, shall fix the place for holding the next council. If the pope fails to name the place, the council must do so.

CONSIDER THIS:

10-7. Explain the significance of the Babylonian Captivity and the Great Schism to Western Christianity. Who was responsible for starting the schism? How did the church justify the authority of the councils?

THEME: THE POWER STRUCTURE

THE REFLECTION IN THE MIRROR

The Vices of the Church

"Luxury Demands Gratifications"

NICHOLAS CLAMANGES

During the fifteenth and sixteenth centuries, the papacy degenerated greatly as popes became involved in the political disputes between various Italian city-states. The papal states were established around the area of Rome and were defended and enlarged especially by

"Luxury Demands Gratifications" is from James H. Robinson, ed., *Readings in European History*, vol.1 (Boston: Ginn and Company, 1904), pp. 508–510.

"The Council of Constance" is from Oliver Thatcher and Edgar McNeal, eds., *A Source Book of Medieval History* (New York: Charles Scribner's Sons, 1905), pp. 331–332.

Pope Alexander VI (1492–1503) and Pope Julius II (1503–1513). Alexander's son, Cesare Borgia, was one of the most infamous and unscrupulous adventurers of the time. Julius II preferred not to fight by proxy, but went into battle himself against the French. The following excerpts testify to the widespread criticism of the papacy during the period. The first is by the cleric Nicholas Clamanges, from his work *The Downfall of the Church*; the second is an anonymous warning about the future. Indeed, it would not be long before Martin Luther broke from the church and began the Reformation movement.

KEEP IN MIND . . .

10-8. What are Nicholas Clamanges's primary criticisms against the Church?

After the great increase of worldly goods, the virtues of our ancestors being quite neglected, boundless avarice and blind ambition invaded the hearts of the churchmen. As a result they were carried away by the glory of their position and the extent of their power, and soon gave way to the degrading effects of luxury. Three most exacting and troublesome masters had now to be satisfied. Luxury demands sundry gratifications—wine, sleep, banquets, music, debasing sports, courtesans, and the like. Display requires fine houses, castles, towers, palaces, rich and varied furniture, expensive clothes, horses, servants, and the pomp of luxury. Lastly is Avarice, which carefully brings together vast treasures to supply the demands of the above-mentioned vices or, if these are otherwise provided for, to gratify the eye by the vain contemplation of the coins themselves.

> "The popes anoint their collectors in every province . . . who would squeeze gold from a stone."
> —NICHOLAS CLAMANGES

So insatiable are these lords, and so imperious are their demands, that the Golden Age of Saturn, which we hear of in stories, should it now return, would hardly suffice to ensure the requirements. Since it is impossible, however rich the bishop and ample his revenue, to satisfy these rapacious harpies with that alone, he must cast about for other sources of income.

For carrying on these exactions and gathering the gains into the [coffers] . . . the popes anoint their collectors in every province,—those, namely, whom they know to be most skillful in extracting money, owing to peculiar energy, diligence, or harshness of temper, those, in short, who will neither spare nor except but would squeeze gold from a stone. To these the popes grant, moreover, the power of anathematizing any one, even prelates, and of expelling from the communion of the faithful every one who does not, within a fixed period, satisfy their demands for money. What ills these collectors have caused, and the extent to which poor churches and people have been oppressed, are questions best omitted, as we could never hope to do the matter justice. . . .

[Excommunication and interdict] were resorted to in the rarest instances by earlier popes, and then only for the most horrible of crimes: for by these penalties a man is separated from the companionship of the faithful and turned over to Satan. But nowadays these inflictions are so fallen in esteem that they are used for the lightest offense, often for no offense at all, so that they no longer bring terror but are objects of contempt.

To the same cause is to be ascribed the ruin of numerous churches and monasteries and the leveling to the ground, in so many places, of sacred edifices, while the money which was formerly used for their restoration is exhausted in paying these taxes. But it even happens, as some well know, that holy relics in not a few churches—crosses, chalices, and other precious articles—go to make up this tribute.

Who does not know how many abbots and other prelates, when they come to die, are, if they prove obnoxious to the papal body on account of their poverty, refused a dignified funeral, and even denied burial, except perchance in some field or garden, or other profane spot, where they are secretly disposed of. Priests, as we all see, are forced, by reason of their scanty means of support, to desert their parishes and their benefices, and in their hunger, seek bread where they may, performing profane services for laymen. Some rich and hitherto prosperous churches have, indeed, been able to support this burden, but all are now exhausted and can no longer bear to be cheated of their revenue.

The Wealth of the Church (1480)

It is as clear as day that by means of smooth and crafty words the clergy have deprived us of our rightful possessions. For they blinded the eyes of our forefathers, and persuaded them to buy the kingdom of heaven with their lands and possessions. If you priests give the poor and the chosen children of God their paternal inheritance, which before God you owe them, God will perhaps grant you such grace that you will know yourselves. But so long as you spend your money on your dear harlots and profligates, instead of upon the children of God, you may be sure that God will reward you according to your merits. For you have angered and overburdened all the people of the empire. The time is coming when your possessions will be seized and divided as if they were the possessions of an enemy. As you have oppressed the people, they will rise up against you so that you will not know where to find a place to stay.

CONSIDER THIS:

10-9. Nicholas Clamanges identifies "luxury, display, and avarice" as the primary vices of the papacy and other clerics such as bishops. What do these specific sins entail? How did the Church use excommunication to fill its coffers?

THE BROADER PERSPECTIVE:

10-10. What specific measures should have been instituted by the papacy to reform the Church and to solve the problems that separated the clergy from its flock?

Disease and History: The Black Death (1347–1351)

The *Black Death* is a general term for a combination of bubonic, pneumonic, and septicemic plague strains. All three raged in the epidemic of 1347 to 1351. By far the most common was the bubonic variety. These bacteria are usually transmitted by the bite of an infected flea; the disease has an incubation period of about six days. The victim has symptoms of high fever (103°–105° F), sweating, chills, rapid pulse, and swelling of the lymph nodes, especially in the groin or armpit. Hemorrhaging then occurs under the skin, producing blackish blotches called buboes, from which the bubonic plague derives its name. This hemorrhaging produces a kind of intoxication of the nervous system that is perhaps responsible for the delusions and psychological disorders that accompany infection. Bubonic plague is the least virulent of the three strains, but nevertheless results in the death of 50 to 60 percent of its victims. Pneumonic plague is more lethal (killing 95 to 100 percent) and more easily transmitted because it is based in the lungs and is spread by simple coughing. Like bubonic plague, septicemic plague usually depends on transference by an insect and is the most virulent strain of all. A rash forms within hours and death occurs in a day. This type of plague is nearly always fatal.

But it is not enough to talk only of the pathology of the strain. Diseases exist in an environment, and conditions may not be conducive to the survival of the bacterium or the transmitting agent. Cold, for example, limits the flea's activity, and humidity of less than 70 percent kills it.

"The Wealth of the Church" is from Oliver Thatcher and Edgar McNeal, eds., *A Source Book for Medieval History* (New York: Charles Scribner's Sons, 1905), p. 336.

Therefore, plague outbreaks were restricted to the summer and early fall. Another important factor in the sweeping devastation of the plague must have been the general health of the population of Europe. From the tenth to the mid-twelfth century, Europe's population increased 300 percent, to about 80 million people—higher than it had been for a thousand years. This was generally the result of improved agricultural techniques and inventions, as well as the greater security of society. But by the late twelfth century, the climate was changing: Europe was growing colder and wetter. The 1290s were an extremely rainy decade; seedlings died and fertile topsoil was washed away. The growing population soon outstripped food production capabilities, and in certain regions of Europe between 10 and 25 percent of the inhabitants died from starvation. Thus the Black Death arrived close on the heels of famine.

Many were in no condition to resist such a virulent disease. To the people who lived in the mid-fourteenth century, the Black Death was an incomprehensible agent of destruction. No one was safe, neither peasant nor aristocrat, priest nor king. In such a spiritual age, many believed that God was rendering His judgment on humanity or that a great cosmic struggle between the forces of Good and Evil was taking place, with the Devil emerging victorious. It was evident to all that Europe was in the throes of change by forces that could not be understood, moving toward a future that could not be guaranteed.

"A Most Terrible Plague"

GIOVANNI BOCCACCIO

Giovanni Boccaccio is best known as a humanist of the Italian Renaissance. The following excerpt is from his most famous work, *The Decameron*. Written during the plague years between 1348 and 1353, it is a collection of stories told intimately between friends while they pass the time away from Florence in the solitude and safety of the country. It begins with a detailed description of the pestilence. Over two thirds of the population of Florence died of the plague.

In the year then of our Lord 1348, there happened at Florence, the finest city in all Italy, a most terrible plague; which, whether owing to the influence of the planets, or that it was sent from God as a just punishment for our sins, had broken out some years before in the Levant, and after passing from place to place, and making incredible havoc all the way, had now reached the west. There, in spite of all the means that art and human foresight could suggest, such as keeping the city clear from filth, the exclusion of all suspected persons, and the publication of copious instructions for the preservation of health; and notwithstanding manifold supplications offered to God in processions and otherwise, it began to show itself in the spring of the aforesaid year, in a sad and wonderful manner. Unlike what had been seen in the east, where bleeding from the nose is the fatal prognostic, here there appeared certain tumors in the groin or under the armpits, some as big as a small apple, others as an egg; and afterwards purple spots in most parts of the body; in some cases large and but few in number, in others smaller and more numerous—both sorts the usual messengers of death. To the cure of this malady, neither medical knowledge nor the power of drugs was of any effect; whether because the disease was in its own nature mortal, or that the physicians (the number of whom, taking quacks and women pretenders into the account, was grown very great) could form no just idea of the cause, nor consequently devise a true method of cure; whichever was the reason, few escaped; but nearly all died the third day from the first appearance of the symptoms, some sooner, some later, without any fever or accessory symptoms. What gave the more virulence to this plague, was that, by being communicated from the sick to the healthy, it spread daily, like fire when it comes in contact with large masses

"A Most Terrible Plague" is from Giovanni Boccaccio, *The Decameron*, in trans. John Payne, *Stories of Boccaccio* (London: Bibliophilist Library, 1903), pp. 1–6.

of combustibles. Nor was it caught only by conversing with, or coming near the sick, but even by touching their clothes, or anything that they had before touched. . . .

These facts, and others of the like sort, occasioned various fears and devices amongst those who survived, all tending to the same uncharitable and cruel end; which was, to avoid the sick, and every thing that had been near them, expecting by that means to save themselves. And some holding it best to live temperately, and to avoid excesses of all kinds, made parties, and shut themselves up from the rest of the world; eating and drinking moderately of the best, and diverting themselves with music, and such other entertainments as they might have within doors; never listening to anything from without, to make them uneasy. Others maintained free living to be a better preservative, and would baulk no passion or appetite they wished to gratify, drinking and reveling incessantly from tavern to tavern, or in private houses (which were frequently found deserted by the owners, and therefore common to every one), yet strenuously avoiding, with all this brutal indulgence, to come near the infected. And such, at that time, was the public distress, that the laws, human and divine, were no more regarded; for the officers, to put them in force, being either dead, sick, or in want of persons to assist them, every one did just as he pleased. A third sort of people chose a method between these two: not confining themselves to rules of diet like the former, and yet avoiding the intemperance of the latter; but eating and drinking what their appetites required, they walked everywhere with [fragrances and nose-coverings], for the whole atmosphere seemed to them tainted with the stench of dead bodies, arising partly from the distemper itself, and partly from the fermenting of the medicines within them. Others with less humanity, but . . . with more security from danger, decided that the only remedy for the pestilence was to avoid it: persuaded, therefore, of this, and taking care for themselves only, men and women in great numbers left the city, their houses, relations, and effects, and fled into the country; as if the wrath of God had been restrained to visit those only within the walls of the city. . . .

I pass over the little regard that citizens and relations showed to each other; for their terror was such, that a brother even fled from his brother, a wife from her husband, and, what is more uncommon, a parent from his own child. Hence numbers that fell sick could have no help but what the charity of friends, who were very few, or the avarice of servants supplied; and even these were scarce and at extravagant wages, and so little used to the business that they were fit only to reach what was called for, and observe when their employer died; and this desire of getting money often cost them their lives. . . .

It fared no better with the adjacent country, for you might see the poor distressed laborers, with their families, without either the aid of physicians, or help of servants, languishing on the highways, in the fields, and in their own houses, and dying rather like cattle than human creatures. The consequence was that, growing dissolute in their manners like the citizens, and careless of everything, as supposing every day to be their last, their thoughts were not so much employed how to improve, as how to use their substance for their present support.

What can I say more, if I return to the city, unless that such was the cruelty of Heaven, and perhaps of men, that between March and July following, according to authentic reckonings, upwards of a hundred thousand souls perished in the city only; whereas, before that calamity, it was not supposed to have contained so many inhabitants. What magnificent dwellings, what noble palaces were then depopulated to the last inhabitant! What families became extinct! What riches and vast possessions were left, and no known heir to inherit them! What numbers of both sexes, in the prime and vigor of youth . . . breakfasted in the morning with their living friends, and supped at night with their departed friends in the other world!

CONSIDER THIS:

10-11. According to Boccaccio, what were the symptoms of the Black Death, and how did people react to the crisis?

10-12. How were the patterns of social interaction and urban production altered by the Black Death? Which passage in Boccaccio's description makes the greatest impression on you and why?

10-13. The "Dance of Death" and the fragility of life were important themes in medieval art during the plague years. A familiar expression of the time was *Media vita in morte sumus* ("In the midst of life, we are in death"). How is the psychological devastation of the plague expressed in the woodcut depicting the "Danse Macabre"?

FIGURE 10.2 The "Danse Macabre" was a common art motif in the fourteenth century. Death seemed to mock the living and the "grim reaper" took his toll indiscriminately. (*Woodcut by Mich. Wohlgemuth, 1493. The Bridgman Art Library International*)

"God's Hand Was Unstrung"

MATTEO VILLANI

Human populations are resilient enough to recover from an isolated epidemic, but pandemic plague gave impetus to the great permanent changes in the Late Middle Ages.

Historians can document some of the changes explicitly; other changes were more ephemeral and are subject to varying opinion. The depopulation of the cities, where the plague hit hardest, caused a crisis in trade and economic exchange. Production of goods was often curtailed with the death of skilled artisans, and those who replaced them offered work of inferior quality. The medieval church grew wealthier from the accumulation of property of those who willed it as a last token of faith before they died. But the church also had difficulty explaining the pestilence and was hard-pressed to defend against the argument that God was taking vengeance for the sins of humanity. The papacy itself was battered by criticism and charges of corruption that were proved daily during its residence in Avignon from 1303 to 1377. What the church gained in wealth, it lost in prestige. The plague also affected the political relationship between church and state that had been under dispute since the eleventh century. The question of whether the secular or spiritual realm had greater authority on earth had already been answered by the mid-fourteenth century, because popes no longer challenged the military might of kings. But this status was confirmed by the results of the Black Death. The traditional containers of monarchical power were the nobility and the clergy. Both groups

"God's Hand Was Unstrung" is from G. G. Coulton, *The Black Death* (London: Ernest Benn Limited, 1929), pp. 66–68. Reprinted by permission of A&C Black Limited.

depended on the strength that numbers and unity gave them in their struggles with the king. The plague reduced their numbers, thus allowing kings to secure their realms more easily.

Matteo Villani was the brother of Giovanni Villani, the first great chronicler of Florence. Giovanni had described the beginnings of the plague before he himself died of it. Matteo continued his brother's work and devoted two chapters to the effects of the plague. He himself succumbed to the disease in 1363. The confused reactions to the plague were often either to lead a very temperate life in hopes that God would approve and lift his ban against humanity or conversely to enjoy life to the utmost before Death knocked on the door. Villani describes the scene in Florence.

Those few discreet folk who remained alive expected many things, all of which, by reasons of the corruption of sin, failed among mankind, whose minds followed marvelously in the contrary direction. They believed that those whom God's grace had saved from death, having beheld the destruction of their neighbors, and having heard the same tidings from all the nations of the world, would become better-conditioned, humble, virtuous, and Catholic; that they would guard themselves from iniquity and sins, and would be full of love and charity one towards another. But no sooner had the plague ceased than we saw the contrary; for, since men were few, and since, by hereditary succession, they abounded in earthly goods, they forgot the past as though it had never been, and gave themselves up to a more shameful and disordered life than they had led before. For, moldering in ease, they dissolutely abandoned themselves to the sin of gluttony, with feasts and taverns and delight of delicate foods; and again to games of hazard and to unbridled lechery, inventing strange and unaccustomed fashions and indecent manners in their garments, and changing all their household stuff into new forms. And the common folk, both men and women, by reason of the abundance and superfluity that they found, would no longer labor at their accustomed trades, but demanded the dearest and most delicate foods for their sustenance; and they married at their will, while children and common women clad themselves in all the fair and costly garments of the ladies dead by that horrible death. Thus, almost the whole city, without any restraint whatsoever, rushed into disorderliness of life; and in other cities or provinces of the world things were the same or worse. Therefore, according to such tidings as we could hear, there was no part of the world wherein men restrained themselves to live

in temperance, when once they had escaped from the fury of the Lord; for now they thought that God's hand was unstrung. . . . Again, men dreamed of wealth and abundance in garments and in all other things beyond meat and drink; yet, in fact, things turned out widely different; for most [luxury] commodities were more costly, by twice or more, than before the plague. And the price of labor, and the work of all trades and crafts, rose in disorderly fashion beyond the double. Lawsuits and disputes and quarrels and riots arose everywhere among citizens in every land, by reason of legacies and successions; the law-courts of our own city of Florence were long filled with such [cases], to our great expense and unwanted discomfort. Wars and scandals arose throughout the world, contrary to men's expectation.

CONSIDER THIS:

10-14. In what ways were the interests of both church and state affected by the Black Death? Religion is often considered a stabilizing force in society. How was faith a casualty of this disease? How did the plague disrupt the balance between religious and secular forces?

THE BROADER PERSPECTIVE:

10-15. What is the role of disease in history? How potent is disease as a force for historical change? How fatalistic are you? Must there be a plague or a war every so often for civilization to survive and for the world's population to remain in proper balance?

10-16. Why do people spend so much time trying to prevent disease or war if it is a natural way of assuring the overall survival of humanity? Discuss the moral implications of this statement with reference to overpopulation in India, Mexico, or China. Is it time for another uncontrollable disease to strike humanity?

Chapter 11

The Age of the Renaissance

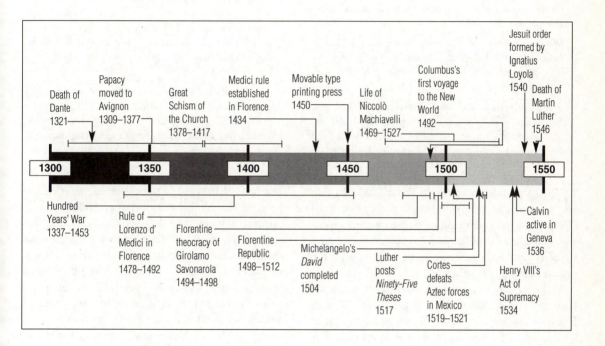

Timeline of events:

- Death of Dante 1321
- Papacy moved to Avignon 1309–1377
- Great Schism of the Church 1378–1417
- Medici rule established in Florence 1434
- Movable type printing press 1450
- Life of Niccolò Machiavelli 1469–1527
- Columbus's first voyage to the New World 1492
- Jesuit order formed by Ignatius Loyola 1540
- Death of Martin Luther 1546

Timeline markers: 1300, 1350, 1400, 1450, 1500, 1550

- Hundred Years' War 1337–1453
- Rule of Lorenzo d' Medici in Florence 1478–1492
- Florentine theocracy of Girolamo Savonarola 1494–1498
- Florentine Republic 1498–1512
- Michelangelo's *David* completed 1504
- Luther posts *Ninety-Five Theses* 1517
- Cortes defeats Aztec forces in Mexico 1519–1521
- Henry VIII's Act of Supremacy 1534
- Calvin active in Geneva 1536

Learning is the only thing the mind never exhausts, never fears and never regrets.

—LEONARDO DA VINCI

What a piece of work is man, how noble in reason, how infinite in faculty; in form and moving, how express and admirable, in action how like an angel, in apprehension how like a god: a beauty of the world, the paragon of animals!

—WILLIAM SHAKESPEARE, *HAMLET*

Apart from man, no being wonders at his own existence.

—ARTHUR SCHOPENHAUER

Man is the measure of all things.

—PROTAGORAS

Man—a creature made at the end of the week's work when God was tired.

—MARK TWAIN

CHAPTER THEMES

- **The Power Structure:** How did the Medici family control Florence? Was their influence based on their "power" or on their "authority"? How could this be compared to the rule of the Roman emperor Augustus? Could the government of Savonarola legitimately be described as a theocracy?

- **Imperialism:** The Renaissance was a period of personal discovery and artistic creativity. It was also a period of brutal conquest of the Americas. Must exploration result in exploitation?

- **Women in History:** The Renaissance was a period in which conventional social, religious, and political structures were being challenged. Did women benefit from this new climate?

- **The Institution and the Individual:** Could the Renaissance papacy be described as primarily secular and not spiritual? Had the Christian Church during the Renaissance become essentially another secular institution in order to compete with European monarchs? Were the Renaissance popes secular rulers?

- **Social and Spiritual Values:** What were the fundamental tenets of humanism, and why were they considered radical, especially to the Church?

- **Revolution and Historical Transition:** The Renaissance has been seen as a period of transition between the "static" Middle Ages and the "vibrant" modern world. Is this a reasonable interpretation? How was progress measured during the Renaissance, and what drawbacks were evident? What debt does our contemporary world owe to the Renaissance?

- **The Big Picture:** Why was the Renaissance period so creative? Is artistic and cultural creativity best served by political and religious stability, or is the progress of civilization best served by the energy that chaos promotes?

The Late Middle Ages, from about 1300 to 1450, was a time of great struggle and calamity in western Europe. The fabric of medieval civilization was gradually torn apart by a plentitude of simultaneous catastrophes that oppressed the spirit and augured the decline of an age of faith.

The great political debacle of the period was the Hundred Years' War, which began in 1337 over English claims to the French throne and did not end until 1453. Although battles were fought only intermittently during this period, the war sapped the economic resources of the developing nation-states and directed the energy of Europe onto a path of self-destruction. No longer were Europeans united in some foreign crusade against the enemies of God; they now tore each other apart in rather mindless confusion. But wars are made by people, and at least they have some foreknowledge of the destruction that inevitably ensues. No one, however, could have predicted the devastating effects of the Black Death. From 1347 to 1351, it raged throughout Europe, destroying one third to one half of the population. Apart from the physical agony of the disease, the mental terror of an unseen, unknown enemy was enough to divert the energy of life into a dance of death. No one was exempt from the potential of its destruction. God seemed to forsake his flock, and the

church was hard-pressed to explain or prevail against the grim reaper. But the church's credibility as the instrument of God had already been called into question by corruption and disunity. In 1309, the papacy was transferred from its traditional seat in Rome to the city of Avignon, France. This Babylonian Captivity, as it was called, deprived the papacy of authority and contributed to its loss of respect as prelates became known for their licentiousness and corruption. In 1378, the papacy was transferred back to Rome. But political maneuvering resulted in a schism that split Western Christianity into two camps, led by two popes, one in Rome and one in Avignon. This spiritual calamity was finally resolved by a series of councils of the church that were empowered to pass judgments on the papacy itself. In effect, they declared their superiority over the pope in spiritual affairs. The reformist zeal of these councils, however, did little but underscore the need for widespread change in the church. The papacy continued to degenerate: Pope Alexander VI fathered several children, and Pope Julius II, bedecked in full armor, led papal armies against the French.

These political, social, and spiritual calamities sapped the energy of medieval civilization and destroyed the spiritual foundation that had inspired people to build the cathedrals and to resist the barbarism that came close on the heels of Rome's decline. The focus of Western civilization was shifting from a dutiful devotion to God to an emphasis on the worth and importance of humanity. This transformation was centered, at the outset, in Italy, and began during the calamitous fourteenth century. By 1450, the Renaissance was in full bloom.

The term *renaissance* means "rebirth"; it was coined by scholars in the fifteenth and sixteenth centuries who felt a new inspiration. They viewed the medieval world as one of mindless chanting and uncreative introspection. According to the people of the Renaissance, the preceding centuries were "Middle Ages" between the brilliance of the ancient Greeks and Romans and the reflection of that light in the culture of fifteenth-century Italy. The Middle Ages became synonymous with the "Dark Ages." For the scholars of the Renaissance, the hope of Western civilization lay in a cultivation of the classical works of antiquity. The masters of thought and erudition were figures like Cicero, Aristotle, Plato, Virgil, and Thucydides. They became models and authorities for argument, insight, and eloquence. No longer was it enough to be able to read Cicero: One was now expected to imitate his Latin style. A cult of the classics developed as people admired the ancient monuments of Roman civilization and sought copies of ancient texts. The Renaissance movement was primarily a scholarly pursuit of the ideals and values of classical civilization.

Chief among those values was the emphasis on human beings; this led to the movement known as humanism. The Renaissance emphasized the most positive aspects of humanity. Rational thought and creative instinct were prized. Humankind was composed of two natures: the brutal force of the animal and some of the divine qualities of God. Most importantly, people had the free will to pursue their own paths. The course of their lives was determined not by God, but by their own ambition, talent, or deceit. The glory of humanity was portrayed in the poetry and astoundingly rich art of the period. The names of Leonardo, Raphael, and Michelangelo evoke mastery of technique and perfection of style. But perhaps the most transparent assessment of reality was made by Niccolò Machiavelli. For him, power and control were the watchwords of existence. This was man, stripped of his embellishment and conscious of the political realities of life. *The Prince* was Machiavelli's manual on practical survival in a chaotic age. Glory could also be attained by strong, competent rule.

Machiavelli made people aware of the realities of power politics, and in doing so he was fulfilling a need in society. For Italy was not a united kingdom but rather a disjointed chaotic grouping of city-states, led variously by despots, oligarchs, and republicans. It is a curious paradox that societal chaos seems to breed creativity; Michelangelo painted the Sistine Chapel while Rome was in peril of being taken by French armies. The relationship between chaos and creativity is a question worth pursuing, for it precedes discussion of a wider issue: the progress of civilization. Why was the Renaissance such a creative period, artistically, technologically, and politically? Is creativity truly an ingredient of progress, or is the progress of civilization best served by solid administration and continuity, as we found during the height of the Roman Empire? This chapter investigates some of the ideas and attitudes that influenced European Renaissance society and continue to influence our lives today.

KEY EVENTS IN THE RENAISSANCE

1434–1466   The Rule of Cosimo de' Medici

Patriarch of the Medici family, banker to the popes, and patron of the arts, Cosimo establishes and consolidates his rule of Florence as a "sham republic." Succeeded by his son, Piero de'Medici (1466–1478).

1435–1455   Johannes Gutenberg

Technology invented for movable type printing press by Johannes Gutenberg. Transforms communication and helps make the Reformation possible.

1452–1519   Life of Leonardo da Vinci

Artist, scientist, musician, and inventor, Leonardo dreams of flight, submarines, tanks, parachutes, siege machines, and . . . the *Mona Lisa*.

1463–1494   Life of Pico della Mirandola

Scholar and philosopher, his *Oration on the Dignity of Man* (1486) is the quintessential expression of humanism.

1478–1492   The Rule of Lorenzo the Magnificent

Grandson of Cosimo, he succeeds Piero de' Medici and maintains family dominance of politics in Florence. A philosopher, poet, effective diplomat, and patron of the arts, Lorenzo survives two assassination attempts to lead Florence at the height of its political and artistic influence.

1492–1494   Florentine Power Vacuum

Pietro de'Medici cannot sustain control in the power vacuum following Lorenzo's death and Florence is in political chaos. Columbus's first voyage to the eastern Bahamas in search of a route to India (1492). Corrupt papacy of Alexander VI (1492–1503).

1494–1498   The Theocracy of Savonarola

The power vacuum in Florence is filled by Dominican friar Girolamo Savonarola, who establishes a theocracy as God's representative. He is excommunicated after a series of sermons condemning the pope. Savonarola welcomes the invasion of Italy by the French king Charles VIII, but loses confidence of Florentines and is executed (1498).

1498–1512   The Florentine Republic

Florence survives Savonarola and a true republic is established and run by civic humanists like Leonardo Bruni. Niccolò Machiavelli is an enthusiastic republican and organizes the Florentine militia, which is defeated by Spanish mercenary forces (1512) as the Medici return to power. Machiavelli is tortured and broken. In retirement, he looks to strong, practical rule and writes *The Prince* (1513).

1503–1513   Papacy of Julius II

The "Warrior Pope" is a patron of the arts who is impressed with Michelangelo's statue of *David* (1501–1504) and commissions him to paint the Sistine Chapel and additional sculptures. Julius II orders a Jubilee Indulgence to pay for the construction of a new Saint Peter's Basilica. Raphael's *School of Athens* completed (1511).

1519–1521   The Spanish Conquest of Mexico

Hernando Cortés lands on the coast of Mexico and brutally defeats Aztec forces, who are devastated by European diseases.

The Humanist Movement

A Humanist Education

LEONARDO BRUNI

An important exponent of the humanist movement in the fifteenth century was the great luminary of the Italian Renaissance, Leonardo Bruni, who is most famous as one of the "civic humanists." These were scholars who not only devoted themselves to the classics

"A Humanist Education" is from G. R. Elton, ed., *Renaissance and Reformation, 1300–1648* (New York: Pearson Education, 1963), pp. 52–53. Copyright © 1963 by Pearson Education, Inc. Reprinted by permission of Pearson Education, Inc.

but also felt a responsibility to be involved in their respective cities and states. Bruni himself served as chancellor of Florence. In the following selection, he offers his ideas about the importance of education in a letter to an aspiring young scholar.

Your recent letter gave me the greatest pleasure. For it demonstrated both the excellence of your spirit and your vigorous and intelligent schooling, the product of study and diligence. Considering your age and the penetration of that letter, it is clear to me that your maturity appears admirable and plainly beyond your years. Nor do I doubt, unless you should be untrue to yourself, that you will become a most distinguished man. Therefore, I beg you, take care, add a little every day and gather things in: remember that these studies promise you enormous prizes in both the conduct of your life and for the fame and glory of your name. These two, believe me, are the way to those ample riches which have never yet been lacking to famous and accomplished men, if only the will was present. You have an excellent teacher whose diligence and energy you should imitate. Devote yourself to two kinds of study. In the first place, acquire a knowledge of letters, not the common run of it, but the more searching and profound kind in which I very much want you to shine. Secondly, acquaint yourself with what pertains to life and manners—those things that are called humane studies because they are perfect and adorn man. In this kind of study your knowledge should be wide, varied, and taken from every sort of experience, leaving out nothing that might seem to contribute to the conduct of your life, to honor, and to fame. I shall advise you to read authors who can help you not only by their matter but also by the splendor of their style and their skill in writing; that is to say, the works of Cicero and of any who may possibly approach his level. If you will listen to me, you will thoroughly explore the fundamental and systematic treatment of those matters in Aristotle; as for beauty of expression, a rounded style, and all the wealth of words and speech, skill in these things you, if I may so put it, borrow from Cicero. For I would wish an outstanding man to be both abundantly learned and capable of giving elegant expression to his learning. However, no one can hope to achieve this without reading a lot, learning a lot, and taking a lot away from everywhere. Thus one must not only learn from the scholars (which is the foundation of all study), but must also get instruction from poets, orators and historians, so that one's style may become eloquent, elegant, and never crude in substance. . . . If you do obtain that excellence which I expect of you, what riches will compare with the rewards of these studies?

Oration on the Dignity of Man (1486)

PICO DELLA MIRANDOLA

Perhaps the supreme statement of the Renaissance idolization of man is an extended essay by Pico della Mirandola, a linguist and philosopher who lived from 1463 to 1494. Note Pico's conception of man's relationship to God in this excerpt from the *Oration on the Dignity of Man.*

At last I understand why man is the most fortunate of creatures and therefore worthy of all admiration and given the highest rank in the universal chain of Being— a rank envied not only by those who are disreputable, but even by the stars and by minds beyond this world. This is a wonderful vision, and even a matter past faith. And why shouldn't it be? For it is because of this that man has been rightly described as a great miracle and a marvelous creature indeed. . . God the Father, the supreme Architect, had already built his cosmic home

Oration on the Dignity of Man is from Edmund G. Gardner, ed., *A Platonic Discourse on Love*, (Boston: The Merrymount Press, 1914). Based on the translation of Thomas Stanley, 1651. Translation modernized by the editor.

that we see all around us, that most sacred temple of His divinity, by the laws of His mysterious wisdom. The region above the heavens He had adorned with Omniscience, the heavenly spheres He had refreshed with eternal souls, and the . . . filthy parts of the lower world He had filled with many animals of every kind. But, when the work was finished, the Craftsman kept wishing that there were someone to ponder and appreciate the plan of so great a work, to love its beauty, and to wonder at its profundity. Therefore, when everything was done, God finally decided to create man. But he had no model—nor was there any treasure that he might give to His son as an inheritance, nor did any place exist where His new son might contemplate the universe. All was now finished and everything had been assigned to the highest, the middle, and the lowest orders . . . At last, this Greatest of Artisans, knowing that man was a creature whose nature was not fully determined, assigned him a place in the middle of the world and addressed him like this: "The nature of all other beings is limited and constrained within the bounds of laws prescribed by Us. You, however, are constrained by no limits, and in accordance with your own free will ... shall determine for yourself the limits of your nature. We have placed you at the world's center so that from here, you may more easily observe all that composes the world. We have made you neither of heaven nor of earth, neither mortal nor immortal, so that endowed with freedom of choice and with honor, and in control of your own life, you may fashion yourself in whatever way you decide. You shall have the power to degenerate into the lower forms of life, which are savage. And you shall have the power, through reflection of your soul, to be reborn into the higher forms, which are divine." What supreme generosity of God the Father! What most wonderful happiness for man! God has granted you the power to have whatever you want, to be whatever you will.

The Soul of Man (1474)

MARSILIO FICINO

The ideas of the Greek philosopher Plato were revived during the Renaissance by Neoplatonists who applied his theory on transmigration of the soul to Christian concepts of resurrection. The leading exponent of this philosophy was Marsilio Ficino. Some of his ideas on God and man follow.

Human beings really are God's chosen vicars since they inhabit the earth and cultivate all of its bounty—the animals, the water, and the air—for food, convenience, and pleasure. . . . Not only does man use the animals, but he also rules them. Now it is true that in using their natural protective gifts, some animals may occasionally attack humans or even escape their control. But with the weapons that man himself has invented, he is generally able to avoid animal attacks, frighten them off, or even tame them. Who has ever seen any human beings kept under the control of animals? In fact, we often see herds of both wild and domesticated animals obeying humans throughout their lives. Man rules animals by force, but he also keeps, tames, and governs them. God, who is the universal cause for all things, alone is omniscient and omnipotent. But man, who generally provides for all things, both living and dead, is a kind of god. Certainly he is the god of animals because he uses them, domesticates and even instructs many of them. It is also evident that man is the god of this earth because he cultivates and uses all the elements on earth. Finally, he is the god of all the materials he handles, for he changes and shapes them to fit his needs. He who controls his body and environment in so many ways,

"The Soul of Man" is from James H. Robinson, ed., *Readings in European History*, vol. 2 (Boston: Ginn and Company, 1906), pp. 52–54. Translation modernized by the editor.

and is representative of the immortal God, is himself no doubt immortal. . . .

Individual animals are not really capable of taking care of themselves or their young. Man alone is of such perfection that he first rules himself (something that no animals do) and then controls his family, administers the state, governs nations, and indeed rules the whole world. . . .

The human soul in everything it does is trying with all its might to attain the principle gift of God— the understanding of truth and the possession of goodness. Does the human soul also see God's second attribute and strive to become everything just as God is everything? Indeed it does in a wonderful way. For the soul lives the life of a plant when it serves to feed and sustain the human body; the life of an animal when its senses are heightened; the life of man when it deliberates on human affairs through its reason; the life of heroes when it investigates the natural world; . . . the life of angels, when it seeks to know the divine mysteries; the life of God, when it does everything for the sake of God. Every human soul experiences all of these things in some way, though perhaps in different ways. Therefore, human beings strive to become all things by living the lives of all things. . . . Man is a great miracle, a creature worthy of reverence and adoration, for he transforms himself into God as if he were God himself.

CONSIDER THIS:

11-1. How would you define humanism? Give examples of its most important tenets from the sources offered in the section entitled "The Humanist Movement." According to Pico della Mirandola, what is man's relationship to God?

11-2. The humanists were criticized by the church for their secular interest at the expense of devotion to God. Do you agree with this criticism? Were the humanists disrespectful of God and irreligious? Note especially Marsilio Ficino on this point. In his opinion, what is man's position with respect to God?

THEME: THE INSTITUTION AND THE INDIVIDUAL

AGAINST THE GRAIN

I, Leonardo

The Notebooks of a Universal Man

LEONARDO DA VINCI

The Renaissance produced several outstanding artists, scholars, and statesmen, but no one seemed to imprint this creative age as did Leonardo da Vinci (1452–1519). Leonardo was a painter of great talent. He was especially innovative in producing naturalistic backgrounds, in his perfection of the techniques of perspective and geometric arrangement of figures, and in the subtle treatment of light and shade. But Leonardo never really considered himself to be primarily a painter. His curiosity for the world around him was too great. He wanted to "learn the causes of things." Toward that end he observed and made notes in a book for future reference and was continually inventing machines that he believed would have military value; his sketches of helicopters, tanks, and submarines were far beyond the realities of his time. Leonardo's notebooks give fascinating insight into the workings of his fertile mind. Some of his comments on birds, flight, sketching, and painting are offered here.

"The Notebooks of a Universal Man" is from Edward McCurdy, ed., *Leonardo Da Vinci Notebooks* (New York: Empire State Book Co., 1922), pp. 150–153, 188–189, 197–199.

11-3. Note Leonardo's methodical attention to detail on both scientific and artistic topics.

FIGURE 11.1 *Self Portrait* by Leonardo da Vinci. (*Library of Congress*)

The Observation of Birds and Thoughts of Flight

The thrushes and other small birds are able to make headway against the course of the wind, because they fly in spurts; that is they take a long course below the wind, by dropping in a slanting direction towards the ground, with their wings half closed, and they open the wings and catch the wind in them with their reverse movement, and so rise to a height; and then they drop again in the same way.

Remember that your bird should have no other model than the bat, because its membranes serve as an armor or rather as a means of binding together the pieces of its armor, that is the framework of the wings.

And if you take as your pattern the wings of feathered birds, these are more powerful in structure of bone and sinew because they are penetrable, that is to say the feathers are separated from one another and the air passes through them. But the bat is aided by its membrane which binds the whole together and is not penetrated by the air. Dissect the bat, study it carefully, and on this model construct the machine . . .

There is as much pressure exerted by a substance against the air as by the air against the substance. Observe how the beating of its wings against the air suffices to bear up the weight of the eagle in the highly rarefied air which borders on the fiery element! Observe also how the air moving over the sea, beaten back by the bellying sails, causes the heavily laden ship to glide onwards! So that by adducing and expounding the reasons of these things you may able to realize that man when he has great wings attached to him, by exerting his strength against the resistance of the air and conquering it, is enabled to subdue it and to raise himself upon it.

The Importance of Sketching

When you have thoroughly learnt perspective, and have fixed in your memory all the various parts and forms of things, you should often amuse yourself when you take a walk for recreation, in watching and taking note of the attitudes and actions of men as they talk and dispute, or laugh or come to blows one with another, both their actions and those of the bystanders who either intervene or stand looking on at these things; noting these down with rapid strokes in this way, in a little pocket-book, which you ought always to carry with you. And let this be tinted paper, so that it may not be rubbed out; but you should change the old for a new one, for these are not things to be rubbed out but preserved with the utmost diligence; for there is such an infinite number of forms and actions of things that the memory is incapable of preserving them, and therefore you should keep those [sketches] as your patterns and teachers.

The Way to Paint a Battle

Show first the smoke of the artillery mingled in the air with the dust stirred up by the movement of the horses and of the combatants . . . The smoke which is mingled with the dust-laden air will as it rises to a certain height have more and more the appearance of a dark cloud, at the summit of which the smoke will be more distinctly visible than the dust. The smoke will assume a bluish tinge, and the dust will keep its natural color. From the side whence the light comes this mixture of air and smoke and dust will seem far brighter than on the opposite side.

As for the combatants, the more they are in the midst of this turmoil the less they will be visible, and the less will be the contrast between their lights and shadows. You should give a ruddy glow to the faces and the figures and the air around them, and to the gunners and those near to them, and this glow should grow fainter as it is further away from its cause. The figures which are between you and the light, if far away, will appear dark against a light background, and the nearer their limbs are to the ground the less will they be visible, for there the dust is greater and thicker. And if you make horses galloping away from the throng make little clouds of dust as far distant one from another as is the space between the strides made by the horse, and that cloud which is further away from the horse should be the least visible, for it should be high and spread out and thin, while that which is nearer should be more conspicuous and smaller and more compact.

Let the air be full of arrows going in various directions, some mounting upwards, other falling, others flying horizontally, and let the balls shot from the guns have a train of smoke following their course. Show the figures in the foreground covered with dust on their hair and eyebrows and such other level parts as afford the dust a space to lodge.

Make the conquerors running, with their hair and other things streaming in the wind, and with brows bent down; and they should be thrusting forward opposite limbs, that is, if a man advances the right foot the left arm should also come forward. If you represent any one fallen you should show the mark where he has been dragged through the dust, which has become changed to blood-stained mire, and round about in the half-liquid earth you should show the marks of the tramping of men and horses who have passed over it. Make a horse dragging the dead body of his master, and leaving behind him in the dust and mud the track of where the body was dragged along.

> "Make the dead, some half buried in dust, others with the dust all mingled with the oozing blood and changing into crimson mud."
> —LEONARDO DA VINCI

Make the beaten and conquered pallid, with brows raised and knit together, and let the skin above the brows be all full of lines of pain; at the sides of the nose show the furrows going in an arch from the nostrils and ending where the eye begins, and show the

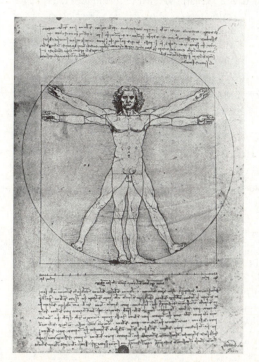

FIGURE 11.2 *Vitruvian Man* by Leonardo da Vinci. (Embassy of Italy)

dilation of the nostrils which is the cause of these lines; and let the lips be arched displaying the upper row of teeth, and let the teeth be parted after the manner of such as cry in lamentation. Show some one using his hand as a shield for his terrified eyes, turning the palm of it towards the enemy, and having the other resting on the ground to support the weight of his body; let others be crying out with their mouths wide open, and fleeing away. Put all sorts of arms lying between the feet of the combatants, such as broken shields, lances, broken swords, and other things like these. Make the dead, some half buried in dust, others with the dust all mingled with the oozing blood and changing into crimson mud; and let the line of the blood be discerned by its color, flowing in a sinuous stream from the corpse of the dust. Show others in the death agony grinding their teeth and rolling their eyes, with clenched fists grinding against their bodies, and with legs distorted . . . but see that there is no level spot of ground that is not trampled over with blood.

CONSIDER THIS:

11-4. Scientific discovery is often based on an inductive process where the observation of particular

experiments in a laboratory leads to the formulation of a general scientific theory. In what ways do Leonardo's notebooks demonstrate this thought process?

11-5. Leonardo's observations of birds and bats led him to conclude that when man "has great wings attached to him, by exerting his strength against the resistance of the air and conquering it, is enabled to subdue it and to raise himself upon it." In other words, human beings linked to a mechanical apparatus and powered by their own physical exertions could fly like birds. Where did Leonardo go wrong in his assumptions? Was this an error based on faulty observation, or was the error tied to Leonardo's confidence that humans could achieve their most fantastic technological dreams? Leonardo never solved the problem of human flight. Why? How necessary is failure in achieving success?

THE BROADER PERSPECTIVE:

11-6. Are you surprised that Leonardo used the same scientific process of observation in painting that he used in inventing? To what extent is a work of art, which may appear so natural and expressive of human emotion and reflection, a process of proportion and mathematical calculation?

The Life of Florence

The Rule of Cosimo de' Medici

VESPASIANO

Florence was perhaps the city most representative of Renaissance activity and inspiration. This was the home of the statesman Leonardo Bruni, the sculptor Michelangelo, the political scientist Machiavelli, and the greatest literary figure of the age, Dante. But during this era, Florence truly belonged to one family—the Medici. They were led by Cosimo de' Medici, who developed the family's financial interests, and they eventually became the bankers of the papacy. Cosimo and his son Lorenzo (the Magnificent) wrote poetry, discussed philosophy, and heavily patronized the great artists of Florence. They were truly humanists in their own right. Although Florence was ostensibly a republic, it was in fact dominated by the

"The Rule of Cosimo de' Medici" is from Vespasiano da Bisticci, *Lives of Illustrious Men of the XV Century*, trans. W. George and E. Waters (London: Routledge and Kegan Paul, Ltd., 1926), pp. 213, 217, 222–224.

Medici family. In their reign, they applied a valuable lesson of "controlled freedom" from the Roman emperor Augustus. In many ways Florence owed her greatness to their efforts. The portrait of Cosimo that follows is by the Renaissance biographer Vespasiano.

Cosimo di Giovanni dé Medici was of most honorable descent, a very prominent citizen and one of great weight in the republic . . .

He had a knowledge of Latin which would scarcely have been looked for in one occupying the station of a leading citizen engrossed with affairs. He was grave in temperament, prone to associate with men of high station who disliked frivolity, and averse from all buffoons and actors and those who spent time unprofitably. He had a great liking for men of letters and sought their society . . . His natural bent was to discuss matters of importance; and, although at this time the city was full of men of distinction, his worth was recognized on account of his praiseworthy qualities, and he began to find employment in affairs of every kind. By his twenty-fifth year he had gained great reputation in the city . . . Cosimo and his party took every step to strengthen their own position . . . Cosimo found that he must be careful to keep their support by being flexible and making believe that [they would] enjoy power equal to his own. Meantime he kept concealed the source of his influence in the city as well as he could . . .

I once heard Cosimo say that the great mistake of his life was that he did not begin to spend his wealth ten years earlier; because, knowing well the disposition of his fellow-citizens, he was sure that, in the lapse of fifty years, no memory would remain of his personality or of his house save the few fabrics he might have built. He went on, "I know that after my death my children will be in worse case than those of any other Florentine who has died for many years past; moreover, I know I shall not wear the crown of laurel more than any other citizen." He spake thus because he knew the difficulty of ruling a state as he had ruled Florence, through the opposition of influential citizens who rated themselves his equals in former times. He acted privately with the greatest discretion in order to safeguard himself, and whenever he sought to attain an object he contrived to let it appear that the matter had been set in motion by some one other than himself and thus he escaped envy and unpopularity. His manner was admirable; he never spoke ill of anyone,

and it angered him greatly to hear slander spoken by others. He was kind and patient to all who sought speech with him: he was more a man of deeds than of words: he always performed what he promised, and when this had been done he sent to let the petitioner know that his wishes had been granted. His replies were brief and sometimes obscure, so that they might be made to bear a double sense . . .

So great was his knowledge of all things, that he could find some matter of discussion with men of all sorts, he would talk literature with a man of letters and theology with a theologian, being well versed therein through his natural liking, and for the reading of the Holy Scripture. With philosophy it was just the same . . . He took kindly notice of all musicians, and delighted greatly in their art. He had dealings with painters and sculptors and had in his house works of diverse masters. He was especially inclined towards sculpture and showed great favor to all worthy craftsmen, being a good friend to Donatello and all sculptors and painters; and because in his time the sculptors found scanty employment, Cosimo, in order that Donatello's chisel might not be idle, commissioned him to make the pulpits of bronze in St. Lorenzo and the doors of the sacristy. He ordered the bank to pay every week enough money to Donatello for his work and for that of his four assistants . . . He had a good knowledge of architecture, as may be seen from the buildings he left, none of which were built without consulting him; moreover, all those who were about to build would go to him for advice.

CONSIDER THIS:

11-7. What personal qualities made Cosimo de' Medici such a successful ruler in Florence?

11-8. Vespasiano notes that Cosimo maintained support in Florence by making all "believe that they would enjoy power equal to his own. Meantime, he kept concealed the source of his influence in the city as well as he could." What was the source of Cosimo's influence? Cosimo, like the Roman emperor Augustus, ruled through his authority, not his power. What is the difference?

"This Will Be Your Final Destruction" (1494)

GIROLAMO SAVONAROLA

In 1492, Lorenzo the Magnificent died and his brother Piero was unable to maintain the family dominance over political affairs in Florence. In 1494, Piero was expelled from the city; the resulting power vacuum was filled by Girolamo Savonarola, the prior of the Dominican convent of San Marco. His preaching against the tyranny of the Medici had a hypnotic effect on the Florentines. His message was directed as well against the corruption of the papacy, and he was soon excommunicated. Nonetheless, he mesmerized Florence for four years. The following excerpt is from a sermon he delivered right after the Medici were overthrown; it was the beginning of Savonarola's own domination. By 1498, the Florentines had become hostile toward Savonarola's restrictive theocracy; he was executed and his body burned at the stake—with the pope's blessing.

Oh, Florence, I cannot tell you everything I feel, for you could not bear it for the present. Oh, if I could tell you all, you would see that I am like a new vessel full of mist that is sealed up, with a seal on every word to prevent it from issuing forth! Many secrets are sealed up there which cannot be told because you would not believe them! Oh, Florence, if you have still been unable to believe, at least believe now; and if you have believed, believe more than ever little man full of sin! God has wished you to see and to know my incapacity so that you may see and realize so much the better that it is He and not I who does all. . . . You know that in these past years while I have preached to you, when everything seemed to be at peace and Florence was so quiet, I predicted to you that you would see much evil and many tribulations; and you did not believe it because you saw no sign of it. Now you have seen it, and you see that they have begun, and you see the beginning of what I told you, and you cannot deny it. Therefore, you must now believe so much the more what I will tell you, since you have seen what was said in the past begin and be verified. And if, then, I predicted evil and you have seen it, now when I speak of good you must believe, because a prophet does not always predict evil. Listen, Florence, this morning to what I am telling you. Hear what God has inspired in me. I trust only in Christ in what I am telling you; and I would fail if I wished to do good to you by myself.

In the first place, I tell you, do those things I have told you to do before: namely, that each one should confess and be purified of his sins, and that all should attend to the common good of the city. And if you will do this, your city will be glorious, because in this way it will be reformed both spiritually and temporally; and from you will come the reformation of all Italy, and Florence will become more rich and more powerful than she has ever been, and she will extend her empire into many places. But if you will not do this that I tell you, this will be your final destruction . . . I have told you before that God wishes to renew his Church; do not doubt that he will renew it with the sword of tribulation, and soon . . .

Above all you must take care lest anyone make himself head and dominate others in the city. Such men are deprived of God's grace and of his special providence, and they are generally the worst men, lacking in understanding and faithless . . . Above all such men have no true friendship with anyone; they do not confide in anyone. True and joyous friendship is necessary in human affairs and conserves you in virtue; but such men have no good virtue, nor do they contract true friendship. They always hate good men and employ only wicked and evil people . . . Furthermore, their rule cannot be long and durable because all the people, even if they do not show it, hate their tyranny. A people under a tyrant is like a body of

"This Will Be Your Final Destruction" is from William J. Bouwsma, trans., in *Major Crises in Western Civilization*, vol. 1 (New York: Harcourt Brace and World, 1965), pp. 165–167. Translated from Mario Ferrara, ed., *Prediche e Scritti Commentati e Collegati da un Racconto Biografico. L'influenza del Savonarola Sulla Letteratura e L'arte del Quattrocento. Bibliografia Ragionata* (Florence: Casa Editrice Leo S. Olschki, 1952), pp. 156–166. Reprinted by permission of Casa Editrice Olschki.

FIGURE 11.3 After ruling Florence as a theocracy, the Dominican friar Giorlamo Savonarola was executed and burned at the stake in the town square. Florence went through many subtle political transformations, at one time a republic, at another an enlightened despotism under the Medici. (*Art Resource, NY*)

water compressed and held back by force, which, when it finds a little hole to escape, bursts forth impetuously and ruinously . . . Have a care, therefore, that such men do not take control in your city, and attend to the common good. And how this should be done I will tell you, as God will inspire me.

I have told you, during the last few days, that when the natural agent wishes to do a thing, it must give every consideration to the form of that thing; therefore, I tell you that you must select a good form for your new gov-

ernment, and above all no one must think of making himself head if you wish to live in liberty . . .

CONSIDER THIS:

11-9. What is the essence of Savonarola's message in his sermon to the Florentines? Why is his oratorical technique so persuasive? In this regard, analyze his words and images. What makes a demagogue like Savonarola so attractive? Why did people follow him? Why did they soon destroy him?

The Prince:
"Everyone Sees What You Appear to Be, Few Perceive What You Are"

NICCOLÒ MACHIAVELLI

Over the centuries, the name of Machiavelli has become synonymous with evil. The adjective *Machiavellian* still evokes images of deceit and political backstabbing. Machiavelli's ideas were condemned by the church as immoral and inspired by Satan himself. In reality, Niccolò Machiavelli (1469–1527) was a loyal citizen of Florence who had been schooled in the classics and had chosen a career in public service. He disliked the rule of the Medici and was a great advocate of republicanism. After Savonarola's fall from power in 1498, his theocracy was replaced by a true republic, led by elected officials of the people. Machiavelli became ambassador to France, and this duty served as a laboratory for the science of politics where he could observe men and governments in action. The Florentine republic was successful until 1512, when a Spanish mercenary army defeated Machiavelli's personally trained Florentine militia. They reinstalled Medici rule, and Machiavelli was tortured on the rack and thrown into prison for a time. He retired to the country and wrote a little book entitled *The Prince*. In it, Machiavelli gives the wisdom of his experience in politics. It is a manual of power: how to obtain it, maintain it, and lose it. In his analysis, Machiavelli is brutally realistic about the nature of human beings and the world of power politics: Learn the rules and you may survive and prosper. In the political chaos of Renaissance Italy, where alliances shifted frequently and distrust prevailed, such a guide proved useful and popular. Some of Machiavelli's most important ideas from *The Prince* are excerpted here.

On Those Who Have Become Princes by Crime

It should be noted at this point that in securing a state by force, its conqueror should consider carefully all the harmful things he must do and do them all at once so he does not to have to repeat them daily. By avoiding such constant brutality, men will begin to feel secure and the prince will gain their loyalty with the benefits he bestows on them. Any ruler who does otherwise, either because he is timid and hesitant, or because he listens to poor advice, must always keep his dagger in his hand. He can never count on the support of his subjects because their continual wounds are always fresh and they will never feel secure with him. The prince, therefore, should inflict all injuries at the same time, for the less often they are imposed, the less they offend. Benefits, on the other hand, should be distributed in small amounts, but continually so that they may be fully appreciated. And a prince should most importantly live with his subjects and be so aware of their attitudes that no unexpected event, whether good or bad, forces him to change his plans. For when emergencies arise, you will not have time to get your subjects to respond through cruelty, and what good you might do will help you little, since they will think that circumstances forced your hand and you will derive no thanks from it whatsoever.

On Cruelty and Mercy

A prince must always be cautious in believing too deeply or in acting too overtly. But he also must never seem timid and hesitant. He should temper his actions with an eye to prudence and a human touch so that too much trust doesn't result in foolish risk, or too little trust make him intolerable.

From this arises the question as to whether it is better to be loved than to be feared, or the opposite. I reply that the prince should be both, but since it is difficult to combine them, it is much safer to be feared than to be loved when one must choose. For it is true

The Prince is from C. E. Detmold, trans., *The Historical, Political and Diplomatic Writings of Niccolò Machiavelli* (Boston, 1882), pp. 51–52, 54–59 (Chapters 8, 17 and 18). Translation modernized by the editor.

FIGURE 11.4 Niccolò Machiavelli: "Let a prince therefore act to seize and to maintain the state; his methods will always be judged honorable and will be praised by all; for ordinary people are always deceived by appearances and by the outcome of a thing; and in the world there is nothing but ordinary people." (*Art Resource, NY*)

about men that they are ungrateful and unfaithful, deceitful and two-faced—bootlicking cowards, who nevertheless are always greedy for their own gain. And while you shower them with benefits, they are all yours and will give you their blood, their property, their lives, and their children—so long as danger is remote. But when danger approaches, they turn away. And that prince who relies exclusively on their empty words, rather than on finding other ways to protect himself, will surely be destroyed. For any friendships that are purchased rather than founded on greatness and nobility of character, are never truly owned—and you can never cash them in at the crucial time.

Besides, men don't mind harming someone who makes himself loved than one who makes himself feared because love is held together by a bond of obligation which, since men are basically a dismal bunch, is broken whenever their own self-interest is threatened. But fear always holds the bond tightly because the dread of punishment never leaves them.

A prince, however, must make himself feared in such a way that, even if he has not won the affection of his people, he has avoided their hatred. For being feared yet not hated is a good combination, if the prince keeps his hands off the property and the women of his subjects. And if he must execute someone, then be sure to do so only when there is manifest cause and proper justification for it. But above all, he should avoid taking the property of others, for men will sooner forget the death of their fathers than the loss of their inheritance. Moreover, there will never be any lack of reason for taking people's property. And a prince who begins to live by stealing will always find a excuses for confiscating property. On the other hand, it is not as easy to find reasons for taking a life, and these justifications dissipate more quickly . . . To come back now to the question of whether it is better to be loved or feared, I conclude that since men love at their own pleasure and fear at the pleasure of the prince, a wise prince should always rely on himself, and not on the will of others. But, above all, he should strive only to avoid hatred, as I have already noted.

How a Prince Should Keep His Word

It must be evident to everyone that it is more commendable for a prince to keep his word at all times and practice integrity rather than live by deceit. And yet, the experience of our own times has shown that the princes who have achieved great things have not cared much for keeping promises but have been expert at manipulating the minds of others. In the end, they have surpassed those rulers whose actions were dictated by loyalty and honesty.

Therefore, you must know that there are two ways of fighting: one according to the laws, the other by force; men practice the first way, and animals the second. But because the first is often insufficient, it becomes necessary to resort to the second. A prince, then, must know how to use both the natures of the beast and of man . . .

Since it is necessary for a prince to know how to make good use of the nature of the beast, he should choose from among animals the fox and the lion; for the lion cannot defend itself from traps and the fox cannot protect itself from wolves. A prince should be a fox in order to recognize the traps laid for him and a lion in order to frighten the wolves. Those who simply employ the nature of the lion do not understand their business. A wise ruler, therefore, cannot and should not keep his word when it is to his disadvantage or when the reasons that made him promise no longer

exist. And if men were all good, this rule would be wrong; but since men are basically bad and will not keep their promises to you, you likewise need not keep yours to them. A prince never lacks legitimate reasons to break his promises. I could offer an infinite number of modern examples that demonstrate this and show how many peace treaties, how many promises have been made null and void by the infidelity of princes. And the ruler who knows best how to play the fox has always been the most successful. But the prince must also know how to disguise this nature well and to be a great hypocrite and a bold liar. For men are so simple and so controlled by their immediate needs that the deceiver will always find a dupe who will allow himself to be deceived . . .

It is not necessary for a ruler to possess all the qualities mentioned above, but it is essential that he should at least seem to have them . . . A prince, therefore, must appear to be all mercy, all faithfulness, all integrity, all kindness, all religion. And it is most necessary for the prince to seem to possess this last quality, since men in general judge more by what they see and hear, than by what they feel. Everyone sees what you appear to be, few perceive what you are, and those few do not dare to contradict the opinion of the many who are protected by the majesty of the state. For the actions of all men, and especially those of princes where there is no other arbiter, are judged by the final result. A prince, therefore, should boldly seize and maintain the state. His methods will always be judged honorable and will be praised by everyone; for ordinary people are always deceived by appearances and by results—and in the world, there is nothing but ordinary people . . .

Consider This:

11-10. Niccolò Machiavelli has been called "the disciple of the Devil." After reading the excerpts from *The Prince*, why do you think this view has prevailed? Is it better for a prince to be loved or feared? Why kill all enemies or potential enemies when you come into power through crime? Interpret the phrase "the ends justify the means." How does Machiavelli's view of human nature compare with that of other Renaissance humanists? Do you see Machiavelli as moral, immoral, or amoral? Why did he write *The Prince*?

THE ARTISTIC VISION

The Dome of Brunelleschi

The Artistic Competition (1420)

GIORGIO VASARI

Filippo Brunelleschi (1377–1446) ranked supreme among Florence's architects. His was a robust personality—confident, innovative, and willing to risk all in creating new solutions to seemingly impossible challenges. His architectural emphasis on mathematics, proportion, and perspective drew glowing praise from his supporters and grudging admiration from his many critics. After losing the competition for the baptistry doors to Ghiberti in 1403, Brunelleschi in 1418 once again put himself on the line in another competition to construct the dome for Florence's cathedral, the Duomo. No architect seemed to be able to solve the many structural complexities of producing an enormous dome, or cupola, over the altar that would not collapse of its own weight. In the following account, Vasari described how Brunelleschi won the competition. His cupola, which remains the most visible public assertion of Florentine brilliance, was praised by Michelangelo, who used it as a model for his dome of Saint Peter's Cathedral in Rome.

At length, in 1420, all these foreign masters and those of Tuscany were assembled at Florence with all the principal Florentine artists, and Filippo returned from Rome. They all met together . . . in the presence of the consuls and wardens and a chosen number of the ablest citizens, so that . . . the method of vaulting the open cupola. They sent for the architects one by one and heard what they had to suggest. It was a remarkable thing to hear the curious and varied opinions upon the subject, for some said that they would build pillars from the ground level to bear arches to carry the beams which would support the weight; others thought it would be good to vault it with pumice stone, so that the weight might be lighter; and many agreed to make a pillar in the middle and construct it in the manner of a tent. . . . Filippo alone said that he could easily vault it without so many beams and pillars or earth, at less expense than would be involved by a quantity of arches, and without a framework. The consuls expected some flighty plan, and the wardens and

all the citizens thought that Filippo had spoken like a madman, and they mocked him, telling him to speak of something else, as his plan was the device of a fool . . .

But there were all routed by Filippo, and it is said that the dispute of the egg arose during these discussion. They wanted Filippo to declare his plan in detail, and to show his model as they had shown theirs, but he refused, and proposed to the masters assembled that whoever should make an egg stand upright on a flat marble surface should make the cupola, as this would be a test of their ability. He produced an egg and all the masters endeavored to make it stand, but no one succeeded. Then they passed it to Filippo, who lightly took it, broke the end with a blow on the marble and made it stand. All the artists cried out that they could have done as much themselves, but Filippo answered laughing that they would also know how to vault the cupola after they had seen his model and design. And so it was resolved that he should have the conduct of the work.

"The Artistic Competition" is from Giorgio Vasari, *The Lives of the Painters, Sculptors, and Architects*, vol. 1 (New York: E. P. Dutton & Co., Inc., 1900), pp. 278–280.

FIGURE 11.5 Filippo Brunelleschi, the cupola of the Duomo in Florence. (*Perry M. Rogers*)

CONSIDER THIS:

11-11. Why did the Florentines often demand competitions for an artistic commission? Can great art be judged as winner and loser? How did Brunelleschi win the competition for the cupola over the Duomo? How important is confidence and pure ego in achieving victory in such a competition? Was Brunelleschi's achievement equal to his boast?

THE BROADER PERSPECTIVE:

11-12. Politically, the Renaissance in Italy was an insecure, chaotic period, with shifting alliances and numerous invasions. Amid all this disunity, an intense cultural creativity was reflected in the art and music of the period. Do you think that chaos is a prerequisite for creativity or at least a contributor to creative energy? Or are great art, literature, and music best fostered in an atmosphere of relative calm and security? Relate this question specifically to the Renaissance, but also give contemporary examples when possible.

Mind and Society in the Renaissance

Renaissance Manners

With the growing emphasis on diplomacy and contact with ambassadors of other states during the Renaissance, rules of etiquette were established. The new age demanded that knights become gentlemen and that the relationship between the sexes be redefined. Baldassare Castiglione provided the instruction for this in his *Book of the Courtier.*

Book of the Courtier (1518)

BALDASSARE CASTIGLIONE

I wish, then, that this Courtier of ours should be nobly born and of gentle race; because it is far less unseemly for one of ignoble birth to fail in worthy deeds, than for one of noble birth, who, if he strays from the path of his predecessors, stains his family name, and not only fails to achieve but loses what has been achieved already; for noble birth is like a bright lamp that manifests and makes visible good and evil deeds, and kindles and stimulates to virtue both by fear of shame and by hope of praise . . .

But to come to some details, I am of the opinion that the principal and true profession of the Courtier ought to be that of arms; which I would have him follow actively above all else, and be known among others as bold and strong, and loyal to whomsoever he serves. And he will win a reputation for these good qualities by exercising them at all times and in all places, since one may never fail in this without severest censure. And just as among women, their fair fame once sullied never recovers its first luster, so the reputation of a gentleman who bears arms, if once it be in the least tarnished with cowardice or other disgrace, remains forever infamous before the world and full of ignominy. Therefore the more our Courtier excels in this art, the more he will be worthy of praise; and yet I do not deem essential in him that perfect knowledge of things and those other qualities that befit a commander; since this would be too wide a sea, let us be content, as we have said, with perfect loyalty and unconquered courage, and that he be always seen to possess them . . .

Therefore let the man we are seeking, be very bold, stern, and always among the first, where the enemy are to be seen; and in every other place, gentle, modest, reserved, above all things avoiding ostentation and that impudent self-praise by which men ever excite hatred and disgust in all who bear them . . .

Then coming to the bodily frame, I say it is enough if this be neither extremely short nor tall, for both of these conditions excite a certain contemptuous surprise, and men of either sort are gazed upon in much the same way that we gaze on monsters. Yet if we must offend in one of the two extremes, it is preferable to fall a little short of the just measure of height than to exceed it, for besides often being dull of intellect, men thus huge of body are also unfit for every exercise of agility, which thing I should much wish in the Courtier. And so I would have him well built and shapely of limb, and would have him show strength and lightness and suppleness, and know all bodily exercises that befit a man of war: I think the first should be to handle every sort of weapon well on foot and on horse, to understand the advantages of each, and especially to be familiar with those weapons that are ordinarily used among gentlemen; for besides the use of them in war, where such subtlety in contrivance is perhaps not needful, there frequently arise differences between one gentleman and another, which afterwards result in duels often fought with such weapons as happen at the moment to be within reach: thus knowledge of this kind is a very safe thing . . .

Book of the Courtier is from Baldassare Castiglione, *Book of the Courtier,* trans. Leonard Opdycke (New York: Horace Liveright, 1903), pp. 22, 25–26, 28–31. Translation modernized by the editor.

It is fitting also to know how to swim, to leap, to run, to throw stones, for besides the use that may be made of this in war, a man often has occasion to show what he can do in such matters; whence good esteem is to be won, especially with the multitude, who must be taken into account withal. Another admirable exercise, and one very befitting a man at court, is the game of tennis, in which are well shown the disposition of the body, the quickness and suppleness of every member, and all those qualities that are seen in nearly every other exercise. Nor less highly do I esteem vaulting on horse, which although it be fatiguing and difficult, makes a man very light and dexterous more than any other thing; and besides its utility, if this lightness is accompanied by grace, it is to my thinking a finer show than any of the others.

On the Nature and Purpose of Women and Men

BALDASSARE CASTIGLIONE

"Now you said that Nature's aim is always to produce the most perfect things, and that she therefore would always bring forth man if she could, and that women are the result of an error or defect in nature rather than of intent. But I deny this completely. Nor do I see how you can say that nature does not intend to produce women, without whom the human species cannot be preserved, which Nature desires more than anything else. For by means of this union of male and female, Nature produces children, who repay the benefits received in childhood by supporting their parents when old; then in turn they have other children of their own, from whom they receive the same support in old age that they offered their parents; thus Nature, as if moving in a circle, fills out eternity and in this way confers immortality on mortals. Women, therefore, are as necessary in this process as men. I do not see how the one was made more by chance than the other.

"It is very true that Nature intends to produce the most perfect things, and therefore always intends to produce human beings, but not male rather than female. Indeed, if Nature always produced men, then she would be imperfect; for just as the unity of body and soul has greater nobility than its parts, so the union of male and female creates a combination that preserves the human species, without which we would all perish. And therefore, men and women are by nature always together, nor can the one exist without the other . . . "

Then Signor Gaspare said: "Let's not go into such subtleties, because these ladies will not understand us, and although I can answer you with excellent arguments, they will believe (or at least pretend to believe) that I am wrong, and immediately declare themselves right. Yet since we are already begun, I will say merely this, that learned men believe that man resembles form, and woman matter; and therefore, just as form is more perfect than matter, and indeed, gives it its being, so man is far more perfect than woman . . . In fact, every woman universally desires to be a man, because it is natural that she desires to achieve her own perfection."

The Magnifico Giuliano at once replied: "The poor creatures do not desire to be men in order to be perfect, but in order to be free of the tyranny that men have imposed on women through their self-serving authority. And the analogy that you give about matter and form does not apply in all cases; for woman is not made perfect by man, as matter by form . . . Woman does not receive her being from man, but rather perfects him just as she is also perfected by him. Therefore, both are necessary for procreation, which neither can pull off without the other.

"Moreover, women have a lasting love for the man who takes her virginity just as men seem to detest their first sexual conquest. . . . And I attribute this to woman's strength and stability and to man's inconstancy. And there is natural reason for this. Because of man's hot nature, he possesses the qualities of lightness, movement, and inconstancy; women, on the other hand, are cold, calm, with a firm gravity and stability that makes them more susceptible to impressions.

"On the Nature and Purpose of Women and Men" is from Baldassare Castiglione, *Book of the Courtier*, trans. Leonard Opdycke (New York: Horace Liveright, 1903), pp. 182–184. Translation modernized by the editor.

11-13. What was a courtier, and what did Castiglione require of him? Why do you think Castiglione's book was so popular? What values of Renaissance society does it promote? According to Castiglione, what should be the relationship between women and men?

THE BROADER PERSPECTIVE:

11-14. In 1929, the British author Virginia Woolf commented in her book *A Room of One's Own* that

"women have served all these centuries as looking-glasses possessing the magic and delicious power of reflecting the figure of man at twice its natural size." How would you compare this idea to Castiglione's view that "woman does not receive her being from man, but rather perfects him just as she is also perfected by him"? Do you agree that the relationship between men and women is symbiotic, or have women been held in lesser esteem throughout the centuries because they have been expected to enhance the image of men? How modern is Castiglione in his thinking?

THEME: WOMEN IN HISTORY

THE REFLECTION IN THE MIRROR

The Hammer of Witches

"All Wickedness Is but Little to the Wickedness of a Woman"

Although the Renaissance period is generally described as an era of creativity and enlightened energy, there certainly existed intolerant attitudes as well. During the sixteenth century, the church established an organization that was designed to maintain purity of doctrine and authority over the faithful. The Inquisition, as it came to be called, was administered by Dominican friars, whose responsibilities had always involved the explanation of doctrine to those who had strayed from the path. Now they were actively to seek out those whose deeds and ideas seemed to contradict established Catholic doctrine. The Inquisition became a vehicle for reform through coercion, with allegiance being obtained through argument, intimidation, and torture if necessary.

Of special concern in the struggle against Satan was the perceived prevalence of witches. Men were accused of employing "black magic" as well, but women, especially elderly women, were often targeted as agents of the Devil. In the following excerpt from a manual entitled *The Hammer of Witches* (1486), two Dominican friars establish the connection between women and witchcraft. Their explanation reveals a common attitude toward women during this era.

KEEP IN MIND . . .

11-15. According to this source, why can the Devil so easily work his evil through women?

Others again have propounded other reasons why there are more superstitious women found than men. And the first is, that they are more credulous; and since the chief aim of the devil is to corrupt faith, therefore he rather attacks them. . . . The second reason is that women are naturally more impressionable, and more ready to receive the influence of a disembodied spirit; and that when they use this quality well they are very good, but when they use it ill they are very evil.

The third reason is that they have slippery tongues, and are unable to conceal from their

---

"All Wickedness Is but Little to the Wickedness of a Woman" is from M. Summers, trans., *Malleus Maleficiarum* (London: John Rodker, 1920), pp. 43–44.

fellow-women those things which by evil arts they know, and, since they are weak, they find an easy and secret manner of vindicating themselves by witchcraft. . . . All wickedness is but little to the wickedness of a woman. And to this may be added that, as they are very impressionable, they act accordingly.

> "Women have slippery tongues, and are unable to conceal from their fellow-women those things which by evil arts they know."

There are also others who bring forward yet other reasons, of which preachers should be very careful how they make use. For it is true that in the Old Testament the Scriptures have much that is evil to say about women, and this because of the first temptress, Eve, and her imitators . . . . But because in these times this perfidy is more often found in women than in men, as we learn by actual experience, if anyone is curious as to the reason, we may add to what has already been said the following: that since they are feebler both in mind and body, it is not surprising that they should come more under the spell of witchcraft.

CONSIDER THIS:

11-16. Compare Castiglione's discussion on the relationship between men and women with this excerpt on witchcraft. Why were women considered more superstitious and susceptible to the spell of Satan?

Chapter 12

The Reformation Era

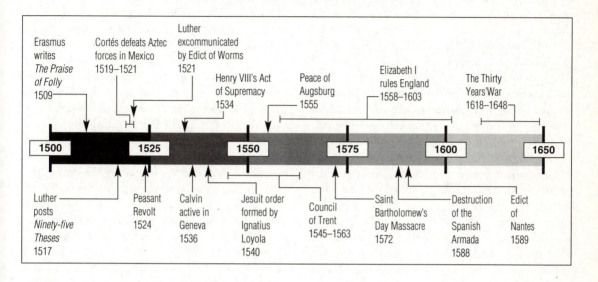

Erasmus writes *The Praise of Folly* 1509

Cortés defeats Aztec forces in Mexico 1519–1521

Luther excommunicated by Edict of Worms 1521

Henry VIII's Act of Supremacy 1534

Peace of Augsburg 1555

Elizabeth I rules England 1558–1603

The Thirty Years' War 1618–1648

1500 · 1525 · 1550 · 1575 · 1600 · 1650

Luther posts *Ninety-five Theses* 1517

Peasant Revolt 1524

Calvin active in Geneva 1536

Jesuit order formed by Ignatius Loyola 1540

Council of Trent 1545–1563

Saint Bartholomew's Day Massacre 1572

Destruction of the Spanish Armada 1588

Edict of Nantes 1589

I am more afraid of my own heart than of the pope and all his cardinals. I have within me the great pope—Self.

—MARTIN LUTHER

Whatever your heart clings to and confides in, that is really your God.

—MARTIN LUTHER

All religions must be tolerated for every man must get to heaven his own way.

—FREDERICK THE GREAT

CHAPTER THEMES

- **Social and Spiritual Values:** Why did the Reformation occur? What led Martin Luther to challenge the belief system of the church? To what extent can faith and personal commitment to a religion change the course of history? Is faith a more powerful force than any army?

- **Revolution and Historical Change:** Was the Protestant Reformation a spiritual revolution that consequently altered the political and economic institutions of Europe? Or was it a spiritually based reform movement that sought limited change in religious matters? Was Luther a revolutionary who was just as influential as Robespierre, Napoleon, or Lenin?

- **The Power Structure:** How did secular rulers benefit from the division of Christianity during the Reformation era? Which monarchs became "defenders of the church" and which aided the reformers? Why? How did King Henry VIII of England solve the competition between church and state? Were his actions based on a sincere spirituality or on pure political expediency?

- **The Institution and the Individual:** Would the Protestant Reformation have occurred without Martin Luther? To what extent can an individual change the course of history? Was the printing press more essential to the success of this transitional movement than was Luther?

- **The Big Picture:** Was the Protestant Reformation ultimately the best thing that could have happened to the Christian church in the West? Do you expect another splinter movement in the contemporary Roman Catholic Church, and if so, what would be the ramifications?

During the Middle Ages, the church was the focal point of society. One's life was inextricably bound to the dictates of religion from the baptism that followed birth to the last rites that accompanied death. But by the sixteenth century, the omnipotence of the church, both in a spiritual sense and in the political realm, had been called into question. The church had lost much of the authority that had allowed it, in the eleventh through the thirteenth centuries, to claim superiority in the ongoing struggle between church and state. Crises such as the Babylonian Captivity (1309–1377) and the Great Schism (1378–1417) had strained the loyalty of the faithful and devastated the unity of the church for over a century. By the middle of the fifteenth century, the papacy was occupied with finding new sources of income that would help it fend off political challenges to its territory and increase its influence in the secular realm. The Renaissance papacy became infamous in its corruption and succumbed to the sensual delights of the world, as well as to the more traditional abuses of simony (the selling of church offices) and pluralism (allowing an individual to hold more than one position). Pope Julius II (1503–1513) was a glaring example of the age as, bedecked in armor, he personally led his armies into battle.

These actions resulted in a plentitude of criticism from within the church and especially from Christian humanists such as Desiderius Erasmus. Perhaps the most controversial practice of the church was the sale of indulgences. An indulgence was a piece of paper, signed by the pope, that remitted punishment in purgatory due to sin. It was based on the theory that all humans are by nature sinful and after death will have to undergo a purgation of sin before being allowed to enter the Kingdom of Heaven. The pope, however, controlled an infinite "treasury of grace" that could be dispensed to mortals, thus removing the taint of sin and freeing the soul from purgatory. By the late fifteenth century, the remission of sin was extended to both the living and the dead, and one could therefore liberate the soul of a relative "trapped" in purgatory by purchasing an indulgence. The sale of indulgences became a routine affair of peddling

forgiveness of purgatorial punishment, and the papacy came to rely on it as a necessary source of income. In 1507, Pope Julius II issued a plenary indulgence to obtain funds for the construction of Saint Peter's Basilica in Rome. Leo X renewed the indulgence in 1513, and subcommissioners actively began selling to the faithful. It was in response to this sale that a young monk named Martin Luther protested and nailed his *Ninety-Five Theses* to the door of the Wittenberg church.

Note that although Luther called into question the sale of indulgences, the main issue was salvation. Salvation, he reasoned, was cheap indeed if it could be purchased. Luther was tortured by the demands of God for perfection and worried that his own righteousness was insufficient for salvation in the sight of God. The church taught that in addition to winning grace through faith, one could also merit God's grace through good works or the remission of sin by indulgence. In fact, the purchase of an indulgence was considered a good work. But to Luther's mind, salvation required more, much more, and had nothing to do with deeds. While studying Saint Paul's *Epistle to the Romans (1:17)*, Luther achieved a breakthrough that freed him from his torment: By the grace of God alone could one be saved, and this salvation was obtained only through faith in Christ. Neither good works nor indulgences could have anything to do with salvation. This stand called into question the very foundation of established Christian belief. Was the pope the true Vicar of Christ who spoke the words of God? If so, why did he advocate indulgences as a means of salvation? Was he in fact infallible on such matters of faith? The corruption of the papacy was also troubling, yet Luther's objective was not to overthrow the church but to reform it from within.

The church replied to such a challenge with what it considered swift and appropriate action. Luther was excommunicated and his writings were condemned as heretical. It became evident to Luther that his desire to reform the church could be achieved only by defying the authority of the pope and starting a new church. Supported by the Holy Roman Emperor Charles V, the church sought to eliminate the root of the controversy. However, Luther was hidden, protected by the secular princes in Germany who, because of their location and traditional independence, were willing to defy their emperor and promote a religion that to them served a secular purpose. Yet Luther's movement was spiritual, and he decried such political connections even as he sought the aid of the princes and nobility.

This chapter explores the spiritual and political foundations of the Reformation and the Protestant movement, from its inception by Martin Luther through its development under John Calvin to its royal imposition in England under Henry VIII and Elizabeth I. The Reformation era must also be viewed in its proper context, noting that during this period the Catholic Church made significant strides toward reform in its own right. The themes presented in this chapter include the role of the individual in changing history and the impact of religion on the political framework and social fabric of the times. The Reformation era was one of transition and instability that eventually led to war and bloodshed as nations fought during the sixteenth and seventeenth centuries in support of a singular conception of the "true religion." This bloody future was far from Martin Luther's mind when he nailed his *Ninety-Five Theses* on the Wittenberg church door in 1517 and thus started a movement that shook the spiritual foundations of Christendom and altered the political face of Europe for centuries to come.

KEY EVENTS IN THE EARLY PROTESTANT REFORMATION

1509 Desiderius Erasmus
A northern humanist, he writes *The Praise of Folly*, a satire that criticizes abuses within the Church.

1517 The Ninety-Five Theses
Luther posts this list of grievances against indulgences and papal corruption on the door of Wittenberg church in hopes of engaging clerical authorities in debate. Document is printed and distributed throughout Germany.

1519–1520 Luther Challenges Papal Authority
At the Leipzig Debate, Luther challenges the authority of the pope and the inerrancy of Church councils (1519). Luther publishes two works critical of the Church: *Address to the Christian Nobility of the German Nation* and *On Christian Liberty* (1520).

1521–1522 Edict of Worms
Luther is excommunicated by order of the pope (1521). Diet of Worms called to question him about his heretical writings. Luther is condemned and secretly leaves Worms aided by his patron, Frederick the Elector. Edict of Worms imposes the "ban of Empire" on Luther, who is hidden by friends at Wartburg Castle, where he translates the New Testament into German.

1523 Ulrich Zwingli
The Swiss soldier and local leader is active as Protestant reformer in Switzerland and issues *Sixty-Seven Articles*.

1524–1525 Peasant Revolt
This rebellion breaks out in Germany as peasants demand freedom from the long-standing feudal obligations of serfdom. Luther sides with aristocracy and condemns violence of peasants.

1529 Marburg Colloquy
A personal meeting arranged by Philip of Hesse, who sought to unite Luther and Zwingli. Luther leaves thinking Zwingli a dangerous fanatic over his vision of communion (a purely

symbolic ceremony). Luther believes that the "real presence" of Christ resides in the ceremony.

1534   Act of Supremacy

Declares Henry VIII of England "the only supreme head of the Church of England." Henry's political need for an heir forces his religious break with the Catholic Church.

1534–1535   The Destruction of Münster

Anabaptists assume political power in the city of Münster. Theocracy imposed and polygamy practiced by unrepresentative Anabaptists. Shocked Protestant and Catholic armies unite to crush the radicals.

1536   John Calvin Arrives in Geneva

Publishes *Institutes of the Christian Religion*, which contains the doctrine of predestination.

The Lutheran Reformation (1517–1546)

The Indulgence Controversy (1517)

Humanism, the state of mind that formed the cornerstone of the Italian Renaissance, spread to the north in the late fifteenth and sixteenth centuries and became popular in the courts of France and England. The emphasis on the wonder, versatility, and individuality of humankind was evident in the art and literature of the period. Humanism also fostered scholarship that, especially in the north, tended to criticize the abuses within the church. The following piece is a satire written by the most famous of all northern humanists, Desiderius Erasmus. In it he criticizes abuses within the church and thereby expresses the hope of promoting a greater spirituality in religion.

"The Cheat of Pardons and Indulgences": The Praise of Folly (1509)

DESIDERIUS ERASMUS

The next to be placed among the regiment of fools are such as make a trade of telling or inquiring after incredible stories of miracles and prodigies. Never doubting that a lie will choke them, they will muster up a thousand several strange relations of spirits, ghosts, apparitions, raising of the devil, and such like bugbears of superstition; which the farther they are from being probably true, the more greedily they are swallowed, and the more devoutly believed. And these absurdities do not only bring an empty pleasure and cheap divertissement, but they are a good trade and procure a comfortable income to such priests and friars as by this craft get their gain.

To these again are nearly related such others as attribute strange virtues to the shrines and images of saints and martyrs, and so would make their credulous proselytes believe that if they pay their devotion to Saint Christopher in the morning, they shall be guarded and secured the day following from all dangers and misfortunes. If soldiers, when they first take arms, shall come and mumble over such a set prayer before the picture of Saint Barbara, they shall return safe from all engagements. Or if any pray to Erasmus on such particular holidays, with the ceremony of wax candles and other fopperies, he shall in a short time be rewarded with a plentiful increase of wealth and riches. The Christians have now their gigantic Saint George, as well as the pagans had their Hercules; they paint the saint on horseback, and drawing the horse in splendid trapping very gloriously accoutered, they

---

The Praise of Folly is from Desiderius Erasmus, *The Praise of Folly* (London: Hamilton Adams and Company, 1887), pp. 90–96, 143–149, 164–169.

scarce refrain in a literal sense from worshiping the very beast.

What shall I say of such as cry up and maintain the cheat of pardons and indulgences? That by these compute the time of each soul's residence in purgatory, and assign them a longer or shorter continuance, according as they purchase more or fewer of these paltry pardons and saleable exemptions? Or what can be said bad enough of others, who pretend that by the force of such magical charms, or by the fumbling over their beads in the rehearsal of such, and such petitions; which some religious imposters invented, either for diversion, or, what is more likely, for advantage; they shall procure riches, honor, pleasure, health, long life, a lusty old age, nay, after death a sitting at the right hand of our Savior in His kingdom.

By this easy way of purchasing pardons, any notorious highwayman, any plundering soldier, or any bribe-taking judge shall disburse some part of their unjust gains, and so think all their grossest impieties sufficiently atoned for. So many perjuries, lusts, drunkenness, quarrels, bloodsheds, cheats, treacheries, shall all be, as it were, struck a bargain for, and such a contract made, as if they had paid off all arrears and might now begin upon a new score.

From the same principles of folly proceeds the custom of each country's challenging their particular guardian-saint. Nay, each saint has his distinct office allotted to him and is accordingly addressed to upon the delivery in childbirth, a third to help persons to lost goods, another to protect seamen in a long voyage, a fifth to guard the farmer's cows and sheep, and so on. For to rehearse all instances would be extremely tedious.

And now for some reflections upon popes, cardinals and bishops, who in pomp and splendor have almost equaled if not [outdone] secular princes. Now if any one consider that their upper crotchet of white linen is to signify their unspotted purity and innocence; that their forked miters, with both divisions tied together by the same knot, are to denote the joint knowledge of the Old and New Testament. That their always wearing gloves represents their keeping their hands clean and undefiled from lucre and covetousness; that the pastoral staff implies the care of a flock committed to their charge; that the cross carried before them expresses their victory over all carnal affection. He that considers this, and much more of the like nature, must needs conclude they are entrusted with a very weighty and difficult office. But alas, they think it sufficient if they can but feed themselves, and as to their flock, either commend them to the care of Christ Himself, or commit them to the guidance of some inferior vicars and curates. [They do] not so much as remember what their name of bishop imports, to wit, labor, pains and diligence, but by base simoniacal contracts, they are in a profane sense . . . overseers of their own gain and income.

The popes of Rome pretend themselves Christ's vicars; if they would but imitate His exemplary life, an unintermitted course of preaching [and] attendance with poverty, nakedness, hunger, and a contempt of this world; if they did but consider the import of the word pope, which signifies a father; or if they did but practice their surname of most holy, what order or degrees of men would be in a worse condition? There would be then no such vigorous making of parties and buying of votes in the conclave upon the vacancy of that see.

And those who, by bribery or other indirect courses, should get themselves elected would never secure their sitting firm in the chair by pistol, poison, force and violence. How much of their pleasure would be abated if they were but endowed with one dram of wisdom? Wisdom, did I say? Nay, with one grain of salt which our Savior bid them not lose the savor of. All their riches, all their honor, their jurisdictions, their Peter's patrimony, their offices, their dispensations, their licenses, their indulgences, their long train and attendants, see in how short a compass I have abbreviated all their marketing of religion; in a word, all their perquisites would be forfeited and lost; and in their [place] would succeed watchings, fastings, tears, prayers, sermons, hard studies, repenting sighs, and a thousand such like severe penalties. . . . The very Head of the Church, the spiritual prince, would then be brought from all his splendor to the poor equipage of a scrip and staff.

CONSIDER THIS:

12-1. Discuss the abuses within the church during the fifteenth and sixteenth centuries. What specifically are the criticisms of Desiderius Erasmus? Does he make a legitimate argument?

Instructions for the Sale of Indulgences (1517)

ARCHBISHOP ALBERT OF MAINZ

The controversy over the sale of indulgences was the spark that set the Reformation in motion. In 1515, Pope Leo X made an agreement with Archbishop Albert to sell indulgences in Mainz and other areas of northern Germany, with half the proceeds going to support Leo's construction of Saint Peter's Basilica in Rome and half going to pay for the debts that Albert had incurred in securing his church offices. In the first selection, Archbishop Albert gives instructions to those subcommissioners who actually sold the indulgences in 1517. One of the most successful subcommissioners was Johann Tetzel, prior of the Dominican monastery at Leipzig. His oratorical ability is evident in the second passage.

Here follow the four principal graces and privileges, which are granted by the apostolic bull, of which each may be obtained without the other. In the matter of these four privileges, preachers shall be careful to recommend each to believers with the greatest care, and, in so far as they can, to explain them as well.

The first grace is the complete remission of all sins; and nothing greater than this can be named, since no man who lives in sin and forfeits the favor of God, obtains complete remission by these means and once more enjoys God's favor: moreover, through this remission of sins the punishment which one is obliged to undergo in Purgatory on account of the affront to the divine Majesty, is all remitted, and the pains of Purgatory completely blotted out. And although nothing is precious enough to be given in exchange for such a grace—since it is a free gift of God and grace is beyond price—yet in order that Christian believers may be the more easily induced to procure the same, we [offer them the following guidance]. . . . Because the conditions of men, and their occupations, are so various and manifold, and we cannot consider and assess them individually, we have therefore decided that the rates can be determined thus, according to recognized classifications: [Then follows a graded schedule of rates: kings and their families, bishops, etc., 25 Rhenish gold guilders; abbots, counts, barons, etc., 10; lesser nobles and ecclesiastics and others with incomes of 500, 6 guilders; citizens with their own income, 1 guilder; those with less, ½. Those with nothing shall supply their contribution with prayer and fasting, "for the kingdom of heaven should be open to the poor as much as the rich."]

The second grace is a confessional letter containing the most extraordinarily comforting and as yet unheard of privileges, and which also retains its virtue even after our bull expires at the end of eight years, since the bull says: "they shall be participators now and for ever. . . ."

The third most important grace is the participation in all the possessions of the church universal; for example, that contributors toward the new Basilica of Saint Peter's, together with their decreased relations, who have departed this world in a state of grace, shall from now and for eternity derive benefit from all petitions, intercessions, alms, fasting, prayers, in each and every pilgrimage, even those to the Holy Land. Furthermore, when in Rome, they may participate in the masses, canonical hours, flagellations, and all other spiritual goods which have brought forth or which shall be brought forth by the universal most holy church militant or by any of its members. Believers who purchase confessional letters will become participants in all these things.

The fourth distinctive grace is for those souls which are in purgatory, and is the complete remission of all sins, which remission the pope brings to pass through his intercession to the advantage of said souls, in this way: that the same contribution shall be placed in the chest by a living person as one would make for himself. . . . Moreover, preachers shall exert themselves to give this grace the widest publicity, since through the same, help will surely come to departed souls, and the construction of the Church of Saint Peter will be abundantly promoted at the same time.

"Instructions for the Sale of Indulgences" is from James H. Robinson, ed., *Translations and Reprints from the Original Sources of European History*, vol. 2, no. 6 (Philadelphia: University of Pennsylvania, 1902), pp. 4–9. Translation modernized by the editor.

"How Many Sins Are Committed in a Single Day?" (1517)

JOHANN TETZEL

Venerable Sir, I pray you that in your utterances you may be pleased to make use of such words as shall serve to open the eyes of the mind and cause your hearers to consider how great a grace and gift they have had and now have at their very doors. Blessed eyes indeed, which see what they see, because already they possess letters of safe conduct by which they are able to lead their souls through that valley of tears, through that sea of the mad world, where storms and tempests and dangers lie in wait, to the blessed land of Paradise. Know that the life of man upon earth is a constant struggle. We have to fight against the flesh, the world, and the devil, who are always seeking to destroy the soul. In sin we are conceived,—alas! what bonds of sin encompass us, and how difficult and almost impossible it is to attain to the gate of salvation without divine aid; since He causes us to be saved, not by virtue of the good works which we accomplish, but through His divine mercy, it is necessary then to put on the armor of God.

You may obtain letters of safe conduct from the vicar of our Lord Jesus Christ, by means of which you are able to liberate your soul from the hands of the enemy, and convey it by means of contrition and confession, safe and secure from all pains of Purgatory, into the happy kingdom. For know that in these letters are stamped and engraved all the merits of Christ's passion there laid bare. Consider, that for each and every mortal sin it is necessary to undergo seven years of penitence after confession and contrition, either in this life or in Purgatory.

How many mortal sins are committed in a day, how many in a week, how many in a month, how many in a year, how many in the whole course of life! They are well-nigh numberless, and those that commit them must needs suffer endless punishment in the burning pains of Purgatory.

But with these confessional letters you will be able at any time in life to obtain full indulgence for all penalties imposed upon you, in all cases except the four reserved to the Apostolic See. Therefore throughout your whole life, whenever you wish to make confession, you may receive the same remission, except in cases reserved to the Pope, and afterwards, at the hour of death, a full indulgence as to all penalties and sins, and your share of all spiritual blessings that exist in the church militant and all its members.

Do you not know that when it is necessary for anyone to go to Rome, or undertake any other dangerous journey, he takes his money to a broker and gives a certain percent—five or six or ten—in order that at Rome or elsewhere he may receive again his funds intact, by means of the letter of this same broker? Are you not willing, then, for the fourth part of a florin, to obtain these letters, by virtue of which you may bring, not your money but your divine and immortal soul safe and sound into the land of Paradise?

CONSIDER THIS:

12-2. What were the advantages of buying indulgences from the church?

12-3. Why were indulgences so detested by critics of the church? Can you construct a logical argument in support of indulgences with which the church could have satisfactorily defended itself against criticism? Is the principle of indulgences at issue here or just the manner in which they were sold?

12-4. Compare the instructions given by Archbishop Albert of Mainz for the sale of indulgences with the actual process of selling them by Johann Tetzel. What made Tetzel such a good "rainmaker" for the church? Was he doing exactly what the pope and archbishops expected of him?

"How Many Sins Are Committed in a Single Day?" is from James H. Robinson, ed., *Translations and Reprints from the Original Sources of European History*, vol. 2, no. 6 (Philadelphia: University of Pennsylvania, 1902), pp. 9–10.

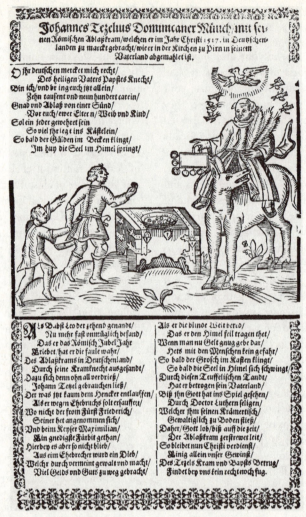

FIGURE 12.1 Caricature of Johann Tetzel, the indulgence preacher who spurred Luther to publish his *Ninety-Five Theses.* The last line of the caption reads, "As soon as gold in the basin rings, right then the soul to heaven springs." (*Corbis/Bettmann*)

THEME: SOCIAL AND SPIRITUAL VALUES

THE ARTISTIC VISION

Saint Peter's Basilica

The focal point for the sale of indulgences throughout Europe in 1517 was the creation of Saint Peter's Basilica in Rome, truly one of the most celebrated edifices in the modern world. Its conception dates back to the reign of Pope Nicholas V (1447–1455), who was dismayed at the deterioration of the Old Saint Peter's Basilica. On April 18, 1506, Pope Julius II laid the first stone for the new cathedral and decided to finance the venture by proclaiming a Jubilee Indulgence. Julius hoped that this special sale of indulgences to the faithful for the remission of sins would provide an income stream to offset the significant cost of his visionary plans. Intended to be the largest cathedral in the world, it was first designed as a Greek cross and eventually evolved into a three-aisle Latin cross with an enormous dome (devised by Michelangelo) fitted directly above the high altar that covered the shrine of Saint Peter. This was the church of the popes, those Bishops of Rome who would be buried in the crypt below the altar.

Little expense was spared in this venture throughout the basilica's construction over the course of nearly 110 years from 1506 to its completion in 1615. The pope, as the Vicar of Christ and spiritual heir to the authority of God, employed the most renowned architects, painters, and sculptors in the creation of this magnificent cathedral.

The decoration of the cavernous interior became the life's work of the great architect and sculptor, Gian Lorenzo Bernini (1598–1680). The impressive bronze Baldachin, or canopy over the altar and above the crypt, was completed in 1633 and is an unprecedented fusion of sculpture and architecture, the first truly Baroque monument.

Bernini's greatest architectural achievement, however, remains the colonnade that encloses the piazza before Saint Peter's Basilica and offsets the enormous facade of the cathedral. Bernini created a series of freestanding columns designed to grant access to visitors as they gathered for the papal benediction on Easter and other special occasions. The encircling design of the colonnade symbolizes the enveloping arms of the church and directs the faithful into the cathedral.

FIGURE 12.2 Gianlorenzo Bernini, Colonnade of St. Peter's, Rome. (*European Tourists Services*)

THE BROADER PERSPECTIVE:

12-5. During the Golden Age of Classical Greece from about 480 to 404 B.C.E., the democracy of Athens established an empire that provided them with a continuous flow of tribute that they used to build the Parthenon and many other monuments that established Athenian cultural supremacy and defined artistic standards for centuries to come. But all this cultural progress was dependent on the maintenance of an empire held by force. Does the beauty and cultural worth of the monuments of a civilization justify the means of obtaining them?

12-6. Similarly, through the sale of indulgences, the Roman church built Saint Peter's Basilica, a testament to the glory of God, the authority of the papacy, and the depository of artistic genius—of Raphael, Bramante, Michelangelo, and Bernini. What price civilization?

Salvation through Faith Alone

MARTIN LUTHER

Martin Luther's transformation from monk to reformer was not a preconceived act; it developed gradually not only as a result of corruption around him, but especially because of a spiritual awakening. Luther struggled with the need to imitate the perfection of Christ, which was important in the eyes of the church for salvation. Luther realized that because of his nature as a human, he was too sinful, and no amount of prayer or good works could help him achieve the Kingdom of Heaven. After much study and pain, he concluded that salvation was a free gift of God and a person was saved by faith in Christ alone. In the first selection, Luther explains his enlightenment. The second document is his answer to the indulgences being sold by Johann Tetzel. When Luther posted the *Ninety-Five Theses* on the church in Wittenberg, the Reformation began in earnest.

I, Martin Luther, entered the monastery against the will of my father and lost favor with him, for he saw through the knavery of the monks very well. On the day on which I sang my first mass he said to me, "Son, don't you know that you ought to honor your father?" Later, when I stood there during the mass and began the canon, I was so frightened that I would have fled if I hadn't been admonished by the prior. . . .

When I was a monk I was unwilling to omit any of the prayers, but when I was busy with public lecturing and writing I often accumulated my appointed prayers for a whole week, or even two or three weeks. Then I would take a Saturday off, or shut myself in for as long as three days without food and drink, until I had said the prescribed prayers. This made my head split, and as a consequence I couldn't close my eyes for five nights, lay sick unto death, and went out of my senses. Even after I had quickly recovered and I tried again to read, my head went 'round and 'round. Thus our Lord God drew me, as if by force, from that torment of prayers. . . .

The words "righteous" and "righteousness of God" struck my conscience like lightning. When I heard them I was exceedingly terrified. If God is righteous [I thought], he must punish. But when by God's grace I pondered, in the tower and heated room of this building, over the words, "He who through faith is righteous shall live" [*Rom. 1:17*] and "the righteousness of God" [*Rom. 3:21*], I soon came to the conclusion that if we, as righteous men, ought to live from faith and if the righteousness of God should contribute to the salvation of all who believe, then salvation won't be our merit but God's mercy. My spirit was thereby cheered. For it's by the

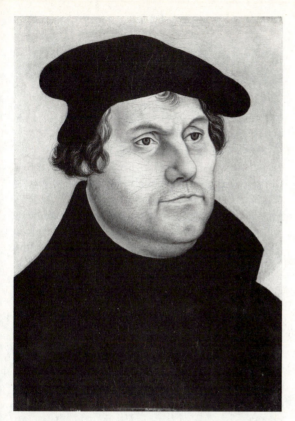

FIGURE 12.3 *Martin Luther* by Lucas Cranach the Elder (1521). This portrait of Luther was painted in the same year that he defied the pope and the Holy Roman Emperor at the Diet of Worms. His complete break with Rome ushered in an age of religious reform. (*Metropolitan Museum of Art*)

righteousness of God that we're justified and saved through Christ. These words [which had before terrified me] now became more pleasing to me. The Holy Spirit unveiled the Scriptures for me in this tower.

God led us away from all this in a wonderful way; without my quite being aware of it he took me away from that game more than twenty years ago. How difficult it was at first when we journeyed toward Kemberg after All Saints' Day in the year 1517, when I first made up my mind to write against the crass errors of indulgences! Jerome Schurff advised against this: "You wish to write against the pope? What are you trying to do? It won't be tolerated!" I replied, "And if they have to tolerate it?" Presently Sylvester, master of the sacred palace, entered the arena, fulminating against me with this syllogism: "Whoever questions what the Roman church says and does is heretical. Luther questions what the Roman church says and does, and therefore [he is a heretic]." So it all began.

CONSIDER THIS:

12-7. In his statement on salvation, Martin Luther argued against the "crass errors of indulgences" and made his mind up to oppose the process actively. But the Archbishop of Mainz in his instructions advocated the sale of indulgences as helping "departed souls" come to Paradise while at the same time promoting the construction of Saint Peter's Cathedral. Sounds like a win/win proposition. Why was Luther so upset?

The Ninety-Five Theses (1517)

MARTIN LUTHER

In the desire and with the purpose of elucidating the truth, a disputation will be held on the underwritten propositions at Wittenberg, under the presidency of the Reverend Father Martin Luther, Monk of the Order of St. Augustine, Master of Arts and of Sacred Theology, and ordinary Reader of the same in that place. He therefore asks those who cannot be present and discuss the subject with us orally, to do so by letter in their absence. In the name of our Lord Jesus Christ, Amen. . . .

The Ninety-Five Theses by Martin Luther is from H. Wace and C. A. Buchheim, eds., *First Principles of the Reformation* (London: John Murray, 1883), pp. 6–13.

5. The Pope has neither the will nor the power to remit any penalties except those which he has imposed by his own authority, or by that of the canons.

6. The Pope has no power to remit any guilt, except by declaring and warranting it to have been remitted by God; or at most by remitting cases reserved for himself; in which cases, if his power were [disregarded], guilt would certainly remain. . . .

20. Therefore the Pope, when he speaks of the plenary remission of all penalties, does not really mean of all, but only of those imposed by himself.

21. Thus those preachers of indulgences are in error who say that by the indulgences of the Pope a man is freed and saved from all punishment.

22. For in fact he remits to souls in Purgatory no penalty which they would have had to pay in this life according to the canons.

23. If any entire remission of all penalties can be granted to any one it is certain that it is granted to none but the most perfect, that is to very few.

24. Hence, the greater part of the people must needs be deceived by his indiscriminate and high-sounding promise of release from penalties.

25. Such power over Purgatory as the Pope has in general, such has every bishop in his own diocese, and every parish priest in his own parish. . . .

27. They are wrong who say that the soul flies out of Purgatory as soon as the money thrown into the chest rattles.

28. It is certain that, when money rattles in the chest, avarice and gain may be increased, but the effect of the intercession of the Church depends on the will of God alone. . . .

32. Those who believe that, through letters of pardon, they are made sure of their own salvation will be eternally damned along with their teachers.

33. We must especially beware of those who say that these pardons from the Pope are that inestimable gift of God by which man is reconciled to God. . . .

35. They preach no Christian doctrine who teach that contrition is not necessary for those who buy souls (out of Purgatory) or buy confessional licenses. . . .

37. Every true Christian, whether living or dead, has a share in all the benefits of Christ and of the Church, given by God, even without letters of pardon. . . .

42. Christians should be taught that it is not the wish of the Pope that buying of pardons should be in any way compared to works of mercy.

43. Christians should be taught that he who gives to a poor man, or lends to a needy man, does better than if he bought pardons. . . .

45. Christians should be taught that he who sees any one in need, and, passing him by, gives money for pardons, is not purchasing for himself the indulgences of the Pope but the anger of God. . . .

50. Christians should be taught that, if the Pope were acquainted with the exactions of the Preachers of pardons, he would prefer that the Basilica of St. Peter should be burnt to ashes rather than that it should be built up with the skin, flesh, and bones of his sheep. . . .

62. The true treasure of the Church is the Holy Gospel of the glory and grace of God. . . .

66. The treasures of indulgences are nets, wherewith they now fish for the riches of men. . . .

86. Again; why does not the Pope, whose riches are at this day more ample than those of the wealthiest of the wealthy, build the Basilica of St. Peter with his own money rather than with that of poor believers. . . .

94. Christians should be exhorted to strive to follow Christ their head through pains, deaths, and hells.

95. And thus not trust to enter heaven through many tribulations, rather than in the security of peace.

THE BROADER PERSPECTIVE:

12-8. What would you identify as the underlying causes for the Reformation, and what was the spark that set things in motion? To what extent was Martin Luther's action directed against abuses within the church?

Breaking with Rome (1517–1525)

Within a period of six months in 1520, Luther finished three important treatises that sealed his break with the Roman church. Excerpts from two of these treatises are presented here. In the *Address to the Christian Nobility of the German Nation*, Luther advocated that the secular authorities in Germany undertake the reform that the church would not. The treatise *On Christian Liberty* describes the liberating effect that pure faith in Christ has on an individual. Luther had written an accompanying letter to Pope Leo X stating that his writings were directed at the false doctrine and corruption surrounding the church and not meant as a personal slight against Leo; nevertheless, the break with Rome was complete, as events in the next year proved.

Address to the Christian Nobility of the German Nation (1520)

MARTIN LUTHER

The Romanists have, with great adroitness, drawn three walls round themselves, with which they have hitherto protected themselves, so that no one could reform them, whereby all Christendom has fallen terribly.

Firstly, if pressed by the temporal power, they have affirmed and maintained that the temporal power has no jurisdiction over them, but on the contrary that the spiritual power is above the temporal.

Secondly, if it were proposed to admonish them with the Scriptures, they objected that no one may interpret the Scriptures but the Pope.

Thirdly, if they are threatened with a Council, they pretend that no one may call a Council but the Pope.

Thus they have secretly stolen our three rods, so that they may be unpunished, and entrenched themselves behind these three walls, to act with all wickedness and malice, as we now see. . . .

Now may God help us, and give us one of those trumpets, that overthrew the walls of Jericho, so that we may blow down these walls of straw and paper, and that we may set free our Christian rods, for the chastisement of sin, and expose the craft and deceit of the devil, so that we may amend ourselves by punishment and again obtain God's favor.

The First Wall

Let us, in the first place, attack the first wall.

It has been devised, that the Pope, bishops, priests and monks are called the Spiritual Estate; Princes, lords, [artisans] and peasants are the Temporal Estate; which is a very fine, hypocritical device. But let no one be made afraid by it; and that for this reason: That all Christians are truly of the Spiritual Estate, and there is no difference among them save of office alone. As St. Paul says (*I Cor. 12*), we are all one body, though each member does its own work, to serve the others. This is because we have one baptism, one gospel, one faith, and are all Christians alike; for baptism, gospel and faith, these alone make Spiritual and Christian people. . . .

It follows then, that between layman and priests, princes and bishops, or as they call it, between spiritual and temporal persons, the only real difference is one of office and function, and not of estate: for they are all of the same Spiritual Estate, true priests, bishops and Popes, though their functions are not the same: just as among priests and monks every man has not the same functions. Christ's body is not double or twofold, one temporal, the other spiritual. He is one head, and he has one body. . . .

The Second Wall

The second wall is even more tottering and weak: that they alone pretend to be considered masters of the Scriptures; although they learn nothing of them all their life, they assume authority, and juggle before us with impudent words, saying that the Pope cannot err in matters of faith, whether he be evil or good; [yet] they cannot prove it by a single letter. That is why the canon law contains so many heretical and unchristian,

Address to the Christian Nobility is from H. Wace and C. A. Buchheim, eds., *First Principles of the Reformation* (London: John Murray, 1883), pp. 20–21, 23, 25–26, 28–30. Translation modernized by the editor.

[even], unnatural laws. . . . If I had not read it, I could never have believed, that the Devil should have put forth such follies at Rome and find a following. . . .

The Third Wall

The third wall falls of itself, as soon as the first two have fallen; for if the Pope acts contrary to the Scriptures, we are bound to stand by the Scriptures, to punish and to constrain him, according to Christ's commandment: ["If your brother sins against you, go and tell him his fault. . . . If he does not listen . . . tell it to the church (*Matt. 18:15–17*)."] . . . If then I am to accuse him before the church, I must collect the church together. Moreover they can show nothing in the Scriptures giving the Pope sole power to call and confirm councils; they have nothing but their own laws; but these hold good only so long as they are not injurious to Christianity and the laws of God. . . .

Therefore when need requires and the Pope is a cause of offence to Christendom, in these cases whoever can best do so, as a faithful member of the whole body, must do what he can to procure a true free council. . . .

And now I hope we have laid bare the false, lying specter with which the Romanists have long terrified and stupefied our consciences. And we have shown that, like all the rest of us, they are subject to the temporal sword; that they have no authority to interpret the Scriptures by force without skill; and that they have no power to prevent a council or to pledge it in accordance with their pleasure, or to bind it beforehand, and deprive it of its freedom; and that if they do this, they are verily of the fellowship of Antichrist and the Devil, and have nothing of Christ but the name.

CONSIDER THIS:

12-9. What are the three walls that Luther argues the Church has constructed to maintain control over its Christian flock? How does he destroy each wall? Do you find his arguments credible?

On Christian Liberty (1520)

MARTIN LUTHER

That I may open, then, an easier way for the ignorant—for these alone I am trying to serve—I first lay down these two propositions, concerning spiritual liberty and servitude.

A Christian man is the most free lord of all, and subject to none; a Christian man is the most dutiful servant of all, and subject to every one.

Although these statements appear contradictory, yet, when they are found to agree together, they will be highly serviceable to my purpose. They are both the statements of Paul himself, who says: "Though I be free from all men, yet have I made myself servant unto all" (*I Cor. 9:19*), and: "Owe no man anything, but to love one another." (*Rom. 13:8*) Now love is by its own nature dutiful and obedient to the beloved object. Thus even Christ, though Lord of all things, was yet made of a woman; made under the law; at once free and a servant; at once in the form of God and in the form of a servant.

Let us examine the subject on a deeper and less simple principle. Man is composed of a two-fold nature, a spiritual and a bodily. As regards the spiritual nature, which they name the soul, he is called the spiritual, inward, new man; as regards the bodily nature, which they name the flesh, he is called the fleshly, outward, old man. The Apostle speaks of this: "Though our outward man perish, yet the inward man is renewed day by day." (*II Cor. 4:16*) The result of this diversity is that in the Scriptures opposing statements are made concerning the same man; the fact being that in the same man these two men are opposed to one another; the flesh lusting against the spirit, and the spirit against the flesh. (*Gal. 5:17*) . . .

And, to cast everything aside, even speculations, meditations, and whatever things can be performed by the exertions of the soul itself, are of no profit. One thing, and one alone, is necessary for life, justification, and Christian liberty; and that is the most holy word of God, the Gospel of Christ, as He says: "I am the resurrection and the life; he that believeth in me shall not die eternally" (*John 11:25*); and also

On Christian Liberty is from H. Wace and C. A. Buchheim, eds., *First Principles of the Reformation* (London: John Murray, 1883), pp. 104–125. Translation modernized by the editor.

(*John 8:36*) "If the Son shall make you free, ye shall be free indeed"; and (*Matt. 4:4*) "Man shall not live by bread alone."

Let us therefore hold it for certain and firmly established that the soul can do without everything, except the word of God, without which none at all of its wants are provided for. But having the word, it is rich and wants for nothing; since that is the word of life, of truth, of light, of peace, of justification, of salvation, of joy, of liberty, of wisdom, of virtue, of grace, of glory, and of every good thing. . . .

Therefore, the first care of every Christian ought to be, to lay aside all reliance on works, and strengthen his faith alone more and more, and by it grow in the knowledge, not of works, but of Christ Jesus, who has suffered and risen again for him. . . . And yet there is nothing of which I have need—for faith alone suffices for my salvation—unless that, in it, faith may exercise the power and empire of its liberty. This is the inestimable power and liberty of Christians.

Nor are we only kings and the freest of all men, but also priests for ever, a dignity far higher than kingship, because by that priesthood we are worthy to appear before God, to pray for others, and to teach one another mutually the things which are of God. For these are the duties of priests, and they cannot possibly be permitted to any unbeliever. Christ has obtained for us this favor, if we believe in Him, that, just as we are His brethren, and co-heirs and fellow kings with Him, so we should be also fellow priests with Him, and venture with confidence, through the spirit of faith, to come into the presence of God, and cry "Abba, Father!" and to pray for one another, and to do all things which we see done and figured in the visible and corporeal office of priesthood. But to an unbelieving person nothing renders service or works for good. He himself is in servitude to all things, and all things turn out for evil to him, because he used all things in an impious way for his own advantage, and not for the glory of God. And thus he is not a priest, but a profane person, whose prayers are turned into sin; nor does he ever appear in the presence of God, because God does not hear sinners. . . .

Here you will ask: "If all who are in the Church are priests, by what character are those, whom we now call priests, to be distinguished from the laity?" I reply:

By the use of these words, "priest," "clergy," "spiritual person," "ecclesiastic," an injustice has been done, since they have been transferred from the remaining body of Christians to those few, who are now, by a hurtful custom, called ecclesiastics. For Holy Scripture makes no distinction between them, except that those, who are now boastfully called popes, bishops, and lords, it calls ministers, servants, and stewards, who are to serve the rest in the ministry of the World, for teaching the faith of Christ and the liberty of believers. For though it is true that we are all equally priests, yet we cannot, nor, if we could, ought we all to minister and teach publicly. Thus Paul says: "Let a man so account of us as of the ministers of Christ, and stewards of the mysteries of God." (*I Cor. 4:1*)

This bad system has now issued a pompous display of power, and such a terrible tyranny, that no earthly government can be compared to it, as if the laity were something else than Christians. Through this perversion of things it has happened that the knowledge of Christian grace, of faith, of liberty, and altogether of Christ, has utterly perished, and has been succeeded by an intolerable bondage to human works and laws; and, according to the Lamentations of Jeremiah, we have become the slaves of the vilest men on earth, who abuse our misery to all the disgraceful and ignominious purposes of their own will. . . .

True then are these two sayings: Good works do not make a good man, but a good man does good works. Bad works do not make a bad man, but a bad man does bad works. Thus it is always necessary that the substance or person should be good before any good works can be done, and that good works should follow and proceed from a good person. As Christ says: "A good tree cannot bring forth evil fruit, neither can a corrupt tree bring forth good fruit." (*Matt. 7:18*) Now it is clear that the fruit does not bear the tree, nor does the tree grow on the fruit; but, on the contrary, the trees bear the fruit and the fruit grows on the trees. . . .

Here is the truly Christian life; here is faith really working by love; when a man applies himself with joy and love to the works of that freest servitude, in which he serves others voluntarily and for naught; himself abundantly satisfied in the fullness and riches of his own faith.

12-10. What are Luther's primary arguments in the treatise *On Christian Liberty* regarding good works and the vision of each Christian as his own priest in the service of God? How does he define Christian liberty? Why were these ideas threatening to the Church?

12-11. What do you consider the most significant passages from Luther's *Address to the Christian Nobility of the German Nation* and treatise *On Christian Liberty*? Why? What was Luther trying to accomplish by writing them? Why did Luther finally break completely with the Roman church?

"Here I Stand": Address at the Diet of Worms (1521)

MARTIN LUTHER

After his excommunication by Leo X in June 1520, Luther was summoned to appear before a diet (assembly) of prelates and officials of the Holy Roman Empire in the city of Worms to answer questions about his heretical writings. His safe conduct to the meeting was guaranteed by the Holy Roman Emperor Charles V, who presided over the diet. Accompanied by his secular protector, Frederick the Wise, Elector of Saxony, Luther appeared on April 17, 1521. When asked whether he wished to defend all his writings or retract some, Luther delivered this famous speech. On April 23, Luther secretly left Worms and was hidden by friends at Wartburg castle. Charles V's edict against Luther is the second selection.

"Most serene emperor, most illustrious princes, most clement lords, obedient to the time set for me yesterday evening, I appear before you, beseeching you, by the mercy of God, that your most serene majesty and your most illustrious lordships may deign to listen graciously to this my cause—which is, as I hope, a cause of justice and truth. If through my inexperience I have either not given the proper titles to some, or have offended in some manner against court customs and etiquette, I beseech you to kindly pardon me, as a man accustomed not to courts but to the cells of monks. I can bear no other witness about myself but that I have taught and written up to this time with simplicity of heart, as I had in view only the glory of God and the sound instruction of Christ's faithful. . . .

"[A] group of my books attacks the papacy and the affairs of the papists as those who both by their doctrines and very wicked examples have laid waste the Christian world with evil that affects the spirit and the body. For no one can deny or conceal this fact, when the experience of all and the complaints of everyone witness that through the decrees of the pope and the doctrines of men the consciences of the faithful have been most miserably entangled, tortured, and torn to pieces. Also, property and possessions, especially in this illustrious nation of Germany, have been devoured by an unbelievable tyranny and are being devoured to this time without letup and by unworthy means. [Yet the papists] by their own decrees . . . warn that the papal laws and doctrines which are contrary to the gospel or the opinions of the fathers are to be regarded as erroneous and reprehensible. If, therefore, I should have retracted these writings, I should have done nothing other than to give strength to this [papal] tyranny and I should have opened not only windows but doors to such great godlessness. It would rage further and more freely than ever it has dared up to this time. Yes, from the proof of such a revocation on my part, their wholly lawless and unrestrained kingdom of wickedness would become still more intolerable for the already wretched people; and their rule would be further strengthened and established, especially if it should be reported that this evil deed had been done by me by virtue of the authority of your most serene majesty and the whole Roman Empire. Good God! What a cover for wickedness and tyranny I should have then become.

"I have written a third sort of book against some private and (as they say) distinguished individuals—those,

"'Here I Stand': Address at the Diet of Worms" is from J. Pelikan, ed., *Luther's Works*, vol. 2, *Career of the Reformer* (Saint Louis: Concordia Publishing House, 1958), pp. 109–112. Copyright © 1958 by Concordia Publishing House. Used by permission of the publisher.

namely, who strive to preserve the Roman tyranny and to destroy the godliness taught by me. Against these I confess I have been more violent than my religion or profession demands. But then, I do not set myself up as a saint; neither am I disputing about my life, but about the teachings of Christ. It is not proper for me to retract these works, because by this retraction it would again happen that tyranny and godlessness would, with my patronage, rule and rage among the people of God more violently than ever before.

"However, because I am a man and not God, I am not able to shield my books with any other protection than that which my Lord Jesus Christ himself offered for his teaching. When questioned before Annas about his teaching and struck by a servant, he said: 'If I have spoken wrongly, bear witness to the wrong' [*John 18:19–23*]. If the Lord himself, who knew that he could not err, did not refuse to hear testimony against his teaching, even from the lowliest servant, how much more ought I, who am the lowest scum and able to do nothing except err, desire and expect that somebody should want to offer testimony against my teaching! Therefore, I ask by the mercy of God, may your most serene majesty, most illustrious lordships, or anyone at all who is able, either high or low, bear witness, expose my errors, overthrowing them by the writings of the prophets and the evangelists. Once I have been taught I shall be quite ready to renounce every error, and I shall be the first to cast my books into the fire.

"From these remarks I think it is clear that I have sufficiently considered and weighed the hazards and dangers, as well as the excitement and dissensions aroused in the world as a result of my teachings, things about which I was gravely and forcefully warned yesterday. To see excitement and dissension arise because of the Word of God is to me clearly the most joyful aspect of all in these matters. For this is the way, the opportunity, and the result of the Word of God, just as He [Christ] said, 'I have not come to bring peace, but a sword. For I have come to set a man against his father, etc.' [*Matt. 10:34–35*] . . . Therefore we must fear God. I do not say these things because there is a need of either my teachings or my warnings for such leaders as you, but because I must not withhold the allegiance which I owe my Germany. With these words I commend myself to your most serene majesty and to your lordships, humbly asking that I not be allowed through the agitation of my enemies, without cause, to be made hateful to you. I have finished."

When I had finished, the speaker for the emperor said, as if in reproach that I had not answered the question, that I ought not call into question those things which had been condemned and defined in councils; therefore what was sought from me was not a horned response, but a simple one, whether or not I wished to retract.

Here I answered:

"Since then your serene majesty and your lordships seek a simple answer, I will give it in this manner, without aggression or prevarication: Unless I am convinced by the testimony of the Scriptures or by clear reason (for I do not trust either in the pope or in councils alone, since it is well known that they have often errored and contradicted themselves), I am bound by the Scriptures I have quoted and my conscience is captive to the Word of God. I cannot and I will not retract anything, since it is neither safe nor right to go against conscience.

"I cannot do otherwise, here I stand, may God help me, Amen."

The Edict of Worms (1521)

EMPEROR CHARLES V

In view of the fact that Martin Luther still persists obstinately and perversely in maintaining his heretical opinions, and consequently all pious and God-fearing persons abominate and abhor him as one mad or possessed by a demon . . . we have declared and made known that the said Martin Luther shall hereafter be held and esteemed by each and all of us as a limb cut off from the Church of God, an obstinate schismatic and manifest heretic. . . .

"The Edict of Worms" is from James H. Robinson, ed., *Readings in European History*, vol. 2 (Boston: Ginn and Company, 1906), pp. 87–88.

And we publicly attest by these letters that we order and command each and all of you, as you owe fidelity to us and the Holy Empire, and would escape the penalties of the crime of treason, and the ban and over-ban of the Empire, and the forfeiture of all regalia, fiefs, privileges, and immunities, which up to this time you have in any way obtained from our predecessors, ourself, and the Holy Roman Empire—commanding, we say, in the name of the Roman and imperial majesty, we strictly order that immediately after the expiration of the appointed twenty days, terminating on the fourteenth day of May, you shall refuse to give the aforesaid Martin Luther hospitality, lodging, food, or drink; neither shall any one, by word or deed, secretly or openly, succor or assist him by counsel or help; but in whatever place you meet him, you shall proceed against him; if you have sufficient force, you shall take him prisoner and keep him in close custody; you shall deliver him, or cause him to be delivered, to us or at least let us know where he may be captured. In the meanwhile you shall keep him closely imprisoned until you receive notice from us what further to do, according to the direction of the laws. And for such holy and pious work we will indemnify you for your trouble and expense. . . .

And in order that all this may be done and credit given to this document we have sealed it with our imperial seal, which has been affixed in our imperial city of Worms, on the eighth day of May, after the birth of Christ 1521, in the second year of our reign over the Roman Empire, and over our other lands the sixth.

By our lord the emperor's own command.

CONSIDER THIS:

12-12. Why was Luther's address at the Diet of Worms considered to be not only an act of principle, but an act of courage as well? What was at risk for Luther?

12-13. In issuing the Edict of Worms, did the Holy Roman Emperor act correctly to stop the incipient reform movement? Did he have any other options as protector of the Church? Was the Protestant Reformation inevitable?

THE BROADER PERSPECTIVE:

12-14. Edward Bulwer-Lytton once said, "A reform is a correction of abuses; a revolution is a transfer of power." Under this definition, would you consider the Protestant Reformation to be a revolution?

Social and Political Aspects of the Lutheran Reformation

The Lutheran Reformation was not simply spiritual or corrective, for it had many political and social repercussions as well. In response to the celibacy demanded of priests by the church, Luther advocated that clergy be allowed to marry. He himself married a former nun. Such defiance in one sphere was confusing for certain elements of society who saw Luther as their champion as well. In 1524, a major peasant revolt broke out in Germany as social and economic conflicts came to a head. The peasants demanded freedom from the long-standing feudal obligations of serfdom. Luther understood that the survival of his movement depended on the political influence and protection of the nobility. Although Luther sympathized with the peasants, he clearly sided with the nobility, and they savagely crushed the revolt.

On Celibacy and Marriage

MARTIN LUTHER

First, not every priest can do without a woman, not only on account of the weakness of the flesh but much more because of the needs of the household. If, then, he is to keep a woman, and the pope grants him permission to do so, but he may not have her in marriage, what is this but leaving a man and a woman alone and

"On Celibacy and Marriage" is from E. M. Plass, ed., *What Luther Says*, vol. 2 (Saint Louis: Concordia Publishing House, 1959), pp. 888–889, 891. Copyright © 1959 by Concordia Publishing House. Used by permission of the publisher.

forbidding them to fall? It is like putting fire and straw together and commanding that there shall be neither smoke nor fire. Secondly, the pope has as little power to give this command as he has to forbid eating, drinking, the natural process of bodily elimination, or becoming fat. No one, therefore, is in duty bound to keep this commandment and the pope is responsible for all the sins that are committed against this ordinance, for all the souls lost thereby, and for all consciences thereby confused and tortured. Consequently, he undoubtedly has deserved long ago that someone should drive him out of the world, so many souls has he strangled with this devilish snare; although I hope that God has been more gracious to many of them at their end than the pope had been during their life. Nothing good has ever come out of the papacy and its laws, nor ever will.

Listen! In all my days I have not heard the confession of a nun, but in the light of Scripture I shall hit upon how matters fare with her and know I shall not be lying. If a girl is not sustained by great and exceptional grace, she can live without a man as little as she can without eating, drinking, sleeping, and other natural necessities. Nor, on the other hand, can a man dispense with a wife. The reason for this is that procreating children is an urge planted as deeply in human nature as eating and drinking. That is why God has given and put into the body the organs, arteries, fluxes, and everything that serves it. Therefore what is he doing who would check this process and keep nature from running its desired and intended course? He is attempting to keep nature from being nature, fire from burning, water from wetting, and a man from eating, drinking, and sleeping.

Whoever intends to enter married life should do so in faith and in God's name. He should pray that it may prosper according to His will and that marriage may not be treated as a matter of fun and folly. It is a hazardous matter and as serious as anything on earth can be. Therefore we should not rush into it as the world does, in keeping with its frivolousness and wantonness and in pursuit of its pleasure; but before taking this step we should consult God, so that we may lead our married life to His glory. Those who do not go about it in this way may certainly thank God if it turns out well. If it turns out badly, they should not be surprised; for they did not begin it in the name of God and did not ask for His blessing.

Condemnation of the Peasant Revolt (1524)

MARTIN LUTHER

In my preceding pamphlet [on the "Twelve Articles"] I had no occasion to condemn the peasants, because they promised to yield to law and better instruction, as Christ also demands (*Matt. 7:1*). But before I can turn around, they go out and appeal to force, in spite of their promises and rob and pillage and act like mad dogs. From this it is quite apparent what they had in their false minds, and that what they put forth under the name of the gospel in the "Twelve Articles" was all vain pretense. In short, they practice mere devil's work, and it is the arch-devil himself who reigns at Muhlhausen, indulging in nothing but robbery, murder, and bloodshed; as Christ says of the devil in John 8:44, "he was a murderer from the beginning." Since, therefore, those peasants and miserable wretches allow themselves to be led astray and act differently from what they declared, I likewise must write differently concerning them; and first bring their sins before their eyes, as God commands (*Isa. 58:1; Ezek. 2:7*), whether perchance some of them may come to their senses; and, further, I would instruct those in authority how to conduct themselves in this matter.

With threefold horrible sins against God and men have these peasants loaded themselves, for which they have deserved a manifold death of body and soul.

First, they have sworn to their true and gracious rulers to be submissive and obedient, in accord with God's command (*Matt. 22:21*), "Render therefore unto

"Condemnation of the Peasant Revolt" is from James H. Robinson, ed., *Readings in European History*, vol. 1 (Boston: Ginn and Company, 1904), pp. 106–108.

Caesar the things which are Caesar's," and (*Rom. 13:1*), "Let every soul be subject unto the higher powers." But since they have deliberately and sacrilegiously abandoned their obedience, and in addition have dared to oppose their lords, they have thereby forfeited body and soul, as perfidious, perjured, lying, disobedient wretches and scoundrels are wont to do. Wherefore Saint Paul judges them saying (*Rom. 13:2*), "And they that resist shall receive to themselves damnation." The peasants will incur this sentence, sooner or later; for God wills that fidelity and allegiance shall be sacredly kept.

Second, they cause uproar and sacrilegiously rob and pillage monasteries and castles that do not belong to them, for which, like public highwaymen and murderers, they deserve the twofold death of body and soul. It is right and lawful to slay at the first opportunity a rebellious person, who is known as such, for he is already under God's and the emperor's ban. Every man is at once judge and executioner of a public rebel; just as, when a fire starts, he who can extinguish it first is the best fellow. Rebellion is not simply vile murder, but is like a great fire that kindles and devastates a country; it fills the land with murder and bloodshed, makes widows and orphans, and destroys everything, like the greatest calamity. Therefore, whosoever can, should smite, strangle, and stab, secretly or publicly, and should remember that there is nothing more poisonous, pernicious, and devilish than a rebellious man. Just as one must slay a mad dog, so, if you do not fight the rebels, they will fight you, and the whole country with you.

Third, they cloak their frightful and revolting sins with the gospel, call themselves Christian brethren, swear allegiance, and compel people to join them in such abominations. Thereby they become the greatest blasphemers and violators of God's holy name, and serve and honor the devil under the semblance of the gospel, so that they have ten times deserved death of body and soul, for never have I heard of uglier sins. And I believe also that the devil foresees the judgment day, that he undertakes such an unheard-of measure; as if he said, "It is the last and therefore it shall be the worst; I'll stir up the dregs and knock the very bottom out." May the Lord restrain him! Lo, how mighty a prince is the devil, how he holds the world in his hands and can put it to confusion; who else could so soon capture so many thousands of peasants, lead them astray, blind and deceive them, stir them to revolt, and make them the willing executioners of his malice. . . .

And should the peasants prevail (which God forbid!),—for all things are possible to God, and we know not but that he is preparing for the judgment day, which cannot be far distant, and may purpose to destroy, by means of the devil, all order and authority and throw the world into wild chaos—yet surely they who are found, sword in hand, shall perish in the wreck with clear consciences, leaving to the devil the kingdom of this world and receiving instead the eternal kingdom. For we are come upon such strange times that a prince may more easily win heaven by the shedding of blood than others by prayers.

CONSIDER THIS:

12-15. What were Luther's arguments against the peasants in 1524? Are they persuasive? What does Luther's condemnation of the Peasants' Revolt tell you about his reform movement? Do you regard Luther as a hypocrite or not?

In the Wake of Luther

John Calvin and the Genevan Reformation (1536–1564)

Although Lutheranism formed the basis of the Reformation, by the mid-sixteenth century it had lost much of its energy and was confined to Germany and Scandinavia. The movement was spread throughout Europe by other reformers, the most influential of whom was John Calvin (1509–1564).

A trained lawyer and classical scholar, Calvin had been a convert to Luther's ideas and was forced to leave France, eventually settling in Geneva in the 1530s. There in the 1540s, he established a very structured society that can best be described as a theocracy. Calvin's strict adherence to biblical authority and his singular strength of personality can be seen in his treatise, *On the Necessity of Reforming the Church*. In it he defines the church as "a society of all the saints, a society spread over the whole world, and existing in all ages, yet bound together by the one doctrine and the one Spirit of Christ." In the words of Saint Cyprian, which Calvin often quoted, "We cannot have God for our Father without having the Church for our mother." The importance of this idea cannot be overestimated in Calvin's understanding of doctrine and of the reform of the church. In the following excerpt from his famous treatise, which was addressed to the Holy Roman Emperor Charles V in 1544, Calvin expressed disgust that the church had become divorced from the society of saints it was supposed to serve. The continuity of the church as a universal embodiment of all believers had to be reestablished through clerical reform and a reconceptualization of Spirit.

On the Necessity of Reforming the Church (1544)

JOHN CALVIN

In the present condition of the empire, your Imperial Majesty, and you, Most Illustrious Princes, necessarily involved in various cares, and distracted by a multiplicity of business, are agitated, and in a manner tempest-tossed. . . . I feel what nerve, what earnestness, what urgency, what ardor, the treatment of this subject requires. . . . First, call to mind the fearful calamities of the Church, which might move to pity even minds of iron. Nay, set before your eyes her squalid and unsightly form, and the sad devastation which is everywhere beheld. How long, pray, will you allow the spouse of Christ, the mother of you all, to lie thus protracted and afflicted—thus, too, when she is imploring your protection, and when the means of relief are at hand? Next, consider how much worse calamities impend. Final destruction cannot be far off, unless you interpose with the utmost speed. Christ will, indeed, in the way which to him seems good, preserve his Church miraculously, and beyond human expectation; but this I say, that the consequence of a little longer delay on your part will be, that in Germany we shall not have even the form of a Church. Look round, and see how many indications threaten that ruin which it is your duty to prevent, and announce that it is actually at hand. These things speak loud enough, though I were silent. . . .

Divine worship being corrupted by so many false opinions, and perverted by so many impious and foul superstitions, the sacred Majesty of God is insulted with atrocious contempt, his holy name profaned, his glory only not trampled under foot. Nay, while the whole Christian world is openly polluted with idolatry, men adore, instead of Him, their own fictions. A thousand superstitions reign, superstitions which are just so many open insults to Him. The power of Christ is almost obliterated from the minds of men, the hope of salvation is transferred from him to empty, frivolous, and insignificant ceremonies, while there is a pollution of the Sacraments not less to be execrated. Baptism is deformed by numerous additions, the Holy Supper [communion] is prostituted to all kinds of ignominy, religion throughout has degenerated into an entirely different form. . . .

In the future, therefore, as often as you shall hear the croaking note—"The business of reforming the Church must be delayed for the present"—"there will be time enough to accomplish it after other matters are transacted"—remember, Most Invincible Emperor, that the matter on which you are to deliberate is, whether you are to leave to your posterity some empire or none. Yet, why do I speak of posterity? Even now, while your own eyes behold, it is half bent, and totters to its final ruin. . . .

But be the issue what it may, we will never repent of having begun, and of having proceeded thus far. The Holy Spirit is a faithful and unerring witness to our doctrine. We know, I say, that it is the eternal truth of God that we preach. We are, indeed, desirous, as we ought to be, that our ministry may prove salutary to the world; but to give it this effect belongs to God, not to us. If, to punish, partly the ingratitude,

On the Necessity of Reforming the Church is from John Calvin, *Tracts and Treatises on the Reformation of the Church*, trans. Henry Beveridge, vol. 1 (Edinburgh: Calvin Translation Society, 1844), pp. 231–234.

and partly the stubbornness of those to whom we desire to do good, success must prove desperate, and all things go to worse, I will say what it befits a Christian man to say, and what all who are true to this holy profession will subscribe: We will die, but in death even be conquerors, not only because through it we shall have a sure passage to a better life, but because we know that our blood will be as seed to propagate the Divine truth which men now despise.

CONSIDER THIS:

12-16. In the treatise *On the Necessity of Reforming the Church*, what is John Calvin's primary message to the Holy Roman Emperor Charles V? Do you think Calvin was exaggerating when he reminded the Emperor that "the matter on which you are to deliberate is, whether you are to leave to your posterity some empire or none"?

Predestination: Institutes of the Christian Religion *(1536)*

JOHN CALVIN

Calvin's doctrines were primarily Lutheran, but he went a step beyond and stressed the doctrine of predestination: One's salvation had already been determined by God, and those elect who had been "chosen" gave evidence of their calling by living exemplary lives. Calvinism became popular in the Netherlands and Scotland, and it formed the core of the Puritan belief that was to be so influential in the colonization of America. The following excerpts reveal Calvin's justification for reform, his concept of predestination, and his strict regulation of lives and beliefs in Geneva.

The covenant of life is not preached equally to all, and among those to whom it is preached, does not always meet with the same reception. This diversity displays the unsearchable depth of the divine judgment, and is without doubt subordinate to God's purpose of eternal election. But it is plainly owing to the mere pleasure of God that salvation is spontaneously offered to some, while others have no access to it, great and difficult questions immediately arise, questions which are inexplicable, when just views are not entertained concerning election and predestination. . . .

By predestination we mean the eternal decree of God, by which he determined with himself whatever he wished to happen with regard to every man. All are not created on equal terms, but some are preordained to eternal life, others to eternal damnation; and, accordingly, as each has been created for one or other of these ends, we say that he has been predestined to life or to death. . . .

We say, then, that Scripture clearly proves this much, that God by his eternal and immutable counsel determined once for all those whom it was his pleasure one day to admit to salvation, and those whom, on the other hand, it was his pleasure to doom to destruction. We maintain that this counsel, as regards the elect, is founded on his free mercy, without any respect to human worth, while those whom he dooms to destruction are excluded from access to life by a just and blameless, but at the same time incomprehensible judgment. In regard to the elect, we regard calling as the evidence of election, and justification as another symbol of its manifestation, until it is fully accomplished by the attainment of glory. But as the Lord seals his elect by calling and justification, so by excluding the reprobate either from the knowledge of his name or the sanctification of his Spirit, he by these marks in a manner discloses the judgment which awaits them. I will here omit many of the fictions which foolish men have devised to overthrow predestination. There is no need of refuting objections which the moment they are produced abundantly betray their hollowness. I will dwell only on those points which either form the subject of dispute among the learned, or may occasion any difficulty to the simple. . . .

CONSIDER THIS:

12-17. How would you define the concept of predestination and why is it so efficient as a device for controlling a congregation? What is the basis for the success of the Calvinist movement?

"Predestination" is from John Calvin, *Institutes of the Christian Religion*, trans. Henry Beveridge, vol. 2 (Edinburgh: Calvin Translation Society, 1845), pp. 529, 534, 540.

Genevan Catechism (1541): Concerning the Lord's Supper

JOHN CALVIN

The minister: Have we in the supper simply a signification of the things above mentioned, or are they given to us in reality?

The child: Since Jesus Christ is truth itself there can be no doubt that the promises he has made regarding the supper are accomplished, and that what is figured there is verified there also. Wherefore according as he promises and represents I have no doubt that he makes us partakers of his own substance, in order that he may unite us with him in one life.

The minister: But how may this be, when the Body of Jesus Christ is in heaven, and we are on this earthly pilgrimage?

The child: It comes about through the incomprehensible power of his spirit, which may indeed unite things widely separated in space.

The minister: You do not understand then that the body is enclosed in the bread, or the blood in the cup?

The child: No. On the contrary, in order that the reality of the sacrament be achieved our hearts must be raised to heaven, where Jesus Christ dwells in the glory of the Father, whence we await him for our redemption; and we are not to seek him in these corruptible elements.

The minister: You understand then that there are two things in this sacrament: the natural bread and wine, which we see with the eye, touch with the hand and perceive with the taste; and Jesus Christ, through whom our souls are inwardly nourished?

The child: I do. In such a way moreover that we have there the very witness and so say a pledge of the resurrection of our bodies; since they are made partakers in the symbol of life.

THE BROADER PERSPECTIVE:

12-18. Should we characterize Calvin as a spiritual leader or a political leader? How could Calvin's vision of predestination or his catechism that was required of all children be used to achieve political authority and control over both the church and Geneva itself? Do these religious documents blur the boundaries of church and state? To obtain effective control over people, must spiritual leaders grant themselves political power and must political leaders claim spiritual authority?

Ordinances for the Regulation of Churches (1547)

JOHN CALVIN

Blasphemy

Whoever shall have blasphemed, swearing by the body or by the blood of our Lord, or in similar manner, he shall be made to kiss the earth for the first offence; for the second to pay 5 sous, and for the third 6 sous, and for the last offence be put in the pillory for one hour.

Drunkenness

1. That no one shall invite another to drink under penalty of 3 sous.

2. That taverns shall be closed during the sermon, under penalty that the tavern-keeper shall pay 3 sous, and whoever may be found therein shall pay the same amount.

3. If any one be found intoxicated he shall pay for the first offense 3 sous and shall be remanded to the consistory; for the second offense he shall be held to pay the same sum of 6 sous, and for the third 10 sous and be put in prison.

"Genevan Catechism" is from James H. Robinson, ed., *Translations and Reprints from the Original Sources of European History*, vol. 3 (Philadelphia: University of Pennsylvania, 1902), pp. 8–9.

"Ordinances for the Regulation of Churches" is from James H. Robinson, ed., *Translations and Reprints from the Original Sources of European History*, vol. 3 (Philadelphia: University of Pennsylvania, 1902), pp. 10–11.

Songs and Dances

If any one sing immoral, dissolute or outrageous songs, or dance the virollet or other dance, he shall be put in prison for three days and then sent to the consistory.

Usury

That no one shall take upon interest or profit more than five percent, upon penalty of confiscation of the principal and of being condemned to make restitution as the case may demand.

Games

That no one shall play at any dissolute game or at any game whatsoever it may be, neither for gold nor silver nor for any excessive stake, upon penalty of 5 sous and forfeiture of stake played for.

How Soon Marriage Must Be Consummated after the Promise Is Made

After the promise is made the marriage shall not be deferred more than six weeks; otherwise the parties shall be called before the consistory, in order that they may be admonished. If they do not obey they shall be remanded to the council and be constrained to celebrate the marriage.

Concerning the Celebration of the Marriage

That the parties at the time when they are to be married shall go modestly to the church, without drummers and minstrels, preserving an order and gravity becoming to Christians; and this before the last stroke of the bell, in order that the marriage blessing may be given before the sermon. If they are negligent and come too late they shall be sent away.

Of the Common Residence of Husband and Wife

That the husband shall have his wife with him and they shall live in the same house, maintaining a common household, and if it should happen that one should leave the other to life apart they shall be summoned in order that they may be remonstrated with and constrained to return, the one to the other.

The Spread of Calvinism (1561)

GIOVANNI MICHIEL

Giovanni Michiel was the Venetian ambassador to the French court when he offered this appraisal of the dangerous spread of Calvinism in France. Notice his comparison of Calvinism to a contagious disease. In Michiel's view, religious disputes would inevitably result in civil war and political chaos.

Unless it otherwise please the Almighty, religious affairs will soon be in an evil case in France, because there is not one single province uncontaminated. . . . This contagion has penetrated so deeply that it affects every class of persons, and, what appears more strange, even the ecclesiastical body itself. I do not mean only priests, friars, and nuns, for there are but few monasteries that are not corrupted, but even bishops and many of the principal prelates, who hitherto had not shown any such disposition. . . . But you Serenity must learn that while the people and the populace show fervent devotion by frequenting the churches and observing the Catholic rites, all other classes are supposed to be disaffected, and the nobility perhaps more than any other class, and, particularly, persons of forty years of age and under. . . . It has now been determined not to proceed against any disaffected persons unless they venture to preach, persuade, and to

---

"The Spread of Calvinism" is from *Calendar of State Papers, Venetian VII*, pp. 322–323.

take part publicly in congregations and assemblies. All other such persons are allowed to live, and some have been set at liberty, and released from the prisons of Paris and of other parts of the kingdom. A great number of these last have still remained in the kingdom, preaching and speaking publicly, and boasting that they have gained their cause against the Papists, as they delight to style their adversaries; so that, now, every one of them is assured against the fear of being questioned; and there exists thus a silent truce because while formerly all suspected persons had to quit the kingdom, and to retire some to Geneva, some to Germany, and some to England, now they not only do not leave the country, but a large number of those who had already emigrated have returned. . . .

Your Serenity will hardly believe the influence and the great power which the principal minister of Geneva, by name Calvin, a Frenchman, and a native of Picardy, possesses in this kingdom; he is a man of extraordinary authority, who by his mode of life, his doctrines, and his writings, rise superior to all the rest; and it is almost impossible to believe the enormous sums of money which are secretly sent to him from France to maintain his power. It is sufficient to add that if God does not interfere, there is great and imminent danger that one of two things will happen in this kingdom; either that the truce which is desire and sought publicly, will end by the heretics having churches wherein they can preach, read, and perform their rites, according to their doctrine, without hindrance . . . or else, that we shall see an obedience to the Pope and to the Catholic rites enforced, and shall have resort to violence and imbrue our hands in noble blood. For these reasons I foresee a manifest and certain division in the kingdom, and civil war as a consequence; and this will be the cause of the ruin both of the kingdom and of religion, because upon a change in religion a change in the state necessarily follows.

CONSIDER THIS:

12-19. After reading the selections on the catechism and the regulation of churches in Geneva, do you think that Calvin was a control freak or a brilliant organizer? What was the basis for the success of Calvinism? Why did the spread of Calvinism seem so dangerous to Giovanni Michiel, the Venetian ambassador to France?

THEME: THE INSTITUTION AND THE INDIVIDUAL

THE REFLECTION IN THE MIRROR
"Beware of Infection" The Abdication of Charles V

"The Wretched Condition of the Christian State" (1556)
EMPEROR CHARLES V

As the Reformation expanded its influence in Germany, Switzerland, and France during the 1530s and 1540s, the Holy Roman Emperor Charles V made several abortive attempts to enforce compromise agreements between Catholics and Protestants. As discussions broke down, he even tried to effect a military solution in 1547 by crushing the Protestant Schmalkaldic League. But the Reformation had become too entrenched to be resolved by brute force. The Emperor was finally forced to relent and accepted the Peace of Augsburg in 1555. This compromise established that the ruler of a region would determine its religion. Lutheranism was finally recognized as a legal form of Christian belief. Lutherans were

"'The Wretched Condition of the Christian State'" is from James H. Robinson, ed., *Readings in European History*, vol. 2 (Boston: Ginn and Company, 1906), pp. 165–167.

allowed to retain church lands seized before 1552 and were permitted to migrate from one area to another without restriction.

But by 1556, Charles V, who had served as king of Spain and Holy Roman emperor since 1519 at the outset of the Reformation, had become a tired and disappointed man. His abdication speech that follows gives insight into his struggles and some political consequences of the Reformation.

Keep in Mind . . .

12-20. Toward the end of his life, what did Emperor Charles V believe he had accomplished and what did he regret?

Soon came the death of my grandfather Maximilian, in my nineteenth year [1519], and although I was still young, they conferred upon me in his stead the imperial dignity. I had no inordinate ambition to rule a multitude of kingdoms, but merely sought to secure the welfare of Germany, to provide for the defense of Flanders, to consecrate my forces to the safety of Christianity against the Turk and to labor for the extension of the Christian religion. But although such zeal was mine, I was unable to show so much of it as I might have wished, on account of the troubles raised by the heresies of Luther and the other innovators of Germany and on account of serious war into which the hostility and envy of neighboring princes had driven me, and from which I have safely emerged, thanks to the favor of God.

> "I was unable to show so much zeal as I might have wished, on account of the troubles raised by the heresies of Luther and the other innovators of Germany."
> —Emperor Charles V

This is the fourth time that I go to Spain, there to bury myself. I wish to say to you that nothing I have ever experienced has given me so much pain or rested so heavily upon my soul as that which I experience in parting from you today, without leaving behind me that peace and quiet which I so much desired. . . . I am no longer able to attend to my affairs without great bodily fatigue and consequent detriment to the affairs of the state. The cares which so great a responsibility involves; the extreme dejection it causes; my health already ruined; all these leave me no longer the strength sufficient for governing the states which God has confided to me. The little strength that remains to me is rapidly disappearing. So I should long ago have put down the burden if my son's immaturity and my mother's incapacity had not forced both my spirit and my body to sustain the weight until this hour.

The last time that I went to Germany I had determined to do what you see me do today, but I could not bring myself to do it when I saw the wretched condition of the Christian state, a prey to such a multitude of disturbances, of innovations, of singular opinions as to faith, of worse than civil wars, and fallen finally into so many lamentable disorders. I was turned from my purpose because my ills were not yet so great, and I hoped to make an end of all these things and restore the peace. In order that I might not be wanting in my duty I risked my strength, my goods, my repose and my life for the safety of Christianity and the defense of my subjects. From this struggle I emerged with a portion of the things I desired. . . .

I have carried out what God has permitted, since the outcome of our efforts depends upon the will of God. We human beings act according to our powers, our strength, our spirit, and God awards the victory and permits defeat. I have ever done as I was able, and God has aided me. I return to Him boundless thanks for having succored me in my greatest trials and in all my dangers.

I am determined then to retire to Spain, to yield to my son Philip the possessions of all my states, and to my brother, the king of the Romans, the Empire. I particularly commend to you my son, and I ask of you in remembrance of me, that you extend to him the love which you have always borne towards me; moreover I ask you to preserve among yourselves the same affection and harmony. Be obedient towards justice, zealous in the observance of the laws, preserve for all that merits it, and do not refuse to grant authority the support of which it stands in need.

Above all, beware of infection from the sects of neighboring lands. Extirpate at once the germs, if they appear in your midst, for fear lest they may spread abroad and utterly overthrow your state, and lest you may fall into the direst calamities.

THE BROADER PERSPECTIVE:

12-21. Some historians have maintained that the success of the Reformation depended on the forces arrayed against it. Without the opposition of figures like Ignatius Loyola and Emperor Charles V, would the Reformation have succeeded? Does opposition help a political or religious movement better define and clarify its doctrine? Does opposition actually strengthen the organization of the movement? In his abdication speech, why does Charles V seem so dejected?

The Radical Reformation: Anabaptism

It is somewhat misleading to speak of the "radical Reformation" as a distinct entity because in a sense the Reformation movement by its very nature was a radical departure from the doctrines of the Western Christian church. Still, within a period of great religious upheaval and change, personal insight and interpretation of scripture often resulted in the establishment of congregations that were formed around derivative issues and channeled through dynamic leadership. These new ideas and leaders, working within a fluid spiritual and political environment, became immediate and even radical threats to authority figures like Luther and Calvin. Indeed, this points up the relative nature of "radicalism." After Luther and Calvin had established their "radical" doctrines and congregations in defiance of papal and imperial decrees, they sought to protect their gains and thus became defenders of their own status quo, suspicious and resistant to alternative interpretations of the Bible. One of the most dramatic movements of the period that challenged both the Catholic and Protestant religious landscape was that of Anabaptism.

Anabaptism arose within the cradle of the Swiss Reformation in Zurich. The most influential local reformer during the 1520s was the contentious Ulrich Zwingli (1484–1531). He and Luther had their own disagreements about the nature of the Eucharist that were never resolved. But Zwingli's influence within Zurich was substantial, and thus he became concerned when in 1523 a few members of the congregation proposed the idea that baptism should not be administered to infants who were unaware of the significance of the act. Baptism, they argued, should be reserved for adults who had made a conscious decision to receive it. Therefore, adults in the community must be "rebaptized" to be truly cleansed of original sin. After much discussion, Zwingli and the Zurich city council pronounced that infant baptism was scriptural and ordered the baptism of all unbaptized children and the prohibition of radical meetings. Anabaptists would not be tolerated in Zurich.

Although Anabaptists believed theirs to be a righteous cause with scriptural support, city governments in southern Germany and Austria disagreed and revived ancient decrees forbidding rebaptism as adults under penalty of death. After 1529, Anabaptists could be sent to prison and even burned at the stake in some communities. Anabaptists, spiritually unified by persecution and driven together by economic need, saw themselves in the mold of early Christians, migrating and endeavoring to found the "true church" in the New Jerusalem.

One such group of Anabaptists succeeded in establishing itself in the town of Münster, Germany, and actually assumed control of the city in 1534. All those who refused to be rebaptized were ordered to leave the city. Under the leadership of two Dutchmen, Jan Matthijs and Jan van Leyden, radical steps were taken to convert Münster to its biblical image as the New Jerusalem. This rather unrepresentative group of radical Anabaptists ordered all books except the Bible to be burned and even introduced communism and polygamy. Condemned by both Catholics and Protestants alike, the town was seized by the forces of Charles V. The Anabaptist leaders were slowly tortured and eventually executed.

The Münster debacle served to cast suspicions on all Anabaptists, because it was thought that the inherent doctrine would lead to immorality and social chaos. Amid a savage European persecution, the movement was refocused by the exhaustive efforts of Menno Simons, who died in 1561. Anabaptism would later arrive in America through the influence of the Mennonites.

The following sources recount the spiritual premise and struggles of this tragic radical sect. Ultimately, their fate confirmed the intolerance of the Reformation era.

On the Mystery of Baptism (1526)

HANS HUT

Now we will speak further about the baptism of rebirth, which is not an exterior sign that Christ shows, but a bath of souls that washes and rinses them clean from all lusts and desires of the heart. That is, baptism is an obliteration of all the lusts and disobedience which are in us and which incite us to oppose God. . . . The whole world . . . is baptized in the same way. But all people do not emerge from baptism alike, nor is baptism equally useful to all. The wicked certainly come to it but do not emerge again, because with their lusts they sink to the very bottom in creaturely things. They have not been able to let go of either worldly things or themselves. But they live continually and happily in lust and the love of creaturely things. . . .

So, to those who live for a renewal of their lives, baptism is not only a submersion and drowning, but a joyous departure from the wavering wishes and impulses of our own desires. We once lived hectically— for these desires and this vehemence are the conflict of the spirit—and the flesh which is in a person. In this conflict, if the desires of the flesh, the lusts, the impulses, and the attraction and repulsions are to be stilled and overcome, then the sweet waters—that is, lust and the desires of the flesh—must become, by contrast and to the same degree, acrid and bitter through the movement of divine justice that sweeps out everything. For the desires were sweet in a creaturely way—coming not from God but from the person himself, for he was inclined to them. Then the vehement conflict in one's consciousness between spirit and flesh arises. Oh, the way to life gets narrow at this point! Then the person, through the dying-out of the old man, must turn to a new life in God. And this is the rebirth in baptism. Here such fears, trembling, and shuddering attack the person as those of a woman in childbirth. When God directs such waters through one's soul, one must be patient, until he has been taught and understand. And peace from the impulses of the flesh is born on this earth. Them, in the patient waiting of his time, in the endurance of God's hand, a person becomes a prepared residence of

God. Then, just as the troubled waters become clear, the bitter sweet, and the turbulent calm, the son of God appears on the waters, stretches out his hand, pulls a person from the turbulence, and lets him se that he unlocks our darkness through his truth—that is, the flow of the living water that is concealed in us. Christ does this in order to prepare us sinful, earthly people for eternal life. The waters which rush into the soul are tribulation, affliction, fear, trembling, and worry. So baptism is suffering. So Christ was also constricted by his baptism before it was perfected in his death. True baptism is nothing but conflict with sin through one's whole life. So the waters of adversity wash from the soul all the lasciviousness and lust which defile and cling to it. . . .

Therefore, baptism has its time and goal and age, just as our first birth has its goal and time and also its age. And thus all creatures are born to their essence and perfection through water; and without baptism nothing is able to live fully and be blessed. Infant baptism, the practice of the existing world, is a pure invention of man, without the word and commandment of God. It is a defrauding of simple people, a pernicious trick on all Christendom, and an arch-villain's cloak for all the godless. For not a single verse in all of Scripture can be brought forth to defend it. Infant baptism is so totally without foundation that the godless must all remain silent about it, no matter how eloquent they wax. According to the words of Christ in the context of Scripture, no one should baptize another unless the baptized person is able, in passionate fidelity, to account for his faith and trust. If this sign of baptism is accepted, it points to the true baptism of suffering which follows, about which I have spoken and without which no one is able to be saved. But the contrived baptism of children is not only useless, it is also the greatest hindrance to truth.

"They Should Be Drowned without Mercy": Measures against Anabaptists

January 1525

There has been much erroneous discussion concerning baptism, most particularly that young children should not be baptized until they have reached an age where they understand the meaning of faith. Some have therefore neglected to baptize their children. Our Lords—the Mayors, Council and Great Council also known as The Two Hundred of Zurich—discussed the matter in with reference to Holy Scripture. They decided that, contrary to erroneous opinion, children should be baptized as soon as they are born. Therefore, all those who have neglected to baptize their children must do so within eight days. Whoever refuses must leave town together with his wife, children, and property, or await prosecution.

March 1562

For a long time, our Lords have earnestly tried to save the misguided Anabaptists from their errors. But some of them, rejecting their oaths and vows, have stubbornly defied the laws and have rejected public authority to the detriment of our Christian community. Many of them—men, women, and girls—have been harshly punished by the Lords with imprisonment. The Lords hereby order that no man, woman, or girl of this town or the surrounding area, can baptize another. Whoever does so will be arrested by our Lords and, according to this decree, drowned without mercy. Whoever defies this pronouncement will have caused his own death.

CONSIDER THIS:

12-22. The nature and process of baptism was a particularly divisive issue during the Reformation. Why? According to Hans Hut in the "Mystery of Baptism," what is the purpose of baptism and why is it important to be "patient" in the process of becoming baptized? Do his arguments seem dangerous? What measures were taken against Anabaptists and why were they so harsh?

"'They Should Be Drowned without Mercy'" is from James H. Robinson, ed., *Readings in European History*, vol. 2 (Boston: Ginn and Company, 1906), p. 180. Translation modernized by the editor.

KEY EVENTS IN THE LATE REFORMATION

1540   The Jesuit Order Formed
Ignatius Loyola, a former soldier, requests recognition of his new order by the pope. The Jesuits became a disciplined organization dedicated to serving the pope with unquestioned loyalty.

1545–1563   Council of Trent
Important council is called to clarify Catholic doctrine and bring about internal reform. Corruption rooted out and discipline restored, but doctrine emerges unchanged. Death of Martin Luther (1546).

1553–1558   Reign of Mary I of England
Daughter of Henry VIII and Catherine of Aragon, Mary restores Catholic doctrine to England. Those who will not accept change are burned at the stake, earning her the nickname "Bloody Mary."

1555   Peace of Augsburg
This agreement recognizes the rights of Lutherans to worship as they please. Principle of *cuius regio, eius religio* is established: "The ruler of a land would determine the religion of the land." Does not apply to Calvinists causing continued conflict in France.

1558–1603   Reign of Elizabeth I of England
Elizabeth fashions a moderate Anglican religious compromise settlement: The Church of England will be Catholic in ritual, but Protestant in doctrine.

1572   Saint Bartholomew's Day Massacre
3,000 Huguenots in Paris and 20,000 throughout France are killed as French Queen Catherine de' Medici tries to "balance" Catholic and Protestant influence at court.

1588   Destruction of the Spanish Armada
Spanish attempt by King Phillip II to destroy the English navy and promote Spanish control in Flanders goes terribly wrong as English ships led by Sir Francis Drake are faster and more manageable than Spanish galleons. Spanish fleet limps home and Spanish influence in Europe begins to wane.

1598   Edict of Nantes
French King Henry IV promotes a moderate policy of religious tolerance by legally recognizing the legitimacy of Calvinism. Henry will be assassinated in 1610.

1618–1648   The Thirty Years' War
Fought between Catholic and Protestant forces primarily in northern Europe. Over one third of German population dies. Peace of Westphalia (1648) ends religious wars by recognizing principle of the Peace of Augsburg (1555).

The English Reformation (1534–1603)

The Protestant Reformation has often been viewed as essentially a spiritual movement that had a fundamental political and social impact throughout Europe. But the motives of some reformers were not purely spiritual, and they sought a more expedient premise. As the Reformation spread to Switzerland, northern Germany, and Scandinavia, it met with little organized opposition. But England, it seemed, was prepared to resist any incursion. Its monarch, Henry VIII, was a gregarious and dynamic king who had grown up amid political intrigue and international power plays in the court of his father, Henry Tudor (VII). Henry VIII knew how to handle himself politically and sought to maintain domestic tranquility by promoting secure alliances abroad.

Henry VIII had himself been a pawn in his father's political accommodations. To preserve an alliance with Spain, Henry had been allowed to marry his brother's widow, Catherine of Aragon, through a special papal dispensation. For a time, this arrangement seemed to work all around. Henry VIII had proved a dutiful son of the church by writing a religious tract supporting the pope that earned him the title "Defender of the Faith." But Henry became concerned when Catherine suffered a series of miscarriages and was unable to provide a male heir to the Tudor throne. Although she bore Henry a daughter named Mary, this did not conciliate the English king. To secure the succession, he needed a male heir, so he turned to a young favorite at court named Anne Boleyn. When Henry wanted an annulment of his marriage to Catherine on the grounds that his union with his brother's widow was incestuous and accursed by God, the pope could not renege on his earlier dispensation. The pathway to a workable solution seemed closed. Henry became increasingly consumed with the need to stabilize the future of England with a male heir. He finally decided to break with Rome and found the Church of England with himself as head. He granted himself a divorce from Catherine and married Anne in 1533. He was excommunicated by the pope "with the sword of eternal damnation" that same year. Henry did not buckle. The break with the Catholic Church had its advantages. Henry confiscated all the wealth and land of the English churches, which helped him stabilize his economy and reward his supporters. Clergy who resisted his authority were executed, and England entered a difficult period of religious and political instability. The Protestant Reformation had come to England, although through political expediency rather than through spiritual commitment.

The following sources are essential in understanding the English Reformation. The first is the Act of Supremacy (1534), which recognized Henry VIII as the supreme head of the Church of England. He had already extorted from the English bishops, abbots, and priests written declaration that the pope had no more authority in England than any other foreign bishop. The next source is an excerpt from the Act of Succession (1534), which declared his marriage with Catherine void and also provided for the royal succession: Anne Boleyn's daughter, the princess Elizabeth, would succeed unless Anne should have sons by the king. Note the harsh provisions should anyone not accept the arrangement. Anne, indeed, failed to produce a son and paid for it with her life as Henry accused her of adultery and moved on to more fertile pastures. Elizabeth was then bumped down the succession ladder.

The Supremacy Act (1534): "The Only Supreme Head of the Church of England"

Albeit the king's majesty firstly and rightfully is and ought to be the supreme head of the Church of England, and so is recognized by the clergy of this realm in their Convocations . . . be it enacted by authority of this present Parliament, that the king our sovereign lord, his heirs and successors, kings of this realm, shall be taken, accepted, and reputed the only supreme head in earth of the Church of England . . . and shall have and enjoy, annexed and united to the imperial crown of this realm, as well the title and style thereof, as all honors, dignities, pre-eminences, jurisdictions, privileges, authorities, immunities, profits, and commodities to the said dignity of supreme head of the same Church; and that our said sovereign lord, his heirs and successors, kings of this realm, shall have full power and authority from time to time to visit, repress, redress, reform, order, correct, restrain, and amend all such errors, heresies, abuses, offenses, contempts, and enormities, whatsoever they be to the pleasure of Almighty God, the increase of virtue in Christ's religion, and for the conservation of the peace, unity, and tranquility of this realm. . . .

The Act of Succession (1534)

If any person or persons, of what estate, dignity, or condition whosoever they be, maliciously, by writing, print, deed, or act, procure or do any thing or things to the prejudice, slander, or derogation of the said lawful matrimony solemnized between your Majesty and the said Queen Anne, or to the peril or slander of any of the heirs of your Highness, being limited by this act to inherit the crown of this realm, every such person and persons, and their aiders and abettors, shall be adjudged high traitors, and every such offense shall be adjudged high treason, and the offenders . . . shall suffer pain of death, as in cases of high treason.

All are to be sworn truly, firmly, and constantly, without fraud or guile, to observe, fulfill, maintain, and keep . . . to the utmost of their powers, the whole effects and contents of this present act.

Good Queen Mary (1553): "Loving Subjects and Christian Charity"

Henry VIII was certainly no Protestant, although he utilized the political and economic advantages of declaring himself a Protestant. He enforced Catholic doctrine in his Church of England while rejecting the control of the pope. But after his death, his son, Edward VI (1547–1553), embraced Protestantism and issued an official Book of Common Prayer and several statutes establishing the primacy of Protestant doctrine. But upon Edward's death in 1553, Henry VIII's daughter by Catherine, Mary Tudor, became queen. She had been raised a Catholic and was married to Philip II, king of Spain. Her brutal attempts to reinstate Catholicism in England by burning heretics earned her the epithet "Bloody Mary." The following accounts offer two perspectives on her reign from 1553 to 1558.

The queen's highness well remembering what great inconvenience and dangers have grown to this her highness's realm in times past through the diversity of opinions in questions of religion, and hearing also that now of late, since the beginning of her most gracious reign, the same contentions be again much renewed,

---

"The Supremacy Act" is from *Statutes of the Realm*, vol. 3, no. 492, in Henry Gee and W. J. Hardy, eds., *Documents Illustrative of English Church History* (London: Macmillan and Co., Ltd., 1896), pp. 243–244.

"The Act of Succession" is from *Statutes of the Realm*, vol. 3, no. 471, in Henry Gee and W. J. Hardy, eds., *Documents Illustrative of English Church History* (London: Macmillan and Co., Ltd., 1896), p. 240.

"Good Queen Mary" is from Henry Gee and W. J. Hardy, eds., *Documents Illustrative of English Church History* (London: Macmillan and Co., Ltd., 1896), pp. 373–374.

through certain false and untrue reports and rumors spread by some light and evil-disposed persons, has thought good to do to understand to all her highness's most loving and obedient subjects her most gracious pleasure in manner and form following.

First, her majesty being presently by the only goodness of God settled in her just possession of the imperial crown of this realm . . . cannot now hide that religion, which God and the world know she has ever professed from her infancy; which as her majesty is minded to observe and maintain for herself by God's grace during her time, so does her highness much desire, and would be glad, the same were of all her subjects quietly and charitably embraced.

And yet she does signify unto all her majesty's loving subjects, her most gracious disposition and clemency; forbidding nevertheless all her subjects of all degrees, at their perils, to move seditions or stir unquietness in her people . . . and therefore wills and charges and commands all her said good loving subjects to live together in quiet sort and Christian charity, leaving those new-found devilish terms of papist or heretic and such like, and applying their whole care, study, and travail to live in the fear of God, exercising their conversations in such charitable and godly doing, as their lives may indeed express that great hunger and thirst of God's glory and holy word. . . .

Bloody Mary: "To Be Burned according to the Wholesome Laws of Our Realm"

Whereas John Hooper, who of late was called bishop of Rochester and Gloucester, by due order of the laws ecclesiastic, condemned and judged for a most obstinate, false, detestable heretic, and committed to our secular power, to be burned according to the wholesome and good laws of our realm in that case provided; forasmuch as in those cities, and the diocese thereof, he has in times past preached and taught most pestilent heresies and doctrine to our subjects there, we have therefore given order that the said Hooper, who yet persists obstinate, and has refused mercy when it was graciously offered, shall be put to execution in the said city of Gloucester, for the example and terror of such as he has there seduced and mistaught, and because he has done most harm there. . . .

The Enforcement of the Elizabethan Settlement (1593): "Divine Service according to Her Majesty's Laws"

After the unsettling reign of Mary Tudor, Henry VIII's daughter by Anne Boleyn came to the throne as Elizabeth I (1558–1603). A talented and diligent queen, she became one of the greatest of all English monarchs, and her reign established England as the most formidable political power of its age. Her religious solution to the struggle between Catholicism and Protestantism was a compromise: The Church of England would be Protestant in doctrine and Catholic in ritual. This "Anglican Settlement" would endure, though Catholic dissent and Protestant attempts at "purifying" or purging Catholic elements from the Church of England would not be settled for nearly two centuries. The following selection demonstrates Elizabeth's commitment to enforcing her religious compromise by demanding Catholic allegiance to the authority of the English crown. Other statutes demanding Puritan obeisance were likewise initiated.

For the better discovering and avoiding of all such traitorous and most dangerous conspiracies and attempts as are daily devised and practiced against our most gracious sovereign lady the queen's majesty and the happy estate of this commonweal, by sundry wicked and seditious persons, who, terming themselves

"Bloody Mary" is from James H. Robinson, ed., *Readings in European History*, vol. 2 (Boston: Ginn and Company, 1906), pp. 151–152.

"The Enforcement of the Elizabethan Settlement" is from *Statutes of the Realm*, vol. 4, part 2, p. 843, in Henry Gee and W. J. Hardy, eds., *Documents Illustrative of English Church History* (London: Macmillan and Co., Ltd., 1896), pp. 499, 506.

Catholics, and being indeed spies and intelligencers, not only for her majesty's foreign enemies, but also for rebellious and traitorous subjects born within her highness's realms and dominions, and hiding their most detestable and devilish purposes under a false pretext of religion and conscience, do secretly wander and shift from place to place within this realm, to corrupt and seduce her majesty's subjects, and to stir them to sedition and rebellion: Be it ordained and enacted by our sovereign lady the queen's majesty, and the Lords spiritual and temporal, and the Commons, in this present Parliament assembled, and by the authority of the same, that every person above the age of sixteen years, born within any of the queen's majesty's realms and dominions . . . shall come to some parish church on some Sunday or other festival day, and then and there hear divine service, and make public and open submission and declaration of his and their conformity to her majesty's laws and statutes. . . .

CONSIDER THIS:

12-23. Did the English Reformation involve personal conscience or political expediency? How was the religious authority of the monarch achieved?

The Catholic Reformation (1540–1565)

The Society of Jesus

During the Protestant movement, the Catholic Church was active in its own efforts to reform from within. The Society of Jesus (Jesuits) was a religious order founded by Ignatius Loyola in 1540. Loyola (1491–1556) was a soldier who had turned to religion while recovering from wounds. Under Loyola's firm leadership, the Jesuits became a disciplined organization dedicated to serving the pope with unquestioned loyalty. The next two selections, from the constitution of the society and the famous *Spiritual Exercises* of Loyola, demonstrate the purity and determination of these Catholic reformers.

Constitution of the Society of Jesus (1540)

He who desires to fight for God under the banner of the cross in our society,—which we wish to distinguish by the name of Jesus,—and to serve God alone and the Roman pontiff, his vicar on earth, after a solemn vow of perpetual chastity, shall set this thought before his mind, that he is a part of a society founded for the especial purpose of providing for the advancement of souls in Christian life and doctrine and for the propagation of faith through public preaching and the ministry of the word of God, spiritual exercises and deeds of charity, and in particular through the training of the young and ignorant in Christianity and through the spiritual consolation of the faithful of Christ in hearing confessions; and he shall take care to keep first God and next the purpose of this organization always before his eyes. . . .

All the members shall realize, and shall recall daily, as long as they live, that this society as a whole and in every part is fighting for God under faithful obedience to one most holy lord, the pope, and to other Roman pontiffs who succeed him. And although we are taught in the gospel and through the orthodox faith to recognize and steadfastly profess that all the faithful of Christ are subject to the Roman pontiff as their head and as the vicar of Jesus Christ, yet we have adjudged that, for the special promotion of greater humility in our society and the perfect mortification of every individual and the sacrifice of our own wills, we should each be bound by a peculiar vow, in addition to the general obligation, that whatever the present Roman pontiff, or any future one, may from time to time decree regarding the welfare of souls and the

"Constitution" is from James H. Robinson, ed., *Readings in European History*, vol. 1 (Boston: Ginn and Company, 1904), pp. 162–163.

propagation of the faith, we are pledged to obey without evasion or excuse, instantly, so far as in us lies, whether he send us to the Turks or any other infidels, even to those who inhabit the regions men call the Indies; whether to heretics or schismatics, or, on the other hand, to certain of the faithful.

Spiritual Exercises (1548)

IGNATIUS LOYOLA

1. Always to be ready to obey with mind and heart, setting aside all judgment of one's own, the true spouse of Jesus Christ, our holy mother our infallible and orthodox mistress, the Catholic Church, whose authority is exercised over us by the hierarchy.

2. To commend the confession of sins to a priest as it is practiced in the Church; the reception of the Holy Eucharist once a year, or better still every week, or at least every month, with the necessary preparation. . . .

4. To have a great esteem for the religious orders, and to give the preference to celibacy or virginity over the married state.

5. To approve of the religious vows of chastity, poverty, perpetual obedience, as well as the other works of perfection and supererogation. Let us remark in passing, that we must never engage by vow to take a state (such e.g. as marriage) that would be an impediment to one more perfect.

6. To praise relics, the veneration and invocation of Saints: also the stations, and pious pilgrimages, indulgences, jubilees, the custom of lighting candles in the churches, and other such aids to piety and devotion. . . .

9. To uphold especially all the precepts of the Church, and not censure them in any manner; but, on the contrary, to defend them promptly, with reasons drawn from all sources, against those who criticize them.

10. To be eager to commend the decrees, mandates, traditions, rites and conduct; although there may not always be the uprightness of conduct that there ought to be, yet to attack or revile them in private or in public tends to scandal and disorder. Such attacks set the people against their princes and pastors; we must avoid such reproaches and never attack superiors before inferiors. The best course is to make private approach to those who have power to remedy the evil.

The Way of Perfection: "Prayer Is the Mortar Which Keeps Our House Together"

SAINT TERESA OF AVILA

The Catholic Reformation was advanced by those, like Ignatius Loyola, who advocated an active and disciplined resistance to Protestantism in the world at large. Others, like Saint Teresa of Avila, worked in the relative seclusion of the cloister. Saint Teresa struggled in poverty behind convent walls to guide her nuns to a pureness of thought to achieve the "Way of Perfection." By writing her autobiography in 1565, she hoped to influence others to choose a simple life of faith and commitment to God.

You see, daughters, upon how great an enterprise we have embarked. . . . Clearly we must work hard; it is a great help to have high aspirations that may cause our actions to become great also. If we endeavor to observe our Rule and Constitutions very faithfully, I hope that God will grant our petitions. I ask you

Spiritual Exercises is from Henry Bettenson, ed., *Documents of the Christian Church*, 2nd ed. (London: Oxford University Press, 1963), pp. 364–365. Reprinted by permission of the publisher.

"The Way of Perfection" is from Saint Teresa of Avila, *The Way of Perfection*, 6th ed., ed. Father Benedict Zimmerman (Westminster: The Newman Press, 1961), pp. 20–21, 22, 24, 115–117. Reprinted by permission of TAN Books, Rockford, IL.

nothing new, my daughters, but only that we should keep what we have professed, which is our vocation and our duty, although there are very diverse ways of observing it.

The first chapter of our Rule bids us "Pray without ceasing": we must obey this with the greatest perfection possible for it is our most important duty; then we shall not neglect the fasts, penances, and silence enjoined by the Rule. As you know, these are necessary if the prayer is to be genuine; self-indulgence and prayer do not go together. Prayer is the subject of which you have asked me to speak; I beg of you, in return, to practice and to read, again and again, what I have already told you. Before speaking of interior matters, that is, of prayer, I will mention some things that must be done by those who intend to lead a life of prayer. . . .

The first of these is love for one another: the second, detachment from all created things: the third is true humility, which, though I mention it last, is chief of all and includes the rest. The first, that is, of fervent mutual charity, is most important, for there is no annoyance that cannot easily be borne by those who love one another: anything must be very out of the way to cause irritation. If this commandment were observed in this world as it ought to be, I believe it would be a great help towards obeying the others, but whether we err by excess or by defect we never succeed in keeping it perfectly.

You might think there could be no harm among us in excessive love for one another, but no one would believe what evil and imperfections spring from this source unless she had seen it herself. The devil sets many snares here which are hardly detected by those who are content to serve God in a superficial way—indeed, they take such conduct for virtue—those however who are bent on perfection understand the evil clearly, for little by little, it deprives the will of strength to devote itself entirely to the love of God. I think this injures women even more than men, and does serious damage to the community. It prevents a nun from loving all the others equally, makes her resent any injury done to her friend, causes her to wish she had something to give her favorite, to seek for opportunities to talk to her

often, to tell her how much she loves her and other nonsense of the sort, rather than of how much we should love God. These close friendships rarely serve to forward the love of God; in fact, I believe the devil originates them so as to make factions among the religious.

In order to guard against these partialities great care must be taken from the very first, and this more by watchfulness and kindness than by severity. A most useful precaution is for the nuns, according to our present habit, never to be with one another nor talk together except at the appointed times, but that, as the Rule enjoins, the sisters should not be together, but each in her own cell. Let there be no work-room in Saint Joseph's for although it is a praiseworthy custom, silence is better kept when one is alone. To accustom ourselves to solitude is a great help to prayer, and since prayer is the mortar which keeps our house together and we came here to practice it, we must learn to like what promotes it. . . .

Take my advice, and let no one mislead you by pointing out any other way than prayer. I am not discussing here whether mental and vocal prayer are necessary for everybody, but I say that you require them both. This is the work of the religious; if anyone tells you it is dangerous, look upon him as your greatest danger and shun his company. Keep my words in mind, for you may need them. A want of humility, of the virtues, may endanger you, but prayer—prayer! Never would God permit that the way of prayer should be a dangerous way! The devil must have originated these fears and so brought about, by crafty tricks, the fall of certain souls that practiced prayer. See how blind men are!

Therefore, sisters, banish these misgivings: take no notice of public opinion. This is no time to believe everything you hear. Be guided only by those who conform their lives to that of Christ; try to keep a good conscience and humility; despise all earthly things; firmly believe that teaching of our holy Mother the Church—then you may feel sure you are on the right way. Cast aside these causeless fears. If anyone tries to frighten you, humbly explain the way to him: tell him that our Rule bids us pray constantly and that you are bound to obey it.

The Council of Trent (1545–1563)

The Council of Trent was an involved effort by the Catholic Church to clarify its doctrine and bring about internal reform. The Church sought to make its own stand in the face of the Protestant threat, and thus its traditional doctrinal views are set forth with firmness and confidence, as the first excerpt indicates. The second excerpt is from the oration by Bishop Jerome Ragozonus, which was delivered during the last session of the Council of Trent and summarized its accomplishments. One of the most significant actions of Trent was the reorganization and codification of laws concerning censorship and the prohibition of books. The last selection, published after the council closed, sets out some of the restrictions. These general rules were in force until they were replaced with new decrees in 1897.

The Profession of Faith

I profess that true God is offered in the Mass, a proper and propitiatory sacrifice for the living and the dead, and that in the most Holy Eucharist there are truly, really and substantially the body and blood together with the soul and divinity of Our Lord Jesus Christ, and that a conversion is made of the whole substance of bread into his body and of the whole substance of wine into his blood, which conversion the Catholic Church calls transubstantiation. I also confess that the whole and entire Christ and the true sacrament is taken under the one species alone.

I hold unswervingly that there is a purgatory and that the souls there detained are helped by the intercessions of the faithful; likewise also that the Saints who reign with Christ are to be venerated and invoked; that they offer prayers to God for us and that their relics are to be venerated. I firmly assert that the images of Christ and of the ever-Virgin Mother of God, as also those of the older Saints, are to be kept and retained, and that due honor and veneration is to be accorded them; and I affirm that the power of indulgences has been left by Christ in the Church, and that their use is very salutary for Christian people.

I recognize the Holy Catholic and Apostolic Roman Church as the Mother and mistress of all churches; and I vow and swear true obedience to the Roman Pontiff, the successor of blessed Peter, the chief of the Apostles and the representative [vicarius] of Jesus Christ.

I accept and profess, without doubting the traditions, definitions and declarations of the sacred Canons and Ecumenical Councils and especially those of the holy Council of Trent. . . .

The Closing Oration at Trent (1563)

BISHOP JEROME RAGOZONUS

"Hear these things, all you nations; give ear all inhabitants of the world!"

The Council of Trent which was begun long ago, was for a time suspended, often postponed and dispersed, now at last through a singular favor of almighty God and with a complete and wonderful accord of all ranks and nations has come to a close. This most happy day has dawned for the Christian people; the day in which the temple of the Lord, often shattered and destroyed, is restored and completed, and this one ship, laden with every blessing and buffeted by the worst and most relentless storms and waves, is brought safely into port. Oh, that those for whose sake this voyage was chiefly undertaken had decided to board it with us; that those who caused us to take this work in hand had participated in the erection of this edifice! Then indeed

"The Profession of Faith" is from Henry Bettenson, ed., *Documents of the Christian Church*, 2nd ed. (London: Oxford University Press, 1963), pp. 364–365. Reprinted by permission of the publisher.

"The Closing Oration at Trent" is from J. Barry Colman, ed., *Readings in Church History*, rev. ed., vol. 2 (Westminster, MD: Christian Classics, Inc., 1985), pp. 699–703.

we would now have reason for greater rejoicing. But it is certainly not through our fault that it so happened.

For that reason we chose this city, situated at the entrance to Germany, situated almost at the threshold of their homes. We have, in order to give them no ground for suspicion that the place is not entirely free, employed no guard for ourselves; we granted them that public security which they requested and which they themselves had drawn up. For a long time we awaited them and never did we cease to exhort them and plead with them to come here and learn the truth. Indeed, even in their absence we were, I think, sufficiently concerned about them. In a twofold respect medicine had to be applied to their weak and infirm spirits, one, the explanation and confirmation of the teaching of the Catholic and truly evangelical faith in those matters upon which they had cast doubt and which at this time appeared opportune for the dispersion and destruction of all the darkness of errors; the other, the restoration of ecclesiastical discipline, the collapse of which they claim was the chief cause of their severance from us. We have amply accomplished both so far as the conditions of the times would permit.

At the beginning, [the Council of Trent] . . . made a profession of faith, in order to lay a foundation, as it were, for subsequent transactions and to point out by what witnesses and evidence the definition of articles of faith must be supported. . . . Through this most extraordinary decree in the memory of man, well-nigh all heresies are strangled and, as darkness before the sun, dispersed and dissipated, and the truth appears with such clearness and splendor that no one can any longer pretend not to see so great a light.

[Most esteemed fathers,] you have thereby removed from the celebration of the Mass all superstition, all greed for lucre and all irreverence; forbidden vagrant, unknown and depraved priests to offer this holy sacrifice; removed its celebration from private homes and profane places to holy and consecrated sanctuaries. You have banished from the temple of the Lord the more effeminate singing and musical compositions, promenades, conversations and business transactions; you have thus prescribed for each ecclesiastical rank such laws as leave no room for the abuse of the orders divinely conferred. You have likewise removed

some matrimonial impediments which seemed to give occasion for violating the precepts of the Church, and to those who do not enter the conjugal union legitimately, you have closed the easy way of obtaining forgiveness. And what shall I say about furtive and clandestine marriages? For myself I feel that if there had been no other reason for convoking the council, and there were many and grave reasons, this one alone would have provided sufficient ground for its convocation. For since this is a matter that concerns all, and since there is no corner of the earth which this plague has not invaded, provision had to be made by which this common evil might be remedied by common deliberation. By your clear-sighted and well-nigh divine direction, most holy fathers, the occasion for innumerable and grave excesses and crimes has been completely removed, and the government of the Christian commonwealth most wisely provided for. To this is added the exceedingly salutary and necessary prohibition of many abuses connected with purgatory, the veneration and invocation of the saints, images and relics, and also indulgences, abuses which appeared to defile and deform in no small measure the beautiful aspect of these objects.

The other part, in which was considered the restoration of the tottering and well-nigh collapsed ecclesiastical discipline, was most carefully performed and completed. In the future only those who are known for their virtues, not for their ambition, who will serve the interests of the people, not their own, and who desire to be useful rather than invested with authority, will be chosen for the discharge of ecclesiastical offices. The word of God, which is more penetrating than any two-edged sword, will be more frequently and more zealously preached and explained.

The bishops and others to whom the *cura animarum* [care of the soul] has been committed, will remain with and watch over their flocks and not wander about outside the districts entrusted to them. Privileges will no longer avail anyone for an impure and wicked life or for evil and pernicious teaching; no crime will go unpunished, no virtue will be without its reward. The multitude of poor and mendicant priests have been very well provided for; everyone will be assigned to a definite church and to a prescribed field of labor whence he may obtain sustenance.

Avarice, than which there is no vice more hideous, especially in the house of God, will be absolutely banished therefrom, and the sacraments, as is proper, will be dispensed gratuitously. From one Church many will be established and from many One, according as the welfare of the people and circumstances demand. Questors of alms, as they are called, who seeking their own and not the things of Jesus Christ, have brought great injury, great dishonor upon our religion, will be completely removed from the memory of men, which must be regarded as a very great blessing. For from this our present calamity took its beginning; from it an endless evil did not cease to creep in by degrees and daily take a wider course, nor have precautionary and disciplinary measures of many councils thus far been able to suppress it. Wherefore, who will not agree that for this reason it was a very prudent undertaking to cut off this member, on whose restoration to health much labor had been vainly spent, lest it corrupt the remainder of the body?

Moreover, divine worship will be discharged more purely and promptly, and those who carry the vessels of the Lord will be so chastened that they will move others to follow their example. In connection with this point plans were skillfully devised whereby those who are to be promoted to sacred orders might in every church be from their youth up instructed in the habits of Christian life and knowledge, so that in this way a sort of seminary of all virtues might be established. In addition, . . . visitations [were] reintroduced for the welfare of the people, not for the disturbance and oppression of them; greater faculties granted to the pastors for guiding and feeding their flocks; . . . plurality of benefices abolished; the hereditary possession of the sanctuary of God prohibited; excommunication restricted and the manner of its imposition determined; . . . a sort of bridle put on the luxury, greed and licentiousness of all people, particularly the clergy, which cannot be easily shaken off; kings and princes diligently reminded of their duties, and other things of a similar nature were enacted with the greatest discernment. . . .

Let [the Protestant Reformers] read with humility, as becomes a Christian, what we have defined concerning our faith, and if some light should come upon them, let them not harden their hearts, and if they should wish to return to the common embrace of mother Church from which they severed themselves, they may rest assured that every indulgence and sympathy will be extended to them. . . .

CONSIDER THIS:

12-24. Read carefully the selections on the Society of Jesus and the Council of Trent. What specifically do Loyola and the Council of Trent demand from the Catholic faithful? How did Saint Teresa of Avila's approach differ? Does the closing oration at the Council of Trent seem to be progressive in its message? Why then does the Tridentine Index of Books seem so repressive (see the following section)? Can faith be enforced in this manner?

THE BROADER PERSPECTIVE:

12-25. Some historians have called the Catholic reform movement the "Counter Reformation." Do you think a reformation of the church would have occurred without Martin Luther? How important was Luther in changing history?

The Tridentine Index of Books (1564)

The holy council in the second session, celebrated under our most holy Lord, Pius IV, commissioned some fathers to consider what ought to be done concerning various censures and books either suspected or pernicious and to report to this holy council. . . .

1. All books which have been condemned either by the supreme pontiffs or by ecumenical councils before the year 1515 and are not contained in this list, shall be considered condemned in the same manner as they were formerly condemned.

"The Tridentine Index of Books" is from J. Barry Colman, ed., *Readings in Church History*, rev. ed., vol. 2 (Westminster, MD: Christian Classics, Inc., 1985), pp. 705–706, 708.

2. The books of those heresiarchs, who after the aforesaid year originated or revived heresies, as well as those who are or have been the heads or leaders of heretics, as Luther, Zwingli, Calvin, Balthasar Friedberg, Schwenkfeld, and others like these, whatever may be their name, title or nature or their heresy, are absolutely forbidden. The books of other heretics, moreover, which deal professedly with religion are absolutely condemned. Those on the other hand, which do not deal with religion and have by order of the bishops and inquisitors been examined by Catholic theologians and approved by them, are permitted. Likewise, Catholic books written by those who afterward fell into heresy, as well as by those who after their fall returned to the bosom of the Church, may be permitted if they have been approved by the theological faculty of a Catholic university or by the general inquisition.

3. The translations of writers, also ecclesiastical, which have till now been edited by condemned authors, are permitted provided they contain nothing contrary to sound doctrine. Translations of the books of the Old Testament may in the judgment of the bishop be permitted to learned and pious men only. . . . Translations of the New Testament made by authors of the first class of this list shall be permitted to no one, since great danger and little usefulness usually results to readers from their perusal. . . .

4. Since it is clear from experience that if the Sacred Books are permitted everywhere and without discrimination in the vernacular, there will by reason of the boldness of men arise therefrom more harm than good, the matter is in this respect left to the judgment of the bishop or inquisitor, who may with the advice of the pastor or confessor permit the reading of the Sacred Books translated into the vernacular by Catholic authors to those who they know will derive from such reading no harm but rather an increase of faith and piety, which permission they must have in writing. Those, however, who presume to read or possess them without such permission may not receive absolution from their sins until they have handed them over to the authorities. . . .

5. Those books which sometimes produce the works of heretical authors, in which these add little or nothing of their own but rather collect therein the sayings of others, as lexicons, concordances, apothegms, parables, tables of contents and such like, are permitted if whatever needs to be eliminated in the additions is removed and corrected in accordance with the suggestions of the bishop, the inquisitor and Catholic theologians. . . .

7. Books which professedly deal with, narrate, or teach things lascivious or obscene are absolutely prohibited, since not only the matter of faith but also that of morals, which are usually easily corrupted through the reading of such books, must be taken into consideration, and those who possess them are to be severely punished by the bishops. Ancient books written by heathens may by reason of their elegance and quality of style be permitted, but may by no means be read to children.

8. Books whose chief contents are good but in which things have incidentally been inserted which have reference to heresy, ungodliness, divination or superstition, may be permitted if by the authority of the general inquisition they have been purged by Catholic theologians. . . .

Finally, all the faithful are commanded not to presume to read or possess any books contrary to the prescriptions of these rules or the prohibition of this list. And if anyone should read or possess books by heretics or writings by any author condemned and prohibited by reason of heresy or suspicion of false teaching, he incurs immediately the sentence of excommunication. . . .

Consider This:

12-26. A critical issue of the Reformation era centered on the diverse means of attaining salvation. How is this issue reflected in the sources? According to Luther, Calvin, Loyola, and the Catholic Church, how is one saved? Be specific in your documentation.

12-27. One of the most important questions of this period that separated the reformers from the church centered on religious authority. In spiritual matters, did religious authority rest in the church (as dictated by the pope), in church councils (such as Trent), in scripture, or in individual conscience? How is this problem reflected in the sources?

Resolution: The Bloody Wars of Religion (1562–1648)

The Saint Bartholomew's Day Massacre (1572):
"A Thousand Times More Terrible than Death Itself"

THE DUKE OF SULLY

It is important to note that Calvinism was not recognized as a legal and therefore protected form of Christianity by the Peace of Augsburg in 1555. After the Council of Trent in 1563, Catholic forces, led by Jesuit-inspired activists, began an offensive against equally dogmatic and aggressive Calvinists, who were determined to secure full religious toleration. The wars of religion that followed were both internal conflicts and international struggles that engaged virtually every major European nation from the 1560s until the resolution of the Thirty Years' War in 1648.

The first selection is an eyewitness account of the Saint Bartholomew's Day Massacre in 1572. Catherine de' Medici, as French regent for her son Charles IX, sought to maintain a precarious balance between Protestant and Catholic influences within her court. When it appeared that the scale was tilting in favor of the Protestants and her position might be threatened, she convinced Charles that a Huguenot plot against the monarchy was afoot.

On the eve of Saint Bartholomew's Day in 1572, 3,000 Huguenots were butchered in Paris and over 20,000 died throughout France during the ensuing three-day massacre. After this, Protestant leaders became convinced that an international struggle to the death must be pursued against a brutal Catholic foe. The Duke of Sully (1560–1641), who later became ambassador and finance minister to King Henry IV and architect of the Edict of Nantes, was only twelve when he viewed the massacre firsthand—but he never forgot it.

If I were inclined to increase the general horror inspired by an action so barbarous as that perpetrated on the 24th of August, 1572, and too well known by the name of the *massacre of St. Bartholomew*, I should in this place enlarge upon the number, the rank, the virtues, and great talents of those who were inhumanly murdered on that horrible day, as well in Paris as in every other part of the kingdom; I should mention at least the ignominious treatment, the fiend-like cruelty, and savage insults these miserable victims suffered from their butchers, whose conduct was a thousand times more terrible than death itself.

I have writings still in my hands which would confirm the report, of the court of France having made the most pressing solicitations to the courts of England and Germany, to the Swiss and the Genoese, to refuse an asylum to those Huguenots who might fly from France; but I prefer the honor of the nation to the satisfying of a malignant pleasure. . . .

Intending on that day to wait upon the king my master [Henry of Navarre, who became King Henry IV of France], I went to bed early on the preceding evening; about three in the morning I was awakened by the cries of people, and the alarm-bells, which were everywhere ringing. . . . I was determined to escape to the College de Bourgogne, and to effect this I put on my scholar's gown, and taking a book under my arm, I set out. In the streets I met three parties of the Lifeguards; the first of these, after handling me very roughly, seized my book, and, most fortunately for me, seeing it was a Roman Catholic prayer-book, suffered me to proceed, and this served me as a passport with the two other parties. As I went along I saw the houses broken open and plundered, and men, women, and children butchered, while a constant cry was kept up of, "Kill! Kill! O you Huguenots! O you Huguenots!" This made me very impatient to gain the college, where, through God's assistance, I at length arrived, without suffering any other injury than a most dreadful fright.

"The Saint Bartholomew's Day Massacre" is from Bayle St. John, ed., *Memoirs of the Duke of Sully*, vol. 1 (London: George Bell and Sons, 1877), pp. 85–87.

The Edict of Nantes (1598)

Henry IV of France came to the throne in 1589, weary of war and religious turmoil. He was a *politique*, who believed that political accommodation and stability could only be obtained through religious toleration. Accordingly, one of his most important acts of reconciliation was the Edict of Nantes, which assured Huguenots of at least partial religious freedom within an officially Catholic France. This truce produced a cold war of sorts between religious factions within France. But the hot war continued throughout northern Europe from 1614 to 1648. This Thirty Years' War, which reflected the hatred and distrust between Protestants and Catholics, was perhaps the worst European catastrophe since the Black Death of the fourteenth century. But at its conclusion, with the Treaty of Westphalia, the Calvinists obtained their long-sought recognition.

We ordain that the Catholic, Apostolic, and Roman faith be restored and re-established in all those districts and places of this our Realm . . . in which its exercise has been interrupted, there to be freely and peaceably exercised. . . .

And to leave no occasion for trouble or difference among our subjects: We permit those of the so-called Reformed Religion to live and abide in all the towns and districts of this our Realm . . . free from inquisition, molestation or compulsion to do anything in the way of Religion, against their conscience . . . provided that they observe the provisions of this Edict. . . .

We also permit those of the aforesaid Religion to practice it in all the town and districts of our dominion, in which it had been established and publicly observed by them on several distinct occasions during the year 1596 and the year 1597 up to the end of August, all decrees and judgments to the contrary notwithstanding.

We most expressly forbid to those of this religion the practice thereof, in respect of ministry, organization, discipline or the public instruction of children, or in any respect, in our realm and dominion, save in the places permitted and granted by this edict.

The practice of this religion is forbidden in our court and suite, in our domains beyond the mountains, in our city of Paris, or within five leagues thereof.

CONSIDER THIS:

12-28. Intolerance is a primary theme during the Reformation era. How was it reflected in the primary sources? Pay particular attention to the Anabaptist episode and the Saint Bartholomew's Day Massacre. To what extent was the Edict of Nantes a progressive vehicle for tolerance?

Chapter 13

"An Embarrassment of Riches": The Interaction of New Worlds

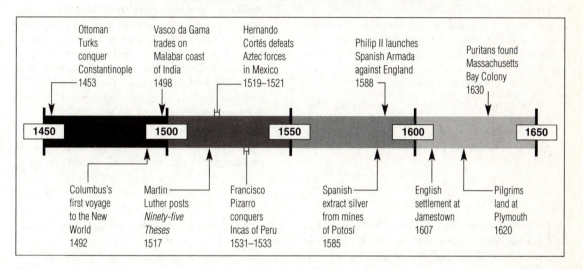

Ottoman Turks conquer Constantinople 1453

Vasco da Gama trades on Malabar coast of India 1498

Hernando Cortés defeats Aztec forces in Mexico 1519–1521

Philip II launches Spanish Armada against England 1588

Puritans found Massachusetts Bay Colony 1630

| 1450 | 1500 | 1550 | 1600 | 1650 |

Columbus's first voyage to the New World 1492

Martin Luther posts *Ninety-five Theses* 1517

Francisco Pizarro conquers Incas of Peru 1531–1533

Spanish extract silver from mines of Potosí 1585

English settlement at Jamestown 1607

Pilgrims land at Plymouth 1620

They are poor discoverers who think that there is no land when they see nothing but sea.

—SIR FRANCIS BACON

Discovery! To know that you are walking where no others have walked; that you are beholding what the human eye has not seen before; to give birth to an idea, to discover a great thought. To be the first—that is the idea!

—MARK TWAIN

The destiny of nations depends on how they nourish themselves.

—JEAN ANTHELME BRILLAT-SAVARIN

It should be noted that when he seizes a state, the new ruler ought to determine the injuries that he will need to inflict. He should then inflict them all at once, and not have to renew them everyday.

—NICCOLÒ MACHIAVELLI

The use of force is but temporary. It may subdue for a moment; but it does not remove the necessity of subduing again— and a nation is not governed, which is perpetually to be conquered.

—EDMUND BURKE

Small pox was the captain of the men of death . . . in that war, typhus fever the first lieutenant, and measles the second lieutenant. More terrible than the conquistadores on horseback, more deadly than the sword and gunpowder, they made the conquest [of the Americas] . . . a walkover as compared with what it would have been without their aid. They were the forerunners of civilization, the companions of Christianity, the friends of the invader.

—P. M. ASHBURN

CHAPTER THEMES

- **The Power Structure:** How did political and economic rivalry among European powers provide motives for exploration and conquest? How did the centralization of absolute monarchies and mercantile economies contribute to the maintenance of empire and the development of a restrictive colonial policy?

- **Imperialism:** Why did Europeans conquer and settle lands in the new worlds of America, Africa, and Asia? Why were they particularly successful in suppressing natives? How important is technology as a factor in progress and destruction? Is imperialism a process that inherently carries the seeds of genocide?

- **The Varieties of Truth:** How did Europeans justify their exploitation of the Americas? To justify conquest or genocide, must the conquered be methodically dehumanized? How has this process been repeated throughout history?

- **The Institution and the Individual:** What role did the Catholic Church and Protestant religious exiles play in the settlement of the Americas? Are missionary motives simply another justification for conquest? Or did religious representatives work for accommodation and coexistence? Were they a positive force in the settlement of the Americas?

- **Revolution and Historical Transition:** What impact did the European exploration and conquest of the Americas have on the cultures of both regions? What are some of the "seeds of change" that ultimately linked these continents? Is the interaction between cultures both a beneficial and dangerous process? In our modern world, can a culture be truly homogeneous? What are the challenges of cultural integration and diversity?

- **The Big Picture:** Must exploration always result in exploitation? How have the European and American worlds been changed through "first contact" over 500 years ago?

"In 1492, Columbus sailed the ocean blue." Often our childhood education is linked to simple expressive phrases that encapsulate important events or ideas adults think are worth remembering. This rhyme does little beyond connecting an event with a date, but the ramifications of Columbus's voyages are vast indeed, for they changed the course of world history. The cultures of Europe and America each existed in old worlds with established societies, religions, and political organizations. Columbus's first contact with Native Americans in the Bahamas began a process of interaction and development that transformed each hemisphere and created a New World where cultures were blended, products exchanged, and societies redefined. This is a story of the transfer of plants and animals that affected the nutrition and movement of peoples, and it is a tragic saga of the decimation of whole Indian populations, the enslavement of African peoples, and the destruction of natural ecosystems. It is difficult to simplify in a phrase what was a complex human drama.

Since the Renaissance, European contact with the rest of the world has gone through distinct phases. The first stage, which ended by the seventeenth century, was one of exploration, conquest, and consolidation of territory in recently "discovered" lands. The second phase during the seventeenth and eighteenth centuries was characterized by the colonial trade rivalry among England, France, Spain, and the Netherlands. The third stage of European contact with the rest of the world occurred in the nineteenth century and saw the establishment of European empires in Africa, India, and Asia. These empires disintegrated in the final stage after 1945 as Britain, France, and Germany, reduced by the destruction of World Wars I and II, retreated from control of their empires and acknowledged the sovereign legitimacy of indigenous governments. This chapter focuses on the first two stages.

There is perhaps no more important or tragic example of the debilitative effects of imperialism than the European domination of the Americas. We often regard the concept of exploration as a positive venture: Europeans took a courageous and imaginative step when Columbus, following the thirteenth-century accounts of Marco Polo, set out to find Chipangu, an outer island of Japan. But exploration was only a means to an end, because Portuguese and Spanish explorers were motivated by the lure of wealth, the spice trade in India, the gold and silver in the Americas, and the slaves of Africa. After Hernando Cortés and Francisco Pizarro conquered, respectively, the Aztecs in 1519 and the

Incas in 1531, the door lay open for the European domination of a continent. Spanish conquistadores, French trappers, Dutch traders, and English religious refugees all sought to establish themselves on territory that was already occupied by indigenous peoples. Europeans ravaged their land, mocked their gods, banished their languages, decimated their populations through disease, and subjugated their children to a subservient and dependent status that is still in evidence today.

This dominance was certainly disproportionate to the geographic size or population of Europe. Although European apologists would concoct theories that explained and justified the domination of supposedly inferior races, their conquest was not the result of racial superiority but of technological supremacy. Gunpowder and naval power proved to be the decisive forces in the eradication of Native American cultures.

The contact between Europeans and American natives also changed the nature of both cultures. Europeans introduced horses, cows, pigs, wheat, barley, and sugar cane to the Americas. Horses alone proved instrumental in extending the horizons and altering the way of life for Indian tribes on the North American plains. Sugarcane has often been seen as the most detrimental contribution of the European world, because the human craving for sweetness resulted in the defoliation of the tropical environment for the establishment of cane plantations and in the methodical integration of slavery into the economies and societies of Africa and the Americas.

American crops such as maize took root in Africa and contributed to better nutrition and a greater population that perhaps promoted the slave trade itself. Likewise, the American potato was introduced to Europe and became the dominant food staple in Ireland. When the potato blight hit that country in 1854, the result was starvation and a new migration of Irish to America.

This interactive relationship might best be noted in the specter of disease. Although the controversy continues about what diseases were introduced by outsiders into the Americas, it is generally held that smallpox, cholera, measles, diphtheria, typhoid fever, some strains of influenza, and the plague came from Europe and Africa. The effect of these diseases on American populations without previous exposure or immunity was devastating. Indian populations may have declined by 75 percent.

The influx of spices into Europe from the Malabar coasts of India and the precious metals delivered by the Spanish treasure fleets from the Americas proved to be a mixed blessing for the economy of Europe. The increase in gold and silver bullion certainly paid for innovations in printing, shipping, mining, textile manufacturing, and weapons development. The influx of bullion alone allowed Spain to launch its powerful naval Armada against England in 1588, France to develop its silk industry, and all of Europe to gorge on the bloody seventeenth-century wars of religion. It also contributed to serious inflation that saw prices doubling in Spain by 1600 and the cost of food and clothing doubling in Germany by 1540.

By the eighteenth century, European trade rivalries for the products and labor of the Americas intensified. European empires existed to enrich the coffers of government and the pockets of the commercial elite. The Americas also provided new opportunities for Europe's disaffected and dispossessed, and a pressure valve for the home government that drained excess population from competitive domestic economies.

The competition between the French and British in Canada, on the North Atlantic seaboard, and along the Saint Lawrence and Mississippi rivers was particularly vicious as Indians and colonists alike fought in bitter rivalry. Although its supremacy on the west coast of North America and in much of South America was secure during the eighteenth century, Spain competed with both France and England for the lucrative sugar trade in the Caribbean. The lesson was clear: National prosperity was directly linked to the protection of foreign trade and the efficient management of overseas empires.

The regulation of these empires in the seventeenth and eighteenth centuries was managed through an informal economic system called *mercantilism*. Mercantilist businessmen believed that the world contained a very limited amount of natural resources and that each country was in dire competition with the others for access to them. A country could only call itself wealthy if it could amass more bullion, grow more crops, and manufacture more goods than any other. The economic well-being of a country was therefore directly tied to the vitality of its colonies and the ability of each nation to control its colonial markets. Laws regulated just what goods colonists could produce and in what quantity. Colonists had to purchase certain raw materials and finished products from Europe, and all colonial goods had to be transported by ships from the mother country. National monopoly was the prime directive.

But mercantilism was an inherently awkward economic system. Ultimately, the home and colonial markets did not mesh, and the colonial governments, especially in America, chafed at the restrictions and grew restive. And there were new economic theories on the horizon. In 1776, Adam Smith in his treatise *The Wealth of Nations* envisioned a world of limitless resources, where the only restrictions were tied to ability and ambition: Capitalism was born.

This chapter explores the political, social, economic, and cultural interactions between different worlds in conflict during the sixteenth through eighteenth centuries. This is not a simple story to be summed up in a cute phrase. History reflects the complexity of human environments and as such is necessarily interactive. This is a bloody tale of the European encounter with the new worlds of Africa, Asia, and America. It is a story of greed, destruction, and ultimately of cultural awareness that affords perspective and presents new possibilities for the progress of world civilization.

KEY EVENTS IN THE AGE OF EXPLORATION

1394–1468   Reign of Portuguese Prince Henry the Navigator
He organized and sanctioned Portuguese exploration of the coasts of Africa and India.

1487–1500   Early Voyages of Exploration
Bartholomew Dias opens spice routes to the East (1487). Columbus's first voyage to the eastern Bahamas in search of a route to India (1492) supported by Ferdinand and Isabella of Spain. Vasco da Gama trades on Malabar coast of India (1498).

1503–1513   Papacy of Julius II
"Warrior Pope" and patron of the arts, Julius commissions Michelangelo's painting of the Sistine Chapel and begins construction of Saint Peter's Basilica.

1517   Protestant Reformation Begins
Martin Luther posts *Ninety-Five Theses* on Wittenberg church door in hopes of engaging clerical authorities in debate.

1519–1600   The Creation of New Spain
Hernando Cortés lands on the coast of Mexico and brutally defeats Aztec forces (1519–1521). Francisco Pizarro conquers Incas in Peru (1531–1533). Silver mines of Potosi, Bolivia, bring extraordinary wealth to Spain (1585). King Philip II launches Spanish Armada against England (1588).

1526   Afonso I, King of Kongo
He writes to Portuguese King Joao III requesting him to condemn slavery. The answer is no.

1585–1630   English Colonization
Colonization of North America proposed to Elizabeth I (1558–1603) by Richard Hakluyt and Sir Walter Raleigh (1585). English settlement of Jamestown (1607). Pilgrims (Separatists) seeking religious freedom land at Plymouth (1620). Puritans establish Massachusetts Bay Colony near Boston (1628–1630).

1600–1680   French and Dutch Colonization
Samuel de Champlain founds Quebec (1608), and Dutch colony of New Netherland established (1624). Jacques Marquette and Louis Joliet explore the Mississippi River (1673).

1754–1763   French and Indian War in America
Called the Seven Years War in Europe. France loses North American empire to Great Britain.

1769   The Settlement of California
Father Junipero Serra begins establishment of California missions on the El Camino Real (The King's Highway) from San Diego north beyond San Francisco.

1776   Adam Smith Publishes *The Wealth of Nations*
The theory of capitalism first expounded and will replace mercantilism as the dominant economic philosophy.

Domination and Destruction

The Ottoman Empire of Turkey

The Ottomans were a Turkish dynasty founded by Osman in about 1280. He led a core of rugged frontier warriors from Asia Minor and fought Christians in the region in about 1291. Within a hundred years, Ottoman control extended from the Danube River east to the Upper Euphrates. Despite a significant defeat at the hands of the Mongol warrior Tamerlane in 1402, which truly shattered the confidence of the Ottoman state, it was restored by the will and efficiency of Mehmed II, who came to power in 1451 and captured the great city of Constantinople in 1453. Under Selim I (1512–1520) and Süleyman "The Lawgiver" (1520–1566), the Ottoman state was established as a major Asian and European power as it annexed North Africa, Egypt, and Syria, as well as Iraq, Kurdistan, and Georgia in the Caucasus. The Ottomans nearly took Vienna by siege in 1526–1529 and controlled virtually all of Hungary by 1540. At this time, no other world power, with the possible exception of China, could match Ottoman strength. The Ottoman state was organized as one great military institution with a discipline and administrative infrastructure that was most impressive, and maintained its influence for centuries before a long decline commenced in the late seventeenth century.

Süleyman "The Lawgiver" and the Advantages of Islam

OGIER DE BUSBECQ

The energy of the Ottoman Empire perhaps reached its zenith under the direction of Sultan Süleyman "the Lawgiver" (1520–1566). One of the most important assessments of Süleyman's influence came from Ogier Ghiselin de Busbecq, the ambassador from Austria to Süleyman's court at Istanbul from 1554 to 1562. Busbecq had been dispatched in the recent wake of the unsuccessful Ottoman siege of Vienna in 1529. His mission was to use his diplomatic skills to prevent another possible attack on the city. Busbecq's letters reveal much about Süleyman, his court, his capital, Islamic traditions, and the treatment of women.

"Süleyman 'the Lawgiver'" is from C. T. Foster and F. H. Blackburne Daniell, *The Life and Letters of Ogier Ghiselin de Busbecq*, vol. 1 (London: Hakluyt Society, 1881), pp. 152–156.

The Sultan [Süleyman "The Lawgiver"] was seated on a very low ottoman, not more than a foot from the ground, which was covered with a quantity of costly rugs and cushions of exquisite workmanship; near him lay his bow and arrows. . . . The Sultan then listened to what I had to say; but the language I used was not at all to his taste, for the demands of his Majesty breathed a spirit of independence and dignity, which was by no means acceptable to one who deemed that his wish was law; and so he made no answer beyond saying in an impatient way, "Giusel, giusel," that is, "well, well". After this we were dismissed to our quarters.

The Sultan's hall was crowded with people, among whom were several officers of high rank. Besides these, there were all the troopers of the Imperial guard, and a large force of Janissaries [the elite infantry corps], but there was not in all that great assembly a single man who owed his position to anything save his valor and his merit. No distinction is attached to birth among the Turks; the respect to be paid to a man is measured by the position he holds in the public service. There is no fighting for precedence; a man's place is marked out by the duties he discharges. . . . It is by merit that men rise in the service, a system which ensures that posts should only be assigned to the competent. Each man in Turkey carries in his own hand his ancestry and his position in life, which he may make or mar as he will. Those who receive the highest offices from the Sultan are for the most part the sons of shepherds or herdsmen, and so far from being ashamed of their parentage, they actually glory in it, and consider it a matter of boasting that they owe nothing to the accident of birth; for they do not believe that high qualities are either natural or hereditary, nor do they think that they can be handed down from father to son, but that they are partly the gift of God, and partly the result of good training, great industry, and unwearied zeal; arguing that high qualities do not descend from a father to his son or heir, any more than a talent for music, mathematics, or the like. . . . Among the Turks, therefore, honors, high posts, and judgeships are the rewards of great ability and good service. If a man is dishonest, or lazy, or careless, he remains at the bottom of the ladder,

an object of contempt; for such qualities there are no honors in Turkey!

This is the reason that they are successful in their undertakings, that they lord it over others, and are daily extending the bounds of their empire. These are not our ideas, with us there is no opening left for merit; birth is the standard for everything; the prestige of birth is the sole key to advancement in the public service.

The Turkish monarch going to war takes with him over 40,000 camels and nearly as many baggage mules, of which a great part, when he is invading Persia, are loaded with rice and other kinds of grain. These mules and camels also serve to carry tents and armor, and likewise tools and munitions for the campaign. . . . The invading army carefully abstains from encroaching on its supplies at the outset, as they are well aware that, when the season for campaigning draws to a close, they will have to retreat over districts wasted by the enemy, or scraped as bare by countless hordes of men and droves of baggage animals, as if they had been devastated by locusts; accordingly they reserve their stores as much as possible for this emergency. . . .

From this you will see that it is the patience, self denial, and thrift of the Turkish soldier that enable him to face the most trying circumstances, and come safely out of the dangers that surround him. What a contrast to our men! . . .

For each man is his own worst enemy, and has no foe more deadly than his own intemperance, which is sure to kill him, if the enemy be not quick. It makes me shudder to think of what the result of a struggle between such different systems must be; one of us must prevail and the other be destroyed, at any rate we cannot both exist in safety. On their side is the vast wealth of their empire, unimpaired resources, experience and practice in arms, a veteran soldiery, an uninterrupted series of victories, readiness to endure hardships, union, order, discipline, thrift, and watchfulness. On ours are found an empty exchequer, luxurious habits, exhausted resources, broken spirits, a raw and insubordinate soldiery, and greedy generals; there is no regard for discipline, license runs riot, the men indulge in drunkenness and debauchery, and, worst of all, the enemy are accustomed to victory, we, to defeat. Can we doubt what the result must be?

CONSIDER THIS:

13-1. What are the most important qualities for success and advancement in the Ottoman Empire?

13-2. Busbecq maintained that between Christians and Muslims, "one of us must prevail and the other be destroyed." Why did he think Christian nations were at a disadvantage? By painting such a picture, was Busbecq hoping to frighten European nations into reform?

Women in Ottoman Society

OGIER DE BUSBECQ

The Turks are the most careful people in the world of the modesty of their wives, and therefore keep them shut up at home and hide them away, so that they scarce see the light of day. But if they have to go into the streets, they are sent out so covered and wrapped up in veils that they seem to those who meet them mere gliding ghosts. They have the means of seeing men through their linen or silken veils, while no part of their own body is exposed to men's view. For it is a received opinion among them, that no woman who is distinguished in the very smallest degree by her figure or youth, can be seen by a man without his desiring her, and therefore without her receiving some contamination; and so it is the universal practice to confine the women to the harem. Their brothers are allowed to see them, but not their brothers-in-law. Men of the richer classes, or of higher rank, make it a condition when they marry, that their wives shall never set foot outside the threshold, and that no man or woman shall be admitted to see them for any reason whatever, not even their nearest relations, except their fathers and mothers, who are allowed to pay a visit to their daughters at the [festival of Bairam].

On the other hand, if the wife has a rather high rank, or has brought a larger dowry than usual, the husband promises on his part that he will take no concubine, but will keep to her alone. Otherwise, the Turks are not forbidden by any law to have as many concubines as they please in addition to their lawful wives. Between the children of wives and those of concubines there is no distinction, and they are considered to have equal rights. As for concubines, they either buy them for themselves or win them in war; when they are tired of them there is nothing to prevent their bringing them to market and selling them; but they are entitled to their freedom if they have borne children to their master. . . . The only distinction between the lawful wife and the concubine is that the former has a dowry, while the slaves have none. A wife who has a portion settled on her [a dowry] is mistress of her husband's house, and all the other women have to obey her orders. The husband, however, may choose which of them shall spend the night with him. He makes known his wishes to the wife, and she sends to him the slave he has selected. . . . Only Friday night . . . is supposed to belong to the wife; and she grumbles if her husband deprives her of it. On all the other nights he may do so as he pleases.

Divorces are granted among them for many reasons which it is easy for the husbands to invent. The divorced wife receives back her dowry, unless the divorce has been caused by some fault on her part. There is more difficulty in a woman's getting a divorce from her husband.

CONSIDER THIS:

13-3. What was the role of women in Ottoman society?

13-4. Why were women completely covered in Ottoman society? What were the expectations for women at this time, and what distinctions were made between wives and concubines?

"Women in Ottoman Society" is from C. T. Foster and F. H. Blackburne Daniell, *The Life and Letters of Ogier Ghiselin de Busbecq*, vol. 1 (London: Hakluyt Society, 1881), pp. 219–221.

The Spanish Conquest of Mexico

A primary area of historical controversy and dissension in the twenty-first century concerns the Spanish conquest of Mexico and Peru and the subsequent administration of Spanish domains in the Western Hemisphere collectively called "New Spain." The role of the Spanish explorers and conquistadors as agents of destruction or purveyors of progress has been hotly disputed in recent years. Subsidized by Spanish royalty, explorers such as Hernando Cortés and Francisco Pizarro landed in Mexico (1519) and Peru (1531), respectively, with lofty dreams and visions of enormous wealth to be extracted from the inhabitants of this mythic land. The Spanish monarchy itself sought the wealth and geopolitical advantage that such a presence in the New World could bring; the church saw an opportunity to spread the Christian faith to new lands without the stifling competition and dissension that the Protestant Reformation had engendered in Europe.

But it is dangerous to narrow the perspective, and the Spanish presence in New Spain surely combined national interest, religious zealotry, and personal greed. This was an encounter of unparalleled importance, and in the process of consolidating their claims, the Spanish destruction of native peoples and their cultures reflected a European arrogance and confirmation of the Machiavellian principle that the "ends justify the means." Indeed, the Catholic Church had difficulty tolerating the exploitation of the native populations it was trying to convert. A "Black Legend" of Spanish abuse and butchery soon developed and, through the propaganda of Anglo-Dutch rivals, colored the Spanish national profile for centuries. This encounter between forces of the Old and New Worlds inaugurated centuries of exploitation and rigid consolidation that set precedents for slaughter and fueled competition among European powers.

The first source describes the initial encounter of the Aztecs with the Spanish explorers in 1519. The Franciscan friar Bernardino de Sahagún was instrumental in preserving information about Aztec culture and the history of this period. His intention was to understand native culture and religious beliefs to more effectively convert the Indians to Christianity. His *General History of the Things of New Spain* was based on information gained from Aztec eyewitnesses and surviving participants of the conquest of Mexico from 1519 to 1521.

The succeeding sources are excerpted from letters by Mexico's Spanish conqueror, Hernando Cortés. They lend a valuable perspective to the motives and methods of Spanish conquest in the New World.

The Aztec Encounter: "This Was Quetzalcoatl Who Had Come to Land"

BERNARDINO DE SAHAGÚN

When the first Spanish ships were seen in this land, Montezuma's stewards and captains who lived along the coast of Veracruz immediately assembled and took counsel among themselves, deciding whether they should give this news to their lord Montezuma, who was in the city of Mexico. The chief among them said, "In order for us to take an accurate report of this matter, it seems to me proper that we should see with our own eyes what this is; this we can do if we go to them on the pretext of selling them some things that they have need of." This seemed like a good idea to the others, and at once they took articles of food and clothing, and loaded into canoes what they were going to sell them and went to them by water. When they arrived at the flagship (to which they directed their canoes because of the banner they saw on it), immediately upon arriving they paid homage and gave signs that they came in peace to sell them food and clothing. [It was thought that this was Quetzalcoatl who had come to land.] The Spaniards asked them where they were from and what they came for. They said, "We are Mexicans." The Spaniards said, "If you are Mexicans, tell us who the lord of Mexico is."

The Indians said, "Gentlemen, the lord of Mexico is called Montezuma." Then the Spaniards answered, "Well, come and sell us some things that we need; climb up here and we shall look at them. Have no fear that we shall do you harm." Then [the Indians] climbed into the ship and took with them certain bundles of rich [capes] that they had brought.

They spread them out in front of the Spaniards, who liked them and agreed to buy them, for which they gave the Indians strings of fake precious stones, some red, others green, some blue, others yellow. As they seemed to the Indians to be precious stones, they accepted them, and gave them the capes. . . . Finally the Spaniards said to them, "God go with you and take those stones to your master and tell him that we are unable to see him now; we will come again and go to see him in Mexico."

With this they departed in their canoes, and upon reaching land they got ready and departed for Mexico to give the news to Montezuma. . . .

Montezuma: "We Shall Obey You and Hold You as Our God"

HERNANDO CORTÉS

After we had crossed this bridge, Montezuma came to greet us and with him some two hundred lords, all barefoot and dressed in a different costume, but also very rich in their way and more so than the others. They came in two columns, pressed very close to the walls of the street, which is very wide and beautiful and so straight that you can see from one end to the other. . . . Montezuma came down the middle of this street with two chiefs, one on his right hand and the other on his left. . . . When we met I dismounted and stepped forward to embrace him, but the two lords who were with him stopped me with their hands so that I should not touch him; and they likewise all performed the ceremony of kissing the earth. . . .

When at last I came to speak to Montezuma himself I took off a necklace of pearls and cut glass that I was wearing and placed it round his neck; after we had walked a little way up the street a servant of his came with two necklaces, wrapped in a cloth, made from red snails' shells, which they hold in great esteem; and from each necklace hung eight shrimps of refined gold almost a span in length. . . . [Montezuma] took me by the hand and led me to a great room facing the courtyard through which we entered. And he bade me sit on a very rich throne and addressed me in the following way:

"For a long time we have known from the writings of our ancestors that neither I, nor any of those who dwell in this land, are natives of it, but foreigners who came from very distant parts; and likewise we know that a chieftain, of whom they were all vassals, brought our people to this region. And he returned to his native land and after many years came again, by which time all those who had remained were married to native women and had built villages and raised children. And when he wished to lead them away again they would not go nor even admit him as their chief; and so he departed. And we have always held that those who descended from him would come and conquer this land and take us as their vassals. So because of the place from which you claim to come, namely from where the sun rises, and the things you tell us of the great lord or king who sent you here, we believe and are certain that he is our natural lord, especially as you say that he has known of us for some time. So be assured that we shall obey you and hold you as our lord in place of that great sovereign of whom you speak; and in this there shall be no offense or betrayal whatsoever. And in all the land that lies in my domain, you may command as you will, for you shall be obeyed; and all that we own is for you to dispose of us as you choose. Thus, as you are in your own country and your own house, rest now from the hardships of your journey and the battles which you have fought. . . . "

"Montezuma" is from Hernando Cortés, *Letters from Mexico*, trans. and ed. A. R. Pagden (New York: Grossman Publishers, 1971), pp. 84–86. Copyright © 1971 by A. R. Pagden. Reprinted by permission of Yale University Press.

Human Sacrifice: "A Most Horrid and Abominable Custom"

HERNANDO CORTÉS

JULY 10, 1519

Most High, Mighty, and Excellent Princes, Most Catholic and Powerful Kings and Sovereigns:

[The Aztecs] have a most horrid and abominable custom which truly ought to be punished and which until now we have seen in no other part, and this is that, whenever they wish to ask something of the idols, in order that their plea may find more acceptance, they take many girls and boys and even adults, and in the presence of the idols they open their chests while they are still alive and take out their hearts and entrails and burn them before the idols, offering the smoke as sacrifice. Some of us have seen this, and they say it is the most terrible and frightful thing they have ever witnessed.

This these Indians do so frequently that not one year passes in which they do not kill and sacrifice some fifty persons in each temple. . . . Your Majesties may be most certain that, as this land seems to us to be very large, and to have many temples in it, not one year has passed, as far as we have been able to discover, in which three or four thousand souls have not been sacrificed in this manner.

Let Your Royal Highnesses consider, therefore, whether they should not put an end to such evil practices, for certainly Our Lord God would be well pleased if by the hand of Your Royal Highnesses the people were initiated and instructed in our Holy Catholic Faith, and the devotion, trust, and hope which they have in these their idols were transferred to the divine power of God. . . . And we believe that it is not without cause that Our Lord God has been pleased that these parts be discovered in the name of Your Royal Highnesses so that Your Majesties may gain much merit and reward in the sight of God by commanding that these barbarous people be instructed and by Your hands be brought to the True Faith. For, as far as we have been able to learn, we believe that had we interpreters and other people to explain to them the error of their ways and the nature of the True Faith, many of them, and perhaps even all, would soon renounce their false beliefs and come to the true knowledge of God; for they live in a more civilized and reasonable manner than any other people we have seen in these parts up to the present.

The Destruction of Tenochtitlán: "And Their Mothers Raised a Cry of Weeping"

BERNARDINO DE SAHAGÚN

The following accounts of the brutal destruction of the Aztec capital of Tenochtitlán, first from the native perspective and then from that of Cortés, demonstrate the advantages that the Spanish enjoyed with their armor, weaponry, horses, and sophisticated manipulation of the rivalries and animosities of Aztec enemies. Cortés had difficulty controlling the anger and brutality of his native allies who were released to fight against their Aztec rulers.

The greatest evil that one can do to another is to take his life when [the victim] is in mortal sin. This is what the Spaniards did to the Mexican Indians because they provoked them by being faithless in honoring their idols. [The Spaniards], catching [the Indians] enclosed [in the courtyard] for the feast [of Huitzilopochtli], killed them, the greater part of whom were unarmed, without their knowing why.

When the great courtyard of the idol, Huitzilopochtli, god of the Mexicans, was full of nobles, priests, and soldiers, and throngs of other people, intent upon the idolatrous songs to that idol, whom they were honoring, the Spaniards suddenly poured forth ready for combat and blocked the exits of the courtyard so that no one could escape. Then they entered with their weapons and ranged themselves all along the inner walls of the courtyard. The Indians thought that they were just admiring the style of their dancing and playing and singing, and so continued the style of their dancing and playing and singing, and so continued with their celebration and songs.

At this moment, the first Spaniards to start fighting suddenly attacked those who were playing the music for the singers and dancers. They chopped off their hands and their heads so that they fell down dead. Then all the other Spaniards began to cut off heads, arms, and legs and to disembowel the Indians. Some had their heads cut off, others were cut in half, and others had their bellies slit open, immediately to fall dead. Others dragged their entrails along until they collapsed. Those who reached the exits were slain by the Spaniards guarding them; and others jumped over the walls of the courtyard; while yet others climbed up the temple; and still others, seeing no escape, threw themselves down among the slaughtered and escaped by feigning death.

So great was the bloodshed that rivers of blood ran through the courtyard like water in a heavy rain. So great was the slime of blood and entrails in the courtyard and so great was the stench that it was both terrifying and heartrending. Now that nearly all were fallen and dead, the Spaniards went searching for those who had climbed up the temple and those who had hidden among the dead, killing all those they found alive. . . .

Seeing themselves hotly pursued by the Mexicans, the Spaniards entered the royal houses and fortified and barricaded themselves as best they could to keep the Indians out. From inside they began to defend themselves, firing off crossbows, [rifles], and cannon, and even aiming stones from the rooftop to drive off the Indians struggling to break down the wall and force their way in.

Having a convenient opportunity, the Spaniards conferred with each other, and also with Montezuma and his courtiers, and decided to put them in irons. Meanwhile, the Mexicans were busy performing burial ceremonies for those who had been killed in the ambush and so delayed a few days before returning to do battle with the Spaniards. Great was the Indians' mourning over their dead. . . . [And their mothers, their fathers raised a cry of weeping. There was weeping for them. There was weeping.]

"We Could No Longer Endure the Stench of Dead Bodies"

HERNANDO CORTÉS

AUGUST 12, 1521

On leaving my camp, I had commanded Gonzalo de Sandoval to sail the brigantines [ships] in between the houses in the other quarter in which the Indians were resisting, so that we should have them surrounded, but not to attack until he saw that we were engaged. In this way they would be surrounded and so hard pressed that they would have no place to move save over the bodies of their dead or along the roof tops. They no longer had nor could find any arrows, javelins or stones with which to attack us; and our allies fighting with us were armed with swords and bucklers, and slaughtered so many of them on land and in the water that more than forty thousand were killed or taken that day. So loud was the wailing of the women and children that there was not one man among us whose heart did not bleed at the sound; and indeed we had more trouble in preventing our allies from killing with such cruelty than we had in fighting the enemy. For no race, however savage, has ever practiced such fierce and unnatural

"'We Could No Longer Endure the Stench of Dead Bodies'" is from Hernando Cortés, *Letters from Mexico*, trans. and ed. A. R. Pagden (New York: Grossman Publishers, 1971), pp. 261–262. Copyright © 1971 by A. R. Pagden. Reprinted by permission of Yale University Press.

cruelty as the natives of these parts. Our allies also took many spoils that day, which we were unable to prevent, as they numbered more than 150,000 and we Spaniards were only some nine hundred. Neither our precautions nor our warnings could stop their looting, though we did all we could. One of the reasons why I had avoided entering the city in force during the past days was the fear that if we attempted to storm them they would throw all they possessed into the water, and, even if they did not, our allies would take all they could find. For this reason I was much afraid that Your Majesty would receive only a small part of the great wealth this city once had, in comparison with all that I once held for Your Highness. Because it was now late, and we could no longer endure the stench of the dead bodies that had lain in those streets for many days, which was the most loathsome thing in all the world, we returned to our camps.

CONSIDER THIS:

13-5. Analyze the sources in the section on the conquest of Mexico. What were Cortés's motives in sailing to Mexico? Why did he decide to destroy the Aztecs after having been accepted as conqueror by Montezuma?

COMPARE AND CONTRAST:

13-6. Compare the two accounts of Cortés and Sahagún regarding the destruction of Tenochtitlán by the Spanish. How do you explain Cortés's statements that "there was not one man among us whose heart did not bleed at the sound" of the slaughter? Who bears the primary responsibility for the Aztec destruction? Cortés? His Indian allies? Or Montezuma himself? Is Cortés's attitude toward the Amerindians consistent with that of Columbus? Were they explorers or exploiters?

The Devastation of Smallpox

BERNARDINO DE SAHAGÚN

It would be narrow and simplistic to view the Spanish conquest of Mexico and Peru from a military or even cultural perspective alone. For there were even more encompassing societal changes that affected both Europe and the Americas as a result of the encounter. Recent research has noted the importance of the Spanish introduction of horses to the Americas and especially the impact of these horses on the Native American cultures of the Southwest and Plains. In addition, the crops that poured into Europe from the Americas after 1492 included maize, potatoes, sweet potatoes, tomatoes, peanuts, and various kinds of peppers, beans, and squashes. When we consider that the four chief staples of the human diet in our contemporary world are wheat, rice, maize, and potatoes, the impact of the Old World on the New World becomes apparent.

But perhaps the most immediate factor in the exchange of European and American cultures was disease. It has been proposed by scholars that syphilis, a disease unknown in Europe before the end of the fifteenth century, was brought to Europe by the Spaniards from America. The Indians suffered from it in a mild form, but it attacked the Spanish more severely. Next to tobacco, it may have been the most harmful gift of the New World to the Old. By the same token, the Spanish brought with them diseases against which the Indians had no resistance. The smallpox as described in the selection by Sahagún certainly devastated the Aztecs and may have been the pivotal factor in Cortés's success.

After the previously mentioned hardships that befell the Spaniards in the year 1519, at the beginning of the year 1520 the epidemic of smallpox, measles, and pustules broke out so virulently that a vast number of people died throughout this New Spain. This pestilence began in the province of Chalco and lasted for sixty days. Among the Mexicans who fell victim to this pestilence was the lord Cuitlahuactzin, whom they had elected a little earlier.

"The Devastation of Smallpox" is from Bernardino de Sahagún, *The Conquest of New Spain*, trans. Howard F. Cline (Salt Lake City: University of Utah Press, 1989), p. 103. Copyright © 1989 University of Utah Press. Reprinted by permission of the publisher.

Many leaders, many veteran soldiers, and valiant men who were their defense in time of war, also died.

During this epidemic, the Spaniards, rested and recovered, were already in Tlaxcala. Having taken courage and energy because of the ravages of the [Mexican] people that the pestilence was causing, firmly believing that God was on their side, being again allied with the Tlaxcalans, and attending to all the necessary preparations to return against the Mexicans, they began to construct the brigantines [ships] that they would need in order to wage war by water.

CONSIDER THIS:

13-7. How was Cortés able to defeat thousands of Aztec warriors with only a few hundred soldiers? What role did smallpox play in the destruction of the Aztec civilization in Mexico? How important is disease as an agent of change in history?

The Advantages of Empire

The Spanish Empire in America

With the exploration of America by Christopher Columbus in 1492, the subsequent Spanish conquest of the Aztecs by Hernando Cortés in 1519 and of the Incas by Juan Pizarro in 1531, perspectives suddenly changed. This New World fired the imagination with the abstraction of discovery—the encounter with strange peoples of different color, perspectives, customs, and religions. But it also presented unique, tangible opportunities to realize immense national and personal power through regional conquest and consolidation, and of untold mythic wealth through the exploitation and extraction of natural resources.

Thus began one of the most brutal episodes in modern Western history. The Spanish *conquistadores* (conquerors) methodically organized the region to extract the gold and silver that would allow Spain to surpass its rivals for European power. This was an economy of exploitation that was primarily focused on mining, agriculture, and shipping. There was little accommodation to the native population on the part of the Spanish, as European language, values, and religion became the dominant culture of what would be called Latin America.

Although the Spanish were particularly attracted to gold, silver became the primary metal of Mexico and Bolivia. Because the Spanish crown received a fifth (the *quinto*) of all mining revenues, it imposed a monopoly over the production and sale of mercury, which was essential in the process of mining silver. The extraction of silver was such a labor-intensive process that the Spanish developed various systems to compel and organize native workers.

One of the most important was the *encomienda*. Influential businessmen (*encomenderos*) received formal grants to the labor of a specified number of Indians for a limited time. In the silver mines of Potosí, Bolivia, the *mita* or labor tax placed on Indians required that they contribute a certain number of days of labor annually to the Spanish authorities. Many of these Indians did not survive their *mita* because conditions in the mines were dangerous and the overseers harsh in their demands.

Antonio Vasquez de Espinosa (d. 1630) was a Spanish friar and missionary in the Americas, who sought to convert the Indians to Christianity. He returned to Spain in 1622 and wrote several accounts of his experiences. In the following excerpt, he describes the *mita* system of forced Indian labor used in the dangerous process of extracting mercury from the mines. He then describes Potosí, the richest silver mine in the world. Such wealth allowed the Spanish government to wage wars in Europe against Protestant forces and contributed to the stability of the Spanish crown.

The Extraction of Mercury

ANTONIO VASQUEZ DE ESPINOSA

And so at the rumor of the rich deposits of mercury . . . in the years 1570 and 1571, they started the construction of the town of Huancavelica de Oropesa in a pleasant valley at the foot of the range. It contains 400 Spanish residents, as well as many temporary shops of dealers in merchandise and groceries, heads of trading houses, and transients, for the town has a lively commerce. . . .

Every two months His Majesty sends by the regular courier from Lima 60,000 pesos to pay for the mita of the Indians, for the crews are changed every two months, so that merely for the Indian mita payment (in my understanding of it) 360,000 pesos are sent from Lima every year, not to speak of much besides, which all crosses at his risk that cold and desolate mountain country which is the puna [high plateau] and has nothing on it but llama ranches.

Up on the range there are 3,000 or 4,000 Indians working in the mine; it is colder up there than in the town, since it is higher. The mine where the mercury is located is a large layer which they keep following downward. When I was in that town (which was in the year 1616) I went up on the range and down into the mine, which at that time was considerably more than 130 stades deep [about 104 miles]. The ore was very rich black flint, and the excavation so extensive that it held more than 3,000 Indians working away hard with picks and hammers, breaking up that flint ore; and when they have filled their little sacks, the poor fellows, loaded down with ore, climb up those ladders or rigging, some like masts and others like cable, and so trying and distressing that a man empty-handed can hardly get up them. That is the way they work in this mine, with many lights and the loud noise of the pounding and great confusion. Nor is that the greatest evil and difficulty; that is due to thievish and undisciplined superintendents. As that great vein of ore keeps going down deeper and they follow its rich trail, in order to make sure that no section of that ore shall drop on top of them, they keep leaving supports or pillars of the ore itself, even if of the richest quality, and they necessarily help to sustain and insure each section with less risk. This being so, there are men so heartless that for the sake of stealing a little rich ore, they go down out of hours and deprive the innocent Indians of this protection by hollowing into these pillars to steal the rich ore in them, and then a great section is apt to fall in and kill all the Indians, and sometimes the unscrupulous and grasping superintendents themselves, as happened when I was in that locality; and much of this is kept quiet so that it shall not come to the notice of the manager and cause the punishment of the accomplices. . . .

This is how they extract the mercury. On the other side of the town there are structures where they grind up the mercury ore an then put it in jars with molds like sugar loaves on top of them, with many little holes, and others on top of them, flaring and plastered with mud, and a channel for it to drip into and pass into the jar or place where it is to fall. Then they roast the ore with a straw fire. . . . Under the onset of this fire it melts and the mercury goes up in vapor . . . until it cools and coagulates and starts falling downward again. Those who carry out the reduction of this ore have to be very careful and test cautiously; they must wait till the jars are cold before uncovering them for otherwise they may easily get mercury poisoning and if they do, they are of no further use; their teeth fall out, and some die. After melting and extracting the mercury by fire, they put it in dressed sheepskins to keep it in His Majesty's storehouses, and from there they usually transport it on llamaback to the port of Chincha . . . where there is a vault and an agent appointed by the royal Council, and he has charge of it there; then they freight it on shipboard to the port of San Marcos de Arica, from which it is carried by herds of llamas and mules to Potosí.

"The Extraction of Mercury" is from Antonio Vasquez de Espinosa, *Compendium and Description of the West Indies* (Washington, DC: Smithsonian Institution, 1942), pp. 621–625.

The Silver Mines of Potosí

ANTONIO VASQUEZ DE ESPINOSA

The famous Potosí range, so celebrated all over the world for the great wealth which God has created unique in its bowels and veins, lies in the Province of the Charcas, 18 leagues form the city of Chuquisaca, which was later called La Plata, on account of the great richness of this range. . . .

According to His Majesty's warrant, the mine owners on this massive range have a right to the mita of 13,300 Indians in the working and exploitation of the mines, both those which have been discovered, those now discovered, and those which shall be discovered. It is the duty of the Corregidor of Potosí [a district military officer] to have them rounded up and to see that they come in from all the provinces between Cuzco over the whole of El Collao and as far as the frontiers of Tarija and Tomina; this Potosí Corregidor [official] has power and authority over all the Corregidors in those provinces mentioned; for if they do not fill the Indian mita allotment assigned each of them in accordance with the capacity of their provinces as indicated to them, he can send them, and does, salaried inspectors to report upon it, and when the remissness is great or remarkable, he can suspend them, notifying the Viceroy of the fact.

These Indians are sent out every year under a captain whom they choose in each village or tribe, for him to take them and oversee them for the year each has to serve; every year they have a new election, for as some go out, others come in. This works out very badly, with great losses and gaps in the quotas of Indians, the villages being depopulated; and this gives rise to great extortions and abuses on the part of the inspectors toward the poor Indians, ruining them and thus depriving the chief Indians of their property and carrying them off in chains because they do not fill out the mita assignment, which they cannot do, for the reason given and for others which I do not bring forward.

These 13,300 are divided up every four months into three mitas, each consisting of 4,443 Indians, to work in the mines on the range and in the 120 smelters in the Potosí and Tarapaya areas; it is a good league [three miles] between the two. These mita Indians earn each day, or there is paid each one for his labor, four reals [Spanish silver coins]. . . .

After each [Indian] has eaten his ration, they climb up the hill, each to his mine, and go in, staying there from that hour until Saturday evening without coming out of the mine; their wives bring them food, but they stay constantly underground, excavating and carrying out the ore from which they get the silver. They all have tallow candles, lighted day and night; that is the light they work with, for as they are underground, they have need of it all the time. . . .

So huge is the wealth which has been taken out of this range since the year 1545, when it was discovered, up to the present year of 1628, which makes eighty-three years that they have been working and reducing its ores, that merely form the registered mines, as appears from an examination of most of the accounts in the royal records, 326,000,000 pesos have been taken out.

Over and above that, such great treasure and riches have come from the Indies in gold and silver from all the other mines in New Spain and Peru, Honduras, the New Kingdom of Granada, chile, New Galicia, New Vzcaya [north central and northwestern Mexico], and other quarters since the discovery of the Indies, that they exceed 1,800 millions.

CONSIDER THIS:

13-8. What was the encomienda system, and how was it and the mita used to exploit Indian labor? How was the mercury extracted from the mines, and why was this a dangerous process? Why were the silver mines of Potosí so important to the Spanish, and what made them such a lucrative operation?

"The Silver Mines of Potosí" is from Antonio Vasquez de Espinosa, *Compendium and Description of the West Indies* (Washington, DC: Smithsonian Institution, 1942), pp. 631–634.

The Barbarians of the New World: "They Are Slaves by Nature"

JUAN GINES DE SEPULVEDA

Juan Gines de Sepulveda (1490–1573) was a scholar and apologist for the Spanish treatment of Indians in the Americas. His argument, in essence, is one that would be echoed by conquerors of later ages, from the nineteenth-century British imperialists and American Social Darwinists, to the Nazis of the twentieth century: Superior peoples have the right to enslave inferior peoples. For Sepulveda, the Aztecs were stupid, cruel, immoral, and deserved destruction; they were "natural slaves." Note how his argument is countered by Bartolomé de Las Casas in the succeeding source.

Turning then to our topic, whether it is proper and just that those who are superior and who excel in nature, customs, and laws rule over their inferiors, you can easily understand . . . if you are familiar with the character and moral code of the two peoples, that it is with perfect right that the Spaniards exercise their dominion over those barbarians of the New World and its adjacent islands. For in prudence, talent, and every kind of virtue and human sentiment they are as inferior to the Spaniards as children are to adults, or women to men, or the cruel and inhumane to the very gentle, or the excessively intemperate to the continent and moderate. . . .

And what shall I say of [Spanish] moderation in rejecting gluttony and lasciviousness, inasmuch as no nation or very few nations of Europe can compare with the frugality and sobriety of the Spaniards? I admit that I have observed in these most recent times that through contact with foreigners luxury has invaded the tables of our nobles. Still, since this is reproved by good men among the people, it is to be hoped that in a short while they may return to the traditional and innate sobriety of our native custom. . . .

As for the Christian religion, I have witnessed many clear proofs of the firm roots it has in the hearts of Spaniards, even those dedicated to the military. . . . What shall I say of the Spanish soldiers' gentleness and humanitarian sentiments? Their only and great solicitude and care in the battles, after the winning of the victory is to save the greatest possible number of vanquished and free them from the cruelty of their allies. Now compare these qualities of prudence, skill, magnanimity, moderation, humanity, and religion with those of those little men [of America] in whom one can scarcely find any remnants of humanity. They not only lack culture but do not even use or know about writing or preserve records of their history—save for some obscure memory of certain deeds contained painting. They lack written laws and their institutions and customs are barbaric. And as for their virtues, if you wish to be informed of their moderation and mildness, what can be expected of men committed to all kinds of passion and nefarious lewdness and of whom not a few are given to the eating of human flesh. Do not believe that their life before the coming of the Spaniards was one of peace—the kind that poets sang about. On the contrary, they made war with each other almost continuously, and with such fury that they considered a victory to be empty if they could not satisfy their prodigious hunger with the flesh of their enemies. . . . But in other respects they are so cowardly and timid that they can scarcely offer any resistance to the hostile presence of our side, and many times thousands and thousands of them have been dispersed and have fled like women, on being defeated by a small Spanish force scarcely amounting to one hundred. . . .

Could there be a better or clearer testimony of the superiority that some men have over others in talent, skill, strength of spirit, and virtue? Is it not proof that they are slaves by nature? For the fact that some of them appear to have a talent for certain manual tasks is no argument for their greater human prudence. We see that certain insects, such as the bees and the spiders, produce works that no human skill can imitate. . . .

I have made reference to the customs and character of the barbarians. What shall I say now of the impious religion and wicked sacrifices of such people, who, in venerating the devil as if he were God, believed that the best sacrifice that they could placate him with was to offer him human hearts? . . . Opening up the human breasts they pulled out the hearts and offered them on their heinous altars. And believing that they had made a ritual sacrifice with which to placate their gods, they themselves ate the flesh of the victims. These are crimes that are considered by the philosophers to be among the most ferocious and abominable perversions, exceeding all human iniquity. . . .

How can we doubt that these people—so uncivilized, so barbaric, contaminated with so many impieties and obscenities—have been justly conquered by . . . a nation excellent in every kind of virtue, with the best law and best benefit for the barbarians? Prior to the arrival of the Christians they had the nature, customs, religion, and practice of evil sacrifice as we have explained. Now, on receiving with our rule our writing, laws, and morality, imbued with the Christian religion, having shown themselves to be docile to the missionaries that we have sent them, as many have done, they are as different from their primitive condition as civilized people are from barbarians, or as those with sight from the blind, as the inhuman from the meek, as the pious from the impious, or to put it in a single phrase, in effect, as men from beasts.

THEME: THE VARIETIES OF TRUTH

THE REFLECTION IN THE MIRROR

The Black Legend of Spain

"They Slaughtered Anyone and Everyone"

BARTOLOMÉ DE LAS CASAS

More than any other single individual, the Dominican friar Bartolomé de Las Casas was responsible for the birth of the Black Legend, the vicious reputation about the Spanish that developed during the sixteenth and seventeenth centuries. Although the Black Legend became primarily an instrument of Anglo-Dutch propaganda against the Spanish that Las Casas probably would never have accepted, his influence in its creation is undeniable. After witnessing the ravages and atrocities of Spanish colonists, Las Casas dedicated himself to the protection and defense of the Indians. He wrote the *Short Account of the Destruction of the Indies* in 1542 and dedicated it to the Spanish king Philip II in an effort to inform the crown of atrocities in the New World that, if not curtailed, would result in God's destruction of Spain. This book, a fierce and deeply atmospheric anatomy of genocide, established the image of the Spanish conquest of America for the next three centuries. It is testimony to the persuasive and enduring influence of the Black Legend that the Spanish government hoped to amend this pejorative image by hosting the 1992 Olympics in Barcelona.

KEEP IN MIND . . .

13-9. Note the brutality of the Spaniards toward the native population of the New World. Is intimidation the most effective way of ruling the conquered?

As we have said, the island of Hispaniola was the first to witness the arrival of Europeans and the first to suffer the wholesale slaughter of its people and the devastation and depopulation of the land.

"The Slaughtered Anyone and Everyone" is from Bartolomé de Las Casas, *A Short Account of the Destruction of the Indies*, trans. and ed. Nigel Griffin (New York and Harmondsworth, Middlesex: Penguin Books, 1967), pp. 14–15. Copyright © Nigel Griffin, 1992. Reprinted by permission of Penguin Books, Ltd.

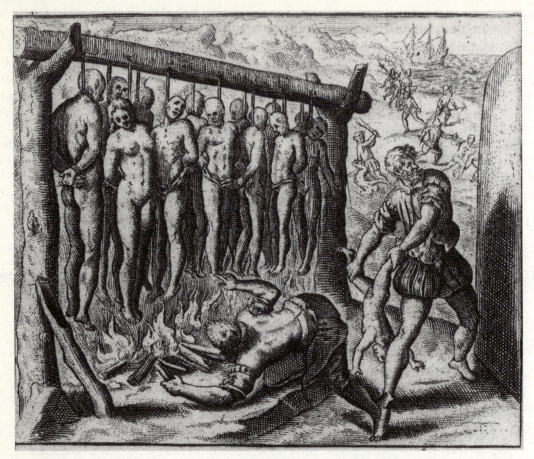

FIGURE 13.1 Bartolomé de Las Casas: "[The Spaniards] spared no one, erecting especially wide gibbets on which they could string their victims up with their feet just off the ground and then burn them alive." (*Illustrations by the Flemish engraver Theodor de Bry taken from a sixteenth-century Dutch edition of the* Short Account of the Destruction of the Indies *by Bartolomé de Las Casas. The British Library*)

It all began with the Europeans taking native women and children both as servants and to satisfy their own base appetites; then not content with what the local people offered them of their own free will (and all offered as much as they could spare), they started taking for themselves the food that natives contrived to produce by the sweat of their brows, (which was in all honesty little enough). . . . Some of them started to conceal what food they had, others decided to send their women and children into hiding, and yet others took to the hills to get away from the brutal and ruthless cruelty that was being inflicted on them. The Christians punched them, boxed their ears and flogged them in order to track down the local leaders, and the whole shameful process came to a head when one of the European commanders raped the wife of the paramount chief of the entire island. It was then that the locals began to think up ways of driving the Europeans out of their lands and to take up arms against them. Their weapons, however, were flimsy and ineffective both in attack and in defense (and, indeed, war in the Americas is no more deadly than our jousting, or than many European children's games) and, with their horses and swords and lances, the Spaniards easily fended them off, killing them and committing all kind of atrocities against them.

They forced their way into native settlements, slaughtering everyone they found there, including small children, old men, pregnant women, and even women who had just given birth. They hacked them to pieces, slicing open their bellies with their swords as though they were so many sheep herded into a pen. They even laid wagers on whether they could manage to slice a man in two at a stroke, or cut an individual's head from his body, or disembowel him with a single blow of their axes. They grabbed suckling infants by the feet and, ripping them from their mothers' breasts, dashed them headlong against the rocks. . . . They slaughtered anyone and everyone in their path, on occasion running through a mother and her baby with a single thrust of their swords. They spared no one, erecting especially wide gibbets on which they could string their victims up with their feet just off the ground and then burn them alive thirteen at a time, in honor of our Savior and the twelve Apostles, or tie dry straw to their bodies

and set fire to it. Some they chose to keep alive and simply cut their wrists, leaving their hands dangling, saying to them: "Take this letter"—meaning that their sorry condition would act as a warning to those hiding in the hills. The way they normally dealt with the native leaders and nobles was to tie them to a kind of griddle consisting of sticks resting on pitchforks driven into the ground and then grill them over a slow fire, with the result that they howled in agony and despair as they died a lingering death.

CONSIDER THIS:

13-10. What was the Black Legend of Spain? What types of atrocities were committed by the Spanish conquistadores? Study the pictures accompanying the accounts of Bartolomé de Las Casas. Were the actions of the Spanish an attempt at genocide, or have these atrocities been blown out of proportion by Las Casas and inflated as anti-Spanish propaganda? Do the arguments of Juan Gines de Sepulveda effectively counter those of Las Casas? How does Sepulveda justify Spanish treatment of the Indians?

Visions of the New World

Utopia

SIR THOMAS MORE

Sir Thomas More (1478–1535) became famous for his opposition to King Henry VIII of England. As Henry's Lord Chancellor, More was expected to support the king's divorce from Catherine of Aragon and his authority as head of the newly created Church of England. But More refused to take an oath impugning the pope's supremacy and paid the price when he was beheaded in 1535. More was made a saint of the Catholic Church 400 years later.

But long before this dramatic climax to his life, Thomas More cultivated his reputation for honesty and intellectual brilliance as a scholar and statesman. The Dutch humanist Erasmus was a good friend and described More as a very engaged and provocative thinker. Nowhere is this in better evidence than in More's most famous work, *Utopia*.

We spend a lot of time in our contemporary world thinking of the perfect society where all the complex problems surrounding us are resolved in harmonious balance. But this fantasy has long been contemplated over the centuries, in the Sumerian epic of *Gilgamesh* and the Elysian fields of Homer, the celestial vision of Saint Augustine's *City of God* and the worker's utopia of Karl Marx. Thomas More, however, was the first to present a detailed

Utopia is from Thomas More, *Utopia*, trans. Valerian Paget (New York: The John McBride Company, 1909), pp. 81–86, 112–116. Translation modernized by the editor.

literary description of the ideal society. He based his conception on Plato's *Republic*, but chose to locate his utopia in the New World. This afforded him an opportunity to comment on the contemporary social and political problems of Europe in a less direct and perhaps safer way.

In More's perfect society, there is a high regard for justice—a few simple laws, assiduously enforced without capital punishment and without lawyers. *Utopia* is a witty exposition of possibilities where society offers material benefits for all, including food, clothing, housing, education, and medical treatment.

All of these bare necessities of life are provided by the state in exchange for a short workday of six hours. However, one must exchange a significant measure of personal liberty for these benefits. There is no private property, but there is virtually no privacy either. In More's utopia, "Everyone has his eye on you so you're practically forced to get on with your job, and make proper use of your spare time." This also was a patriarchal society where each month women had to confess "all their sins of omission and commission, and ask to be forgiven." Yet men were apparently exempt from this provision. In sexual matters, consequences were unforgiving. Premarital sex was punished by compulsory celibacy for life, and adultery by slavery and even death for repeated offenses. More's vision was of a moral landscape, free from want, attuned to need, but cognizant of moral obligation.

The following excerpt is a dialogue between Raphael Nonesenso, who had just returned from the New World, and Thomas More as they discuss the parameters of utopian society.

Raphael: To tell you the truth, my dear More, it would be difficult, if not impossible, to govern a state justly and make it prosperous, as long as private property exists and everything is judged with an eye to profit—unless, of course, you think justice should flourish where all things are controlled by cheats, or that you are willing to call a country prosperous in which all wealth is owned by a tiny minority, and with those few not really happy and everyone else simply miserable.

On the other hand, when I think how wise and just things are here in Utopia, where things are run so smoothly, even with so very few laws, and where individual character is greatly esteemed and yet everyone is prospering—well, when I compare Utopia with those other capitalist nations that are always making new regulations, but could never be called well-regulated, where several laws are passed everyday, but none of them ensure that people can buy or protect private property—I have to agree with Plato when he refused to legislate for a city that rejected absolute equality of rights in the first place. Such a wise man certainly understood that the essential condition for a healthy society was the equal distribution of goods—clearly an impossibility under capitalism. For when anyone, on some pretext or other, tries

to grab as much as he can for himself, and the few who succeed divide among themselves the whole wealth of the nation, no matter how rich the nation is, the rest of the people are bound to be poor. And these poor are generally more deserving of wealth. The rich tend to be greedy, unscrupulous, and worthless characters, while the poor, because of their daily labor, are simple, unaffected people who are of greater service to the community than they are to themselves. Therefore, I am convinced that you'll never be able to distribute goods fairly or organize human society satisfactorily unless you abolish private property altogether. As long as it exists, the lower classes will inevitably have to bear the greatest poverty and hardship. Although this burden can be reduced, it will never be lifted from their shoulders. . . .

More: I disagree. In fact, I believe that you can never prosper under a communist system. How could there be any prosperity where people simply don't work hard enough? Where there is no profit incentive, everyone would become lazy, and rely on everyone else to do the work for him. Then, when things really got tight and the masses grew upset about their sustained poverty, the inevitable result would be a series of murders and riots, since there would be no legal recourse to protect the products of their own labor—no respect for the rule of law, or I can't imagine any in a classless society.

Raphael: Oh, I don't wonder that you doubt this. You simply can't imagine what it would be like. But if you'd been with me in Utopia, and seen it all for yourself, as I did over a five year period, you'd admit that you had never before seen a country so well governed. . . .

In Utopia they have a six-hour working day—three hours in the morning, then lunch—then a two-hour break—then three more hours in the afternoon, after which they go to dinner. About 8 o'clock in the evening they go to bed and sleep for about eight hours. The rest of the time they spend as they like, not with the idea that want to waste time doing nothing or just indulging themselves, but in making good use of it in some worthy activity. Most people spend these free periods furthering their education. . . .

But here you must guard against getting the wrong idea. Perhaps you think that since they only work six hours a day, they cannot produce enough essential goods. On the contrary, it is more than enough time to provide an abundance of all that's needed for a comfortable life. And you'll realize why if you consider for a moment how many people in other countries are unemployed. First, almost all the women (who are half the population) don't work, and in countries where they *do* have jobs, the men

just hang around instead. Besides this, what about all the priests or members of so-called religious orders? What do they actually accomplish? Add to that the wealthy landowners, commonly called gentlemen and nobles, and their servants—I mean that gang of armed brawlers and braggarts that I noted before. Finally, throw into the mix all the beggars who are perfectly healthy and strong, but who pretend to be sick as an excuse for their laziness. Taken altogether, you will find that far fewer people than you ever imagined actually produce the necessary goods for the whole country. . . . This is clearly illustrated in Utopia where out of all the able-bodied men and women who live in a town, or in the country around it, five hundred at the most are exempted from ordinary work.

CONSIDER THIS:

13-11. In the dialogue, Raphael argues that "the one essential condition of a healthy society [is] the equal distribution of goods," which he believed was impossible under capitalism. Do you agree? How does More counter this argument?

13-12. According to Raphael, why is a six-hour day sufficient to provide all that's needed for "a comfortable life"? For Utopians, what is a comfortable life? How do they spend their free time? What assumptions does Raphael make about human beings that might make his vision of utopia problematic?

On Cannibals

MICHEL DE MONTAIGNE

Michel de Montaigne (1533–1592) was born the son of a lawyer and landowner in Bordeaux, France. He studied philosophy and law amid the general religious disorder that was ravaging France during the middle of the sixteenth century. The contending Huguenot and Catholic factions produced a barbaric chaos as justice was sought in extreme action—the slaughter of innocents, the execution by fire at the stake. Montaigne became skeptical of understanding the world, but sought to find balance through a personal quest for truth. He rejected easy theories and sought to test himself through a series of "trials" or "essays" that forced him to set out on a voyage of self discovery without the protection of an egotistical spirit or fear of religious condemnation. Montaigne wrote on many subjects: cruelty, friendship, the imagination, repentance, and in the following selection, on cannibals.

On Cannibals is from Michel de Montaigne, *The Essays of Montaigne*, trans. E. J. Trechmann (London: Oxford University Press, 1927), pp. 205–210. Translation modernized by the editor.

As the exploration of the New World produced great wealth and opportunity, it also presented moral dilemmas about the horrors of conquest and the treatment of peoples from new and exotic lands with strange customs and social expectations. Were these "noble savages" or vicious barbarians? And could their barbaric acts of cannibalism compare with the atrocities that attended European religious rivalries? In the following selection, Montaigne struggles with the question of human depravity.

Now, to return to my subject, from what I have heard of that nation, I can see nothing barbarous or uncivilized about it, except that we all call barbarous anything that does not fit with our own habits. And indeed, we have no other criterion of truth than the kinds of opinions and customs that currently exist in our own countries. There we always see the perfect religion, the perfect government, and accomplished way of doing all things. Those people, on the other hand, are wild in the same way that fruits are wild that Nature has produced by herself and in her ordinary way. But we should really call wild only those things that we have altered artificially and diverted from the natural order. In the first, we still see, alive and vigorous, the genuine and most natural and useful virtues and properties, which we have bastardized in the latter, and only adapted to please our corrupt taste. . . . These nations, then, seem to me barbarous in the sense that they have received very little molding from the human intelligence, and are still very close to their original simplicity. They are still ruled by the laws of Nature, and very little corrupted by ours; but they are still in such a state of purity, that I am sometimes saddened that they were not known earlier, at a time when there were men who could have appreciated them better than we do. . . .

Theirs is a country in which there is no kind of commerce, no knowledge of letters, no science of numbers, no title of magistrate or statesman, no use of slaves, neither wealth nor property, no contracts, no inheritance, no property divisions, no occupation but that of idleness, a general respect for parents only, no clothing, no agriculture, no metals, no use of wine or corn. The very words denoting lying, treachery, deceit, greed, envy, slander, and forgiveness, are unknown. . . .

For the rest, they live in a land with a very pleasant and temperate climate, so that, according to my witnesses, one rarely sees a sick man; and they assured me that they had never seen any man shaking with palsy, or with bleary eyes, toothless or bent with age. They are settled along the sea coast, and closed in on the land side by a range of high mountains, which leave a strip of land about a hundred leagues wide between them and the sea. They have a great abundance of fish and meat which bear no resemblance to ours, and they eat them roasted, without any other preparation. The first man who brought a horse there, although he had associated with them on some earlier voyages, so terrified them when up in the saddle, that they shot him to death with arrows before recognizing him. . . .

They spend the whole day dancing. The younger men hunt animals with bows. Some of the women meanwhile spend their time warming their drink, which is their principal duty. In the morning before they begin to eat, one of their old men preaches to the whole barnful of people in common, walking from one end to the other, repeating the same words several times, until he has finished the round (for the buildings are quite a hundred yards long). He recommends only two things: courage against the enemy and love for their wives. And he never fails to emphasize this obligation, which forms their refrain—that it is the women who keep their wine warm and seasoned for them. . . .

They have their wars against the people who live further inland, on the other side of the mountains, to which they go quite naked, with no other arms but their bows or their wooden swords. . . . It is incredible with what obstinacy they fight their battles, which never end without great slaughter and bloodshed. They don't know what flight or terror are. Each man brings back as a trophy the head of an enemy he has killed, and hangs it over the entrance to his house. After treating his prisoner well for a considerable time, and giving him every bit of hospitality imaginable, his captor assembles a great gathering of his acquaintances. He then ties a rope to one of the prisoner's arms, holding him at some distance for fear of being hurt, and gives the other arm to be held in the same way by his best friend; and these two, in full view of the whole assembly, kill him with their swords. Then they roast and eat him together, and send bits of him to their friends who couldn't join them. They do this not, as one might suppose, for nourishment, but in order to demonstrate extreme vengeance.

The proof of this is that when they saw the Portuguese, who had allied themselves with their enemies, inflicting a different kind of death on their prisoners, which was to bury them to the waist, to shoot the rest of their bodies full of arrows, and then to hang them, they concluded that these people from another world (who were much more skilled than they in all sorts of evil), chose this form of revenge for a reason. So, thinking that it must be more painful than their own, they began to give up their old practice and follow this new one.

I am not so much concerned that we should note the horrible savagery of these acts as concerned that, while correctly judging their faults, we should be so blind to our own. I think it more barbarous to eat a man alive than to eat him dead; to tear on the rack and torture a body still full of feeling, to roast it by degrees, and then give it to be mangled and eaten by dogs and swine—a practice which we have not

only read about, but seen within recent memory not between old enemies, but between neighbors and fellow-citizens and, what is worse, under the cloak of piety and religion—than to roast a man and eat him after he is dead.

CONSIDER THIS:

13-13. Montaigne describes these natives as "wild." What did he mean? What were Montaigne's criticisms of his contemporary European society?

13-14. Why did the natives eat their enemies? Can a society that commits such an act truly have any civilized qualities? What are the standards of "civilization"? How did Montaigne's essay test his personal beliefs on the subject?

COMPARE AND CONTRAST:

13-15. What did the natives learn from the Portuguese treatment of their enemies? What point was Montaigne trying to make here? Were the natives "noble savages"?

13-16. Compare Montaigne's description of the way the natives live with Thomas More's description of life in Utopia. How is the "natural environment" of the New World idealized? What were the drawbacks?